Indonesia

Edited by Eric Oey
Designed by Hans Johannes Hoefer

APA PUBLICATIONS

THE INSIGHT GUIDES SERIES RECEIVED SPECIAL AWARDS FOR EXCELLENCE FROM THE PACIFIC AREA TRAVEL ASSOCIATION.

APA PUBLICATIONS

Publisher: Hans Johannes Hoefer
General Manager: Henry Lee
Marketing Director: Aileen Lau
Editorial Director: Geoffrey Eu
Editorial Manager: Vivien Kim
Editorial Consultants: Adam Liptak (North America)
Brian Bell (Europe)
Heinz Vestner (German Editions)

Project Editors

Helen Abbott, Diana Ackland, Mohamed Amin, Ravindralal Anthonis, Roy Bailet, Louisa Cambell, Jon Carroll, Hillary Cunningham, John Eames, Janie Freeburg, Bikram Grewal, Virginia Hopkins, Samuel Israel, Jay Itzkowitz, Phil Jarratt, Tracy Johnson, Bèn Kalb, Wilhelm Klein, Saul Lockhart, Sylvia Mayuga, Gordon MaLauchlan, Kal Müller, Eric Oey, Daniel P. Reid, Kim Robinson, Ronn Ronck, Robert Seidenberg, Rolf Steinberg, Sriyani Tidball, Lisa Van Gruisen, Merin Wexler.

Contributing Writers

A.D. Aird, Ruth Armstrong, T. Terence Barrow, F. Lisa Beebe, Bruce Berger, Dor Bahadur Bista, Clinton V. Black, Star Black, Frena Bloomfield, John Borthwick, Roger Boschman, Tom Brosnahan, Jerry Carroll, Tom Chaffin, Nedra Chung, Tom Cole, Orman Day, Kunda Dixit, Richard Erdoes, Guillermo Gar-Oropeza, Ted Giannoulas, Barbara Gloudon, Harka Gurung, Sharifah Hamzah, Willard A. Hanna, Elizabeth Hawley, Sir Edmund Hillary, Tony Hillerman, Jerry Hopkins, Peter Hutton, Neil Jameson, Michael King, Michele Kort, Thomas Lucey, Leonard Lueras, Michael E. Macmillan, Derek Maitland, Buddy Mays, Craig McGregor, Reinhold Messner, Julie Michaels, M.R. Priya Rangsit, Al Read, Elizabeth V. Reyes, Victor Stafford Reid, Harry Rolnick, E.R. Sarachandra, Uli Schmetzer, Ilsa Sharp, Norman Sibley, Peter Spiro, Harold Stephens, Keith Stevens, Michael Stone, Desmond Tate, Colin Taylor, Deanna L. Thompson, Randy Udall, James Wade, Mallika Wanigasundara, William Warren, Cynthia Wee, Tony Wheeler, Linda White, H. Taft Wireback, Alfred A. Yuson, Paul Zach.

Contributing Photographers

Carole Allen, Ping Amarand, Tony Arruza, Marcello Bertinetti, Alberto Cassio, Pat Canova, Alain Compost, Ray Cranbourne, Alian Evrard, Ricardo Ferro, Lee Foster, Manfred Gottschalk, Werner Hahn, Dallas and John Heaton, Brent Hesselyn, Hans Hoefer, Luca Invernizzi, Ingo Jezierski, Wilhelm Klein, Dennis Lane, Max Lawrence, Lyle Lawson, Philip Little, Guy Marche, Antonio Martinelli, David Messent, Ben Nakayama, Vautier de Nanxe, Kal Müller, Günter Pfannmuller, Van Philips, Ronni Pinsler, Fitz Prenzel, G.P. Reichelt, Dan Rocovits, David Ryan, Frank Salmoiraghi, Thomas Schollhammer, Blair Seitz, David Stahl, Bill Wassman, Rendo Yap, Hisham Youssef.

While contributions to Insight Guides are very welcome, the publisher cannot assume responsibility for the care and return of unsolicited manuscripts or photographs. Return postage and/or a self-addressed envelope must accompany unsolicited material if it is to be returned. Please address all editorial contributions to Apa Photo Agency P.O. Box 219, Orchard Point Post Office, Singapore 9123.

Advertising and Special Sales Representatives

APA PHOTO AGENCY PTE. LTD.

The volume you now hold in your hands represents a major milestone for its creators at Apa Productions. Indeed, the publication of *Insight Guide: Indonesia* in 1985 not only marked the 15th anniversary of Apa's award-winning series of Insight Guides, now numbering over thirty titles; it marked a homecoming, too. For it was Bali, now the most-visited part of the Indonesian archipelago, that breathed life into the very first Insight Guide. Apa's founder-publisher, German-born designer and photographer **Hans Hoefer**, was first captivated by the island's mystique in 1970. Living in Ubud, and painting, reading and bicycling his way under Bali's skin, he began to appreciate the island's tremendous cultural vitality. Influenced especially by Miguel Covarrubias, Beryl de Zoete, Walter Spies and Vicki Baum, who wrote about Bali in the 1930s, Hoefer's dream was to put Bali within reach of the traveller of the 1970s, without losing sight of its unique heritage. This all prompted a new kind of guide book—one that emphasised the "why" of travelling to a particular place and not simply the "how." When *Insight Guide: Bali* was published, it received unanimous praise and along with it came the recognition that a new generation of guide book had indeed arrived.

Following quickly in the footsteps of Bali was *Insight Guide: Java.* More than 18 months of travel by photographer Hoefer and writer Peter Hutton produced a book that was just as warmly received. And the photojournalistic format of these two titles, though it has undergone various modifications through the years, continues to provide the window through which Insight Guides look out onto destinations worldwide, earning Apa Productions a growing reputation.

Insight Guide: Bali, benefiting from the regular updating it receives, continues to be an international bestseller while at the same time ensuring that its namesake remains in the limelight. With the arrival of *Insight Guide: Indonesia* some of the farthest corners of the Indonesian archipelago now receive Apa's distinctive and much acclaimed coverage—offering a broad overview where the two earlier titles continue to provide that much needed fine focus.

Not that a book on the whole of Indonesia would have been feasible in 1970. Bali was just about the only part of Indonesia with the kind of infrastructure for anyone other than the genuinely intrepid traveller. But times have changed, and though the majority of visitors still make Bali the centrepiece of an Indonesian sojourn, there has developed over the years, a corpus of travellers who enjoys the unique experience of straying from Indonesia's beaten tracks.

Since the early 1970s, Indonesia's stature as an exotic Southeast Asian destination has grown, and it was in 1982 that Apa Productions invited an old colleague. **Eric Oey**, to accept the task of putting together a new Indonesia book.

Hoefer   *Oey*

Oey had been with Apa previously in 1978 and 1979 as Marketing Manager. When he was asked to take the helm of the Indonesia book, he was a graduate student at the University of California, Berkeley, undertaking doctoral studies in the field of Malay Philology and linguistics. Having travelled extensively in Indonesia already, his credentials for overseeing work on *Insight Guide: Indonesia* were more than sound.

This project was very much a cooperative effort that owes a considerable debt to some of Indonesia's most distinguished writers, who ensure that the book boasts genuine native expertise. No other guide to Indonesia benefits from the dual perspectives of "insiders" and "outsiders" and Oey was well placed to orchestrate the necessary editorial cooperation over the three years it took for this book to evolve, through judicious editing and a significant personal contribution.

Part One—History—benefits from the expertise of two leading Indonesian academics, **Satyawati Suleiman** and **Dr. Onghokham**. Satyawati is currently Senior Researcher with the Archaeological Publishing Department in Jakarta. She was previously head of the Archaeological Service of Indonesia and has published several books on Indonesian history, among them: *A Concise History of Indonesia; Monuments of Ancient Indonesia;* and *The Art of Srivijaya.* Her writing appears regularly in many of Indonesia's best-known periodicals.

Onghokham, whose special interest is the social history of Java, has been lecturing at the University of Indonesia in the Department of History since 1963. His writings appear regularly in Indonesian newspapers and magazines, including: *Tempo, Kompas, Sinar Harapan* and *Prisma.*

Three writers were involved in Part Two: Geography and People—**Kathy MacKinnon, William Collins** and **Dewi Anwar**. MacKinnon, a zoologist, gained her doctorate in 1976 from Oxford, after which she worked for seven years with the World Wildlife Fund's Indonesia programme. With her husband, she has written books on Asian wildlife and contributed to scientific journals. Having spent most of the last 10 years in Indonesia as a traveller and scientist, she was a welcome source of expertise in "The Mightiest Archipelago." "Indonesia's Incredible Wildlife" (Part Four—Features) was also penned by her. During her time with the World Wildlife Fund, MacKinnon spent two years working in Tangkoko Batuangus Reserve in North Sulawesi.

In Part Three a number of writers and resources were brought together by the editor, who himself penned the Jakarta piece. *Insight Guide: Java,* written by **Peter Hutton**, served as a major resource, though all of the material was revised and updated for this more compact volume. Hutton returned to his native Australia early in 1985 after nearly two decades in Southeast Asia. His earlier peregrinations had seen him as a stockman and papaya-pollinator in Queensland, a shearers' cook in New Zealand, a truckdriver and dishwasher in London, a seller of the *New York Herald Tribune* in Paris, and a film extra in Rome. Between times he had wandered in and out of the world of journalism before settling into a long stint in advertising which took him to Kuala Lumpur in 1967 and to Singapore in 1969.

The pages on Bali and Lombok are the work of **Made Wijaya** and **Professor Willard Hanna**. Wijaya, an Australian by birth who has spent the past decade in Bali, revised and updated the 1984 edition of *Insight Guide: Bali.* His contribution to that book has been used wherever appropriate. Hanna's historical introduction to the 1984 edition of *Insight Guide: Bali* was

also an important source of reference for the coverage in this book on Bali. A member of the American Universities Field Staff Inc., Hanna has been writing about Asia since 1930.

Nusa Tenggara came under the sole proprietorship of **Kal Müller**—itinerant (and widely published) photojournalist and doctor of anthropology. Müller wrote much of the *Insight Guide: Mexico* in 1981 and 1982. Since then his travels have taken him on regular trips to Indonesia. His articles on Nusa Tenggara have appeared in *National Geographic Magazine* and *Geo.* He is currently working on an illustrated book on Indonesia. **Liz Mortlock**, a freelance writer now living in Bangkok, also helped edit these last two sections.

The pages on Sumatra are the efforts of two writers—**Michel Vatin** and **Frederic**

Onghokham

Suleiman

Abdurachman

MacKinnon

Collins

Hanna

Lontcho. Free-lance journalist and photographer Vatin has lived and worked in several countries and has travelled frequently in Indonesia. Publisher, author and doctor of anthropology, Lontcho has written extensively on Sumatra and Sulawesi.

Bob Monkhouse, a native Australian, penned the Kalimantan pages. Originally arriving in Indonesia as an English teacher, he has lived here for ten years and can claim substantial knowledge of the nation he has adopted as his home. Making a living as a technical writer for an LNG plant in East Kalimantan, he has travelled extensively in Indonesia, spent four years of the last decade in East Kalimantan working in the oil industry, and written and published articles on a variety of Indonesian topics.

Both Sulawesi and Maluku, and the feature on Indonesian textiles, were written by **Paramita Abdurachman**—one of Indonesia's leading writers in the field of Indonesian culture and history. She is currently a Senior Researcher at the Indonesian Institute for cultural studies where she specializes in Portuguese and Spanish documents from the 16th and 17th centuries as they relate to Indonesian and Southeast Asian history. Her travels have taken her worldwide, while at home her concentration on the eastern portion of the Indonesian archipelago has earned her a reputation as an expert in that field. Paramita has for a long time been active in the arts as well, having helped establish a cultural foundation and a foundation for the promotion of Indonesian textiles. She has published widely in professional journals, books and popular magazines on

Wijaya   *Müller*   *Tirta*

Tenzer   *Soedarsono*   *Monkhouse*

historical subjects, textiles and dance for both an academic and a general readership.

The feature on *batik* was penned by **Iwan Tirta**—Indonesia's foremost Batik designer. Tirta qualified originally as a lawyer and taught International Law in Indonesia before working at the United Nations in New York. A research project he undertook on the Sacred Dances of the Court of the Susuhunan of Surakarta brought him into contact with Javanese fabrics, notably *batik*. The interest soon became a major preoccupation and a book on *batik* followed in 1967. In 1970, returned from a trip to the United States, Tirta embarked on a career as a *batik* designer and formed his own atelier. Since then, Tirta's creations have earned him a sound

reputation in fashion circles around the world. In 1974, he was involved in a documentary film on *batik* made by the state oil company Pertamina. Tirta has combined his career as a fashion designer with his role as a promoter of the art of *batik;* he gives exhibitions, lectures and slide shows on the historical and sociological background of *batik*.

The performing arts in Indonesia are covered by two features on *gamelan* music and dance and drama respectively. Three writers—**Michael Tenzer, Bernard Suryabrata** and **Soedarsono**—contributed their expertise. Tenzer received his doctorate in music from the University of California, Berkeley, in 1985. A classical musician by training, Tenzer also studied *gamelan* in Bali for two years. His fascination with this musical form prompted him to set up Sekar Jaya, his own *gamelan* orchestra—not in Bali but in San Francisco, where his efforts are causing a not inconsiderable stir. And in a tribute to the homeland of this unique musical form, Tenzer took his *gamelan* orchestra to perform in Bali in July 1985.

Suryabrata, a professor of ethnomusicology at the School of Folk Art in the National University, Jakarta, has the special distinction of having studied under Jaap Kunst—the best-known name in the field of *gamelan*. Soedarsono, an academic expert on the history of Southeast Asian Performing Arts, contributed his knowledge to the piece on "Dance and Drama in Indonesia." Presently Senior Lecturer in the History of Arts at Gajah Mada University in Yogykarta, he has contributed to a wide range of academic journals and written three books on Indonesian performing arts.

The Travel Advisories were prepared by Oey and Apa Editor in Singapore, **Stuart Ridsdale**, using travel notes supplied by the contributing writers. Jakarta-based freelance journalist **Jeremy Allan** also contributed with his own research. Throughout the six months it took to compile these travel notes, **Patricia Chin** of the Indonesian Tourist Promotion in Singapore lent a helping hand—providing a constant stream of answers to Apa Productions' enquiries.

Apa Productions

TABLE OF

CONTENTS

Colour maps by Nelles Verlag GmbH,
Munich, West Germany
monochrome maps by Apa Productions

OTHER INSIGHT GUIDES TITLES

COUNTRY/REGION

ASIA
Bali
Burma
Hong Kong
India
Indonesia
Korea
Malaysia
Nepal
Philippines
Rajasthan
Singapore
Sri Lanka
Taiwan
Thailand
Turkey

PACIFIC
Hawaii
New Zealand

NORTH AMERICA
Alaska
American Southwest
Northern California
Southern California
Florida
Mexico
New England
New York State
The Pacific Northwest
The Rockies
Texas

SOUTH AMERICA
Brazil
Argentina

CARIBBEAN
Bahamas
Barbados
Jamaica
Puerto Rico
Trinidad and Tobago

EUROPE
Channel Islands
France
Germany
Great Britain
Greece
Ireland
Italy
Portugal
Scotland
Spain

MIDDLE EAST
Egypt
Israel

AFRICA
Kenya

GRAND TOURS
Australia
California
Canada
Continental Europe
Crossing America
East Asia
South Asia

GREAT ADVENTURE
Indian Wildlife

CITYGUIDES
Bangkok
Berlin
Buenos Aires
Dublin
Istanbul
Lisbon
London
Paris
Rio de Janeiro
Rome
San Francisco
Venice
Vienna

UNITY IN DIVERSITY

Indonesia. Insulinde. Nusantara. The East Indies—13,677 sun-drenched tropical isles, "girding the equator like a string of emeralds." More than 160 million people speaking hundreds of distinct tongues—an ethnic mosaic of kaleidoscope proportions.

Known to anthropologists and naturalists as "The Malay Archipelago" and famed throughout much of history as the eagerly-sought "Spice Islands" of the East—Indonesia is still today an inexhaustible storehouse of historical marvels and the single most extraordinary collection of peoples, places, sights, sounds and natural wonders in the world.

Collectively, these islands constitute one of the most exciting and rewarding travel destinations on earth.

Today's visitor to Indonesia joins a long line of distinguished voyagers. The intrepid Chinese monk Fa Hsien was the first to pen a travelogue to these isles, after being shipwrecked off Java in 412 AD on his way home from India. Marco Polo sojourned along the northeastern shores of Sumatra in 1292 en route back to Italy. Ferdinand Magellan plotted his historic round-the-world voyage in 1520 specifically to reach the eastern Indonesian islands of Maluku. And in 1770, Captain Cook sailed into Batavia (Jakarta) harbour for repairs, having charted the little-known coasts of remote New Guinea (Irian Jaya).

The discoveries continue. Though arriving now in ever-increasing numbers, modern visitors from abroad have absolutely no need to fear that all has been seen and done here before. This archipelago today constitutes one of the world's largest nations, and the potential for personal exploration and adventure is truly limitless. Superimposed on a map of North America, Indonesia stretches from Oregon all the way to Bermuda. On a map of Europe, the islands extend from Ireland to the Caspian Sea.

Found along the way is a breathtaking variety of landscapes: smouldering blue-grey volcanoes, verdant rice paddies, azure seas, dazzling white beaches, teeming coral reefs, pristine rainforests, rolling meadows, dense mangrove swamps and lush, cool hill country.

This is the land of Krakatau and *kretek,* of the Borobudur and *batik*, the metropolitan urbanity of Jakarta juxtaposed with the "Stone Age" tribes of Irian Jaya, the proud nobility of the Central Javanese court with the magic ritual of a Balinese peasant village, and the primeval 'dragons' of Komodo with the brightly-plumed 'Birds of Paradise.' All take their special place in the cornucopia that is Indonesia.

Indonesia's diversity owes much to its long history and spectacular geography. But above all, it owes much to the hundreds of tribes and ethnic groups who today call themselves Indonesians—the inhabitants of a proud and independent nation whose motto, quite understandably, is *Bhinneka Tunggal Ika* — "Many are One."

INDONESIA'S PROUD PREHISTORY

Recent excavations at two sites in northern Thailand have revealed that a metal-age culture was underway there in the 4th millennium B.C.—much earlier than in either China or India. This discovery has already overturned the conception of Southeast Asia as a prehistoric backwater, and some scholars are now speculating that this region was in fact one of the great prehistoric cradles of human cultural development.

Such speculation is somewhat premature in the case of Indonesia, where relatively few Neolithic sites have been excavated and

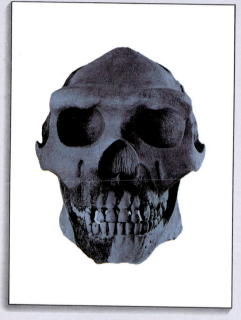

dated with precision. But numerous excavations being undertaken here are expected to turn up new and exciting discoveries.

Java Man

Indonesian archaeological findings have contributed more than their share of controversy in the past. In 1890, a Dutch military physician by the name of Eugene Dubois discovered a fossilized primate jawbone in Central Java that possessed distinctively human characteristics. The jawbone was found in association with fossils of mammalian species thought to have died out several hundred thousand years ago, and was at first discounted by Dubois as belonging to an extinct species of apes. But when, in the following year, he discovered two more hominoid fossils in similar circumstances, he became convinced that he had unearthed the world's first evidence of Darwin's long-sought "missing link." He named his discovery *pithecanthropus erectus* (upright ape-man), and published his findings in 1894.

Unfortunately for Dubois, Darwin's evolutionary theories were still being hotly disputed at this time and his discovery, dubbed "Java Man," was vehemently denounced by religious groups. Crushed, Dubois withdrew his specimens and thereafter ceased to work in the field of paleoanthropology. It was not until more than two decades later, with the discovery of similar fossils outside Peking in 1921, that he was eventually vindicated.

"Java Man" and "Peking Man" are now recognized as members of the species *Homo erectus*, a direct ancestor of man who inhabited the Old World from about 1.7 million until 250,000 years ago. The body skeleton of *Homo erectus* was essentially modern, but his skull was thick, long and low and he possessed a massive face with strongly protruding brow ridges. Many fossils of this type have been discovered in central Java since Dubois' time, some of which are more than a million years old. Replicas are on display at the Geological Museum in Bandung and the Sangiran site museum, outside Surakarta.

Recent research has shown that *Homo erectus* probably could not speak, but that he could utter sounds with which to communicate. He was an omnivore and a food gatherer who lived in caves as well as in open camp sites and was apparently the first creature to know the use of fire. He also produced an extensive stone tool kit that included flaked choppers, axes and hand-adzes. Thousands of stone tools dating from between 500,000 and 250,000 years ago have been collected from the bed of the Baksoka River near Pacitan, in south-central Java. Similar tools have also been found in Flores and Timor, which raises the intriguing possibility that *Homo erectus* may have spread to the eastern islands. Unfortunately these tools cannot be accurately dated.

Preceding pages: Legong dancer; contemporary dance; Balinese *kecak* dance; horsemen from Sumba; Borobudur; an oil rig in the South China Sea. Left, reconstructed skull of Java Man. Above, Central Javanese neolithic stone tools.

Modern Man

The classification of more recent hominoid fossils is still very much in doubt, particularly for the transitional species between *Homo erectus* and modern man. Central to the problem of classification is the question of whether modern man evolved in a single place (thought by some to be sub-Saharan Africa) and then spread to other areas, or whether parallel evolutions occurred in various places and at different rates.

Fossil records can be interpreted to support both views. In the Indonesian sphere, the controversy is centered around the dating and classification of the so-called "Solo Man" fossils discovered between 1931 and 1933 next to the Solo River at Ngandong, in central Java. Some scholars classify "Solo Man" as an intermediate species dating from perhaps 250,000 years ago, and claim him as evidence of a distinct Southeast-Asian evolutionary descent from *Homo erectus* to modern man. Others insist that "Solo Man" was simply an advanced *Homo erectus*" species who survived in isolation and then died out completely. More accurately dated discoveries will be needed to resolve the issue.

Fossil records of modern man (*Homo sapiens*) dating from as early as 60,000 years ago have been found in China and mainland Southeast Asia, and this compares favourably with the appearance of *Homo sapiens* in other parts of the world, though two imprecisely dated African fossils are said to be more than 90,000 years old. Modern man also inhabited Indonesia, New Guinea and Australia by about 40,000 years ago and perhaps even earlier.

All Southeast Asian *Homo sapiens* fossils prior to about 5,000 B.C. have been identified as members of the Australoid group of peoples who survive in isolated pockets in

Malaya and the Philippines today as the black-skinned, wiry-haired negritos. It is thought therefore that Australoid peoples were the original inhabitants of the entire region, and then were absorbed, driven to the uplands or pushed eastward by subsequent "waves" of Mongolian migration. According to this view, Australoid physical traits found today among the predominantly Mongolian populations of Indonesia, such as curly hair and dark skin, are evidence of an Australoid genetic contribution that becomes increasingly marked as one moves eastward in the archipelago.

From the little evidence we have it appears that early *Homo sapiens* continued and refined the flaked-stone tool-making industries of *Homo erectus*, also fashioning instruments of bone, shell and bamboo. They gathered and hunted, eating a great variety of fruits, plants, molluscs and animals, including tapirs, elephants, deer and rhinoceri. It seems that they were also cannibals, because crushed human bones have been found alongside discarded shells and animal debris. Beginning about 20,000 years ago, there is evidence of human burials and partial cremations; several cave paintings (mainly hand stencils but also human and animal figures) found in southwestern Sulawesi and New Guinea may be 10,000 or more years old.

The Neolithic or New Stone Age is characterized here as elsewhere by the advent of village settlements, domesticated animals, well into this century.

In southwestern Sulawesi and eastern Timor, plain pottery pots and open bowls dating from about 3000 B.C. have been found, together with shell bracelets, discs, beads, adzes, and the bones of pig and dog species that may well have been domesticated. Isolated Neolithic findings of incised and cord-marked pottery have been made in Sulawesi, Flores, Timor, Irian and Java, but well-dated Neolithic sequences are notably lacking, particularly in western Indonesia.

The first agriculturalists in Indonesia must have grown taro before the introduction of rice. In fact rice came to much of Indonesia only in recent centuries, and taro is still a staple crop on many eastern islands, together with bananas, yams, breadfruits,

polished stone tools, pottery and food cultivation. Its first appearance is everywhere being pushed back in time by new archaeological findings, but worldwide it appears to have begun soon after the end of the last ice age around 10,000 B.C. In northern Thailand, one recently discovered Neolithic site has been reliably placed in the seventh millennium B.C. For Indonesia, however, there is no evidence prior to the third millennium B.C. and most sites are of a more recent date. This situation is likely to change as new discoveries are made, but it must be remembered too that cultural development in such a geographically fragmented area was highly uneven, and that remote tribes in New Guinea were still living in the Stone Age coconuts and sugarcane. The dog, goat, buffalo, chicken and pig were all domesticated by the first millennium B.C., and most animals were probably slaughtered only for ritual sacrifices and communal feasts. Chicken entrails were employed for the art of augury, examined by a priest or shaman to determine auspicious dates for important undertakings such as a hunt or a marriage. Barkcloth clothing was produced with stone beaters, and pottery was shaped with the aid of a wooden paddle and a stone anvil tapper. Two major categories of stone adzes were

Above, an early 20th Century photograph records a surviving megalithic culture on Nias. Right, *Dong-son* bronze-age ceremonial drum.

known: quadrangular and round, and the remains of early workshops producing the former have been found in south Sumatra and Java.

Neolithic Indonesians were undoubtedly seafarers, like their Polynesian cousins who spread across the Pacific at this time. Nautical terms bear significant similarity throughout the Austronesian family of languages, and stylized boat motifs are depicted on early pottery and in early bronze reliefs, as well as on the houses and sacred textiles of primitive tribes. Today the outrigger is found throughout Indonesia and Oceania.

At the end of the Neolithic, megaliths (stone monuments) were constructed on many islands. These were variously places of worship or tombs, in the shape of dolmen,

however the discovery of 5000-year-old copper and bronze tools at Ban Chiang and Non Nok Tha in northern Thailand has raised the possibility of related developments elsewhere in the region. Nevertheless, all early Indonesian bronzes known to date are clearly of the *Dong-son* type and probably date from between 500 B.C. and 500 A.D.

The finest *Dong-son* ceremonial bronze drums and axes are distinctively decorated with engraved geometric, animal and human motifs. This decorative style was highly influential in many fields of Indonesian art, and seems to have spread together with the bronze casting technique, as old stone moulds have been found at various sites in Indonesia. The sophisticated "lost wax" technique of bronze casting was employed,

menhirs, terraced sanctuaries, stepped pyramids, spirit seats and ancestor statues. The most striking of these are the carved stone statues of men riding and wrestling animals, found on the Pasemah plateau in southern Sumatra. No definite date can be given for these and other megaliths, though it has been suggested that they are less than 2,000 years old. Stone-slab tomb megaliths are still being made on islands like Nias and Sumba.

The *Dong-son* Bronze Culture

It was once thought that Southeast Asia's Bronze Age began with the Chinese-influenced *Dong-son* bronze culture of North Vietnam in the first millennium B.C.,

and bronzes of this type have been recovered as far east as New Guinea and Roti.

Who were the Indonesian producers of *Dong-son* type bronzes? It is difficult to say for sure, but it seems that small kingdoms based on wet-rice agriculture and foreign trade flourished already in the archipelago during this period. Articles of Indian manufacture have been found at several prehistoric sites in Indonesia, and a panel from a bronze drum found on Sangeang Island near Sumbawa, depicts figures in ancient Chinese dress. Early Han texts mention the clove-producing islands of eastern Indonesia, and it is certain that by the second century B.C. (if not earlier), trade was widespread throughout the archipelago.

AN AGE OF EMPIRES

Beginning in the 2nd Century A.D., a number of highly sophisticated civilizations emerged in Southeast Asia—civilizations whose cosmology, literature, architecture and political organization were all closely patterned on Indian models. These kingdoms are best known for the wonderful monuments which they created: Borobudur, Prambanan, Angkor, Pagan and others, many of which were "rediscovered" in the 19th Century, and have now been visited by millions. Yet their creators remain largely an enigma. Who built these Indian monuments and how is it that Southeast Asians came to have such a profound knowledge of Indian culture in ancient times?

Part of our bewilderment is undoubtedly the product of a longstanding and erroneous conception of Southeast Asia as a prehistoric backwater. This view forced many earlier scholars to conclude that nothing short of massive Indian invasions and migrations to the region could have effected the sort of changes necessary for Indianized kingdoms to flourish as they did. The problem with this hypothesis is that there is absolutely no evidence to support it. Southeast Asia was actually a thriving trade and cultural centre in prehistoric times.

While the reality of the Indianization process was far more complex than will probably ever be known, the most recent and most plausible theory is that Southeast-Asian rulers Indianized their own kingdoms, either by employing Indian Brahmans or by sending their own people to India to acquire the necessary knowledge. The motivation for doing this is clear—Sanskrit writing and texts, along with sophisticated Indian ritual and architectural techniques, afforded a ruler greater organizational control, wealth and social status. It also enabled him to participate in an expanding Indian trading network.

Support for this hypothesis has come from detailed studies of Hindu period temples, which show that they not only employ many diverse Indian architectural and artistic styles in an eclectic fashion unknown in India, but that they also incorporate pre-Hindu indigenous design elements.

Left, Loro Jonggrang—the main Shiva temple of Prambanan. Erected by Rakai Pikatan in the 9th Century, it can be considered the Hindu counterpart of Buddhist Borobudur.

The First Indianized Kingdoms

Knowledge of the early Indonesian kingdoms of the Classical or Hindu period is very shadowy—gleaned solely from old stone inscriptions and vague references in ancient Chinese, Indian and Classical texts. The island of Java, for example, was mentioned in the *Ramayana* (as Yawadwipa) and in the *Almagest* of Ptolemy (as Yabadiou). However, the first specific references to Indonesian rulers and kingdoms are found in written Chinese sources and Sanskrit stone inscriptions dating from the early 5th Century.

The stone inscriptions (written in the south-Indian *Pallawa* script), were issued by Indonesian rulers in two different areas of the archipelago—Kutei on the eastern coast of Kalimantan, and Tarumanegara on the Citarum River in West Java (near Bogor). Both rulers were Hindus whose power seems to have derived from a combination of wet-rice agriculture and maritime trade.

Also, in the early 5th Century, there is the interesting figure of Fa Hsien, a Chinese Buddhist monk who journeyed to India to obtain Buddhist scriptures and was then shipwrecked on Java on his way home. In his memoirs (translated into English by James Legge as, *A Record of Buddhistic Kingdoms*), Fa Hsien noted that there were many Brahmans and heretics on Java, but that the Buddhist Dharma there was not worth mentioning. His comments highlight a fascinating feature of Indianized Indonesia—that while some early kingdoms were mainly Hindu, others were primarily Buddhist. As time went on the distinction became increasingly blurred.

Another fact of life for the Hinduized states of Indonesia was that their power depended greatly on control of the maritime trade. It appears that Tarumanegara in West Java first controlled the trade for two centuries or more, but that at the end of the 7th Century a new Buddhist kingdom based at Palembang took over the vital Malacca and Sunda Straits. This kingdom was Srivijaya and it ruled these seas throughout the next 600 years.

Srivijaya and the *P'o-ssu* Trade

The kingdom of Srivijaya left behind no magnificent temples or monuments because it was a thalassic (maritime) kingdom that relied for its existence not on agriculture, but on control of the trade. Most of its citizens were therefore sailors who lived on boats, as do many of the coastal Malay *orang laut* (sea people) today. Knowledge of Srivijaya is consequently very sketchy, and the kingdom was not even identified by scholars until 1918. Four stone inscriptions in Old Malay, several in Sanskrit and a handful of statues and bronze icons are all that remain of one of the most powerful maritime empires in history.

Prof. O.W. Wolters has speculated that Srivijaya rose to prominence as a result of a substitution of some Sumatran aromatics for expensive Middle Eastern frankincense and myrrh—the so-called *P'o-ssu* (Persian) goods then being shipped to China in great all over the world.

Though Srivijaya controlled all coastal ports on either side of the Malacca and Sunda straits (eastern Sumatra, western Java and the Malay peninsula), none of these areas was suitable for wet-rice agriculture. The nearest such area was in central Java, and from the early 8th Century onward, great Indianized kingdoms established themselves here. They first supplied Srivijaya with rice and later began to compete with her for a share of the maritime trade.

The Sailendras and the Sanjayas

From the beginning, a tension developed in central Java between competing Buddhist and Hindu ruling families. The first central-

quantities. Be that as it may, Srivijaya was also located in an extremely strategic position and is said to have developed large ships of between 400 and 600 tons. These were by far the largest ships in the world at this time, and they appear to have achieved regular direct sailings to India and China by at least the late 8th Century.

It is significant that the *P'o-ssu* trade consisted mainly of incense and other rare substances used by Buddhists in China. Srivijaya's rulers were also Buddhists, and a passing Chinese monk by the name of I-Ching stopped here for several months to study and copy Buddhist texts. There he found a thousand Buddhist monks and noted that it was a meeting place for traders from

Javanese temples and inscriptions, dating from 732 A.D., were the work of a Hindu ruler by the name of Sanjaya. Very soon thereafter, however, a Buddhist line of kings known as the Sailendras (Lords of the Mountain) seem to have come from the north coast of Java to impose their rule over Sanjaya and his descendants.

The Sailendras maintained close relations with Srivijaya (both rulers were Buddhists) and ruled Java for about 100 years. During this relatively short period they constructed

Above, from the mid 5th Century, inscription and footprints of Purnavarman—Hindu ruler of Tarumanegara in West Java. Right, temple relief from Borobudur.

22

the magnificent Buddhist monuments of Borobudur, Mendut, Kalasan, Sewu and many others in the shadow of majestic Mt. Merapi. Still today this area is blessed with unusually fertile soils, and already in ancient times it must have supported a vast population, who all participated in the erection of these state monuments.

The decline of the Sailendras began around 830 A.D. culminating with their ouster, in 856 A.D., by a descendant of Sanjaya. Apparently the Sanjayan line of kings ruled continuously over outlying areas of the realm as vassals of the Sailendras, and during this time they built many Hindu temples in remote areas of Java such as the Dieng Plateau and Mt. Ungaran (south of Semarang). Around 850

A succession of Hindu kings ruled in central Java, then suddenly the capital was transferred to east Java around 930 A.D. No satisfactory explanation has been given for this move, though a number of factors might account for it.

As mentioned before, the Sailendran kings, once installed at Srivijaya, were successful in shutting off the vital overseas trade from Java's north coast, and may even have been threatening to re-invade central Java. An eruption of Mt. Merapi at about this time may also have closed the roads to the north coastal ports and covered much of central Java in volcanic ash. A partially completed temple has been unearthed at Sambisar, near Prambanan, from under five metres of volcanic debris.

A.D., a prince of the Sanjaya dynasty, Rakai Pikatan, married a Sailendran princess and seized control of central Java. The Sailendras fled to Srivijaya, where they prospered and successfully blocked all Javanese shipping in the South China Sea for more than a century.

The Mysterious Move to East Java

Rakai Pikatan commemorated his victory by erecting the spendid temple complex at Prambanan, which can be considered a Hindu counterpart of Buddhist Borobudur. Both are terraced ancestor sanctuaries, highly elaborate versions of those constructed by Indonesian rulers in prehistoric times.

Then, too, there is the possibility of epidemics and of mass migrations to the more fertile lands of East Java.

Whatever the reason for the move, an eastern Javanese empire prospered in the 10th Century and actually attacked and occupied Srivijaya for two years 990–1A.D. Srivijaya retaliated a quarter of a century later with a huge seaborne force that destroyed the Javanese capital, killed the ruler King Dharmawangsa, and splintered the realm into numerous petty fiefdoms. It took nearly 20 years for the next great king, Airlangga, to fully restore the empire.

Airlangga was King Dharmawangsa's nephew and he succeeded to the throne in 1019 after the Srivijayan forces had departed. With the help of loyal followers and advisors he reconquered the realm and restored its prosperity. He is best known, though, as a patron of the arts and as an ascete. Under his rule the Indian classics were translated from Sanskrit into Javanese, thus marking the flowering of indigenous Javanese arts.

Shortly before his death in 1049, Airlangga changed his name and became an ascetic without, however, abdicating. To appease the ambitions of his two sons he then divided his empire into two equal halves, Kediri and Janggala (or Daha and Koripan). Kediri became the more powerful of the two, and it is remembered today as the source of numerous works of Old Javanese literature—mainly adaptations of

the Indian epics in a Javanese poetic form known as the *kekawin*.

Singhasari and Majapahit

In subsequent centuries Java prospered as never before. The rulers of successive east Javan empires were able to combine the benefits of a strong agricultural economy with income from a lucrative overseas trade. In the process, the Javanese became the master shipbuilders and mariners of Southeast Asia. During the 14th Century, at the height of the Majapahit Empire, they controlled the sea lanes throughout the Indonesian archipelago as well as to faraway India and China.

Despite this, our knowledge of the two great empires of the 13th and 14th centuries, Singhasari and Majapahit, would be very sparse were it not for two Old Javanese texts dating from the 14th Century. The first, the *Pararaton* (Book of Kings), tells of the founding of the Singhasari dynasty by Ken Arok in 1222.

Ken Arok was an adventurer who managed to marry the beautiful Ken Dedes (heir to the throne of Janggala) after murdering her husband. As ruler of Janggala he next revolted against his sovereign, the ruler of Kediri with the full support of the clergy, and set up his new capital at Singhasari, near present-day Malang.

The *Pararaton* goes on to tell of Ken Arok's successors, particularly of the last king of the Singhasari line, Kertanagara. He was eventually murdered in 1292 by the king of Kediri. Kertanagara was an extraordinary figure, a scholar as well as a statesman, who belonged to the Tantric Bhairawa sect of Buddhism. In 1275 and again in 1291 he sent successful naval expeditions against Srivijaya, thus wresting control of the increasingly important maritime trade.

So powerful did he become, in fact, that Kublai Khan, the Mongol emperor of China sent ambassadors to him to demand tribute. Kertanagara refused and disfigured the Chinese ambassador, a gesture which so enraged the great Khan that in 1293 he sent a powerful fleet to Java to avenge the insult. The fleet landed only to discover that Kertanagara had already died at the hands of Jayakatwang, one of his vassals.

The Chinese remained on Javanese soil for about a year, just long enough to defeat the murderous Jayakatwang. Battles raged back and forth across the Brantas valley for many months, eventually producing victory for Kertanagara's son-in-law, Wijaya, and his Chinese allies. In the end Wijaya entrapped the Mongol generals and chased the foreign troops back to their ships. The Chinese fleet returned to China, and its commanders were severely punished by the great Khan for their failure to subdue Java.

Wijaya married four of Kertanagara's daughters and established a new capital in 1294 on the bank of the Brantas River between Kediri and the sea (near present-day Trowulan). This was an area known for its *pahit* (bitter) maja fruits, and the new kingdom became known as Majapahit. The capital city was constructed entirely of red bricks, only the foundations of which now remain. Aerial photographs reveal that the city had an extensive system of canals and barges were probably used to transport rice and other trade goods down the river from Majapahit to the seaports at the mouth of the Brantas.

The Glory of Majapahit

Majapahit was the first empire to truly embrace the entire Indonesian archipelago. Later Javanese rulers, ancient and modern, have always looked upon this kingdom as their spiritual and political forerunner. Majapahit reached its zenith in the middle of the 14th Century under the rule of Wijaya's grandson Hayam Wuruk and his brilliant prime minister *Patih* Gajah Mada.

One of the most important passages concerns an oath taken by Gajah Mada (the so-called *sumpah palapa*) to bring all the major islands of the archipelago (the *Nusantara* or 'other islands'), under Majapahit's control. This is said to have been accomplished by Gajah Mada, but historians feel that the subjugation of Nusantara actually involved a kind of trading federation with Majapahit as the dominant partner.

Nevertheless, the trading ports of Sumatra as well as the Malay peninsula, Borneo, Sulawesi, Maluku and Bali all seem to have acknowledged Majapahit's sovereignty. Not until the end of the 19th Century was a comparable attempt made to unify these disparate areas under a single banner.

Knowledge of Majapahit comes partly from stone inscriptions found among hundreds of temple ruins discovered in the vicinity of the capital, but mainly from a panegyric poem written by the court poet Prapanca following the death of Gajah Mada in 1365. This text, known as the *Negarakertagama*, records all kinds of interesting details about the court and the royal family.

Left, a sculpture of Ken Dedes, the wife of Ken Arok, representing her as a goddess. Above, the so-called *wayang-kulit* style of temple sculpture of Candi Jago.

Majapahit's decline set in almost immediately after Hayam Wuruk's death in 1389. In a vain attempt to forestall the inevitable sibling conflict, Hayam Wuruk had divided his kingdom between his son and his daughter. However, a smouldering struggle for supremacy erupted into civil war between 1403 and 1406 and though the country was reunited in 1429, Majapahit had by this time lost control of the western Java Sea and the straits to a new Islamic power located at Malacca. Toward the end of the 15th Century, Majapahit and Kediri were conquered by the new Islamic state of Demak on Java's north coast, and it is said that the entire Hindu-Javanese aristocracy then fled to Bali.

ISLAM IN INDONESIA

Islam first arrived in the Indonesian archipelago not through a series of holy wars or armed rebellions, but rather on the coat-tails of a peaceful economic expansion along the major trade routes of the East. Although Muslim traders had visited the region for centuries, it was not until the important Indian trading centre of Gujarat fell into Muslim hands in the mid-13th Century that Indonesian rulers began to convert to the new faith. The trading ports of Samudra, Perlak and Pasai on the northeastern coast of Sumatra—ports that guarded the en-

trance to the economically strategic Straits of Malacca—became the first Islamic kingdoms in Indonesia. Marco Polo mentions that Perlak was already Muslim at the time of his visit in 1292, and the tombstone of the first Islamic ruler of Samudra, Sultan Malik al Saleh, bears the date 1297.

The dominant sect of Islam during this period was the mystical brotherhood of Sufism. The Sufis were peripatetic mediums and mystics who propagated charismatic traditions of ecstasy, asceticism, dance and poetry. Such teachings probably accorded well with the existing political and cultural climate of the Hinduized Indonesian courts—whose God-Kings, Brahmin gurus and Tibeto-Buddhist mystics had held sway for

many centuries. Perhaps for this reason, the arrival of Islam seems not to have disturbed the social and political structure of these courts, even though Islam, by stressing the equality of all men before God, would seem to be more egalitarian than the caste-oriented Indian religions that existed in many forms in Indonesia prior to this.

Trade and Islam

But conversion to Islam was not accomplished on the basis of faith alone—there were compelling worldly benefits to be obtained. Islamic traders were at this time becoming a dominant force on the international scene. They had controlled the overland trade from China and India to Europe via Persia and the Levant for some time, and with the major textile-producing ports of India in their hands, they began to dominate the maritime trade routes through South and East Asia as well. Conversion thus ensured that Indonesian rulers could participate in the growing international Islamic trade network. And equally importantly, it provided these rulers with protection against the encroachments of two aggressive regional powers, the Thais and the Javanese.

To clarify the process of Islamization in Indonesia, an understanding of the basic political and economic structure of the region at this time is necessary. In the pre-colonial period, there were essentially three important types of kingdoms: 1) the coastal (riverine) states around the Straits of Malacca that produced little food and few trade goods of their own but relied on trade and control of the seas for their existence; 2) the vast inland states on Java and Bali that produced surplusses of rice in irrigated paddies and possessed large manpower reserves; and 3) the tiny kingdoms on the eastern Maluku islands that produced valuable cloves, nutmegs and mace but little food.

All of these kingdoms imported some "luxury" goods from abroad—textiles and porcelains, precious metals, medicines, and gems, to name but a few. The coastal and spice-producing states also needed to import rice. And the trade was not only inter-

Left, tombstone of Sultan Malik al Saleh—the first Islamic monarch. Right, a page from a Koran in Aceh, Sumatra—for more than four centuries a powerful Muslim sultanate.

سورة الفاتحة

بسم الله الرحمن الرحيم

الحمد لله رب العالمين الرحمن

الرحيم مالك يوم الدين

إياك نعبد وإياك نستعين

اهدنا الصراط المستقيم صراط

الذين أنعمت عليهم غير المغضوب

عليهم ولا الضالين

روح اسل

insular, but involved foreigners as well—principally Indians and Chinese, but also Arabs, Siamese and Burmese.

Many of these trading patterns were the result of physical limitations on the trade itself. Sailing ships were at the mercy of the annual monsoon winds. Sea voyages to and from China or India could only be made once a year in each direction, so that certain ports came to serve as havens and trading emporiums where traders could gather to exchange their goods while waiting for the winds to shift.

Conversion of Malacca

Islam received its greatest boost when, in 1436, the shrewd ruler of the port of Malacca

capitalize upon the commercial successes of the Islamic world, while maintaining ties with other traders as well. By 1500, Malacca was to become the greatest emporium in the East, a city comparable in size to the largest European cities of the day.

During the 15th Century, all of the trading ports of the western archipelago were brought within Malacca's orbit. The most important of these were the ports along the north or *pesisir* coast of Java. Traditionally these ports owed their allegiance to the great inland Hindu-Javanese kingdoms, acting in effect as import-export and shipping agents, exchanging Javanese-grown rice for spices, silks, gold, textiles, medicines, gems and other items in a complex series of transactions which vastly increased the ori-

suddenly converted upon returning from an extended stay in China. Up to this time, Malacca had been a vassal of China—ruled by descendants of the prestigious Hindu line of Palembang (Srivijaya) and Singapore kings who had been attacked and evicted by the Javanese and the Thais during the 14th Century. China had proved a valuable patron of Malacca ever since its founding in 1402, but by 1436, China's influence in the region was on the wane, and the Thais were once again demanding tribute. By embracing Islam, the ruler of Malacca gained protection against Thai advances. And as a port ruled by a dynasty with a long-standing tradition of catering to overseas traders, Malacca was then in an excellent position to

ginal value of the goods. After about 1400, however, the power of the inland Javanese rulers was rapidly declining, and the rulers of the coastal cities were seeking ways to assert their independence and thereby retain more of the profits of the trade for themselves. Gradually, through intermarriage between leading Islamic traders and local aristocrats, relations were cemented with the Muslim world centred at Malacca.

Islam on Java

If Islamization at first occurred peacefully in the coastal kingdoms of Java, a turning point was reached sometime in the early 16th Century when the newly founded Islamic kingdom of Demak (on the north central coast) attacked and conquered the last great Hindu-Buddhist kingdom of Java. They drove the Hindu rulers to the east and annexed the agriculturally rich Javanese hinterlands. Demak then consolidated its control over the entire north coast by subduing Tuban, Gresik, Madura, Surabaya, Cirebon, Banten and Jayakarta—emerging as the master of Java by the 16th Century.

The traditional account of the Islamization of Java is quite different, but equally interesting. According to Javanese chronicles, nine Islamic saints—the so-called *wali sanga*, propagated Islam through the Javanese shadow play (*wayang kulit*) and *gamelan* music. They introduced the *kalimat shahadat* or Islamic confession of faith and the reading of Koranic prayers to performances of the Ramayana and Mahabarata epics. No better explanation could be given for the origins of Islamic syncretism in Java.

Islam in this period, was the faith of traders and urban dwellers, firmly entrenched in the maritime centres of the archipelago. Many of these towns were quite substantial; Malacca is estimated to have had a population of at least 100,000 in the 16th Century—as large as Paris, Venice and Naples but dwarfed by Peking and Edo (Tokyo) which then had roughly 1 million inhabitants each. Other cities in Indonesia were comparably large: Semarang had 2,000 houses; Jayakarta had an army of 4,000 men; Tuban was then a walled city with 30,000 inhabitants. Such statistics indicate that the urban population of Indonesia in the 16th Century at least equalled the agrarian population. Thus the typical Indonesian of that period was not a peasant as he is today, but a town dweller engaged as an artisan, sailor or a trader.

Indonesian cities were also physically different from cities in Europe, the Middle East, India or China. Built without walls for the most part, Indonesian cities were located at river mouths or on wide plains, and relied on surrounding villages for their defence. An official envoy from the Sultanate of Aceh (in north Sumatra) to the Ottoman empire, explained that Acehnese defences consisted not of walls, but of "stout hearts in fighting the enemy and a large number of elephants." Indonesian cities tended also to be very green. Coconut, banana and other fruit trees were everywhere, and most of the

widely spaced wooden or bamboo houses had vegetable gardens. The royal compound was the centre for defence and might have walls and a moat. With perhaps no more than 5 million people in the entire archipelago, land had no intrinsic value except what man made of it. Thus in 1613, when the English wanted some land to build a fortress in Makassar, they had to recompense the residents not for the space but for the coconut trees growing there (at the rate of half a Spanish dollar per tree).

During the 16th Century, Islam continued to spread throughout the Indonesian archipelago, but the whole system of Islamic economic and political alliances was swiftly overturned in the dramatic conquest of Malacca in 1511 by a small band of Portu-

guese. Though the Portuguese, as we shall see, were never able to control more than a portion of the total trade in the region, the capture of Malacca itself had far-reaching consequences. Never again was an Islamic state able to exert the sort of regional influence once exercised by Malacca. Instead, a number of competing Islamic centres vied with each other and with the Europeans for the trade, with the end result that the Dutch were eventually able to divide and conquer almost all of them.

The Islamic kingdom of Aceh, at the northern tip of Sumatra, was best situated to benefit from the fall of Malacca. Islamic traders resorted increasingly to Aceh's harbour after 1511, and a succession of aggres-

Left, print of the historic mosque at Banten—one of the towns subdued by the Islamic kingdom of Demak. Right, Muslim traders had a crucial role in the expansion of Islam.

sive Acehnese rulers slowly built an empire by conquering lesser ports all along the eastern coast of Sumatra. Although repeated attacks on Portuguese Malacca and Islamic Johor were unsuccessful, Aceh nevertheless established itself as the major seapower in the archipelago under the reign of Sultan Iskandar Muda (1607-36). The Acehnese remained powerful and fiercely independent long after that "Golden Age," resisting the Dutch right down into this century. Today Aceh is one of the most devoutly Muslim regions in Indonesia.

In Java during the second half of the 16th Century, the centre of power abruptly shifted from the north coast to an area of central Java near Borobudur, Prambanan and the other Hindu-Buddhist monuments

of many centuries earlier. The new kingdom was called Mataram, the name both of the area and the classical Javanese kingdoms once located here. Mataram first conquered Demak; the eastern half of Java and other north coastal ports were subdued by about 1625. Although the Mataram dynasty was Muslim, it patterned itself after the great Hindu-Javanese empires of previous centuries. Court chroniclers traced the lineage of the Mataram line to the *deva-rajas* of Majapahit rather than to the Islamic rulers of Demak. In fact, the fall of Majapahit to Demak was described in these chronicles as, "the disappearance of the Light of the Universe," a rather odd viewpoint for a Muslim writer who describes the demise of an infidel

kingdom at the hands of an Islamic saint! Clearly, identification with the prestigious Majapahit royal house was of greater importance than religious solidarity with the coastal powers. And indeed the Islam of the central Javanese courts became an extremely eccentric one—a potpourri of ancient mystical practices, European pomp and Islamic circumstance.

Islam came to the remaining islands of eastern Indonesia only sporadically. The trading port of Makassar, now the city of Ujung Pandang in south Sulawesi, became an important Islamic centre. It expanded rapidly towards the end of the 16th Century. It captured a substantial share of the eastern spice trade for several decades, until it was finally forced to submit to the Dutch in 1667. Makassar was very cosmopolitan, with kings and nobles who spoke Arab and Portuguese and were the patrons of scholars. Portuguese reports speak of the Islamic conversion of Makassar in the following way: undecided whether to adopt Islam or Christianity, the Makassarese sent emissaries to both Aceh and Portuguese Malacca to request that religious teachers be sent. The Acehnese, according to this account, simply arrived first.

In the Spice Islands of Maluku—Ternate, Tidore, Hitu, Ambon and Banda—most of the native rulers converted to Islam fairly early (in the 15th Century) and maintained close ties with first Malacca, then Makassar. However, in the 16th and 17th centuries these kingdoms were brutally conquered by a succession of European powers and those people who survived were then converted to Christianity.

On other islands, Jesuit missionaries arrived even before the Muslims, and together with later Dutch Calvinists established many Christian strongholds. Thus most peoples in the eastern archipelago are today either animist or predominantly Christian, and there is a sense in which Christianity put a stop to Islam's eastward advance in the 17th Century. The Philippines, for example, were colonized and actively converted to Catholicism by the Spanish, so that only a few southern islands ever became Islamic. However, in terms of numbers if not geographically, Islam continues to be a growing force throughout the archipelago, with over 80 per cent of Indonesians declaring themselves disciples of Mohammed.

Islam is today the driving force in Indonesian religious life. Left, worshippers in a mosque. Right, the Koran receiving this young man's studious attention.

ARRIVAL OF THE PORTUGUESE

When Portuguese vessels sailed into Indonesian waters in 1509, just 12 years after Vasco da Gama's pioneering voyage to India, Europeans were not wholly unknown in the archipelago. In fact a stream of European monks, adventurers and merchants had passed through Southeast Asian ports from the 13th Century onward.

The first Portuguese mission, four ships under the command of Diogo Lopes de Sequeira, ended in failure. Muslim merchants convinced the Sultan of Malacca that the newcomers posed a grave threat and de Se-

for much of the 16th Century. This was accomplished with fewer than 3,000 fighting men and despite debilitating epidemics, official corruption and a chronic shortage of ships! In Indonesia, however, after their initial successes, the Portuguese simply became one of several competing regional powers.

The conquest of Malacca in 1511 by Portuguese forces under Alfonso de Albuquerque was part of a carefully orchestrated plan to monopolize the spice trade and undermine Islamic influence in the East.

quiera was driven off. The Portuguese returned two years later, however, with more ships and men, and managed to pull off the greatest coup in Southeast Asian history—the capture of Malacca.

In the past, colonial historians have tended to view the Portuguese arrival as a major turning point in Indonesian history —as the beginning of a "modern" period. In fact, the Portuguese brought with them relatively little that was new. This is not to belittle their achievements—they conquered three major Asian entrepôts (Goa, Malacca and Hormuz) and established a chain of forty trading settlements within as many years, and then went on to dominate maritime commerce in the Indian Ocean

To this end, the Portuguese relied heavily on the sword—partly because they had been charged by the Pope to wage holy war against the infidels, but also because there was for them no other way to break open the tightly knit Muslim trading network. Not that the Portuguese possessed overwhelming military or technological superiority—in fact, Portugal was one of the smallest and most backward nations of Europe, and Europe and Asia were on roughly equal footing at this time. Their only material advantage was a number of

Above, Portuguese ships at Ternate. Near right. Alfonso de Albuquerque—conqueror of Malacca. Far right, St. Francis Xavier, who prostelytized in Indonesia for several years.

large oceangoing *carracks* fitted with many noisy but inaccurate cannon—the first floating artillery. The Malaccans, though, had firearms too, and vastly superior numbers. So it was Portuguese determination that decided the contest for Malacca; with only 1,200 men and 17 or 18 ships, de Albuquerque successfully stormed the largest and most prosperous trading port in Asia.

Though the Portuguese remained in control of Malacca until 1641, and also established numerous trading settlements in the Spice Islands of Maluku and in the lesser

The Portuguese legacy in Indonesia is therefore largely cultural rather than political or economic. Mixed Portuguese-Indonesian and Portuguese-Indian descendants of the original settlers formed separated communities in many coastal towns of Indonesia, and for two centuries or more, a creole form of Portuguese was the *lingua franca* of the archipelago. Many words of Portuguese origin found their way into Malay/Indonesian, such as *sepatu* (shoe), *pesta* (party), *sabun* (soap), *meja* (table) and *Minggu* (Sunday).

Sunda islands, they came under almost continual attack and were never able to obtain the desired monopoly in spices. Much of the spice trade passed through rival Muslim ports: Aceh, Johor, Banten, Demak, Jepara, Surabaya and Makassar. Malacca continued to prosper after 1511, but as a fortified waystation for Portuguese shipping rather than a gathering point for international traders. And with time, the Portuguese themselves slowly became more settled and less aggressive, until finally all their possessions except for one were overtaken by the Dutch and the English in the 17th Century. The single exception was Portuguese Timor, which like Macao remained a colony of Portugal into this century.

Of even greater import was the conversion of roughly 20,000 Indonesians to Catholicism during the 16th Century. Though these converts at first lived only in the shadow of Portuguese garrisons and many later switched to Protestantism under Dutch rule, the existence today of large Christian communities in Ambon, Flores and Timor may be traced to the efforts of a handful of early Portuguese missionaries. Foremost among them was Saint Francis Xavier (1506–52), a co-founder with Saint Ignatius Loyola of the Jesuit order. He visited Ambon in 1546–7, and though disgusted by the rapaciousness of Portuguese officials there, helped lay the foundations for what is today the largest Christian community in Indonesia.

THE DUTCH IN INDONESIA

The saga of the Dutch in Indonesia began in 1596, when four small Dutch vessels led by the incompetent and arrogant Cornelis de Houtman anchored in the roads of Banten, then the largest pepper-port in the archipelago. Repeatedly blown off course and racked by disease and dissension, the de Houtman expedition had been a disaster from the start. In Banten, the sea-weary Dutch crew went on a drinking binge and had to be chased back to their ships by order of an angry prince, who then refused to do business with such unruly *farang*. Hopping from

following year five consortiums dispatched a total of 22 ships to the Indies.

The Dutch East India Company

The Netherlands was at this time rapidly becoming the commercial centre of Northern Europe. Since the 15th Century, ports of the two Dutch coastal provinces, Holland and Zeeland, had served as entrepots for goods shipped to Germany and the Baltic states. Many Dutch merchants grew wealthy on this carrying trade, and following the out-

port-to-port down the north coast of Java, de Houtman wisely confined his sailors to their ships and managed to purchase some spices. But upon arriving in Bali, the entire crew jumped ship and it was some months before de Houtman could muster a quorum for the return voyage.

Arriving back in Holland in 1597 after an absence of two years, with only three lightly laden ships and a third of their crew, the de Houtman voyage was nonetheless hailed as a success. So dear were spices in Europe at this time, that the sale of her meagre cargos sufficed to cover all expenses and even produced a modest profit for the investors! This touched off a veritable fever of speculation in Dutch commercial circles, and in the

break of war with Spain in 1568, they began to expand their shipping fleets rapidly, so that by the 1590s they were trading directly with the Levant and Brazil.

Thus when a Dutchman published his itinerary to the East Indies in 1595-6, it occasioned the immediate dispatch of the de Houtman and later expeditions. Indeed, so keen was the interest in direct trade with the Indies, that all Dutch traders soon came to recognize the need for cooperation—to minimize competition and maximize profits.

Above, early Dutch expedition to Java. Right: Van Linschoten—author of the first "guide book" to the Indies; Jan Pieterszoon Coen, architect of Dutch empire in the East.

In 1602, therefore, they formed the United Dutch East India Company (known by its Dutch initials—VOC), one of the first joint-stock corporations in history. It was capitalized at more than 6 million guilders and empowered by the states-general to negotiate treaties, raise armies, build fortresses and wage war on behalf of the Netherlands in Asia.

The VOC's whole purpose and philosophy can be summed up in a single word—monopoly. Like the Portuguese before them, the Dutch dreamed of securing abso-

VOC operations, and promptly embarked on a series of military adventures that were to set the pattern for Dutch behaviour in the region.

The Founding of Batavia

Coen's first step was to establish a permanent headquarters at Jayakarta on the north-western coast of Java, close to the pepper-producing parts of Sumatra and the strategic Sunda Straits. In 1618, he sought and received permission from Prince Wijayakrama

lute control of the East Indies spice trade, which traditionally had passed through many Muslim and Mediterranean hands. The profits from such a trade were potentially enormous, in the order of several thousand per cent.

In its early years the VOC met with only limited success. Several trading posts were opened, and Ambon was taken from the Portuguese (in 1605), but Spanish and English, not to mention Muslim, competition kept spice prices high in Indonesia and low in Europe. Then in 1614, a young accountant by the name of Jan Pietieszoon Coen convinced the directors that only a more forceful policy would make the company profitable. Coen was given command of

of Jayakarta to expand the existing Dutch post, and proceeded to throw up a stone barricade mounted with cannon. The prince protested that fortifications were not provided for in their agreement and Coen responded by bombarding the palace thereby reducing it to rubble. A seige of the fledgling Dutch fortress ensued, in which the powerful Bantenese and a recently arrived English fleet joined the Jayakartans. Coen was not so easily beaten, however (his motto: "Never Dispair!"), and escaped to Ambon leaving a handful of his men in defence of the fort and its valuable contents.

Five months later, Coen returned to discover his men still in possession of their post. Though outnumbered 30-to-1 they had rather unwittingly played one foe against another by acceding to any and all demands, but were never actually required to surrender their position due to the mutual suspicion and timidity of the three attacking parties. Coen set his adversaries to flight in a series of dramatic attacks, undertaken with a small force of 1,000 men that included several score of fearsome Japanese mercenaries. The town of Jayakarta was razed to the ground and construction of a new Dutch town begun, eventually to include canals, drawbridges, docks, warehouses, barracks, a central square, a city hall and a church—all protected by a high stone wall and a moat—a copy, in short, of Amsterdam itself.

The only sour note in the proceedings

tionary force there, and within a few weeks rounded up and killed most of the 15,000 inhabitants on the islands. Three of the islands were then transformed into spice plantations managed by Dutch colonists and worked by slaves.

In the years that followed, the Dutch gradually tightened their grip on the spice trade. From their base at Ambon, they attempted to "negotiate" a monopoly in cloves with the rulers of Ternate and Tidore. But "leakages" continued to occur. Finally, in 1649, the Dutch began a series of yearly sweeps of the entire area, the infamous *hongi* (war-fleet) expeditions deislands other than Ambon and Ceram, where the Dutch were firmly established.

was struck by the revelation that during the darkest days of the seige, many of the Dutch defenders had behaved themselves in a most unseemly manner—drinking, singing and fornicating for several nights in succession. Worst of all, they had broken open the company storehouse and divided the contents up amongst themselves. Coen, a strict disciplinarian, ordered the immediate execution of those involved, and memories of the infamous siege soon faded—save one. The defenders had dubbed their fortress "Batavia," and the new name stuck.

Coen's next step was to secure control of the five tiny nutmeg- and mace-producing Banda Islands. In 1621, he led an expedi-

So successful were these expeditions, that half of the islanders starved for lack of trade, and the remaining half were reduced to abject poverty.

Still, the smuggling of cloves and clove trees continued. Traders obtained these and other goods at the new Islamic port of Makassar, in southern Sulawesi. The Dutch repeatedly blockaded Makassar and imposed treaties theoretically barring the Makassarese from trading with other nations, but were unable for many years to

Above, natives bring nutmegs for sale to a Dutch trading post at Banda Neira. Right, on the site of Jayakarta, the new town of Batavia had many of the features of Amsterdam.

enforce them. Finally, in 1669, following three years of bitter and bloody fighting, the Makassarese surrendered to superior Dutch and Buginese forces. The Dutch now placed their Bugis ally, Arung Palakka, in charge of Makassar. The bloodletting did not stop here, however, for Arung Palakka embarked on a reign of terror to extend his control over all of southern Sulawesi.

The Dutch in Java

By such nefarious means the Dutch had achieved effective control of the eastern archipelago and its lucrative spice trade by the end of the 17th Century. In the western half of the archipelago, however, they became increasingly embroiled in fruitless in-

back outside the walls in a last-ditch effort led by Governor-General Coen. The Javanese were not prepared for such resistance and withdrew for lack of provisions. A year later, in 1629, Sultan Agung sent an even larger force, estimated at 10,000 men, provisioned with huge stockpiles of rice for what threatened to be a protracted siege. Coen, however, learned of the location of the rice stockpiles and captured or destroyed them before the Javanese even arrived. Poorly led, starving and sick, the Javanese troops died by the thousands outside the walls of Batavia. Never again did Mataram pose a threat to the city.

Relations between the Dutch and the Javanese improved during the despotic reign of Amangkurat I (1646-77), one

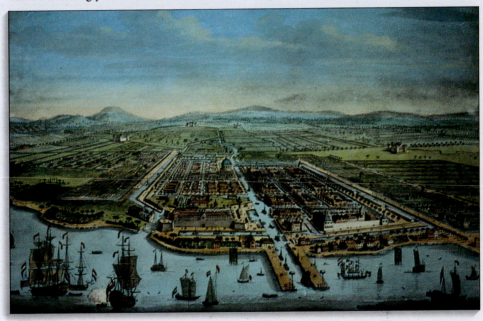

trigues and wars, particularly on Java. This came about largely because the Dutch presence at Batavia disturbed a delicate balance of power on Java.

As early as 1628, Batavia came under Javanese attack. Sultan Agung (1613-46), third and greatest ruler of the Mataram kingdom, was then aggressively expanding his domain and had recently concluded a successful five-year siege of Surabaya. He now controlled all of central and eastern Java, and next, he intended to take western Java by pushing the Dutch into the sea and then conquering Banten.

He nearly succeeded. A large Javanese expeditionary force momentarily breached Batavia's defences, but was then driven

reason being that they had common enemies—the *pesisir* trading kingdoms of the north Java coast.

It was ironic, then, that the Dutch conquest of Makassar later resulted, albeit indirectly, in the demise of their 'ally'.

The Makassar wars of 1666-69, and their aftermath, created a diaspora of Makassarese and Buginese refugees. Many of them fled to eastern Java, where they united under the leadership of a Madurese prince, Trunajaya. Aided and abetted by none other than the Mataram crown prince, Trunajaya successfully stormed through Central Java and plundered the Mataram capital in 1676-7. Amangkurat I died fleeing the enemy forces.

Once in control of Java, Trunajaya renounced his alliance with the young Mataram prince and declared himself king. Having no one else to turn to, the crown prince pleaded for Dutch support, promising to reimburse all military expenses and to award the Dutch valuable trade concessions. The bait was swallowed, and a costly campaign was promptly mounted to capture Trunajaya. This ended, in 1680, with the restoration of the crown prince, now styling himself Amangkurat II, to the throne.

But the new king was then in no position to fulfil his end of the bargain with the Dutch—his treasury had been looted and his kingdom was in ruin. All he had to offer was territory, and although he ceded much of western Java to the VOC, they still suf-

Chinese residents of Batavia, and ended 15 years later, only after many bloody battles, broken alliances and kaleidoscopic shifts of fortune had exhausted (or killed) almost everyone on the island. Indeed Java was never the same again, for by the 1755 Treaty of Giyanti, Mataram had been cleft in two, with rival rulers occupying neighbouring capitals in Yogyakarta and Surakarta. Nor did the VOC ever recover from this drain on its resources, even though it emerged at this time as the pre-eminent power on Java.

Daendels and Raffles

It is one of the great ironies of colonial history that to fully exploit their colony, the Dutch had to first lose their shirts. The

fered a heavy financial loss.

On December 31, 1799, Dutch financiers received stunning news—the VOC was bankrupt! During the 18th Century, the spice trade had become less profitable, while the military involvement in Java had grown increasingly costly—this at least is the broad outline of events leading to one of the largest commercial collapses in history.

It was a great war in Java (1740-55), however, which dealt the death blow to delicate Dutch finances. And once again, through a complex chain of events, it was the Dutch themselves who inadvertently precipitated the conflict. The details of the struggle are too convoluted to follow here, but it began in 1740 with the massacre of the

domination of Java—achieved at the expense of VOC bankruptcy—profited the Dutch handsomely in the 19th Century.

In the traumatic aftermath of the VOC bankruptcy, there was great indecision in Holland as to the course that should be steered in the Indies. In 1800, the Netherlands government assumed control of all former VOC possessions, now renamed Netherlands India, but for many years no one could figure out how to make them profitable. A number of factors, notably the Napoleonic Wars, compounded the confusion.

A new beginning of sorts was finally made under the iron rule of Governor-General Marshall Daendals (1808-11), a follower of

Napoleon who wrought numerous administrative reforms, rebuilt Batavia, and constructed a post road the length of Java.

The English interregnum—a brief period of English rule under Thomas Stamford Raffles (1811-16)—followed. Raffles was in many ways an extraordinary man: a brilliant scholar, naturalist, linguist, diplomat and strategist, "discoverer" of Borobudur and author of the monumental *History of Java*. In 1811, he planned and led the successful English invasion of Java, and was then placed in charge of its government at the tender age of 32. His active mind and free-trade philosophy led him to promulgate reforms almost daily, but the result was bureaucratic anarchy. Essentially, Raffles wanted to replace the old mercantilist sys-

Yogyakarta in 1812 led ultimately to the cataclysmic Java War of 1825-30.

From Carnage to 'Cultivation'

So numerous were the abuses leading to the Java War, and so great were the atrocities committed by the Dutch during it, that the Javanese leader, Pangeran Dipanagara (1785-1855), has been proclaimed a great hero even by Dutch historians. He was indeed a charismatic figure—crown prince, Muslim mystic and man of the people—who led a series of uprisings against the Dutch and his own ruling family. His guerilla rebellion might have succeeded but for a Dutch trick; lured to negotiate, Dipanagara was captured and exiled to Sulawesi. The cost of

tem (from which the colonial government derived its income through a monopoly on trade), by one in which income was derived from taxes, and trade was unrestrained. This enormous task was barely begun when the order came from London, following Napoleon's defeat at Waterloo in 1815, to restore the Indies to the Dutch. Raffles' legacy lived on, however. Many of his land taxes were eventually levied by the Dutch, and they in fact made possible the horrible exploitation of Java in later years. And his invasion of

Left, two 19th Century prints capture some of the adjuncts of colonialism. Above, the Dutch Army poses after a victory over Acehnese forces.

the conflict in human terms was staggering—200,000 Javanese and 8,000 Europeans lost their lives, many more from starvation and cholera than on the battlefield.

By this time, the Dutch were indeed in desperate economic straits. All efforts at reform had ended in disaster, to put it mildly, and the government debt had reached 30 million guilders! New ideas were sought, and in 1829, Johannes van den Bosch submitted a proposal to the crown for what he called a *Cultuurstelsel* or "Cultivation System" of fiscal administration in the colonies. His unoriginal notion was to levy a tax of 20 per cent (later raised to 33 per cent) on all land in Java, but to demand payment not in rice, but in labour or use of the land. This, he pointed out, would permit the Dutch to grow crops that they could sell in Europe.

Van den Bosch soon assumed control of Netherlands India, and in the estimation of many, his Cultivation System was an immediate, unqualified success. In the very first year, 1831, it produced a profit of 3 million guilders and within a decade, more than 22 million guilders were flowing annually into Dutch coffers, largely from the sale of coffee, but also from tea, sugar, indigo, quinine, copra, palm oil and rubber.

With the windfall profits received from the sale of Indonesian products during the rest of the 19th Century, almost a billion guilders in all, the Dutch not only retired their debt, but built new waterways, dikes, roads and a national railway system. Indeed, observers like Englishman J. B. Money, whose book *Java, Or How To Manage A Colony* (1861) was received in Holland with a great fanfare, concluded that the system provided a panacea for all colonial woes.

In reality, of course, the pernicious effects of the Cultivation System were apparent from the beginning. While in theory the system called for peasants to surrender only a portion of their land and labour, in practice certain lands were worked exclusively for the Dutch by forced labour. The island of Java, one of the richest pieces of real estate on earth, was thus transformed into a huge Dutch plantation. As noted by a succession of writers, beginning with Multatuli (*nom de plume* of a disillusioned Dutch colonial administrator, Douwes Dekker) and his celebrated novel *Max Havelaar* (1860), the system imposed unimagineable hardships and injustices upon the Javanese.

The long-range effects of the Cultivation System were equally insidious and are still being felt today. The opening up of new lands to cultivation and the ever-increasing Dutch demand for labour resulted in a population explosion on Java. From an estimated total of between 3 and 5 million in 1800 (a figure kept low, it is true, by frequent wars and famines), the population of Java grew to 26 million by 1900. Today the total has topped 110 million (on an island the size of New York State or England!), and the Malthusian time bomb is still ticking.

Another effect is what anthropologist Clifford Geertz has termed the "involution" of Javanese agriculture. Instead of encouraging the growth of an urban economy, as should have occurred under a free-market system, Javanese agricultural development only encouraged more agriculture, due to Dutch intervention. This eventually created a two-tier colonial economy in which the towns developed apart from the vast majority of rural peasants.

Rhetoric and Conquest

Though a great deal of acrimonious debate took place in Holland after 1860, and a few significant reforms were gradually instituted under the Liberal Policy of 1870, there was more rhetoric in the colonies than progress. True, peasants were paid wages for their labour and given legal titles to their land, but the wages were miniscule, taxes were high, and the land belonged to a few. Privately managed plantations largely replaced government ones after 1870, but in fact some government coffee plantations continued to employ forced labour well into the 20th Century.

Outside of Java, military campaigns were undertaken, throughout the 19th Century, to extend Dutch control over areas still ruled by native kings. The most bitter battles were fought against the powerful Islamic kingdom of Aceh, during a war which began in 1873 and lasted more than 30 years. Both sides sustained horrendous losses. In the earlier "Padri War" between the Dutch and the Minangkabau of west-central Sumatra (1821-38), the fighting was almost as bloody, as here too, the Dutch were pitted against Indonesians inspired by Islam. In the east, Flores and Sulawesi were repeatedly raided and finally subdued and occupied by about 1905-6. And the success of a renegade Englishman, James Brooke, in establishing a private empire in northwestern Borneo in the 1840s caused the Dutch to pay more attention to the southern and eastern coasts of that island thereafter. But the most shocking incidents occurred on Lombok and Bali, where on three occasions (1894, 1906 and 1908), Balinese rulers and their courtiers stormed headlong into Dutch gunfire armed only with ceremonial weapons—after ritualistically purifying themselves for a *puputan* (royal suicide) and avoiding the humiliation of defeat. In some ways, these tragic *puputans* symbolize the abrupt changes wrought by the Dutch at this time, for by the end of the first decade of this century they had achieved the unification of the entire Indonesian archipelago, at the expense of her indigenous kingdoms and rulers.

Right, Susuhunan Pakubuwana X of Surakarta poses with a Dutch administrator. Relations between the Dutch and natives frequently led to tragic conflicts however.

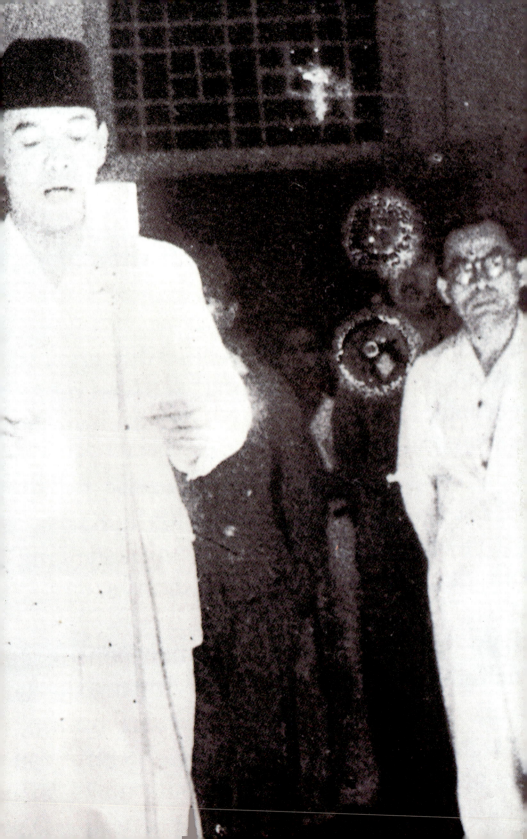

THE ROCKY ROAD TO INDEPENDENCE

At the beginning of the 20th Century, signs of change were everywhere in the Indies. Dutch military expeditions and private enterprises were making inroads into the hinterlands of Sumatra and the eastern islands. Steam shipping and the Suez Canal (opened in 1869) had brought Europe closer, and the European presence in Java was growing steadily. Gracious new shops, clubs, hotels and homes added an air of cosmopolitan elegance to the towns, while newspapers, factories, gas lighting, trains, tramways, electricity and automobiles receiving Dutch educations, and by the turn of the century came the remarkable figure of Raden Ajeng Kartini (1879-1904), the daughter of an enlightened Javanese aristocrat whose ardent yearnings for emancipation were articulated in a series of letters written in Dutch (now published in English as *Letters of a Javanese Princess*, with a foreword by Eleanor Roosevelt).

The irony is, from a Dutch point of view, that 19th Century European idealism provided much of the intellectual basis of Indonesian nationalism. As early as 1908, Indonesians

imparted a distinct feeling of modernity. Indeed, thousands of newly arrived Dutch immigrants were moved to remark on the extremely tolerable conditions that greeted them in the colonies—that is to say, it was just like home or even better.

But if Netherlands India was becoming increasingly Europeanized, elsewhere in Asia turn-of-the-century modernization was bringing with it a new spirit of nationalism—reflected in the Meiji Restoration and the Japanese victory over Russia (1898), the revolution in China (1911) and the Chulalongkorn reforms in Thailand (1873-1910).

In the Indies, nationalism was slow in developing, but just as inevitable. A small but growing number of Indonesians were attending Dutch schools began to form a number of regional student organizations dedicated to the betterment of their fellows. Though small, aristocratic and extremely idealistic, such organizations nonetheless spawned an elite group of leaders and provided forums in which a new national consciousness was to take shape.

A National Awakening

In 1928, at the second all-Indies student conference, the important concept of a single Indonesian nation (one people, one language, one nation) was proclaimed in the so-called *sumpah pemuda* (youth pledge). The nationalism and idealism of these students later spread in the print media and through the non-government schools. By the 1930s as many as 130,000 pupils were enrolled in these "wild" (i.e. non-government) Dutch and Malay-medium schools—twice the total attending government schools.

The colonial authorities watched the formation of the Dutch-educated urban elite with some concern. Two political movements of the day provided much greater cause for alarm, however. The first and most important of these was the pan-Islamic movement which had its roots in the

came to see in the Islamic movement some hope of relief from oppressive economic conditions.

The Indonesian communist movement was also founded around 1910 by small groups of Dutch and Indonesian radicals. It soon moved to embrace both Islam and international communism. Many of its leaders gained control of local Islamic workers' unions and frequently spoke at Islamic rallies, but after the Russian revolution of 1917, also maintained ties with the Comintern and increasingly espoused

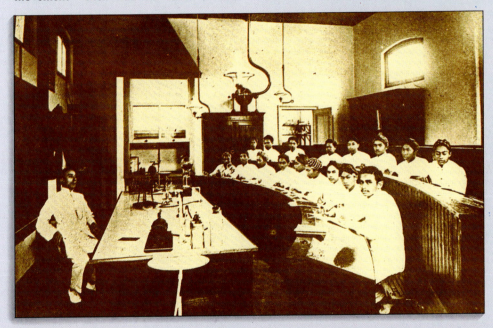

steady and growing stream of pilgrims visiting Mecca from the mid-19th Century onwards, and in the religious teachings of the *ulama* (Arabic scholars). What began in Java in 1909 as a small Islamic traders association (*Sarekat Dagang Islamiyah*) soon turned into a national confederation of Islamic labour unions (*Sarekat Islam*) which claimed 2 million members in 1919. Rallies were held, sometimes attracting as many as 50,000 people, and many peasants

Marxist-Leninist doctrine.

The period from 1910 to 1930 was a turbulent one. Strikes frequently erupted into violence, and while at first the colonial government took a liberal view of these rebellious activities, many Indonesian leaders were eventually arrested and moderate Muslim leaders soon disassociated themselves from political activities. The rank-and-file deserted their unions, and while the communists fought on for several years, staging a series of poorly organized local rebellions in Java and Sumatra up through 1927, they too were crushed.

Leadership of the anti-colonial movement then reverted to the student elite. In 1927, a recently graduated engineer by the

Preceding pages, Sukarno reads the declaration of independence. Left, members of a Dutch household. Opposition to the Dutch found a voice in groups such as these medical students, above.

name of Sukarno, together with his Bandung Study Club, founded the first major political party with Indonesian independence as its goal. Within two years his so-called *Partai Nasional Indonesia* (PNI) had over 10,000 members, due in large part to Sukarno's gifted oratory. Shortly thereafter, Sukarno was arrested for "openly treasonous statements against the state." Though publicly tried (in Bandung) and then imprisoned, he was later released. A general crackdown ensued and after 1933, Sukarno and all other student leaders were exiled to distant islands where they remained for almost ten years. Ringing in their ears as they were sent off was the statement by then Governor-General de Jonge that the Dutch had "been here for 350 years with stick

this as a liberation from Dutch rule.

The immediate effect of the Japanese invasion of Java in January, 1942 was to show that Dutch military might was basically a bluff. The Japanese encountered little resistance and within just a few weeks they rounded up all Europeans and placed them in concentration camps. Initially there was jubilation, but it immediately became apparent that the Japanese had come to exploit the Indies not to free them.

Throughout the occupation all imports were cut off and Japanese rice requisitions steadily increased, creating famines and sparking peasant uprisings which were then ruthlessly put down by the dreaded *Kempeitai* or Japanese secret police.

and sword and will remain here for another 350 years with stick and sword." The flower of secular nationalism, it would seem, had been effectively nipped in the bud.

The Japanese Occupation

There was a king of 12th Century Java, Jayabaya by name, who had prophesied that despotic white men would one day rule but that following the arrival of yellow men from the north (who would remain just as long as it takes the maize to ripen), Java would be freed forever of foreign oppressors and would enter a millennial golden age. When the Japanese invasion came, it is not suprising that many Indonesians interpreted

Still, the Japanese found it necessary to rely on Indonesians and to promote a sense of Indonesian nationhood in order to extract their desired war material Indonesians were placed in many key positions previously held by Dutchmen. The use of the Dutch language was banned and replaced by Indonesian. And nationalist leaders were freed and encouraged to cooperate with the Japanese, which most of them did. All these factors contributed to a growing sense of Indonesian confidence.

Left and right, the movement for independence spawned marches and gatherings. Despite Dutch intentions to return to Indonesia after the Japanese defeat, independence came in 1950.

When it eventually became apparent, in late 1944, that Japan was losing the war, the Japanese began to promise independence in an attempt to maintain faltering Indonesian support. Nationalist slogans were encouraged, the nationalist anthem (*Indonesia Raya*) was played, the Indonesian "Red and White" flew next to the "Rising Sun," Indonesian leaders were brought together for discussions and close to 200,000 young people were hurriedly mobilized into para-military groups. By this point there was clearly no chance of turning back.

Revolution: 1945-50

On Aug. 9, 1945, the day the second atomic bomb was dropped, three Indonesian

fire and millions of Indonesians enthusiastically echoed the call for *merdeka*! The Dutch eventually returned, but Holland was at this time in a shambles and world opinion was against them.

The nationalist leaders, too, were hesitant and divided, awed by the swift course of events and undecided whether to press for full victory or negotiate a compromise. The ensuing struggle was thus a strange combination of bitter fighting, punctuated by calm diplomacy.

In the end, heroic sacrifices on the battlefield by tens of thousands of Indonesian youths placed the Dutch in an untenable position. Three Dutch "police actions" gave the returning colonial forces control

leaders were flown to Saigon to meet with the Japanese Commander for Southeast Asia, Marshal Terauchi. The marshal promised them independence for all the former Dutch possessions in Asia and appointed Sukarno chairman of the preparatory committee with Mohammed Hatta as vice-chairman. They arrived back in Jakarta on August 14th and the very next day Japan surrendered unconditionally to the Allies. Following two days of debate, Sukarno and Hatta were persuaded to proclaim *merdeka* (independence) on August 17th and the long process of constructing a government was begun.

The following months were chaotic. News of the Japanese surrender spread like wild-

of the cities, but each time the ragtag Indonesian army valiantly fought back, and to all foreign observers it became clear that the revolution would drag on for years if a political solution were not achieved.

Finally in January, 1949, the United States halted the transfer of Marshall Plan funds to the Netherlands and the UN Security Council ordered the Dutch to withdraw their forces and negotiate a settlement. This done, Dutch influence in Indonesia rapidly crumbled, and on Aug. 17, 1950—the fifth anniversary of the *merdeka* proclamation—all previous governments and agreements were unilaterally swept away by the new government of the Republic of Indonesia.

INDONESIA SINCE INDEPENDENCE

Euphoria swept through the cities and towns of Indonesia following the withdrawal of Dutch forces and the secural of Indonesian sovereignty. Mass rallies and processions were held; flag-waving crowds thronged the streets shouting the magical words: "*Merdeka, merdeka!*" (Freedom, freedom!). Independence had come at last, and though many obstacles remained, Indonesians felt that nothing was impossible now that they held their destiny in their own hands.

Meanwhile, in Jakarta, the slow and called for a system of government in which a variety of interests could be represented. Largely due to the high profile of Dutch-educated intellectuals among the nationalists, a western-style parliamentary system of government was adopted.

From the beginning, however, the existence of more than 30 rival parties paralysed the system. A string of weak coalition cabinets rose and fell at the rate of almost one a year, and attempts at cooperation were increasingly stymied not only by a growing ideological polarization, but also by

arduous process of constructing a peacetime government had begun. And while the unifying power of the revolution had done much to forge a coherent state, the fact of Indonesia's remarkable ethnic, religious and ideological diversity remained. Moreover, massive economic and social problems faced the new nation—a legacy of colonialism and war. Factories and plantations were shut down, capital and skilled personnel were scarce, rice production was insufficient to meet demand, the Indonesian people were overwhelmingly poor and illiterate, and the population was growing at an unprecedented rate.

The inability of any single political group to effectively dominate all others clearly religous and regional loyalties. Parties became more and more preoccupied with ensuring their own survival and less and less attentive toward the nation's pressing economic and social needs, frustrating those who wished to see the revolution produce more tangible results. Most impatient of all were Sukarno, whose powers as President had been limited by the provisional constitution of 1950, and the army leadership, who felt that their key role during the revolution entitled them to a greater political say

A series of uprisings by disaffected groups in Sumatra, North Sulawesi and West Java in the late 1950s gave them their cue. The ever-popular Sukarno declared martial law and gave the army a free hand to crush the rebels. By 1959, with the rebellions under control, Sukarno resurrected the "revolutionary" constitution of 1945 and declared the beginning of Guided Democracy.

"Guided Democracy": 1959-65

Under the new political system, power was focused in the hands of the President and the army leadership, at the expense of political parties, whom Sukarno now regarded as counter-revolutionary. Militant nationalism became Sukarno's new recipe

In the early 1960s Sukarno's anti-colonial sentiments took a more militant turn. A long and successful campaign to wrest control of western New Guinea from the Dutch was followed closely by military confrontation with newly independent Malaysia, in 1963. Sukarno's audacity and growing contempt for the United States ("To hell with your aid!" he told the Americans) earned him the reputation of *enfant terrible* among Asian leaders.

Sukarno's nationalistic élan was in some ways just what Indonesia needed. Many

for national integration, and the blame for all sorts of economic and political problems was placed squarely at the feet of foreign imperialism and colonialism. In the international arena, Sukarno had, in 1955, made a significant impact by convening the Asia-Africa Conference in Bandung. Attended by leaders such as Chou En-lai, Nehru and Nassar, the conference led to the formation of a non-aligned movement and placed Indonesia in the forefront among emergent Third World nations.

Above, Jakarta's Gunung Sahara Street in the early fifties, a time of national reconstruction. Sukarno (centre) with his first cabinet, of which Hatta (right of Sukarno) was vice-president.

Indonesians saw in him a kind of father figure—a natural leader who offered a vision of a strong and independent Indonesia not seen since the 14th Century, during the reign of the powerful empire of Majapahit.

Yet Sukarno's reliance on his charisma, and his lack of attention to day-to-day administration created a vacuum in which the government and the nation floundered. While Sukarno attempted to offset the growing influence of the military by identifying himself more closely with the most active of the civilian parties, the communist PKI, the nation's economy ground to a halt. Foreign investment fled, deficits left the government bankrupt and inflation skyrocketed to an annual rate of 680 per cent. By 1965, the year that Sukarno christened, "The Year of Living Dangerously," social, cultural and political ferment was intense.

The 1965 Coup

The political tinderbox was ignited in the early hours of Oct. 1, 1965 when, with the apparent encouragement of the PKI, a group of radical young army officers kidnapped and brutally executed six leading generals, claiming that they were plotting against the President. Failing to gain Sukarno's backing, however, the rebel officers soon lost the initiative to General Suharto, then head of the elite Army Strategic Reserve. In the space of a few hours, Suharto moved to assume command of the army and to crush

broke out between the army, supported by students, intellectuals, Muslims and other middle-class groups on the one hand, and Sukarno, with his considerable populist/nationalist following on the other. Finally on March 11th, 1966, Sukarno was persuaded to sign a document bestowing wide powers on General Suharto.

Although Suharto was not formally installed as Indonesia's second president until 1968, immediate reforms were carried out under his direction. Martial law was declared and order was restored. The communist party and all Marxist-Leninist teachings were outlawed. The civil administration was radically restructured and restaffed by military personnel. A major realignment in foreign policy restored relations

the attempted coup.

The nation was shocked by news of the generals' execution, and, although the exact extent to which PKI leaders were involved is still not clear, the communists were charged with attempting to overthrow the government. A state of anarchy ensued, in which moderate, Muslim and army elements sought to settle the score. Thousands upon thousands were killed as long-simmering frustrations erupted into mob violence first in northern Sumarta, then later in Java, Bali and Lombok. The bloodletting continued for months, and the period 1965-66 is remembered today as the darkest in the Republic's history.

Meanwhile, in Jakarta, a political struggle

with the United States and the West, while severing ties with China and the Soviet Union.

Economic 'New Order'

Building its political legitimacy upon promises to revive the moribund Indonesian economy, the new Suharto administration wasted no time in addressing the fundamental problems of inflation and stagnation. American-trained economists were called upon to oversee the rapid reintegration of Indonesia into the world economy, and in a short space of time, foreign investment laws were liberalized, monetary controls were imposed, and western aid was sought and received to replenish the nation's exhausted foreign exchange reserves. These measures formed the cornerstones of Suharto's economic "new order," and served to dramatically curb inflation and to set the nation on a course of rapid economic growth by the early 1970s.

Indonesia's first five-year plan, *Repelita I*, was designed to encourage growth by attracting foreign investment. Most of the targets of the plan were achieved—a first wave of investors moved in to take advantage of Indonesia's vast natural reserves of copper, tin, timber and oil, setting up facilities to extract these raw materials in Sumatra, Sulawesi, Kalimantan and Irian Jaya.

As the political stability of the region seemed more assured, a second wave of

where a black viscous substance lay thick across the water. The discovery soon led to the formation of Royal Dutch Shell Company, and eventually to the establishment of Indonesia as the world's fifth largest OPEC producer.

From a total of US$323 million in 1966, oil exports rose to US$5.2 billion in 1974, largely due to the steep OPEC price hikes of the early 1970s. Today oil has come to account for roughly 60 per cent of the state's total revenues, and the flood of petrodollars has been used to fund not only a number of capital works programmes but also a significant upgrading of the nation's huge civil service. The most impressive advances have been in education, particularly at the primary level. Between 1972 and 1978, no less

investors, largely Japanese and local Chinese, set up a wide variety of urban-based manufacturing industries. By 1975, textile manufacturing alone accounted for US$708 million worth of investments, and the economy was rocketing.

By far the greatest benefits, however, came from oil. The story began in northern Sumatra in 1883 when a Dutch planter took shelter from a storm in a native shed and noticed a wet torch burning brightly. Inquiring about this, he was led to a nearby spring

Left, Nehru (left) standing with Sukarno (right) during a state visit of 1957. Right, Sukarno reads a statement to the press handing over power, while his successor Suharto looks on.

than 26,677 primary schools were built, bringing the percentage of children enrolled from 69 to 84. Primary school teachers today account for roughly a third of the nation's 2.3 million government employees.

Indonesia's civil service though is not without its problems. Despite 100 per cent across-the-board wage hikes in the early 1970s, pay levels remain low. In 1983, over 70 per cent of civil servants were receiving less than US$20 per week. Inefficiency and corruption are the result, compounding a serious lack of expertise and training. Only 26 per cent of all government employees (including teachers) have more than a junior high school education.

A different sort of problem arose within

the government body responsible for the oil bonanza, the State Oil and Natural Gas Corporation, Pertamina. In the early 1970s, under the direction of Colonel Ibnu Sutowo, Pertamina poured huge sums of money into projects intended to reduce Indonesia's dependence on foreign technology and imports. These included a floating fertilizer plant to be anchored over offshore gas fields, the massive Krakatau steel mill in West Java, a three-million-ton tanker fleet, petrochemical and refining plants, as well as several non-industrial projects such as a first-class hospital, a sports stadium, a chain of hotels, an airline and a golf course.

Ibnu Sutowo's flamboyant spending came to an abrupt halt in 1975, when Pertamina announced that it was defaulting on one of

its foreign bank loans. Sutowo, it turned out, had recklessly borrowed money that he had no chance of repaying, clocking up over $10 billion in foreign debts in the process! In the end, the Indonesian government was saddled with one of the largest peacetime losses any country has ever suffered, and many industrial projects had to be scrapped or rescheduled.

Peace and Progress

Despite these and other problems, the 1970s and early 1980s have been characterized by relative political stability. The tenor of the Suharto regime and its supporters is well caught by the slogan, "Development

yes, politics no!" Opposition political parties have been restricted and closely supervised, managing to poll only 40 per cent in the 1971 election and even less in 1977 and 1982. The big winner, meanwhile, has been the government's political "functional" group, *Golkar*, consisting of representatives chosen from various professional, religious, ethnic and military constituencies.

Yet politics refused to go away entirely. A proposed secular marriage law brought an angry response from Indonesia's Muslim majority in 1973 and had to be dropped. And pressure has mounted for the government to provide for a greater distribution of the wealth and benefits of economic growth, to curb the level of foreign debt, to contain inflation and to eradicate corruption. Frustration, particularly over economic matters, has erupted in the past, notably on the occasion of Japanese Prime Minister Tanaka's visit to Jakarta in 1974, when the capital was rocked by two days of violent student demonstrations.

Among the influential middle class, however, opposition has been muted by the very prosperity the "New Order" has helped to generate. Most Indonesians consider themselves better off today than ever before—there are far more cassette players, motorbikes, cars, telephones, televisions and other consumer goods around than there have ever been.

Striking advances have also been made in the vital areas of population control and agriculture. In 1980, Indonesia's population was counted at 147 million. Java and Bali are the most seriously overcrowded islands, representing only seven per cent of Indonesia's total land area, while housing two thirds of her people—equivalent to the entire population of the United States occupying the state of California.

The government first attempted to ease the pressure with transmigration—the resettlement of Javanese and Balinese villagers to the sparsely populated islands of Sumatra, Kalimantan and Sulawesi. Transmigration has proved slow and costly, though, and since 1970 has been complemented by an intensive family planning campaign, that has managed to reduce the birth rate from over two per cent to around 1.8 per cent per annum.

Directly linked to the population situation is the challenge of food production. The

Left, in Jakarta, the monument commemorating the "liberation" of Irian Jaya. Right, early oil exploration in Sumatra—where Indonesia's vital oil revenue originated.

highest priority has been given to rice, Indonesia's staple food. The introduction of new high-yield plant strains, multiple croppings, better irrigation, chemical fertilizers and pesticides has resulted in a spectacular 50 per cent increase in rice production between 1974 and 1984. A government rice stockpiling and distribution network has also reduced the threat of famine, stabilized prices and provided credits and subsidies to farmers.

The problem has not yet been solved, however. Bad weather and insect infestations caused serious shortfalls in 1977, forcing Indonesia to import one third of the world's surplus rice. Since then, the introduction of a new pest-resistant rice strain and further intensification has raised aver-

imports in 1981, increased cultivation and higher price incentives reduced the figure to US$261 million in 1982 and Indonesia is now a nett exporter of sugar.

On the intensely cultivated island of Java, it is estimated that only a quarter of the population own land. And as the population expands, so agriculture absorbs a progressively smaller percentage of the total labour force. In 1960 the figure was over 75 per cent, while today only about 55 per cent of Javanese are engaged in food production. This has created a massive unemployment problem, in which millions of landless labourers have moved into the cities to seek work.

Some of these migrants have been absorbed into the budding manufacturing sector. Yet despite the priority afforded the

age yields by 21 per cent, making Indonesia virtually self-sufficient in rice. Whether levels of production can keep pace with the rapidly increasing demand is the central question. The weather, of course, remains a key variable, though increased irrigation is reducing some of the uncertainty.

Other food and export crops have not fared so well. Production of vital crops such as rubber, copra, peanuts, oil palms, soybeans, cassava and maize has remained virtually stagnant over the past decade, and in some cases has actually declined. Sugar has been the notable exception, and is a possible model for future governmental intervention in other areas. Whereas Indonesia spent US$700 million on sugar

development of an urban industrial base in the government's second five-year plan, *Repelita II,* job opportunities in industry have not managed to keep pace with a labour force that is growing by 1.4 million a year. As a result, these young people lead a hand-to-mouth existence in the cities—driving pedicabs, peddling noodles and fried bananas, selling cigarettes, shining shoes and scavenging from garbage dumps. Their plight represents one of the major challenges facing Indonesia today.

Above and right, as the world's fifth largest OPEC producer, the nation's economy is heavily dependent on oil. Indonesia is also the world's top exporter of natural gas.

Unfortunately, the world economic recession and oil glut of the early 1980s has created financial circumstances which have temporarily pushed all other problems to the rear. Indonesia has recently been forced to cut back oil production and to reduce prices significantly. The resulting drop in oil revenues exacerbated by the declining value of other key exports and reductions in foreign industrial investment, has led to a critical shortage of foreign exchange and a drop in the economic growth rate to only two per cent in 1982.

The guiding principles of the government's present economic strategy are export promotion and import substitution—selling more abroad and importing less. Oil refining is one area in which significant advances

In the realm of exports, Indonesia's most promising source of revenue is natural gas. Massive reserves totalling over 73 trillion cubic metres were discovered in east Kalimantan and in Aceh, northern Sumatra, in 1971. Since then, liquid natural gas (LNG) plants have been set into operation at both sites, and Indonesia now ranks as the world's number one exporter of LNG, with 1982 revenues of over US$2.6 billion.

Yet another industrial priority has been cement production. In the past decade the number of plants has more than trebled, and production has risen twelvefold.

Indonesia's other manufacturing industries are more embryonic. Almost 90 per cent of those employed in this sector work in small-scale cottage industries, producing

have been made towards the goal of self-sufficiency. Indonesia now boasts eight state-run refineries, the largest of which are in central Java and east Kalimantan, and refining capacity is now supplying all of the domestic demand for kerosene and gasolene.

Significant savings have also been realized through domestic fertilizer production. Indonesia's first plant was opened at Palembang, South Sumatra, in 1964 with a capacity of 100,000 tons per year. Fed by abundant supplies of local natural gas, the state-owned plant has over the years developed into the world's largest urea-producing complex, now turning out more than 1.6 million tons a year.

basic items such as salt, coconut oil and furniture. Larger factories more dependent upon imported machinery and capital have had some success in supplying consumer goods for the local market in recent years. In 1982, for example, Indonesia produced 847,000 television sets, assembled 210,000 cars and trucks and over half-a-million motorbikes.

The government has pinned its future hopes on labour-intensive, export-oriented manufacturing and they are predicting an industrial "take-off" for Indonesia during the latter half of the 1980s. It is hoped that this will provide jobs and prosperity for a population that is expected to reach 212 million by the year 2,000.

THE MIGHTIEST ARCHIPELAGO

The Indonesian archipelago is by far the world's largest—13,677 islands strewn across 5,120 kms (3,200 miles) of tropical seas. When superimposed on a map of North America, this means that Indonesia stretches from Oregon all the way to Bermuda. On a map of Europe, the archipelago extends from Ireland past the Caspian Sea.

Of course, four-fifths of the intervening area is occupied by ocean, and many of the islands are tiny, no more than rocky outcrops populated, perhaps, by a few seabirds. But 3,000 Indonesian islands are large enough to be inhabited, and New Guinea and Borneo rank as the second and third largest in the world (after Greenland). Of the other major islands, Sumatra is slightly larger than Sweden or California; Sulawesi is roughly the size of Great Britain, and Java alone is as large as England or New York State. With a total land area of 2.02 million sq kms (780,000 sq miles), Indonesia is the world's fourteenth largest political unit.

Befitting its reputation as the celebrated Spice Islands of the East, this archipelago also constitutes one of the most diverse and biologically fascinating corners of our planet. Unique geologic and climatic conditions have created spectacularly varied tropical habitats—from the exceptionally fertile ricelands of Java and Bali to the luxuriant rainforests of Sumatra, Kalimantan, Sulawesi and Maluku, to the savannah grasslands of Nusa Tenggara and the snow-capped peaks of Irian. Found here are an amazing variety of spice, aromatic had hardwood trees (clove, nutmeg, sandalwood, camphor, ebony, ironwood and teak, among others), many unusual fruits (durian, rambutan, lengkeng, salak, blimbing, nangka, manggis, jambu), the world's largest flower (the *Rafflesia*), the largest lizard (Komodo's monitor), many rare animal species found nowhere else (like the orangutan, the Javan rhinoceros and the Sulawesian *anoa*—a dwarf buffalo), thousands of varieties of butterflies and wild orchids, and many exquisite plumage birds—like the cockatoo and the bird of paradise.

The geological history of the region is

complex. All of the islands are relatively young; the earliest dates only from the end of the Miocene, 15 million years ago—just yesterday on the geological time scale. Since that time, the whole archipelago has been the scene of violent tectonic activity, as islands were torn from jostling supercontinents or pushed up by colliding oceanic plates, and then enlarged in earth-wrenching volcanic explosions. The process continues today—Australia is drifting slowly northward, as the immense Pacific plate presses south and west to meet it and

the Asian mainland. The islands of Indonesia lie along the lines of impact, a fact that is reflected in their geography and in the great seismic instability of the region.

The islands fall into three main categories. Firstly, the large islands of western Indonesia: Sumatra, Kalimantan (Borneo) and Java, together with several smaller adjacent ones (the Riau chain, Bangka, Billiton, Madura and Bali) all rest on the broad Sunda continental shelf that extends down from the Southeast-Asian mainland. The intervening Java Sea is thus very shallow, no more than 100 metres (328 feet) deep at its lowest point, and in fact these islands were often connected to each other and to the mainland during the Ice Ages, when sea levels receded as much as 200 metres worldwide and the entire Sunda shelf was exposed as a huge subcontinent. Today these islands are fringed with broad plains that are continually expanding, as new alluvial deposits collect and reclaim the shallow sea.

Vast New Guinea and the tiny islands that dot the neighbouring Arafura Sea, are connected in a similar way by the Sahul continental shelf to Australia. New Guinea was in fact torn off from Australia long ago during a rift movement of the earth's crust.

In between these two continental shelves lie Sulawesi (The Celebes), Maluku and Nusa Tenggara (the Lesser Sundas)— several rugged island arcs which rise from a deep geosyncline that drops as much as 4,500 metres (15,000 feet) below the water's

Timor, and Tanimbar farther to the east. Parallel to this is an inner, highly volcanic fold that forms the central mountain spines of Sumatra, Java, Bali, Lombok, Sumbawa, and Flores, running through Alor and Wetar to the Banda islands in the east.

Though structurally less well defined, a similar non-volcanic outer fold in the east forms the central ranges of New Guinea, Seram, Buru, and eastern Sulawesi, while an inner volcanic range runs up the western and northern sides of Sulawesi and Halmahera to the Philippines. Within this schema, Borneo forms, along with the Malay peninsula and the mainland, an old and stable non-volcanic core and Sulawesi, due to its intermediary position, is geologically the most confused— a young volcanic arc (the southwestern-

surface.

Geologically all these islands were created along fault lines where the various tectonic plates of the earth's crust collided and folded at the edges. Subsequently, volcanoes arose along several of these same fault lines.

It is possible to distinguish between two sets of symmetrical folds for each island chain in the archipelago: an older, non-volcanic outer fold and a younger, intensely volcanic inner fold. Running down the west coast of Sumatra is a non-volcanic outer range known as the Mentawai chain of islands. This continues as the southern coastal ranges of Java, Bali, Lombok and western Sumbawa, and then splits off to form the non-volcanic islands of Sumba, Roti, Sawu,

central-northern range) welded onto an older, non-volcanic one (the eastern and southeastern arms).

A Volcanic Legacy

The importance of volcanoes in Indonesia cannot be overstated. Not only do they dominate the landscape of many islands with majestic smoking cones, they also fundamentally alter their size and soils— spewing forth millions of tons of ash and

Above, early 16th Century Portuguese map of Southeast Asia with much of the Indonesian archipelago undrawn. Right, early Dutch painting depicts a Sumatran volcano.

debris at irregular intervals. Much of this eventually gets washed down to form gently sloping alluvial plains. Where the ejecta is acidic, the land is infertile and practically useless for agricultural purposes. But where it is basic, as on Java and Bali and in a few scattered localities on other islands, it has produced the most spectacularly fertile tropical soils in the world.

Of the hundreds of volcanoes, in Indonesia, over 70 remain active and hardly a year passes without a major eruption. On such a densely populated island as Java, this inevitably brings death and destruction. When Mt. Galunggung erupted in West Java in 1982, many were killed and about 4 million were directly affected through loss of home, land and livelihood.

ejected material blocked out the sun for many months, producing the famous "years without summer" of 1816. Geologists say that even greater explosions created Sumatra's Lake Toba and Lake Ranau eons ago.

Climate

All of the islands in the archipelago lie within the tropical zone, and the surrounding seas exert everywhere a homogenizing effect on temperatures and humidity, so that local variables like topography, altitude and rainfall produce more variation in climate than do latitude or season. Mean temperatures at sea level are uniform, varying by only a few degrees throughout the region, and throughout the year (25-28 C/78-82 F).

Yet Galunggung was only a small eruption. Tiny Mt. Krakatau off Java's west coast erupted in 1883 with a force equivalent to that of several hydrogen bombs, creating tidal waves that killed more than 35,000 people on Java. The bang of this eruption, 18 times larger than that of Mt. St. Helens, was heard as far away as Colombo and Sydney, and the great quantities of debris hurled into the atmosphere caused vivid sunsets all over the world for three years afterwards.

Even the Krakatau explosion, however, was dwarfed by the cataclysmic 1815 eruption of Mt. Tambora on Sumbawa—the largest in recorded history, in which 90,000 people were killed and over 80 cubic kms of

In the mountains, however, the temperature decreases about one degree C (two degrees F) for every 200 metres (656 feet) of altitude, which makes for a cool, pleasant climate in upland towns like Bandung (in West Java: altitude 900 metres [2,950 ft]) and Bukit Tinggi (in West Sumatra: altitude 1,000 metres [3,280 ft]).

Much of the archipelago also lies within the equatorial everwet zone, where no month passes without several inches of rainfall. Most islands receive considerably more than this during the northeast monsoon, which blows down over the South China Sea picking up moisture, then veers to the northwest across the equator, unleashing drenching precipitation wherever it touches land from November through April. Moreover, the tropical sun and the oceans combine to produce continuously high humidity everywhere, and due to local wind patterns, a few places, like Bogor in West Java, receive rain almost daily—as much as 400 cm (200 inches) of it annually!

The Southeast Monsoon nevertheless tends to counteract this generally high humidity by blowing hot, dry air up from over the Australian landmass between May and October. Though much depends on local topography, on most islands this produces a dry season of markedly reduced precipitation, and as one moves south and eastward in the archipelago, the influence of this dessicating Southeast Monsoon increases dramatically. Thus, for example, Sumba and

Beneath this grows a tangle of palms, lianas, epiphytic ferns, rattans and bamboos, covered by innumerable lichens, mosses and lower plants.

One would imagine that to support such growth the soils would have to be very rich, but this is generally not so. The rainforests of Sumatra, Kalimantan, Sulawesi and Irian typically thrive on very poor and thin soils, that have been heavily leached of minerals by the incessant rains. Cleared of their forest cover by shifting agriculturalists, they support only two or three meagre crops before being exhausted, eroded or choked with weeds.

How does the rainforest flourish in such circumstances? The answer lies in the nature of its ecosystem, which has brilliantly

Timor in the Nusa Tenggara chain have an extremely long dry season, with occasional two-year droughts. Similarly, the southern Bukit peninsula in Bali is much drier than the rest of the island, as are parts of Java east and south of Surakarta.

Arboreal Canopies

The vegetation found in different parts of the archipelago varies greatly according to rainfall, soil and altitude. On the wetter equatorial islands, the luxuriance of the rainforests is simply amazing. The main canopy of interlocking tree crowns may be 40 metres (130 ft) from the ground, with individual trees rising as high as 70 metres (230 ft).

adapted over millions of years to just such conditions. Essentially, the system holds most of its minerals and nutrients in the form of living tissues. As these die and fall to the ground, they are immediately decomposed and absorbed back up into the system once again. In effect, then, the rainforest is a self-fertilizing system largely independent of the soil.

On each level, various plants play unique roles in the ecosystem. The upper tree canopy absorbs sunlight and photosynthe-

Above, mangroves along the Cihandeuleum River at Ujung Kulon in West Java. Near right, montane forest at Cibodas in West Java. Far right, fruit of the cacao tree.

sizes it, while maintaining low temperatures and high humidity below. Growth is very slow on the shady lower levels. Lianas wind up from the ground; rattan canes use hooked barbs to grapple and climb; epiphytes simply settle on the branches of big trees.

All plants in the system face shortages of minerals and water, and have therefore developed water storage tubers and other strategies, such as providing shelter and special fluids for ants who in turn deposit their nutrient-rich faeces for the plant to use. Some plants resort to piracy, living as parasites—like the garish *Rafflesia* flower found only in south-central Sumatra, which has no leaves and lives on the ground-trailing *Tetrastigma* vine. Its cabbage-like buds swell and eventually burst open in

hardwood, aromatic and spice trees flourish—including teak, ebony, sandal-wood, camphor, clove and nutmeg trees, as well as exotic fruit-bearing species: durian rambutan, jackfruit, salak, jambu, tamarind, breadfruit and hundreds of varieties of banana and fruit-bearing palms. In New Guinea more than 2,500 species of wild orchids are found in the rainforest, including the world's largest—the tiger orchid (*Grammatophyllum Speciosum*) with its three-metre-long spray of yellow-orange blooms.

Alpine Forests and Mangrove Swamps

At high altitudes, temperatures drop and cloud cover increases, resulting in slower growth, fewer species and less complex

enormous blooms, five reddish-brown petals splashed with white that can measure one metre across and sometimes weigh nine kgs (20 lbs).

Carnivorous pitcher plants lure unsuspecting insects into liquid-filled cups, where they are dissolved to provide essential nutrients. And the strangler fig settles on a lofty branch, putting down aerial roots that eventually strangle the host tree itself.

Lowland rainforests display the greatest diversity. Stands of a single tree are rare, rather the lowland forest is composed of a fantastic mosaic of different species, so that in Borneo alone, for example, 3,000 different tree species are known. On this and other islands, many economically valuable

structure. Rainforests give way to more specialized montane forests, dominated by chestnuts, laurels and oaks. Higher up, one finds rhododendrons and stunted moss forests—dwarf trees draped in lichens. Higher still, there are alpine meadows with giant edelweiss and other plants more reminiscent of Switzerland than Indonesia. This unexpected habitat can be seen at Mt. Gede National Park, only 100 kms (62 miles) south of hot, humid Jakarta. Indonesia's highest peaks, the Lorentz mountains of Irian Jaya, rise to over 5,000 metres (16,000 feet), and are clad in permanent snowfields and glaciers, the only icefields in the eastern tropics.

Other specialized forests grow on ultrabasic rocks, on limestone karsts, in young volcanic areas and in poorly drained swamps where lack of aeration leads to the build-up of acid peat. In the vast tidal zones of eastern Sumatra, Kalimantan and southern Irian, specialized mangrove trees with looping roots and air-breathing nodules flourish. These trap silt washed down by rivers and creep slowly forward behind a wall of growing coral, forming new land. Mangrove swamps are inhabited by fiddler crabs, fish that skip out of the water, dancing fireflies and the amazing proboscis monkey unique to Borneo.

Moving east from central Java across Bali and Nusa Tenggara, the climate becomes drier and lowland jungles are replaced by deciduous monsoon forests and open savan-

man has created exceptionally productive agricultural environments on islands like Java and Bali. This was accomplished through the introduction of irrigated wet-rice cultivation to areas that already possessed soil and climatic conditions ideal for agriculture.

Not only are Java and Bali among the few islands where volcanic ejecta is basic and not acidic, so that frequent volcanic eruptions have in fact continually improved the soils by adding mineral-rich nutrients, but they are also areas which achieve something of a golden mean in climate, between the incessant rainfall of the equatorial islands and the extended droughts of Nusa Tenggara. Java and Bali receive plentiful rainfall and sunshine during alternating dry and wet sea-

nah grasslands. Depending on how dry the climate is, these forests are partly or wholly deciduous, with fewer species and many broad-leaf trees like teak, which shed their leaves during the dry season. This renders them highly vulnerable to forest fires, and indeed most of the natural forests on Sumbawa, Komodo, Flores and Timor have been either cut or burned off in recent centuries by man. The exposed land has then been devoured by voracious *alang-alang* (elephant grasses), so that today there are only useless grasslands and scrub where once there were valuable hardwood forests.

Man's presence in the archipelago has not always had an adverse impact on the environment. Indeed, since prehistoric times,

sons, each of which lasts half of the year.

It remained, then, for man to harness these natural blessings to his advantage, through the construction of elaborate irrigation networks and labour-intensive wet-rice paddies. The results have been astounding—rice yields under traditional conditions (i.e. before the use of chemical fertilizers and miracle rice strains) that are by far the highest in the world.

Such extraordinary fecundity, responsible in great measure for the numerous cultural

Above, a wet-rice paddy in Sumba is "ploughed" by water buffalo. Near right, climbing a lontar palm for tuak. Far right, a tea plantation in the cool uplands of Java.

64

achievements of the Javanese and the Balinese, has now resulted in runaway population growth. Java today supports 100 million people, two-thirds of Indonesia's population, on only seven per cent of the nation's total land area. This represents an average of over 750 persons per sq km (2,000 per sq mile)—more than twice that of densely populated industrial nations like Japan and Holland. And in many areas of Java, average rural population densities actually soar to an incredible 2,000 persons per sq km (5,000 per sq mile)!

The situation on other islands stands in marked contrast to this. The remaining 50 million Indonesians live spread over more than 90 per cent of the archipelago, with an average population density of only 35 per sq

ine trading networks. Today, the Outer Islands are also the source of almost all valuable exports: rubber and palm oil (from Sumatran estates), petroleum, copper, tin and bauxite (from Sumatra, Bangka, Billiton and Irian Jaya) and timber (from Kalimantan).

In a sense, the serious ecological problems of over-populated Inner Indonesia are now being exported to the Outer Islands. Java has already suffered for some time from problems of erosion, soil exhaustion and pollution. Now, as the nation's export resources are increasingly being called upon to support a burgeoning population, there are the beginnings of massive deforestation, leading to erosion and the replacement of rainforest by useless grassland.

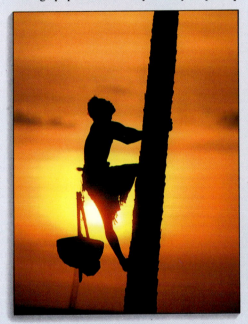

km (90 per sq mile). On some islands, like Kalimantan and Irian Jaya, this figure drops to around 10 per sq km.

Partly in view of this dramatic population imbalance and partly because of the historical importance of Java as a political centre of gravity within the archipelago, many observers tend to distinguish between an Inner Indonesia (i.e. Java and Bali, including Madura and West Lombok) and an Outer Indonesia (all other islands).

Whereas Inner Indonesia has been characterized for centuries by high population densities and labour-intensive irrigated agriculture, Outer Indonesia is the home, traditionally, of dense rainforests, thinly-spread shifting agricultural communities and river-

These problems have been recognized by the Indonesian government. Realizing, for example, that if indiscriminate clear-felling in Kalimantan timber concessions continues at its present rate, there will be no lowland forest left by the end of the century, they are taking steps to encourage selective cutting and reforestation. Moreover, six per cent of the nation's land has been set aside as nature reserves and national parks. These are not just for the protection of a few wild animals—they safeguard a genetic treasure trove containing many species that may be valuable to man, as well as providing watershed protection and recreational facilities. (*See* Part IV, "Indonesia's Incredible Wildlife.")

THE INDONESIAN MELTING POT

The kaleidoscopic array of peoples, languages, customs and material cultures found in the Indonesian archipelago is truly astounding, for living here are over 100 distinct ethnic groups, each with its own cultural identity, who together speak a total of more than 300 mutually unintelligible languages! These figures are in fact rather conservative estimates, developed by Dutch scholars during the 1930s on the basis of highly incomplete data, and lively debates continue to rage as to just how Indonesian cultural units ought to be defined.

cording any and everything that came to their attention. The result is a series of invaluable books, encyclopaedic in their breadth, that still make for absorbing reading today.

Francois Valentyn's compendious *Oud en Nieuw Oost-Indien* (1726), for example, is chock-filled with anecdotes, oddities and perceptive observations recorded during the author's many years as a missionary in the Moluccas. William Marsden's *History of Sumatra* (1783), compiled while Marsden was employed at the tiny English outpost of

A number of questions are often posed: how can each group best be characterized; in what ways are they related to one another; and where did they come from? Yet even after decades of work and hundreds of studies, the picture is still far from complete. Scores of ethnic groups and languages have yet to be investigated in detail.

Ethnographic surveys were first undertaken in Indonesia by colonial missionaries and administrators during the 18th and 19th centuries, as part of much broader investigations into the nature of the islands and their inhabitants. Confronted at the time with such a profusion of hitherto undocumented peoples, places and things, these pioneering Europeans began by re-

Benkulu on Sumatra's southwest coast, contains a similarly broad range of delightful tidbits concerning the geography, wildlife and people of that enormously varied island. And Sir Stamford Raffles' monumental *History of Java* (1817)—the product of years of work by a team of scribes, taxidermists and artists in the author's personal employ—contains the first detailed look at that island's elaborate civilization, including such fascinating trivia as the traditional Javanese recipe for fermented shrimp-paste (*trasi*).

Preceding pages, Niasian children at play. Above, a classic Javanese face; woman from south Sumatra. Near right, a Minangkabau woman. Far right, a Dayak woman.

The Question of Race

Toward the end of the 19th Century, however, Europeans investigating Indonesia's peoples and cultures began to focus almost exclusively on questions of socio-cultural evolution and typology. It was perhaps inevitable, given the nature of the investigations and the intellectual tenor of the times, that such questions came to be seen largely in terms of the rather nebulous concept of race.

Anyone travelling widely in Indonesia is

the Malay peninsula, in the Andaman Island north of Sumatra and on several of the Philippine Islands. Because of their resemblance to the Pygmies of north-central Africa, it has commonly been suggested that the negritos somehow migrated the length of the Eurasian continent eons ago.

The second wave, too, were thought to have arrived possibly from Africa or perhaps India. These peoples—dark-skinned with woolly or kinky hair, pronounced brow-ridges and broad, flat noses—were dubbed the "Australoids," and are the native inhabi-

soon made aware of the enormous physical differences exhibited by peoples from one end of the archipelago to the other—differences in pigmentation, hair type, stature and physiognomy, among other things. To explain this observable range of racial types, scholars began by postulating a wave theory of racial migrations to the archipelago. According to this theory, various Indonesian groups arrived from the Asian mainland in a series of discrete but massive migratory waves, each separated by a period of several centuries.

The first wave of migrants, it was thought, were the primitive dark-skinned, wiry-haired negritos—peoples of pygmy stature who today inhabit remote forest enclaves on

tants of New Guinea, Melanesia and Australia. They traditionally lived in semi-settled villages in remote areas, where they hunted and gathered but also raised crops and animals and produced a variety of handicrafts, including pottery and vegetable-fibre cloths.

The third wave, termed "proto-Malays," were thought to have migrated from China via Indochina. They are essentially "Mongolians"—light-skinned people with almond-shaped eyes, who somehow acquired an admixture of certain Australoid features, such as curly hair and brown skin. Examples often cited include the Batak and Kubu tribes of Sumatra, the Badui and Tenggerese of Java, the Aga tribes of Bali, the Dayaks of Borneo, the Toalans and Torajans of Sulawesi and several peoples of the eastern archipelago. Most of these groups still inhabit highland or remote inland regions, though they are by no means primitive. They have long possessed highly sophisticated ritual and material cultures, including elaborate religious rites and sacrificial feasts, dances, music, textiles, carpentry, metalworking, traditions of storytelling and sometimes also the use of writing.

The last wave, the "deutero-Malays," were described as pure Mongoloids, hence related to and much resembling the Chinese. These peoples today inhabit the plains and coastal regions of all the major islands, and many developed large hierarchical kingdoms, attaining a level of pre-modern civi-

great variety of physical traits to the similarly broad range of cultural types found in Indonesia. Yet in fact these two concepts—"race" and "culture"—do not correlate as easily as previously believed. The basic problem is that no one knows exactly what is meant by the term "race." As ideal types they are fine, but in practice of course sharp racial boundaries do not exist, and distinguishing features have a way of dissolving into meaningless abstractions. It is now clear that in Indonesia, as elsewhere, physical appearance does not correlate in any systematic fashion with language or culture.

In fact the real picture is very much more complex than this. First of all, the existence of *Homo erectus* (Java Man) fossils in Indonesia—million-year-old remains of one

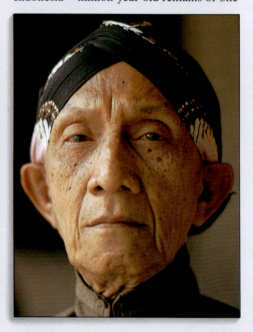

lization comparable to that found anywhere in the world. Examples of so-called deutero-Malay groups, who today constitute a majority of Indonesians, include the Acehnese, Minangkabau and Malays of Sumatra; the Sundanese, Javanese, Balinese and Madurese of Java, Madura and Bali; the Sasaks of Lombok, and the Makassarese and Buginese of Sulawesi. As these Mongoloids arrived, they are said to have forced all earlier groups to move on to marginal mountain fastnesses, dense upriver jungles and dry eastern islands—and to have monopolized the best agricultural lands and the most strategic river estuaries for themselves.

One virtue of this now-rejected theory, is that it does at least attempt to connect the

of modern man's earliest ancestors— suggests that the so-called negrito and Australoid-type peoples, with their sun-screening skin pigmentation, actually evolved partially or wholly in the tropical rainforests of Southeast Asia, just as the light-skinned Mongoloid types evolved in the cold, temperate regions of East and Central Asia. Of course during the last Ice Ages, when land bridges linked the major islands of the Sunda shelf to the mainland, these peoples circulated freely and even

Above left, a Balinese. Above right, a Javanese. Near right, a Minang *haji*. Far right, a Batak from the region around Lake Toba in Sumatra.

crossed the oceans, populating Australia by about 50,000 years ago. There can be no doubt that Mongoloid-type peoples did migrate to the region much later, but the question is how.

The wave theory of co-ordinated, coherent mass movements seems unlikely for a number of reasons. In a fragmented region like the Indonesian archipelago, village and tribal groups have always been constantly on the move, at least in historic times, dissolving and absorbing each other as they go. It is more realistic therefore to conceive of a situation in which small groups of Mongoloid hunters, gatherers and shifting cultivators percolated into the region slowly—absorbing and replacing the original Australoid inhabitants over a period of many mil-

have been adequately studied. Languages such as Javanese, Balinese and Indonesian (the national language, which derives from a literary dialect of Malay) are closely related, belonging to the Malayo-Polynesian branch of the Austronesian language family, but they are as different from one another as are French, English and Spanish.

The Austronesian family is an enormous grouping of about 800 tongues spoken over more than half the globe—from Madagascar in the west to the eastern Pacific islands. About 200 or so are spoken in Indonesia, the rest being found mainly in the Philippines and the islands of Oceania. Another linguistic family, the Papuan group, contains almost as many distinct languages even though it is spoken by only

lennia. The end result can best be described as a clinal gradation of physical types, with more Australoid traits in evidence in more remote mountain or jungle areas, particularly moving eastward in Indonesia. Support for this complex, multi-dimensional conception of Indonesian ethnic origins has come from comparative linguistic studies.

The Indonesian Babel

Indonesians speak such a variety of different languages that the exact number would largely depend on an arbitrary definition of what constitutes a distinct language, as opposed to a dialect. Most estimates place the total above 300, only a handful of which

about 3 million people, most of whom live on the huge island of New Guinea.

Statistical studies have revealed that linguistic diversity actually increases moving eastward across the archipelago, so that not only are there more languages in the eastern islands, but these languages are also increasingly distinct from one another. This seems to tie in with the physical evidence, but it also has another, rather surprising implication.

Linguists have long postulated that great linguistic diversity means an area has been settled and stable for a very long time. In fact, one of the purposes of lexico-statistical studies (the comparison of related languages to determine the percentage of words they share) is to locate the ancestral homeland of a language family—assumed to lie in the region of greatest diversity. Within the scattered Austronesian family, this ancestral homeland appears to be located in western Melanesia (an area between the north coast of New Guinea and the Soloman Islands)—at least according to a massive study undertaken by Isidore Dyen in the early 1960s with the aid of computers.

For this reason, some scholars have begun to speculate that the Mongoloid inhabitants of Indonesia migrated not via mainland Southeast Asia (Indochina), as had previously been thought, but rather from southern China via Taiwan, Hainan and the Philippines to Melanesia. From here, so the theory goes, there occurred a diaspora of

speak quite different languages (and conversely, some very different peoples speak closely related dialects). For a clearer exposition of the whole problem of Indonesian ethnic typologies we must turn to the complex and rather controversial field of cultural anthropology.

The Typological Debate

When it comes to defining and classifying ethnic groups, there are basically two schools of thought. One school holds that each group, tribe or people should be treated as a unique case, and that a complex, holistic view of the group's culture should be sought. Only when enough Indonesian cultures are adequately documented, according to this

Austronesian speakers, some of whom sailed east to populate the Pacific Islands, others of whom travelled west to Indonesia and even across the Indian Ocean to Madagascar. No definite time frame is given for these migrations, but they are thought to have begun around 7,000 years ago, and to have greatly accelerated over the 3,000 years leading up to the Christian era.

This is an interesting hypothesis, one which needs to be examined and tested in detail, but it still does not yield very much about Indonesia's ethnic groupings. In fact, linguistic boundaries often have a way of confusing rather than clarifying the issue of ethnic distinctions in Indonesia, for the simple reason that closely related peoples often

view, can any meaningful typologies or comparisons be made.

There is much to recommend such a cautious approach. Of course, the problem is that ethnographic information is by its very nature never complete. What we know about a foreign culture is largely determined by the questions we ask. An opposing view therefore says that we should begin by establishing certain general guidelines for classifying Indonesian ethnic groups, then work to refine and revise them.

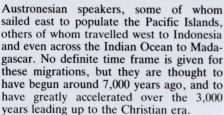

A picture gallery taken from the eastern end of the Indonesian archipelago. Moving from left to right, natives from Timor, Flores, Siberut and Irian Jaya.

One important distinction, which has been developed in the work of Clifford and Hildred Geertz, focuses on the two main agricultural patterns found in Indonesia: *ladang* and *sawah*. *Ladang* agriculture, also referred to by the Old English word "swidden" and by the descriptive phrase "slash-and-burn," is practised in marginal or heavily forested terrains, generally outside of Java and Bali. The *ladang* farmer utilizes fire as a tool, along with his axe and bush knife, to clear a forest plot. By carefully timing the burn to immediately precede the onset of rains, the farmer simultaneously fertilizes and weeds the land.

Depending on local soil conditions and tastes, the main staple crop planted might be a grain like rice or corn, a tuber like yams or

rious Iban and Dayak tribes, the average density is less than 10 persons per sq km. The size and complexity of social organization within such *ladang* communities is also limited. Nuclear families are generally autonomous, labour is exchanged with fellow villagers or kinsmen on a carefully calculated basis, and warfare, headhunting and slave raiding traditionally kept villages isolated and distant from one another.

While these semi-nomadic swidden farmers now comprise less than a tenth of Indonesia's total population, they are scattered throughout more than two-thirds of the nation's land area. Most Indonesians, by contrast, inhabit the narrow plains and coastal regions of the major islands, where the principal farming method employed is *sawah*

taro, or a starch-producing palm like sago or lontar. Rice is the preferred crop in the western islands—tubers and sago palms predominate in the eastern and southeastern archipelagoes. In addition to the staple, farmers also plant a great variety of other food crops, thereby in effect recreating the symbiotic system of a tropical forest found in nature, while also providing a more varied diet for themselves. After several years, however, the land in these areas, never rich to begin with (most nutrients are provided by ash from the burn), is depleted and new plots must be cleared.

For obvious reasons, the swidden method can support only a small population. In Kalimantan for instance, home of the noto-

or wet-rice paddy cultivation. In fact, two-thirds of Indonesia's population (over 100 million people) live on Java and Bali, which between them comprise only about seven per cent of Indonesia's land. Here the average rural population densities can soar as high as 2,000 people per sq kilometre (5,000 per sq mile)—by far the world's highest! *Sawah* cultivation is a highly labour-intensive form of agriculture that can be successfully practised only under very special conditions (rich soil and adequate water supply), but one which seems capable of producing seemingly limitless quantities of food. The sedentary farmers who plant wet-rice paddies actually reshape their environment over a period of many generations—

CUSTOM AND RELIGION IN INDONESIA

While all of Indonesia's more than 160 million people are officially listed as adherents of one or another of four great "World Religions" practised in the archipelago: Islam, Christianity, Hinduism and Buddhism—with the vast majority, about 140 million, registered as Muslims (which, incidentally, makes Indonesia by far the world's largest Muslim nation), Indonesians actually exhibit almost infinite variety in what they do and believe in spiritual matters. The reason is that here, as elsewhere, religious beliefs and practices are strongly Balinese. And among the Javanese, children not yet familiar with the social values and mystical sensibilities of their elders are considered *durung Jawa*—not yet Javanese.

An Eclectic Tradition

To the great consternation of religious purists (and much to the confusion of foreign observers), the *adat* and religion of any given Indonesian group tend to be remarkably eclectic. The classic example cited is that of the average Javanese, a self-declared

tinged, if not entirely dominated, by local traditions—the corpus of private rites, public rituals, communal knowledge and customary laws that is passed from generation to generation and forms the distinctive fabric of each society—known throughout Indonesia as the *adat* (custom) of an ethnic group or community.

So great is the identification of most Indonesians with their respective *adat* and religion, that these are commonly said to constitute ethnic identity. To a Malay, for example, conversion to Islam is regarded as *masuk Melayu*—becoming a Malay. Likewise, a Balinese who leaves off worshipping with his fellow villagers, and converts to Islam or Christianity, is said to be no longer

Muslim who yet firmly believes in the existence of Indian deities and indigenous folk heroes portrayed in the ever-popular *wayang kulit* shadow play, as well as in a host of goddesses, ghosts, spirits, demons and genies said to inhabit his worldly environment. Typically, in addition to fulfilling the requirements of the Islamic faith, he will engage in a number of other activities: burn incense and leave small offerings to local spirits; hold frequent communal feasts (*sela-*

Preceding pages, entranced participants in a Balinese temple festival. Above, the final day of the Sekaten feast. Right, a procession in the Eka Desa Rudra rite, Bali.

matan) to celebrate major holidays, births, marriages or business successes and to mitigate the disruptions of unsettling events, moves or changes; seek and heed the advice of a local *dukun* or mystic in times of distress; trust to the magical potency of an inherited *keris* dagger and a variety of other talismans; and make occasional pilgrimages to a sacred spring, tomb or hilltop sanctuary, there to accumulate the potent spiritual emanations (*semangat*) of the place, meditate or otherwise augment his own inner spiritual "capital."

and island-wide temple celebrations; to obey the ritual instructions and provide the sacrificial offerings prescribed by temple priests and village mediums; and to perform elaborate rites of passage marking birth, puberty, marriage and death, many of which are undoubtedly much older than the presence of Hinduism on the island.

Similarly, among many Christian communities in Indonesia, one finds that shamans and mediums are still frequently consulted; that births, marriages, deaths and communal feasts are still celebrated in the

A similar situation obtains among Balinese: self-declared Hindus (a term which is by no means well defined in its Indian context) whose temples are filled with a multitude of shrines dedicated not only to the Hindu trinity (Siva, Brahma, Vishnu) and a host of their lesser manifestations and acolytes, but also to native Balinese mountain spirits, deified ancestors, rice- and water-goddesses, heavenly "spokesmen" and other supernatural beings. Few Balinese are familiar with the more exalted Hindu deities, much less knowledgable about their worship—this is left to the learned brahmanic specialist in such matters. For most, it is sufficient to participate in the busy calendar of village-

traditional fashion; and that Christian services and holy celebrations have more often than not incorporated many local elements, such as the famous Black Virgin who walks in the yearly Easter parade at Larantuka. (*See* Part III, "Nusa Tenggara.")

Some scholars liken these syncretic *adat* and religious patterns to cultural layer cakes, and interpret the layers historically. In this view, the native animism is seen as predating and underlying later Indic, Islamic, Christian and other foreign accretions. Sociologists prefer to analyze these patterns structurally, categorizing various beliefs and practices according to the class of people who espouse them and to their apparent or supposed purpose. A common conclusion is that aristocrats are rather mystically inclined and the majority of rural peasants are superstitious, while the urban middle class is more inclined to Muslim or Christian orthodoxy.

Feasts and Sacrifices

What is undeniable, however, is that these are not merely academic notions but living traditions; their fluidity, complexity and even their inherent contradictions are what make them so fascinating and colourful. More than this, of course, many local Indonesian rites are extraordinary dramatic spectacles and exceptional occasions in the life of the community. Some of them could even be said to rank among the more extraordinary ritual events to occur at any

host. A *selamatan* may be given at any time and for almost any reason—most commonly to celebrate a birth, a marriage, a circumcision or an anniversary; to commemorate a death; to initiate a new project or dedicate a new building; to dispel bad luck; or to invite good fortune.

More elaborate *selamatan* are held annually by the royal courts of Yogyakarta and Surakarta in Central Java. The largest of these is known as Sekaten and coincides with the prophet Mohammed's birthday. For a month before the appointed day, tens of thousands of Javanese throng to these cities to attend a carnival set up in the square before the palace. During the final week, two sacred royal *gamelan* sets are alternately played in the adjacent mosque, and villagers

time, anywhere.

Central to the *adat* observances of most Indonesians is the ritual sacrifice and communal feast, in which ceremonial foods (generally including freshly slaughtered meats) are offered up to the spirits and blessed, then publicly consumed, in order to ensure the well-being of the participants and strengthen the solidarity of the group.

The most common example of such a feast is the ordinary Javanese *selamatan* (literally: "safe-guarding"), in which special foods are eaten (most commonly, a *tumpeng* or inverted cone of coloured rice accompanied by various meat dishes), incense is burned, Islamic prayers are intoned and formal announcements or requests are made by the

believe that listening to them can prolong one's life, while small whips purchased here are said to have the power to fertilize cattle.

On the final day of Sekaten a long procession composed of elegantly dressed noblemen, court officials, palace guards, dancers and musicians accompany two impressive *gunungan*—mountains of rice and vegetables in the shape of *lingga* and *yoni* (representing the male and female reproductive organs)—from the palace to the mosque. Here the *gunungan* are blessed through the reading of Koranic prayers, and the food is

Above, Hindu cremation of a Balinese raja. Right, a wedding is considered an important step of the life cycle.

then distributed to the gathered masses, in what is essentially an ancient fertility rite co-opted by Islam. Peasants eat and deposit morsels of the *gunungan* in their fields, to ensure good health and harvests.

A Communal Birthday

In Bali, festive activities centre about the village temple, where every 210 days a communal birthday feast (*odalan*) is held on the anniversary of its consecration. For several days beforehand, the entire village is engaged in preparing elaborate decorations, altars and offerings; in praying and receiving blessings of sprinkled holy water from the *pemangku* or temple priest. On the day of the festival, delicately carved sandalwood idols

the *pemangku* leads the village in a ritual adoration of the sun, and everyone goes home to bed.

Nurturing the Life Force

These and other types of feasts frequently have to do with enhancing the fertility and prosperity of the participants by strengthening, purifying or augmenting something known to many Indonesian peoples as *semangat*—the life forces or vital principles thought to inhabit and animate not only humans but plants, animals, sacred objects and also entire villages, kingdoms, islands or nations. These forces are negative as well as positive, bringing bad as well as good consequences, and it is generally believed that

are brought out of their special compartment, wrapped in sacred weavings and then infused with the protective spirits of the village, who are then escorted to the seashore or the riverbank in a colourful procession. Symbolic ablutions are performed and everyone receives a blessing of holy water, and the procession returns to the temple, where the spirits receive their offerings and possess mediums who tell if the celebrations and offerings have been satisfactory, answer questions and give advice. The villagers feast, and various entertainments are staged throughout the night—a chance for young dancers, puppeteers and *gamelan* musicians to star. Finally, as the first rays of dawn break over the horizon,

by boosting their own life-giving *semangat*, men are able to achieve and maintain a fragile balance between them.

The *semangat* of human beings is thought to be concentrated in the head, and in the past, many Indonesian peoples (like the Toraja of Sulawesi, the Dayak of Kalimantan and the Dani of Irian Jaya), sought to promote their own *semangat* at the expense of an adversary through headhunting raids. Skull trophies were once regarded as powerful talismans that would enhance the prosperity of a community, promote the fertility of its fields, and ward off sickness, war or ill fortune.

The hair of the head is likewise considered to contain large concentrations of *semangat*.

A ceremonial first haircutting often serves to initiate an infant into human society, while the exchange of snippits of hair or the ceremonial knotting of the hair of a bride and groom together is an integral part of many Indonesian marriage rites. Almost universally in traditional Indonesia, hair clippings are disposed of carefully (as are nail trimmings) lest they fall unknowingly into the hands of an enemy sorceror, and human hair curiously features in the costumes of many supernatural characters—such as the huge *Rangda* and *Barong* dance masks of Bali.

Power of Blood

Blood, too, is thought to be infused with *semangat*, which can be especially easily nan, Bali), the chief goal of which seems to be to draw human blood to be used for talismanic purposes.

The Soul of Plants

According to many Indonesians, this soul substance is found also in plants. The most common example is that of the powerful but sensitive *semangat* associated with the rice plant. There are many versions of the legend accounting for the origins of domesticated plants, but most describe a beautiful woman who is given the choice of death or sexual submission to her step-father, her twin brother or a gruesome ogre. She chooses death, and out of her buried remains grow rice, palm trees, fruits and edible tubers. In

transmitted or conferred. On many islands, the pillars of a new house are annointed with the sacrificial blood of animals to render them strong and durable. Among the Makassarese of Sulawesi, royal weapons and other regalia (*pusaka*) were once bathed regularly in blood to keep them spiritually "charged." And it used to be widely reported that victors in battle in many parts of the archipelago drank the blood or gall of their slain enemies, or smeared these fluids over themselves, to augment their own *semangat* with that of the fallen. Still today on many islands, ritual battles are enacted (such as the *caci* whip duels of Flores, the Pasola cavalry wars of Sumba, and the Perang Pandan [pandanus wars] of Tenga-

some areas, she is known as Dewi Sri and is described variously as the wife of Vishnu or the daughter of Batara Guru—the protectress or embodiment of the sacred rice spirit. In Bali, special temples are dedicated to Dewi Sri and her image—the triangular *cili* delicately cut from palm fronds or formed of coloured rice-dough, adorns most temples and offerings on festive occasions.

Throughout the cultivation cycle, ritual precautions are taken to ensure that the rice soul is carefully shepherded into the field,

Above, buffalo are kept by the Toraja only for ceremonial purposes. Here, one is sacrificed as part of a funeral rite. Right, the Torajan dead are "buried" in caves outside of which effigies of the departed stand on display.

tenderly nurtured and assiduously protected. If harmed or even startled, she might leave and the crop would fail, producing famine. When the grain is being harvested, special care is taken to treat the grain-laden plants with respect. Short, curved blades are often used, concealed in the palm of the hand so that the rice spirit cannot "see" that she is about to be violated. Soothing incantations or apologies are often muttered as the rice is cut—traditionally, music was played, dances performed and poetry was recited in some communities while the harvest was in progress. Grains that are to become next year's seed are often wrapped in swaddling and treated as newborn infants. Representative sheafs of rice are sometimes "married" and then hung up in the granary until the

thought to be imbued with a special *semangat* or soul. Some rock crystals, for instance, are regarded as "windows" into the spirit world, and neolithic polished stone adzes are spoken of in some areas as "thunder teeth." Bezoar stones, mineral deposits found in animals and in the nodes of certain bamboos, are used for magic and healing, while more generally, any object that is designated a *pusaka* or sacred heirloom is credited with harbouring a vital spiritual essence that requires special veneration and care. Antique *keris* daggers, lances, spear heads, cannon, gems, jewellery, textiles, ceramics, manuscripts, gravestones, sculptures and masks can all become *pusaka* and may contain a soul of their own or that of a previous owner. Such objects are often in the custody

next planting cycle begins.

Other economically important plants are also said to possess a soul. In the Moluccas (Maluku), a clove tree in bloom is treated as a pregnant woman. In Sumatra, collectors of camphor speak a secret language among themselves so that the trees will not conceal their valuable crystals. The hunters of aromatic resins and beehives must similarly take elaborate ritual precautions to appease the trees in which these products are found. And many leaves are used in Indonesia in mystical healing seances and medicinal concoctions, because of the reputed strength of their vital principles.

All ancient and curious objects, mountains and bodies of water are likewise

of a king, a priest, a chief or an elder, who forms a link between the living and the powerful ancestral spirits.

Souls, Shamans and Demons

Human spirits are, of course, considered to be important, and much of a community's private and public ritual life often centres around the management of its souls, both living and dead. In this, there are invariably certain individuals in the community who possess specialized knowledge or skills in such matters. Special attention is always devoted to funerary rites, in which the dead are ritually venerated and can be "transformed" into protective clan or village deities.

It is commonly believed, for instance, that the soul of a person may become detached during life, and that this can result in diminished strength or illness. Even under normal conditions, it is thought that the soul wanders during sleep, thus giving rise to dreams. Sorcery can entice unwitting souls away; a sudden fright may jar and disorient them. Certain trees are said to be able to snatch the spirit of careless and preoccupied individuals. Prolonged yearning, craving or discontent are thought to loosen the soul, producing illness or insanity. The shaman, often a woman, must then be called upon to retrieve or comfort the lost or disturbed soul. It may be gathered up in a beautiful cloth, a small doll, a basket or a bowl. Or,

pregnant women. This so-called *pontianak* can also assume the shape of a beautiful maiden, who waits at night beneath a banyan tree to seduce and emasculate passing men. Elaborate rituals must then be performed by a shaman to mollify the evil *hantu* and banish it from the area.

In Bali, mass exorcisms are held annually to drive evil witches and demons from the villages. For several days before the spring equinox, there is great excitement all over the island as houses are cleaned, village gods are processed to the water for a symbolic bath, great altars and offerings are prepared, and cockfighting and gambling are prevalent. The day before the Balinese New Year, evil spirits are lured by priests into a large offering in the shape of an eight-pointed star

the shaman may enter a trance and journey to the spirit world to determine the proper diagnosis and cure for the afflicted person.

'Good' and 'Bad' Spirits

A distinction is made virtually everywhere between "good" spirits and "bad" spirits, resulting respectively from "good" and "bad" deaths. A "bad" death, generally premature or violent such as a murder or an accident, releases a vengeful ghost or *hantu* that may bring considerable misfortune on a household or community. The soul of a woman who dies at childbirth, for example, is pictured as a bird with long talons that jealously stabs and rents the stomachs of

(*mecaru*), after which all hell breaks loose as the villagers beat drums, shriek and shout to drive them away. This is followed by a day of complete stillness (Nyepi), in which all fires and normal activities are suspended, lest the newly banished evil spirits should return.

Mortuary Rites

"Good" deaths must also, of course, be attended by a lengthy sequence of elaborate funerary rites. When a person dies, it is universally thought that the soul is at first resentful and potentially harmful. Some rites are therefore specifically designed to confuse the soul and to dissuade it from returning to seek the company of the bereaved. It is a widespread custom in Sumatra, Kalimantan, Southern Sulawesi and Halmahera, for instance, to send the corpse out of the house through a gap in the wall or floor of the house, which is then sealed so the shade cannot find its way back. The path on the way from the graveyard is sometimes also strewn with obstacles, to impede the soul's return to the village. Likewise, mourning customs often involve the substitution of unusual foods and clothing in the household or in the community, so as not to excite the envious attention of the deceased.

There is a wide variety of beliefs in Indonesia concerning the fate of a person's soul after death. For three days, according to one widespread view, the soul is not conscious of its death; though when it leaves

living descendants must pool their resources, call in communal obligations and take on additional debts in order to put on the best possible showing. These arrangements take many months and often years to complete. Meanwhile the corpse lies wrapped in special shrouds in the house, in a special death house or pavilion, in a tree, or buried temporarily in a grave.

Eventually, the bones are unwrapped or exhumed and cleaned, and then given a final burial or cremation in a festive ceremony that is accompanied by many lavish offerings—often including the sacrifice of valuable livestock. This is followed by feasting, dancing, processions, music and rites performed by funeral specialists. The most famous Indonesian funeral feasts are those

the corpse, it often does so through the mouth, in the form of an insect or a bird. It is very commonly believed, however, that a soul cannot make the final journey to the land of the ancestors (usually pictured as a boat voyage or a flight atop a sacred bird) until a suitable mortuary feast has been held, one that both honours the deceased and provisions his spirit for a safe and orderly passage to the world of the dead.

Assembling the requisites for such a mortuary feast is generally a complicated and expensive undertaking, one in which the

Left: Christian of Flores at Easter; a Balinese trance ritual. Right, a purification birth rite takes place over a pig carcass.

of the Toraja of South Sulawesi (see Part III, "Visiting Torajaland"), though for most visitors, the dramatic and colourful cremations of the Balinese are more memorable.

The final burial may be in a cave (as among the Torajans), or in a great stone urn or huge sarcophagus (as among the Batak, the Niah and the Sumbanese). Following a cremation, the ashes are either kept in a clay pot or strewn in the ocean (as among the Balinese). The skulls and bones of the deceased are preserved and honoured among many tribes in Kalimantan and Irian Jaya, And for many Indonesians, graves or representative effigies, statues, stones or masks are thought to be inhabited by the benevolent spirits of powerful ancestors.

TRAVEL IN INDONESIA

Selamat Datang! Welcome to Indonesia! Indonesia is not your typical tropical paradise populated by smiling friendly peoples. It is much, much more. Indonesia can indeed claim to be the only nation on earth to span such a broad spectrum of world history and human civilization—from its ancient Hindu-Javanese temples to its modern luxury hotels, and from the Stone Age lifestyle practised by some highland tribes in Irian Jaya to the modern metropolis that is Jakarta. It will come as no surprise, then, that travelling in Indonesia yields eye-opening and sometimes startling contrasts—a fascinating juxtaposition of East and West, rich and poor, old with new, the familiar and the exotic. This can be an exciting experience; it can also be a disturbing one. Most of all, however, it is a chance to learn—to observe the intricacies of traditional cultures, and to see how they are adapting to the modern world.

Many have come to see and learn already. Anthropologists, artists, musicians, writers and statesmen have visited the archipelago for decades. Since the late 1960s, tourism has also come—in 1984 some 600,000 foreigners visited Indonesia. While this is not a substantial figure by international standards, it is one that has quadrupled over the last decade and is growing steadily. Moreover, the government has announced recently that it is giving high priority to tourism development in an attempt to boost foreign exchange earnings. In Bali alone, 5 new hotels were slated to open in 1985.

The Impact of Tourism

All of this, fortunately, does not mean that Indonesia in being overrun. Far from it. Unlike many other tropical tourist destinations, Indonesia is a huge country, both in terms of population and land area. Foreigners constitute an almost insignificant presence in most parts of the archipelago. Even Bali, the small island which absorbs more than half the nation's foreign visitors, has 3 million inhabitants of her

own—a people whose ancient and resilient culture has withstood several foreign "invasions" in the past. Even here, outside of those very narrow areas where they tend to congregate, Westerners are still a novelty.

Keep in mind, as you plan your itinerary, that there are many Indonesias. Most visitors stick to the tried and trued tour route leading from Jakarta through Yogyakarta (Central Java) and on to Bali; and they do so not least of all because of the superb sights and excellent transport services that encourage this itinerary. Other sizeable, but lesser known islands are equally fascinating, if less accessible to the average visitor.

Travel services and facilities are rapidly improving—convenience and comfort are becoming less and less the exception. Every provincial capital and major city in the nation now has at least one first-class air-conditioned hotel and a range of other accommodation.

Daily air connections have brought all the islands within a few hours of each other. This complex air network provides an easy first step into seldom-visited corners of the archipelago, so that the door to some truly adventurous travel is now open. In the more heavily populated regions, the local network of buses, jitneys and taxis is both fast and inexpensive. Language, too is no longer a problem—you can find more and more Indonesians who are able to speak English and who will gladly act as guides or otherwise assist you in making travel arrangements.

As a result of all this, more visitors are venturing out from the "core" tourist areas on Java and Bali to more remote regions such as South Sulawesi's Tanah Toraja, North Sumatra's Lake Toba, Bali's neighbour, Lombok, and tiny Komodo Island. Even within Java and Bali, many people are finding accessible, and, more importantly, exciting alternatives to the conventional tourist fare. Literally hundreds of other islands and destinations are just waiting to be discovered; this book shines a little more light on them so as to help you on your way.

JAKARTA: INDONESIA'S METROPOLIS

Capital to the world's fifth most populous nation and home to 7 million Indonesians, Jakarta is a metropolis by any measure. Yet apart from several skyscrapers and monuments in and around the city centre, it is made up almost entirely of small one- and two-storey structures. Most of these have sprung up rather haphazardly over the past few decades: shops, offices and factories are found in residential districts; market gardens and makeshift *kampung* dwellings impart something of a village atmosphere to many back alleys, and the people live just about everywhere.

Partly as a result, the city has not much of a reputation among tourists. In the words of one local wag: "Jakarta is a wonderful place to live but I wouldn't want to visit." Why the negative publicity? Partly, it's the heat, the traffic and the overcrowding. But basically this is a *big* city and many visitors are not prepared for that.

Jakarta's attractions, nonetheless, are abundant. Ask the locals. Those with an interest in Indonesian history and culture will tell you about Jakarta's fine museums, her colonial architecture, her performing arts and her rich intellectual life. Adventurous types will probably regale you with tales of traditional temples and bustling markets in obscure corners of the city. Bon vivants will more likely speak of a favourite antique shop, an excellent seafood restaurant or an exciting discotheque. Most residents will also express a sense of being in the thick of things, of living at the epicentre of the nation's commercial, cultural and political life. And everyone will tell you about their friends: funny, funloving, irreverent, irrepressible—Jakartans are the city's greatest asset. So give Jakarta a chance. Get to know her. Who knows, you may decide to leave Bali to the tourists.

Queen City of the East

The mouth of the Ciliwung River where Jakarta is located has been settled since very ancient times; it developed into a major pepper port during the 15th and 16th centuries. In 1618, the architect of Dutch empire in the Indies, Jan Pieterszoon Coen, transferred his headquarters here. Coen subsequently attacked and razed the town of Jayakarta—the name by which the port was then known—and ordered construction of a new town, that was subsequently dubbed Batavia.

The fortunes of Batavia under the Dutch East India Company (VOC) (1602-1799) rose and then fell. Batavia grew rich throughout the 17th Century on an entrepôt trade in sugar, pepper, cloves, nutmegs, tea, textiles, porcelains, hardwoods and rice. But after 1700, a series of disasters befell her. Declining market prices, epidemics of malaria, cholera and typhoid, and an unfortunate massacre of the Batavia Chinese (1740), combined with the frequent wars and official corruption—that had plagued the VOC since its inception—to cast a pall over the city that had once fancied herself "Queen of the East."

At the beginning of the 19th Century, Batavia received a much-needed facelift under Governor-General ("Iron Marshal") Willem Daendels, a follower of Napoleon. The old city was demolished

Preceding pages, President Suharto and his wife tour Borobudur after reopening it; train near Cirebon. Left, Jakarta. Right, National Monument.

93

to provide building materials for a new one to the south, around what are now Medan Merdeka and Lapangan Banteng. Two fashionable architectural styles of the period—French Empire and Neo-Classical—blended with many tree-lined boulevards and extensive gardens laid out by Daendels to impart a certain grace and elegance to the city. And with the economic success of the exploitative Cultivation System on Java, the colony was once again extremely prosperous. By the turn of the century, Batavia's homes, hotels and clubs were in no way inferior to those of Europe.

During the brief Japanese occupation (1942-5), Batavia was renamed Jakarta and dramatically transformed—from a tidy Dutch colonial town of 200,000 to an Indonesian city of more than 1 million. Following independence, hundreds of thousands more Indonesians flooded in from the countryside and the outer islands, and Jakarta quickly outstripped all other Indonesian cities in size and importance to become what scholars term a "primate" city: the unrivalled political, cultural and economic centre of the new nation.

City Tour: The Old Harbour

Beginning at sunrise if possible (or at sunset if not), visit the picturesque port of **Sunda Kelapa**. This is the name of the original Hindu spice-trading post that was conquered and converted to Islam more than four and a half centuries ago. The flavour of ancient times is today preserved in the form of traditional wooden *pinisi*—sailing vessels that continue to play a vital role in the commerce of modern-day Indonesia. Each day some 70 or 80 of these Buginese craft arrive laden with sawn timber from Kalimantan (Borneo), which is off-loaded at a 2-km (1.2-mile) long wharf that has been in continuous use since 1817. A brisk morning walk amidst this nautical bustle to the sea, to witness mammoth sails unfurling to the wind, is one of the unforgettable experiences of Jakarta.

The area around Sunda Kelapa is rich in history. Directly across the river stands a 19th-Century Dutch lookout tower (the Uitkijk), constructed upon the site of the original customs house (Pabean) of Jayakarta. This is where traders once rendered their gifts and

The church in Batavia, 1811.

94

tribute to the native ruler in return for the privilege of trading here. The tower is sometimes open and offers a panoramic view of the city and the coast.

Behind the lookout stands a long, two-storey structure dating from VOC times, now the *Museum Bahari*. This warehouse was erected by the Dutch in 1652 and used for many years to store coffee, tea and Indian cloth. Inside are displays of traditional sailing craft from all corners of the Indonesian archipelago, as well as some old maps of Batavia. Down a narrow lane and around a corner behind the museum lies the fish market (Pasar Ikan), beyond numerous stalls selling nautical gear.

Sights of Old Batavia

Batavia came to life in the 1620s, as a tiny walled town modelled after Amsterdam. Most of the original settlement—Old Batavia—was demolished at the beginning of the 19th Century. Only the town square area survived. It has been restored and renamed **Taman Fatahillah**, and three of the surrounding colonial edifices have been converted into museums: the Jakarta History Museum, the Fine Arts Museum and the Wayang Museum. They are all open Tuesday through Thursday, 8:30 a.m. to 2:30 p.m.; Friday 8:30 a.m. to 11 p.m. and Saturday 8:30 a.m. to 1 p.m. (Closed Monday.)

Start at the **Jakarta History Museum** on the south side of the square. This was formerly the city hall (Stadhuis) of Batavia, a solid structure completed in 1710 and used by successive governments right up through the 1960s. It now houses fascinating memorabilia from the colonial period, notably 18th-Century furnishings and portraits of the VOC governors, along with many prehistoric, classical and Portuguese period artifacts. Dungeons, visible from the back of the building, were used as holding cells where prisoners were made to stand waist-deep in sewage for weeks awaiting their trials. Executions and public tortures were once commonplace, performed daily in the main square as judges watched from the balcony above the main entrance.

The **Wayang Museum** on the western side of the square contains many puppets and masks, some of them quite

A view of Jakarta today.

95

rare. There are buffalo-hide shadow puppets (*wayang kulit*), round-stick puppets (*wayang golek*), flat-stick puppets (*wayang klithik*), Chinese hand puppets (*potehi*), Thai shadow puppets (*wayang siam*), patriotic shadow puppets (*wayang Suluh*), Biblical shadow puppets (*wayang wahyu*), and even a puppet of Batavia's founder, J.P. Coen. Interesting, too, are the simple puppets made of rice straw and bamboo. There is also a collection of *topeng* masks, and tombstones of several early Dutch governors are on display. Every Sunday morning a puppet performance is staged between 10 a.m. and 11 a.m.

The Fine Arts Museum (**Museum Seni Rupa**) on the east side of Fatahillah square is housed in the former Court of Justice building (completed in 1879). The museum has collections of paintings and sculptures by modern Indonesian artists, and an important exhibition of rare porcelains, including many Sung celadons from the Adam Malik collection, ancient Javanese waterjugs (*kendhi*), and terracottas dating from the Majapahit period (14th Century).

Before leaving the area, walk over to the cannon mounted on the north side of Taman Fatahillah. Si Jago, as he is called, is regarded by many as a fertility symbol, perhaps because of the fist cast into the butt end of the cannon, whose thumb protrudes between its index and middle fingers (an obscene gesture in Indonesia). Occasionally, young couples are seen approaching with offerings. The wife then straddles the cannon's barrel, in the hope of thereby conceiving a child.

Next, walk behind the Wayang Museum to view two Dutch houses dating from the 18th Century. Across the canal and to the left stands a solid red-brick townhouse (Jl. Kali Besar Barat No.11) that was built around 1730 by the then soon-to-be Governor-General Van Imhoff. The design and particularly the fine Chinese-style woodwork are typical of old Batavian residences. Three doors to the left stands the only other house from the same period, now the offices of the Chartered Bank. Several blocks to the north, an old wooden drawbridge straddles the canal, recalling the days when Batavia was a Dutch town laced with waterways.

As is the case in most post-colonial

Ships in Jakarta harbour.

Asian cities, Jakarta's Chinatown is immediately adjacent to the old European town centre—here just to the south of the old city in an area now known as **Glodok**. Give yourself an hour on foot to tour Jakarta's busiest district. Begin at the Glodok Plaza/City Hotel (Jl. Pancoran) and walk back through the maze of narrow lanes to the canal. Turn left (south), past busy shopfronts selling clothing, food, medicine, electronic and household goods, to arrive at the Jin-de Yuan temple on Gang Petak Sembilan. This is the oldest of Jakarta's more than 70 Chinese temples (founded ca. 1650), and in it are enshrined numerous Buddhist, Taoist and popular deities, including several deified Chinese notables of Old Batavia.

Central Jakarta

A circumnavigation of central Jakarta begins at the top of the **National Monument** (Monas), a 137-metre (450-foot) marble obelisk set in the centre of Freedom Square (Medan Merdeka). The monument is surmounted by an observation deck and a 14-metre (45-foot) bronze flame sheathed in 33 kg (73 lbs) of gold. It was commissioned by Sukarno and completed in 1961—a combination Olympic Flame/Washington Monument with the phallic overtones of an ancient Hindu-Javanese *lingga*. In the basement is a series of dioramas depicting historical scenes from a nationalistic viewpoint. A high-speed elevator shoots you to the observation deck. (Open 9 a.m. to 5 p.m. daily)

From Monas, travel north along Jl. Gajah Mada to the splendid villa that now houses the **National Archives**. This is the last out of scores of 18th-Century mansions built by rich Dutch officials of the East India Company. Unfortunately, special permission is needed to tour the building, but even from the street the beautiful woodwork and manicured gardens that were once the hallmark of Batavia are visible.

Double back to Medan Merdeka and pass behind the **Presidential Palace**, situated between Jl. Medan Merdeka Utara and Jl. Veteran. The palace building consists of two 19th-Century neo-classical-style villas back-to-back. The older of the two, the Istana Negara, faces north and was built by a wealthy Dutch merchant around 1800. It was

National Museum.

taken over some years later to serve as the town residence of the governor (whose official residence was then located in Bogor). The southern-facing Istana Merdeka was added in 1879, as a reception area. Whereas President Sukarno resided in the palace and frequently gave lavish banquets in the central courtyard, President Suharto prefers to stay in his more modest home in the Menteng area and commutes to work.

Proceeding eastward, one encounters the imposing white marble **Istiqlal Mosque** with its massive dome and rakish minarets—said to be the largest mosque in East Asia. Opposite it are the ultra-modern headquarters of Pertamina, the state oil monopoly that supplies a tenth of OPEC's oil and well over half the state's revenue.

Lapangan Banteng (Wild-Ox Field) lies just to the east, bounded on the north by the neo-Gothic National Cathedral (completed in 1901), on the east by the Supreme Court (1848) and the Department of Finance (1982), and on the south by the monstrous Borobudur Hotel. In the centre of the square stands a muscle-bound giant bursting from his shackles. This is the **Irian Jaya Freedom Memorial**—placed here in 1963 by Sukarno to commemorate the annexation of Irian Jaya (West New Guinea). When the statue was first erected, Jakartans joked that the giant was crying "empty"—with reference to the Finance Department behind.

Returning to the eastern side of Medan Merdeka, one passes two more colonial structures: the Gedung Pancasila (1830) where Sukarno unveiled his five principles of the Indonesian state, and the small Emmanuel Church (1835), meant to resemble a Greek temple. The Jakarta Fair (an exhibition complex) and an amusement park called Taman Ria occupy the southern quadrant of the square.

On the western border of Medan Merdeka lies one of Indonesia's great cultural treasures: the **National Museum**. Opened in 1868 by the Batavian Society for Arts and Sciences—the first scholarly organization in colonial Asia (founded 1778)—the museum houses enormously valuable collections of antiquities, books and ethnographic artifacts acquired by the Dutch during the 19th and early 20th centuries. Un-

Istiqlal Mosque.

fortunately the displays are not well labelled, though the objects exhibited are fascinating. Hindu-Javanese stone statuary, prehistoric bronzewares and Chinese porcelains are among the exhibits that take hours to see properly. The star collection, however, is housed in the Treasure Room, open only on Sunday mornings (10 a.m. to 12 noon)— a plundered hoard of royal Indonesian heirlooms. The museum itself is open Tuesday to Sunday, 8:30 a.m. to 2:30 p.m., but closes early on Friday (11 a.m.) and Saturday (1 p.m.). Closed Monday.

Joyride to Kebayoran Baru

Hail a cab and brace yourself for the high-speed cruise down Jl. Thamrin and Jl. Sudirman to the new satellite city of **Kebayoran Baru**. Along the way, you'll pass many monuments to Indonesia's recent economic development: banks, hotels, shopping centres and office blocks. Twenty years ago, this was a ceremonial boulevard with nothing on either side. Today, it is lined with high-rise buildings.

In Kebayoran, which is the upper-

class residential suburb of the city, visit a supermarket or department store near **Blok M**, just to examine the range and prices of goods available to affluent Indonesians. The World Bank rates Jakarta one of the most expensive cities in the world, for a person living a western, consumer-oriented lifestyle. Then try one of the trendy restaurants or pubs in the area. Lastly, tour an adjacent residential neighbourhood, where an air-conditioned western-style home rents for US$1500 a month paid three years in advance!

Indonesia in Miniature

The idea behind **Taman Mini**, the "Beautiful Indonesia In Miniature Park," is to compress the entire archipelago into a single attraction. While this is surely an impossible feat, the park does at least permit you to see something of the thousands of Indonesian islands you will not visit.

Located about 10 kms (six miles) south of Jakarta and encompassing nearly 100 hectares (247 acres), Taman Mini has 27 main pavilions—one for each of Indonesia's provinces. These are clustered around a lake containing a three-dimensional relief map of the Indonesian archipelago. The pavilions have been constructed using authentic materials and workmanship to exhibit a traditional style of architecture from each province. Inside are displays of handicrafts, traditional costumes, musical instruments and other artifacts for which the region is known. Many items are sold as souvenirs.

In addition, there are at least 30 other attractions, including a Tropical Bird Park, an Orchid Garden, a mock-up of Borobudur (one-quarter scale), a swimming pool, and the splendid new **Museum Indonesia**—a three-storey air-conditioned Balinese palace filled with traditional textiles, houses, boats, puppets, jewellery and wedding costumes.

On Sundays, many of the pavilions schedule dance and theatrical performances, and the crowds are correspondingly large. During the week, Taman Mini is eerily deserted, and many pavilions are closed. Whenever you go, be sure to bring along your swimming gear for a cool dip in the new pool behind the museum—wonderfully refreshing after a hot day of sightseeing. Open between 9 a.m. and 5 p.m. daily.

West Sumatran wedding regalia on display in a traditional house from Jakarta's Taman Mini.

JAVA: INDONESIA'S HEARTLAND

The fabulously fertile island of Java, home of one of man's earliest ancestors, today virtually constitutes a world unto itself. Over 100 million people live here on an island the size of England, which means that the population density (800 per sq km/2,000 per sq mile) is at least double that of any other area of comparable extent on the planet.

Beyond sheer weight of numbers, however, the Javanese also possess a rich historical record and a unique cultural heritage. Java's dance and dramatic traditions, *wayang* puppets, *gamelan* music and *batik* textiles are famous the world over, as are her ancient temples and elegant palaces.

The island's physical beauty is less widely renowned, perhaps, but no less captivating. From the tropical rainforests of Ujung Kulon, to the alpine meadows of Mt. Gede Pangrango, to the black sand dunes of Parangtritis and the unforgettable moonscapes of Mt. Bromo—Java has a private place for almost everyone.

The Garden of the East

Since ancient times, Java has been known as a lush island paradise. Rich volcanic soils, watered by the yearly monsoonal rains and baked by the equatorial sun, produce what must once have been (before man felled it) the world's most luxuriant tropical rainforest—a tangle of exotic flowers, palms, fruits, ferns, lianas, epiphytes and towering hardwood trees.

For thousands of years, this was the land of the rhinoceros (*badak*), the Javan tiger, the wild ox (*banteng*), the mousedeer (*kancil*) and the Javan gibbon, which together with numerous palm civets, flying foxes, coconut squirrels, monitor lizards, crocodiles, pythons, hornbills, kingfishers, egrets, terns, starlings and peacocks, still inhabit the island's few remaining jungle refuges. The great naturalist Alfred Russel Wallace was so struck by the abundance and dizzying diversity of floral and faunal types on Java, that he proclaimed it, "that noble and fertile island —the very Garden of the East."

Physically, Java is distinguished by her many volcanoes, and indeed volcanoes are such a dominant feature of the Javan land-

scape that one of the island's 121 cones is nearly always within view—its weathered, blue-grey outline rising majestically skyward, commonly to a height of 3,000 to 4,000 metres (10,000 to 13,000 feet). Approximately 30 of these behemoths are still active, and in several parts of the island they produce cauldrons of bubbling mud (solfataras), vented jets of gas (fumaroles) and hot sulphur springs. Every few years, a subterranean convulsion produces massive eruptions of ash and lava, unleashing poisonous gases, clouds of scorching dust (*ladoes*)

and avalanches of boiling mud (*lahars*) which wipe out entire villages, sometimes killing hundreds and rendering thousands homeless.

Yet despite their awesome destructiveness, volcanic eruptions are in fact the ultimate source of Java's legendary fecundity. For while volcanic ejecta in many parts of the world is acidic, here it is chemically basic, rich in soluble plant nutrients such as calcium, magnesium, nitrogen and phosphorus. Thus the thousands of tons of ash periodically spewn into the atmosphere and onto the surrounding countryside with such devastating results, are actually a blessing in disguise. Where the ash settles, or is later transported by the vigorous action of mon-

Left, Sri Sunan Pakubuwana XII at coronation anniversary. Right, a farmer working in Central Java—one of the most fertile regions of the Indonesian archipelago.

soonal rains, the soils are fertilized to an extraordinary degree.

Geologically, the island and her volcanoes are exceptionally young. They began to form only 2 to 3 million years ago (Upper Pliocene/Lower Pleistocene times), as a result of tectonic pressures along a major fault between two rigid plates of the earth's crust. Soft sedimentary rocks resting over the fault were folded and uplifted, so that the island's basic structure consists of two almost parallel lengthwise folds, separated by a deep medial trough which is narrow in the west and broadens to the east, eventually submerging in the Straits of Madura.

It is through this medial trough that most of Java's volcanoes have thrust upwards, erecting a lofty array of peaks and sculpting the lowlands generally with deposits of igneous material. In the west, closely packed festoons of volcanoes have created a tangle of uplands and two large basins (Bandung and Garut), that remained relatively isolated from the rest of the island until Dutch roads and railways opened them for cultivation in the 19th Century.

In the central and eastern regions, the greater width of the trough and the 30-to-50-km (20-to-30-mile) spacing of the major volcanic clusters produced a spectacular series of five gently sloping interstitial valleys, which have hosted, since very early times, one of the great civilizations of humankind. These valleys are separated from the north coast by the folded Kendeng Range, and from the Indian Ocean by a band of elevated limestone plateaus, but internal communication among them is not seriously hindered and today each has developed large urban centres (Yogyakarta, Surakarta, Madiun, Kediri and Malang).

Given the ideal agricultural and climatic conditions found on the island, it is no surprise that Java has been populated and cultivated for centuries. After all, this is where the world's first *Homo erectus* or "Java Man" fossils were discovered. (*See* Part I: "Pre-History".) What *is* remarkable, however, is the intensity of cultivation on the island and the enormous population that it now supports. This is a fairly recent phenomenon, largely the result of 19th Century Dutch colonial policies.

Around 1800, it is estimated that Java had about 3.5 million inhabitants—a figure, it is true, which was kept low by frequent wars and famines, but one which had nevertheless remained relatively stable since the time of the great Hindu-Buddhist empires a millennium earlier. Wet-rice cultivation has al-

ways, of course, formed the basis for Javanese civilization, and as long as the population was still fairly small and only the choicest land was tilled, the Javanese were able to produce vast surpluses.

The earliest rulers of Java based their power upon the resources which surplus rice afforded, provisioning armies of warriors and labourers to do their bidding. Later, with the general increase in world commerce during Hindu and Islamic times, surplus rice was shipped overseas and traded, often passing through several hands, but always bringing a wealth of precious metals, gems, textiles, ceramics and manufactured goods home to Java from abroad.

All of this changed dramatically following the intervention of the Dutch in Javanese economic and political affairs, culminating with the institution, from 1830 to 1870, of the infamous Cultivation System (*Cultuurstelsel*) of forced labour and land-use taxes. Under this system, more and more Javanese lands were opened to cultivation, the products of which the Dutch sold at such a handsome profit overseas.

An unforeseen side-effect of these colonial policies was uncontrollable Javanese growth. By 1900, the population of Java had soared by 28 million and today it stands at about 110 million.

Not everyone on the island is Javanese. In the uplands of West Java, the inhabitants are mainly Sundanese, a people with their own language and identity. The Javanese themselves constitute about two-thirds of the total population and inhabit the fertile plains of Central and East Java plus much of the island's northern coast, with the exception of the island of Madura and the adjoining shores of East Java—home of the Madurese people. There are, in addition, small pockets of Tenggerese and Badui peoples living in isolated highland sanctuaries at the far eastern and western ends of Java respectively. Lastly, the trading ports of the north Java coast also harbour cosmopolitan communities of immigrant Chinese, Arabs and Europeans, as well as seafarers and traders from islands of the Indonesian archipelago.

Each group has its own heritage, language and culture—the capital city of Jakarta has in fact become such a melting pot that Indonesians no longer consider it a part of Java (which is why it is treated separately here). Although *Bahasa Indonesia*, the Indonesian national language (a variant of Malay), is the lingua franca throughout the island, in most towns and villages, day-to-day conversations are still carried on in

Sundanese, Javanese and Madurese.

Culturally, Java is also a giant pot-pourri. There is a repertoire of dance, drama and comedy which draws its inspiration alternatively from the Hindu epics, from the exploits of Islamic warriors, and from the tales of ancient Javanese folk heroes. There are mosques where white-capped *hajis* finger their prayer beads, Chinese temples where stone lions guard the gates, and churches where choirs sing. There are trance rituals whose origins are as misty as mankind's own beginnings and puppets in leather and wood who entrance local audiences through all-night performances. More than that, there is a music of gongs and chimes which is as glistening and fluid as quicksilver, yet as textured as the face of the land. (*See* Part

IV, "Dance and Drama" and "Gamelan.")

An island of such depth and complexity naturally has a darker side to its personality. No country in the world, after hundreds of years of domination by a foreign power, has ever been able to achieve social and economic justice in a quarter of a century. And, it would be ridiculous to suggest that over-populated Java is without its problems. The distance between the privileged and the poor is obvious. There is a need for more jobs, schools and medical facilities. And there are signs of youthful alienation and religious discontent—an overt rejection of older communal and cultural values, and at the same time a dissatisfaction with newer imported ones.

Yet despite these social and economic problems, there is an underlying current of hopefulness. Desperate people cannot laugh with the spontaneity of the Javanese nor can they find real pleasure in simple things. Least of all can they be as generous in action and in spirit as the people of Java.

Java is a wonderful place for the explorer who wants to get off the beaten track. The arrival of a foreigner in remote towns and villages is an entertainment, an event which adds spice and flavour to an otherwise ordinary day. You'll be greeted with shrill cries of "Londo, Londo" (which originally meant "Hollander" and now applies to any pale-face). A boisterous crowd of children trail after you down village paths screaming "Hallo Mister." Eyes fix on you as you tuck into a plate of fried rice at a food stall. Giggles, cheekiness and laughter follow.

Sometimes, tired and fretful after the rigours of a journey, you may feel like screaming. And often, when voices are raised and tempers fray, it is a frenetic Westerner who is at fault—not in tune with the gentle flow of Javanese time, but obsessed with the seconds, minutes and hours of schedules. The average Westerner, enmeshed in a private world, also shrinks from physical contact. The Javanese do not. A seat meant for two will always take three, buttocks to thigh. Proximity means friendliness and warmth; people are people.

So, though you may already have a long list of temples, dances and places that you want to see, or may quickly develop one while reading through the pages that follow, keep in mind that it is a mistake to try to do too much on Java—to keep yourself on a rapid-fire itinerary of planes, trains, tour-buses, sights and performances. Take a few days off instead and retreat for hikes in the cool mountains; or visit the secluded south shore; or tour the north coast—as yet virtually undiscovered by tourists; or seek out one of the several dozen more rarely visited Hindu temples on the island. But above all, take your time, for in Java, perhaps more than in any place else in the world, the travel experience offers the chance to be spontaneous and personal. Take the chance. You will find yourself engulfed in a world of extraordinary variety and vitality. You may also become the happy victim of a great and enduring passion for one of the world's last bastions of serendipity.

Above, working in a padi field in Central Java. Even though more than 50 per cent of Java is under cultivation, Java still has to import food. Right, ubiquitous smiling Javanese children.

WEST JAVA

The exigencies of time and the search for more relaxing climes generally press the traveller onward to Yogyakarta and Bali after only a brief stopover in Jakarta. Little do most visitors suspect, however, that within West Java itself, and only hours from the capital city, are sandy beaches and breathtaking landscapes as attractive as any in the more heavily visited destinations to the east.

And while it may be true that the Sundanese of West Java lack the courtly sophistications and architectural monuments of a high civilization—they are certainly no cultural paupers. Their rhythmically complex *gamelan* and *angklung* music, popular *jaipongan* dances and lively *wayang golek* puppet performances have achieved every bit as much recognition as similar art forms in Central Java or Bali.

Above all, the "Sunda Lands" are among the most beautiful and most accessible highlands in all of Indonesia. So if you prefer the exhilaration of a mountain climb, or the thrill of glimpsing rare wildlife species, to the endless round of temples, palaces and dance performances, then you should consider spending some time in West Java.

Encompassing much of the western third of Java, the so-called "Sunda Lands" (Tanah Sunda) are where the Sundanese people live. Although physically indistinguishable from the Javanese of Central and East Java, they are culturally quite different—known for their mellifluous language, hardy individualism and staunch adherence to Islam.

West Java may be roughly divided into two distinct regions: the Parahyangan (Abode of the Gods) or volcanic highlands, and the northern coastal plain. The coast is much more mixed, culturally, having absorbed a multitude of immigrants and influences via its trading ports for many centuries, and in certain coastal areas (notably around Jakarta and Banten), Javanese and Indonesian are more commonly spoken than Sundanese.

The Sundanese highlands, though relatively impenetrable and very sparsely populated until the 19th Century, have

West Javanese padi patterns.

also been inhabited for many millennia. Neolithic stepped pyramids, pottery shards and stone tools have been found in several areas. And from the 5th Century onwards, Hindu kingdoms such as Tarumanagara, Galuh and Pajajaran flourished here, leaving behind a handful of temples and inscriptions.

During the early 16th Century, the coastal ports of Banten and Jayakarta (later Batavia, now Jakarta) were conquered by Islamic forces from Demak and Cirebon, and Banten then rose to prominence as a major trading emporium. The prosperity and influence of Banten was founded upon control of the pepper trade, pepper being a commodity that was then produced in abundance in southern Sumatra (Lampung).

The Dutch, when they arrived, sought to corner the market on pepper, and for several years Batavia and Banten competed fiercely, until finally the Dutch attacked and subdued Banten in 1683. At about this time also, the Dutch were ceded much of the rugged Priangan (Parahyangan) highlands by the ruler of Central Java, Amangkurat II. For many years, however, they remained unable to penetrate these tangled uplands and a number of local rulers administered them autonomously.

The great trans-Java post road, constructed by order of Governor-General Daendels between 1808 and 1811, finally opened up the Sundanese hinterland by linking Batavia (Jakarta) with what is now Bandung, via Bogor and Sukabumi. From 1830 onwards, and especially after 1870, when the Dutch allowed certain enterprising Englishmen to operate tea, cinchona (quinine) and rubber estates here, the highlands of West Java became the cornerstone of the colonial economy. Eventually, 5,000 sq kms (2,000 sq miles) or over 10 per cent of all land in West Java was cleared and planted with cash crops, of which coffee was the most important.

The cool highland climate attracted European residents as well, and first Bogor (Buitenzorg) then Bandung became Dutch administrative centres. Today these cities continue to attract new residents at a rate disproportionate to their size, and modern industry has followed. Many textile and pharmaceutical plants, even an aircraft factory, operate here with the result that the province of West Java, together with Jakarta, is economically the most advanced region in Indonesia.

Escape From Jakarta

There are a number of ways to escape from Jakarta without actually leaving western Java. The easiest option is to hop a boat or plane to one of the 600 islands clustered offshore to the north of the city, known collectively as the **Thousand Islands** (Pulau Seribu). Several of the closer islands, notably Onrust, were used by the East India Company as warehousing and drydocking stations, and the ruins of these colonial installations, from the 17th and 18th centuries, can still be seen.

Many other islands are privately owned as weekend hideaways. One of them, **Pulau Putri**, has been developed as a tourist resort with air-conditioned bungalows and an airstrip. All the islands are encircled by coral reefs, and this is an excellent place for aquatic sports of all sorts: snorkeling, scuba diving, water skiing, wind surfing and sailing.

Another quick getaway, soon to be made even quicker with the opening of the new Jakarta-to-Merak expressway, is the jaunt to Java's sandy and secluded

The old city walls of Banten providing fun for Javanese children.

West Coast Beaches. Depending on the method of transportation, the route taken and the traffic, you can enjoy a swim and a cool ocean breeze within three to five hours of leaving the city.

History buffs will want to stop along the way at the village of **Banten**—the site, during the 16th Century, of one of Asia's largest and most cosmopolitan trading emporiums. Banten town was razed by order of Dutch Governor-General Daendels in 1808, and is today but a tiny fishing village straddling a tidal creek, but the ruins of two massive palaces and a Dutch fortress, plus the interesting old mosque (with its adjacent museum) and a famous Chinese temple are all well worth the detour. (*See* "Guide in Brief.")

The Western Beaches

About 110 kms (68 miles) west of Jakarta, at Cilegon, the main road branches off to the right (north) and brings you, after 13 more kms (8 miles), to the small harbour of **Merak**, where ferries depart hourly for Bakauhuni on Sumatra. There is a narrow beach and an efficiently run motel at Merak, but the more spacious beaches between Anyer and Carita to the south are more inviting. The area around **Cilegon** itself is dominated by the vast Krakatau Steel Mill complex, with its adjoining country club, 18-hole golf course and guesthouse.

There are pretty bays and long stretches of deserted beach past the village of **Anyer**, 20 kms (12 miles) to the west and south of Cilegon—also an old lighthouse and a luxurious seaside motel, complete with bowling alleys and a swimming pool. Six kms (4 miles) past the motel, at **Karang Bolong**, a huge rock forms a natural archway to the sea and this has become a popular (and crowded) weekend swimming spot for Jakartans. Twenty-two kms (14 miles) farther down the coast, around the village of **Carita**, two beachside bungalow resorts offer good accommodation, swimming, sailing, diving and dining.

In addition to sun, sea, sand and solitude, this palm-fringed coast is famous for its sunset views out across the uninhabited volcanic islands of **Krakatau**. Though dormant for centuries, this volcano achieved instant and lasting infamy in 1883 when it erupted with

Krakatau and "Anak" Krakatau.

cataclysmic force, ripping out a huge chunk of the earth's crust to form a monstrous 41-sq-km (16-sq-mile) submarine caldera. The sea rushed in, and tidal waves up to 30 metres (100 feet) high swept the coast, claiming more than 35,000 lives. In the decades that followed, undersea activity continued and a new cone with a gaping half-crater has emerged from the sea—Anak Krakatau ("Son of Krakatau"). Today the four tiny islands of the Krakatau group may be visited by chartering a boat from the port of **Labuan** for the smooth four-hour voyage.

Boats can also be chartered from Labuan to **Ujung Kulon National Park** at Java's southwestern tip, for a tramp through pristine tropical rainforests and a first-hand look at some of Java's rare wildlife species. (*See* Part IV, "Indonesia's Incredible Wildlife.") And there is a scenic backroad, leaving Labuan to the east, that winds through the Parahyangan foothills to Rangkasbitung and Bogor, skirting the highland home of the mysterious Badui people. (*See* "Guide in Brief.")

The third, and perhaps most scenic, of West Java's "escape routes" from

Jakarta is the ascent into the dramatic Parahyangan highlands to the south of the city. First stop, along this route, is the town of **Bogor**—now only an hour's drive from the city via the new Jagorawi Expressway. Situated about 80 kms (50 miles) inland and 290 metres (900 feet) above sea level in the foothills of Mt. Salak, Bogor is appreciably cooler (and wetter) than Jakarta.

The main attraction here are the glorious **Botanical Gardens** (Kebun Raya), originally opened by the Dutch in 1817 and world renowned, during the 19th Century, for its range of tropical botanical specimens and its research into cash crops such as tea, cassava, tobacco and cinchona. The vast park, with its rolling lawns, lily ponds and forest groves, now contains over 15,000 species of trees and plants (including 400 different types of palms), and special orchid nurseries house more than 5,000 orchid varieties from Indonesia and abroad. There is also an excellent zoological museum and a library of richly illustrated botanical tomes. The elegant white presidential summer palace, constructed by the Dutch in 1856 as the official residence for governors-general of the Dutch East Indies, stands at the northern end of the gardens. (Open daily 9 a.m. to 5 p.m. very crowded on Sundays.)

The road east from Bogor up to **Puncak Pass** climbs steadily, winding its way through a manicured landscape of tea plantations. Stop at the Rindu Alam Restaurant on the right just before the peak to enjoy a spectacular view (on a clear day) down to Jakarta and the coast. Walk across the road and downhill a short distance to find a path leading to tiny **Telaga Warna** ("Lake of Many Colours.")

Seven kms (4 miles) beyond Puncak Pass, a turn-off to the right leads to the **Cibodas Botanical Gardens**, an extension of Bogor's Kebun Raya famous for its collection of montane and temperate-climate flora from around the world. This is also the starting point for the six-hour climb up to the peaks of Mt. Gede and Mt. Pangrango, with their fine views, hotsprings, waterfalls and interesting wildlife. (*See* Part IV, "Indonesia's Incredible Wildlife.") Excellent accommodation and food are available in the nearby mountain resort of **Cipanas** and this is a lovely place to spend a few days, hiking through the highland forests and tea estates.

The southern coast of West Java, beautiful but dangerous, is also within easy reach of Bogor (about two hours by car). A good road winds south from Ciawi over the pass between Mt. Pangrango and Mt. Salak, where the valleys and hillsides are a lush garden of rubber trees, tea plantations and terraced rice-fields. A scenic sideroad branches off to the right at Cibadak and meanders down to the fishing village of **Pelabuhan Ratu**, where the ragged, wind-lashed Indian Ocean foams and crashes onto smooth black-sand beaches.

The village itself is unspoilt and vital—when the boats moor in the morning, the fish market does a roaring trade in fresh tunafish, prawns, whitebait, sharks, stingrays and other delicacies. A number of good swimming beaches and hotels line the coast for several kms past the town (*See* "Guide in Brief"), but be warned that the surf and the undertow here can be treacherous, so don't venture in farther than waist-deep. From the village of Cisolok, 15 kms (9 miles) beyond Pelabuhan Ratu, a small road leads inland to a sulphur spring gushing from a tiny streambed. With a sturdy vehicle and a sense of adventure, you can then continue on to the goldmines at Cikotok and beyond—ending up eventually at Labuan on the west coast.

Bandung: 'City of Flowers'

Only three hours from Jakarta by train, four or more by road, the highland city of **Bandung** offers a cool alternative to the capital's oppressive heat. Located in a huge basin 700 metres (2,300 feet) above sea level and surrounded on all sides by lofty peaks, Bandung is now the population and cultural centre of the Sunda Lands, a burgeoning city with over 1.5 million inhabitants. Before the war, it was a quaint Dutch administrative and university town of about 150,000—then known as the Paris of Java because of its broad, shady boulevards and elegant homes. Today, although a rapidly growing industrial city with snarled traffic and often-polluted air, Bandung is still green and attractive; and is popularly referred to by residents as Kota Kembang—the "City of Flowers."

Aside from the charming colonial

Tangkuban Prahu.

ambience imparted by numerous Dutch mansions, shops and hotels dating from the 1920s and 1930s, Bandung's sights are actually quite few. The **Geological Museum** on Jl. Diponegoro (opposite the imposing Gedung Sate provincial government headquarters) is definitely worth a visit, for a look at the extraordinary array of rocks, maps and fossils displayed here—including replicas of the famous "Java Man" *Homo erectus* skulls found in Central Java. Incidentally, the Publications Department, upstairs in the back building, makes and sells copies of detailed Dutch survey maps for nearly all places in Indonesia.

The campus of Bandung's **Institute of Technology (ITB)**, Indonesia's oldest and finest university, is also interesting. The institute's library, built in the 1920s, is a honeycomb of massive wooden girders, and ITB students have a reputation for outspokenness and activism. Spend some time, too, wandering in the old Dutch shopping district downtown around Jl. Braga, and have a look into the newly remodelled art-deco Savoy Homann Hotel on Jl. Asia-Afrika. The town's large flower market is nearby (on Jl. Wastukencana)

Driving through Bandung.

and if you are interested in the Sundanese performing arts, then spend a morning observing classes at the Music Conservatory (Jl. Buah Batu 212) or at Pak Udjo's private *angklung* school (Jl. Padasuka 118) in Bandung's suburbs. In the evenings, attend one of several local theatres and clubs to observe traditional music, dance or puppet performances. (*See* "Guide in Brief.")

Bandung's most exciting excursion, though, is a visit to one of the neighbouring volcanic highlands. The nearest and most frequently visited peak is **Tangkuban Prahu**, the "Upturned Boat" volcano lying 32 kms (20 miles) to the north of the city. A steep, narrow road turns off to the left a short distance past the vegetable-growing town of **Lembang**, and winds right up to the crater's 1,830-metre (5,700-foot) rim. Here, cold mountain mists and sulphurous fumes swirl up around jagged, scrub-covered ridges, and souvenir sellers offer you strange monkey-like objects fashioned from tree-fern fibres. After this rather chilling experience, make your way quickly down to the **Ciater** hot springs, 7 kms (4 miles) beyond the Tangkuban Prahu exit, for a meal and a soothing soak in one of their piping-hot pools. Accommodation is available at Ciater, as well as at Lembang and at nearby **Maribaya**—where there are also hot springs and numerous nature trails.

Several peaks to the south of Bandung are even more spectacular but, higher and more rarely visited, they are somewhat difficult to find. At **Ciwidey**, 30 kms (19 miles) to the southwest of the city, you'll find blacksmiths turning out a fascinating range of hand-forged knives and daggers, and then you can continue on up through the tea estates to scenic Lake Patenggang or to Ciwidey Crater. Alternatively, the town of **Pengalengan**, with its seemingly endless vista of manicured rolling hills, 40 kms (25 miles) due south of Bandung, is the jumping-off point for visits to the Cileunca Lakes, to the rim of Mt. Wayang, and into the "Golden Crater" of sulphurous, steaming, sputtering Mt. Papandayan. Add to all of these the old Dutch hill station of **Garut**, with its hot springs and reconstructed Hindu temple, and you could easily spend weeks exploring the beautiful southern Parahyangan mountains. (*See* "Guide in Brief" for further details.)

JAVA'S NORTH COAST

The northern coastal (*pesisir*) ports of Java were once the busiest and richest towns on the island; they served, in effect, as exporters of agricultural produce from the fertile Javanese hinterland, as builders and outfitters of large spice-trading fleets, and as trading entrepôts frequented by merchants from all corners of the globe. Between the 15th and 17th centuries, when Islam was a new and growing force in the archipelago, these ports also flourished as political and religious centres for powerful rulers who spread the word of the prophet at home and abroad.

Most of the *pesisir* harbours have long ago silted up, and their major monuments are few. Consequently, foreigners seldom visit the north coast, even though it is one of the finest areas for handicrafts in Indonesia and contains many unique sights: eccentric palaces, holy graves, ancient mosques, bustling markets and colourful Chinese temples. Perhaps the coast's greatest attraction, however, is that it is completely off the beaten tourist track.

Eclectic Cirebon

The first port of call if you are taking the northern route is the ancient sultanate of **Cirebon**—once a powerful court centre and still a fascinating pot-pourri of Sundanese, Javanese, Chinese, Islamic and European influences. It's a rather sleepy place now, with a small harbour and a sizeable fishing industry. While it is famous for its seafood, it is physically indistinguishable from many other mid-sized Javanese cities. As you begin to explore Cirebon's byways, however, the town's colourful past quickly comes to life.

Cirebon's two major palaces were both built in 1678 in order that each of two princes could have his own court. The **Kraton Kesepuhan** (palace of the "elder brother") was raised upon the site of the 15th Century Pakungwati palace of Cirebon's earlier Hindu rulers, and one of the royal pavilions occupying the forecourt bears the date 1425. This complex, with its split red-brick gate (*candi bentar*) and several elaborately carved audience pavilions,

is undoubtedly one of the finest ex-Hindu-Javanese architecture in existence.

The palace itself is Javanese in design, but thoroughly composite in its execution. A Romanesque archway framed by mystical Chinese rocks and clouds gives onto a spacious, pillared Javanese *pendopo* furnished with French period pieces. And the walls of the Dalem Ageng (ceremonial chamber) behind it are inlaid with blue-and-white Delft tiles exhibiting biblical scenes. To top it all off, the small adjoining museum contains a coach carved in the shape of a winged, horned, hooved elephant grasping a trident in its trunk; it's a glorious fusion of Javanese, Hindu, Islamic, Persian, Greek and Chinese mythological elements.

Just next to the Kesepuhan palace stands the **Mesjid Ageng** (Grand Mosque) constructed ca. 1500. Its two-tiered "meru" roof rests on an elaborate wooden scaffolding, and the interior contains imported sandstone portals and a teakwood *kala* head pulpit, together with the Demak mosque, it is one of the oldest remaining landmarks of Islam on Java.

Kraton Kanoman (the palace of the "younger brother") is nearby, reached via a bustling marketplace. Large banyan trees shade the peaceful courtyard within, and as at Kesepuhan, the furnishings are European and the walls are studded with tiles and porcelains from Holland and China. The museum here contains a collection of stakes still used to immolate the flesh of Muslim believers on Mohammed's birthday each year (*seni debus*), as well as a pair of fine coaches and relics from Cirebon's past.

Further evidence of Cirebon's extreme cultural eclecticism is to be found among the restored ruins of **Taman Arum Sunyaragi**, about 4 kms (2.5 miles) out of town on the southwestern bypass. Though originally built as a fortress in 1702 and used as a base for resistance against the Dutch, this stone, mortar and coral-rock folly was cast in its present form in 1852 by a Chinese architect, to serve as a pleasure palace-cum-hermitage for Cirebon's rajas. With its many nooks, crannies, tunnels, pools, gardens, gates and sentry cages, it is at once reminiscent of Taoist meditational grottoes and Hindu representations of Nirvana.

Five kms (three miles) north of the city along the main Jakarta road, lies the hilltop **tomb of Sunan Gunung Jati**, a 16th Century ruler of Cirebon and one of the nine *walis* who helped propagate Islam on Java. Pilgrims come to burn incense and pray in a shrine at the foot of the hill. Its guardians are said to be descendants of a sea captain who was shipwrecked here, and their shifts are still assigned like watches on a ship. The mausoleum of Gunung Jati's mentor, Sheik Datu Kahfi, sits on another hillside across the road to the east, and at the summit of this hill the grave of Gunung Jati's fifth wife, the Chinese princess Ong Tien, overlooks the sea.

Before leaving Cirebon, be sure to visit one of several artisan villages located just to the west of the city. In keeping with the area's eclectic past, these villages maintain highly distinctive traditions of calligraphic painting, *wayang* puppetry, *gamelan* music and *topeng* mask dancing, in addition to producing some of Java's most unique *batik* textiles. (*See* "Guide in Brief.")

Travelling east along the coast, the prospect is generally dull. Occasionally there are small estuarine towns where colourful boats ride easily on the tide, and rolled fishing nets shimmer in the bright sunlight like giant cocoons of raw silk. Except as a road junction, **Tegal** has little to recommend it, though pottery and handicraft enthusiasts may be tempted by the excellent ochre and brass wares produced and sold about 10 kms (6 miles) to the south of the town.

Pekalongan: Batik City

What the north coast lacks in scenic beauty it makes up for in *batik*. About 220 kms (138 miles) and four hours east of Cirebon, you arrive at **Pekalongan**, a medium-sized town that announces itself on roadside pillars as "Kota Batik"—*batik* city. Quite apart from the many factories and retail stores lining its streets, Pekalongan justifies this sobriquet by producing some of the finest and most highly prized *batik* on Java. The Pekalongan style, like Cirebon's, is unique—a blending of Muslim, Javanese, Chinese and European motifs, executed in pastel tones of mustard, ochre, olive, mauve, rose, orange and blue. Pekalongan's hallmark is the floral bouquet with hovering humming-

Taman Arum
Sunyaragi.

113

birds and butterfiles, a design deriving ultimately from 18th Century Dutch porcelains. To see the finest hand-drawn *tulis* work, visit the homes of individual *batik* artists. (*See* "Guide in Brief.")

Another 90 kms (55 miles) and two hours to the east, the large city of **Semarang** overflows out across a narrow coastal plain and up onto steeply rising foothills. Known during Islamic times for its skilled shipwrights and abundant supplies of hardwood, this otherwise insignificant town was subsequently chosen as an administrative and trading base by the Dutch, and was one of the few *pesisir* ports to successfully make the transition to steam shipping at the turn of this century. Today it is the commercial hub and provincial capital of Central Java, and the island's fourth largest city—a smaller version, in short, of Jakarta and Surabaya.

Modern Semarang possesses but few relics from the past. Most of them bear witness to the presence, in bygone days, of a large population of Dutch traders and officials, and a generous sprinkling of affluent Chinese merchants. The old **Dutch Church** on Jl. Suprapto downtown, with its copper-clad dome and Greek-cross floorplan, was consecrated in 1753 and stands at the centre of the town's 18th Century European commercial district. During the 19th Century, the Dutch built elegant mansions to the west of here, along what is now Jl. Pemuda ("Bojong"), but most of these were later torn down and replaced by shopfronts. One of the shops, **Toko Oen**, is now a charming cafe with wicker chairs, ceiling fans and a menu that has remained unchanged since colonial times.

Semarang's most interesting district, however, is its **Chinatown** (Pacinan)—a grid of narrow lanes tucked away in the centre of the city, reached by walking due south from the old church along Jl. Suari to Jl. Pekojan. Here some old townhouses retain the distinctive Nanyang style: elaborately carved doors and shutters, and delicately wrought iron balustrades. Half a dozen colourful Chinese temples and clan houses cluster in the space of a few blocks, the largest and oldest of which is on tiny **Gang Lombok** (turn to the right just by the bridge from Jl. Pekojan). This is the Thay Kak Sie temple, built in 1772,

A lion dance ‹ Gedung Batu

114

which houses more than a dozen major deities. Those with time and an interest in things Chinese will also want to visit the famous grotto **Gedung Batu**, of the deified Ming admiral Cheng Ho (Sam Po Kung), on the western outskirts of Semarang. (*See* "Guide in Brief.")

From Semarang, there are several towns to the east that may be visited either as day-trips from the city, or as stops along the coastal route to Surabaya and Bali. During the early 16th Century, a Muslim kingdom centred at **Demak** was the undisputed nonpareil amongst the coastal states of Java—now only the town's old mosque remains. Neighbouring **Kudus** was then Demak's holy city, and its Muslim quarter has beautifully carved teakwood houses and an early 16th Century mosque whose red-brick *candi bentar* gate and minaret are distinctly Hindu-Javanese in design. Today Kudus is better known as "Kota Kretek," the Kretek cigarette capital of Java.

The village of **Jepara**, 33 kms (21 miles) north of Kudus, has long been famous for its teak woodcarvings. Faithful copies of antique chairs and tables are still dowelled, slotted, tongued and joined without a nail, and there is apparently also a heavy demand for extremely detailed panels depicting scenes from the Ramayana and other Hindu-Javanese tales. Today some 4,000 carpenters work in 500 shops here.

Farther to the east, the twin towns of **Rembang** and **Lassem** are perhaps the oldest Chinese settlements on Java. Gracious Chinese country homes with upturned eaves, central courtyards and whitewashed outer walls, border on a honeycomb of narrow lanes. Both towns have exquisite Chinese temples.

The road south from Semarang climbs quickly up through the stylish Dutch residential suburb of **Candi Baru** into the foothills of Mt. Ungaran. If you have time, make a detour from the town of Ambarawa to the cool mountain resort of **Bandungan**, to visit the **Gedung Songo** temples—some of the oldest and certainly the most spectacularly situated antiquities in Java. These nine Sivaitic shrines were built sometime in the 8th Century, and perch on a series of collines overlooking the majestic peaks and verdant valleys of Central Java.

Woodcarver at Jepara.

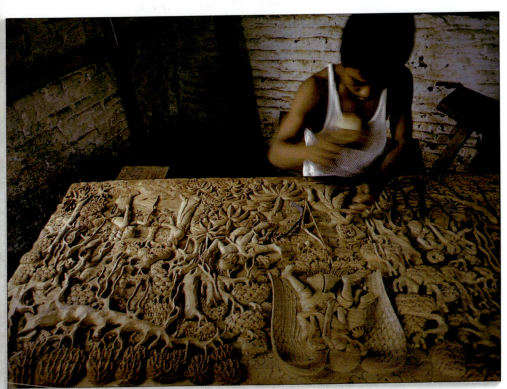

YOGYAKARTA

The broad, green crescent of fertile ricelands that blankets Mt. Merapi's southern flanks—with the historic city of Yogyakarta as its focal point—is today inhabited by about 10 million Javanese. Rural population densities here soar above 1,000 people per sq km (2,500 per square mile) and in some areas a sq km of land feeds an astounding 2,000 people (5,000 per sq mile), under the most labour-intensive cultivation conditions found on earth.

The area also embraces a seemingly disproportionate number of cultural attractions. The somber stillness of its beautiful Hindu and Buddhist temples, from the 8th, 9th and 10th centuries, is found again in the sequestered courtyards of its 18th Century Islamic palaces, where the liquid cadences of the stately Central Javanese *gamelan* provide a measured counterpoint to the boisterous clamour of colourful city streets and crowded village markets.

Most of the "official" tourist sights are concentrated in and around the twin court cities of Yogyakarta (Jogja) and Surakarta (Solo), for it was here, on the well-irrigated banks of several adjacent rivers, that Central Java's two great Mataram empires (one ancient and one modern) flourished. The role of the Javanese courts as cultural "centres of gravity"—taxing and patronizing scores of satellite villages—has long been recognised, but their vast catalogue of artistic wealth has only begun to be explored.

Though it was founded only in 1755, the sprawling city of Yogyakarta (pop. 500,000) is situated at the very core of an ancient region known as Mataram—site of the first great Central Javanese empires. From the 8th until the early 10th centuries, this fertile, sloping plain between the Progo and the Opak Rivers, was ruled by a succession of Indianized kings—the builders of Borobudur, Prambanan and dozens of other elaborate stone monuments. (*See* Part I, "An Age of Empires.") In about 928, however, these rulers suddenly and inexplicably shifted their capital to eastern Java, and for more than six centuries thereafter, Mataram remained rel-

Preceding pages, *wayang kulit* shadow play at Yogyakarta. Below, Bedoyo dancers in Yogya Kraton circa 1860.

atively deserted.

At the end of the 16th Century, the area was revived by a new Islamic power based at Kota Gede, just to the east of present-day Yogyakarta. This New or Second Mataram dynasty was founded around 1584 by Panembahan Senapati, and his descendants have ruled Central Java up until the present day, though with wildly varying degrees of power and influence.

Muslim Mataram achieved its greatest territorial extent under Senapati's grandson, Sultan Agung (r. 1613-45), but thereafter became embroiled in an endless series of bitter and bloody disputes that involved not only rival court factions, but the Dutch and the Madurese as well. In 1680, following the sacking of Mataram by Madurese forces, the capital was moved 50 kms (30 miles) to the east, to the basin of the Solo River near present-day Surakarta. The intrigues and fighting continued, however, and peace was finally achieved only after the kingdom was literally rent in two. By the Dutch-negotiated Treaty of Giyanti (1755), the Mataram ruler's rebellious brother was given half of the lands, appanages and incomes of the court, and the new ruler, now styling himself Sultan Hamengkubuwana I (r. 1749-92), proceeded to construct an elaborate palace complex near the graves of his dynastic forebears, at Yogyakarta.

The subsequent history of the Yogyakarta sultanate is notably one of resistance to ever-increasing colonial influence in Central Java. The court was twice invaded for failure to comply with colonial instructions—once by the Dutch in 1810 and again by the British in 1812. It was thereafter swept up in a vortex of violence during the Great Java War of rebellion (1825-30), led by the charismatic crown prince of the Yogyakarta ruling family, Pangeran Dipanagara.

In more recent times, Yogyakarta served as the capital of the beleaguered Indonesian republic for four long years during the revolution against the Dutch, from January, 1946 until December, 1949. This was a time of extraordinary social ferment—when 6 million refugees, more than 1 million young fighters and an enlightened young Sultan (Hamengkubuwana IX), transformed the venerable court city into a hotbed of

Sultan Hamengkubu-wana IX, 1946.

Sri Sultan Hamengkubuwono IX.

revolutionary zeal and idealism.

In many ways, Yogyakarta is still young and restless, despite her traditional Javanese past. Gajah Mada University was founded here during the revolution and is now the largest and one of the most respected schools in the nation.

Yogyakarta's Heart

Despite all the extraordinary changes that have taken place here during the past few decades, still it is Yogya's traditional attractions that tourists come to see—the ancient temples, the palaces, the *batik* workshops, the *gamelan* orchestras, the court dances and the *wayang* puppet performances.

The first stop for all visitors to Yogyakarta is the royal **Kraton**—a two-centuries old palace complex that stands at the very heart of the city. According to traditional cosmological beliefs, the Javanese ruler is literally the "navel" or central "spike" of the universe—anchoring the temporal world and communicating with the mystical realm of powerful deities. In this scheme of things, the *kraton* is both the capital of the kingdom and the hub of the cosmos, and indeed brings the two into coincidence through the application of certain elaborate design principles. It traditionally housed not only the sultan and his family, but also the powerful dynastic regalia (*pusaka*), private meditational and ceremonial chambers, a magnificent throne hall, several audience and performance pavilions, a mosque, an immense royal pleasure garden, stables, barracks, an armaments foundry and two expansive parade grounds planted with sacred banyan trees—all in a carefully conceived complex of walled compounds, narrow lanes and massive gateways, bounded by a fortified outer wall measuring two kms (1.25 miles) on every side.

Construction of Yogyakarta's *kraton* began in 1755 and continued for almost 40 years, throughout the long reign of Hamengkubuwana I. Structurally, in fact, very little has been added since his death in 1792. Today only the innermost compound is considered part of the *kraton* proper, while the maze of lanes and lesser compounds, the mosque and the two vast squares, have been integrated into the city. Long sections

Throne hall of the Kraton.

of the outermost wall (*beteng*) still stand, however, and many if not most of the residences inside it are still owned and occupied by members of the royal family.

To step within the massive inner *kraton* walls (open daily 8:30 a.m. to 12:30 p.m.; closed at 11 a.m. on Fri. and Sat.) is to enter a patrician world of grace and elegance. In the first half of this century, the interior was rather anachronistically remodelled along European lines, incorporating Italian marble, cast-iron columns, crystal chandeliers and rococo furnishings into an otherwise classically Javanese setting. Architecturally, the *kraton's* central throne hall (Bangsal Kencana) is its most striking feature—a *pendopo* or open pavilion consisting of an ornately decorated and dramatically sloping roof supported at the centre by four massive wooden columns. This is a development from the ancient tribal meeting-pavilion (*balai*), echoes of which may be seen throughout the Austronesian world including Japan. The Javanese have imbued the structure with certain symbolic design precepts of Indian origin, so that the *pendopo* has become at once a symbol of temporal authority and a microcosm of the universe—a Mt. Meru standing at the very centre of the cosmos.

There is much else to see within the *kraton*—including the museum, the ancient *gamelan* sets, two great *kala* head gateways and several spacious courtyards. If possible, try to visit on a Sunday at 10 a.m., when dancers rehearse to the otherworldly melodies of the *gamelan*.

An Ingenious Pleasure Palace

Behind and just to the west of the kraton stand the ruins of the opulent and architecturally ingenious royal pleasure gardens, **Taman Sari**, constructed over a period of many years by Hamengkubuwana I, and then abruptly abandoned after his death. Dutch representatives to the sultan's court marvelled at its construction: a large artificial lake, underground and underwater passageways, meditational retreats, a series of sunken bathing pools, and an imposing, two-storey mansion of European design. They referred to the latter as the *waterkasteel* (Water Castle) as it was apparently fortified and was originally surrounded on all four sides by a man-made lake.

The **Water Castle** occupies high ground at the northern end of the huge Taman Sari complex, and today overlooks a crowded bird market and a colony of *batik* painters. Though its stairways have collapsed, one can still scramble atop the crumbling walls to gain a commanding vista of Yogya town and beyond.

A tunnel behind the "castle" leads to a complex of three partially restored **Bathing Pools** (*umbul-umbul*). The large central pool with a naga-head fountain was designed for the use of queens, concubines and princesses, while the small southernmost pool was reserved for His Highness. A tower with several interior chambers overlooks the female bathing area—this is where the sultan rested during the day.

Farther to the south, tucked amid a crowded *kampung*, lies the interesting **Pesarean Pertapaan**, a royal retreat—reached by passing through an ornate archway to the west of the bathing area, then following a winding path to the left. The main structure is a small Chinese-style temple with a forecourt

Sumur Gumuling.

and galleries on either side, and is said to have been where the sultan and his sons meditated for seven days and seven nights at a time.

The most remarkable structure at Taman Sari is the **Sumur Gumuling** (circular well), commonly referred to by locals as the *mesjid* (mosque) but more likely intended as a trysting place for the Sultan and Kyai Loro Kidul, the powerful Goddess of the South Sea to whom all rulers of Mataram had been promised in marriage by the dynasty's founder (and from whom they are said to derive their mystical powers). Access is by means of an underground (formerly underwater) passageway, whose entrance lies immediately to the west of the water castle. The "well" is in fact a sunken atrium—circular galleries facing onto a small, round pool.

Before leaving the area, stroll through the Pasar Ngasem **Bird Market**, where Javanese bird lovers browse and haggle over a multitude of parrots, cockatoos, macaws, parakeets, thrushes, lories, minivets, sunbirds, guineafowl and more.

Next to the bird market is a **Batik Painters Colony**, home to scores of young and unsung artists of the cloth. Motifs here fall into two distinct categories: traditional Ramayana scenes (in non-traditional colours), and attempts at primitive expressionism. Most of it is kitsch, even if of a rather exotic variety; talented artists who make it quickly move out to set up their own studios elsewhere. Bargain hard if you are buying.

A Stroll Up 'Garland Bearing' Street

Yogyakarta's main thoroughfare, **Jalan Malioboro**, begins directly in front of the royal audience pavilion, at the front of the palace, and ends at a phallic lingga some two kms (1.25 miles) to the north—a shrine dedicated to the local guardian spirit, Kyai Jaga. It was laid out by Hamengkubuwana I as a ceremonial boulevard for colourful state processions, but also as a symbolic meridian along which to orient his domain. Local folk etymologists insist that the street somehow takes its name from the Duke of Marlborough, perhaps as a consequence of the humiliating English assault on Yogyakarta in 1812. But in fact "Malioboro" derives from Sanskrit terms meaning "garland bearing"—the

royal processional route was always adorned with floral bouquets.

Today, Jalan Malioboro is a bustling avenue lined with shopfronts and teeming with vehicles and pedicabs—primarily a shopping district but also an area of historical and cultural interest. Begin at the town square (*alun-alun*) and stroll up this latter-day processional, stopping first at the **Sana Budaya Museum**, just on the northwestern side of the square. It was opened in 1935 by the Java Institute, a cultural foundation composed of wealthy Javanese and Dutch art patrons, and today houses important collections of prehistoric artifacts, Hindu-Buddhist bronzes, *wayang* puppets, dance costumes and traditional Javanese weapons. (Open Tue. to Thur. 8 a.m. to 1:30 p.m.; Fri. to Sun. until 10:30 a.m. Closed Mondays and holidays). The royal library is behind the museum. Visit also the nearby **Grand Mosque** (completed in 1773), and notice the two fenced-off banyan trees standing on either side of the road in the square's centre. These symbolize the stable balance of opposing forces within the Javanese kingdom.

Proceed northward from the square

Bird Market.

through the main gates and out across Yogya's main intersection. Immediately ahead on the right stands the old Dutch garrison, **Fort Vredeburgh**, which is slated to become a cultural centre, complete with exhibition and performance halls. Opposite it on the left stands the former Dutch Resident's mansion, used during the revolution as the presidential palace, now the Governor's residence. Farther along on the right, past the fort, is the huge, covered central market, **Pasar Beringan**—a dimly lit women's world of small stalls.

Back out on Malioboro, both sides of the street are lined with handicraft shops selling a great range of traditional textiles, leather goods, baskets, tortoise shell, jewellery and endless knick-knacks. Many restaurants here also cater especially to foreign tourists, serving refreshing iced fruit juices, Chinese, Indonesian and Western fare. (*See* "Guide in Brief" for shopping and dining information.) The **Tourist Information Office** faces onto Malioboro not far from the Hotel Mutiara. Stop in to get a copy of their up-to-date information sheet about temple tours and dance performances.

Yogyakarta silversmith.

Yogya's Peerless Performing Arts

In between visits to the palace and the temples, take time off to investigate Yogya's sophisticated performing arts. Of all Java's many art forms, the *wayang kulit* or shadow-puppet play undoubtedly lies closest to the heart of the Javanese. The *dalang* or puppeteer is the key to the performance: a masterly stage hand, actor, impersonator, singer, orchestra conductor, historian, counsellor, comedian and storyteller all in one. The basic outlines of the ancient tales, generally episodes from the Mahabarata epic, are familiar enough to the audience. But the *dalang* breathes new life into each re-telling of them, introducing the present in bawdy asides and outrageous satires, while continually reaffirming the harmony and balance between antagonists and protagonists that is a central motif in the Javanese worldview.

Despite the increasing encroachment of films and television, *wayang kulit* still flourishes in and around Yogya. Performances for *selamatan* ritual feasts, weddings or circumcisions occur regularly, often in modest village com-

pounds. The performance always starts around 9 p.m. and continues till dawn. There is a full eight-hour presentation of *wayang kulit* on the second Saturday of every month at the **Sasana Inggil** performance pavilion, just south of the *kraton*. Short *wayang* excerpts are also performed for the benefit of visitors at several locations. (*See* "Guide in Brief").

Chances are that your most vivid memory of the *wayang*, and indeed of Yogya itself, will be aural—the gentle music of the *gamelan. (See* Part IV, "The Sound of Moonlight.") You'll hear its insinuating, liquid melodies floating over white-washed walls on quiet sunlit streets, or bursting forth from a transistor radio at roadside stalls; you may also hear it as you stroll through the *kraton* (where there is a regular rehearsal on Mon. and Wed. between 10 a.m. and noon), or in the lobby of your hotel. Pre-recorded cassette tapes are available at shops on Jl. Malioboro, and entire orchestras may be ordered from *gamelan* foundries in Yogya, where these ancient bronze instruments are still cast, forged and polished using age-old tools and methods. (*See* "Guide in Brief.")

Classical Javanese Dance is another highlight of Yogya's cultural scene. Having originated in the *kratons* (*See* Part IV, "Dance and Drama"), where they still thrive, court dances are now also taught at a number of private dance schools and government art academies in the city. The weekly rehearsal within the *kraton* itself (Sundays, 10 a.m. to noon) should not be missed, but there are also a number of regular evening performances, and interested visitors are welcome to observe dance classes at the schools. (*See* "Guide in Brief" for details.)

Perhaps the ultimate in Javanese dance spectaculars, though, is the **Ramayana Ballet**—a modernized version of the lavish *wayang orang* dance-drama productions, performed monthly over four consecutive nights during the dry season (May to October), under the full moon in front of the elegant, 9th Century Lara Jonggrang temple at Prambanan.

Boutiques and *Batiks*

The list of traditional crafts still practised in the suburbs and towns around

Below: *wayang klitik* (a variation of *wayang kulit* without the use of shadow); a Yogyakarta batik factory.

Yogyakarta is practically endless, both because skilled labour is cheap and plentiful here, but also because the court once patronized these village craftsmen. Most villages are specialized, some producing earthenware pottery, others turning out delicate filagree silverwork, and yet others leather bags, weavings, baskets, cane furniture or hand-forged ceremonial *keris* blades. These products are generally available from shops and boutiques in Yogyakarta, but it is also interesting to visit the villages, if you have the time, to observe how they are made. (*See* "Guide in Brief.")

Of course Yogya's most famous handicraft is still *batik*, and unless you class yourself with the connoisseurs of this extraordinarily involved textile art, it's a good idea to first visit the **Batik Research Centre** (Balai Penelitian Batik) at Jl. Kusumanegara 2, a 15-minute walk to the east of the main Post Office. (*See* also Part IV, "The World of Javanese Batik.") Here, an individual guided tour costs nothing, and you are introduced to the craft's painstaking manufacturing process as well as to the staggering variety of patterns and colours to be found throughout Java. One-month courses are offered here for a nominal fee. For three hours a day; six days a week, you help other students design, draw, wax, dye and clean the cloth.

Batik cloth is produced and sold all over Yogya, but especially on **Jalan Tirtodipuran** in the south of the city, a street with over 25 factories and showrooms, most of which are happy to let you observe their production. But if you want to see a range of finished *batik* from all over Java, then visit the large **Toko Terang Bulan** shop on Jl. Malioboro (near the central market). Here you can see and buy a great variety of yardgoods, *sarungs*, tablecloths, shirts and dresses at reasonable fixed prices.

Many of the city's better-known artists, and a number of aspiring ones, also produce *batik* **paintings**, made with the same resist-dyeing method but specifically designed for framing and hanging. Three of the most famous (and expensive) boutiques are: Amri Gallery (Jl. Gampingan 67); Bambang Oetoro (Jl. Taman Siswa 55); and Saptohudoyo (opposite the airport).

Dance-school performance at Dalem Pujakusuman.

ANTIQUITIES OF CENTRAL JAVA

For the Javanese, the *candi* or ancient stone monuments of Java are tangible evidence of the great energy and artistry of their ancestors. For the foreign visitor, communion with one of these 1,000-year-old shrines provides an opportunity to ponder the achievements of a culture other than one's own. For just about anyone, a visit to one of the hundred-odd *candi*, major and minor, that lie scattered about the dramatic volcanic landscapes of Central Java, is an unforgettable event.

A great deal of effort has been expended since 1900 to excavate, reconstruct and restore their reliefs, study their iconography and decipher their inscriptions. Still, we know little more than the most basic symbolism of these structures. Fundamental questions as to their stylistic affinities with Indian art and their function within ancient Indonesian society remain unanswered—even their chronology is in doubt. What we do know is that they are among the most technically accomplished structures produced in ancient times; and that the awe inspired by their very presence has always formed a substantial part of their message.

The World's Largest Buddhist Monument

A leisurely one-hour's drive across the river beds and rice fields of the Kedu plain, brings you to the steps of fabled **Borobudur**, 42 kms (26 miles) to the northwest of Yogyakarta. This huge stupa, the world's largest Buddhist monument, was built sometime during the relatively short reign of the Sailendra dynasty in Central Java, between 778 and 856—300 years before Angkor Wat and 200 years before Notre Dame. Yet within little more than a century of her completion, Borobudur and all of Central Java were mysteriously abandoned. (*See* Part I, "An Age of Empires.") At about this time, too, neighbouring Mt. Merapi erupted violently, covering Borobudur in volcanic ash and concealing her for the greater part of a millennium.

The story of Borobudur's "re-

Borobudur Temple at sunset.

126

discovery" begins in 1814, when the English Lieutenant-governor of Java, Thomas Stamford Raffles, visited Semarang and heard rumours of "a mountain of Buddhist sculptures in stone" near the town of Magelang. Raffles dispatched his military engineer, H.C.C. Cornelius, to investigate. What Cornelius discovered was a hillock overgrown with trees and shrubs, but curiously scattered with hundreds of cut and carved andesite blocks. For two months, he directed a massive clearing operation, removing vegetation and a layer of earth, until it became clear that an elaborate structure lay beneath the surface. Cornelius dug no further, for fear of damaging the ancient monument.

In the years that followed, Borobudur was fully laid bare and subsequently suffered almost a century of decay, plunder and abuse, during which thousands of stones were "borrowed" by villagers and scores of priceless sculptures ended up as garden decorations in the homes of the rich and powerful. Typical of the attitude of Dutch officials was the presentation, in 1896, of eight cartloads of Borobudur souvenirs to visiting King Chulalongkorn of Siam—including 30 relief panels, five Buddha statues, two lions and a guardian sculpture. Many of these and other irreplaceable works of Indo-Javanese art ended up in private collections, and now reside in museums around the world.

Finally, in 1900, the Dutch government responded to cries of outrage from within its own ranks, and established a committee for the preservation and restoration of Borobudur. The huge task of reconstruction was accomplished between 1907 and 1911 by Dr. Th. Van Erp, a Dutch military engineer with a keen interest in Javanese antiquities. Scattered stones were replaced, collapsed walls and *stupas* were straightened, weak spots were reinforced and the drainage system was improved. It was at this time, too, that Borobudur was discovered to be a fragile mantle of stone blocks built upon a natural mound of earth. Van Erp soon realized that his efforts at reconstruction were insufficient: rainwater was seeping through the stone mantle and eroding the soft foundation from within, while mineral salts were collecting on the monument's surface, where they acted in conjunction with sun, wind, rain and fungus to destroy it. But Van Erp's grandiose plans for a permanent restoration were never realized, due to the intervention of two world wars and a depression.

During the 1950s and 1960s, it became increasingly evident that Borobudur was structurally endangered. Parts of the north wall on the lowest terrace began to bulge as a result of internal pressures, and two earthquakes in May of 1961 created severe cracks and dislocations. Some lower balustrades were dismantled in 1965, but within a year work was discontinued for lack of funds. In 1967, an appeal was made by Professor Soekmono (head of the Indonesian Archaeological Institute) at the International Congress of Orientalists in Ann Arbor. To his surprise, the Indian delegates proposed a motion that UNESCO be called upon to direct a rescue operation; it passed unanimously. "Save Borobudur" became a rallying cry among art lovers around the world, technical assistance and financing became available, and the project officially got underway in 1973.

The scale of the Borobudur Restoration Project was spectacular. It took 700

Borobudur under repair.

men, working six days a week, fully 10 years to dismantle, catalogue, photograph, clean, treat and reassemble a total of 1,300,232 stone blocks. In addition, a new infrastructure of reinforced concrete, tar, asphalt, epoxy and tin has been constructed to support the entire monument, and a system of PVC drainage pipes installed to prevent further seepage. IBM donated the use of a computer to keep tabs on the stones and to coordinate various phases of the operation. Each stone had to be individually inspected, scrubbed and chemically treated before being replaced.

In the end, the work was completed on time, but at a cost of US$25 million, or more than three times the original estimate. In his dedication address at the official re-opening of Borobudur on Feb. 23, 1983, President Suharto explained that his government had decided to underwrite the additional expense, so that the Indonesian people would not be deprived of their ancient and glorious heritage. "It is now to be hoped," he said, "that Borobudur will live a thousand years more."

It is unlikely that we shall ever know the full import of Borobudur as a religious monument. It is estimated that 30,000 stonecutters and sculptors, 15,000 carriers and thousands more masons worked anywhere from 20 to 75 years to build the monument. At a time when the entire population of Central Java numbered less than 1 million, this represents a commitment of perhaps 10 per cent of the total workforce to a single production. Was it spiritual faith or coercive force that drove so many men to create this statement in stone? We shall never know.

What is clear is that the Sailendran rulers of Java were able to command a surplus of rice and labour from the populace. The easiest way to accomplish this was of course to convince the cultivators that it was in their own best interest to donate a part of their production to the gods. When we look for the meaning, then, in the monument of Borobudur, we must recognize that its primary function was to embody and reinforce the very beliefs which created it.

Seen from the air, Borobudur forms a *mandala*, or geometric aid for meditation. Seen from a distance, Borobudur is a *stupa* or reliquary, a model of the

A 17th Century etching of Borobudur.

cosmos in three vertical parts—a square base supporting a hemispheric body and a crowning spire. As one approaches along the traditional pilgrimage route (from the east), and then ascends the monument, circumambulating each terrace clockwise in succession, every relief and carving contributes to the symbolism of the whole.

There were originally 10 levels at Borobudur, each falling within one of the three divisions of the Mahayana Buddhist universe: *khamadhatu*, the lower spheres of human life; *rupadhatu*, the middle sphere of "form"; and *arupadhatu*, the higher sphere of detachment from the world. The lowest gallery of reliefs, now covered, once depicted the delights of this world and the damnations of the next.

The next five levels (the processional terrace and four concentric galleries) show, in their reliefs (beginning at the eastern staircase and going around each gallery clockwise), the life of Prince Siddharta on his way to becoming the Gautama Buddha, scenes from the Jataka folktales about his previous incarnations, and the life of the Bodhisattva Sudhana (from the *Gandavyuha*).

These absorbing and delightful tales are illustrated in stone by a parade of commoners, princes, musicians, dancing girls, ships, saints and heavenly throngs, with many interesting ethnographic details about daily life in ancient Java. Placed in niches above the galleries are 432 stone Buddhas, each displaying one of five *mudras* or hand positions, alternately calling upon the earth as witness and embodying charity, meditation, fearlessness and reason.

Above the square galleries, three circular terraces support 72 perforated *dagobs* (miniature *stupas*) which are unique in Buddhist art. Most contain a statue of the meditating *dhyani* Buddha. Two statues have been left uncovered—to gaze over the nearby Menoreh mountains, where one series of knobs and knolls is said to represent Gunadharma, the temple's divine architect. These three terraces are in fact transitional steps leading to the 10th and highest level, the realm of formlessness and total abstraction (*arupadhatu*), embodied in the huge crowning *stupa*, now missing its spire and sunshades.

Borobudur was thus erected for the glorification of the Ultimate Reality— the serene realm of the Lord Buddha— and as a tangible, tactile lesson for priests and pilgrims, an illustrated textbook of the path to Buddhist enlightenment. It was also likely a massive mausoleum, and may have once contained the remains of a Buddhist ruler or saint.

Mendut and Pawon

Two smaller, subsidiary *candi* lie along a straight line directly to the east of Borobudur. The closer of the two is tiny **Pawon** (meaning "kitchen" or perhaps "crematorium"), situated in a shady clearing 1,750 metres (one mile) from the *stupa's* main entrance. It is often referred to as Borobudur's "porch-temple" because of its proximity, and may well have constituted the last stop along a brick-paved pilgrimage route. Though many theories have been advanced, we know very little about Pawon's actual function or symbolism, other than that the outer walls are covered with heavenly "money trees" and celestial musicians, and that a bearded dwarf above the entrance pours out riches from his bag, perhaps for the benefit of visiting pilgrims.

Just 1,150 metres farther to the east, across the confluence of two holy rivers (the Progo and the Elo), lies beautiful **Candi Mendut**. A large banyan tree shades the forecourt, and unlike most other Central Javanese monuments (which face east), Mendut opens to the northwest. The large central *dagob* and a series of smaller ones that once crowned the temple's roof are now missing, so that its broad base and high body now seem rather plain from a distance. As you approach, however, the delightful bas-reliefs on the outer walls come to life.

The base and both sides of the staircase are decorated with scenes from moralistic fables and folktales, many of which concern animals. The main body of Mendut contains superbly carved panels depicting *bodhisattvas* and Buddhist goddesses—the largest reliefs found on any Indonesian temple. The walls of the antechamber are decorated with money trees and celestial beings, and contain two beautiful panels of a man and a woman amid swarms of playful children. It is thought that these represent child-eating ogres who converted to Buddhism and became protectors instead of devourers.

The Mendut panels are decorative, but they hardly prepare one for the stunning interior, which contains three of the finest Buddhist statues in the world: a magnificent three-metre (10-foot) figure of the seated Sakyamuni Buddha, flanked on his left and right by Bodhisattva Vajrapani and Bodhisattva Avalokitesvara, each about 2.5 metres (8 feet) high. The central or Sakyamuni statue symbolizes the first sermon of the Buddha at the Deer Park near Benares, as shown by the position of his hands (*dharmacakra mudra*) and by a small relief of a wheel between two deer. The two *bodhisattvas* or buddhas-to-be, have elected to stay behind in the world to help all of Buddha's followers. Four niches around them probably once held meditating *dhyani* buddhas.

(For the **Dieng Plateau** temples, *see* "Guide in Brief.")

Prambanan: 'Valley of the Kings'

To the east of Yogyakarta, past the airport, the main Yogya-Solo highway slices through a plain that is literally littered with ancient ruins. Because these *candis* are considered by the Javanese to be royal mausoleums, this region is known by them as the "Valley of the Kings" or the "Valley of the Dead." In the centre of the plain, 17 kms (10.5 miles) from Yogya, lies the small town of **Prambanan**, and a sign at one intersection points north along a rutted road towards a major temple complex of the same name. For many, this is the finest monument in Java.

Prambanan was completed sometime around 856, to commemorate the victory of Sanjaya's Sivaitic descendant, Rakai Pikatan, over the last Sailendran ruler of Central Java, Balaputra (who fled to Sumatra and became the ruler of Srivijaya). It was deserted within a few years of its completion, however, and eventually collapsed. Preparations for the restoration of the central temple began in 1918, work started in 1937, and it was completed only in 1953.

The central courtyard of the complex contains eight buildings. The three largest are arrayed north-to-south: the magnificent 47-metre (155 foot) central or Siva temple, flanked on either side by slightly smaller shrines dedicated to Vishnu (to the north) and Brahma (to

Temples on the Dieng Plateau.

the south). Standing opposite these, to the east, are three smaller temples which contained the "vehicles" of each god: Siva's bull (*nandi*), Brahma's gander (*hamsa*) and Vishnu's sun-bird (*garuda*). Only *nandi* remains. By the northern and southern gates of the central compound are two identical court temples, standing 16 metres (52.5 feet) high.

The largest temple, the masterpiece dedicated to Siva, is also known as Loro Jonggrang (Slender Maiden), a folk-name sometimes given to the temple complex as a whole. Local legend has it that Loro Jonggrang was a princess wooed by an unwanted suitor. She commanded the man to build a temple in one night, and then frustrated his nearly-successful effort by pounding the rice-mortar, prematurely announcing the dawn. Enraged, he turned the maiden to stone, and according to the tale she remains here in the northern chamber of the temple—as a statue of Siva's consort, Durga. In the other three chambers are statues of: Agastya, the "Divine Teacher" (facing south); Ganesa, Siva's elephant-headed son (facing west); and a 3-metre (10-foot)

figure of Siva (in the central chamber, facing east).

One aspect of Loro Jonggrang's appeal is her glorious symmetry and graceful proportions. Another is her wealth of sculptural detail. On the base of the main terrace are the so-called 'Prambanan Motifs'—little lions in niches, flanked by trees of life bearing a lively menagerie of endearing animals.

Above these, on the outer balustrade, are panels of celestial beings and 62 scenes from the classical Indian dance manual, the *Natyasastra*. Finally, on the inner walls of the balustrade, beginning from the eastern gate and proceeding around clockwise, the wonderfully vital and utterly engrossing tale of the *Ramayana* is told in bas-relief (and completed on the balustrade of the Brahma temple). The movement within each panel is free-flowing, filled with fascinating detail. Even the most tumultuous scenes contain lovingly rendered touches—monkeys in a fruit tree, birds raiding a granary, kitchen scenes. Prambanan's beauty and variety demand more than a single visit. (For other temples in the vicinity of Prambanan, *see* "Guide in Brief.")

Loro Jonggrang Temple during a total eclipse of the sun in 1983.

SURAKARTA

Noble **Surakarta** (also known as "Solo" or "Sala"), located just 60 kms (38 miles) to the east of Yogyakarta, generally receives far less attention from foreign visitors than her distinguished neighbour. This is a curious state of affairs from the point of view of most Javanese, for whom Surakarta is the elder and more refined court centre—the arbiter of cultivated speech and aristocratic elegance in traditional Java.

This is partly because Surakarta and her rulers have themselves generally preferred to remain out of the limelight. Indeed, throughout the tumultuous 18th Century they had little choice, for in those years, Solo's reigning Pakubuwana line were dependent upon the Dutch for military and economic support. Thereafter, the royal family became well-to-do landowners and sugar magnates—styling themselves, as did all 19th Century Javanese aristocrats, after the manner of European royalty. During the Indonesian revolution, the anti-colonial movement was notable in Surakarta by its absence.

Despite some carping (by Yogyakartans in particular), the Susuhunan of Surakarta (a titular Muslim prince) can nevertheless claim, with good reason, to be the true and rightful heir to the Central Javanese Mataram throne. The court was moved to the Solo River valley in in 1680 from the Yogya area, first to Kartasura and later (in 1745) to Surakarta. Here the Mataram line has ruled uninterruptedly, despite losing half of the Kingdom to the "upstart" ruler of Yogyakarta in 1755, as the price of a Dutch-negotiated peace.

Perhaps the real reason that Surakarta is less known than Yogyakarta, is that she has fewer connecting flights and is farther from the ancient monuents of Borobudur and Prambanan. But in fact it is only an hour from Yogya by rail or road, and is certainly worth visiting, even if for a single day.

The **Kraton** or palace of Surakarta was constructed between 1743 and 1746 on the banks of the mighty Bengawan Solo, Java's longest river. As with the Yogyakarta palace, Surakarta's *kraton* simultaneously defines

the centre of the town and the kingdom, as well as, metaphysically, the hub of the cosmos. Indeed the similarities between the two courts, built within 10 years of each other, are striking. Both have a thick outer wall enclosing a network of narrow lanes and smaller compounds, two large squares, a mosque and a central or inner royal residential complex. Perhaps the major difference is that Surakarta has no north-south processional boulevard or pleasure palace.

Entering the *kraton* precincts from the north gate, one crosses the main square (*alun-alunlor*) between two royal banyan trees and stops in front of the pale blue Pagelaran performance pavilion, with its shining expanse of cool marble tiles. Behind the Pagelaran is the royal audience pavilion (*Sitinggil*), and behind that is an immense gate leading to the front or north door of the palace.

Casual visitors are never permitted to enter this north door, which is kept closed except on special occasions, but must walk around to the east and pay a small fee for a guided tour of the museum and the inner sanctum. Here,

shaded by groves of leafy trees, between which flit the bare-shouldered *abdidalem* or female attendants, is the large throne hall of the Susuhunan. The inner columns supporting the roof are richly carved and gilded, crystal chandeliers hang from the rafters and marble statues, cast-iron columns and Chinese blue-and-white vases line the walkways. As if to underscore the sanctity of this place, you are instructed to remove your shoes (to walk on the finely swept dirt) and refrain from photographing. Notice the phallic-looking royal meditation tower to one side—if it looks familiar, that's because it's essentially a Dutch windmill without the arms.

The museum associated with the *kraton* was established in 1963 and contains ancient Hindu-Javanese bronzes, traditional Javanese weapons and three marvellous coaches. The oldest—a lumbering, deep-bodied carriage built around 1740—was a gift from the Dutch East India Company to Pakubuwana II. The museum also displays some remarkable figure-heads from the old royal barges, including Kyai Rajamala, a giant of surpassing ugliness, who once adorned the bow of the Susuhunan's private boat and is said even now to emit a nasty fishy odour when daily offerings are not forthcoming. (Open daily 8:30 a.m. to 12:30 p.m. Fridays until 11:00 a.m.).

After visiting the *kraton*, stroll through the narrow lanes outside and be sure to pay a visit to nearby **Sasana Mulya**—the music and dance pavilion of the Indonesian Performing Arts Academy (ASKI), located just to the west of the main or north palace gate. This is an art school with an illustrious history, for it was here that the first musical notation for *gamelan* was devised at the turn of the century. Serious students of *gamelan* music, traditional dance and *wayang kulit* attend classes and rehearsals here daily. You are welcome to listen and observe, provided you do so unobtrusively.

Surakarta's 'Other' Palace

About one km (half-a-mile) to the west and north of the main *kraton*, a branch of the Surakarta royal family has constructed their own smaller, more intimate palace. Begun by Mangkunegara II at the end of the 18th Century and completed in 1866, the

View of the main hall of Surakarta Kraton.

Pura Mangkunegaran is also open to the public. Upon entering the grounds (via the east or west gates), report to the reception office just inside the east gate and pay a small fee for a guided tour. (Open 8:30 a.m. to noon daily).

The outer *pendopo* or audience pavilion of the Mangkunegaran is said to be the largest in Java—built of solid teak wood and jointed and fitted in the traditional manner, without the use of nails. Note the brightly painted ceiling, with the eight mystical Javanese colours in the centre, highlighted by a flame motif and bordered by symbols of the Javanese zodiac. The *gamelan* set in the southwest corner of the *pendopo* is known as Kyai Kanyut Mesem (Enchanting Smiles.) Try to visit the palace on Wednesday mornings, when it is struck to accompany an informal dance rehearsal between 10 a.m. and noon.

The museum is in the ceremonial hall of the palace, directly behind the *pendopo* and it houses mainly the private collections of Mankunegara IV: dance ornaments, *topeng* masks, jewellery (including two silver chastity belts), ancient Javanese and Chinese coins, bronze figures, and a superb set of ceremonial *keris* blades.

Solo is an excellent place for the unhurried shopper who likes to explore out-of-the-way places in the hope of finding hidden treasures. To begin with, there is a sizeable "antique industry" here—many dealers collect and restore old European, Javanese and Chinese furniture and bric-a-brac. The starting point for any treasure hunt is **Pasar Triwindu**, just to the south of the Mangkunegaran palace (behind the electronics shops on Jl. Diponegoro). Five minutes here will whet your appetite: old bottles, candelabras, Japanese teacups, Chinese coins, Dutch oil lamps, photographs, picture frames, marble-top tables and other odds and ends clutter more than a dozen stalls. Bargain hard, and don't be carried away by the sales pressure. There are many more shops in town where the dealers are more reputable, the selection just as good and the prices not necessarily any higher. (*See* "Guide in Brief.")

Solo is also the home of Indonesia's largest *batik* manufacturers, three of whom have showrooms in town with reasonable fixed prices for superb yard goods, shirts and dresses. (*See* "Guide in Brief" for locations.) Many smaller *batik* shops also line the main streets, but to discover why Surakarta calls itself the "City of Batik," pay a visit to the huge textile market, **Pasar Klewer**, beside the Grand Mosque (near the *kraton*.) This is where village vendors and housewives converge to buy their cloth, mostly of medium to lower quality, from scores of narrow stalls that are stacked to the rafters with a bewildering array of *batik*. Just be sure you know what you are doing if you buy here—*batik* can sell for as little as US$1 a yard or US$100 a piece, and it takes some experience to know what is what.

As the acknowledged centre for the traditional Javanese performing arts, Solo is also the place to see an evening *wayang orang* dance performance or a *wayang kulit* shadow play, or to listen to live *gamelan* music. It is also the place, not surprisingly, to buy the costumes, puppets and instruments associated with these arts. Ornately carved and painted hide puppets, contorted wooden masks, gilded headdresses and even monstrous bronze gongs are available and make highly distinctive gifts or house decorations. (*See* "Guide in Brief" for details.)

asar
riwindu
ntique seller
waits another
ustomer.

EAST JAVA
AND MADURA

Though East Java lacks many of the more usual tourist sights and amenities, it is a paradise for unorthodox travellers—rugged individualists who relish the search for obscure but exquisite antiquities, or the breathtaking views from the rims of desolate volcanic craters.

Geographically and historically, the province may be divided into three regions: the north coast (including the island of Madura), with its old Islamic trading ports; the Brantas River Valley, with its ancient monuments and colonial hill stations; and the eastern salient (known to history as Blambangan), with its spectacular volcanoes, secluded nature reserves and unparallelled scenic beauty.

The broad Brantas River traces a circular path through the ancient and fertile ricelands of eastern central Java, around several adjacent peaks—Mt. Arjuna, Mt. Kawi and Mt. Kelud. For five centuries after 930 A.D., this valley was the undisputed locus of power and civilization on the island. The great kingdoms of this period—Kediri, Singhasari and Majapahit—have bequeathed a rich heritage of temple art, literature, music and drama.

With the arrival of Islam as a political force in the 15th Century and the great florescence of the spice and textile trade, a struggle arose between the rice-growing kingdoms of the interior and the new Islamic trading powers of the coast. The Brantas valley was conquered by Muslim forces circa 1527, and many Hindus then fled eastward to Blambangan and Bali. Even today, the highland Tenggerese tribes around Mt. Semeru claim to be the living descendants of these Indo-Javanese exiles, and of course Bali's most powerful rulers trace their genealogies back to the 14th Century kings of East Java's Majapahit empire.

Surabaya: City of Heroes

Up until the turn of the century the East Javanese capital of **Surabaya** was the largest and most important seaport in the archipelago. It still ranks second

Old Dutch warehouses overlooking th Kalimas Cana

(after Jakarta's Tanjung Priok), and with more than 400 years of colourful history behind it, one would expect to find much of interest here, though unfortunately, this is not so.

Surabaya's rise to prominence began around 1525, when her rulers converted to Islam and then rapidly subdued all neighbouring coastal states. However, in the final years of the 16th Century, the Central Javanese kingdom of Mataram expanded eastward and joined a bloody and protracted struggle with Surabaya for control of the area. Dutch descriptions of the city in 1620 paint her as a formidable adversary surrounded by a canal and heavily fortified bastions measuring some 37 kms (23 miles) in circumference. And her army is said to have numbered 30,000. In the end, Surabaya succumbed (in 1625) only after Sultan Agung's armies had devastated her rice-lands and diverted her mighty river.

In the mid-18th Century, Surabaya was ceded to the Dutch, and soon developed into the greatest commercial city of the Indies—the chief sugar port and rail head on Java. Immortalized in many of Joseph Conrad's novels, this era was characterized by square-riggers in full sail, wealthy Chinese and Arab traders, eccentric German hoteliers and lusty seamen brawling over the likes of Surabaya Sue (who really existed).

Today's reality is mundane by comparison—Surabaya is a hot, sprawling city of almost 4 million. It is known as the "City of Heroes" because of the momentous first battle of the revolution, fought here in November 1945. Though the ragtag Indonesian rebels were driven from the city at this time by better-equipped British troops, they inflicted heavy casualties and proved to the world (and themselves) that independence could be, and would be, fought for.

The most interesting areas of Surabaya are the old Arab and Chinese quarters at the northern end of the city, not far from the harbour. Spend some time wandering the narrow lanes to the east of Jl. K.H. Mas Mansyur, around the mosque and the **Holy Grave of Sunan Ampel**, one of the "nine saints" who propagated Islam on the island. Many stalls around the mosque sell handmade textiles from all over Java.

Just to the south of here, at Jl. Dukuh

Bull races at Madura.

II/2, is the **Hong Tik Hian Temple**, where Chinese hand-puppet (*potehi*) performances are put on daily for the benefit of the assembled deities. And just across Jl. Kembang Jepun, on Jl. Selompretan, stands Surabaya's oldest Chinese shrine—the 18th Century **Hok An Kiong Temple**—built entirely of wood in the traditional manner by native Chinese craftsmen. The temple's central deity is Ma Co, the protectress of sailors.

From the Chinese quarter, walk westward along Jl. Kembang Jepun to the famous "Red Bridge" straddling Kali Mas canal. This lies at the very heart of the 19th Century commercial district, where many dilapidated Dutch warehouses and office buildings still stand.

'Fat Boy' and a Dragon

Travel south from here, parallel to the river past the new **Heroes Monument**, to see how Surabaya has expanded. From Jl. Tunjungan, the main shopping street, turn left down Jl. Pemuda to see the former Dutch **Governor's Mansion**. This stood at what was then the new centre of colonial Surabaya, constructed after the turn of the century, and is now a major hotel district. There is a centuries-old statue of King Kertanegara (died 1292) enshrined in a small park directly opposite—called **Joko Dolog** but affectionately known as the "fat boy." From here, continue south through fashionable suburbs to the **Surabaya Zoo**—home of many exotic species, including the famous "Komodo Dragon."

Beer-Drinking Bulls

Most visitors, eager to escape Surabaya's heat and bustle, head for the cool and inviting hills to the south of the city, but a few also cross the narrow straits to the neighbouring island of **Madura**—particularly during August or September, time of the exciting annual bull races.

It's a strange sport, this *kerapan sapi*. According to the Madurese, it began long ago when plow team was pitted against plow team over the length of a rice field. Today's racing bulls are never used for plowing, but are specially bred; they represent a considerable source of regional pride. Only bulls of a certain standard (condition, weight, colour)

may be entered, and they are judged according to appearance as well as speed. In August, district and regency heats are held all over Madura and East Java, building up to the grand finale in September in **Pamekasan**, the island's capital.

The main event is a thundering sprint down a 100-metre field lined by throngs of screaming spectators. Fed on a special diet of beer, eggs and chili peppers, these huge and normally slow-moving creatures attain speeds of over 50 kph (nearly 30 mph). Some half-crazed spectators consider it good sport to stand at the end of the track, directly in the path of the onrushing bulls. Accidents do occur.

The Madurese have long enjoyed a reputation for toughness, and Madura's dry limestone terrain may account for this. The major industries here are fishing, tobacco growing and salt-panning. The southern coastal fishing villages exude a solid but slightly jaded Mediterranean air. There are some good beaches here and to the east, where a modest palace at **Sumenep** has a small museum and an important library of manuscripts attached.

A quest for antiquities can be one of

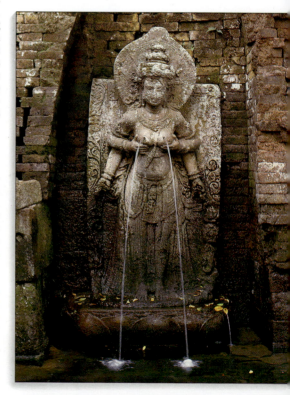

11th Century Belahan bathing pools.

the great joys of East Java. And even if old stones leave you cold, you'll be on the trail to some beautiful and remote countryside here, with ne'er a tour bus in sight. One of the best bases for temple-tripping (or explorations of any sort) is the delightful mountain resort of **Tretes** just 55 kms (35 miles) south of Surabaya.

The air here is fresh, the nights are cool and the mountain scenery is superb. Walk or ride on horseback in the morning to one of three lovely waterfalls in the vicinity. Then spend the afternoon by a bracing spring-fed swimming pool, or curled up with a good book and a huge pot of tea or coffee. More active souls will perhaps want to hike up **Mt. Arjuna** (3,340 metres/10,950 feet) behind Tretes, through lush montane casuarina forests, or across the Lalijiwa Plateau along a well-worn path to neighbouring **Mt. Welirang**, where sulphur is collected by villagers from hissing fumeroles.

This area is also studded with ancient monuments, beginning with **Candi Jawi**, just by the main road 7 kms (4 miles) below Tretes. This slender Buddhist shrine was completed around 1300, and is one of several funerary temples dedicated to King Kertanegara, who died in 1292, of the Singhasari dynasty.

Candi Jawi overlooks Mt. Penanggungan to the north—a perfect cone surrounded on four sides by smaller peaks and regarded, because of its shape, as a replica of the holy mountain, Mahameru. Penanggungan is littered with dozens of terraced sanctuaries, meditation grottoes and sacred pools—about 81 sites in all (most of which are on the mountain's northern and western faces). The most accessible and charming of these is **Belahan**, a bathing pool situated at Penanggungan's eastern foot, that is thought to be the burial site of King Airlangga (died 1049). The pool is reached by a dirt road from the main Surabaya highway, only a few minutes' drive north of Pandaan.

Traces of the Past

From Tretes or Surabaya, it's about an hour to the village of **Trowulan** near Mojokerto, once the seat of Java's greatest empire: 14th Century Majapa-

Tretes:
Candi Jawi.

hit. Unfortunately, most of Majapahit's monuments were built of wood and soft red brick, so that only the foundations and a few gateways remain. The **Trowulan Museum** (open 8 a.m. to 1 p.m. daily), by the main road, nevertheless has a fascinating collection of terracotta figures and fragments, and a useful table-top map of the area. From here, seek out several nearby ruins: **Candi Tikus** (a royal bathing complex); **Candi Bajang Ratu** (a tall brick entryway); and **Wringin Lawang** (a palace gate). Visit also the cemetery at **Tralaya**, two kms (about 1½ miles) south of Trowulan, site of the oldest Muslim graves on Java. The most impressive pieces of statuary, however, are kept in the **Mojokerto Museum**, including the famous "portrait sculpture" of King Airlangga as Vishnu mounted on a formidable *garuda*—once the centrepiece at Belahan. (Open 7 a.m. to 2 p.m. Mon. to Thurs., 7 a.m. to noon Fri. to Sun.).

Many other antiquities are found outside the attractive city of Malang—a thriving coffee and tobacco centre to the south of Surabaya. Turn west next to the Garuda Cinema on the northern outskirts of Singosari, 10 kms (6 miles) north of Malang, and follow a narrow lane to **Candi Singhasari**. This unfinished monument was probably the main funerary temple for King Kertanegara, whose palace must also have been nearby. It is noted for its unusual design (the chambers are built into the temple's base instead of its body) and for two monstrous guardian figures (*raksasas*).

Malang

Malang itself is very pleasant, with a cool climate and a colonial atmosphere. (*See* "Guide in Brief.") Just east of here are two interesting temples. From the village of Blimbing on the northern outskirts of Malang, take a signposted road to Tumpang, about 20 kms (12 miles) away. Just before the Tumpang market, a small road to the left leads to **Candi Jago**—a terraced shrine begun in 1268 as a memorial to another Singhasari king—Vishnuvardhana. All around the terraces are reliefs in the distinctive *wayang* or Javanese shadow-puppet style depicting scenes from the Mahabharata, and a frightening procession of demons in the underworld (from

Sundoro: Watching the sunrise from Mt. Bromo.

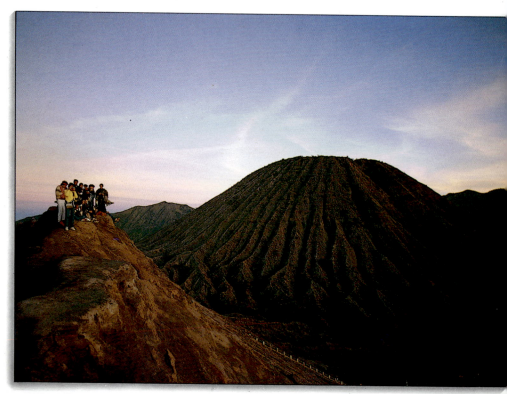

the Kunjarakarna). A little over 5 kms (3 miles) to the southwest of Tumpang is **Candi Kidal**, a tall, slender gem of a temple honouring yet another Singhasari monarch, Anushapati, who died in 1248.

East Java's only sizeable temple complex is **Candi Penataran**, located 80 kms (50 miles) to the west of Malang, just north of the city of Blitar (best reached by taking the longer but more scenic route over the mountains via Kediri). This was apparently the "state temple" of Majapahit, assembled over a period of some 250 years, between 1197 and 1454. It has no soaring pinnacle or massive stupa but rather a series of shrines and pavilions arranged before a broad platform. It is assumed that the pavilions were originally roofed with wood and thatch, as was the body of the main temple, now partially reconstructed at ground level alongside its massive three-tiered base.

It is interesting that Penataran's architects no longer aimed at formal symmetry, in imitation of Indian models, but instead laid out their temple essentially in the manner of an indigenous palace, with audience pavilions in the forecourt and an ornately decorated bathing pool at the rear. The main temple is at the back of the complex, closest to the mountain (as in Bali), and its terraces are lined with bold *wayang* reliefs—scenes from the ever-popular Ramayana and the Krishnayana, and with many unique animal medallions.

Near Penataran (on the road to Blitar) stands **President Sukarno's Mausoleum**, the final resting place of the famous "Father of Indonesian Independence" who died in 1970. And on the way to or from Blitar via the scenic Malang-Kediri highroad, make a detour north from Batu to the mountain resort of **Selekta**—famous for its colonial bungalows, swimming pools and apple orchards.

Wildlife on the Way to Bali

The eastern salient of Java is formed by three highly active volcanic clusters, each of which now contains a nature reserve or national park. The most frequently visited of these is **Mt. Bromo**, a cone inside the huge Tengger Caldera, that has a hotel conveniently situated on its lip. (*See* Part IV "Indonesia's Incredible Wildlife.") The other two, the **Yang Plateau** and the **Ijen Crater** are also accessible, but require somewhat more preparation. (*See* "Guide in Brief.")

There are, in addition, three coastal game reserves in this area, that can be visited on the way to or from Bali (connected to Java by the Ketapang-Gilimanuk ferry). The most accessible of these is the **Baluran Game Reserve** at Java's northeastern tip. (*See* Part IV, "Indonesia's Incredible Wildlife.") The protruding southeasternmost tip of Java has also been designated a reserve, the **Banyuwangi Selatan Reserve**, and though there are no roads leading into it, surfers have constructed bamboo shacks on the western shore and often charter boats over from Bali to take advantage of the excellent waves here. More enticing, perhaps, for non-surfers is the **Meru Betiri Reserve** on the southern coast around Sukamade, where giant sea turtles lay their eggs on black sand beaches and a rain pocket has created unusually dense jungles. This area is also the last refuge of the nearly extinct Javan tiger. (*See* "Guide in Brief.")

Malang.

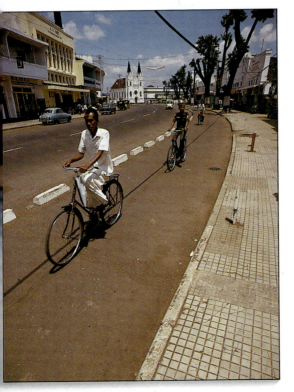

BALI: EMERALD ISLE

Bali is, in many ways, the star jewel in the treasure chest of marvels that comprise the Indonesian archipelago. The island is first and foremost a masterpiece of nature, formed by an east-west range of volcanoes and dominated by two towering peaks (Batur and Agung) that are sculpted by a magnificent series of deep north-south ravines. Bali's volcanic soils are exceptionally fertile and the reliable northwest monsoon brings abundant rainfall from December to April. Months of uninterrupted tropical sunshine complete the vision of paradise by blanketing the island in a luxuriant mantle of green.

The Balinese have done much to turn such natural blessings to their advantage. All but the steepest land has been painstakingly terraced with rice paddies that hug the hilly contours and mount the volcanic slopes like steps. Each watery patch is efficiently irrigated through an elaborate system of aqueducts, dams and sluices that have been regulated since ancient times by intra-village agricultural organizations (*subak*). The land repays these efforts with abundant harvests, which in turn have given the Balinese the leisure and the energy to devote to their justly renowned cultural pursuits. Periods of intense labour and a high degree of cooperation are essential to ensure this bounty. The Balinese are ever mindful of this fact, and their culture may indeed be seen as a primary ingredient in their agricultural success— enhancing a fruitful cooperation with the land, the gods and with each other.

The Balinese take a spiritual view of their environment. Abundant harvests are attributed to the benign efforts of the goddess of rice and fertility, Dewi Sri. Her symbol is the *cili*, two triangles connected in the form of a shapely woman, and she appears in various forms on all temple offerings, on rooftops and even on earthenware ashtrays. Divine spirits dwell in the lofty mountains; dark and inimicable forces lurk in the seas. Man's rightful place is in the middle ground between these two extremes, and each home, village and kingdom in Bali has traditionally been aligned along this mountain-sea axis.

Preceding pages, Besakih Temple is regarded as Bali's holiest spot. The first record of the temple's existence is an inscription dated 1007 A.D. Left, morning in Tampaksiring. Right, Sanghyang Dedari dancer in trance.

The Children of Myth

When the world was ready for human habitation, the Great Teacher Batara Guru debated with his other self, Brahma, regarding the need for man and the nature of a human. The divine duality engaged in sporting competition, fashioning figures of clay. Each admitted that he worked on the basis of trial and error. Each ridiculed the other's efforts. When they experimented with baking the figures in an oven, the first came out in an underdone white finish, the next an

overbaked black. The last batch of people— the Balinese—were just right, a golden brown. By meditation, Batara Guru and Brahma infused the creatures with life.

This whimsical account of The Creation is certainly well suited to the Balinese, themselves a blend of various Mongolian peoples who immigrated to the island several thousand years ago. Their language is closely related to that of the Sasaks (on Lombok), but also to Javanese, from which it has borrowed the usage of honorific levels of speech. Bali was settled and civilized relatively early, as evidenced by stone megaliths like Gunung Kawi and the sophisticated Moon of Pejeng bronze drum, which is thought to date from the first centuries B.C.

Almost a millennium ago, Bali became a vassal of the great Hinduized empires of East Java, one of whose earliest rulers, Airlangga (r. 1019-49), was in fact the son of a great Balinese king, Udayana, by a Javanese wife. Long before this, however, the Balinese had already begun to transmute their native animism by adopting Hindu rites, learning and cosmology, in a process of centuries-long cultural osmosis.

Hindu-Javanese influence reached its zenith at the turn of the 16th Century, when the entire Hinduized aristocracy of Java is said to have fled before the onslaught of Islam and to have taken refuge here. Indeed, much of what is known about ancient Javanese language and customs derives from texts and traditions preserved only on Bali.

Yet Balinese culture developed a glittering and sophisticated persona all its own. Following the Islamic conquest of Java, Bali was united in 1550 under an independent ruler, the fourth great god-king or *Dewa Agung* of Gelgel, Batu Renggong. Though the political unification lasted only two generations, Bali at this time entered a cultural "golden age" in which an elaborate ceremonial life and its associated arts flourished.

Under Batu Renggong, the spiritual and temporal Balinese worlds were fused through the construction of nine great temples (the Pura Agung or Sad Kahyangan), with Pura Besakih high on Mt. Agung's slopes as the central or "mother" temple. At the same time, the *saka* calendar of Hindu

Java and the 30-week Balinese *wuku* calendar were combined, thus defining the complex Balinese schedule of ritual observances as it exists today.

The domain and absolute authority of the *Dewa Agung* diminished under Batu Renggong's son and grandson, and thereafter there emerged a dozen more or less clearly defined rajadoms, who ruled Bali for the next 300 years. Eight of these still survive today as administrative districts: Bandung, Bangli, Tabanan, Gianyar and Klungkung in the south and central regions; Buleleng, Karangasem and Jembrana in the north, east and west respectively.

Due to their traditional fear of the sea and a now-forgotten suspicion of foreigners, the Balinese lived in virtual isolation from the rest of the world from about 1600 to 1900 A.D. Throughout this period her traditions of dance, music, painting, sculpture, poetry, drama and architecture were refined and elaborated, ostensibly for the benefit of Bali's numerous gods and god-kings.

Largely spared the ravages of the 19th Century (due, in part, to Dutch respect for the Balinese and their fierce pride), Bali was the scene of a succession of horrific mass suicide battles (*puputan*) at the turn of this century, in which Balinese kings and their courtiers threw themselves on their *keris* or ran headlong into Dutch gunfire rather than face the humiliation of surrender.

The Dutch conquest of Bali was complete by 1908, and a number of rulers were given regent status under the new colonial order. A few rulers, such as the king of Karangasem in East Bali, even retained a degree of autonomy, and in general the authority and wealth of the native rulers lasted up into the 1950s, when land reform and a republican government finally stripped them of their lands and feudal powers. Today Balinese aristocrats still command a good deal of respect, however, in their role as *pengamong*—guardians of the island's 5,000 or more major temples.

Into the Modern World

Since its discovery by Dutch scholars and Western artists in the early decades of this century, Bali has become synonymous with Shangrila—the last paradise on earth. Hollywood movies, exotic cigars, restaurants, wines and a super-deluxe line of chandeliers

Left, Bali's soft volcanic rock means that sculpture such as this is ubiquitous. Right, a close-up of an intricate and painstakingly made rice-paste offering.

147

have all borne the name—conveying a feeling of the wondrous so often associated with the island's culture. The flinging of "fabled island" Bali epithets has indeed been so promiscuous as to arouse no uncertain fears in the minds of paradise seekers. Has the world's most glamorous traditional culture lost some of its glitter?

Bali's rapid entry into the 20th Century and the subsequent tourist invasion of the 1960s and 1970s has unfortunate parallels in other tropical idylls, where the usual result has been a loss of cultural identity and native charm. But history shows that Bali has resisted major cultural invasions in the past, essentially by integrating and adapting foreign elements into her own incredibly resilient and flexible living traditions.

The polyglot nature of Balinese art, with Indian, Hindu-Javanese, Chinese, Islamic and European influences all in evidence, is a striking example of the Balinese ability to digest and absorb—a fan here, a gold arabesque there, new deities everywhere—and to reject those elements not compatible with their sophisticated, conservative, integrated way of life.

A popular misconception among foreigners is that the Balinese arts have lost much of their lustre—that *gamelans* are rusting in their pavilions and dancers have left the stage for a job on the juice blender. Nothing could be farther from the truth. In many ways, Bali is currently undergoing a cultural renaissance, with bigger and brighter temple festivals, ancient artforms being revived and more musical ensembles active than ever before in the island's history.

A Faith of Harmony

Religious beliefs, rites and festivals guide a Balinese from birth to death and into the world thereafter. They provide a cohesive force within the family and form the basis for village social interaction and cooperation. Religious custom defines the plan of a town, the design of a temple, the structure of a home and the distribution of responsibilities within the community. Holidays, entertainments and social gatherings are all determined by the religious calendar and occur within the context of ritual observances. Some might find such a situation confining, but for the Balinese these observances are a rich source of inspiration, providing a life of unending pageantry and an outlet for their considerable artistic talents.

Each person finds himself born into a complex web of social bonds. Children are privileged in Bali, for it is believed that the younger a person is, the closer his soul is to heaven and the purer is his spirit. A baby is not permitted to touch the impure earth and is carried everywhere. Never are Balinese children alone, nor are they ever beaten, and rarely are they upset. Ceremonies are held at prescribed intervals, notably on the child's first birthday (210 days), when offerings are made by a priest. Thus begins a life-long cycle of rites-of-passage, which will later include ceremonies to mark puberty, marriage, childbirth and death. These are interspersed with regular offerings to the ancestors, at a household shrine.

Communal activities revolve around the three temples possessed by every village: the *Pura Puseh* or temple of origin dedicated to Vishnu; ceremonies for the living; and the *Pura Dalem* or sanctuary for the ancestors.

Wondsoredjo

Java

Menjagan Is.

Banyuwedang

Ketapang

Sumberkerta

Pulaki

Gilimanuk

Banjuwangi

Belimbingsari

Nusasari

Bali Strait

Negara

Puluka

Djawa

India

20 km

Bali

148

Each has a separate calendar of local ceremonies in addition to the regional and island-wide schedule of temple festivals.

Within the village (*desa*) are smaller communities, the *banjar*: cooperative groups of neighbours bound to assist each other in marriages, festivals and especially during funeral cremations. Every adult belongs both to his *desa* and to his *banjar*, where he carries out most of his responsibilities to the village. The *banjars* control community property—a *gamelan* orchestra and dance properties—and have a kitchen for preparing banquets, a signal drum tower (*kulkul*) to call meetings, and a communal temple. The *banjar's* meeting hall is an open pavilion with a large porch, called the *bale*. It serves as a local clubhouse, where men gather in their leisure hours to practise with their *gamelan* ensemble, watch dancers rehearse, hold council, or just sit and smoke and chat.

Fortunately, the 20th Century Balinese harbour no anxieties about the preservation of their old, traditional customs. The traditional way of life is to each new generation as fresh and dynamic as it was to the last. By the same token, the Balinese are not precious about their religion, which they regard simply as custom (*adat*). And as the Mexican artist Covarrubias so astutely noted in his book, *Bali* (1937), "what is the rule in one village is the exception in the next." This makes Bali a place which is unendingly new and fresh for visitors, too—for no matter how well you may know the island, there is always more. (For a description of Balinese religious practices, *see* Part II, "Customary Life.")

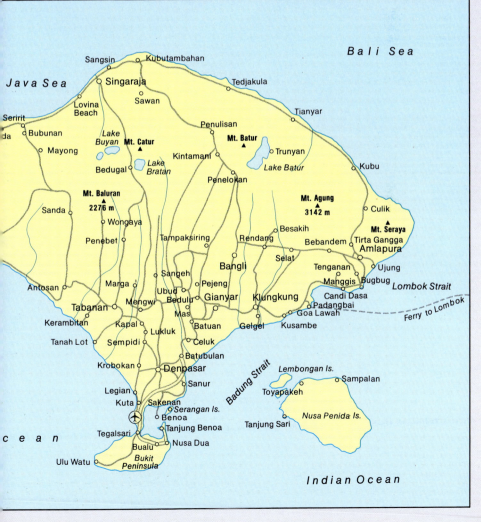

SOUTH AND WEST BALI

As the focus for Bali's tourism, commerce and government, the south is by far the island's busiest region. Screaming Garuda jets disgorge hundreds of visitors daily at Ngurah Rai International Airport, set astride the narrow isthmus that connects the southern *Bukit* peninsula with the rest of the island. Most of these paradise-seekers then retire to one of the three nearby beach resorts—Kuta, Sanur or Nusa Dua. Denpasar, the provincial capital, has experienced unprecedented economic and population growth during the past decade partly as a result of this tourist influx.

But don't be deceived by south Bali's patina of development. The south's temple festivals are legendary for the intensity of their trance dances and the earthiness of their ritual. Denpasar's palace ceremonies rank amongst the most regal on the island, and Kuta Beach—more St. Tropez than Manda-lay—hosts highly professional dance performances nightly. Meanwhile, Sanur's loyal band of hirsute and holy priests continue to maintain cosmic order amidst the condominia.

The region's most illustrious temple, Pura Uluwatu, chosen by the Balinese saint Pedanda Sakti Wawu Rauh as the "stage" for his *moksa* reunion with the godhead, is unrivalled on the island for sheer grandeur of site and elegance of architecture. Giant sea turtles swim in the ocean 300 metres (984 feet) below the temple's clifftop perch, and a nearby beach is at the same time gazetted in the top ten Indonesian surfing spots. Moreover, during Nyepi (the Balinese New Year), south Bali becomes a pilgrimage point—as thousands upon thousands of villagers, arrayed in their ceremonial finery, flood to southern shores bearing offerings of food for the performance of *melis* purification rites.

Sybaritic Sanur Beach

It is the south's beaches, however, that have captivated generations of foreign tourists. **Sanur**, ten kilometres (six miles) to the southeast of Denpasar at the lagoonside end of the fertile Renon-Kepaon-Legian rice crescent,

was once an enclave of fishermen and holy Brahman priests, more famous for its demons and magic than its scenic delights. During the 1930s, however, Sanur's spectacular beaches attracted a colony of western intellectuals and artists that included anthropologist Margaret Mead and painter Walter Spies.

Mass tourism began in the early 1960s with the construction of the massive **Hotel Bali Beach** complex, but the real boom got under way only during the 1970s, with the construction of over a dozen exceptionally comfortable accommodation. These range in size from the **Bali Hyatt Hotel**, a regal complex sprawling across many acres of tastefully landscaped beachfront, and the medium-but-friendly sized **Sanur Beach Hotel**, to more intimate cottage-style establishments like the **Tanjung Sari Hotel**—nominated, for the 1982 Aga Khan Award for Excellence in Islamic Architecture, a dream-garden of Balinese antiques and grottoes, (*See* "Guide in Brief" for detailed hotel and restaurant listings.)

Mountainwards, north of the Hotel Bali Beach, where sands turn myster-

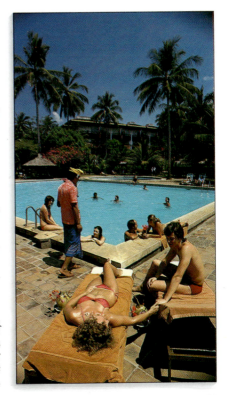

iously black (and the last stop on many of the south's processional trails), nestles the **Le Mayeur Museum**. Once the home and studio of the talented Belgian impressionist and his dancer wife, Ni Pollock, the museum now contains luscious images and vivid colours on canvasses framed in an Edwardian chamber with a breathtaking view over Sanur Bay to East Bali, with majestic Mt. Agung rising in the background.

Over the Water

Sanur's main attraction is leisure—a facet of life not unknown to those who live here. Strolls up and down the beach can easily occupy your day, capped by a fine meal and an evening dance performance. For a bit more activity catch one of the sailing *prahus* that ply the hotel shores, and sail across the narrow strait (two hours) to Lembongan Island, spending the day snorkeling in the crystal waters of this idyllic island off an idyllic island. The architecture and culture of the Lembongan's two or three small adjacent villages are still very medieval: pure and strong.

Cross to the neighbouring big brother island, Nusa Penida and take a stroll through the forgotten mountain villages of Bali's former penal colony—the views to Bali are unforgettable. The island is celebrated as the home of the demon king, Ratu Gede Mencaling, who once terrorized much of southern Bali. The demon-king lives on in the legends and ceremonies of the island, especially the giant puppet dance, *Barong Landung*, performed in village streets and temple squares on festival days. Nusa Penida is incidentally where Bali's best lobster is caught and sold.

Sail farther south to Desa Tanjung, a picturesque fishing village on the far side of Benoa harbour. Bronze icons, survivors from a 15th Century Chinese shipwreck, are still worshipped in an annex of the village's Chinese temple-Bali's oldest.

If you return to Sanur and visit Belanjong temple, you'll see an inscription on a low pillar that commemorates the victories of the great king, Sri Kesari Warmadewa, over his enemies in 913 A.D. Tours can be arranged, or *prahus* easily hired to visit the beautiful Pura Sakenan temple on **Pulau Serangan** (turtle island). Twice a year at Kuning-

an, a holiday which caps the festive Galungan season, hundreds of thousands of Balinese converge on the temple—gliding across the narrow shoal in outriggers, conveying offerings, *barong* masks and even entire *gamelan* orchestras. Giant sea turtles lay their eggs here at night, and villagers on the island hatch and raise them for their meat and shells. Beautiful seashells are collected and sold to visitors.

Bali's Southern Tip

South of the airport, a bulbous appendage fans out to form the Bukit Peninsula, once the hunting grounds of Denpasar's rajas. Geologically and climatically this area is Mediterranean—a dry, mostly barren plateau lying well above sea level. The western and southern shoreline is rimmed with sharp, jutting cliffs, site of **Pura Uluwatu**—a sublime place to watch the sunset.

The mangroves lining Benoa harbour give way to superb beaches along the northeastern shore of the peninsula. This is the Nusa Dua Tourist Development Area, created in 1970 with help from the World Bank. A new highway

The cliffs at Uluwatu.

has been constructed, connecting Bualu village to the airport, Kuta and Sanur, and eleven luxury hotels have been licensed for operation. The first of these opened in 1983—the palatially baroque Nusa Dua Hotel and the 50-room deluxe Hotel Bualu Beach—valiantly proving to the sceptics that it will work.

Fun-loving Kuta Beach

Whereas Sanur and Nusa Dua cater to visitors in search of relaxed seclusion and comfort, **Kuta** on Bali's southwestern coast, has blossomed recently into a bargain basement beach party.

"Discovered" by Aussie surfers in the early 1970s, Kuta's chief natural attractions are a broad, sloping beach, a pounding surf and a technicolour sunset. Kuta's accommodations are delightfully informal—often no more than a concrete block hastily thrown up behind a villager's home. Rooms rent for as little as US$1 a night. There are also increasing numbers of up-scale bungalow resorts, and the streets of Kuta and neighbouring Legian are lined with a staggering array of restaurants, cafes, pubs, boutiques, discos, bike rentals, artshops and tour agencies. The result is a kind of tinseltown with a cosmopolitan feel—during peak season (July, August and December, January), Kuta roars into the fast lane.

Deserted stretches of sandy beach and the serenity of the Balinese countryside are, thankfully, never more than a few minutes away. Walk or drive north from Kuta through Legian to Seminyak and beyond. Crowded beaches and raucous traffic give way to empty space. Past the **Bali Oberoi Hotel**, built of coral rock in a handsome traditional style, you reach the important estuary temple of Peti Tenget. By divine coincidence, this is the spot where the first Hindu-Javanese priest and the first Dutchman both set foot on Bali.

Farther along the main road lies **Kerobokan Village**, an outpost of rural charm and as instant a trip into the "real" Bali as one can hope to find. Kerobokan's main road, leading to the richly carved palace, is lined by a series of three score and ten temples: tall gates define a ridge of decorative precipices unique in Bali. See the "art nouveau" temple in the nearby village of **Kaji** on

Taking it easy
on Kuta Beach.

the back road to Sempidi—itself a shangrila of mossy gulleys, fast flowing streams, miniature dams and waterfalls.

Downtown Denpasar

Denpasar has swollen some tenfold, to a mini-metropolis of 200,000 since replacing the northern port of Singaraja as the island's capital in 1945. The last decade has been one of extraordinary change—some ten blocks of shops at the town's centre get busier by the year, suburban sprawl is swallowing up once autonomous satellite villages and the capital's formerly packed hotels now cater only to *domestik* visitors from neighbouring Java.

But Denpasar has its hidden attractions. If you are lucky enough to pass an inner-city ceremony, stop for a moment and observe how the basically rural Balinese cope with patterns of urban life. The *pasar malam* (night market), riverside in the carpark of the smart new multi-level Kusumasari shopping complex, is the area's best nocturnal treat. Feast on *babi guling* (roast suckling pig), Javanese goat *sate* or Chinese noodles.

Denpasar's **main square** was the scene of the horrific mass suicide of 1906, when almost the entire royal house of Denpasar, dressed in white and armed with ceremonial daggers and lances, rushed headlong into blazing Dutch guns. Successive governments have erected monuments commemorating the event. In the middle of a main intersection at the northwest corner of the square is a five-metre (16-foot) statue of Bhatara Guru, teacher and lord-protector of the realm. On the square proper towers a triple life-size bronze executed in the Sukarno School of social realism—idealizing the role of ordinary men and women in the nation's struggle for independence.

To the east of the square stands the town's state temple, Pura Jagatnata, a figurine of Tintya, the almighty godhead, glinting from its seat high on the temple's central shrine. The **Bali Museum** nextdoor houses a fine collection of archaeological artifacts and examples of Balinese craftsmanship.

In the morning visit Bali's foremost conservatory of dance, music and puppet theatre, kokar/SMKI on Jalan Ratna, to see the island's graceful and

Denpasar's new Cultural Centre.

handsome teenage stars rehearsing in polyester midis and drainpipe jeans—*de rigueur* for the 1980s.

The tertiary level of the school, ASTI, is located inside the sprawling grounds of the performing arts centre, Werdi Budaya, located at Abian Kapas. A masterwork of baroque Balinese recreational architecture, the complex contains museums, open stages and recital halls. Visitors are welcome to observe dance and music classes in progress. In 1979 the first island-wide **Arts Festival** was held here, encompassing a monster programme of *gamelan* competitions, art contests, theatre revivals, craft exhibitions, and a seven-part production of the ever-popular Ramayana Ballet. It has now become an annual affair, held between May and July, and tens of thousands of art lovers come from around the world to witness the glamour of Bali's cultural heritage.

West Bali

Compared with the compact, temple-encrusted valleys of central and southern Bali, the sweeping horizons of the west unfold most dramatically. Geographical ups-and-downs and twists-and-turns impart a slightly different character to each of the three western districts: **Mengwi**, **Tabanan** and **Jembrana**. Together they make up almost half of Bali, and are noted for their beautiful garden temples, *gamelan* orchestras, dancers, bull races and traditional weavers.

Don't swallow the west in one trip. Instead, base yourself in the south and plan mini-excursions to points of special interest. Visit the **monkey forest** of Sangeh, the moated **Pura Taman Ayun** temple, or the island temple **Tanah Lot**. Longer day trips can be made to the mountain sanctuary at **Batukau** or to the bull races at **Negara**.

The neighbouring villages of **Sempidi**, **Lukluk** and **Kapal** to the west of Denpasar are noted for their decorative temple reliefs depicting domestic as well as mythic scenes, mischievously executed in exuberant colours. The most important temple in this area, dating from the 12th Century, is **Pura Sada** in Kapal. It has 64 stone seats resembling megalithic ancestral shrines—these are believed to commemorate loyal warriors who fell in battle.

Mengwi

Past Kapal, a turnoff towards the mountains leads to **Mengwi**, which until 1981 was the capital of the powerful Gelgel kingdom. In 1634, the Raja of Mengwi, I Gusti Agung Anom, built the magnificent garden temple, **Pura Taman Ayun**. The temple's spacious compound is surrounded by a moat and is adjacent to a lotus lake, with a pagoda-like community hall or *wantilan* in its expansive forecourt. Among the *pelinggih*, rows of wooden shrines that serve as seats for visiting deities during temple feasts, stands a brick *paibon* or royal ancestral altar, which faces east. In the surrounding pavilions, priests recite their vedic incantations, village elders hold council, offerings are prepared and the temple's *gamelan* orchestra is stored.

Northeast of Mengwi, at Sangeh, is Bali's famed **monkey forest**. According to Balinese versions of the Ramayana epic, this is where part of Hanuman's monkey army landed when the monkey king lifted the sacred mountain, Mahameru, and broke it apart in order

Temple offerings at Taman Ayun.

to crush Rawana. Tall nutmeg trees are unique to this region and are considered sacred. A moss-covered temple lies hidden deep in the jungle. In its courtyard is the 17th Century **Pura Bukit Sari**, containing a large statue of the mythical *garuda* bird. The mischievous monkey tribe normally appears whenever there are visitors, in order to divest them of any and all edibles. Hold on tight to your belongings.

Snakes in Caves

Continue along the main highway toward Tabanan, then turn left (south) at the town of Kediri along a small but well-marked lane which leads after some kilometres to a parking lot and a walkway down to the beach. Here, perched on a large rock just offshore, sits the remarkable temple of **Tanah Lot**, founded by the proselytizing Hindu saint, Naratha, during his wanderings. Like many temples in Bali it has animal guardians, in this case snakes who live in caves nearby. At high tide, waves lash the islet, but at other times it is possible to cross over the rocks and ascend to the temple, which appears at sunset strikingly silhouetted against a flaming sky.

Farther west, the district capital of **Tabanan** was once the seat of a powerful independent kingdom, founded in the 17th Century. **Puri Tabanan**, the traditional home of the raja, is a striking reminder of the immense wealth once possessed by the Balinese rulers. The town itself has been overshadowed economically by Denpasar, but still boasts many famous music ensembles, dance troupes and a lively night market. The regional cultural centre, Gedung Mario, takes its name from the most celebrated dancer of the 1930s and 1940s, the legendary I Nyoman Mario.

The fabulous beaches of Tabanan regency, reached by taking any side-road to the sea, are remarkably little known. One such side-road, southwest of Tabanan, passes through the village of Kerambitan, famous for its beautiful maidens and *joged* dancers. The palace, **Puri Kerambitan**, is another example of the region's ornate architectural style, its *merajan* house shrine encrusted with strands of old Chinese porcelain.

Kerambitan is currently governed by

Tanah Lot.

156

identical twins, grandsons of the late raja, and in 1974 they created a dance, the *Tektekan*, which combines the clatter of a spirit-appeasing bamboo ensemble with the high drama of a *Calonarang* play. Held in the handsome forecourt of the palace, the dance's finale finds the entire orchestra entranced, armed with *keris* and throwing themselves upon the evil Rangda.

Batukaro and Negara

All temples in west Bali have shrines dedicated to the spirit of Mt. Batukaro, the highest peak of the western volcanic range. A turnoff to the right some kilometres west of Tabanan leads up past the hot springs at Yeh Panas to Wongaya Gede, the village closest to the temple sanctuary, Pura Luhur, high on Batukaro's slopes.

Uninhabited jungle encloses the solitary temple, whose single seven-tiered *meru* is the symbolic abode of the mountain deity. Nearby is a square pool, symbolizing the ocean, and from the adjacent village of Jati Luwih, a stunning panorama of the sea and the coast presents itself.

Back down to the highway and many kilometres farther west, the district capital of Negara is famed mostly for its bull races. A secular entertainment introduced from east Java and Madura less than a century ago, bull racing takes place regularly between July and October. Bulls are specially bred for speed and colour (no ordinary plowing bulls, these), then decked out in silk banners and enormous wooden bells, and paraded before being raced down a two-km (1.25-mile) track. They are judged for speed and style. It is remarkable to see such ordinarily slow-moving creatures thunder down to the finish line at speeds of up to 50 km (32 miles) per hour!

As one approaches the western tip of Bali, the landscape changes to thick savanna, and villagers live by hunting or fishing rather than farming. Avid skin-divers will want to explore the coral gardens ringing the island of **Menjangan** in the **Bali Barat Nature Reserve**, just north of Gilimanuk. From Gilimanuk, a ferry crosses on the half hour to Banyuwangi in Java.

Batukaro Temple.

CENTRAL BALI

With more gold leaf per square inch than imperial China, more artists than Montmartre and the most glamourous traditional culture in the modern world, the magical middle kingdom is Bali's most exotic and artistic region. Ever since the great Hindu-Balinese renaissance of the 17th Century, the realm within a 15-km (nine-mile) radius of the village of Ubud has been the centre for Bali's arts.

The star villages of Singapadu, Batubulan and Batuan support a full spectrum of dance and drama groups, while Ubud and Mas have produced, over the last decade, enough master painters and sculptors to satisfy the next century of connoisseurs and collectors. Balinese lucky enough to be re-born (according to their belief) in this region are presented with numerous sources of inspiration, and plenty of outlets for their considerable talents.

Leaving Denpasar and heading first east then north toward Ubud, the road climbs slowly, past bountiful rice fields and super-ornate temples, into villages where bright smiles and laughter are as universal as are the gentle tones of the *gamelan*.

The highway crosses the River Sasagan (the boundary between Badung and Gianyar districts) at Tohpati, and turns into the village of **Batubulan**. Though performed here daily before busloads of world-weary tourists, the villages' *Barong* dance remains a great piece of professional theatre, and is an accurate synopsis of the morality play that is central to Balinese social education. Local folklore has it that the *Barong* loves to dance everyday, and can be heard rattling in protest whenever rain or lack of tourists forces a cancellation!

Another more verifiable tale recounts the birth, in Batubulan, of the popular *kecak* dance. In 1928, German artist Walter Spies, and Baron von Messon, director of the first feature film on Bali, were watching a performance of the village's *Sanghyang Dedari* trance dance, when a member of the male chorus flew into a wild impromptu *Baris* dance. Spies took the idea of a formal dance to the accompaniment of the

Rice fields at Batubulan.

chanting *Sanghyang* chorus, and together with authoress Kathryn Myerson, fresh from the Martha Graham school in New York, created the *Kecak* for the Baron's film.

Batubulan is also an area of beautiful temples. The soft soapstone quarried in nearby ravines is an ideal medium for Balinese stonecarvers, who love to smother their temples and shrines in ornate carvings. Of particular note here is the **Pura Puseh** temple, a one-minute walk from the main road. Etched into the massive temple gate, are the Hindu pantheon on one side and a meditating Buddha on the other.

Gold, Silver, Puppets and Dances

A silver dragon twice encircles the wrist to form a bracelet sold in the village of **Celuk**, a centre for gold and silver work. Original designs in delicate filigree give Balinese jewellery a distinctive appearance.

Although the results are sophisticated, methods of production are primitive. Craftsmen use a tree stump with a protruding metal spike for an anvil, and a manually operated bellows to produce smelting and forging temperatures. As with most crafts in Bali, gold and silver smithing is a hereditary trade. Son-apprentices begin young, and by the time they are 12 they are already producing exquisite ornaments and settings.

After crossing the Oos River, you enter the village of **Sukawati**, once an important kingdom and centre for Chinese traders during the Dalem dynasty period. A phalanx of shops and a market now conceal the grand Puri Sukawati palace. Behind the palace live some of Bali's greatest shadow puppet masters. Sukawati is the undisputed custodian of the Balinese *wayang kulit* shadow puppet tradition, and a performance by a Sukawati *dalang* (puppeteer) at a wedding or temple festival is considered a major event.

The views of distant Mt. Agung become more spectacular as one turns the corner into **Batuan** village just north of Sukawati. Truly gifted in all the arts, the residents of Batuan are best known for their painting and dance. Under the patronage of Walter Spies, the Batuan School of the 1930s was the first to produce secular Balinese paintings—

Invitation to the popular *kecak* dance.

semi-realistic village-scapes and sensitive studies of costumed dancers and musicians.

Batuan's young dancers regularly win the island-wide competitions held in Denpasar, and if you are lucky enough to be present during the *odalan* anniversary rites of the village temple, you are treated to a round-robin of superb *Baris, Legong, Arja* and *Gambuh* dances, *Topeng* mask plays and shadow puppet performances. As many as six music ensembles may play at any given moment, and in the forecourt of the temple, groups of entranced grandmothers go through the mesmerizing *mendek* ritual used to welcome the gods. It is truly one of the high points of the Balinese festive calendar.

Woodcarvers, Dancers and Painters

After omni-talented Batuan, villages once again become more specialized. The Rajas of old, who orchestrated village activities, seem to have parcelled out artistic responsibility like today's corporate bosses—with each village as a separate sub-division of the corporation.

For historical reasons, the village of **Mas** is an almost exclusively Brahman enclave, the order of its town planning and the exquisiteness of its festivals reflecting the high-born status of its inhabitants. It is a village of **master carvers**. In former times, woodcarvers worked only on religious or royal projects, but now they also produce decorative and "art" works for export. The village's most famous carver was Ida Bagus Nyana, whose visionary modernist sculptures of the 1940s—ethereal maidens with twisted torsoes—are now on display in the vast gallery of his son, Ida Bagus Tilem, himself a talented carver. Farther north is the gallery of Ida Bagus Anom, whose expressive *topeng* masks are much sought after by the island's 100 or so *topeng* dance troupes.

The quiet village of Pengosekan is known for its Community of Artists, a **painter's cooperative** founded in 1969 by Dewa Nyoman Batuan. Aided by ideas and sponsors from abroad, and taking their inspiration from nature and day-to-day life, the artists have moved, like the English school of William Morris, from the decorative to the industrial

The tranquility of a Lotus pond in the centre of Ubud.

arts—doing a booming trade not only in paintings but also in screens, kitchenware and umbrellas, two metres (six feet) across, decorated with painted scenes from the Ramayana. The founder's brother, Dewa Mokoh, has developed a wide following on account of his beautifully simple depictions of Balinese flora and fauna.

On the threshold of Ubud, the village of **Peliatan** is the home of an especially active **dance troupe** and its *semar pegulingan* orchestra. In 1953, in preparation for a tour of Europe and America (organized following the troupe's cameo appearance in the Lamar-Hope-Crosby film, *Road to Bali*), the great choreographer and dancer Mario created the *Oleg* dance specifically for Peliatan's tiny star, Gusti Ayu Raka. She subsequently took Paris by storm, and a famous photograph shows the troupe at the President's Palace, with Raka looking for all the world like Eloise at the Ritz.

The village *Puri* (palace) continues the tradition of fine performing arts, with private dance lessons for aspirants from the age of five under the direction of A.A. Mandera. It is delightful to watch a graceful *legong* teacher glide through the formations of the dance, trailed by a bevy of young girls, who strain intently to imitate her every movement.

Ubud

For many years, **Ubud** has been a mecca for foreign and local artists who enjoy the creative atmosphere in this area of Bali. Although Ubud's main street is now lined with shops selling all manner of paintings, carvings, weavings and bric-a-brac, the surrounding villages and countryside are as charming as ever, and most artists gladly welcome visitors into their home or studio.

Artists have thrived in Ubud since the 1930s, when a local aristocrat named Cokorda Sukawati formed the Pita Maha art society together with German painter Walter Spies and Dutch artist Rudolf Bonnet. Many of the finest works of the early Pita Maha years, which show clearly the transition from traditional to modern Balinese painting styles, are exhibited in the **Puri Lukisan Museum**.

Among the Pita Maha artists, I Gusti Nyoman Lempad was probably the greatest. His ink drawings, cremation towers, *Barong* heads and temple stone carvings are greatly admired. Lempad died in 1978 at the age of 121 and some of his works are on display in his home, at the eastern end of Ubud's main street. Others may be seen at the excellent Neka Gallery to the West of Ubud.

Many other well-known artists have homes and galleries in Ubud, including American Antonio Blanco, Dutch-born Hans Snel, Javanese Abdul Azziz, and Balinese stone carver Wayan Cemul. A pleasant ten-minute walk through the rice fields (follow the main street of Ubud west over the bridge and turn left opposite the Campuan Hotel) leads to the village of **Penestanan**, where a community of young artists, inspired by Dutchman Arie Smit, works on brightly coloured "naive" paintings of dancers, rice harvests and village scenes.

In fact the finest work of art in Ubud is the surrounding countryside, and the only way to see it properly is on foot. Take a walk in the early morning or late afternoon to any of the neighbouring villages, or catch a minibus north from Ubud's main intersection for the

A young Balinese girl.

breathtaking ride to Pujung, then walk up to Sebatu village and admire the split-bamboo roofs, coloured spirit boxes and carved temple plinths. While away the hot midday hours in one of Ubud's charming cafes, such as Murni's next to the bridge or the Cafe Lotus overlooking the ponds of the Puri Saraswati palace.

Antiquities of Central Bali

Most of Bali's ancient remains and artifacts are to be found in the narrow region bounded by two holy rivers, the Pekrisan and the Petanu. Crossing the Petanu River immediately to the east of Peliatan on the road to Bedulu, the mysterious **Goa Gajah** (elephant cave) is just visible on the lower side of the road, opposite a row of souvenir stands. The cave's gaping mouth is fantastically carved with leaves, rocks, animals, waves and demons, and when it was discovered in 1923 these carvings were apparently mistaken for an elephant, hence the cave's name. Adjacent baths were discovered and excavated in 1954, and in fact the site was probably a hermitage used by early Hindu-

Buddhist holy men, as the cave contains three joined *lingga* (Shivaitic fertility symbols). Two Buddha statues, as well, have been found only a short distance away. All are believed to date from about the 8th or 9th Century. After a visit to the cave, the Puri Suling restaurant next door is highly recommended for refreshments or a meal.

Just beyond Goa Gajah, the crossroad village of Bedulu was formerly the centre of the powerful and cultured Pejeng dynasty. On the southern side of Bedulu, a dirt track leads to the rarely frequented ruins of Yeh Pulu—another small hermitage dating from the 14th Century. A unique frieze, two metres (6.5 feet) high and 25 metres (81 feet) long, is said to have been etched by the thumbnail of a giant. At the end is a small niche and a spring.

Two km (1.25 miles) north of Bedulu on the main road is the **Archaeological Museum**, which houses a collection of neolithic axe heads, sarcophagi, weapons, bronze jewellery and Chinese ceramics. And in 1981, villagers digging in this area discovered the tip of a stone ziggurat which may answer many of the

Left, a Balinese woodcarver. Right, the ornately carved entrance to Gao Gajah.

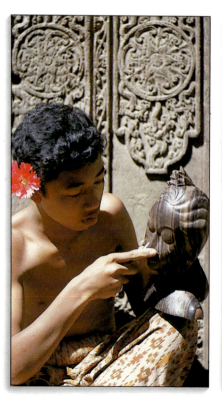

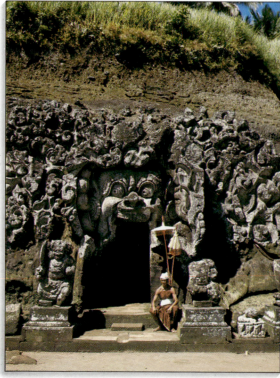

questions concerning the origins and culture of the Pejeng dynasty.

Several temples just to the north of the museum contain objects of interest. The Pura Kebo Edan (crazed water buffalo) temple houses a 3.6-metre (12-foot) statue. The Pura Pusering Jagat (cosmic navel) temple contains a remarkable stone vessel carved with the tale of the churning of the ocean by gods and demons to obtain *amrta*, the elixir of life.

And the Pura Penataran Sasih (lunar governance) temple contains Indonesia's most important bronze-age antiquity, the 2,000-year-old **Moon of Pejeng** drum. Shaped like an hourglass, beautifully etched and over three metres (10 feet) long, it is the largest drum in the world to be cast as a single piece. According to Balinese legend it fell from the sky, but the discovery of an ancient, similarly shaped stone mould in Bali proves that sophisticated bronze-casting techniques were known here from an early time.

A Tomb and a Spring

From Pejeng, the road winds up towards the crater of Mt. Batur, but about halfway to the peak, just at the source of the Pakrisan River, are two of Bali's holiest spots. The first, **Gunung Kawi**, is a spectacular and ancient royal tomb reached by descending a long, steep stairway through a stone arch into a watery canyon. On the far wall, ghostly shrines are hewn out of solid rock, probably memorials to the deified 11th Century Balinese ruler, Anak Wungsu. A complex of monk's cells also line the canyon walls.

The Balinese refer to their religion as *Agama Tirta*—the religion of the waters. It is not surprising then that a pilgrimage to the Pura Tirta Empul spring at **Tampaksiring**, 2 km upstream from Gunung Kawi, is an essential part of every major Balinese ceremony. For according to Balinese folklore, this spring was created when the god Indra pierced a stone (really Indra's enemy, the proud King Mayadanawa in disguise) to produce a source of *amrta* with which to revive his poisoned army. To this day, the waters of Tampaksiring are believed to have magic curative powers. Ivory, bone and coconut shell carvings can be easily purchased and are another reason why the village is well known.

unung Kawi.

NORTH BALI ROUND TRIP

One of Bali's greatest attributes is its compactness. In only a few hours one can travel from the island's sandy southern shores to the spectacular rim of an active volcano, 1,450 metres (4,750 feet) above sea level, and in so doing observe a broad spectrum of natural and historical wonders.

Up and Over Mt. Batur

In Bali there are two passes over the scenic central mountains, via Kintamani and via Bedugul, and the two roads rendezvous on Bali's secluded north coast. Most tours simply take you up to Kintamani and back in a single day, but it is more fun to leisurely circumnavigate the island. The entire round trip is ideally accomplished in three stages, with overnights in Ubud and Lovina Beach (just west of Singaraja—see below). Indeed, the journey can easily be stretched out over a week or more, and many people find this to be their most

memorable Bali experience.

Get an early start for the ascent of Mt. Batur, to arrive before the inevitable mountain mists descend to obscure the view. After Tampaksiring (see previous section), the road climbs sharply, until bursting finally upon one of the most dramatic sights in Bali: expansive **Lake Batur**, 100 metres (328 feet) below with the smoking, black cone of Mt. Batur rising in the background. This is the village **Penelokan** (the lookout), perched on the lip of an immense, 20-km (12.5-mile) wide caldera. Lava-laden Batur is a much younger, active volcano set in the centre of the old volcanic basin, and the adjacent lake is moon-shaped, covering about a third of the basin's area.

From Penelokan the main road follows the rim of the crater northward, but there is also a small road that winds down to the lake's edge. If the mists have not yet rolled in, descend and hire a motorized canoe across the lake to the curious village of Trunyan, one of the few pre-Hindu Bali Aga (original Balinese) enclaves on the island. These mountain people still maintain many ancient customs, the most famous of which is the practice of exposing their dead to the elements in a skeleton-filled graveyard by the lake. On the way back, stop for a hot sulphur-spring bath at **Toya Bungkah**, by the foot of Mt. Batur.

Continue north along the caldera's rim to **Kintamani**, the village closest to Batur's menacing cone. In 1917, the volcano erupted violently, claiming 1,000 lives and destroying a village that clung to its slopes, but miraculously leaving the village temple intact. The survivors took this as an auspicious sign and continued to live there. In 1926, another eruption buried the village and the temple, sparing only the shrine to Dewi Danu, goddess of the lake. The villagers resettled higher up at Kintamani, where the shrine now stands in the Pura Ulun Danu temple.

A short distance past Kintamani, the road veers left and begins the precipitous descent to the north coast. Before descending, however, stop and climb up a long flight of steps visible on the right, to the peak of **Mt. Penulisan**. This is the site of Bali's highest temple, and is believed to have been the mountain sanctuary of the kings of Pejeng. The temple is almost always shrouded in

Left, ornamental *kala* head gateways are a distinctive feature of Balinese temples. Below, in the background is Mt. Batur— Bali's most impressive panorama.

fog, but on a clear day you have a spectacular view all the way to Java.

The North Coast

Bali's criss-crossing network of paved roadways was constructed by the Dutch only in the 1920s. Before that time the people of Buleleng regency on the island's north shore were relatively isolated from their southern cousins. North Bali, always a centre for foreign trade, was annexed by the Dutch in 1848, some 60 years before they subdued the rest of Bali, and Buleleng's rulers converted to Christianity at this time.

The culture of the north is thus different in several ways: the language is faster and less refined, the music more *allegro* and the temple ornamentation more fanciful. The port city of **Singaraja**, the capital of Bali under the Dutch, has sizeable communities of Chinese and Muslims.

From Penulisan, the winding road seems to drop straight out of the sky, flattening out several miles before the village of **Kubutambahan**, on the coast. This village's main temple, Pura Maduwe Karang, is dedicated to the animistic ground spirits that ensure good harvests. Partly because the local raja converted to Christianity early this century, leaving temple affairs in the hands of villagers, the carvings at Pura Maduwe Karang are "popular" in the way they depict startling ghouls, domestic scenes, lovers and even an official riding a bicycle.

Other temples in the region have equally unusual carvings. A temple at **Jagaraga**, a short distance inland from the coast, has reliefs depicting Europeans riding in a Model-T Ford, a single-propeller plane diving into the sea, and a steamship attacked by sea monsters. And the Pura Beji temple at **Sangsit** just to the west of Kubutambahan by the sea, is known for its Rabelaisian scenes—complete with flames, arabesques and spirals all executed in pink sandstone.

From Kubutambahan you may want to make a detour east to **Air Saneh**, a holy spring and bathing place situated at the edge of the sea. It is said that the spring is for lovers—here you can sharpen the libido and do laps at the same time! There are also small guest houses

A Balinese temple relief records the age of the automobile.

and restaurants.

The best facilities, however, are to be found at **Lovina Beach**, 11 kms (7 miles) west of Singaraja on the scenic coast road. Here a calm sea laps the sandy shore and tidy bungalows rent for only a few dollars a night. This is the ideal hideaway for tired travellers.

The town of **Singaraja**, once a bustling centre of commerce and government, is now rather sleepy (pop. 25,000). Its tree-lined boulevards and colonial residences tell something of its former glory, but there is relatively little to see or do. The **Gedung Kertya**, on Jl. Veteran near the colonial Hotel Singaraja (once the Dutch governor's mansion), houses a valuable collection of palm-leaf *lontar* (manuscripts). And at the port, you can see sailing vessels unloading wood and loading coffee, corn or rice.

Heading due south from Singaraja, the road climbs up and up into the lush Bratan plateau, an area fed by numerous mountain lakes and streams where the earth is covered with thick moss and creepers. At Pancosar, you pass the anomalous **Bali Handara Country Club**, built by the state oil monopoly, Perta-

mina, during the halcyon days of Ibnu Sutowo's administration in the early 1970s. Its 18-hole golf course is on the list of the world's top 50!

The road continues through dense jungle terrain, skirting serene **Lake Bratan**, veiled in mists and filling the ancient crater of Mt. Bratan. People in the surrounding villages honour Dewi Danu, the goddess of the lake, in the temple of Ulu Danu on a small promontory by the western shore. Around on the southern shore there is a small, government-run guest house and restaurant, where recently they have begun renting motorboats and waterskis. This is a cool, peaceful place. Children fish for minnows and canoes cross the still waters, carrying firewood to villages on the far bank.

Just below the lake is the village of **Bedugul**, where wild orchids, tree ferns and fresh vegetables are sold at the **Bukit Mungsu market. Three kms (1.9 miles) to the west along a marked sideroad, there is a botanical garden, Lila Graha, where mountain orchids are raised. From Bedugul the road drops down again to the cultivated plains, emerging at Mengwi.

Relaxing at Lovina Beach.

EAST BALI

The direction "east" is greatly revered by the Balinese, as the realm of the Hindu god Siwa in his manifestation as Surya, the sun god. Balinese myth tells how the gods set towering Mt. Agung in the east and placed their thrones upon it. Some millennia later, divine providence and a sense for proprieties led a party of East-Javanese nobles, priests, architects and craftsmen to establish the sanctuary of Besakih, where all Balinese castes and creeds could worship, high on the slopes of this sacred mountain.

East Bali was also the home of Bali's most powerful kingdoms. Courts at Gelgel, and later at Klungkung and Karangasem, were places of refinement and grandeur, where rajas and noblemen patronized the arts and created traditions of music and dance that flourish today. And as the only area where the aristocratic high Balinese dialect still survives as the *lingua franca*, the Golden East is somehow in a class by itself.

The grand tour of the eastern realm begins in the palace of Klungkung, leads up to the "mother" temple of Besakih, follows the coastline past the Goa Lawah (bat cave) to the isolated village of Tenganan and to the water palaces of Karangasem, and ends with a breathtaking return drive across the emerald foothills of Mt. Agung. At least two days (with an overnight in Candi Dasa) are required to see everything.

Heaven and Hell in Klungkung

Coming from Ubud or the south, all roads to Klungkung pass through **Gianyar**, the centre for Bali's famous weaving industry. Many workshops and factories still produce a variety of beautiful hand-woven and hand-dyed textiles, although the use of machine-spun cotton thread, quick chemical dyes and tinsel foil cannot possibly match the quality of the older cloths, with their hand-spun threads, elaborate vegetable dyes and gold and silver ornamentation.

Beside the town square of Gianyar is the royal palace, one of the few that is

Bima Suarga—a Balinese epic of crime and punishment in the Kerta Gosa.

still inhabited by a royal family. The intricately carved wooden pillars, the stonework and generous proportions of its various courtyards are representative of the style to which all Balinese rulers were once accustomed. The Gianyar market has many shops selling traditional gold jewellery, and a food-stall of nationwide acclaim specializing in *babi guling gianyar*, a local version of roast suckling pig.

The town of **Klungkung**, 20 kms (12.5 miles) to the east, was once the political centre of Bali. The descendants of the great Hindu-Javanese Majapahit court settled in this area after fleeing Java in the 15th Century. Their first capital was at Gelgel, 3 kms (1.9 miles) to the south, but in 1710 the palace was moved to Klungkung. The raja of Klungkung was regarded, by virtue of his illustrious genealogy, as the most senior of all Balinese rulers, and played an influential role in government and the arts.

At the very centre of modern Klungkung sits the 18th Century Kerta Gosa hall of justice and the Bale Kambang floating pavilion. The Kerta Gosa is known for its concentric ceiling murals, painted in the traditional *wayang* style.

The lower panels depict gory scenes of retribution in hell, while higher up, the virtuous are shown reaping their heavenly rewards. These murals were once used by judges to influence witnesses and defendants during hearings.

While in Klungkung, visit the central market, where a great variety of baskets and other housewares are sold. Four kms (2.5 miles) to the south, past Gelgel, the villagers of **Kamasan** produce gold and silver work and *wayang*-style paintings like those in the Kerta Gosa, illustrations from the Hindu-Javanese classics.

Besakih: Holiest of the Holy

The mountain road north from Klungkung climbs up for about an hour through some of Bali's most spectacular rice terraces, passing through several villages on the way to the island's holiest spot, **Pura Besakih** temple. With the massive peak of Mt. Agung, the Balinese Olympus, as a backdrop, the broad, stepped granite terraces and slender, pointed black pagodas of this 60-temple complex are a fitting residence for the gods.

Regarded as a holy place since pre-

Besakih Temple, site of the Eka Dasa Rudra ceremony.

historic times, the first record of Besakih's existence is an inscription dating from 1007 A.D. From at least the 15th Century, when Besakih was designated as the sanctuary of the deified ancestors of the Gelgel god-kings and their very extended family, the temple has been the central, "mother" temple for the entire island. All the allegiances of the Balinese come together here: all gods in the extensive Balinese pantheon are represented, gathered here in one vast meeting place in the clouds, and all Balinese make periodic pilgrimages to worship them.

All of Bali's many caste groups, even the non-Hindu Bali Aga tribes, have their own *pedarmaan* shrine off to the side of the main courtyard. Each shrine is afforded individual *odalan* anniversary rites, and everyone joins in the general *turun kabeh* (they all descend) ceremony held on the day of the full moon, which marks the anniversary of Besakih's consecration.

Once a century, the Balinese hold the *Eka Dasa Rudra* rite at Besakih—a ceremony of truly cosmic proportions aimed at purifying and stabilizing the entire universe. The ceremony involves millions of man-hours of labour in the preparation of offerings, thousands of animal sacrifices and the participation of every high priest and indeed every Balinese on the island in a 3-month sequence of rituals. An attempt was made to hold the ceremony in 1963, but was aborted when Mt. Agung erupted violently after lying dormant for several centuries. Two thousand people were killed, thousands more were left homeless and the temple was enclosed in clouds of black volcanic ash for several months. The *Eka Dasa Rudra* was finally held again over six months in 1979, this time without incident.

The East Coast

East of Klungkung the road descends to the shore at **Kusumba**, where sea-salt is mined in large fields. Palms dip their branches over the waves of the strait separating Bali from distant Nusa Penida island, and fishing boats line the shore.

Several kilometres after Kusumba, at the foot of a rocky escarpment, gapes the entrance to **Goa Lawah**, one of the nine great temples of Bali. Goa Lawah

An early morning fisherman.

is said to be the terminus of an underground passageway leading to distant Besakih temple up on Mt. Agung. Many Balinese temples have resident beasts, the so-called *duwe* (possession) of the temple, and apart from the thousands of small, black bats that inhabit Goa Lawah and give it its name, the cave is also believed to be the abode of Naga Basuki, the legendary sacred dragon of Mt. Agung. One of many fascinating tales surrounding Naga Basuki tells of a group of visiting Dutch soldiers who sighted and shot him in the cave. They were rushed away before the horrified locals got a chance to stone them to death, but that night a bright white light crossed the courtyard of the Denpasar Hotel and the soldiers vanished without a trace.

About 15 kms (nine miles) past Goa Lawah, a side-road to the right leads to the picturesque harbour town of **Padang Bai**. This is where the Lombok ferry departs, and where cruise ships anchor—a perfectly shaped bay, cradled by white sand coves and grassy hills.

Continue east through the pretty coastal village of Manggis, where wooden puppets and gargoyles gaze down at you from atop white-washed walls. Then just after the Tenganan road T-intersection, stop and have a swim and a meal at **Candi Dasa** (10 temples), a romantic lagoon and bay that is just beginning to be developed into a resort. The roomy beach-side cabanas here are simple, cheap and quiet—the favourite retreat of the island's cognoscenti.

Tenganan Village

Candi Dasa is also the perfect base for an exploration of the fascinating village of **Tenganan**, home of a pre-Hindu Bali Aga tribe. Located several kilometres inland, in a hilly area of lush bamboo forests and mystical banyan trees, Tenganan was for some reason never assimilated to the island's Hindu-Balinese culture and has retained its own traditions of architecture, kinship, government, religion, dance and music, supplying the rest of the island with several valuable items, notably the sacred *geringsing* fabrics.

The main village is rectangular and enclosed by walls, with tall gates at the four cardinal points. Only about 200 families live here and the living compounds are all arranged symmetrically around two wide, terraced stone lanes—a design principle used in many primitive megalithic areas of Indonesia such as Sumba and Nias. There are central meeting pavilions, and the strong sense of community and a ready defence against the outside world. Indeed, until recently, no outsiders were permitted, and most villagers still seem rather ambivalent about the intrusion of foreigners, despite the fact that several operate shops selling drinks as well as handicrafts.

The villagers own, communally, large tracts of cultivated land but traditionally the fields were worked by the residents of neighbouring villages. The Tenganese, meanwhile, concerned themselves primarily with the production of *tuak bayu* palm beer and *kamben geringsing* cloths. The latter, much sought after throughout Bali, is a fabric believed to immunize the wearer against evil influences and disease. (*See* Part IV, "Threads of Tradition.") Tenganan is also famous for its annual *usaba sembah* festival, when many unusual ceremonies, dances and musical

Balinese woman dressed in *kain gerinsing*.

performances are held, including the *perang pandan* (pandanus-leaf wars) and the playing of the *gamelan selunding* (an iron metallophone orchestra).

Explore the village quietly, and if offered, take the opportunity of observing one of the learned village elders producing illustrated *lontar* palm-leaf books in the old-Balinese script. Books such as these were once used throughout India and Southeast Asia. Walk up behind the village to an old, black-roofed temple shaded by two huge banyan trees, and continue on for lovely walks through the countryside to adjacent villages.

The Palaces of Karangasem

Twenty-five kms (16 miles) farther east, the road crosses a wide lava bed and enters **Amlapura**, a medium-size town formerly known as Karangasem and once the capital of Bali's most cultured king. Following the bloody Dutch conquest at the turn of the century, the ruler of Karangasem was the only Balinese raja allowed to retain his title and powers. Subsequently he became active in colonial commerce and

prospered, expanding his residence in Karangasem and building two elaborate pleasure palaces outside the town.

The traditional home of the Karangasem kings, Puri Agung Karangasem, is an austere compound surrounded by a thick red-brick wall, penetrated only by a three-tiered main gate.

Puri Kanginan, the palace where the last raja was born is an eclectic creation reflecting the strong European influence of his education, and of his architect—a Chinese by the name of Tung. The main building, with its lavish Edwardian mouldings and long veranda, is called the Bale London. The furniture, curiously, bears the crest of the British royal family. Above a doorway hangs a photograph of the late king, Anak Agung Anglurah Ketut, whose passion in life was to build opulent water palaces for frequent excursions with his wives and children to the country.

Eight kms (five miles) to the south, in **Ujung**, are the ruins of his first creation, a vast pool bordered by small pavilions representing the sun and the moon. In the centre "floats" the king's large stained-glass and stone bungalow, perhaps a latter-day Mt. Meru sur-

Tenganan village, home of a pre-Hindu *Bali Aga* tribe.

rounded by the calm seas of the Hindu cosmos, in which case the raja is symbolically deifying himself as resident of the sacred mountain. This retreat was completed in 1921 and the king retired in his old age to pursue his religious studies, but it was badly damaged after his death by the eruption and earthquake of 1963.

In 1946, the king finished a new project: the Tirta Gangga (Ganges water) pool located 15 kms (nine miles) to the north of Amlapura, at the site of a sacred spring and temple formerly known as Embukan. It was acclaimed as a masterwork of hydraulic engineering at the time, and was the source of some considerable pride to the much-decorated raja and his wives. Like the palace at Ujung it is a polymorphic follie of various royal modes. One can still swim in its three clear, fresh ponds, which flow out from under the umbrella of a huge banyan tree, with lovely views over the eastern hills to towering Mt. Agung. From here, a track leads north along the barren, uninhabited north-eastern coast to Singaraja, but this route is not particularly recommended.

From Subagan, a village in the solidified lava flows on the western outskirts of Amlapura, the mountain road climbs due west through **Sibetan**, a village famous for its *salak* — a teardrop-shaped fruit with the sweet-sour texture of an apple and skin resembling that of a cobra. Past Sibetan, the road levels out, winding across an exciting landscape of sculpted rice-terraces and river valleys of great dramatic beauty.

Stop at the village of **Putung**, where a road to the left leads to a small government-run guest house and restaurant perched on a cliff overlooking Padang Bai and the coast. From Putung, the road forks. Either continue straight on through Selat to Rendang and thence up to Besakih (about an hour's drive), or turn left on the road through Iseh to Klungkung.

The idyllic mountain village of **Iseh** was chosen by painter Walter Spies as the site for his country home. After Spies' untimely death, the Swiss painter, Theo Meier, lived in the house for many years. It gazes over an uninterrupted vista of mighty Mt. Agung—acclaimed by many as the great Bali view.

LOMBOK

To the east of Bali, across a deep strait seething with whirlpools and swimming with dolphins lies Lombok—an island whose history and culture are intimately intertwined with those of her illustrious neighbour. Yet in many important ways, Lombok is quite different from Bali. It's climate is drier and her land more rugged. And with 1.6 million inhabitants, a majority of whom are Muslim Sasaks, Lombok is only about half as densely populated.

Like Bali, Lombok is dominated by a towering northern volcanic range, with

3,800-metre (12,300-foot) Mt. Rinjani, the second highest peak in Indonesia, at its centre. Another non-volcanic range traverses the barren southern side of the island (corresponding to Bali's southern Bukit Peninsula), and most of Lombok's arable land and the majority of her population occupy a narrow 25-km (16-mile) wide strip of land in between.

The western third of this plain, similar in many ways to east Bali, which it faces across the strait, is well fed by mountain streams and artesian springs. Here, Balinese and Sasaks have sculpted handsome rice terraces into the fertile, sloping alluvial fan at the foot of Mt. Punikan, and Hindu temples vie for attention with glistening white mosques

amidst the picturesque rural villages. The island's two large towns, Mataram and Ampenan, are located here, within close proximity of the stately old court centre of Cakranegara. And the port, the secluded mountain resorts, and Lombok's spectacular southern beaches are an hour away,

A Touch of History

Early native chronicles confirm that Lombok was colonized from East Java, and the Sasak people perhaps take their name from a type of bamboo raft (*sesek*) used to cross the straits. According to a 14th-Century Old Javanese lontar-leaf text found here in 1894 (the famous *Negarakertagama*, which incidentally is the main source of information concerning the ancient empires of East Java), the island was brought under direct Javanese control by Patih Gajah Mada, powerful prime minister of the great Majapahit empire, before his death in 1365. No trace of this conquest remains, with the possible exception of an isolated group of peoples living near Sembalun, high on Rinjani's slopes, who claim to be descended from Hindu-Javanese settlers and who guard the grave of a brother of Majapahit's king.

In the 17th Century, Lombok was invaded and colonized from two directions. The western plain was annexed by the Balinese ruler of Karangasem, who was to exert a controlling influence over this part of the island up until the Dutch Conquest of 1894. The east coast, meanwhile, which was at this time the political centre of the native Sasak inhabitants, was conquered by groups of Muslim Makassarese traders operating from Sumbawa, and the Sasak aristocracy was thereafter converted to Islam.

In 1677, Balinese and Sasak forces succeeded in defeating the Makassarese and expelling them from eastern Lombok, and for the next 150 years the native Sasak aristocracy successfully resisted numerous Balinese advances, maintaining a series of independent Muslim kingdoms in the East. In west Lombok, the 18th Century was a Balinese-inspired "golden age." Hindu temples were given face-lifts and the local raja,

Above, the *kecodak* dance. Right, fishing boats line up on a Lombok beach at dawn.

Agung Made Gege Ngurah, established an architectural style and court pageantry that rivalled Bali's own. In 1744, he moved the palace to a new site at the town of Cakranegara. A mighty state temple, the Pura Meru, and a splendid water garden, the Taman Mayura, were erected at this time.

Finally in 1849, all of Lombok and east Bali were united under the rule of the Balinese raja of Karangasem, Ratu Agungagung K'tut. Balinese hegemony lasted less than half a century, however, because in 1894 a large Dutch military expedition land-

tants are Sasaks and they divide themselves into two more or less distinct groups: the Waktu-telu—mountain villagers who were ruled by Islamic leaders but whose customs are still basically pagan with some Muslim influence; and the Waktu-lima who inhabit the lowlands and the coasts and are today fervent Muslims.

The patchwork layout of west Lombok's Hindu and Sasak communities, between whom there is some smouldering antagonism (do not ask to be served alcohol in a Muslim Sasak restaurant), has given rise to

ed at Ampenan, and aided by East Lombok Sasak leaders who were at this time trying to liberate themselves from Balinese rule, the superior Dutch forces managed to wrest control of the island. This was accomplished only after much bitter fighting, in which the Dutch suffered over 1,000 casualties (out of a force that originally numbered 4,400) and the Balinese at least twice that number—including a ritual mass suicide attack (*puputan*) undertaken by the Balinese royal family and courtiers of Sasari.

Only about 10 per cent of Lombok's inhabitants are Hindu Balinese and almost all of them live in towns and villages in the tiny western-central plain of the island.

The vast majority of Lombok's inhabi-

an interesting spectrum of customs and juxtaposition of architectural modes. On the one hand, there are formal walled Balinese villages (including Mataram and Cakranegara) with their *kulkul* drum towers, central meeting pavilions and *banjar* system of community organization. And on the other hand, there are white-washed Muslim Sasak kampungs with their open compounds.

And in the mountain tribal villages (of the Waktu-telu), such as Pujung and Sengkol in southern-central Lombok, one finds still another type of village—traditional hyperbolic-shaped thatched huts supported by roughly hewn wooden beams, with wide strips of bamboo and tree branches interwoven to form walls and partitions.

TOURING LOMBOK

Compared with Java, bulging at the seams from overpopulation, and the newly cosmopolitan but ever-civilized Bali, Lombok exudes an aura of the staid and the rural—a genteel way of life in a quiet backwater. An island of startling contradictions and contrasts: Hindu rituals incorporated into Muslim ceremonies; lush rainforests backing arid plains, Lombok has been spared, to a great extent, the more vulgar intrusions of Western culture. The island's polyglot populace—Sasak, Balinese, Chinese and Arabs—continue their slow, traditional ways. Tourism is still in its infancy here, which means that a lack of amenities are more than offset by a relatively unspoilt culture rich in attractions, but without the "hard sell."

Best of all, for the visitors, is the fact that most of Lombok's sights and activities—temples, palaces, and villages, are still very much concentrated in West Lombok, within a 15-km radius of Cakranegara, the former royal capital. Catch the dawn at Puri Mayura in Cakranegara and watch a sea of water lilies unfold as the reflection of the towering Pura Meru pagoda swims slowly into focus. Then spend the morning investigating the Cakranegara bird market and the Arab-owned weaving factories. Visit the harbour and Maritime Museum in Ampenan, then retire to the cool hill resort of Suranadi. Take a day trip to the southern beach at Kuta, stopping along the way to visit traditional Sasak villages. All of this may easily be done in three days. More time is needed to make the spectacular climb up Mt. Rinjani, Indonesia's second highest peak.

Maritime Memories

Lombok's three largest towns—Ampenan, Mataram and Cakranegara—bunch together on a six-km (four-mile) stretch of road running from the western coast inland. **Ampenan**, formerly the main port of Lombok and once a vital link in the spice trade, is now little more than a broken-down wooden jetty with rows of deserted warehouses. At the main crossroads

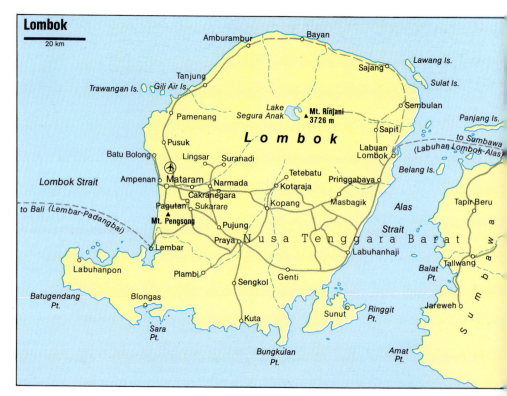

stands the **Maritime Museum**, which attempts to recount the colourful history of Ampenan's overseas trade. Stop at the Regional Tourist Office , (Diparda, Jl. Langka 70) to find out if there are any major festivals on the island.

Neighbouring **Mataram** is the modern provincial capital, with government buildings and large, well-kept houses to prove it. Yet other than providing banking, ticketing and other services, the town offers little for the visitor.

Cakranegara, a short distance to the east of Mataram, is the most interesting of the island's towns. It was the royal capital up until the turn of the century, and is still the major market town of Lombok. Cakranegara's crowded Arab quarter bustles with activity—this is the place to shop for an intricately patterned cotton *sarung*. And the Balinese quarter, to the north of the town across the Ancar River, has many splendid courtyard homes in the unique Lombok-Balinese style.

Pura Meru, the central temple for Lombok's Hindus, overlooks Cakranegara's main crossroads. It was built in 1720 to unify the various Hindu factions on the island, and the three courts of the temple symbolize the *tri loka* or three-tiered division of the Hindu cosmos: the earth, the human realm and the divine. In the innermost courtyard stand three pagodas representing the Hindu trinity—Brahma, Vishnu and Siva. Each of the 33 smaller shrines in this temple is cared for by a different Hindu community in Lombok.

Opposite the temple, a vast pond filled with lilies surrounds a pavilion, which may be reached by crossing over a stone causeway. This is the **Puri Mayura** royal garden, constructed in 1744. The pavilion is known as the Bale Kambang and formerly served as both a court of justice and a meeting hall for Lombok's lords. The leader of the Dutch military expedition of 1894, General Van Ham, was killed here with all his men.

The **Royal Palace** behind the garden is surprisingly modest—a part Dutch, part Balinese-style bungalow surrounded by a moat. The house is now a kind of museum, filled with old photographs and memorabilia from the Dutch times.

To the north and south of Mataram and Ampenan there are several sights

Below, the *kecodak* dance in Tanjung. Right, the Odalan ritual at Pura Meru.

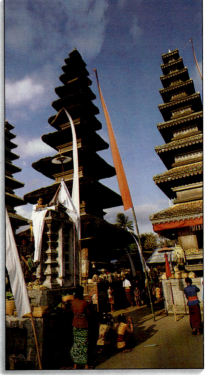

worthy of investigation, though few tourists take the time to seek them out. Seven kms (4.5 miles) south of Mataram, white shrines glint like calcified stalagmites on the rocky outcrops of **Mt. Pengsong**. The temples are reached by climbing a long flight of stairs that rises from the road between ancient banyan trees, and the 360-degree view from the top is superb. Tribes of monkeys, the temple guardians, play on the slopes below.

The small village temple in nearby **Pagutan** once housed a priceless 14th Century palmleaf manuscript version of the *Negarakertagama*—the major source of knowledge concerning the great Majapahit empire in Java. The manuscript was discovered here by a Dutch scholar in 1898 and now resides in the National Museum in Jakarta.

From Ampenan, a small road leads north across river estuaries and through coconut groves to the **Batu Bolong cliff temple**. Situated high upon a rock formation that juts out into the Lombok Strait, the temple is reached by passing over a natural stone arch. From this unique vantage point you may experience the magnificent setting of the sun

as it picks up specks of colour from the sails of passing boats.

Skindivers will be tempted to visit **Pemenang beach**, about an hour from Mataram on the northwestern coast. Dive in the coral gardens offshore, or hire a boat for the 30-minute sail to **Gili Air island** for even more spectacular coral formations and marine life.

Narmada and Suranadi

Small white mosques speckle the terraced ricefields between Cakranegara and **Narmada**, 10 kms (six miles) to the east. Stop at the sprawling market on the right, reputed to be Lombok's largest, and shop for baskets, earthenware and other village handicrafts.

The small town of Narmada is dominated by a man-made plateau, upon which stands the late 19th Century summer palace that was designed and built by the king of Karangasem. It is a vast complex of tiered gardens that descends sharply into a river valley below. Western-style ponds, fountains and arbors are built into traditional Balinese compounds of interlocking courtyards and pavilions. The king was

Crater Lake, Mt. Rinjani.

evidently influenced by wealthy Dutch merchants, who told him of the great palaces of Europe, and his eclectic summer palace ranks as one of the great achievements in the history of Balinese architecture.

The temple at **Suranadi**, seven kms (4.5 miles) above Narmada, is a pilgrimage point for Hindus from Lombok and Bali on account of its holy springs. Like Tampaksiring in Bali, the waters here (Suranadi is the name of the river that flows through Nirvana) are sought for the performance of important rituals. The springs were created, according to local legend, by the Hindu saint, Niratha, who led a group of village elders to the spot and thrust his staff in the ground five times.

The neighbouring **Suranadi Hotel**, once a royal pleasure garden, is the most delightful hostelry on the island, with a large spring-fed swimming pool and an excellent restaurant. There are trails from here leading up into mountain villages, where traditional stilt houses line small clearings in the rainforest. And just to the west, at the temple of **Lingsar**, albino fish swim in the ponds of the inner sanctum, a sure sign of elevated spirituality according to ancient Javanese belief.

To the South Shore

From Narmada, travel south through Mangang and Praya to the sandy shores of the southern coast. The round trip takes between 4 and 5 hours so you should get an early start in order to make stops on the way and still spend time on the beach. At **Sukarere**, stop to see traditional Lombok *ikat* and *lambung* cloths being woven.

By prior arrangement, made through your hotel, you may also stop in **Bayan** to see the frenzied *cekapung* and *cupak* dances, and hear a performance of the *tawa tawa* orchestra. Or in **Tanjung**, ask for Mr. Martinom, who can arrange a performance of the *kecodak* war dance.

Farther south the road gently rolls through miles of wet-rice paddies — a sea of lime-green shoots or cracked brown earth, depending on the season. Finally you arrive at **Kuta**, a small solitary village that guards access to a magnificent 100-km (62-mile) stretch of deserted golden beach.

On the way home from Kuta, or on your way to the east, visit the Dutch hill station of **Tetebatu**. Here in the midst of fruit orchards and vegetable gardens, a pre-war villa with a spring-fed pool has been transformed into a small hotel and picnic stop.

Scaling the Heights

Those who have made the climb to the top of 3,800-metre (12,300-foot) **Mt. Rinjani** claim that it's the ultimate Bali/Lombok experience. Be that as it may, the climb is a strenuous one and is certainly not for everyone — it takes time and preparation, and can only be attempted during the dry season (April to October).

First of all, you need a police permit from the main office in Mataram. Then be sure you have enough warm clothing, food and water for the two-day expedition. The favoured approach is from the village of **Sapit** in eastern Lombok, where you can hire a guide and porters. Ascend the slopes just below the caldera, then camp and climb the last stretch in the pre-dawn hours in time for the sunrise — an unforgettable "unveiling" of the eastern islands of the archipelago.

Narmada.

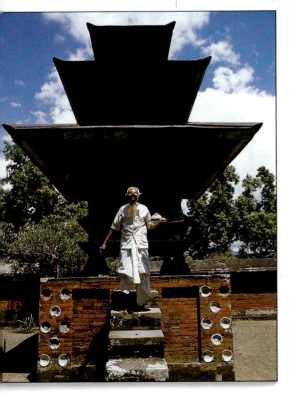

NUSA TENGGARA (THE LESSER SUNDAS)

The term Nusa Tenggara (meaning south-eastern islands in Old Javanese) refers to the tightly packed necklace of sparsely inhabited islands to the east of Bali. In Dutch times, these islands were known as the "Lesser" or "Eastern" Sundas—a grouping which then included Bali. But in 1951, Bali was made a separate province of the new Republic of Indonesia, and the other islands were organized into two distinct provinces: West Nusatenggara (comprising Lombok and Sumbawa) and East Nusatenggara (Sumba, Flores, Timor and the adjacent islands). When, in 1976, Indonesia annexed the former Portuguese colony of East Timor, Indonesia gained its 27th province.

The islands of Nusa Tenggara are formed by the protruding peaks of a mountain range that begins at the northern tip of Sumatra and extends down across the length of Java through Bali to the east. In fact to the east there are two ranges: a southerly one which is older and non-volcanic (forming the island Sumba, Sawu, Roti and Timor) and a northerly, intensely volcanic range that dominates

Sumbawa, Flores and a chain of smaller islands.

Whereas Java, Sumatra and Borneo (the "Greater Sundas") are bordered by a very shallow Java Sea (maximum depth: 100 metres [328 feet]) and have increased their area through the build-up of vast alluvial deposits over geological time, the islands to the east of Bali rise from a deep seabed. The interstices between them have not been "filled in," and this has created a stepping-stone effect of small, adjacent islands with steep slopes, high mountains and very narrow coastal plains.

Moving eastward in the Sunda archipelago, the climate becomes markedly drier due to the action of hot, dessicating winds that blow up from the Australian land mass. The moisture-laden northwest monsoon fights against these dry winds in November and December, reaching the easterly island of Nusa Tenggara relatively late and sometimes only for a period of weeks. Year-long droughts are common on Sumba and Timor. Rainfall is deposited mainly on the wind-

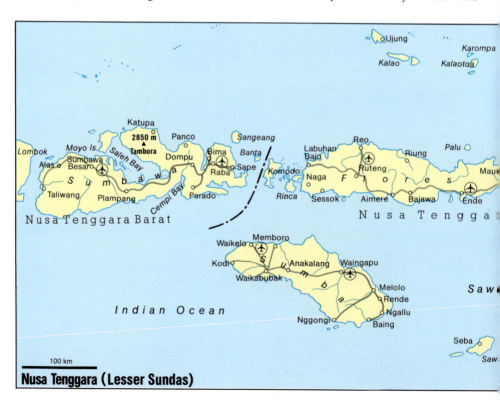

Nusa Tenggara (Lesser Sundas)

ward slopes of mountains, creating pockets of lush forest and vegetation amidst parched expanses of scrub grassland and savannah.

Strange Beasts of Wallacea

The depth of the seas and straits separating the islands of Nusa Tenggara is such that even at the height of the Ice Age, when world sea levels were about 200 metres (456 feet) lower than today, there were no land bridges to these islands. The great 19th Century naturalist Sir Alfred Russell Wallace spent several years studying these islands and noted a marked difference between the Eurasian animal species of the Greater Sundas (monkeys, elephants, tigers, pigs, rhinoceroses, buffalo, deer, etc.) and the Australian species of the eastern islands. He drew a line (now known as the Wallace Line) separating Bali and Borneo from Lombok and the Celebes, and postulated this as a boundary between two faunal groups.

More recent studies have shown that many Eurasian species, particularly birds and insects, persist throughout the islands of Nusa Tenggara and disappear only in New Guinea and Australia. Nusa Tenggara thus lies within a transitional zone (now known as Wallacea), in which the fauna of Eurasia and Australia coexist.

There is in these islands a great variety of interesting wildlife: Australian marsupial species, colourful New Guinean plumage birds (parrots, cockatoos) and large primitive reptiles—the most spectacular being the so-called Komodo dragon (*Varanus Komodoensis*).

An Underpopulated Region

Nusa Tenggara is among the poorest and least fertile regions of Indonesia. The population is very unevenly distributed—for example the large island of Timor is home to only 1.3 million people due to its mountainous terrain, poor soils and dry cli-

mate. By contrast, the tiny island of Sawu supports a population of over 10,000 thanks to the widespread cultivation of the *lontar* palm which, when tapped, furnishes a carbohydrate-rich beverage.

Most of the almost 10 million inhabitants of Nusa Tenggara are subsistence farmers or fishermen. Fish, livestock and some agricultural products (coffee, copra, rice, beans, onions) are exported to other islands, while manufactured goods and some food products are imported, mainly from Java.

Recently the Indonesian government has invested heavily to improve communications, establish schools and provide health facilities. This is bringing rapid change to some of the urban areas, but partly because the population is so scattered, many hinter-

Tenggara by the 11th or 12th centuries.

In the 14th Century, the Majapahit empire on Java claimed the entire Nusa Tenggara chain as part of its realm. Undoubtedly this was a case of vassal-sovereign trading relations and not direct political control, for there is little evidence today of "Hinduization" in the region. Islam arrived in the 15th and 16th centuries, via Java and Ternate (in Maluku), later also from Makassar, and slaves became a major export item.

The first Portuguese explorer to the Spice Islands, Antonio de Abreu, sailed past Flores in 1512 and gave the island its present name. During the 16th Century, the Portuguese muscled in on the Timorese sandalwood trade, and established fortresses on Flores and Solor. Dominican friars con-

land villages remain remote and relatively untouched by modern civilization.

A Rich History

Coastal areas of Nusa Tenggara have participated in the trade of the archipelago since very early times. Though these islands produce no spices, they have been a major source of sandalwood and other aromatic and hardwood products for almost 2,000 years. Small coastal kingdoms have sprung up at river mouths to handle this export trade and to import metal goods, textiles and porcelains. Chinese and Arab traders ventured beyond Borneo and Sulawesi to Maluku and probably reached areas of Nusa

verted many islanders to Roman Catholicism in the vicinity of their trading establishments, and today large Christian communities are found on Flores and Timor as a result.

The ruthless Dutch, with their superior ships, managed to wrestle much of the spice trade away from their rivals in the 17th Century, but the eastern-island's supplies of sandalwood were nearly depleted by this time. Consequently the Dutch never took much interest in Nusa Tenggara until the

Preceding pages, the serene far-away feel of the sparsely inhabited islands to the east of Bali. Left, faces from an archipelago. Right, Roman Catholic missionary at Lela, South Flores.

mid-19th Century. Instead it was the Portuguese, the mestizos and the Muslim Makassarese who were most active here in the 18th Century.

This complacent Dutch attitude changed rather dramatically at the turn of the 20th Century, when a series of military expeditions were dispatched to impose Dutch rule on all islands in the Indies. On several islands these measures met with armed resistance, but the Dutch prevailed with superior forces and by the early 1910s all areas were subdued. Though the Dutch built roads, schools and administrative facilities throughout the islands of Nusa Tenggara, many villages in remote areas had few contacts with the outside world until very recently.

beings are thought to control harvests, bring disease and guard against disaster. Chickens, pigs and water buffalo are frequently sacrificed to the spirits, and then consumed in huge communal feasts. Human blood often flows in ritualized contests—boxing matches, whip duels or cavalry bouts—associated with planting, harvesting and marriage.

Most peoples of Nusa Tenggara fitted, until recently, into one of three distinct social categories: noble, commoner or slave. The ruler of a trading port frequently styled himself "raja" or "sultan," though in most areas a kind of tribal organization prevailed and the leaders were often quite indistinguishable from the other members of the community.

While the peoples of Nusa Tenggara are backwards by many standards (health, calorie intake, education), they certainly are not uncivilized. Indeed, they possess highly elaborate material, social, economic and spiritual cultures: traditions of music, dance, literature, crafts and complex kinship systems strictly regulated by rituals of exchange and religious practices.

The Strength of Tradition

Indigenous beliefs in the spirits of nature and ancestral spirits are still widely held on Sumba and Timor. Elsewhere they are disguised by what is often a very superficial layer of Islam or Christianity. Supernatural

Nobles have always been distinguished instead by ritual practices and status items. The bride price was an essential cultural and economic factor—an aristocrat would need to provide money and exotic items such as bronze drums (on Alor), ivory tusks (on Flores and Lembata), or ivory bracelets and water buffalo (on Sumba) in order to secure a bride of high social standing. The bride's family would reciprocate with fine woven *ikat* cloths, which often had ritual significance. Indeed the *ikat* weavers of Nusa Tenggara are famed throughout the archipelago, and their products are now highly prized by textile collectors around the world. (*See* Part IV, "Threads of Tradition" for more information on textiles.)

SUMBAWA

The island of Sumbawa is larger than Bali and Lombok combined. Its contorted form is the result of violent volcanic explosions, and indeed it appears on the map as two or three islands thrown hastily together. It is now divided into three administrative districts or regencies that correspond roughly to the island's former sultanates: Bima in the east, Sumbawa in the west and Dompu in the middle.

Most of Sumbawa's 800,000 inhabitants are farmers or fishermen. The island's exports are almost entirely agricultural: rice, peanuts, beans and cattle, although raw timber is now being exported as part of a joint venture with the Philippines.

The people of Sumbawa are devout Muslims. Indeed, the eastern regency of Bima sends a higher percentage of pilgrims to Mecca than any other area in Indonesia. Of course, this reflects prosperity as well as piety. The government-sponsored one-month *haj*

cost US$3,800 in 1983, equivalent here to the price of 10 water buffalo. The *kerundung* or orthodox Islamic dress for women is very much in evidence in Bima, and powerful loudspeakers amplify the *muezzin's* 4 a.m. call to prayer in all major towns on the island.

Yet even though Islam is firmly implanted on Sumbawa, here as elsewhere in Indonesia, there is a strong undercurrent of traditional customs and beliefs. One of the most important is the belief in the power of the *dukun* or shaman, who can cure disease, make water-buffalo run faster and enable a young man to deliver a "100-ton punch" in the traditional post-harvest boxing matches.

Sumbawa Besar and Bima

Very few visitors spend more than a minimum of time in either Sumbawa Besar or Bima, the island's two main towns (with populations of 30,000 and 40,000 respectively.) Nevertheless, each town has a royal palace museum where the sultan's sacred *pusaka* or insignia of power can be seen. And at the ports outside of each town, skilled ship-

Market at Sape.

186

wrights still construct large wooden vessels with the most primitive of tools.

In **Sumbawa Besar** the sultan's former residence is made entirely of wood. Built in 1885 and called the Dalem Loka, it is raised on stilts in the traditional manner and crowned by two unusual carvings. A complete restoration is underway and is scheduled to be completed in 1986.

The palace in **Bima** will house a fantastic collection: the royal crown and many *keris* with gem-studded gold and ivory hilts. It is possible to see these already, but you must contact the city government and negotiate a fee. Near Bima, there are several important Muslim tombs. The most important is the Dantara, grave of the first sultan to embrace Islam, located at the village of Tolobali.

The Hinterlands

Fertile river valleys with shimmering velvet-green rice fields surround the towns, but as one moves out across Sumbawa along the single paved trans-island highway, the monotony of rolling scorched-brown hills is alleviated only

by a stretch of dramatic coast. Here picturesque bays and harbours shelter *bagans*, twin-sailed catamaran fishing boats with a small hut in the middle. These vessels set out to sea at night, using powerful lanterns to attract fish.

Outside of the cities, most houses are made of wood and raised one or two metres above the ground on stilts, to avoid the mud of the rainy season. Men and women wear wrap-around *sarungs*, and on the easternmost coast, around Sape, it is not unusual to see conical, brilliantly painted, plaited-leaf sunhats.

From Sumbawa Besar's harbour, one can charter a motorized fishing boat for the three-hour voyage to **Pulau Moyo**, an island populated by deer, wild boar and other game. Hunting is permitted, but requires a police permit. For non-hunters, there is excellent skindiving. There are no facilities on the island, so bring food, water and bedding to sleep on the boat. Fresh fish and coconuts may be purchased at small villages.

Hikers and climbers may want to ascend to the crater of **Gunung Tambora**, site of the world's greatest volcanic explosion. In 1815, approximately 100 cubic kilometres of debris were ejected into the atmosphere with a force equivalent to that of several hydrogen bombs, creating the famous "year without summer" of 1816. Today the gaping, 2,820-metre (9,250-feet) high caldera offers a spectacular view of the island and the sea. It is a day's walk to the rim from Dempu, but jeeps can negotiate a dirt track part of the way.

Archaeology buffs will be interested to know that the hills east of Sumbawa Besar contain many large stone sarcophagi carved in low relief with human forms and crocodiles. These are scattered near the village of **Batu Tering** in the district of Semamung and villagers can guide you on the hour-and-a-half walk to the massive, raised sarcophagi. It is assumed that these megaliths are the royal tombs of a late Neolithic culture which thrived here, perhaps 2,000 years ago. Regular *bemos* run almost into Batu Tering and can be chartered all the way.

While waiting for the weekly Komodo ferry in **Sape**, it is possible to charter a minibus for the 25-km (15.5-mile) ride northward to several small villages by the sea. Here white sand beaches, crystal-clear water and coconut trees contribute to an idyllic setting.

Past royal glory pictured at the Dalem Loka.

KOMODO: ISLAND OF DRAGONS

Directly in the centre of the island-strewn strait between Sumbawa and Flores lies the island of **Komodo**, home of the world's largest reptile, the so-called Komodo Dragon (*varanus komodoensis*). This giant monitor lizard (called *ora* by the natives) is one of the world's oldest species, a close relative of the dinosaurs who roamed the earth 100 million years ago.

Komodo island lies some 500 km (312 miles) to the east of Bali and is 30 km (19 miles) long on its north-south axis and 16 km (10 miles) at its widest point. The island's parched hills (highest point: 735 metres [2,410 feet]) sprout skinny *lontar* palms and scruffy undergrowth.

There is but one native village on Komodo, a small community of 500 souls clinging precariously to the shore. Some say they arrived several hundred years ago from Sumbawa, others claim they are the descendants of exiled criminals. Little grows on the

on Komodo. The adult males can reach three metres (ten feet) in length and weigh 150 kgs (330 pounds). Females attain only two thirds of this size and lay up to 30 eggs at a time.

The greatest threat to the monitors comes now from deer poachers who kill off the animals upon which the lizards feed. Dogs are sometimes abandoned on the island and compete with the dragons as scavengers and eat their eggs.

The highlight of a Komodo visit is to see the dragon in its natural habitat. Though you may spot one by walking around the island, a safer and surer way is to let the Indonesian Directorate of Nature Conservation (known by its Indonesian initials: PPA) arrange your visit. For $30 they will bring a goat to the PPA campsite on Komodo, and from there walk you to a vantage point some 2 km (1.25 miles) away. Here the goat will be slaughtered, and from the shade and safety of an elevated hut you'll have an excellent opportunity to photograph a group of dragons devouring the bait. Be sure to bring a telephoto lens and keep well away from the

dry coast of this barren island. Having been requested by the government to abandon their inland gardens, the natives now make a living fishing by night from graceful catamarans.

Apart from its renowned lizards, Komodo has several other exotic species, such as the mound-building *megapode* bird, the sulfur-crested cockatoo and the noisy friar bird. Deer, wild pig and water buffalo also inhabit the island and serve as prey for the monitors.

Several hundred adult lizards live

lizards—their tails are lethal weapons and their saliva is extremely toxic.

Aside from the "dragon tour," there are designated trails which you may follow, accompanied always by a guide. These take you into the hills where, especially towards **Mt. Ara**, there are exquisite panoramas of the surrounding emerald-blue seas to be enjoyed. You may also hire a boat to **Red Beach** east of Loho Liang, or to **Lasa Island** across from Komodo village. The snorkeling and swimming here are superb.

SUMBA ISLAND

Sumba Island lies well to the south of the other islands of the central and east Nusa Tenggara chain and has always been one of the major backwater regions of the archipelago. Mostly flat, and barren throughout the long dry season, with few tourist facilities, Sumba does offer the opportunity to see remnants of an ancient pagan Indonesian culture. Because Sumba never had much historical significance and few resources, it escaped the Hindu, Muslim and Christian waves of influence that successively washed over neighbouring islands. Known in past centuries primarily as a source of sandalwood, slaves and horses, and as a land of cannibal tribes and rugged horsemen, Sumba is famous today for its sculptured megalithic tombs, its tribal war-game rituals and its painstakingly made hand-woven *ikat* textiles.

Sumba is almost oval in shape, about 300 kms (188 miles) long and 80 kms (50 miles) wide, and is divided politically and climatically into two quite distinct halves.

East and West

West Sumba, with a population of 350,000, is the more prosperous half of the island, lush and green during the rainy season and culturally diverse, with two separate linguistic groups speaking a total of at least eight dialects. West Sumbans live in traditional thatched huts with conical roofs raised on stilts. Here agricultural communities flourish, and ancestral and land worship is still strong, with about two-thirds of the population observing traditional religious practices such as the *pasola* (in which hundreds of mounted warriors fling spears at one another) and the communal construction of stone slab tombs.

East Sumba, which is dry, rocky and inhospitable, has 250,000 inhabitants all of whom speak the same language. Most people live near or on the coast, and an extensive hand-loom industry has flourished for several centuries, producing distinctive, high-quality *ikat* weavings.

Left, a goat serves as bait to lure these "dragons." Below, a weaving such as this can take several months to complete. Right, megalithic carving.

Megaliths of West Sumba

There are many traditional villages with elaborate megalithic tombs scattered throughout West Sumba. Right in **Waikabubak**, the small district capital with a population of 8,000, you can see the following tombs (named for their location): Kadung Tana, Hatu Karagate and Bulu Puka Mila.

Tarung village, an important ceremonial centre located on top of a hill a short walk to the west of Waikabubak, also has several tombs, and the facades of many traditional houses are decorated with huge water-buffalo horns—souvenirs of past sacrificial feasts.

In the district of **Anakalang** 22 km (14 miles) east of Waikabubak on the main road to Waingapu, there is a tomb with unusual carvings at the village of Pasunga. A bit farther east and a few minutes off the road, the Resi Moni grave is the burial site of a former raja of Anakalang—one of the largest megaliths on the island. Nearby, in the traditional village of Lai Tarung, there are many old graves and an important ceremony called the *Purunga Ta Kadonga* is held here every two years.

In the district of Wanukaka, 18 kms (12 miles) south Waikabubak, the traditional village of Prai Goli boasts the oldest megaliths in the area, called the *Hatu Kajiwa* (spirit stones).

Sodan, near the south coast, is perhaps the most interesting traditional village in West Sumba. It is located 25 kms (16 miles) southwest of Waikabubak, a few kms from Lamboya. Here, as well as at Tarung, an important lunar new year ceremony takes place each October. The village possesses a sacred drum whose playing surface is covered with human skin.

Ordinary pick-ups (*bemos*) from Waikabubak will get you quite close to all the places mentioned above, and it is perhaps best to ask which village is holding its weekly market and head in that direction. Adventurous visitors may want to hike to even more remote villages away from the roadways. Your best bet is to head south from Waikabubak towards Hanokaka, Lamboya or Padedewatu. From these places, villages are as close as half an hour away, and if you feel fit, keep going for three hours or more to the very fringes of civilization.

Traditional Sumban village.

The Pasola

The *pasola* is West Sumba's most exciting ritual—scores of colourfully arrayed horsemen on bareback, battling with lances. The ceremony is held during February in **Lamboya** and **Kodi** (on the western tip of the island), and during March in **Gaura** and **Hanokaka**. It begins several days after the full moon, and coincides with the yearly arrival to the shore of strange, multihued sea-worms. During the war ritual riders charge one another flinging spears. The government has now decreed that the spears must be blunt, but deaths do occur occasionally.

To relax in West Sumba while waiting for the *pasola* or other rituals, swim at the white sand beach at Rua 21 km (13 miles) south of Waikabubak, or at the spring-fed pools at Haikelo Sawah 10 km (6 miles) west of the town. Both places may be reached by *bemo*.

East Sumban Weavings

East Sumba has been known for centuries as a centre for its warp-*ikat*—weavings patterned by dyeing the warp threads before the weft is introduced. The entire process is long and tedious, taking several months to complete a single piece. First the cotton is carded and spun, then the threads are stretched on a frame and tied with dye-resistant fibres to create the pattern. Then they are immersed in pots of dyestuff, such as locally-grown indigo, and sun-dried.

Subsequent re-bindings and re-dyeings create the final design—bands of blue and red with bold animal and human figures. Sumban *hinggi* come in pairs, one as a body-wrap and one as a shawl. Small scarves are also produced.

You can observe women dyeing and weaving in Praliu village just outside of **Waingapu**. Other major *ikat* production centres are down on the southeast coast. Take a bus from Waingapu to **Rende**, 69 km (43 miles) and two hours to the southeast, where megalithic tombs with unusual carvings may be seen. Farther down the coast, in the vicinity of Ngallu and Baing, 125 km (78 miles) from Waingapu, whole villages produce the famous *hinggi kombu* weavings. There is also great surfing at **Kalala Beach**, 5km (3 miles) from Baing between December and May.

he pasola.

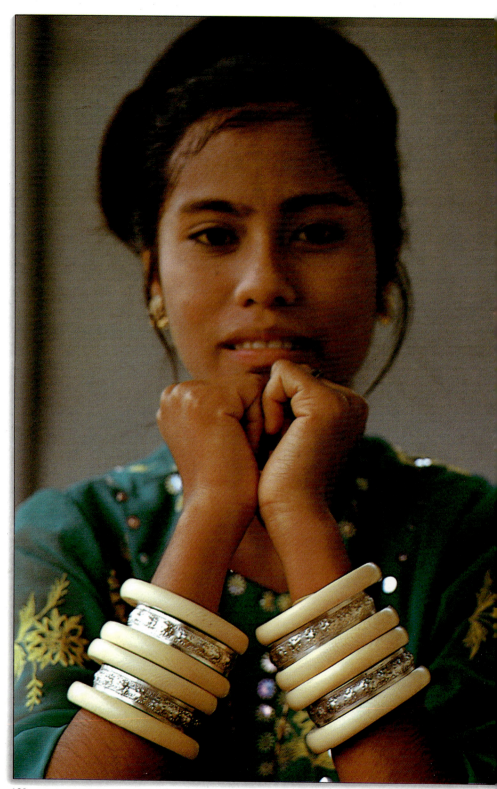

FLORES AND THE EASTERN ISLANDS

At the eastern end of the Sunda archipelago lie two large islands, Flores and Timor, and a number of smaller ones: Solor, Adonara, Lembata, Pantar and Alor (to the east of Flores), as well as Sawu and Roti (to the south and west of Timor). The inhabitants of all these islands have been in contact with each other since ancient times, and have developed over the centuries sophisticated cultures based on palm and taro cultivation, and trade in sandalwood, textiles and slaves.

Because it is the most readily visited island, more space is devoted here to Flores, with only brief mention of Timor and the smaller islands.

Invaders and Missionaries

Flores, the largest island in the eastern Nusa Tenggara chain, received its present name in 1512 from passing Portuguese explorers, who called it *Cabo das Flores* (Cape of Flowers). Before this it was known to Javanese traders as Stone Island.

Flores has received foreign influences from many quarters. For centuries its ports formed a vital link in the eastern inter-island trade, and during the 14th Century it was drawn into the commercial and political sphere of the Hindu-Javanese empire of Majapahit. Some coastal communities began to convert to Islam in the 15th and 16th centuries, as a result of contacts with the far-flung trading Sultanate of clove-producing Ternate.

Then in the mid-16th Century, the Portuguese arrived. They established a mission at Larantuka and built a fort on Solor Island to the east of Flores (1566), primarily to protect their trading interests in Timor. By the 1570s there was already a seminary in Larantuka and Catholicism was spreading quickly to other areas.

In 1664, Muslim invaders from Goa in South Sulawesi took control of Ende, ostensibly to stem the tide of Catholic conversions. Subsequent Makassarese immigrations created a strong Islamic community here, and the Endenese raided Sumba for slaves and traded sandalwood from Timor.

The Dutch took control of Portuguese settlements on Flores in 1859, with the proviso that the Catholic church be encouraged. They also bombarded Muslim Ende twice and exercised increasing authority there, but fully controlled the island only after subduing a bloody rebellion in 1907-8. Catholic missionaries flooded into Flores in this century, sparking a new wave of conversions that continues up to the present.

A Catholic Tradition

At present, Catholicism claims 90 per cent of Flores' 1 million inhabitants. The church has placed heavy emphasis on improving living conditions through its schools, health services and agricultural programmes. And although the clergy in Flores is well aware of the continued existence of many traditional beliefs and customs, they make no systematic efforts to eliminate them. The traditions which have survived are many and varied, and constitute much of Flores' fascination for the visitor.

Ancient tradition states that *nitu* or ancestral spirits reside in trees, stones, rivers and mountains. These spirits once were — and perhaps still are — propitiated with offerings to ward off illness and encourage bountiful harvests. The *nitu* employ snakes to warn their descendants of impending danger, and pythons were once worshipped on Flores, giving the island its former name: Snake Island.

In many areas, the bride price is still of paramount social importance. Items given to the father of a bride determine the status of all individuals involved, and can include fine hand-woven textiles, money, water buffalo, horses, pigs and ivory tusks. Church wedding or no, a marriage cannot be consummated until the bride price has been paid and certain ancient rituals have been performed.

And in various parts of Flores, one can still find traditional-style houses, called *kada*, where offerings are made and relics are preserved. In one such *kada*, the beams are carved with serpents and life-sized male and female figures. These are interpreted variously as Jesus and the virgin Mary, or as the male principle of the sun and the female principle of the earth, showing clearly the coexistence of Catholicism and traditional cosmology.

Flores girl wearing ivory bracelets. Flores is an ivory carving centre.

193

A 667-km (417-mile) road, almost none of it paved, runs the length of Flores, from Labuhanbajo in the west to Larantuka in the east. To travel the entire route is long and exhausting, but can also be exciting, particularly if you time your visit to coincide with a major ritual somewhere on the island.

The western third of Flores is called **Manggarai** and contains almost half the island's population. Manggarai is self-sufficient in rice and exports fine coffee and livestock. The agricultural economy suffers somewhat from a lack of adequate roads, as will become painfully obvious during your journey, but progress is being made.

Labuhanbajo is the westernmost of three main port towns on the island, a beautiful harbour filled with native catamarans.

From here, the road winds up to **Ruteng**, a pleasant, cool town situated in the western hills at an altitude of 1,100 metres (3,600 feet). There are fairly good hotels in Ruteng, and in the market you will find many colourful embroidered *sarung*.

With luck, you may see a spectacular *caci* whip duel, held here occasionally as part of a wedding or other important ceremony. Combatants are outfitted with head-wrappings and buffalo-hide shields and they attack each other with long leather whips. The aim is to overcome the physical and spiritual defences of one's opponent. Resulting welts and scars are admired, and blood drawn during the *caci* becomes an offering to the ancestral spirits.

Next stop, following a scenic but back-wrenching 8-hour ride, is the town of **Bajawa**, scene of the annual Maha Kudus mass. The mass itself is essentially Catholic in form and content, yet afterwards swordsmen lead a lively procession of dancing villagers around the town bearing the holy cross. The date of this event is determined according to the traditional calendar, and it immediately precedes a ritual deer hunt in nearby So'a, to the north.

The deer hunt is a fertility ritual associated with puberty rites: circumcision for the boys and tooth filling for the girls. Strong taboos against sex are in force throughout the hunt, including a prohibition against the consummation of recent marriages. After the hunt, young women dip their hands into the

Kelimutu.

blood of slain deer to enhance their fertility.

The area around Bajawa is one of the most traditional of Flores, and several old megaliths are in evidence. Exquisite yellow-on-black embroidered *sarungs* are also produced here. The accommodations are basic, as is the food— dog meat is a local delicacy.

From Bajawa, it is 125 kms (78 miles) and about five hours to **Ende**, the principal city of Flores. Ende has a distinctly Islamic flavour—it was an important Islamic trading port from the late 17th to the 19th centuries. During the Japanese occupation, the city was the regional capital for the eastern archipelago. Sukarno was exiled here for a time, and the town was later bombed by the Allies. Today, Ende's commerce is largely in Chinese hands. Good accommodations and delicious Chinese food are available.

Keli Mutu, three adjacent multi-coloured volcanic lakes located a couple of hours northeast of Ende (off the main road to Maumere), are considered the island's chief tourist attraction. The lakes are separated only by low ridges, and curiously they are of different col-

ours. Recently, two of them were a dark, burgundy red while the other was a light turquoise green, but chameleon-like they appear to be changing all the time.

Sorcerers, Sinners, Infants and Virgins

No scientific study of the lakes has been made, but one possible explanation is that the colouration results from dissolved minerals and that the water eats through different mineral layers at varying rates, perhaps due also to changes in acidity. The natives of this area say that one red lake holds the souls of sorcerers, the other the souls of sinners, while the third lake holds the souls of infants and virgins.

Ende to Larantuka

Twelve kms (7.5 miles) to the east of Keli Mutu, at Wolowaru, turn south to the coastal village of **Japo** to see superb weavings being produced, often with vegetable dyes. Similar weavings are available in Ende, but the quality is often lower and the prices higher than

Left, a whip warrior. Right, Easter procession.

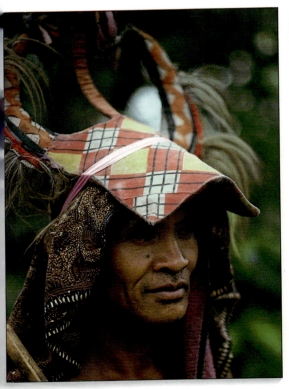

in the village.

From Ende to **Maumere**, the road cuts diagonally across the island toward the north coast. The distance is 148 km (92 miles), but the ride could easily take seven hours.

Maumere is experiencing something of an economic boom, as a result of increased copra and coffee exports. The Catholic Church, with its large coconut and coffee holdings, is behind much of the development. There is a large seminary and regional church headquarters here. The surrounding area looks like a gigantic coconut factory, with vast groves and drying racks. Trucks pass to and fro, carrying copra to the harbour.

The last leg of your journey is a hot and dusty 137-km (86-mile) stretch of road to **Larantuka** on the easternmost tip of Flores. Count on a 10-hour ride.

Larantuka's history is intimately bound up with the fortunes of the Portuguese and the spread of Catholicism on the island. It was a Portuguese colony for about 300 years, and Catholic rituals here reflect a great deal of Iberian influence. As in Seville, men dressed in white hoods carry the black coffin of the saviour through the streets during the daytime Easter procession. At night, another procession bears Christ's coffin through the eery blackness, stopping along the way for prayers and hymns, in a modified form of the *Via Dolorosa*. There are many local Christian elements—a black Virgin Mary statue said to have been washed ashore at a spot designated by a beautiful woman in a local man's dream. Another statue of the Lord Jesus is washed each year before Easter, and the water is kept to cure sick children and to ease difficult childbirths.

Islands East of Flores

Larantuka is the gateway to the tightly packed chain of islands to the east. Many small boats of all shapes and sizes leave daily from Larantuka harbour, plying the inter-island, inter-village trade routes. You need plenty of time and patience to explore this area, but the fares are at least cheap. We mention only a few highlights below.

On the island of **Solor**, you can see the old Portuguese fort, constructed in 1566 and still in surprisingly good shape. Massive stone walls, some two metres

A Portuguese cannon at Solor.

(seven feet) thick and four metres (13 feet) high, encircle a rectangular interior. The entryway is covered by an impressive arch, and in one corner of the fort rusting cannon have survived and stand guard over the approaches from the sea.

Lembata Island (also known as Lomblen) is famous primarily for its primitive whaling industry. Shallow-draught sail- and oar-propelled wooden boats are used for whale hunting. When a whale is sighted, a harpooner balances precariously on a narrow plank extending from the bow of the boat and then jumps with his harpoon, thrusting it accurately into the whale's back. The islanders also weave fabulously intricate *ikat* cloths from home-spun threads.

The islands of **Pantar** and **Alor** farther to the east are known for their bronze kettle drums. Hundreds and perhaps thousands of these drums, called *moko* by the natives, are still kept as heirlooms today and are used to pay the bride price. They are similar to 2,000-year-old *Dong-son* bronze drums unearthed in these islands; the local bronze culture and its associated customs are of great antiquity.

Turbulent Timor

The island of **Timor** has been known throughout its history as a source of fragrant sandalwood. Chinese, Javanese and Islamic traders frequented the island for many centuries to obtain the wood; the Portuguese and the Dutch later fought to control the trade and subsequently divided the island into two: Dutch west Timor and Portuguese east Timor.

After Indonesia's independence, east Timor remained a Portuguese possession up until 1975. Political events overtook the island in 1976, when a left-wing movement threatened to take control of a newly-independent east Timor, and Indonesia decided to step in and annex the territory. Isolated fighting continues on the island, and travel to east Timor is still banned. Though technically possible, visits to the west Timorese capital of **Kupang** are difficult to arrange in practice. When Timor finally opens up, it will be a fascinating place to visit. Kupang is only a short flight from Darwin, Australia, and is also the gateway for the famous *ikat* islands of **Sawu** and **Roti**.

SUMATRA: INDONESIA'S BACKBONE

The great island of Sumatra—third largest in the archipelago and fifth largest in the world (roughly the size of California or Sweden)—is Indonesia's most important territory. In just about every way—strategically, economically and politically—Sumatra has always formed a kind of pivotal "backbone" for the nation. Second among the major islands in population (with 30 million inhabitants) but first in exports (principally oil, natural gas, rubber, tin and palm oil, but also tobacco, tea, coffee and timber), it stands at the crossroads of Asia—heir to an ancient and illustrious past and home to a broad spectrum of dynamic and fiercely independent peoples. Today Sumatra is also the third most popular tourist destination in Indonesia—after Bali and Java.

A Volcanic Chain

Like Java, Sumatra is formed by a longitudinal range of mountains—a double fold in the earth's crust with a central trough through which towering volcanoes have thrust upwards. This so-called **Bukit Barisan Range** extends for about 1,600 kms (1,000 miles) in a northwest-southeasterly direction rising at several points above 3,000 metres (10,000 feet), but with peaks generally around 2,500 metres (8,000 feet) high. There are about 90 volcanoes in this range, 15 of which are active, but unlike in Java and Bali they frequently eject material of an acidic nature which does nothing to improve the fertility of the surrounding soils. There are several notable exceptions: on the northern Batak Plateau (around Lake Toba) and in the Minangkabau Highlands (around Bukittinggi), the volcanic ejecta is primarily neutral-basic and the land here is correspondingly more productive.

Whereas to the west, this mountain range drops rather precipitously into the sea, producing little or no coastal plain along the island's western shore, the eastern face descends rather more gradually through a series of foothill ranges. Over many millennia, a vast alluvial plain has developed along

Sumatra's east coast—narrow in the north and broadening to the south. Unfortunately, this plain is very poorly drained (the adjoining Straits of Malacca and South China Sea being only 50 metres [160 feet] deep), and more than half of it, indeed almost a third of Sumatra, is covered in inhospitable mangrove swamps—a malarial band of acid peat that is a few miles wide in the north but commonly 100 to 150 miles (160 to 240 kms) wide in the south.

Agriculturally, then, the central foothills and highlands of Sumatra are generally more productive than the lowlands. The one great exception to this rule is the so-called *Cultuurgebied* (Plantation Area) around the huge city of Medan in northeastern Sumatra. Here the band of coastal swamps is narrow and the alluvial soils brought down from the Batak Plateau (Lake Toba area) are rich. This area was exploited on a large scale beginning in 1863 by enterprising Dutch and British planters, who cleared the land and introduced cash crops—first tobacco then later coffee, rubber, tea and oil palms. They also imported Javanese, Chinese and Indian labourers to work the estates, and Minang, Batak and Malay migrants soon followed, so that today this is the most densely populated region in Sumatra.

Oil was also discovered in this area in 1883, and led to the formation of the Royal Dutch Shell Company in 1902. Additional oil finds were subsequently made all up and down the eastern coast and Sumatra now produces about three-quarters of Indonesia's crude oil and a host of refined petrochemical products: gasolene, kerosene, urea and even plastics. This has created an economic boom in the large coastal cities—Medan, Pekanbaru, Jambi and Palembang—where the foreign oil companies and the Indonesian State Oil Monopoly (Pertamına) are well represented.

In other coastal areas, shipping, trading and fishing have traditionally formed the mainstays of the local economy. As early as the 7th Century A.D., Sumatra's southeastern coast was the site of Southeast Asia's greatest trading empire—the Buddhist kingdom of Srivijaya, which had its capital somewhere in the vicinity of present-day Palembang. Srivijaya had no agricultural lands to speak of, but existed solely by controlling the flow of ships and goods through the narrow Sunda and Malacca Straits—then, as now, strategic gateways linking the Pacific and Indian Oceans.

There was a good reason for Srivijaya's success as a maritime power: the eastern coast of Sumatra has probably been populated for several millennia by hardy seafarers—the Malays and the Orang Laut ("Sea Gypsies")—who still today fish and trade along these swampy shores from fragile sailing craft. Whereas the Orang Laut live a nomadic existence onboard their boats, the Malays are settled peoples, living in villages raised on stilts over the water at river estuaries, but also now in inland village settlements scattered throughout southeastern Sumatra, the Riau Archipelago and the Malay peninsula. Though they have taken up farming in some areas, their primary

dominated the entire area.

Islam obtained its first Southeast Asian foothold on Sumatra at the end of the 13th Century, with the conversion of several small trading ports on the island's northeastern shore. The name of one of them, Samudra, has come to refer to the island as a whole. And from the late 16th Century onward, this northern coastal area became the home of Indonesia's most powerful modern kingdom—the Sultanate of Aceh.

Like Srivijaya, Aceh was strategically located to take advantage of the sea trade passing through the Straits of Malacca, and during the "Golden Age" under Sultan Iskandar Muda (r. 1607 to 1636), Aceh expanded to include all the major ports of eastern Sumatra and several on the Malay peninsu-

connection has always been to the sea, and as the great traders of the western archipelago, their language, Malay, eventually developed into a regional *lingua franca* (and is now the national language of both Malaysia and Indonesia).

Srivijaya maintained its control over the straits for about seven centuries, though not without experiencing a good deal of outside competition and several severe setbacks. Her final defeat at the hands of Majapahit forces from East Java in 1377 then set the stage for Islam's rapid advance into the archipelago from India, and from this time up until the late 19th Century, the coasts of Sumatra were ruled by river-based Islamic trading kingdoms, not one of whom ever

la. Though the Acehnese were unable to hold on to these conquered areas for long, they maintained a strong fleet and an active trading economy for many centuries, and later proved to be a major thorn in the side of the Dutch.

The Dutch finally invaded Aceh in 1873 with the largest military force they had ever mustered in the Indies (more than 10,000 troops), and though they soon occupied Banda Aceh, the Acehnese capital, they suffered horrendous losses of men and mate-

Left, Dutch officers survey the field of battle during the Aceh Wars. The Dutch lost thousands of men in the holy war of attrition waged by Acehnese Muslims. Right, King Adityawarman's rebuilt palace at Batusangar.

rials for over a quarter of a century afterwards as a result of a *jihad* (holy war) of attrition waged by Acehnese guerilla fighters inspired by Islam. Today, the Acehnese—still devoutly Muslim and fiercely independent—occupy Sumatra's northern coasts, and because of their long record of resistance to Dutch rule, this area (like Yogyakarta) has been designated a Special Autonomous Region with provincial status.

Highland Cultivators

The majority of Sumatrans do not, however, live along the coasts, but in the long range of undulating foothills, plateaus, river basins and highland lakes along the island's spine, where they make a living as subsistence cultivators. Here are found two major ethnic groups—the Minangkabau and the Bataks—and a number of minor ones (the Gayo, Alas, Kubu, Kerinci, Rejang, Lampung and others), in an area that was once covered in dense rainforest and inhabited by many exotic Asian mammals (elephants, tigers, rhinos, gibbons, langurs, orangutans, mousedeer, tapirs, flying foxes, pangolins et al), but which is now increasingly being cleared and planted with food crops.

The traditional method of agriculture employed—"slash-and-burn" also known as "swidden"—in which the forest cover is cleared and burned just before the rains to fertilize the land—is likewise giving way to the use of ploughing, irrigation and fertilizers. In certain areas, though, this is nothing new, and indeed the Minangkabau tribes of the western Sumatran highlands have long practised such sophisticated farming methods.

The Minangkabau are settled peoples who are related to the Malays of the east Sumatran coast and are thought to be descended from an inland or western branch of the later Srivijayan empire. Their language is similar to Malay; their large, ornately carved highland homes have up-curved gables in the shape of boats (also said to resemble buffalo horns). Buddhist sculptures and monuments, dating from between the 12th and 14th centuries, are also found in this area.

In other ways, however, the Minangkabau are quite different from any other Sumatran

peoples. They are in fact one of the few remaining matrilineal societies in the world, upholding a social system in which property and responsibilities are distributed through the mother's family—and men are therefore responsible for their sisters' children more than their own. Since their conversion to Islam in the 16th Century, however, this system has been gradually eroding, particularly now that more Minangs (more than 4 million of them) live in large towns and cities, scattered all over Sumatra and Indonesia, than in their traditional homeland of the Padang highlands (where about 3 million remain).

This is partly the result of another distinctive Minang trait: the traditional tendency for women to stay at home and tend the fields, and for the men to roam far and wide as itinerant traders and craftsmen. And because of their high rate of literacy and formidable managerial skills, the Minangkabau have played a vital role in Indonesia's political, economic and intellectual development. Many famous Indonesian leaders and writers have been Minangs.

The other great highland people of Sumatra, the Bataks, inhabit a fertile volcanic plateau, roughly oval in shape, that covers much of northern central Sumatra. In the middle lies lovely Lake Toba, situated at an altitude of 900 metres (3,000 feet) in a huge caldera covering some 2,100 sq kms (800 sq miles), with the lush, green island of Samosir at its centre. Geologists tell us that this

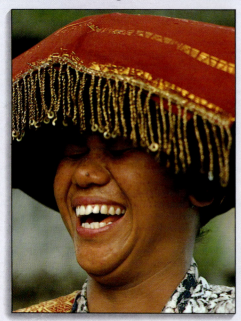

crater lake was created by the world's greatest volcanic explosion many eons ago, and this entire area was once very remote.

The Bataks, when they were discovered at this time by the Dutch, were heralded as primitive cannibals isolated for centuries from the rest of the world. In fact, they are sophisticated and settled agriculturalists who possess elaborate crafts, calendars and cosmological texts written in an Indic alphabet. Buddhist stupas and statues dating from between the 11th and 14th centuries and perhaps earlier have been discovered on the southern edges of the plateau, and it seems that the Bataks were in close contact with the Hinduized empires of Sumatra and Java.

There are numerous Batak tribes, each

with its own dialect, customs and architectural style. As with the Minang and other highland Indonesian tribes, their houses are massive, multifamily wooden dwellings raised on stilts with tall thatched roofs that recall the shape of a boat or a sail. The Batak reputation for aggressiveness dates back to a time in the not-so-distant past when these tribes were engaged in a perpetual state of ritual warfare with their neighbours and headhunting and cannibalism were common. Since the 1860s, European missionaries have been active in this area and most Bataks are now officially Christians, though the role of traditional *adat* law and custom is still prominent among them.

Provinces and Islands

Sumatra today is divided into eight provinces: Aceh, North Sumatra, West Sumatra, Riau, Jambi, Bengkulu, South Sumatra and Lampung. These administrative units often include a number of smaller islands lying some distance offshore. The east Sumatran Province of Riau, for instance, includes not only the Riau Archipelago (home of many interesting tribal groups) to the southwest of Singapore but also the oil-rich Anambas and Natuna Islands in the middle of the South China Sea between East and West Malaysia. The province of South Sumatra likewise includes the two "tin islands"—Bangka and Belitung (Billiton)—who between them produce about 20 per cent of the world's tin and are inhabited by the descendants of Hakka Chinese coolies brought in by the Dutch to work the mines in the 19th Century.

The long chain of islands running down Sumatra's west coast—Simeulue, Nias, the Mentawai Chain and Enggano—are geologically much older than Sumatra herself, and inhabited by truly isolated and primitive peoples who until recently still produced stone implements and megalithic monuments. Unfortunately, these peoples were decimated by epidemics carried to the islands in this century by European missionaries, who have also contributed to a loss of their languages and distinct cultural identities. The rocky, forested island of Nias is nevertheless still a stronghold of traditional *adat* practices—ancient war dances and stone-jumping rituals that are now enacted for shiploads of camera-toting tourists.

A Karo Batak woman. When the Bataks were "discovered" by the Dutch they were heralded as primitive cannibals. They were in fact sophisticated and settled agriculturalists.

Sumatra

MEDAN AND ACEH

From the booming industrial metropolis of Medan to the forested, volcanic Alas River Valley (haunt of primitive tribes), or to the fiercely independent Islamic stronghold of Aceh, Sumatra's northernmost segment is easily its most diverse.

Most visitors enter this region via Medan, a sprawling and crowded city of about 1.5 million. Once the marshy suburb of a small court centre, Medan developed into a commercial city after the Dutch overran the Deli Sultanate in 1872. It became the regional capital in 1886.

Modern Medan has retained many architectural anachronisms from its colonial days. Rococo, art-deco and art-nouveau styles were especially popular. The largest concentration of commercial buildings is found along Jalan Jendral A. Yani, and around Merdeka Square: the General Post Office, the former Witte Societet (now Bank Negara), Hotel de Boer (now Hotel Dharma Bhakti), Grand Hotel Medan (now the Granada Medan), and the estate offices of Harrison & Crossfield's (now P.T. London Sumatra Indonesia).

Left, a guard at Medan palace. Below, Medan Grand Mosque.

Chinese shops line Jalan A. Yani. Here also is the mansion of millionaire Chong Ah-tie, who, it is said, committed suicide by eating gold dust. In fact, he died of malnutrition in a concentration camp during the Japanese occupation; his mausoleum stands in the Pulau Brayan cemetery.

The central marketing district is just adjacent to the downtown area, and an ever-increasing flow of buses, trucks, cars, motorcycles and pedicabs converges about the main markets: Pasar Kampung Keling, Pasar Ramas, Pasar Hongkong and the Central Market.

At the southern end of Medan's longest street, Jalan Sisingamangaraja, stands the imposing **Masjid Raya**. Built in a rococo style in 1906 to match **Istana Maimun**, (the sultan's palace just opposite), and constructed by an Italian architect in 1888, it is still the residence of the sultan's descendants and may be visited during the day. Inside are memorabilia such as Dutch furniture and lamps, portraits and old weaponry.

Across the Deli River, on the west side of Medan, is the European town. Its wide avenues, flanked by huge colonial villas, are planted with flowering trees. The art-deco **Immanuel Protestant Church**, erected in 1921, is on Jalan Diponegoro, while on Jalan Hang Tua is **Vihara Gunung Timur**, Indonesia's largest Chinese temple. It is said to be such a powerful place that photographs taken within will remain unexposed. Nevertheless, cameras are not permitted. Both Buddhists and Taoists worship here, while Vihara Borobudur, next to the Danau Toba Hotel, is used solely by devotees of the Buddha. Its clergy is Javanese. A Hindu temple off Jalan Arifin is the spiritual centre for Medan's sizeable Indian community.

Elsewhere in Medan, the **Taman Margasatwa Zoo** has a varied collection of native Sumatran wildlife. **Medan Fair** has permanent cultural and agricultural exhibits and an amusement park. And the **Bukit Kubu Museum** surveys Sumatra's tribal lifestyles.

North of Medan, 26 kms (16 miles) down the Deli River, is **Belawan**, Indonesia's third largest port. Foreign interests are funding a harbour expansion to relieve a bottleneck on the export of

plantation commodities and the import of essential goods.

Well off the main road 97 kms (60 miles) west of Medan, past the orchard city of **Binjai** (famous for its rambutans and durians), is **Bohorok**, a World Wildlife Fund rehabilitation centre for orangutans. Experts train domesticated apes to re-adapt to the jungle environment before releasing them in the wild.

The Resistant, Resilient Acehnese

Aceh—Sumatra's (and Indonesia's) northern and westernmost province— has traditionally been the archipelago's first point of contact with external influences. Hinduism and Buddhism were here absorbed via passing Indian traders in the 7th and 8th centuries; Islam was introduced through Arab and Indian Muslims in the 13th Century.

The Portuguese landed here at the beginning of the 16th Century, followed by the Dutch and the English in the next century. Except for a period during the so-called "Golden Age" under Sultan Iskandar Muda (1604 to 1637), when Aceh briefly expanded its influence to the Malay Peninsula, subsequent centuries were marked by defensive resistance to Dutch colonial expansion through acts of trade, foreign diplomacy and guerrilla warfare.

The Dutch officially declared war on Aceh in 1873, but it took 10,000 troops, and thousands of casualties, to finally defeat the sultan and overrun his fortress at Banda Aceh. A subsequent Islamic "holy war" to oust the Dutch ended in defeat in 1878. Guerrilla activities then spread inland to Gayo tribal territories, where the rebel-controlled pepper trade financed the purchase and smuggling of arms from the British. The Dutch resorted to a counter-insurgency force of native troops armed with rifles and *klewang* sabres used to slice off their enemies' heads.

These *mareechausee* troops made steady progress, enabling the Dutch to build a railroad along the coast from Medan to Banda Aceh via Langsa, Sigli and Bireuen. Colonial officials entrenched themselves in these towns and used them as bases of control. Despite a setback in 1896, when Tungku Omar, a local chief highly trusted by the Dutch, joined the guerrillas (he is revered today as an Acehnese hero), relative peace came to Aceh after about 1903.

But the Dutch maintained strong garrisons here up until the Japanese invasion of 1942. In recognition of Aceh's resistance to outside domination, the province has been granted the status of Daerah Istimewa (Special Autonomous District).

Today, Aceh's economy relies largely on trade and vast reserves of natural gas and oil at Lhokseumawe. Cement and urea plants are scheduled for development.

Aceh: the Grand Tour

Though the coastal road to Aceh is better and shorter, it is also flat and excessively busy. The route suggested here follows the Alas Valley through the spectacular Mt. Leuser Nature Reserve. Starting from Medan the first stop is **Brastagi**, a hill resort and market town 68 kms (42 miles) to the south. The Dutch built guest houses, villas and an imposing hotel, the Bukit Kubu, in a park at the entrance to the town. Brastagi has a cool climate, ideal for growing French beans, carrots, tomatoes, passion fruit, flowers and oranges. Nearby Karo Batak villages,

Fruit market at Brastagi.

208

with their massive wooden clan houses, may also be visited from here.

The next town, **Kabanjahe**, stands at a crossroads between Aceh province and the Lake Toba region. Southern Aceh, including portions of the Batak plateau, has rich swamp-free, volcanic soils, and rubber palms, oil palms, tea and tobacco all flourish. In the surrounding area are the Karo Batak villages of **Barus Jahe** and **Lingga**, as well as two impressive waterfalls: **Sikulap** and **Sipisopiso**.

Gayo and Alas country starts at **Kutacane**. The Bataks were vassals of these mountain tribes when the Acehnese Sultan first conquered the region in the 17th Century and then imposed Islam and made the Gayos and the Alas his own vassals. Some Gayos, called Orang Lingga, retain their animistic beliefs and practices high in the mountains, far from the main roads. They believe natural harmony is achieved by sacrificing buffaloes and fowl, and offering fruit and vegetables to the spirits of trees, rocks, mountains, lakes and streams.

Kutacane, set amid rice paddies and coconut trees and surrounded by high, jungle-covered mountains, is a small market town with a traditional shop-lined main street, and bus station.

Proceeding north, a narrow road winds up the Alas River valley through a jungle corridor in Mt. Leuser Nature Reserve. Surrounding sputtering 3,466-metre (11,372-foot) Mt. Leuser, Sumatra's second highest peak, this reserve reaches all the way to the west coast and is probably one of the most accessible in Indonesia.

Just north of the park boundary is **Blangkeseren**, with numerous century-old Gayo and Alas houses. Long and low, they shelter as many as 60 people from several families with a common male ancestor; unmarried men, pubescent boys and travellers stay in a communal house. The area is known for its high-grade cannabis; today the authorities are trying to eradicate it in swift actions known as *Operasi Narkotika*.

A Japanese-supervised World-War-Two track built by slave labour connects Blangkeseren to **Takingeun**, the Gayo capital. Takingeun is built on the banks of 25-km (15-mile) long Danau Laut Tawar. The water is clean, cool and refreshing but local people do not swim. Fearing they may be pulled into the

ipisopiso
aterfall.

underwater realm of a seductive fairy, they opt instead for the public baths and hot springs at **Kampong Balik**.

The east-coast town of **Bireuen** is the chief marketplace for Gayo coffee, cinnamon, cloves and tobacco. Like many towns and villages north of Banda Aceh, Bireuen is an Acehnese settlement. Traditional Acehnese villages are surrounded by rice fields or coconut groves. The rectangular houses are built on stilts of solid *bangka* wood and covered with *nipah* palms; a hole carved in the roof lets smoke escape. Extended families build their houses within the same compound and every village has a mosque and a *balairong* (communal house), used during the day as a meeting place and at night as a dormitory.

While the Acehnese social system is patriarchal, residence is matrilocal. When a man gets married, he lives with his wife's family—a practice which contradicts conventional Muslim practices (though not native *adat* tradition).

Civil War and Rail Ruins

Sigli, at the estuaries of the Krong Baru and Krong Tuka rivers, was known as Padri when it was the principal port from which Acehnese *hajis* (pilgrims) to Mecca departed. The tragic Padri War started here in 1804; the Dutch took the town and completely destroyed it in the process. Remains of the *padri kraton* (fortress) can be seen on the outskirts of town along the road to Banda Aceh. At nearby Kampong Kibet is the grave of Sultan Maarif Syah, the first Islamic sultan of Aceh, who died in 1511.

Sigli was rebuilt and became a major stop along the rail line. Although the track, which runs parallel to the coast road, has not been used in over 20 years, the town's most impressive sight is still the station, a wooden colonial building now deserted except for goats grazing between rails and children at play in the empty coal yard. In the abandoned hangars, locomotives and wagons are rusting, while rows of machine tools lay idle in the workshops.

The climate is mild and the town has the look of a turn-of-the-century European resort. At one end of the villa-lined sea promenade stands a kiosk; at the other stands the skeleton of what was once the harbour master's home.

Banda Aceh' Grand Mosque.

Three cemeteries—one Muslim, one European and one Chinese—with their white and gray tombstones set among coconut trees, grace a neck of land across the Krong Baru river.

Banda Aceh, the capital of the province, is also built on two rivers, Krong Aceh and Krong Daroy. Although the fortress and palace of the Sultan of Aceh were destroyed along with the great mosque when the Dutch invaded in 1874, vestiges of Aceh's glorious past can still be found. Jalan Tengku Umar is the site of the **Gunungan**, a palace built by Iskandar Muda or his son at the beginning of the 17th Century, and of the royal princesses' baths of the same period. On Jalan Kraton are the tombs of a dozen 15th Century and 16th Century sultans of Aceh, while another series of royal tombs on Jalan Mansur Sjah includes that of Iskandar Muda. They in turn surround the **Rumoh Aceh Awe Gentah Museum**, a former aristocrat's house displaying *kris*, daggers, textiles and jewellery.

Most of the Dutch killed in the Aceh War are buried at the Christian cemetery on Jalan Iskandar Muda. With wrought-iron art-nouveau gates, the entrance stands between two marble plates on which are engraved the names of all the soldiers killed in Aceh. Many graves are works of sepulchral art; most impressive is the stele to the *mareechaussee*, erected by the East Sumatran Tobacco Planters Association.

The **Masjid Raya**, or great mosque, though built of wood, was constructed without a single nail. At night, the huge white structure, with its black domes, is illuminated. The interior is marble and may be visited by non-Muslims except during prayer times. Behind, and to the west, are the market and the Chinese quarter along Jalan Perdagangan.

The centre of Banda Aceh's "night life" is Penayung, a small square on the other side of the Krong Aceh. This is the place to sit in a low chair, talk with friends, and order drinks or a meal from surrounding hawkers.

A nearby village, **Kampung Kuala Aceh**, is a place of pilgrimage. Among mangroves and fish ponds facing the sea lies the grave of Teungku Sheikh Shah Kuala (1615 to 1693), a holy man who translated the Koran into Malay and who wrote religious books. Today Aceh's famous university bears his name.

The wind-and-wave-battered beaches of **Lohong**, **Lampuk** and **Lhokinga**, on the west coast about 20 kms (12 miles) from Banda Aceh, are not for swimming. They receive the full force of the Indian Ocean and have an extremely strong undertow. At Lampuk, you'll have a hard time even standing knee-high in the water.

Stranded Portuguese

Some 60 kms (37 miles) farther down the coast and a short distance inland, is the village of Lamno. Its inhabitants, said to be descended from Portuguese stranded there three centuries ago after a shipwreck, do indeed have green eyes and faces that are recognizably Iberian.

Banda Aceh is not Indonesia's "Land's End." That distinction belongs to **Pulau Weh**, an island reached by plane or ferry. The island's main town, **Sabang**, is a duty-free port linked to Calcutta, Melaka, Penang and Singapore. The local Chinese temple (Tua Peh Kong Bio) is the northernmost in Indonesia, and Pulau Weh is renowned for its gin-clear waters, ideal for scuba diving.

THE BATAK LANDS AND LAKE TOBA

Sumatra's finest sight is blue-green Lake Toba, a vast crater lake surrounding steep-backed Samosir Island. Located on a high plateau 160 kms (100 miles) south of Medan, it is the focus of the Batak Highlands. More than 3 million members of six major Batak tribes make their homes in the highlands, which stretch north-south 500 kms (310 miles) and east-west 150 kms (93 miles) around Lake Toba. The Toba, Karo, Pakpak, Simalungun, Angkola and Mandailing Batak each have their own dialect and customs.

The Batak migrated from the Himalayan foothills of upper Burma and Thailand over 1,500 years ago, settling in these mountains because of similarities to their ancestral homelands. Contact with coastal peoples led to the adoption of wet-rice agriculture, the plough and water buffalo, cotton and the spinning wheel, Sanskrit vocabulary and writing system, and a pantheistic religious hierarchy.

Wedged in between two fervently Muslim peoples, the Minangkabau and the Acehnese, the Bataks somehow remained isolated, animistic and cannibalistic until the middle of the last century, when German and Dutch missionaries converted many of them to a mystical sort of Christianity. (Northern Bataks are still animists, while southern Bataks, especially the Mandailing, are Muslim.) Cemeteries display stone sculptures of dead ancestors, shamans communicate with spirits, and priests consult astrological tables to make decisions for their clans.

A Batak clan (*marga*) consists of several close-knit communities (*huta*) tracing descent from a single male ancestor. The web of kinship is as strong as any in Indonesia, with weddings and funerals often drawing 1,000 kinsfolk or more. Genealogies, going back five centuries are carefully kept, as they determine status in personal relations and formal ceremonies.

Traditional Batak houses are multi-family dwellings about 18 metres (60 feet) long. Built with rope and wooden pegs, without nails, they are so sturdy they can withstand a century of wear. The roof is higher on the ends than in the middle; although it was originally thatched, corrugated iron is increasingly used, requiring less frequent replacement but drowning out conversations when it rains. Mosaics and woodcarvings of mystical patterns and mythical creatures decorate gable ends. Between 10 and 12 families live in separate areas surrounding a central corridor and four fireplaces where people work, play, cook and visit.

Medan to Lake Toba

The main route from Medan to Lake Toba runs east and south along the coast through the market towns of **Tebingtinggi** and Pematang Siantar. Side-roads along the first 50 kms (31 miles) offer access to fine beaches like **Pantai Cermin** (Mirror Beach) and **Sialangbuah**, renowned for its "mud skipper" amphibians that swim like fish and climb trees.

Pematang Siantar, 128 kms (80 miles) from Medan, is the second largest city in North Sumatra. This cool highland-rubber and palm-oil centre is notable for its Simalungun Museum (open daily except Sunday) on Jalan Sudirman, containing an excellent display of Batak artifacts, including woodcarvings.

Exactly 176 kms (110 miles) from Medan, the road reaches Lake Toba at **Prapat**. A tourist resort (hotels, golf course, water-ski boats, etc.) with a refreshingly brisk climate and a fine Saturday market, Prapat is nestled midway up the lake's eastern shore.

A longer, more westerly **Medan-Prapat** route runs through Brastagi and the **Karo Batak** highlands, described in the preceding chapter on Aceh. Only a short bus trip from Kabanjahe is a spectacular viewpoint near the northern tip of Lake Toba that overlooks the remote Tongging Valley and the Sipisopiso Waterfall. From here, the road skirts Toba's eastern shore, passing through the Monday-market village of **Haranggaol**, and continuing to Prapat.

Sumatra's Beauty Mark

The largest lake in Southeast Asia (1,707 sq kms [635 sq miles]), **Lake Toba** (Danau Toba) was formed by a prehistoric volcanic eruption. It is one of the highest (900 metres [2,953 feet]) and deepest (450 metres [1,476 feet]) lakes on earth. Enclosed by pine-covered mountain slopes and cliffs, the climate is cool but not bracing, and sometimes rainy but rarely saturated.

The best place to experience Toba's spell is 1,055-sq-km (392-sq-mile) Samosir Island. Boats depart from Prapat for Samosir daily, starting at 9 a.m. and take visitors directly to the Tuk Tuk Hotel or to the dozens of *losmen* scattered in Tomok, Ambarita and on the Tuk Tuk Peninsula.

Most lakeside *losmen* have no electricity and there are few vehicles on the island. Samosir is regarded as the original home of the Batak in Sumatra, and the Toba Batak are considered the ''purest'' Batak tribe. Most tourists restrict their exploration to the central east coast, but there are many untouched villages on the west coast and the remote central plateau of the island.

The main entry point for boats from Prapat is Tomok—a 30-minute cruise away. The tomb of animistic King Sidabuta is here—carved like a boat, with a fine head, and suspiciously blood coloured. In an enclosure opposite the tomb are ritual statues of a buffalo sacrifice with a *gondang* band, a *raja* and queen, and executioners who have

lost their knives. A small museum in the royal house nearby is kept by a dignified old aristocrat. At the end of an avenue of souvenir booths leading from the jetty are dozens of stands selling *ulos kain* (a beautiful woven fabric), two-stringed mandolins, ornate woodcarvings, Batak calendars and more.

Tuk Tuk is a tourist village and the Tuk Tuk Hotel is Samosir's premier resthouse; it has electricity, tennis courts and its own beach. On the peninsula are a new community hall for Batak dances and a few traditional houses, as well as many *losmen*, the most popular (and expensive) of which is Carolina's.

Since the arrival of Christianity on Samosir in 1848, the tuneful Bataks have taken enthusiastically to hymnals. Sunday church services are fine entertainment, though there are many other opportunities to hear tribal ballads (*ture ture*) in village cafes (*warung*).

Ambarita, an hour's walk from Tuk Tuk, has three megalithic complexes. The first is just up from the jetty and is notable for its 300-year-old stone seats and the tomb of Laga Siallagan, first *raja* of Ambarita. If an enemy were captured in Ambarita, neighbouring

Ambarita village on Samosir.

rajas were invited to this hilltop complex for a conference before moving to the second megalithic cluster—stone chairs where *rajas* and headmen met to decide the fate of the prisoner. The meeting place is now enclosed in a large courtyard in the village proper; sharing its terrace is a mound used for animistic prayers. South of Ambarita is the third complex, which includes a cannibal's breakfast table. The prisoner was beaten to death here, decapitated, chopped up on a flat stone, cooked with buffalo meat for the *raja's* breakfast, then washed down with blood.

Simanindo, at Samosir's northern tip and a half-day walk from Tuk Tuk, is 16 kms (10 miles) from Ambarita. (Ferries run to Simanindo from Tigaras on the eastern shore north of Prapat.) The village has a huge former king's house, which has been restored and is now a traditional Batak museum. Look for the buffalo horns out front, one for each generation, and the fine sculptures outside. A 10-minute boat ride off Simanindo is little **Tao Island**, where a few tiny bungalows offer escape to those who find even Samosir too hectic.

Though **Pangururan** on Samosir's west coast can be reached in half a day by the coastal path from Simanindo, a hike across the island's forested central plateau offers unforgettable views. From Tomok, you can climb past the king's tomb to the plateau above in about three hours. Pangururan is another 13 kms (8 miles) beyond and can be reached in less than 10 hours. On top, stay the night at one of the villages before pressing on to Roonggurni Huta and the swimming lake. It may be necessary to ask directions from locals frequently. In the wet season this climb is extremely muddy and slippery. Because the terrain is steep, it's easier to take a ferry to Pangururan and hike back to Tuk Tuk.

Pangururan is so close to the Sumatran mainland that it is connected by a short stone bridge. Its main attraction is an hour's walk away—the *air panas*, hot springs. On turning right at the bridge you'll find the springs halfway up the hill, commanding a fine view of the lake.

Every Sunday, a nine-hour round-island cruise departs from several villages. There's food on board, and the boat stops at the hot springs.

WEST SUMATRA

Just as northern Sumatra is dominated by the Batak and Acehnese peoples, West Sumatra is the land of the Minangkabau. From the hill station of Bukittinggi to the bustling port of Padang, the gentle and sophisticated Minangkabau culture pervades the region and provides a striking contrast with the rougher Bataks of the hinterland.

Anthropologists are fascinated by the Minangkabau, who despite their staunch Islamic devotion comprise the largest matrilineal society on earth. According to tradition, the Minangkabau derive their name from victory (*menang*) in an ancient fight between Sumatran and Javanese water buffalo (*kerbau*) over land ownership. The Sumatrans entered a calf, starved it for 10 days before the fight, and bound an iron spike to its nose. Frantic in pursuit of its mother's milk, the calf impaled and killed its Javanese counterpart. Today the buffalo is the Minangkabau tribal symbol.

Minangkabau villagers are skilful *padi* farmers and craftsmen as well as competent merchants. The Minangkabau traditionally live in multi-family longhouses (*rumah gadang*). Every man and woman maintains lifetime membership in his or her maternal *rumah*. Children grow up in the mother's longhouse. While a man has little influence in his wife's longhouse, he inherits property through his mother and may wield control and even become a clan chief (*pangulu*) through his natal *rumah*. Although Islamic property law favours males over females as heirs, observance of this religious dictum has been quite rare among Minangkabau, despite their conversion to Islam many centuries ago.

Traditional Minangkabau clans include the Melayu, Tanjung, Chaniago and Jambak. Further subdivision among clans has led to the creation of numerous, locally autonomous sub-clans, some of whom have rejected tribal customs. The *pangulu*, who inherits his position from a brother or maternal uncle, decides property, ritual, marital and other disputes for his clan.

These valley and cliffs are characteristic of the landscape of the Padang highlands.

The Minangkabau Highlands

Travellers heading south from Lake Toba on the Trans-Sumatran Highway reach Sumatra's west coast at **Sibolga**, a port town and terminus for boats to Nias, 73 kms (45 miles) south of Prapat. Inhabitants of this region are mainly Mandailing Batak farmers. The next major town to the south is Padang Sidempuan, noted primarily for its succulent *salak* fruits.

Hidden in the jungle about two hours' drive east of Sidempuan, 15 kms (9 miles) from the market town of Gunung Tua, are the 39 isolated **Padanglawas** ruins—11th Century and 12th Century red-brick Hindu temples. At least four temples are well preserved, others are being restored, and fragments of religious statuary and other artifacts are scattered around the area.

At the village of **Bonjol**, the highway crosses the Equator. A large globe and sign by the side of the road give ample notice. Here also the island of Sumatra is at its widest. The village is also known as the headquarters of 19th Century Padri leader Tunku Imam Bonjol, who led a bloody rebellion against the Dutch.

The Minangkabau Highlands begin just south of here, rising to a highpoint below Padang at 3,850-metre (12,483-foot) Mt. Kerinci—Sumatra's highest peak. Eons of faulting have resulted in the creation of numerous mountain lakes, including deep and beautiful Maninjau, Singkarak and Kerinci.

The delightful hill town of **Bukittinggi**, nestling amid mountain greenery at 920 metres (3,018 feet) above sea level, is the Minangkabau "capital." Government offices, a museum and a small university make it the administrative, cultural and educational centre of the region. The climate is cool and sunny; people are relaxed and friendly. Music pulses from taxis and shopfronts as handsome horse-pulled *dokars* ply the hilly streets.

The market is a fine place to bargain for Minangkabau crafts, antiques and souvenirs. On Saturdays, it overflows up and down steep hillside steps throughout the centre of the city. Behind huge baskets of farm produce, weavers from Kota Gadang display their colourful embroidered shawls and silver and gold-filigree jewellery.

The central landmark in Bukittinggi is the clock tower, with its stylized roof, standing in the town square. Geographically, the town's highest point is the **Rumah Adat Baandjuang Museum**. ("*Bukittinggi*" means "high hill"; the museum is its peak.) The 140-year-old building is a classic *rumah adat* (clan house). Exhibited are old and traditional Minangkabau wedding and dance costumes, head-dresses, musical instruments, various village crafts and historic weaponry.

The museum shares the grounds with the Bukittinggi Zoo. The variety of caged Sumatran birds and mammals, is impressive, even if the conditions in which they are kept, and the attitude of zoogoers toward the beasts, are deplorable. Huge tigers and orangutans, for instance, are penned behind bars so restrictive their muscles deteriorate, while they are continually subjected to the indignity of rubber bands shot at them by schoolchildren.

On another hilltop on the western side of town stands **Fort de Kock**, built by the Dutch in 1825. The fortress itself doesn't contain much of interest, but it provides a good vantage point to look

lock Tower at ukittingi.

out over the surrounding farmland to smouldering 2,440-metre (8,005-foot) Gunung Merapi and Ngarai Canyon.

This rocky, steep-sided gorge, 4 kms (2½ miles) long, is sometimes grandiloquently called the "Grand Canyon of Indonesia." A narrow path leads from a lookout on the south side of Bukittinggi through the chasm to **Kota Gadang**, a village famed both for its silver and gold filigree and hand-embroidered shawls. It has also produced a number of leading intellectuals, including two former Indonesian prime ministers—Haji Agus Salim and Mohamed Natsir.

Giant Flowers and Stalactites

An easy day trip 36 kms (22 miles) west of Bukittinggi, Lake Maninjau is a crater lake renowned for its serenity and remote beauty. Canoes and motorboats can be rented at the lakeshore. About 12 kms (8 miles) north of town at **Batang Palapuh**, the giant Rafflesia flower blooms in July and August. **Ngalau Kamang**, 15 kms (9 miles) away, is a cave two kms (1.25 miles) in length and boasts a dazzling array of stalactites and stalagmites. **Payakumbuh**, 39 kms (24

miles) east, is the gateway to the cliffs and waterfalls of **Harau Canyon**.

A car can cover the 92 kms (57 miles) south from Bukittinggi to Padang in 2½ hours; the railway journey takes eight. Both routes pass through **Padang Panjang**, site of a conservatory of Minangkabau dance and music. A short distance south is Lake Singkarak, larger than Maninjau and easily accessible by rail or road, and Solok, a mountain town famous for its woodcarvings and high-roofed houses. East of Padang Panjang is **Batusangkar**, once the residence of the Minangkabau kings. A magnificent preserved *rumah adat* is in the town, while 5 kms (3 miles) east, a palace replica is under construction.

Padang, West Sumatra's provincial capital, is the third largest city on the island with a population approaching 250,000. Its wide streets, traditional architecture and horse-drawn *dokars* give it the feel of a sleepy backwater—despite the presence of a bustling seaport at Teluk Bayur, 6 kms (4 miles) from the centre of town. Spicy-hot *nasi padang* is the city's claim to fame—a smorgasbord of between 10 and 20 dishes eaten cold with rice.

Padang's museum has fine exhibits of Minangkabau artifacts, and Andalas University features an Institute of Minangkabau Studies. Otherwise, there are few "sights" in Padang, other than the brief river crossing and hike up through a Chinese cemetery to Padang Hill, overlooking the ocean.

About 10 hours to the south of Padang, the new 1.5 million-hectare (600,000-acre) **Kerinci-Seblat Reserve**, covers a 345-km (214-mile) stretch of mountains, dominated by the volcanic cone of Gunung Kerinci. You can turn off the coast road at Tapan and proceed inland (in a four-wheel-drive vehicle) to **Sungai Penuh**, the main town at the heart of the reserve.

Footpaths lead in all directions from here—to Gunung Tujuh and its beautiful crater lake; to the high-altitude marsh surrounding Danau Bentu; and to the wild rain forests around Gunung Seblat, the last such woodlands in southern Sumatra. Elephants, rhinos, tigers, tapirs, clouded leopards and sun bears still roam the region. There are no orangutans, but there *are* occasional sightings of the mysterious *orang pendek* (a hairy, squat, strong "man") and the mythical *cigau* (half lion, half tiger).

Left, spicy Padang food

NIAS ISLAND

Running parallel to Sumatra's west coast, about 100 kms (62 miles) offshore, are a string of ancient islands—the peaks of an undersea ridge separated from Sumatra by a deep trench. These islands, which include Simeulue, Nias, the Batu and Mentawi groups, and Enggano, have been worlds apart for half-a-million years; their wildlife and human inhabitants have developed in isolation.

Nias is the largest, best known and most accessible island. One hundred kms long and 50 kms (31 miles) wide, it is home to one of Southeast Asia's most unique cultures, expressing itself today mainly in an ancient architectural style, stone sculptures and remarkable stone-jumping rituals.

A rice-growing society, Nias seems to have been primarily influenced by the Bronze Age *Dong-son* culture of Annam (North Vietnam) and by Hindu, Chinese and Muslim traders. The first missionaries set foot on the island

Stone jumper of Nias.

in 1865 and now half the inhabitants are nominal Christians.

While dances are still performed, they are primarily for paying tourists. *Fahombe* is the most memorable performance; acrobatic tribesmen leap feet-first over stone columns between two and 2.5 metres (6.5 and eight feet) high and half-a-metre (20 inches) broad. *Tulotolo* is a warrior dance in which young men make huge leaps and engage in ritual combat. Niasan villages are veritable fortresses, with great stone-paved central "runways." Stilt houses stand in parallel rows on hillsides, a bamboo barricade protecting them from outside attack.

Northern Nias, raided by Acehnese slave traders for centuries, has few cultural remnants, though the Nias capital, Gunungsitoli, is here. The remote centre of the island is culturally rich, however; in its jungle stand ruins of abandoned villages with huge statues. The south has retained its traditional villages and some folklore, and is the best area for casual visitors.

Teluk Dalam is the port of entry for regular boats from Sibolga and Padang. There's a tourist office here. Visitors can use the town as a base and travel out to the villages by bus.

An impressive 150-year-old royal palace, standing 15 metres (50 feet) high, is preserved in **Bawomataluwo**, a 15-km (nine-mile) drive from Teluk Dalam. Ornamental motifs on posts and panels are finely carved to represent crocodiles, boatmen and princesses. In front of the palace, and throughout the village, are carved stone megaliths—287 of them.

The 4,500 residents of **Hilisimaetano** live in 140 traditional houses, though their "great house" was destroyed by war. **Hilimondegaraya's** great house was dismantled and shipped off in 1922 by a Danish professor who also took a Nias wife. **Gomo** is the original home of the Nias people; there's a fine village with traditional houses nearby.

Of the other islands off Sumatra's west coast, **Siberut**, in the Mentawai chain, is worthy of note. Missionary influence and rapid deforestation by loggers have irrevocably changed the face of the island, but a World Wildlife Fund campaign has been launched on behalf of the people, and their unique fauna and flora.

SOUTHERN AND EASTERN SUMATRA

The southern half of Sumatra is at once the island's richest and its most primitive region. Lampung province alone accounts for 40 per cent of Indonesian government revenues through its oil and rubber resources, yet man-eating tigers can still be seen on the main highways. And while Javanese migrants have resettled and cultivated previously remote jungles, there are still animistic tribes like the Kubu and Sakai that roam the swamplands and hunt birds and monkeys.

Four huge provinces: Lampung, South Sumatra, Bengkulu and Jambi cover roughly the southern half of Sumatra. Nearly all of Jambi, and the eastern two-thirds of Lampung, are broad alluvial lowlands no more than 30 metres (100 feet) above sea level and as much as 200 kms (124 miles) wide. The whole area is drained by numerous meandering rivers, including the Batang Hari, navigable for nearly 500 kms (310 miles) inland, and the Musi, Sumatra's largest. Western Lampung province is mountainous, rising to volcanic peaks of more than 3,000 metres (above 10,000 feet) before dropping sharply to the Indian Ocean at the former British outpost of Bengkulu.

The new Trans-Sumatran Highway runs the full length of the island, from Telukbetung to Aceh. With the recent completion of unfinished sections in South Sumatra, the region now has a fine transportation network.

Crossing the Sunda Strait from West Java, the Sumatran port of entry is Bakauhuni, the harbour for Teluk Betung. The ferry passes within view of Krakatau, the enormous island volcano that erupted in 1883, killing 30,000 people and dramatically affecting the climate worldwide for over a year.

About two-thirds of the residents of central and southern Lampung province are Javanese farmers who migrated here—either voluntarily or assisted by the government—to relieve overcrowded conditions in Java. Although the policy was begun by the Dutch over 50 years ago and accelerated since 1970, its effectiveness is debatable: the Javanese still tend to overpopulate the

East coast refinery.

rice land they work.

The south Sumatran railway, which has its terminus at Teluk Betung's twin city of **Tanjungkarang**, wends its way north as far as Palembang, with a western branch to Lubuklinggau. There is little of real visitor interest in this part of Sumatra; archaeological remains are few and far from main routes, and many settlements are Javanese.

Tanjungkarang is the gateway, however, to the Way Kambas Reserve. Comprising river mouths, marshes and open grasslands along the southeast coast, it is the best place on the island to see wild elephants. Tigers and wild boars are also plentiful, and bird watching is a delight. (*See* Part IV, "Indonesia's Wildlife.")

Yet it has been an uphill battle to conserve this rich coastal land. Migrant farmers, loggers, Jakarta-based developers and other entrepreneurs have claimed tens of thousands of hectares; three disastrous fires nearly eliminated what once was a substantial forest; and tigers were legally hunted until 1974. Park authorities in Tanjungkarang can arrange for visitors to take a four-hour (one-way) boat trip from **Labuhan Meringgi**, 12 kms (7.5 miles) south of the reserve, to the Way Kambas estuary, navigable for 25 kms (16 miles) inland.

Oil Cities

South Sumatra's metropolis, **Palembang**, is second in Sumatra only to Medan. A city of 600,000 has grown on the banks of the Musi River about 200 kms (124 miles) from the coast. A major port for well over 1,200 years, Palembang was, up until the 13th Century, the major focus of trade in the Indonesian archipelago and a great international bazaar. It was also a spiritual centre where thousands of Mahayana Buddhist monks studied and translated texts.

Palembang was nurtured during the Dutch colonial era as a tin entrepôt, servicing the tin mines found on Bangka Island, beyond the mouth of the Musi. Forest products, rubber and coffee plantations in the vicinity contribute to the city's economy today, but oil is the real source of the wealth that has made Palembang Indonesia's richest city. There is a US$200 million petrochemical complex at Plaju, and a massive refinery (daily capacity: 75,000 barrels) at Sungei Gerong. Pertamina, the state oil monopoly has shown its gratitude to Palembang by constructing a television station, a sports stadium, a clock tower and an elegant minaret for the main mosque.

Palembang has houses and shops raised on piles above the Musi, with river merchants plying their trade from boats, not unlike the *klongs* of Bangkok. Jalan Sudirman is the best street for shopping, and Jalan Veteran for dining. The city's red-light district has made its home in Kampung Baru. The region produces fine woven fabrics and has unique dances—including the Gending Srivijaya, dating from the 7th Century, and resembling classic Thai forms. The **Rumah Bari Museum**, occupying several buildings, contains important megalithic statuary, Hindu and Buddhist sculptures, primitive ethnic crafts and weaponry, Chinese porcelain, and a division for natural history.

Jambi, a lush jungle riverport on the Batang Hari about 200 kms (125 miles) north of Palembang, is a surprisingly cosmopolitan city; 160,000 Chinese, Japanese, Arabs, Indians, Malaysians, Javanese and other nationalities live here. Occasionally a tiger wanders in from the surrounding jungle and carries off an unwary victim. As with Palembang, oil supports the economy to a great extent and there are large exploratory camps belonging to Caltex, Japex, Jambi Oil and Huffco in western Jambi province.

Road and water connections between Jambi and Palembang are slow and rugged; most inter-city commuters wisely choose to fly. Those who opt for an overland (or river) journey, however, will come across some remarkably isolated tribes. In the swamps along the Batang Hari and Musi rivers, and between them along the Rawas and Tembesi, the Kubu people live in bamboo lean-tos with leaf roofs. Despite their water-logged environment, they avoid contact with water, convinced it will make them sick. They gather bananas and other fruits in bamboo baskets, and hunt wild pigs and apes.

North of Jambi, near the Kuantan and Indragiri rivers, the Orang Mamaq dwell in pile houses above the swamps. Traditionally hunters and fishermen who gather fruit from the jungle to supplement their diets, they have begun cultivating rice in recent times.

Farther north, as far as Pekanbaru, live the nomadic Sakai people. Their name in Malay means "subordinate," but they refer to themselves as Orang Batin, "the inner people." Like their southern neighbours, the Sakai people support themselves mainly by hunting and fishing—their favourite food is monkey. A strong belief in magic is intrinsic to Sakai culture.

Megaliths and Forts

West of Palembang, not far off the rail line to Lubuklinggau, is the town of Lahat, gateway to the Pasemah Highlands. Dotting this mountain plateau are carved megaliths, tombs, pillars and other stone ruins thought to date from about 100 A.D. These are considered the best examples of prehistoric stone sculpture in Indonesia. Oddly shaped rocks have been fashioned into figures of armed warriors either riding elephants, wrestling buffaloes or fighting snakes. There are dolmens, sanctuaries, coloured paintings and other works of art in the area of volcanic Mt.

Dempo.

The rail line's northwestern terminus is **Lubuklinggau**. You should plan a stopover here to see some of the region's many transmigration schemes at work. From here you can continue by bus onto Padang or to Bengkulu on the west coast of Sumatra.

Bengkulu (Bencoolen) was founded in 1685 by the British. Fort York, built in 1690, was destroyed but Fort Marlborough, constructed in 1762, has survived splendidly. Built as a castle, there's a gatehouse which contains old gravestones with English inscriptions. Today the Indonesian army maintains a post within the fort.

Sir Stamford Raffles, who later founded Singapore, was lieutenant governor of Bengkulu from 1818 to 1823. He introduced coffee and sugar cultivation, established schools, and fought a royal decision to hand control of Sumatra over to the Dutch in 1824. His scientific zeal (as first president of the Zoological Society of London) led to the naming of the giant Rafflesia flower in his honour. This botanical wonder can be found in Bengkulu at the **Dendam Taksuda Botanical Gardens**.

Fort Marlborough a Bengkulu.

222

RIAU

Between the swampy shores of Sumatra and the Malay peninsula stretches a chain of 1,000 small islands. These and the eastern Sumatran lowlands comprise the province of **Riau**.

Fishing and timber sustain the economy, although tin, bauxite and oil are of increasing importance. Varied island cultures make it a rich ethnographic region. Historically, the Riau chain was the centre of the Malay civilization from the 16th through to the 18th centuries.

The mainland is populated by Coastal Malays, while the island populations include Malays, Bugis *orang laut* (sea gypsies) Chinese, Arabs, Indians and others. The dominance of the Malay language as lingua franca in the region led to its adoption (as *Bahasa Indonesia*) as the official languages of both Indonesia and Malaysia.

The Bugis are renowned seamen in self-imposed exile from their native Sulawesian homeland, living aboard

cally situated at the intersection of sea lanes connecting Singapore, Sumatra, Java, Madura and Sulawesi. The harbour is a port of call for all sorts of boats: junks, cargo ships, fishing vessels, indigenous craft from Sulawesi and Madura, and the Sumatran *nade*, a freighter with large sails modelled after old Portuguese and Spanish caravels. Across the harbour on a small island is the Snake River Chinese temple. Water taxis—*kapal motor* or *spetboat* (a longboat with an outboard motor)—are easily hired.

Twenty minutes from Tanjung Pinang harbour on Pulau Penyengat, is the former capital of the Malay kingdom. High Malay is supposedly still spoken by the 2,000 fishermen who live here. In the middle of a small jungle are the ruins of the sultan's palace, built in 1808 and now overgrown with banyans. Nearby stands the mausoleum of the Malay *rajas*, and a mosque, both dating from the second half of the 16th Century.

Pulau Batam has been earmarked for industrial development and already there is an airstrip connecting the island with Jakarta. A country

The harbour at Tanjung Pinang.

wooden *pinisi* sailing craft and trading throughout the archipelago on adjacent seas. The *orang laut* are seafaring nomads who are born, live and die on their small boats. Although they have maritime settlements from Burma to the Philippines they more commonly sail or row their boats through a labyrinth of inter-island channels and mangrove swamps, fishing and trading.

All these races can be found in Tanjung Pinang, the main town of the Riau archipelago, located on Pulau Bintan a quick 6-hour ferry ride from Singapore. This active port is strategi-

club opened recently, and there are plans for hotels along the white-sand beaches on the northeastern shore.

The province's biggest city is **Pekanbaru**, a Siak River port 160 kms (100 miles) from the coast. This friendly Caltex oil town, with a large foreign population, is a good base for exploring nearby jungle abodes of the *durian*-loving Sumatran rhinoceros, tigers, elephants and birds. Four hours downriver, at the village of **Siak Sri Indrapura**, is the Balai Rung Sari, a palace built in 1723 and last occupied by Sultan Syarief Kassim II until 1968.

KALIMANTAN: INDONESIAN BORNEO

Dense jungles and steaming swamps. Headhunters and riverboats. The *Wild Man of Borneo*. Many exotic and often frightening images are traditionally associated with Kalimantan, the immense Indonesian portion of Borneo. But Kalimantan today is not the god-forsaken outpost it once was.

The island's vast reserves of oil, natural gas, timber and even diamonds (the name Kalimantan is derived from Malay words meaning "diamond river") have drawn a great deal of attention in recent years and are now responsible for a hefty chunk of

743,000 sq kms (287,000 sq miles), about a third larger than France and slightly bigger than the State of Texas. Yet the island's population totals only about 7 million, about the same as that of the city of Jakarta—making this one of the most sparsely inhabited regions of Southeast Asia. About 5.5 million people live in Kalimantan, the majority in settlements on the banks of mighty rivers.

Geologically, Borneo is one of the oldest islands in the Indonesian archipelago. Unlike most other Indonesian islands, it

Indonesia's total foreign exchange exports, in addition to supplying many products for the domestic market. Consequently, there are daily jet flights to the major coastal cities, where fine tourist-class hotels and restaurants are to be found. But the dedicated explorer will still have no difficulty finding primitive Dayak villages and wild orangutans in remote up-river jungles.

Kalimantan comprises the southern and eastern portions of Borneo—roughly three-quarters of what is the world's third largest island. The remaining quarter of Borneo, the northwestern portion, is occupied by the Malaysian states of Sarawak and Sabah and the independent oil sultanate of Brunei. Altogether Borneo has a land area of

has no volcanoes. Instead, the island's core is formed by a fold in the earth's crust—a central mountain range which has been heavily eroded over millennia. This western-central range is not very high—Kalimantan's highest peak, Mount Raya in the Schwaner Range, stands at only 2,205 metres (7,234 ft)—but it feeds Kalimantan's major river systems, long and broad waterways with numerous inter-connecting tributaries which have traditionally formed the

Preceding pages, rainforest in Kalimantan. Above, Dutch engraving depicting the natives of Borneo. Right, wooden craftwork from Central Borneo. The climate means that little woodcraft survives—this figure has deteriorated badly.

island's "roads." These rivers are also largely responsible for Borneo's immense size, for they carry down enormous quantities of silt and deposit it into the shallow South China Sea, thereby forming new land and pushing the coastlines steadily outward. Because of poor drainage and constant rainfall, however, the result is a broad rim of dense, inhospitable mangrove swamps all along the island's outer shores; swamps that make cultivation and communication difficult.

Most of the native population consequently lives inland. The large cities, located generally 20 to 50 kms (12 to 30 miles) from the sea on the banks of major rivers, are inhabited by Chinese, Malays, Javanese and other groups whose ancestors came to Borneo centuries ago as miners, traders, fishermen or pirates. These townspeople generally survive on some form of trading or manufacturing, not agriculture, and much of Kalimantan's food is in fact imported from Java or Singapore. Recently, thousands of Javanese and Balinese families have been resettled in Kalimantan from their overpopulated homelands, under the Indonesian government's ambitious transmigration programme. Some of them are now enjoying financial success as farmers, supplying the townspeople with rice and vegetables. Much farther up-river, in the remote and wild hinterlands, live the 1 million or so members of more than 200 indigenous Bornean tribes—peoples who live in small, shifting villages, practise swidden (slash-and-burn) agriculture and are collectively known to outsiders as the Dayaks.

History in Plinths and Ceramics

Kalimantan's recorded history begins in the early 5th Century, with an inscribed stone plinth discovered near Kutei on the east coast of the island. This inscription, written in the South Indian Pallawa script, records the existence here of an Indianized kingdom which probably prospered as a vital link in the chain of ancient spice-trading ports. Roman and Hindu-Javanese relics and coins have also been discovered in Kalimantan, together with many old Chinese ceramics.

Chinese communities appear to have flourished on the northwest coast of Borneo toward the end of the first millennium A.D. and this in fact became a ceramic-producing

centre for several centuries during the Sung period. In later centuries, the Chinese also immigrated to the south and west coasts of the island, drawn there to mine the gold and diamonds that were for many years Borneo's chief claim to fame.

The coastal ports were Islamized in the 15th and 16th centuries, and small, independent Sultanates such as Kutei, Banjar, and Pontianak flourished for many years as cosmopolitan communities ruled by Malay, Buginese, Makassarese and Middle Eastern trading elites with strong ties to the Islamic

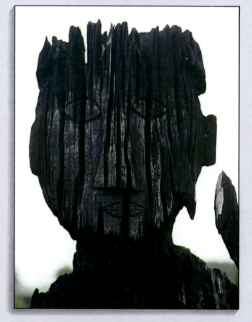

ports of Java and the eastern archipelago. This era ended late in the 19th Century, when treaties with the Dutch forced the native rulers into the colonial sphere of trading relations, thus eroding and eventually removing altogether their main sources of income. This twilight period of the Bornean sultanates and the ascendency of the European traders is romantically captured in several of Joseph Conrad's novels, notably *Lord Jim*.

Borneo remained as something of an economic backwater until, in recent years, her natural resources were finally exploited on a grand scale, making her an indispensable part of the Indonesian economy as a whole. Large enclaves of Western expatriates have blossomed, mainly in the east-coast cities of Balikpapan and Bontang, to help extract the island's enormous reserves of oil, natural gas and timber. This has created something of a boomtown atmosphere and these coastal regions now enjoy a modern transportation system which includes new roads, waterways, and extensive air connections.

The Dayaks

Upriver, however, the scattered and relatively primitive Dayak tribespeople continue to live as they have for centuries. The collective term "Dayak" is somewhat misleading because it is never used by these tribes themselves, in fact they find it rather insulting. Each of the 200 or so tribes has its

own name and dialect, and they exhibit a wide variety of customs and lifestyles.

These tribespeople are generally light-skinned—descended from Mongolian immigrants who arrived in this region beginning around 5,000 B.C., and thus greatly resemble the Chinese. But since that time their cultures have evolved in isolation. With the arrival of Malays and Chinese in the coastal regions, the Dayaks have moved farther and farther inland. As the outer "civilized" world has penetrated deeper and deeper into the hinterlands of Kalimantan in this century, the Dayaks have begun a slow but certain process of assimilation. Today the government is encouraging them to produce cash crops such as cloves and pepper,

and many tribesmen have settled on the fringes of the cities, towns and timber or oil camps, in the hopes of finding employment.

The most distinctive feature of traditional Dayak villages is the longhouse (*lamin*), a massive wooden building elevated on stilts that might house as many as 50 families. Some longhouses are 20 metres (65 feet) wide and 180 metres (600 feet) long. Architectural styles vary greatly from tribe to tribe, but most longhouses have magnificently carved door frames, posts and railings—with elaborate dragon, snake, bird and demon motifs. Each longhouse has a sacred herb garden and a collection of ancestral stone images. Most have large verandas, where daily necessities such as paddles, nets, traps and blowpipes are stored. Kitchens are normally in a separate structure, connected to the main house by a wooden bridge.

The Dayaks have a remarkably vibrant and graphic sense of design. Crafts are adorned with geometric patterns—anthropomorphic and stylized animal designs for the most part. Birds and reptiles are most commonly depicted. Spirals, hooks and meanders weave through every creation. A variety of barkcloth and *ikat* vegetable fibre cloths are produced. (*See* Part IV "Threads of Tradition.")

The Dayaks are also famed for their beadwork and basketry. Thousands of tiny glass beads are used to decorate purses, tobacco pouches, scabbards, baby carriers, basket lids, caps and headbands. Many types of shoulder bags and backpacks are produced from rattan and bamboo strips, usually elegantly decorated with two-tone geometric patterns.

Not long ago it was common to see human skulls hanging in woven baskets under the verandas of longhouses. In some remote villages, the Kalimantan traveller may still come across them. Headhunting no longer exists in Kalimantan, but formerly, the capture of a head was cause for villagers to celebrate. The powerful magic of a skull, placed in a basket and cured over a fire, was believed to protect the village from harm. The spirit of the head would have to be "fed" from time to time with regular offerings of food and even given cigarettes. Dayaks believed that as skulls became older, their magic power decreased and new skulls were needed. Tribes without skulls were considered weak and prone to pestilence.

Left, a women's hands show the intricate tattoo work of the Dayaks. Right, Dayak graphic design is remarkable; their beadwork is especially well known for its colour and intricacy.

228

Kalimantan (Indonesian Borneo)

200 km

Palawan
○ Quezon
Malabuñgan ○
○ Iwahig

South China Sea

Sulu Sea

Balabac ○
Balabac Strait
Mahalu ○
Kudat ○
○ Senaja
Cagayan Sulu ○
Kinabalu
Tuaran ○
Lingkabau
▲
Kota Kinabalu ○
4101 m
Labuk Bay
○ Ranau
○ Sandakan
Mempakul ○
○ Bingkor
S a b a h
Banda Seri Begawan ○
Muara
○ Baka
Lahad Datu
Brunei
○ Bangar
Badas ●
○ Pensiangan
Semporna
Miri ○
Lumbis ○
○ Tawau
Sibuti ○
Marudi ○
○ Nunukan
Bunyu Is.
Bintulu ○
Long Akah ○
Hulu Bahau
Nature Reserve
○ Tarakan
Mukah ○
Belaga ○
Lemutan ○
Kaj an R.
○ Tanjung Selor
Daro ○
Long
Murum ○
Bahau R.
Sibu ○
S a r a w a k
Kayan R.
○ Longsegan
Berau R.
○ Tanjung Redep
Paloh ○
Lundu
Kabong
Rajang
○ Kapit
Baleh
○ Longnawan
○ Dumaring
○ Lundu
Kuching
Pakan ○
Simanggang ○
○ Kelolokan
Talok ○
Sambas ○
Lupar
Rengkang ○
Putussibau ○
Kapuas R.
2998 m
Kalimantan Timur
Singkawang ○
Mualang ○
Bunut ○
Nangaraun ○
○ Longpahanghai
Bengkajang ○
Temangga ○
Selimbau ○
○ Longbangun
Kutei Nature
Reserve
Mandor ○
Sidas ○
Sanggau ○
Silat ○
○ Longiram
○ Bontang
Pontianak
Tayan ○
Sintang ○
Nangamuntatai ○
Melak ○
Muarakaman
Tenggarong
Limbung ○
Sebedau ○
Kapuas R.
Melawi
Mahakam R.
○ Samarinda
Selat-
pampang ○
Pati ○
Raja ▲
2278 m
Kalimantan Barat
Mt. Palung
Nature Reserve
Tewah ○
Butong ○
Barito R.
○ Samboja
Simpang ○
Sandai ○
Balikpapan
Karimata
Islands
Sukadana ○
Bakumpai ○
Buntok ○
Ketapang ○
Serengka ○
Panahan ○
Memala ○
○ Tanahgrogot
Kuala Pesaguan ○
Sukaraja ○
Kalimantan Tengah
Tuanan ○
○ Tanjung
Jangeru ○
Kendawangan ○
Sampit ○
Pilang ○
Amuntai ○
Bawal Is.
Pangkalanbun ○
Arut R.
○ Barabai
Galam Is.
Kumai ○
○ Kandangan
Matua ○
Cape Puting
Nature Reserve
Rantau ○
Pantai
○ Kotabaru
Kampungtengah ○
Kalimantan
Selatan
Banjarmasin
○ Martapura
Pagatan ○
Batibat ○
Laut
Pleihari ○
○ Karambu
Batakan ○
○ Jorong

Laut Kecil Is. ○
○ Matasiri
○ Lima

J a v a   S e a

Makasar Strait

Karimun Is. ○
Bawean ○
Masalembo ○

Kepulauan
Natuna

230

CITIES OF THE KALIMANTAN COAST

Coastal Kalimantan has entered and embraced the 20th Century. The three major coastal cities—Pontianak in the west, Banjarmasin in the south and Balikpapan in the east—are the island's major harbours and the natural starting points for visits to any part of Kalimantan. For those with limited time, south and east Kalimantan are the most interesting areas. Banjarmasin and Balikpapan are also the best jumping-off points for visits to the interior (see subsequent section). All three cities have airports with regular connections to Jakarta and Surabaya. (*See* "Guide in Brief.")

Pontianak, the rubber capital of West Kalimantan, sits astride the equator on the Landak River. A trading centre with about 250,000 inhabitants, most of them Chinese, Pontianak is only about 200 kms (125 miles) from the Malaysian (Sarawak) border and 25 kms (15 miles) north of the mighty Kapuas River.

The Kapuas is the longest river in Indonesia, measuring more than 1,000 kms (620 miles) from its mouth to its headwaters, and while Indonesian authorities recommend otherwise, occasionally travellers do journey up the Kapuas, cross the jungle, and continue down the Mahakam River to Samarinda in East Kalimantan.

A good road runs north of Pontianak through the town of **Sambas**, well known for its hand-woven *kain sambas* cloth. En route the road passes through Singkawang, noted for its Chinese temples and golden beaches—a rarity in Kalimantan. Just 40 kms (25 miles) north and east from Pontianak (an easy day-trip), lies the **Mandor Nature Reserve**—a 2,000-hectare (5,000-acre) botanical park with a neighbouring war memorial and orchid gardens.

Indonesia's Venice

Banjarmasin, the largest city in south Kalimantan, is set on an island formed where the Martapura River enters the Barito River, 22 kms (14 miles) upstream from the Barito's mouth. This river system and its associated canals provide the major thoroughfares of Banjarmasin, carrying thousands of watercraft in and out of the city daily, and earning it the nickname "Venice of Indonesia." The water is blood-red from the peat bogs through which the Barito passes en route to the sea. About 25 per cent of south Kalimantan's land area is occupied by swamp and bog.

Most of the native Banjarese—pirates as recently as three decades ago—are devout Muslims. The fasting month of Ramadan is strictly observed, and there are probably more *hajis* (returned pilgrims) per capita than in any other Indonesian city. These *hajis* play a major role in the trading life of the city, many of them taking local gemstones on their annual pilgrimages to Mecca and returning with goods from around the world.

As the centre of the Indonesian gemstone trade, Banjarmasin is the place to buy semi-precious stones such as amethysts, sapphires and agates. Diamonds are also abundant, though these are best purchased in nearby Martapura. Several excellent souvenir shops along Jl. Simpang Sudimampir deal in Dayak handicrafts, hand-woven cloth purses, and traditional Banjar brassware of Hindu-Javanese design. Museum-goers

Right, Mandor Nature Reserve houses fine orchid gardens.

will want to visit the Ceramic Museum on Jl. Kuripan to see their fine collection of porcelain—old Japanese and Chinese as well as Dutch Delft blue.

Two hours' river journey west of Banjarmasin lies the community of **Mandomai**, gateway to primitive Dayak villages near **Kandangan**. Prices of handicrafts are much lower than in Banjarmasin. And those who visit nearby **Pandu** are almost guaranteed a few sightings of the famous wild orangutans (*orangutan*: man of the jungle) of Borneo.

Several wildlife reserves are readily accessible from Banjarmasin, including the **Kaget Island Reserve**, a small island in the middle of the Barito River, 12 kms downstream from Banjarmasin, home of many long-nosed proboscis monkeys. The **Pleihari Martapura Reserve**, 30,000 mountainous hectares (74,000 acres) 50 kms (31 miles) east of Banjarmasin, is reached by road and PHPA (National Park Authority) launch across the Riam Kanan reservoir. And some 350 kms (220 miles) west is the **Cape Puting Reserve**, 305,000 hectares (752,000 acres) of faunal-rich swampland, including the Camp Leakey Orangutan Rehabilitation Station. (*See* Part IV, "Observing Indonesia's Wildlife.") To visit any of these reserves, contact the PHPA office in Banjarmasin.

Diamonds of Martapura

Chartering a motorized canoe is a rewarding way to travel to **Martapura**, the diamond capital of Kalimantan located some 40 kms (25 miles) east of Banjarmasin. The canoes cruise through the waterways to the Martapura wharves, nowadays used by small Indonesian coastal freighters and sailing ships manned by Buginese crews from South Sulawesi.

More than 30,000 people are employed in the diamond mines of Martapura. Hundreds more work in polishing factories, using centuries-old techniques. Martapura lies on a major highway juncture of South Kalimantan, where roads from Banjarmasin and Batakan, Borneo's southernmost town, join. Travellers may proceed north from here to Balikpapan, the major metropolis of East Kalimantan.

Barabai, 165 kms (100 miles) from Banjarmasin.

Banjarmasin, offers access to the beautiful hill country around Batu Benawa. In **Amuntai**, another 25 kms (16 miles), inquire about the buffalo sacrifices which are an integral part of local Dayak funerals. Then head north to Magantis and proceed two kms on foot to **Tamianglayang**. Dayak villages here still practise age-old burial rites, and if no funeral is scheduled, the ancient burial grounds are worth visiting. Tamianglayang also has a fascinating weekly market, when throngs of tribespeople arrive from some of the outlying villages.

Bustling Balikpapan

Balikpapan is Kalimantan's oil town—the busy, bustling focus of East Kalimantan. It features a modern oil refinery and harbour. Thousands of expatriate "oilies" (oil workers) and "chippies" (loggers) live in company housing complexes, shop in modern supermarkets, send their children to private schools and have access to good medical and dental facilities here. There has been a parallel improvement in facilities available to local workers.

Modern amenities include an international-standard hotel, a large number of clubs and bars (including several discos) and even a bowling alley.

But most travellers don't stay long in Balikpapan, preferring instead to head inland in search of remote trading posts, wild jungles and Dayak villages. Their first major stop is Samarinda, about 200 kms (125 miles) from Balikpapan, and 60 kms (37 miles) upriver from the mouth of the broad Mahakam River. A new ferry moves vehicles across the river, giving access to the network of timber tracks and oil/gas pipeline roads that reach to Bontang. Regularly scheduled buses ply the route between Balikpapan and Samarinda for about US$2. Light aircraft provide several daily flights between the two towns. Alternatively, travellers can take a taxi or bus from Balikpapan to **Handil II** on the Mahakam delta, then catch a speedboat upriver.

Samarinda was established as a trading post in 1730 and remains the provincial capital despite the fact that Balikpapan is now the economic centre of the region. Sawmills line the river through

Balikpapan.

the town, evidence of the dozens of timber companies (many of them foreign-owned) based here. The Mahakam is busy with large and small vessels taking sawn timber and logs to Java and other Indonesian islands. Most of the logs come from upriver and are floated down to Samarinda on huge rafts.

The town itself, located on the northern bank of the Mahakam across the river from the bus terminal, is dirty and not particularly interesting. Most travellers continue directly to **Tenggarong**, transferring at the Samarinda bus station. Founded nearly two centuries ago, Tenggarong was the court town of the Sultan of Kutei, **Kartanegara**, in the days before Indonesian independence. The sultan's residence is now the **Mulawarman Museum**, housing an amazing collection of ceramics from China, Vietnam and Japan. Also displayed are Kutei royal heirlooms and examples of tribal beadwork and jewellery. The palace is surrounded by a garden full of Dayak woodcarvings.

Tenggarong is the principal starting point for trips into Dayak country. The town's tourist office, just outside the palace, has information on scheduled activities upriver and visitors are urged to inquire here before proceeding up the Mahakam. (*See* the following section "Visiting the Dayaks.")

Bontang, the Gas Capital

About 80 kms (50 miles) from Samarinda, just a few miles north of the equator, lies **Bontang**, headquarters for a massive (US$1 million daily production) liquified natural gas (LNG) project jointly run by the state-owned oil monopoly, Pertamina, and a number of foreign investors. Several shanty towns have sprung up on the outskirts of the complex, providing cheap accommodations and meals for manual labourers employed on the site. Nearby is **Lokh Tuan**, where a newly completed joint venture fertilizer plant is operating.

Roads connect Bontang and Lokh Tuan with Samarinda, but no regular transportation is available and the road is impassable during the rainy season. It is best to catch speedboats which leave Samarinda every morning about 6 a.m. The trip takes five to 10 hours, depending upon the type of speedboat.

Cessna "Sky-van" flights from Balik-   Samarinda.

234

papan to Bontang and Sanggala must be arranged through one of the oil companies in Balikpapan; most are willing to take passengers if extra seats are available. Inquiries can be made at Balikpapan airport.

Built out over the bay near Bontang is an enormous recreation centre catering to the single workers from the LNG plant. It has literally hundreds of bars, and is a pleasant place to drink and dance and get to know some of the locals. Dozens of taxi motors—young men offering to transport visitors on motorbikes—hang out at this wharf.

Kutei National Park

Bontang and Lokh Tuan are the gateways to **Kutei National Park**, 200,000 hectares (500,000 acres) of coastal forest rich in plant and animal species. Kutei's lowland dipterocarp forest is regarded as the largest rainforest reserve of its type on Earth, richer than anything found in Africa or the Amazon. The game reserve is home to a multitude of wildlife, including orangutans, monkeys, gibbons, wild pigs, herds of wild buffalo, feral cats, more than 300 species of plumage birds . . . and perhaps even the rare Sumatran rhino, though none has been sighted in many years.

Kutei National Park cannot yet be considered a tourist attraction, though it has tremendous potential. Exotic animals are easily visible to the casual observer on abandoned roads and landings. There are river trips through rapids and pools, jungle walks and panoramic views, cold streams and coal seams. The Indonesian government, in conjunction with the World Wildlife Fund, is presently conducting a study on future use and development of the reserve. Those intending to visit it should first obtain permission from the PHPA office on Jl. Kesuma Bangsa in Samarinda, and then report on arrival to the local PHPA office in Bontang Baru. Officials there are very helpful and will generally assist travellers to reach the park by road (during the dry season) or by launch via Teluk Kaba.

The Tarakan Coast

The oil-rich island of **Tarakan**, just off the east coast of Kalimantan near the border with Sabah (Malaysia), is a waystation for those travelling on to Malaysia or across the Makassar Strait to Sulawesi. Daily flights connect Tarakan and Balikpapan; boats to and from Samarinda, Balikpapan, Banjarmasin, Manado and Ujung Pandang stop here.

Tarakan has an interesting market, dealing in many goods from Sabah in Malaysia, but not much else. Fifty-seven kms (35 miles) south of Tarakan (four hours by boat), is **Tanjung Selor**, a town on the Kayan River from which river launches operate (see next section) for visits into Dayak country. The neighbouring community of **Tanjung Palas** is known for its *Jepen* dance, performed for visitors by village girls, and for an old cannon dating from the 16th Century.

Farther south and 59 kms (37 miles) up the Berau River, is **Tanjung Redep**, now a small harbour town but formerly the capital of a prosperous kingdom. From the 14th Century until 1960, when the kingdom was abolished by parliamentary decree, the autonomous ruler (actually two rulers since 1883) governed from here. There are small private museums in the palaces at Sabaliung and Gunung Tabur.

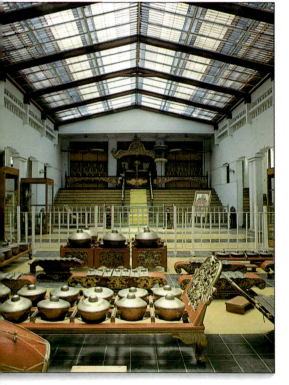
This gamelan is from the Mulawarman Museum.

VISITING THE DAYAKS

A river journey into Dayak country is an unforgettable experience. Travellers can stay in the famous longhouses, marvel at the beadwork and woodcarvings, study the religious rituals, meet a *wadian* (shaman) and perhaps even join in a traditional dance. All that is needed is plenty of time, some money and a sense of adventure. It is also a good idea to have camping equipment (mosquito netting and repellant are a must!) and a letter of introduction (*surat jalan*) from the regional authorities (obtainable in the police headquarters of provincial capitals or in Jakarta).

Tenggarong, near Samarinda in East Kalimantan, is the principal starting point for trips up the Mahakam River. Though this is the most popular upriver adventure, similar voyages can also be made up the Barito and Kapuas rivers from Banjarmasin and Pontianak (see below), as well as up the Kayan and Bahau Rivers from Tarakan and Tanjung Selor.

Independent travellers can book passage aboard the regularly scheduled passenger boats which ply the river, allowing them to stop off in various places of interest. Time is needed, however, because most boats are slow, especially in the wet season when the currents are running. Those who prefer the convenience of organized tours can arrange this in Tenggarong. Three- to seven-day tours are available on riverboats reminiscent of the *African Queen*, and everything is provided, including food and sleeping gear. The Tenggarong tourist office, just outside the Mulawarman Museum, has information on scheduled activities upriver, including local festivals.

Whether you go it alone or take an organized tour, the following is a fairly representative itinerary:

Day One: Coming from Balikpapan by bus, transfer to the Tenggarong bus either at Samarinda or Loa Janan (before Samarinda). Limited accommodations are available at Tenggarong, and you may want to catch a slow boat directly to **Muara Muntai**, a small village just upriver, where even the roads are made of hardwood. Here you can either sleep on a boat or find lodging in the village.

Many of the Dayak longhouses in this area have been abandoned in favour of small *kampung* houses. However, as you come into contact with your first Dayak community, note the spirit of mutual help which is still so strong. Dayaks are monogamous. A man traditionally seeks a wife in another village and sets up his household there. Meals are taken communally with the family or together with a group of families. They squat around mounds of steaming rice heaped on banana leaves, and pick bits of corn, fish, fresh vegetables and meat with sauce from communal pots.

Lakeside Dancing

Day Two: Beyond **Longbangun**, about 140 kms (90 miles) upriver from Tenggarong, the Mahakam passes between two vast lakes: Jempang and Somayang. These lakes are shallow, and in May and June, at the height of the dry season, it is often impossible to cross them by motorboat.

Take a slow boat or canoe across 6,000-hectare (15,000-acre) **Lake Jempang**, home of unique freshwater dol-

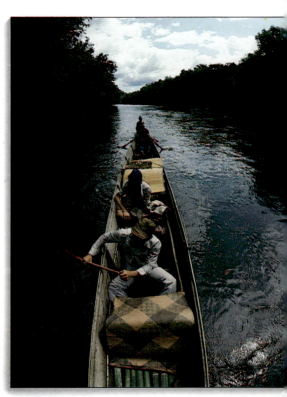

River journey in Dayak country.

phins who will escort your boat to the lakeshore village of **Tanjung Isuy**. This village is inhabited by the Banuaq Dayaks, famous for their colourful *ulap doyoh* weavings, their dancing and their warm hospitality. The Banuaq often welcome guests with dances performed by girls in traditional costumes, and more often than not, the village chief will invite visitors to dine and spend the night with him.

Dancing is generally reserved for nights and is accompanied by a number of musical instruments, including the *kledi* (a kind of bamboo bagpipe), *gamelan*-type percussion instruments and a lute with twisted rattan strings. Ritual dances are exuberant occasions, accompanied by a good deal of shouting and excitement. The men sport animal skins and adorn themselves with feathers while brandishing highly decorative swords, rattles and staffs. Especially popular in the interior, these dances were traditionally held to celebrate victory in battle or a child's coming of age, at harvest time (February/March), for marriages or births, to welcome guests and for whenever protection is sought against natural disasters and evil influences.

In the centre of Lake Jempang is the **Tanjung Haur** floating village—a picturesque spot which the local inhabitants share with hundreds of egrets.

Orchids and Phallic Totems

Day Three: Take a boat or canoe to Jantur and hence on to **Melak**, home of the Tanjung Dayaks. Nearby, close to the village of **Kersik Luwai**, is a 2,000-hectare (5,000-acre) orchid reservation where rare black orchids (*Cologeneia pandurata*) grow in profusion. Most visitors stay in the village of **Sekolak Darat**.

Look for the huge phallic totem poles (*belawang*) erected just outside the village to ward off evil spirits, who are said to be shy of anything sexual. Fiendish-looking carved images adorn the poles. Called *hampatong* (slaves of the dead), they have deformed faces, long protruding tongues, and wild beasts (usually a tiger) sitting on their heads. The poles are hung with a mass of rubbish, including such things as rotten eggs, pig bones, chicken carcasses and bales of wilting grass.

Progress in Dayak country is slow and hazardous.

Despite efforts by Christian missionaries, the Dayaks remain fundamentally animistic. Most Dayak tribes revere Belare, a thunder spirit who rides in storm clouds, creating thunder by opening his mouth and lightning by winking. Said to have large claw-like hands, Belare is held responsible for storm damage to villages and crops. Dayaks also worship rain spirits and river spirits. After the annual rice harvest, special ceremonies are held to float the river spirits home from whence they came.

Corpses are sent to the Land of the Dead in coffin-shaped canoes called Ships of the Dead. Splendidly carved to represent water snakes (for men) and hornbills (for women), these ships are sent drifting downriver to the sea. On the eve of the launching, the male dancers don grotesque masks and straw cloaks.

An important figure in Dayak society is the *wadian* (also *balian*) —a female sorceror. Most Dayak shamans are elderly women who heal the sick and perform ritual chants and dances. During self-induced trance states, the *wadian* are believed to communicate with the spirits, dancing for days on end to the haunting melodies of the *kledi*. The *wadian* is also the village historian and storyteller, passing on her knowledge to younger shamans under her tutelage.

Earrings and Tattoos

Day Four: Back to Tenggarong or, for the adventurous, farther upriver to **Muara Wahau**, passing along the way the villages of Tanjung Manis, Long Noran and Long Segar—homes of the Kenyah and Bahau Dayak tribes. You will notice certain differences in the handicrafts, dances and ceremonies of these villages. The best time to visit is February/March, when the ritual calendar is busiest. Farther upstream is **Tanjung Jone**, where there are six more Dayak villages, noted for weaving both the Samarinda- and Dayak-style *sarung*. The latter is reddish in colour and short.

Travel upriver to these areas becomes more difficult, and boats are irregular. It is possible, however, to travel all the way up to **Longnawan** by boat and then overland to the Kayan Valley, where the isolated Apo-Kayan tribes live. From here, one can descend to the coast

Dayak war dance.

at Tarakan via the Kayan River.

As you venture into these more remote regions, you are likely to find Dayak women wearing large, heavy silver earrings in their pierced earlobes. More rings are added with age, and it was once common to see a middle-aged Dayak woman with earlobes extended as low as her shoulders, sometimes to her chest. Missionary doctors have sometimes been successful in convincing women to lop off these extended lobes as proof of their conversion to Christianity.

Most Dayaks chew betelnut and *sirih* (a narcotic leaf), believing that white teeth are only for animals. If their teeth do not become dark from chewing betel, they will often blacken them with varnish.

Both men and women also consider tattoos attractive. Tattoo designs are initially stamped on the body with handmade wooden blocks. The tattooing is then normally done by women. While some tattoos are purely decorative, others convey social rank or status. Tattooing begins when a child is about 12. More tattoos are added as he or she grows, often following some physical or spiritual event. In certain areas, a man's body is tattooed after his death with designs that relate biographical details. Old tattoo blocks can be purchased very easily in almost every Dayak village.

Though the Mahakam is the most commonly travelled river, boats can also be chartered from Banjarmasin or Mandomai in South Kalimantan to carry visitors up the Barito River as far as **Mauratewe**. From here, you can go by canoe to the river's headwaters, trek four to six days across swamps and jungle via Intu to **Longiram** on the Mahakam River, thence proceed downstream to Samarinda. The full trip takes at least two weeks.

The Kayan and Kenyah Dayaks live near the headwaters of the Kayan River in East Kalimantan, which can be reached from **Tanjung Selor**, just south of Tarakan. Boats leave regularly from Tanjung Selor for Mara I and Mara II, homes of the Kenyah Dayaks. These tribes still practise tooth filing and Kenyah art is distinctive among the Dayaks—the *aso* dragon, a symbol of prosperity, and curling tendrils, are the predominant patterns found on homes, walls, pillars and shields.

It is often possible to arrange flights with some of the missionary airlines to places like **Longbawang** and **Longberini** from Tarakan. These remote settlements lie close to the proposed **Hulu Bahau-Sungai Malinau Reserve**, 950,000 hectares (2.3 million acres) of steep forested ridges around the rugged headwaters of the Bahau River, a tributary of the Kayan. Punan Dayak tribesmen can be hired as guides here for about US$2 a day, for a full-scale nature expedition into the wilds of this reserve. If you visit a Punan village, keep in mind that these people are famed throughout Kalimantan for their yellow-and-black beadwork.

From Pontianak in West Kalimantan, the Kapuas River is also navigable by small boats for more than 900 kms (560 miles). With maybe six weeks to spare, the intrepid traveller can travel upstream to the village of **Putussibau** (where there is an old Dutch Mission), proceed overland through the jungle for about two weeks to the headwaters of the Mahakam River, then board a riverboat for the journey downstream to Samarinda. Few attempt this trip, one of the great adventures remaining on Earth today.

Hunting with a blow pipe.

SULAWESI: AN ISLAND CROSSROAD

Though primarily known as the home of two flamboyant ethnic groups—the highland Torajans and the sea-faring Buginese—the oddly shaped island of **Sulawesi** contains a great variety of exotic peoples, landscapes and natural wonders.

To begin with, Sulawesi's steep mountains, deep gorges, fast flowing rivers, blue highland lakes, lush rainforests, *lontar* palm savannahs and white-sand beaches house a fascinating range of unusual flora and fauna—including many species found nowhere else: the black macaque, the *babirusa* wild boar, the *anoa* dwarf buffalo, the eccentric *maleo* bird, the saucer-eyed tarsier, and many beautiful butterflies. The island's 9 million human inhabitants are equally diverse and between them speak a total of 40 to 50 different languages!

Such astonishing diversity is partially a product of Sulawesi's tortured geography. The island's four outstretched "arms" are in a sense all separate; they rise from a deep seabed formed by contiguous folds in the earth's crust but are isolated from one another by steep ravines, dense forests and forbidding peaks. Unlike many other Indonesian islands, only Sulawesi's northeastern and southwestern extremities (the Minahasa and Makassar regions) are volcanic, and instead of gently sloping contours and broad plains, most of the island consists of jagged uplands and rugged plateaus lying 500 metres (1,600 feet) or more above sea level. The central peaks of Sulawesi are 3,400 metres (11,000 feet) high.

Sulawesi's central position within the archipelago has contributed greatly to her heterogeneity. The northern Sangihe-Talaud archipelago forms a natural link with the Philippines, while the eastern Banggai and Sula archipelagos connect Sulawesi to the spice islands of Maluku. Borneo and the Lesser Sunda islands (Flores, Sumbawa, Lombok) lying directly to the west and south are separated by deep straits, but are reached in only a few days' sail from southern Sulawesi's excellent natural harbours. Over the centuries, this island has therefore received numerous influences from abroad, serving as a focus for inter-island migrations and trading operations.

A Complex History

A neolithic settlement has recently been discovered on Sulawesi's west coast—evidence, together with numerous cave stencils, megaliths, sarcophagi and other prehistoric artifacts, of man's long presence on the island. Highly developed native traditions of textile manufacture, woodcraft,

shipbuilding and metalworking bear witness to a long process of civilization.

Buddhist bronze images dating from the 4th or 5th Century have been found in South Sulawesi, and this region, with its many excellent anchorages, was a key stop on the international spice trading routes for more than a millennium. Indeed, the Bugis peoples of the island's Southern coast are famed to this day as boatbuilders and mariners.

Although the coastal states of South Sulawesi officially converted to Islam only in the 17th Century, they must have maintained trading relations with the emerging Muslim kingdoms on Java's north coast from the early 16th Century, judging from traditional lore. And the "clove" sultanate of

Preceding pages, a verdant panorama from Sulawesi. Left, a traditional Bugis house on stilts. Right, the hat worn by this horseman is a reminder of the past Portuguese and Spanish colonial presence.

Ternate (in the neighbouring Maluku archipelago) also rose to power at this time, bringing all of northern and eastern Sulawesi within its orbit.

When the Islamic conversions began, at the end of the 16th Century, there were already a dozen major ports established on the island—cosmopolitan entrepots where Chinese, Indian, Siamese, Malay, Javanese and Portuguese traders came to exchange their fine textiles and manufactured metal goods for the equally precious cloves, nutmegs, pearls, gold, copper and camphor of the eastern islands.

The first western visitors were the Portuguese, who ventured in this direction soon after their conquest of Malacca in 1511. A number of Portuguese ships, in fact, were

wrecked on reefs north of the Minahassa coast on their way to Ternate in 1521, hence that region became known as the Ponto dos Celebres (Cape of the Infamous). Initially, it seems, the Portuguese thought that Sulawesi was an archipelago and not a single island, and the name they applied to it— The Celebes—was adopted thereafter.

Spanish missionaries followed the Portuguese, preaching in Minahassa and the neighbouring islands from their base in the Philippines. But early in the 17th Century the Dutch arrived and eventually drove out all competing foreigners—European and Asian. At first the Dutch attempted, somewhat unsuccessfully, to impose monopolistic treaties on the powerful South Sulawesi

trading sultanates. Finally in 1666-7, a large Dutch fleet under the command of Admiral Cornelis Speelman managed to subdue the Makassarese forces of Sultan Hasanuddin and put a stop to the "smuggling" of spices.

Though the Dutch were able to enforce an external trading monopoly on the island thereafter, it was not until the early 20th Century that they secured political control over the interior of the island, through treaties endorsed by local rulers. Dutch administrators were assisted in these efforts by Calvinist and other missionaries who converted many Toraja, Minahassa, Sangihe and Talaud peoples.

Most of the other coastal peoples—those of Gorontalo, Kendari, Buton, and South Sulawesi, are ardent Muslims, however. Pockets of pagan peoples also survive in the central and southern highlands—and it is these disparate tribes, generically known as the Toalans and the Torajans, with their colourful funeral rites and sacrificial feasts, that have most fascinated foreign visitors.

Today Sulawesi and its adjacent islands are divided into four provinces.

South Sulawesi, the most developed area, includes the densely populated Bugis coastal areas of Luwu and Bone on the east coast of the peninsula, Bantaeng and the island of Salayar to the south, and Ujung Pandang (formerly Makassar—now the provincial capital) and Pare-Pare on the west coast. In the northern-central uplands live the renowned Torajan peoples. (*See* "Visiting Torajaland.")

Southeastern Sulawesi, including the islands of Buton and Muna, is fairly heavily populated by a number of peoples who speak about a dozen different languages. Kendari is the provincial capital, and nickel is mined near Kolaka on the western shore.

Central Sulawesi, a vast underdeveloped and little known area, plus the Banggai archipelago, comprises the rugged central highlands and eastern "arm" of the island. Its capital is Palu and the newly completed trans-Sulawesi roadway now links this town with the south via spectacular Lake Poso.

North Sulawesi, though less developed than South Sulawesi, is in many ways the most civilized and scenic area on the island, wth dramatic volcanic landscapes, forested highland lakes and an exotic complement of wildlife. Manado, the provincial capital, is famous for its cleanliness and its mixed Indonesian-Chinese-European population.

Sulawesi's varied geography provides a habitat for many endemic species. Its fascinating flora and fauna is notable for its variety of butterflies.

Sulawesi (The Celebes)

100 km

Sangihe

Archipelago

Maratua

Talok

Santigi
Lanu   Biau   **Sulawesi Utara**
Tompo   Likupang
                                    Pimpi   Tangkoko
                        Kuandang Kotamobagu   MANADO Reserve
Siboa   Tomini   Bone-Dumoga Tondano Bitung
                            Marisa Tilamuta Gorontalo Lombagin
Tinombo   Taludaa Reserve Dumoga Mt. Ambang
Sabang   Reserve

Toribulu   *Togian Islands*

Cape   *Tomini Bay*   *Moluku Sea*
Karang   *Sulawesi Tengah* *Walea Strait*
Donggala Parigi   Teku
PALU   Ampana   Boalang Luwuk
Pasangkayu Lore Lindu   Batui   Palam
          Wuasa Tojo Bongka   Peleng
Palu   Sidaunta Reserve   Kembani
     Watukama Posso   *Bangkulu*   Taliabu Mantarara
Kakali   Ratodena   Morowali
          Lake   Reserve Kolonodale   Lekitool *Sula Islands*
          Posso   *Tolo Bay*
    Sulawesi Lake Matana   *Banggai Archipelago*
Karama   Saroako Sokita
Mamuju   Masamba Bonebone Malili *Lake*
       Sulawesi Selatan   *Towuti* Labota
Talapang Rantepao Paloppo   Tolala   Lindu
Cenrana Makale   Mondeodo
Balangnipa Polewali   *Konaweha* **Sulawesi Tenggara**
Majene **Rantekombola** Enrekang   Kolaka **KENDARI**
     Mandar ▲ 3455 m Siwa   Baula   Benua Monse
     Bay   Pinrang Pangkajene
Parepare   Sengkang-
          Lake   soppeng
Sumpangbinangae *Tempe* Watangsoppeng   Towari Raha
     Baru   Watampone   Samak Muna Bone
          Pangkajene   Pising   *Buton*
     Maros   Balangnipa   Kabaena Mawasangka Pasarwajo
UJUNG PANDANG Camba Sinjai
        Malino Tanette   *Tukangbesi*
Takalar Bantaeng Bulukumba
     Djeneponto   Bira   *Batuata*
                                        Banda Sea
          Benteng Bonelohe
          Barangbarang *Selayar*

     Tanahjampea Ujung

               Kalaotoa

                    Komba

Makassar Strait

Bone Bay

Woworii Strait

245

UJUNG PANDANG AND SOUTH SULAWESI

Dramatic landscapes and remarkable peoples are the hallmarks of South Sulawesi—a province that is rapidly becoming one of Indonesia's major tourist destinations. This is a region of steep volcanoes, fast flowing rivers, fertile plains, broad savannahs, uneven coasts and white sand beaches.

Such geographic diversity has led to the development of divergent lifestyles among the province's 6 million inhabitants—and indeed South Sulawesi is one of the most heavily populated regions of Indonesia, with an average density of more than 125 persons per sq km (300 per sq mile)—considerably lower than in Java and Bali but much higher than in most other areas. The staple food here is rice, grown in lowland irrigated paddies; but maize and in some areas, sago, is the preferred highland crop. Tall pandanus, lontar and banana palms abound, as do wild pineapples—providing a varied diet as well as many natural fibres for the highly developed native arts of weaving and plaiting.

The many natural harbours of South Sulawesi have long been settled by seafaring peoples. Cave-paintings at Leang-Leang north of Ujung Pandang are thought to be 5,000 years old. As new immigrants arrived, they often forced earlier settlers to the highlands.

The Sea-Faring Bugis

The coastal and lowland regions of South Sulawesi are today inhabited by many Mongoloid-type peoples—generically known as the Bugis. It is generally assumed that they settled along these shores well over 1,000 years ago, and since that time they have had one of the more colourful histories of any Indonesian ethnic group.

The Bugis have always been great seafarers and shipbuilders. From South Sulawesi, it is thought that they sailed as far afield in ancient times as Madagascar and northern Australia, leaving behind artifacts and loanwords and returning with foreign trade goods and treasures. Buginese settlers almost certainly lived in some of the region's great Hindu-period maritime capitals such as Sumatra's Srivijaya (7th-13th centuries) and East Java's Kediri, Daha and Majapahit (11th-14th centuries), bringing new beliefs and practices back to Sulawesi after their sojourns abroad.

These connections lasted for many centuries, and various Bugis kingdoms—Luwu (Paloppo), Bone, Soppeng, Goa, Supa and Mandar—rose to power in South Sulawesi between the 12th and 15th centuries as a result. After 1500, trading relations with the Islamic sultanates on Java's north coast were strong, and with the emergence of the Makassarese kingdom of Goa-Tallo as the preeminent power in the early 17th Century, South Sulawesi officially converted to Islam.

Though the Bugis kingdoms were later subdued and dominated by the Dutch, their influence was felt throughout the Malay world. Even in the 18th and 19th centuries, Bugis groups were still founding new sultanates on the Malay peninsula and in the Riau archipelago. Today there is hardly an estuary or a bay in Indonesian waters without a Buginese settlement.

The Bugis courtly heritage is preserved today only imperfectly in South Sulawesi's villages. And visitors often misinterpret their traits of aggressiveness, outspokenness, perseverance and pride. Most tourists therefore bypass the Bugis homelands route to the highland Torajan communities in the north. There is much to see in the south, nonetheless, and the dynamism of the Bugis is serving them well in the modern world, gearing the province for rapid economic development.

The 'Pandanus-Palm Cape'

Ujung Pandang is today a modern, bustling city of 700,000—the business and administrative centre of Sulawesi. Called Makassar by the Dutch after they conquered the Kingdom of Goa and established a fortified trading post here in 1667, the current name (which means "Pandanus Cape") was restored following Indonesian independence. Like all major Indonesian cities, it has undergone its share of growing pains in recent years, as the grandeur of the colonial town has given way to concrete boxes, roads and drainage ditches that create a rather bland contemporary look.

The town flourished as the port and

trading centre for the medieval kingdom of Goa. The old fort (*benteng*) of Ujung Pandang was one of eleven Goanese strongholds when it was first erected in 1545. The Dutch conquered and reconstructed it in 1667, renaming it **Amsterdam Castle**. With its interior church and trading offices, it today stands as one of the outstanding examples of 17th Century Dutch fortress architecture. The fort now houses the **Ujung Pandang Provincial Museum**, with many fine displays of old ceramics, manuscripts, coins, musical instruments and ethnic costumes. The Conservatory of Dance and Music is also located here—drop in to observe rehearsals in progress. And there is a famous dungeon where one of Indonesia's national heroes, Prince Diponegoro of Yogyakarta (1785-1855), was imprisoned for 27 years.

Prince Diponegoro's grave and that of his family and followers are located in the middle of town on a street named after him. He was exiled after defying both the Dutch and his own royal family, leading a series of popular uprisings in Central Java between 1825 and 1830. None of the prince's relatives or descendants ever returned to Java. His grave is now a pilgrimage point for many Indonesian visitors.

Another interesting stop is the residence of Dutchman C.L. Bundt at No. 15 Jalan Mochtar Lufti. His house, with its spacious gardens, contains a private collection of seashells, coral rocks and rare orchids.

In the late afternoon, it is pleasant to stroll along the Makassar Strait and watch the sunset from the **Pantere Anchorage** along Jalan Penghibur at the north end of the city, berth for many *pinisi* schooners.

Just to the south of Ujung Pandang lies **Sungguminassa**, the former capital of the Sultanate of Tallo. Today the wooden palace is the **Ballompoa Museum**, containing many weapons and royal costumes. The royal regalia, which includes a gem-studded gold crown weighing 15.4 kgs (34 lbs), may be seen on request.

Near Sungguminassa are the tombs of the kings of Goa, of whom Sultan Hasanuddin (1629-1670) is the most famous, for his bravery and leadership in the struggle against the Dutch. Just outside the walls of the cemetery, a small

Prahu in the Java Sea.

fenced-off plot contains the **Tomanur-ung stone** upon which the kings of Goa were once crowned. On a side road nearby lies the tomb of Aru Palakka, the King of Bone—related to and yet the arch enemy of Sultan Hasanuddin.

Southern Round-Trip

To escape the lowland heat of Ujung Pandang, travel 71 kms (44 miles) to **Malino**, on the slopes of Mt. Bawakar-aeng, some 760 metres (2,500 feet) above sea level. This cool, quiet resort in a pine forest is noted for its orchards of *markisa* (passion) fruit trees. The fruit is pressed locally to produce a refreshing drink that is marketed all over Indonesia. The lovely **Takapala Waterfall** is an easy 4-km (2.5-mile) walk south of the town.

A road from Malino leads across to **Sinjai** on the eastern coast of the peninsula, facing the Gulf of Bone. From there, a coastal road—breathtaking for its steep precipices and spectacular views— leads south to the tip of **Cape Bira**, heart of the Bugis shipbuilding industry. Round-bellied *prahu* are still fashioned here with ancient tools and

without the use of metal or nails of any sort. Teak logs are hewn into planks then fastened with wooden pegs according to an ancient design engraved in the communal memory. Sails were once made of plaited banana and pineapple fibres, later of woven cotton and ironed silk. Rituals are employed in all phases of the construction, from the selection of the tree to the final launching, to ensure that the craft will be seaworthy. The huge 200-ton *pinisi* and a lighter vessel called the *bago* are unstable and ungainly till fully loaded with copra or timber—then they are one of the best ships afloat and may be seen today from one end of the archipelago to the other carrying vital cargoes just as they did centuries ago.

Turning westward along the southern **Bulukumba Coast**, the road leads back to Ujung Pandang through small towns like Bontain (Bantaeng), Jeneponto and Takalar, whose names were mentioned six and seven centuries ago in Chinese texts. The road then passes through Barongbong, a popular seaside resort with white sand beaches.

A mountainous 180-km (112-mile) road takes one northeast from Ujung

This Bugis prahu *is being built to specifications introduced by the Dutch centuries ago*

Pandang toward **Watampone**, the former capital and port city of the Bugis Kingdom of Bone. En route, it passes a new telecommunications station at Maros and a series of gushing waterfalls at Bantimurung. Nearby are the Leang-Leang Caves containing 5,000-year-old blood-red henna hand stencils. To the east is the brisk mountain resort of **Camba**, where the views are superb and there are many mysterious caves. A side-road north from Camba leads to **Ujunglamuru**, noted for its holy graveyard—site of the tombs of Bone's early Muslim teachers and rulers. The main road descends to the coast.

The once-bustling port town of **Watampone** is quiet now, but retains its dignity. Notice the architecture of the houses in the Bugis section of town. The tympanum-like triangles over the doorways are composed of three, five, seven, or nine parts, indicating the social rank of the inhabitants. Nine parts were reserved only for royalty.

The **Museum Lapawawoi** houses the regalia of the kings of Bone, as well as a copy of the 1667 Treaty of Bonggaya with the Dutch that ended their economic dominance over the area. Both may

Laeng Pataere Caves.

be seen only on request. Watampone's harbour is still a centre for inter-island shipping, and a ferry leaves here for Kolaka in Southeast Sulawesi, across the bay of Bone. Boatbuilding and fishing are the principal industries. Beautiful cotton and silk weavings are also produced, as well as some unusual plaitings made with orchid fibres.

South Sulawesi's largest cave system, **Goa Mampu**, is located about 30 kms (19 miles) away. Stalactites and stalagmites here resemble animals and humans, and give rise to local legends.

On a mountain plateau northwest of Watampone, nestled on the shores of Lake Tempe, lies **Sengkang-Soppeng**, seat of another feudal kingdom of old. It is best known today for its hand-loomed silk weavings. Fishing in Lake Tempe was formerly an important industry until the lake began to dry up in recent years. South of Sengkang in the hill country is the town's twin court centre, **Watang-Soppeng**. The regalia of the kings of Soppeng are kept in a small pavilion and may be seen on request.

From Watang-Soppeng a road leads northwest to the coast and the port town of **Pare-Pare**. This was once the site of the powerful trading kingdom of Supa, connecting Ujung Pandang in the south and the ports of the Kingdom of Mandar in the north with the highlands. In the days of sailing *pinisi* and Portuguese galleons, Pare-Pare's deep natural harbour was busier than Ujung Pandang's.

Farther to the north and west, the old kingdom of Mandar once stretched all along the coast of what is now Mandar Bay. The Mandarese, who are distinct from the Bugis yet often confused with them, are also great sailors. Their shipbuilding tradition still rivals that of their southern neighbours, centred now around **Balangnipa** between Polewali and Majene.

The last Bugis stronghold to the northeast of Pare-Pare before entering Torajaland is **Enrekang**, separated from neighbouring towns by a deep ravine. On the east coast of the peninsula, the Bugis Kingdom of Luwu with its harbour, **Paloppo**, is Toraja's closest neighbour. Luwu is regarded as the oldest of all Bugis Kingdoms, and Paloppo is still today a busy commercial centre—gateway to southern Central Sulawesi and to the nickel-mining areas around Malili.

THE TORAJA: HIGHLAND PEOPLE

Tucked away amid the rugged peaks and fertile plateaus of south-central Sulawesi live many isolated tribes, who share a common ancestry with the sea-faring Bugis, Mandar and Makassar peoples of the coasts, conservatively maintaining many ancient crafts and customs. Coastal dwellers refer to these tribes collectively as the Toraja or "highland peoples."

According to traditional accounts, the Toraja left the island of Pongko, located to the southwest, some 25 generations ago and crossed the ocean in canoes (*lembang*). Arriving in Sulawesi, they made their way up the Sa'dan River (which now cuts diagonally across Torajaland) and settled on its banks.

The Toraja have remained in this landlocked region, growing rice and vegetables. During this century clove trees and coffee were also introduced as cash crops. A certain degree of outside influence was brought by traders and missionaries, but for the most part Torajan tribal customs and social structures endure as before.

The Toraja traditionally lived in small settlements perched on hilltops and surrounded by stone walls. Each village is composed of several extended families, who inhabit a series of houses, called *tongkonan*, arranged in a circular row around an open field. In the middle stands a sacred stone or banyan tree used for ritual offerings, and granaries (*lumbung*) face the dwellings.

The roofs of *tongkonan* rise at both ends like the bow and stern of a boat; ritual chants today compare these dwellings to the vessels that carried their ancestors here. House panels are exquisitely carved with geometric and animal motifs executed in the sacred colours of white, red, yellow and black. The house symbolizes the universe. The roof represents the heavens, and it is always oriented northeast to southwest—the directions of the two ancestral realms, according to Torajan cosmology.

Though villages were self contained and often warred with one another, larger federations called *wanua* eventually formed. These were headed by a council of elders (*puang*). At one time there were as many as 40 *wanua*, dominated by the powerful southeastern *wanua* of Sangalla. This Torajan super-state maintained relations with the Buginese coastal kingdoms, and even later converted to Islam.

In the early 20th Century, Dutch missionaries penetrated to the highlands of *Tana Toraja* (Torajaland), and in 1905 many Torajan villages were brought under direct Dutch control. To facilitate their administration, they were ordered to remove from their hilltop perches and settle in more accessible valleys and plateaus. Instead of stone walls, these villages are now ringed by hedges. In the post-independence era, the Toraja were organized into a single *kabupaten* (district), with Makale as its capital.

Travelling in Torajaland

Since the late 1970s, travelling in Torajaland has become much easier due to the installation of new roads and transportation systems. Tana Toraja is generally reached from Ujung Pandang via Pare-Pare and the inland river town of Enrekang. From here the road enters a land of steep terraced slopes, tall

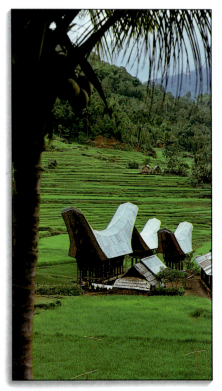

Left, an entire Torajan "graveyard" with galleries for effigies of the dead. Right, the architecture of Ke'te village is typical.

251

bamboo forests and high mountain peaks. Across the Sa'dan River from Salubarani, the road passes under a large boat-shaped arch, marking the entrance to Tana Toraja. The road continues through Bambapuang Valley and past the shapely Buttu Kabobong (Erotic Hills). After 310 kms (190 miles) and eight hours, the traveller arrives at **Makale**, the district capital.

Eighteen kms (11 miles) farther on lies **Rantepao**, the centre of the Torajan tourist trade. Small hotels, restaurants and shops cater now to foreign visitors. The surrounding villages contain bustling markets and traditional houses, where Torajans practise their native crafts of weaving and woodcarving and stage rituals and folk dances for themselves and for the tourists. There are several cave tombs (*liang*) in the vicinity, with effigies that stare out from suspended balconies like guards.

The best-known grave site is at **Londa**, about two kms (1.25 miles) off the main road connecting Makale with Rantepao. Here the effigies are those of noblemen and other high-ranking community leaders. Similar tombs can be seen at **Lemo**, about five kms (three miles) from Rantepao, where the burial chambers are carved out of a sheer rock face. On a hillside behind nearby **Ke'te**, coffins are guarded by life-size statues.

Especially beautiful *tongkonan* houses grace the village of **Palawa**, on a small hill facing *lumbung* granaries. This village, which has a traditional feel to it, is located about nine kms (5.5 miles) from Rantepao.

All these places are easily reached by hired four-wheel-drive vehicles. Unfortunately though, because of the proximity to Rantepao, many traditions in this locality seem to be waning. Travellers with more time and stamina are urged to go farther afield: Tana Toraja offers many exciting excursions.

A journey from Makale to **Sangalla** is worth the effort. Older *tongkonan* houses here provide a more traditional atmosphere. And the 80-km (50-mile) trek west through the mountains to **Mamasa**, or 120 kms (75 miles) north to **Rongkong**, will introduce the traveller to other facets of Torajan life. Mamasa is the only place in Sulawesi where copper is worked. Here is produced a dazzling array of jewellery with unique *Dongson* type designs. Rongkong weavings,

Torajan burial ceremony.

with their characteristic colours and bold motifs, are used throughout the area as ancestor cloths.

Torajan Feasts
For the Dead

The Toraja are perhaps best known for their elaborate, colourful feasts for the dead, offered to ensure that souls of the dead may pass to the afterworld (*puya*) in a manner appropriate to the status they enjoyed in this world. Only when these rites have been performed, it is believed, will the ancestors bestow their blessings upon the living, thus maintaining the fragile balance between the various realms of the cosmos.

These feasts require an enormous outlay of material wealth—kin groups will often save and work for many years to prepare a suitably elaborate funeral. Many are thus held from August to October, following harvest time. Visitors should be sure to contribute food, cigarettes, soap or money to assist the family.

A man is considered dead only when his funeral feast is held. In the meantime, the deceased is regarded as mere-ly "sick" and the corpse is kept in the southern end of the *tongkonan*, where he is fed and visited as if he were still alive. The corpse is first ritually cleansed and dressed in fine weavings, and made to sit up. After some days, it is wrapped in specially woven fabrics and lain in a westward-facing position.

When enough goods have been set aside to send the soul off, the funeral ceremonies are performed in two stages over a period of about a week, presided over by a "death" specialist or *tomaba-lu*. Buffaloes and pigs are first slaughtered, and offerings of betelnut, fruits and *tuak* (palmwine) are made. The corpse is then moved to face north and is now officially dead. The kinfolk must observe a number of taboos, including a rice fast that lasts several days, as dances and chants are performed.

The *ma'bolong* ceremony follows, for which a pig and a buffalo are again slaughtered and the relatives wear black. The body is placed in a sandal-wood coffin in the shape of a *tong-konan*, then brought out of the house draped in a glittering death shroud and placed on an open platform beneath the granary. Meanwhile, an effigy (*tau-tau*) and funeral tower (*lakkian*) are prepared, and a large stone is placed in the centre of the village ceremonial field (*rante*).

The second phase of the funeral takes place in the *rante*, decorated for the occasion with banners and the funeral tower. The coffin is borne from the house to the field and suspended in the *lakkian*.

All the guests have now arrived. Feasting, chanting and dancing continue through the night and buffalo fights and boxing matches take place during the day.

The funeral culminates with the ritual slaughter of up to 50 water buffalo, each by a single stroke of the sword. The blood is collected in bamboo containers to be cooked along with the buffalo meat, and distributed among the guests. On the last day of the feast, the coffin is lowered from the funeral tower and run up to the mountainside family gravesite amidst great shouting and excitement. From here the soul of the deceased ascends to the realm of the deified ancestors (*deata*) and its *tau-tau* effigy is installed on a high balcony overlooking the beautiful green valleys of the Toraja homeland.

At Kete village a coffin is hoisted up a rock face.

MANADO AND NORTH SULAWESI

North Sulawesi is something of an anomaly—a fertile, snake-like volcanic peninsula outstretched in the middle of the vast Maluku Sea, more than 1,000 kms (600 miles) from the nearest major population centre, it is nevertheless one of the most thoroughly Christianized places in Indonesia.

About 2.3 million people make their homes here, more than 200,000 of them in the overcrowded provincial capital of Manado. This city lies at the tip of the lovely mountainous **Minahasa** region, with its active volcanoes, clear highland lakes, hotwater springs and sandy beaches. Coconut plantations stretch for miles along the coasts (18,000 tons of copra are produced in North Sulawesi every month!), and inland there are terraced ricefields, vegetable gardens and patches of cultivated maize. Minahasans also love flowers, and brightly coloured bunches line the roads of the region, relieving the monotony of the grey asphalt.

The Minahasans

The Minahasan peoples are originally of Mongoloid stock, and as with most coastal Indonesians, they migrated here several thousands years ago. Their languages most closely resemble those spoken in the Philippines, however, and over the past few centuries large numbers of Chinese and Europeans have settled in the area and intermarried with the native inhabitants.

It is said that the earliest Minahasan port was situated on Manado Tua, an extinct volcanic island on the north side of Manado Bay. Perhaps 500 years ago the town was moved across to the site of modern-day Manado and flourished thereafter as a stop on the spice route.

Portuguese traders arrived here early in the 16th Century, and were soon followed by Spanish missionaries from Manila, who landed at Manado and persuaded many Minahasans to convert to Catholicism. Dutch Calvinist missionaries in turn converted most of them to Protestantism in the mid-19th Century, when colonial administrators made Manado the capital of the Residency of Ternate and attempted to break the power of the North Moluccan sultanates from their base here. The town has grown in importance ever since that time.

Most of the traditional crafts of Minahasa have been lost, including the Bentenan weavings for which the area was once renowned. Folk dances are the most attractive of the surviving arts, though they lose much of their meaning when performed out of context for tourists. The Cakalele war dances are often performed today, a rather pale imitation of what they once must have been. A harvest dance called Maengket is still popular in the villages, together with flirtatious "scarf" dances that are obviously Malay-derived.

In agricultural areas, various seasonal events are well worth watching for. At the beginning of the planting season and at harvest time, villagers march to the fields singing songs in a festival known as the Mapalus. Following the harvest, thanksgiving feasts last for several days and nights. They are inaugurated with a religious convocation, but consist mainly of eating, *saguer* (palm toddy) drinking and dancing. Adults prefer the traditional European waltz, polka and quadrille, while the younger generation indulges in more modern gyrations. The lack of a dance hall is no problem—an open coconut-palm clearing or sandy beach provides an ideal setting.

Visiting Manado

Once a quiet, elegant city with broad seaside boulevards and swaying palms, **Manado** has now assumed the character of many other overcrowded urban centres. Old colonial facades have been renovated in an attempt to give the city a contemporary appearance. The central marketplace, where products from the surrounding countryside and the islands of Sangihe and Talaud were once bought and sold, is no longer the bargainer's delight it once was. Instead, it resembles more a large supermarket with many imported goods. Local housewives prefer to do their marketing at **Ranotana** on the outskirts of the city, and for visitors too this is a good place to observe the traditional Minahasan lifestyle.

Manado has no sightseeing attractions like museums or cultural events.

It is best regarded as a base for trips to the inland mountains and offshore coral islands. Spread over several hills overlooking the sea, it is served by good roads and public transport, and travellers can escape in any direction.

One interesting road runs due east from Manado through the Tonsea area to the port town of **Bitung** on the east coast of the peninsula, a distance of 55 kms (35 miles). Along the way it passes through **Airmadidi** (Boiling Water) and the coastal town of **Kema**, populated by *burghers* (Minahasan-Dutch settlers) who all have Dutch surnames.

South of Kema there is a lovely stretch of coastline that is ideal for water sports, with many coral gardens in the neighbourhood of **Nona Island**. Beyond Bitung lies **Aertembaga**, focus for the region's tuna fishing industry. From Bitung, one may hire a boat for the journey up the coast to Batuputih Village gateway to the **Tangkoko-Batuangus-Dua Saudara Nature Reserve** (*See* Part IV, "Observing Indonesia's Wildlife" for details).

A road south from **Lembeyan** (near Airmadidi) winds up through the Mina-

Large numbers of Chinese have settled in North Sulawesi. Below, Toapekong Chinese festival.

hasan hills to the lakeside district capital of **Tondano**, an attractive town with wide boulevards and surrounded by rice fields and forested hills. Just before Tondano, the road passes a park full of *waruga*—1.5-metres (5-foot) stone sarcophagi engraved with interesting reliefs and capped with statues. From prehistoric times into the early 20th Century, Minahasans buried their dead in such sarcophagi in a crouching position, together with their most valuable possessions. Traditionally they were placed around the family house; now they have been assembled in one place to preserve them.

On a hill just outside of Tondano lies the mausoleum of Kyai Maja, a Javanese leader who fought in Diponegoro's army during the Java Wars (1825-1830) and was exiled here by the Dutch along with his relatives and retinue. Even now, his **Kampung Jawa** is a Muslim enclave in an otherwise Christian region.

There are a number of interesting towns around **Lake Tondano**, including **Passo** and **Remboken** (noted for their hotsprings and ceramics), **Tandengan** and **Eris**. At the southern end of the lake is the village of **Kolongan Kawang-**

Large numbers of Chinese have settled in North Sulawesi. Below, Toapekong Chinese festival.

koan, site of *kolintang* performances, bullock-cart races and an underground Japanese fortress.

Southwest of Lake Tondano, near
Langowan, a sign gives directions to
the ancient megalithic monument
known as **Watung Pinabetengan,** a
short distance off the main road. A
huge, anvil-shaped stone thought to
mark the territorial boundary of three
tribal areas, it is covered with hitherto
undeciphered hieroglyphics. Pre-Chris-
tian traditional heroes are still worshipped here.

Beaches and Springs

West from Tondano, the road cuts
through more hills on the way to **To-
mohon**, a busy centre for trade, education and missionary activities. There
are hotsprings nearby, at **Lahendong**,
amidst a clove-tree forest, and at **Kini-
low**. From here the road descends to
the coast at **Tanawangko**, a popular
beach resort.

Travelling south along the coast, you
soon arrive at **Amurang**, a small harbour
town 80 kms (50 miles) from Manado
that has a thriving trade with East
Kalimantan, across the Sulawesi Sea.

Surrounded by lovely hills, this is the
gateway to southern Minahasa and
Gorontalo (a day's drive west) via the
newly completed Trans-Sulawesi Highway. And the **Mt. Ambang Nature Reserve** near the town of **Kotamobagu**
(two hours' drive south) offers excellent
hikes amidst an area of montane forests,
lakes and coffee plantations.

Returning to Manado from Amurang
via the coastal road, you pass through
many seaside villages—ideal spots for
picnicking and swimming. The fishing
village of **Malalayang** is now developing as a beach resort, and from here
you can rent boats for excursions to
offshore islands that are surrounded by
reefs and coral gardens. **Bunaken
Island** is the closest, perfect for a short
visit. **Manado Tua** has a crater lake in
the centre of its extinct volcano.

Starting at **Pineleng** as you enter
Manado, villages and houses become
tightly packed and this is the most
heavily populated rural area in the
region. Near Pineleng, a side-road leads
to the mausoleum of Tuanku Imam
Bonjol, a Sumatran leader who led a re-
volt against the Dutch in the mid-19th
Century and was exiled here.

North
Sulawesi war
dance.

SOUTHEASTERN AND CENTRAL SULAWESI

Sulawesi's southeastern and central provinces (Sulawesi Tenggara and Sulawesi Tengah) are rarely visited and have not developed tourist facilities of any significance. Because of their distance from the beaten track, however, they retain a charm and a traditional lifestyle not found in more developed areas.

The capital of southeastern Sulawesi is **Kendari**, whose craftsmen were famed for their silver filigree work. This town, situated on the east coast facing the Banda Sea, is a port of some importance and a gateway to Maluku. Sheltered by myriad small islands, the town gives the appearance, when viewed from the sea, of lying on a lake.

The boat trip from Kendari to **Baubau** on Buton Island is highly recommended. This smooth 12-hour passage through several straits separating in numerable islands, is a joy.

Atop the town on a hill stands the *Kraton*—a huge centuries-old fortress with a commanding view of the sea and adjacent islands. Inhabiting remote shorelines all along these coasts as far north as the Salabangka Islands, the Bajau people hunt the giant stingray, using its poisonous spine as a point for their harpoons.

A good road from Kendari leads across the peninsula to the nickel-mining area of **Kolaka**, where a ferry crosses over the Bay of Bone to Watampone in South Sulawesi.

At the northern end of the bay, on the border between Southeastern and Central Sulawesi, lie the nickel-mining townships of **Malili** and **Saroako**. The latter is the headquarters for the International Nickel Co. (INCO) mining operations. About 45,000 tons of nickel—nearly 10 per cent of the world's total supply—are extracted here each year. The mine site is 52 kms (32 miles) inland by an all-weather road, on the shores of huge Lake Matana.

The best reason to visit this area is to see the two lakes, Matana and Towuti. INCO has a recreational camp on **Lake Matana** with sailboats and speedboats, water skiing and swimming. Visitors are sometimes permitted to use the facilities. There are ancient burial caves around the lake, especially near Saroako village (accessible by boat).

Lake Towuti, at 48 kms (30 miles) wide the largest lake in Sulawesi, is surrounded by mountain rainforest and elephant grass. INCO can sometimes arrange launches. Otherwise, it can be reached by bus from Malili via Timampu.

The provincial capital of Central Sulawesi is **Palu**, a trading city located on the west coast at the tip of a deep, narrow bay. There are daily flights here from many cities; and overnight boats to Samarinda depart weekly from the harbour, 25 kms (15 miles) to the north. Palu is also the gateway to the beautiful Lore Lindu Nature Reserve. (*See* Part IV, "Observing Indonesia's Wildlife.") **Donggala**, a quaint sea port at the mouth of the bay, is 35 kms (22 miles) away.

Most of central Sulawesi takes the form of isolated peaks, rainforests and remote tribal settlements. The Trans-Sulawesi roadway now connects **Tentena** and **Pendolo** above spectacularly scenic Lake Posso, so that it is now possible to drive the length of Sulawesi, from Ujung Pandang to Manado, in a week.

A horse and cart is still a common form of transport.

MALUKU: THE SPICE ISLANDS

Every schoolchild has heard of the fabled, faraway Spice Islands, that Oriental source of exotic cloves, nutmegs, pepper, cinnamon and mace which changed the course of history. The search for a passage to these isles touched off the expansive Age of Discovery, and the lucrative spice trade contributed greatly to the rise of European mercantile and colonial empires that have shaped the modern world.

Fewer people realize that there were in fact two distinct groups of "spice islands" when the European lust for spices was at its peak in the 16th and 17th centuries. Cinnamon and pepper were then produced primarily on Ceylon and Sumatra (but also in India and on Java), while cloves, nutmegs and mace were exclusively grown on certain of the eastern "Moluccan" islands—tiny volcanic specks of land now contained within the Indonesian province known as Maluku.

Cloves, Nutmegs and Trade

The name Moluccas (or Maluku—from an Arabic term meaning "land of kings") applied originally only to a chain of five small islands (Ternate, Tidore, Moti, Mare and Makian) lying just off the west coast of relatively gigantic Halmahera. Located just north of the equator, this mini-archipelago with a total land area of less than 525 sq kms (200 sq miles) supported in early times a population of 25,000 persons (as compared with about 60,000 today), most of whom were engaged in tending and harvesting the world's supply of prime cloves.

The key elements in the clove trade were the closely adjacent twin islands of Ternate and Tidore, each about 104 sq kms (40 sq miles) in area—symmetrical volcanic cones, ringed by coral reefs and rising from the ocean depths to heights of 1.6 kms (one mile) above sea level. They were the seats of rival kingdoms, whose dominions extended for hundreds of miles in every direction during the 15th and 16th centuries. Sought out since ancient times by Chinese, Javanese and Arab traders, and visited in the year 1512 by the pioneer Portuguese navigators in

the Pacific, these islands were destined thereafter to become the focus for sanguinary East-West conflicts in the area.

Six hundred and fifty kms (400 miles) to the south, the first Portuguese voyagers found also the cluster of five yet smaller Banda islands—Neira, Lonthor, Run, Ai and Rosengain—that with a population of just 15,000 people (25,000 today) then produced the world's supply of prime nutmeg and mace (two parts of the same fruit). Because they freely sold their spices to all visiting European and Asian merchants, the

Bandanese were to suffer a brutal conquest in 1621 at the hands of the newly arrived Dutch, who sought to monopolize the spice trade in the East. These islands thereafter became a rigidly regulated Dutch horticultural preserve.

One hundred and sixty kms (100 miles) north of Banda, and 480 kms (300 miles) south of Ternate and Tidore, the Portuguese also visited the great island of Ceram (or Seram), and its tiny but much more celebrated neighbour, Ambon. These islands then produced few if any spices, and until late in the 16th Century were of no special interest to Westerners other than a few Portuguese and Spanish missionaries (among them St. Francis Xavier). But in

1574, their posts in Ternate and Tidore having become precarious, the Portuguese built a new fortress on the splendidly spacious and well-sheltered Ambon Bay, at the site of the as yet to be built Ambon City, and made it their regional headquarters. In 1605 the Dutch expelled the Portuguese, began planting extensive clove orchards on the island, and expanded the settlement, so that thereafter it became the linchpin for Dutch control over the eastern islands.

Other of the Moluccan islands played more minor roles in regional history. Halmahera (then known as Gilolo) remained the great Ternate-Tidore hinterland. But since it produced only minor quantities of inferior spices and few other marketable commodities, even the methodical Dutch

various of the long-forgotten spice islands again made international news when they were first overrun by the Japanese (in 1942) and then retaken by the Allies (in 1945). And just after the transformation of the Dutch East Indies into the Republic of Indonesia, many of the Moluccans paradoxically looked to the Dutch to support them against their new nationalist liberators. There are now, as a result, some 40,000 self-exiled Moluccans residing in the Netherlands, a majority of whom were born in Holland and have never seen their homeland. A few cling romantically to the dream of an independent Moluccan republic, and sporadically command world attention through public acts of defiance, such as the simultaneous seizure of an Indonesian Con-

never made the effort to impose very effective controls. Ceram was the preserve primarily of the fierce Alfuru headhunters, against whom the Dutch launched occasional forays. The big island of Buru, just west of Ambon, produced eucalyptus oil; and the Aru and Kai islands beyond Banda yielded pearls and trepang. But once the region was pacified by the Dutch, none of these islands received very serious attention. It was only within the very recent past that Maluku's important deposits of minerals (notably petroleum), extensive stands of timber, and fabulously wealthy fishing grounds have begun to attract national and international interest.

During World War Two, the names of

sulate and a Dutch commuter train in 1977.

Despite their illustrious past, today the 999 islands of Maluku constitute one of the most remote and least known of Indonesia's 27 provinces. They are scattered over an area larger than the island of Borneo, yet together they make up only 87,000 sq kms (33,200 sq miles) of territory—about two-thirds the area of Java. The two largest islands (Halmahera and Ceram) each measures over 17,000 sq kms (6,500 sq miles), about three times the size of Bali, but sever-

Above, women of Ambon performing a welcome dance. Right, a welcome of a different, yet no less endearing, kind is provided by the gentlemen of this conch orchestra from Ambon.

al hundred others are no more than tiny atolls, inaccessible and sparsely inhabited because of the area's deep seas, coral reefs, mangrove swamps and dense jungles.

Maluku is subdivided administratively into three units. North Maluku includes the five original clove islands, together with octopus-shaped Halmahera, the Bacan archipelago (noted for its cocoa production), and the lush timber-producing islands of the Obi and Sula archipelagoes that extend westward toward Sulawesi.

Central Maluku consists of the large and primitively beautiful islands of Buru and Ceram, Ambon Island (site of the provincial capital, Ambon City), and the volcanic nutmeg-producing Banda group to the south.

made between the Muslim and Christian majorities who inhabit the old coastal spice-trading towns (now roughly equal in numbers), and the numerous minority tribes who populate the more remote areas. The island of Halmahera alone, for example, is home to more than 30 tribes speaking almost as many distinct languages. There are, furthermore, many groups of peripatetic "sea gypsies" (*orang laut*) who live on boats and roam the shores of the archipelago.

The northern and central islands are wet, green and often volcanic—covered by dense jungles housing a rich variety of tropical flora and fauna, including many exotic marsupial mammals, orchids, butterflies and plumage birds. These islands still produce large quantities of spices.

Southeast Maluku (not included here) is a long chain of smaller and even more infrequently visited islands stretching from the tip of Timor to the underside of New Guinea—from Wetar in the west to the Aru archipelago in the east.

Maluku now has a total of about 1.5 million inhabitants, who belong to a great number of different tribal and linguistic subgroups (no one is quite sure how to accurately identify and classify them all). Physically they fall somewhere in between the light-skinned, straight-haired "Mongoloid" peoples of western Indonesia and the dark-skinned, frizzy-haired "Australoids" of New Guinea.

Culturally, a rough distinction may be

Maluku's fishing grounds are among the richest in the world, with an abundance of shrimp, tuna and crabs (seafood lovers take note!).

Though the climate, the sandy beaches, the many historical sites, the spectacular marine life and the relaxed and friendly populace create an ideal setting for foreign holiday-seekers, tourism is still in its infancy here. Part of the reason for this is that Maluku is still little known and rather far (and therefore expensive to reach) from the well-worn Java-to-Bali tourist track. But who knows, with such a long history of foreign involvement, the "spice islands" may be destined to be discovered once again by the outside world.

AMBON AND CENTRAL MALUKU

The centre for government, commerce and communications in the far-flung island province of Maluku is **Ambon**, a tiny tropical idyll that has seen Muslim, Portuguese and Dutch rule, and is today heavily populated and predominantly Christian. Known locally as Nusa Yapoona or "dew island" because of frequent evening fog cover, Ambon Island is composed of two parallel peninsulas, Leihitu and Leitimor, joined at the end by a narrow isthmus. (*See* Ambon Island map in "Guide in Brief.")

Sights of Ambon City

Kota Ambon or Ambon City, the bustling provincial capital (pop. 220,000), lies on the southern or Leitimor side of the bay and was founded here by the Portuguese in 1574. Once a delightful town with many tall trees shading its sloping cobblestone streets, Kota Ambon was heavily bombed in

1945. It has since recovered, but has suffered the concrete-box fate of other expanding Indonesian towns. Nonetheless, the city possesses remnants of its former charm and even now the pace of life here is still markedly slower than on urban Java.

Fort Victoria at the town's centre is the most visible reminder of Ambon's colonial past, an old Dutch fortification raised on Portuguese foundations. Because it is now a military installation, a pass must be obtained at the local tourist office to gain entrance. In the town square facing the fort stands a statue of Kapitan Pattimura, the leader of an 1817 rebellion against the Dutch. Another statue, of Martha Tiahahu (a "freedom fighter" in Pattimura's army), stands in front of the provincial parliament building overlooking Ambon Bay.

Other colonial-era monuments on Jl. Batu Gajah, include: the former Dutch governor's mansion; the former residence of Javanese Prince Dipanegara (exiled here for a time); and the mausoleum of Sunan Pakubuwana VI of Surakarta (the Central Javanese ruler), who died here in exile in 1849.

More interesting than these, perhaps,

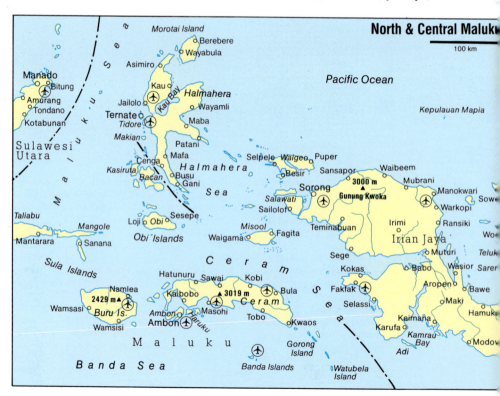

North & Central Maluku

100 km

Pacific Ocean

is the **Museum Siwalima** which stands up on a hill on the eastern edge of town (in the suburb of Karang Panjang), and contains an extensive collection of traditional tribal artifacts, mainly from the Kai and Tanimbar islands: carved canoe bowsprits, ancestor figures, magic and sacrificial objects, talismanic skulls, Chinese ceramics and other treasures. It is best to make an appointment to see it at the Ministry of Education (PDK) offices on Jl. Ahmad Yani.

Touring the Island

A picturesque road skirts the bayshore to the west of Ambon City and passes through a string of old villages (**Amahusu**, **Eri** and **Latuhalat**), whose clove orchards, churches and Portuguese family names are all legacies of the 16th and 17th centuries. There are some fine beaches near the southern tip of the peninsula, and the reef-protected cove at **Namanlatu**, once an excursion spot for Ambon's rajas, is a perfect place for snorkeling.

Another road leaves Ambon City in a southeasterly direction and climbs steeply up toward the interesting old village of **Soya**, where a Dutch church (built in 1817) and a residence of the former raja may be seen. Soya rests on Mt. Sirimahu, famous for its prehistoric megaliths, and above the village near the peak stands a stone table known as the "ancestor's throne."

Lower down the slopes, by Soya, are many huge boulders and a square marked off by stones, said to be an old assembly hall (*baileu*). An adjacent flight of stone steps is used by local shamans to communicate with the ancestors buried in nearby graves, and a festival is held on the second Friday of each December to ritually cleanse the church and the *baileu*.

The narrow lane leading up beyond Soya forks into a number of other footpaths (locally known as the "Roads of Golgotha") that lead to the villages of **Ema**, **Kilang**, **Naku** and **Hatalai** on the southern slopes of Mt. Sirimahu. Each has its own ancient and sacred megalith. The physical strains of the climb are rewarded by breathtaking views of the island. These tidy, friendly villages have remained almost unchanged since St. Francis Xavier first converted them to Catholicism in the mid-16th Century.

he harbour at
mbon.

Caves near **Kusukusu Sereh** are full of megaliths, further evidence of the area's antiquity.

A short distance northeast of Ambon City, on the road to Passo, lies the Muslim village of **Batumerah**, famous for its shell crafts and its old mosque. Factories are also now springing up along the harbour's edge here, bringing jobs and change to these once-sleepy hamlets. The Heroes Cemetery and the Allied Forces Cemetery lie next to one another just to the east of Batumerah.

The town of **Galala**, located at the neck where Ambon's outer bay slips into the inner bay, is the terminus for a ferry crossing to **Pokka** on the Leihitu side, home of Pattimura University. Students prefer to use small dugout canoes with multi-coloured sails rather than the costlier ferry. Galala is known for its smoked tunafish, sold here from bamboo racks. Ambonese returning to Jakarta always stop here on the way to the airport to stock up on this local delicacy.

All roads meet at **Passo** and **Baguala**, located on opposite sides of the narrow isthmus joining Ambon's two halves. **Natsepa Beach**, located just to the east of Baguala, is an excellent spot for picnicking and swimming. Farther to the east, across the Leihitu plateau, lies **Tulehu**, a busy Muslim port town— gateway to the neighbouring islands of "The Lease" and Ceram (*See* below).

To the north of Tulehu along the coast, **Waai** (which means "water" in the local language), is a prosperous Christian village known for its sacred white eels, who inhabit a large pond. Beyond Waai, at the easternmost tip of the island, boats can be hired to cross to **Pombo** ("Pigeon") **Island**, a nature reserve surrounded by spectacular coral gardens. A visit pass should be obtained first, however, from the Oceanographic Institute at Pokka.

The Leihitu peninsula takes its name from the historic village of **Hitu**, reached by travelling west from Passo and then crossing to the island's north shore.

On the coast to the east of Hitu lies **Mamala**, where every year, a week after Ramadan (the end of the Muslim fasting month), villagers stage the traditional *baku pukul sapu*. In this ritual warfare, combatants strike their foes with long coconut-fibre whips to the accompaniment of gongs. A shaman treats their open wounds periodically with special ointment, and that evening the entire village joins in a communal feast.

Northeast of Mamala, beyond Morela, a footpath stumbles into the hills along a precipitous ravine past caves with mysterious rock formations to an old stone fortress known as **Kapahaha**. Stone steps give access to the fortress, protected on three sides by a sheer drop, and within are a spring and the graves of the last Leihitu defenders. The fortress was overrun by the Dutch in 1646.

To the west of Hitu, an easy road leads to the twin villages of **Hila** (Muslim) and **Kaitetu** (Christian). The island's oldest mosque (built in 1646) is in Hila. At Kaitetu, a 16th Century Portuguese fort (now known as **Fort Amsterdam**) stands crumbling and overgrown. Old cannon are planted among the flower gardens of a neighbouring school. The town's Dutch church dates from 1780.

Visits to Neighbouring Islands

The three small islands scattered to the east of Ambon, **Haruku**, **Saparua** and **Nusalaut**, are collectively known as "The Lease." Many coastal villages on these islands are five centuries old, and were important spice-trading centres. Consequently, they are littered with old Dutch fortifications. Recently restored **Fort Duurstede** in the town of Saparua is famous because it came under attack from Pattimura's army.

The large and mountainous island of **Ceram**, with peaks reaching to 3,000 metres (nearly 10,000 feet), is dotted with villages and old fortifications, but has few major towns and even fewer roads. It is regarded as the homeland of the Hituese aristocracy, though the interior of the island has still not been fully explored and primitive native tribes like the Nalulu and the Alfuru were headhunters until quite recently.

The sizeable island of **Buru** to the west is similarly unknown, surrounded by reefs and swamps, densely forested and inhabited by huge insects and fiercely independent tribesmen. Today logging is the principal industry, and since 1969 Buru has served as a government "rehabilitation centre." Special permission from the military authorities in Ambon is thus needed to visit the island.

BANDA: THE NUTMEG ISLANDS

The diminutive size and tiny population of the volcanic Banda group of islands strewn in the middle of the ocean, 160 kms (100 miles) southeast of Ambon, belie their importance through many centuries of world history. From very early times up until the late 18th Century, they were the world's principal source of valuable nutmeg and mace—the kernel and pit-covering of a fruit that is endemic to this region.

It seems that Hindu-Javanese traders were responsible for introducing these two spices to international markets, and they first reached Europe about the 6th Century A.D., where they became increasingly popular. Thus when the Portuguese arrived in the East a millennium later, they made a beeline for the Bandas, and thereafter the islands became the object of a good deal of unfriendly competition between rival trading nations, until finally the Dutch sent in a large fleet and ruthlessly secured control of them in 1621. Eventually, nutmeg seedlings were smuggled out by the French and the English, and after about 1800, their nutmeg exports reduced to a trickle, the tiny Bandas faded into obscurity.

The Banda Sea is deep and incredibly blue. Indeed, all colours seem to be accentuated here and there is a certain surreality to these islands, as if you have suddenly been transported to the coast of southern Italy.

The main island, **Banda Neira**, simply oozes history. The principal town (of the same name) rises dramatically up a slope from the water's edge and faces out across a narrow strait to **Gunung Api Island**. The large mansions of the *perkeniers* (Dutch estate managers) and wealthy Arab and Chinese traders, many of them two or three centuries old, have been well preserved. An old Dutch Reform church stands in the centre of town, its weathered tombstones recounting the 350 years of Dutch presence on the island.

Two old Dutch forts are located here—**Fort Belgica** (above the town) and **Fort Nassau** (below it next to the church). Walk up to Belgica for a superb view.

The town's Mediterranean-style stone houses were purposefully built low to the ground because of frequent earthquakes. Several of them were once occupied by Indonesian nationalists like Mohammad Hatta (first vice-president of the Republic), who spent many years in exile here during the 1930s. The Baadillah family, descendants of Arab sea captains, have converted their home into a small museum containing a variety of interesting heirlooms.

Boats may easily be hired for visits to neighbouring islands. The smoking 650-metre (2,000-foot) peak of **Gunung Api Island** can be climbed in a few hours, yielding a panoramic view of the entire Banda chain. The strait in between these two islands is like a large crater lake, site of some of the world's most beautiful coral gardens. And the larger island of **Lonthor** just behind Banda Neira is covered in nutmeg orchards and crowned by an old hilltop sanctuary known as **Fort Hollandia**.

Nutmeg trees on Banda.

TERNATE AND TIDORE: THE CLOVE ISLANDS

Though little known today, the tiny twin islands of Ternate and Tidore, two perfectly shaped volcanic cones measuring less than 10 kms (six miles) in diameter, but each rising to a height of about 1,700 metres (5,600 feet) above sea level, were for centuries the most important parcels of real estate in eastern Indonesia. Like the Banda islands, they achieved early prominence as the source of a rare and highly prized spice, in this case cloves.

Moluccan cloves, known locally by the Chinese-derived term *cengkeh*, were an ingredient in the ancient Egyptian embalming process and were employed more than 2,000 years ago as breath-sweeteners by Chinese courtiers. They were produced for many millennia in a limited area of western Halmahera and the adjacent islands, but after the 13th Century the trade in this exceedingly valuable spice (the dried flower bud of a tree) centred on Ternate and Tidore, two powerful rival kingdoms

who later converted to Islam.

The Portuguese arrived, or rather were escorted to, Ternate from Hitu (Ambon) aboard royal *kora-koras* (large native vessels rowed by upwards of 100 men) in 1512 and promptly declared an "alliance" with the Ternatean king. Several years later, in 1521, the Magellan expedition landed at Tidore via the Pacific, thus touching off a fierce and bloody foreign rivalry.

For a time, at the end of the 16th Century, the Ternateans under Sultans Baabullah and Said managed to reassert their authority, expelling the Portuguese from their island (in 1574) and sending substantial *kora-kora* fleets as far afield as Cebu and Flores to negotiate alliances and demand tribute. But in 1606 a huge Spanish force arrived from Manila and conquered both islands.

Presently, the Dutch and the English also became involved in the struggle. The Dutch eventually prevailed; their legacy is today apparent

The towering peaks of Ternate and Tidore stand in a row of 10 similarly shaped volcanoes that form a line up and down the west coast of Halmahera like so many chimneys. The area's only

An engraving showing the King of Tidore putting on a show for visiting traders

airstrip and main harbour are on Ternate; the arrival, whether by air or sea, is a dramatic one.

Crumbling Fortresses

The main town of **Ternate**, located on the southeastern side of the island facing Tidore, is a small port and growing commercial centre. It has grown up around **Benteng Oranye**, a fortified trading post built here by the Dutch in 1606-7.

The 19th Century **Kedaton** located up above the town, with a majestic view over the straits, was designed by an English architect and resembles more a colonial villa than a sultan's palace. The last sultan passed away in 1974 and has not been replaced—the palace is now a museum housing artifacts, dating back some four centuries, including old weapons and armour, porcelains and books. The jewelled Crown of Ternate, made of human hair and said to be seven centuries old, is exhibited on special request.

A circuit of the island is easily accomplished in a day, with numerous stops at forsaken fortresses, sparkling beaches

Women picking cloves.

and other points of interest. Just south of Ternate town, an English bulwark known as **Kayu Merah** lies mouldering by the seaside. Farther along is a subterranean fortress, **Kota Janji**, where Ternatean Sultan Hairun was murdered by the Portuguese in 1570.

A short drive out of Ternate, past Laguna (a spring-fed lake covered with lotuses), the road turns up the mountain to **Foramadiaha**, site of the original Ternatean court. Only the palace foundations and tombs of the great sultans remain. Down by the shore and to the west on the main road lies **Kastela**, formerly the principal Portuguese-Spanish fortress on the island, now an overgrown ruin.

At nearby **Akerica**, a sacred spring, the Portuguese and Dutch reported finding the oldest clove tree in Maluku. From here the road weaves past pebbled beaches and along the steep western cliffs to the village of **Aftador**, scene of a Japanese atrocity during World War Two.

Ternate's northernmost point is **Sulamedeha**, where boats leave for Hiri Island. At nearby **Batu Angus** (Burnt Rock), a lava trail traces a black line from the mountain to the sea. The still-active volcano last erupted in 1983. The northeastern coast, down to **Dufa-Dufa**, is a long stretch of white sand and coral reefs, beckoning beachcombers and divers. Between Dufa-Dufa and Ternate town stands the well-preserved fort of **Toloku**, with a four-centuries-old Portuguese seal still legible on its walls.

The 20-minute boat ride from Ternate to **Tidore** is spectacular, and brings with it quite a change of atmosphere as the Tidoreans seem markedly more relaxed than their cousins on Ternate. Private taxis take visitors from the old port of **Rum**, known for its Portuguese fort and Sunday market, around to the eastern shore.

Soa-Siu, Tidore's principal town, has the feel of a Mediterranean fishing village. Built up against the slopes of cloud-wreathed Mt. Tidore, its houses are white washed with gates formed in the shape of gabled Iberian archways, a legacy of Spanish times. The old sultan's palace, now in ruins, and the restored mosque stand above the town. There are two crumbling Spanish fortresses, one by the sea and one high on a cliff, with a lovely vista across to sparsely inhabited Halmahera.

IRIAN JAYA: THE LAST FRONTIER

Irian Jaya, the Indonesian or western half of the immense island of New Guinea, undoubtedly ranks as the most isolated and primitive region on earth today. Impenetrable mangrove swamps seal much of the island's extensive coastline while dense jungles and rugged peaks, some of them snow-capped and towering above 5,000 metres (16,400 feet), dominate and subdivide the interior. Roads are almost non-existent; air and sea connections are few and far between, and most villages in the interior can be reached only by walking up and down

treacherous paths, sometimes for weeks. Partly as a result of this extraordinary fragmentation, the province is home to a wildly diverse assortment of peoples and cultures. More than 100 mutually unintelligible languages are spoken in Irian by scores of distinct and colourful tribes, many of whom are barely emerging from the Stone Age.

Not counting Australia, New Guinea is the world's second largest island (after Greenland), with a land area of 785,000 sq kms (303,000 sq miles). The eastern half, formerly a British and German colony and then an Australian protectorate, has since 1975 become an independent nation of 3 million people, called Papua New Guinea. The western half of the island, formerly Dutch New Guinea, was ceded to Indonesia in 1963 following a brief but boisterous military campaign undertaken by President Sukarno, thus expanding the territory of his young nation by some 25 per cent.

A remarkable flora and fauna thrive on the island. Epyphitic ferns, orchids and climbing lianas intertwine beneath the towering canopy of the lowland *dipterocarp* rainforests. About 700 species of birds have been identified, including the huge flightless cassowary and the fabled Bird of Paradise (*Paradisea apoda*), whose brilliant golden plumes have made it much sought after by hunters and collectors for centuries. Marsupial mammals such as the tree kangaroo, the wallaby and the flying phalanger inhabit the forests and grasslands. A variety of fierce reptiles, including the crocodile and the "death" adder, are much feared by natives.

Papuans and Austronesians

The native inhabitants of Irian Jaya number just over 1 million and are generally divided, on linguistic grounds, into two distinct subgroups: the coastal Austronesians and the highland Papuans. The two groups are similar in appearance—dark skinned, woolly haired and heavily bearded, with facial features similar to the Australian aboriginals, to whom they are closely related. It is believed that these peoples (known typologically as *Australoids*) have inhabited this region for more than 40,000 years, and that before the immigration of *Mongoloid* peoples several thousand years ago, they inhabited much of Southeast Asia.

The Austronesian settlements, composed of peoples who speak languages related to other Indonesian and Polynesian tongues, are found along the north and western coasts—in the vicinity of Jayapura (the provincial capital, located in the northeastern corner of Irian Jaya), along the top of the Vogelkop ("Bird's Head") peninsula near Manokwari, and on the neighbouring islands of Biak and the Schouten archipelago. These peoples have long been in contact with the outside world and they are skilled agricultur-

Preceding pages, the shields of these Asmat tribesmen are prized by connoisseurs of "primitive art." Left, the bow and arrow is still both a tool and weapon. Right, many tribes live in the swampy southern river basins of the island.

ists and fishermen, as well as traders.

Today the Papuans, who speak tongues belonging to a unique language family found only on New Guinea, Australia and a few neighbouring islands, live in small communities scattered throughout the highlands and in the swampy southern river basins of the island. They are kept apart from one another not only by the difficult terrain and the limited productivity of the land, but also by a long tradition of inter-tribal warfare, headhunting and cannibalism. The result is a degree of linguistic and cultural diversity

graphic shields, masks, ancestor totems and carved war canoes.

The highland Dani people of the Great Baliem Valley, by contrast, are adept cultivators who have probably been terracing and irrigating their well-manicured fields and raising domesticated pigs for centuries. And they in turn are quite distinct from numerous neighbouring tribes who are still primarily hunters and gatherers, or who rely on a trade in arrowheads, cowry shells, animal skins, pigs teeth or Bird of Paradise feathers.

unheard of in other areas of the world. Each village averages only a few hundred inhabitants, yet several villages will together often constitute a separate people, with their own distinct language and customs.

The material culture practised by these tribes depends very much on their environment. For example, the Asmat people of the southern coast live in wooden houses raised on stilts over the mangrove swamps and lack even stone out of which to fashion tools. They traditionally obtained ready-made stone adzes and choppers from traders in exchange for dried fish and forest products. The Asmat staple is sago, which grows abundantly in this area; the people are skilled woodcarvers known for their strikingly

Change is coming to the highlands, largely in the form of Indonesian-government and foreign-missionary presence. Though the construction of roads is in most cases out of the question due to the distances involved and the rugged terrain, the government has managed to construct several thousand primary schools and village medical stations, supplying them by air through a network of tiny airstrips and frequent commercial flights. Missionaries are just as influential, operating numerous Dutch- and American-staffed schools and clinics serviced by a private fleet of Cessnas. Together these have brought literacy and greater life expectancy to many villages, but many others remain largely untouched by the modern world.

JAYAPURA AND THE COAST

While large numbers of Irianese continue to stubbornly resist the transition into the Metal Age, much less the 20th Century, rapid changes are afoot throughout much of the province. Progress has been particularly dramatic along the coasts, where valuable mineral deposits, vast reserves of timber and rich fishing grounds are increasingly being exploited by multinational and Indonesian concerns. New harbours and airfields are springing up along the island's perimeter to make these resources more accessible, and a steady stream of labourers and transmigrants is arriving from Indonesia and elsewhere.

Boom Towns

Oil was discovered at the western tip of New Guinea 50 years ago by the Dutch and the port of **Sorong** has boomed from a settlement of just a few thousand two decades ago to a small city of over 40,000 today, with its atten-

dant hotels, bars and expatriate workers. From Sorong, the **Raja Empat Islands Nature Reserve** can be reached by boat. Each isle in this group, most notably Waigeo, has its own endemic species of birds and small marsupials, and this is the best place to see the fabulous Bird of Paradise in its natural habitat.

The area around **Manokwari**, a town nestled on top of the "Bird's Head" peninsula, has for several centuries been settled by a mixture of Irianese, Chinese, Filipinos, Buginese and Moluccans, and is today predominantly Christian. Manokwari is now an oil town too, and the site of a growing sawmill industry.

The growing town of **Biak** located on a crowded island of the same name, 200 kms (125 miles) from Irian's north coast, is prospering today as a supply centre for offshore drilling operations in nearby waters, and as the base for an international tuna fishing industry. There is a fascinating market here, a large Indonesian naval base, and some ruggedly beautiful villages, landscapes and beaches. A dirt track leads from the town to the island's north shore, where

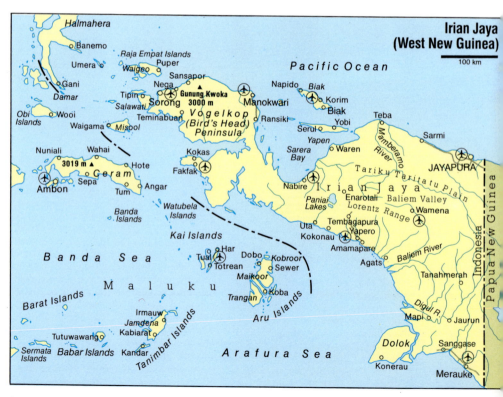

Irian Jaya (West New Guinea)

the **North Biak Nature Reserve** harbours many beautiful parrots and cockatoos. Adjacent **Superiori Island**, several hours away by boat, has an even larger reserve, and incidentally, Biak is the centre for the illegal trade in rare Irianese plumage birds.

And the town of **Amamapare** on the south central coast, though still small, has prospered because of the discovery and development of a massive copper deposit in the neighbouring Sudirman (Carstenz) Mountains. The Freeport Copper Company has poured millions of dollars into the area, building a deepwater port, an airstrip and a spectacular 112-km (70-mile) highway leading from the coast up to the new copper town of **Tembagapura**, perched 3,700 metres (12,136 feet) up snow-capped Mt. Jaya, Irian's highest peak.

Not all urban development is related to mining, fishing and forestry, however. **Jayapura**, Irian's capital and largest city, with over 50,000 inhabitants, was originally founded here by the Dutch to lay political claim to New Guinea's beautiful north-central shore. It now exists primarily as an administrative centre, with thousands of government employees and a provincial university. Like the towns of Manokwari, Biak and Merauke, Jayapura is also developing an extensive agricultural hinterland with a population that is steadily growing due to the government's resettlement of thousands of Javanese and Balinese peasants.

The hills around Jayapura form a dramatic amphitheatre, with excellent views out over the town to the sea. General MacArthur's Pacific headquarters were located here during 1944 and 1945; today the old Base G is known as "Bestiji" and MacArthur's former command post forms part of a fish farm. **Yotefa Nature Reserve**, east of Jayapura along Yos Sudarso (Humboldt) Bay, contains many beautiful beaches, rare birds and butterflies, and the wreckages of several World-War-Two ships. Boats may be chartered from **Hamadi**, five kms (3.2 miles) to the east of Jayapura, out to Holteken beach and beyond. The Sepik people who live along these shores are known for their primitive bark paintings and their carved ancestor figures.

To the west of Jayapura, along the shores of **Lake Sentani** (where the airport is located), live a people who are accomplished sculptors and potters. They dive in the lake to set fish traps for food; the chieftains' houses are elaborately ornamented with carved fish, birds, reptiles and human figures.

Striking woodcarvings and handicrafts: shields, spears, masks, baskets, boats and clothing, are produced by many Irianese tribes, and many are on display at the **Anthropological Museum** of Cendrawasih University in Abepura, between Sentani airport and Jayapura. The main attraction is a collection of distinctive red, white and black Asmat artifacts acquired through a grant from the John D. Rockefeller III Fund. Asmat figures and weapons are executed with a keen, dramatic sense of balance and beauty, and are prized by connoisseurs of "primitive art" around the world. Since 1969 the Indonesian government, in a UN-initiated project, has undertaken to train and support Asmat artisans, and though the Asmat live more than 800 kms (500 miles) away, on the south Irian coast around the town of **Agats**, a large selection of Asmat carvings is available in Jayapura, either from the Asmat Handicraft Project warehouse or from shops.

native of an Jaya earing a ombination of odern and rimitive garb.

Into The Central Highlands

It may seem paradoxical that the oldest inhabited regions in Irian Jaya are also the most inaccessible, but the reasons for this become clear as you fly from the hot, humid coast to the mountainous interior; tangled jungles and impenetrable mangrove swamps give way to forested foothills and jagged, cloud-wracked peaks. Then as your plane narrowly traverses a cleft in the mountains, the clouds part to reveal another world—a green valley, neatly cultivated, dotted with thatched huts, and watered by pebbly streams. When western explorers first stumbled upon these hidden highlands in the 1930s, it is no wonder that they thought they had discovered the lost paradise of Shangri-La.

The largest and most accessible now of these highland areas is the **Grand Baliem Valley** of central Irian Jaya—a mile-high, 72-km (45-mile) corridor formed by the Baliem River. It is inhabited by about 100,000 primitive Dani tribesmen, who live in tiny settlements scattered evenly throughout the broad valley floor. The only way in and out is by air, unless you plan to walk for a month. Due to the active presence of the Indonesian government and missionary groups, there are regular scheduled flights from Jayapura to an airstrip by the village of Wamena.

Cannibals and Missionaries

Christian missionaries are extremely active in this area, though their efforts began on a rather inauspicious note, in 1933, when a number of pioneer Dutch clergymen were cannibalized by their erstwhile converts, for reportedly trying to deprive the natives of their valued skull trophies, ancestor fetishes and penis sheaths. There are about 25 Protestant and Catholic groups now in Irian Jaya and most rightly take a more tolerant view of traditional Irianese beliefs and practices. They operate schools, churches and clinics, and a private air service that is the most extensive on the island. Reports of confrontations between zealous missionaries (mostly southern American Protestants) and

Huts in the Baliem valley—the most accessible c the highland areas.

276

hostile tribespeople persist, however, and violence is not unknown—four Dutch families were killed and eaten southeast of the Baliem Valley on Christmas Day, 1974.

There is little danger of being eaten in the Baliem Valley today, however, even if some still remember it as the infamous Cannibal Valley described in a number of books and films that appeared during the 1950s and early 60s. The Dani people who live here then still engaged in regular warfare and cannibalism. Groups allied by marriage and kinship maintained a constant state of hostilities with one or more neighbouring alliances, building high watchtowers and going on periodic forays into enemy territory to kill unsuspecting victims. The government has now succeeded in stamping them out.

The Dani are slash-and-burn agriculturalists who for centuries have farmed this between-16-and-32-km-wide (10 and 20 miles) valley, and now raise pigs, sweet potatoes, ginger, cucumbers, sugar cane and bananas in checkerboard gardens surrounded by neat stone fences. They live in domed-roof huts clustered within womb-like compounds,

and their intricately constructed dwellings, elaborate suspension bridges and extensive irrigation ditches display a high-degree of engineering skill.

Even when temperatures are cool, and at this altitude they can drop to as low as 5C (40F), the Dani wear virtually no clothing. Girls wear reed skirts, married women wrap themselves with a braided cord, and men sport only long tubular penis sheaths made of dried yellow gourds. Armbands and throat patches fashioned from pigs' scrotums, barkcloth or matted spider webs, ward off evil spirits.

Villages throughout the valley are connected with Wamena by footpaths and an increasing number of crude vehicular tracks. Be sure to bring along warm clothing, sturdy shoes and a rucksack. Porters and guides may be hired through hotels in Wamena, and can also arrange local feasts or dance rituals.

Many interesting day hikes can be made using Wamena as a base. Just south of the airstrip, a rickety suspension bridge crosses the Baliem River. Without crossing, follow the river for several hours to the brine pool at **Hetigima** where the Dani extract salt by soaking banana-palm sheets, drying and then burning them. Farther south, the valley narrows to a deep gorge, with spectacular views, at **Kurima**.

Travelling north from Wamena, many visitors cross over the river and make the three-hour trek to **Akima**, where the chief's grandfather has been mummified and may be seen on payment of a small fee. It is several hours farther to **Ywika**, home of a renowned village chief and site of a Catholic mission offering comfortable lodgings. Farther north, but on the west side of the river, the village of **Woogi** is known for its wedding dances. About two hours beyond Woogi, a symmetrical hill, known here as the **Pyramid**, offers a panoramic view over the entire valley floor.

It is possible to continue north and west from here, literally hiking for weeks up and down wild mountain trails through the Bokodini Valley to **Illaga** and eventually to **Enrotali**, on the shores of enchanting Lake Paniai. These places can be more conveniently visited by air, however, through arrangement with the missionary air services. (*See* "Guide in Brief" for details of missionary air services.)

Dani men wearing penis sheaths fashioned from dried yellow gourds.

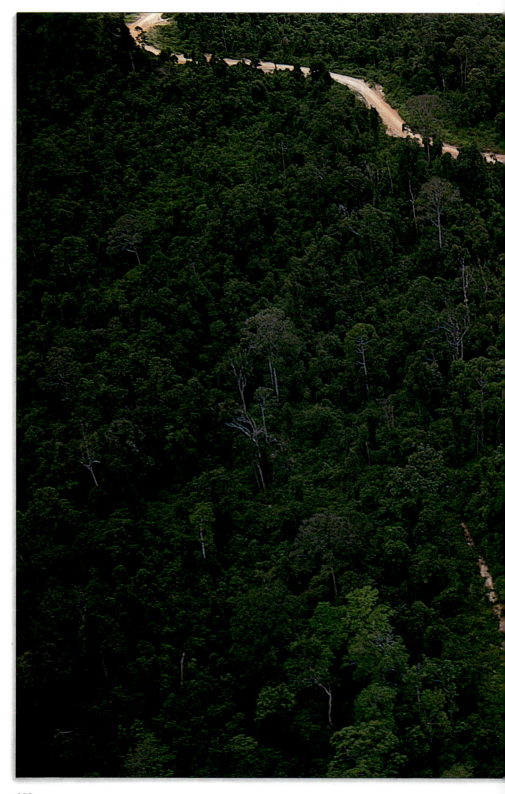

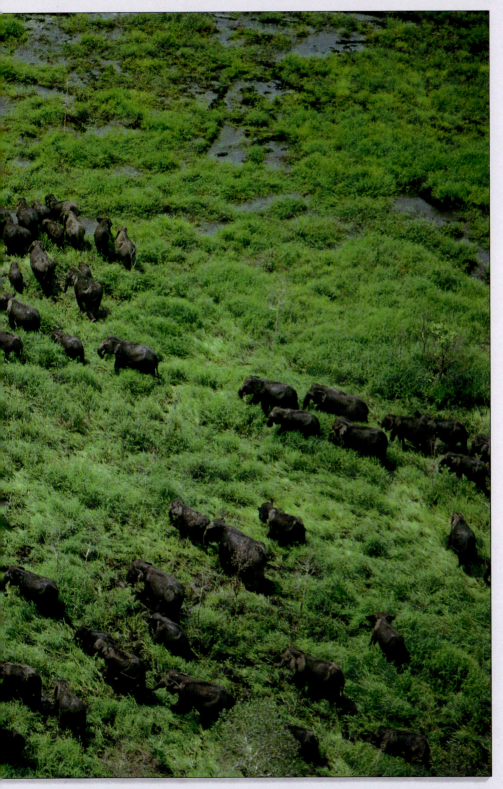

INDONESIA'S INCREDIBLE WILDLIFE

Though man's impact on his environment has been severe in the more heavily populated areas of Sumatra, Java, Bali and Nusa Tenggara, much of Indonesia remains in a pristine wilderness state. Highly conscious of the need to preserve this unique natural heritage, and of the necessity of maintaining good forest cover on hilly areas to prevent flooding and erosion, the Indonesian government has recently embarked upon a highly ambitious conservation programme.

Of particular interest to tourists is the very extensive system of National Parks, Nature Reserves and Protected Forests, now numbering over 300 distinct reserve areas comprising some 120,000 sq km (46,000 sq miles), roughly 6.5 per cent of the nation's total land area. Sixteen of these are National Parks, now being developed for recreational use, and many of the smaller Nature Reserves and Protected Forests are also accessible and well worth visiting.

The National Parks vary greatly in size, habitats, wildlife and visitor facilities. Some are quite remote and require weeks to visit, while others are extremely accessible. For example, the huge forested Mt. Leuser National Park in northern Sumatra, the home of tigers, elephants, orangutan and a long list of other mammals, is only a few hours from the city of Medan. And in the mountains, just two hours' drive south of Jakarta, one can visit botanic gardens established and laid out by the Dutch over a century ago, then climb up to the peak of Mt. Gede and its alpine meadows and edelweiss for a view over the entire western third of Java.

To visit the small Ujung Kulon National Park on the western tip of Java, however, takes a week. Ujung Kulon is the abode of the world's last herd of Javan rhinoceri and contains vestiges of the dense rainforest that once covered the entire island before man conquered and cultivated it.

For spectacular scenery, few places can match the primordial volcanic landscapes of Bromo-Tengger National Park in East Java—an overnight excursion from Surabaya or Bali. Here a lodge has been built on the lip of a massive caldera, literally suspended above the clouds, and as the sun rises over the famous "sand sea," there is the feeling of being at the "world's first morning."

For naturalists, however, the ultimate thrill is to make the two-week pilgrimage out to Komodo Island National Park located between Flores and Sumbawa, here to witness the legendary dragons of Komodo—latter-day relatives of the dinosaurs—in their arid, rocky natural habitat.

Several parks also have special marine areas with excellent snorkeling and scuba

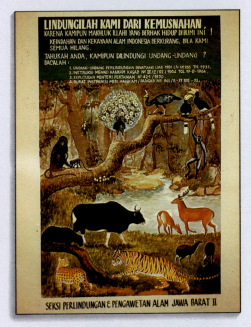

diving, where one can observe fabulous coral reef marine communities or swim with grim-faced whales.

Exotic Species

The plant life of Indonesia derives almost exclusively from the Asian mainland, and is abundant, exotic and incredibly diverse—consisting of almost 40,000 different species belonging to 3,000 different families: about 10 per cent of all plant species in the world are found here. Most of these are natives of the fantastically varied equatorial rainforest, with its thousands of varieties of wild orchids, palms, ferns, fruits, spice trees, and oddities such as the *Rafflesia*—the world's

Preceding pages, a "logging" road penetrates the forest; World Wildlife Fund "operation Ganesha," Sumatra. Left, orang utan, Mt. Leuser National Park. Right, conservation poster.

largest parasitic bloom. (*See* Part II, "The Mightiest Archipelago.") Many of these plants can be seen in the Botanic Gardens in Bogor and Cibodas, just south of Jakarta, but there is surely no substitute for a hike through a pristine tropical rainforest.

The animals of Indonesia are just as diverse, having come from two quite different sources at opposite ends of the archipelago. From the west came the Asian or Oriental mammalian fauna—apes, monkeys, civets, pigs, cats, tapirs and elephants. These species predominate on Sumatra, Java, Borneo and Bali—islands connected to the Asian mainland by a land bridge during the Ice Ages.

From the east came the pouched marsupial species and plumage birds so typical of less cassowary, the cockatoo, numerous parrots and the more than 40 species of birds of paradise found in Maluku and Irian. In addition, countless reptiles, amphibians and invertebrates populate the seas and coasts, including giant sea turtles that lay eggs on many Indonesian beaches and the huge, carnivorous monitor lizards that have survived for millions of years on the island of Komodo.

The boundaries of the Asian and Australasian faunal regions are far from clear—the islands of Sulawesi, Maluku and Nusa Tenggara lying between them are in fact transitional and therefore of great interest to zoologists. Here are found both Asian and Australasian species, as well as many endemic species found nowhere else in the world.

Australia. These are naturally found in Irian Jaya and the Aru Islands of the Sahul continental shelf, all of which were once connected to Australia.

Because of its legacy of animals from these two major zoo-geographical realms, Indonesia has a wealth of animal life not matched anywhere else in the world. More than 500 mammals are found here (Sumatra has the greatest variety), from the tigers, orangutans and elephants of Sumatra to the freshwater dolphins and proboscis monkeys of Kalimantan to the tree kangaroos and wallabies of Irian.

Fifteen hundred species of birds are known, many of them beautiful and rare Australasian plumage species, like the flight-

Today this area is known as Wallacea. in honour of the great 19th Century naturalist, Sir Alfred Russel Wallace, who was the first to recognize the break in faunal types that occurs to the east of Borneo and Bali.

Of all the islands of Wallacea, Sulawesi is, biologically, the most interesting. Most of the island's mammals, which include deer, pigs, civets, squirrels and tarsiers, are of obvious Asian origin, however the two types of cuscus found here are marsupial and typically Australasian.

Left, black-capped lory, (*Lorius lory lory*). Above, lesser bird of paradise, (*Paradisea minor*). Right, blue-throated bee eater, (*Merops viridis*).

But Sulawesi has many curious animals uniquely its own—including the *anoa* dwarf buffalo; the *babirusa*, a "deer" pig with curved tushes growing from the top of its snout; the giant palm civet; and the heavy-set black macaque, which despite its resemblance to a miniature gorilla, is actually a monkey—a close cousin of the pig-tailed macaques of neighbouring Borneo. Sulawesi has a rich avifauna, too, made up of both Asian and Australasian species: hornbills, drongos, kingfishers, babblers, sunbirds, cockatoos and the amazing *maleo* bird, which buries its eggs in warm sandy areas, leaving its young to hatch themselves, like reptiles.

Touring the Parks and Reserves

All Indonesian National Parks and Nature Reserves come under the jurisdiction of the Directorate-General of Forest Protection and Natural Conservation (known by its Indonesian initials—PHPA), based in Bogor. Though a few of the reserves, like Pangandaran in south-central Java, can be entered on payment of a small entrance fee, most require that you first obtain a permit from PHPA headquarters at Jl. Juanda 9 in Bogor, just to the left of the main gate of the Botanic Gardens (bring along your passport). There are also PHPA field offices in all 27 Indonesian provinces, where visitors must make travel arrangements and reservations to visit the parks.

Although the wildlife of Indonesia is spectacular, it is not always easy to observe. Good preparation and planning are essential. Many reserves have difficult access. and almost all involve walking, so good health and sensible shoes and clothing are a must. Horses are available in some reserves (e.g. Lore Lindu in Sulawesi and Bromo in East Java); others must be approached by air, by river or by sea. Plane or boat hire can be expensive—US$100 a day for a boat to Ujung Kulon on Java's westernmost tip is representative. Travel in small groups is recommended.

Accommodation facilities, if provided, are usually primitive and you must bring along bedding and provisions in many cases, as well as essentials like first aid kits, mosquito netting and repellant. It is also recommended that you take anti-malarial prophylactics and obtain all necessary vaccinations some weeks in advance of a trip into wilderness areas.

Local porters can be hired and park guards may often accompany visitors as guides. They should be tipped at a rate of US$3 to $5 per day, plus expenses. To avoid misunderstandings, it is always advisable to negotiate all fees clearly before setting out.

The National Parks: A Capsule Guide

The list below, though not comprehensive, covers *some* of Indonesia's finest reserves and parks. For additional information, apply for a copy of *Indonesia*, *National Parks & Nature Reserves* from the Directorate-General of Tourism, Jl. Kramat Raya 81, Jakarta.

Java

Ujung Kulon National Park at Java's western tip is Indonesia's premier reserve—the

nation's first National Park. You will have to be lucky to see one of the park's rare Javan rhinos, only about 60 of which remain, but there are many other fascinating animals including leopards, gibbons, long-tailed macaques, leaf-monkeys, crocodiles, muntjaks, mousedeer and herds of grazing wild oxen (*banteng*).

There are two accommodation facilities in the park: most visitors stay at the new guesthouses on Peucang Island, but it is worthwhile to stop over for a night or two at the older guesthouse on Handeleum Island to visit the Cigenter river just across the strait, a favourite rhino haunt. Bedding, furniture and cooking facilities are provided at both guesthouses, but you must bring your own food. Make reservations and arrangements at the PHPA office in Labuan, a port town on the west coast easily accessible from Jakarta or Bogor by bus or taxi.

Ujung Kulon is accessible by motorbike track from Labuan via Sumur to Taman Jaya, where the park headquarters is located (about a six-hour ride). From here it is a leisurely two-day hike to Kalejetan and Peucang Island via the south coast. Or, charter a boat from Labuan directly to Peucang or Handeleum, a 4 to 5 hour voyage each way. Boat charters run about US$100 per day.

While you are there, visit the famous volcanic island of Krakatau, 40 km (25 miles) northwest of Labuan in the middle of the Sunda Strait separating Java from Sumatra.

where leaf-monkeys and rare Javan gibbons are often spotted. The surrounding forest is rich in bird species—more than 245 have been recorded. To witness the spectacular sunrise, camp overnight at a hut in the saddle between Mt. Gede and Mt. Pangrango and climb the final stretch just before dawn. Excellent accommodations can be had in the Botanic Gardens and also at near Cipanas, a weekend mountain resort.

Bromo-Tengger National Park is a volcanic area of incredible scenic beauty, about four hours from Surabaya in East Java. It is usually approached from the northeast (turn south just west of Probolinggo) via a small road which leads to Ngadisari, three km (two miles) below the caldera's rim. There is a lodge and a restaurant, with guides and

(*See* Part III, "West Java.")

Cibodas/Mt. Gede-Pangrango National Park is a spectacular mountain reserve just two hours south of Jakarta along the main Bogor-Bandung road. (Take the marked turn-off to the right at Pacet, after Puncak Pass and just before Cipanas.)

The well laid-out Cibodas Botanic Gardens are an extension of the Bogor Gardens, specializing in sub-montane, montane and alpine species. From the garden climb to the summit of Mt. Gede (5 to 6 hours each way), passing through several interesting vegetation zones along the way, including alpine meadows and thickets of Javan edelweiss near the peak. About halfway up there is a side trail leading to the Cibeureum waterfall,

horses for hire at the top. Descend on horseback into the Tengger caldera and climb a flight of steps to the summit of Mt. Bromo to watch the sun rise over the sand sea, or simply watch the sunrise from the caldera's edge. Bring plenty of warm clothing.

Baluran National Park is located at the northeastern tip of Java, 32 km (20 miles) north of the Java-Bali ferry at Ketapang, four hours from Denpasar (including the ferry crossing) and two hours from Surabaya. Report first to the PHPA office in Banyuwangi (Jl. Jendral A. Yani 108), eight km (5 miles) south of the ferry. This reserve, with its monsoon forests, acacia bushes and open grasslands, dominated by the volcanic cone of Mt. Baluran, reminds one of Africa. There is a guesthouse and a lookout tower at Bekol, twelve km (7.5 miles) into the reserve from the main road (turn north at Wonorejo), with marvellous views over grazing lands where herds of *banteng*, feral buffalo and deer feed. Along the coast are nice beaches and mangroves where mudskippers can be seen.

Bali and Nusa Tenggara

Bali Barat National Park lies in the western part of Bali, accessible from the Gilimanuk-Singaraja north coast road, with temporary accommodations and a guard post at Terima Bay, 20 km (12.5 miles) east of the ferry terminal at Gilimanuk. This is

cess is still difficult, however, and almost two weeks are needed to visit the island. (*See* Part III, "Komodo.")

Sumatra

Mt. Leuser National Park contains some of Sumatra's most spectacular forest, centering around the Alas River valley on the western side of North Sumatra. The park harbours orangutans, Sumatran rhinos, gibbons, leaf-monkeys, macaques, elephants, tigers, and countless other animals, birds, butterflies and plants. For a day trip from Medan, visit the Bohorok Orangutan Rehabilitation Centre near Bukit Lawang (two hours from Medan via Binjai), where confiscated pet orangutan are encouraged to re-

the last refuge of the endangered Rothschild's starling and of wild oxen. The marine portion of the reserve around Terima Bay and neighbouring Menjangan Island has some spectacular reefs, particularly on Menjangan's north shore, and there are no strong currents to contend with. There is a shelter for divers on Menjangan Island's western tip and more facilities are planned.

Komodo National Park is the home of the famous Komodo monitor lizards and is now being developed as a tourist attraction. Ac-

Left, the Javan rhinocerous. Ujung Kulon is the abode of the last herd of this breed. Above, the Sumatran tiger, if sighted, can be the highlight of a trip to a National Park.

turn to the wild. Visitors are welcome twice a day at feeding times, but you must get a permit first from the PHPA office in Medan (J. Sisingamangaraja Km 5.5). This office can also help plan extended trips into other parts of the reserve

Way Kambas Reserve is located on Sumatra's southeast coast, just across the Sunda Strait from Java and only a few hours' journey from Jakarta. Though much of the original swamp forest has been felled and replaced by open grassland, this is the best place to see wild elephants and the reserve is packed with interesting animals—gibbons, tapir, leaf-monkeys, macaques, otters and many birds. Fly from Jakarta to Tanjung Karang or take the Merak-Bakauheni ferry, report to the PHPA office at Tanjung Karang, then drive via Sukadana right to the reserve guesthouse at Way Kanan. Hire canoes to explore the river; travel to the estuary of the Kambas River with its sand-spit and fishing village, or visit the swamps and mudflats at Wako where elephants graze and shorebirds feed.

Kalimantan

Mt. Palung Reserve in West Kalimantan is one of the best and most accessible reserves on this vast island. It offers a complete range of rainforest vegetation types including man-grove and swamp forests. It also offers a good chance to see orangutan, gibbons and the strange-looking, silver-and-red proboscis monkeys found only on this island. Check-in with the PHPA office in Pontianak and travel south along the coast by boat from Pontianak to Melanu Bay (a day's journey). Here charter a river barge for the four-hour journey up-river, to a point where you can walk up Mt. Palung (a ten-hour hike) for a closer look at the rainforest.

Tanjung Puting Reserve on the south coast of Kalimantan is a bit more remote but equally accessible. At the northern end of the reserve, on the banks of the scenic Sekunir River, lies Camp Leakey—a re-search station and orangutan rehabilitation centre with a guesthouse and a splendid network of forest trails. See orangutans, gibbons, macaques and crocodiles. Fly first to Pangkalanbun via Banjarmasin and check here with the PHPA office. From here travel by road 15 km (9.5 miles) to Kumai and by boat (about three hours) to Camp Leakey. Bring your own provisions and allow at least four days from Banjarmasin. (*See* Part III "Kalimantan" for trips up the Mahakam and other rivers to remote Dyak areas.)

Sulawesi

Tankoko-Batuangus-Dua Saudara Reserve in northeastern Sulawesi just a few hours from the city of Manado, is the most convenient place to see a cross-section of Sulawesi's most unique animal species. Here are found crested macaques, tarsiers, cus-cus, anoas and maleo birds, all in a geologi-cally interesting area of volcanic craters and hot springs. Make arrangements at the PHPA office in Manado and then travel by road to Bitung, a port town about one hour to the east. Hire a boat from Bitung up the coast to Batuputih village, 25 km (15 miles) away, on the reserve's northern fringe and stay at the nearby guest bungalow. Bring

your own food and spend several days walk-ing around the reserve.

Mt. Ambang Reserve is a picturesque re-gion of montane forests, crater lakes and sulphur fumeroles (hot mud pools) at an altitude of between 1,100 and 1,800 metres above sea level. There are many well-used paths among the forests, which are filled with lovely tree ferns, *Pigafetta* palms and flowering shrubs. Stay in the town of Kota-mobagu (two hours by bus from Manado) and make day-hikes to the beautiful crater lakes: Moaat, Alia and Payapaya, and through the surrounding coffee plantations.

Lore Lindu National Park is the largest reserve at 2,500 sq. km (970 sq. miles) in Sulawesi, located only a few hours south of Palu, the provincial capital of Central Sulawesi. Lore Lindu has it all: high, heavily forested mountains and a large highland lake (Lake Lindu) in the north; and gently-sloping open grasslands, home of the in-teresting Torajan peoples, in the southern valleys. See black macaques and many birds, perhaps also *anoa* (dwarf buffalo) and wild *babirusa* pigs.

Make arrangements at the PHPA office in Palu (Jl. S. Parman). Depending on whether you want to see the northern mountains or the southern valleys, travel to Sidaunta on the western side of the park or Wuasa on the eastern side, both about three hours by good roads from Palu. Bring along camping gear, provisions and hire porters/guides to camp at many excellent sites along the rivers of the area. At least a week is needed to explore the southern valleys of Besoa and Bada (where there are ancient megaliths and wa-ter cisterns), but it is possible to cross the park from Sidaunta to Wuasa via Lake Lin-du in two or three days.

Maluku and Irian Jaya

These two provinces contain many fine reserves, but have few roads or facilities. To reach them is therefore expensive and time-consuming. The really keen traveller who wants to visit Manusela Reserve on Seram, Aru Reserve or Banda Reserve should con-tact the PHPA office in Ambon (Jl. Kapa-tia). To visit the many vast and remote reserves on Irian Jaya, including the mountain-top glaciers and snowfields of the Lorentz Reserve at 5,000 metres (16,400 feet) above sea level, contact the PHPA office in Jayapura.

A celebrated oddity of Indonesia's equatorial rain-forest is the *Rafflesia*—the world's largest parasi-tic bloom.

Gamelan: The Sound of Moonlight

Gamelan music is comparable to only two things: moonlight and flowing water. It is pure and mysterious like moonlight and always changing like flowing water.

Since 1893, when Claude Debussy first heard a Javanese ensemble perform at the Paris International Exhibition, the haunting and hypnotic tones of the *gamelan* have fascinated the West. Although once ignorantly dismissed as primitive, or simply admired for its exoticism, this music has since been sensitively studied by scholars such as Jaap Kunst and Colin McPhee, and is now indisputably recognized as one of the world's most sophisticated musical arts. In Indonesia, of course, *gamelan* music has always been simply the sound of everything civilized—the music of art, religion and government.

Karawitan is the Indonesian term coined in the 1950s by Ki Sindusawarno, the first director of the music conservatory in Surakarta, to encompass the entire range of Javanese and Balinese performing arts that incorporate the use of *gamelan* music—from dance to drama to puppet shows to sung poetry. Though *gamelan* ensembles most commonly perform as an accompaniment to dance or theatre, the music is also enjoyed for its own sake, often in connection with royal or religious festivities. Today *gamelans* frequently perform for radio and television, as well as on national and other significant occasions. Cassette recordings have become readily available, so that the liquid tones of the instruments frequently accompany one down the back lanes of Javanese towns or while eating at village *warungs* in Bali. Yet despite the current ubiquity of the music, it very much retains its associations with festive and ritual events.

The term *gamelan* derives from *gamel*, an old Javanese word for handle or hammer, appropriately so since most of the instruments in the orchestra are percussive. The interlocking rhythmic and melodic patterns found in *gamelan* music are said by some to

originate in the rhythms of the *lesung*—stone or wooden mortars used for husking rice. Others ascribe these patterns to the rhythmic chanting of frogs in the ricefields after dusk, or the wonderful cacophony of roosters crowing at dawn.

No one knows exactly when the first *gamelan* orchestra came into being. Metallophones (bronze, brass or iron percussion instruments) date back to prehistoric times and the manufacture of bronze gongs and drums associated with the *Dong Son* bronze culture that is thought to have reached Indonesia in about the third Century B.C. Since then, large bronze gongs have formed the very heartbeat of this distinctive music, with a deep and penetrating sound that can be heard for miles on a quiet night.

Javanese *Gamelan*

In Java, *karawitan* and its related arts reached its height of refinement in the Islamic courts of the 18th and 19th centuries, despite the fact that renowned instrument sets supposedly date from the Majapahit era centuries earlier in East Java and that there are references to the instruments from the 10th Century A.D. The aristocratic refinement of the *gamelan* in Java has resulted in a

Preceding pages, *wayang kulit* (leather shadow-puppet performance accompanied by a *gamelan* orchestra). Left, and right, Royal *gamelan* at Surakarta.

music that is slow, stately and mystical in feeling, designed to be heard in the large audience hall of the aristocratic home and to convey a sense of stately, awesome power and emotional control.

Anywhere from five to 40 instruments make up a *gamelan* orchestra, and most of them are never played otherwise than as part of an ensemble. In fact the two instruments that do see regular solo use, the *rebab* (a two-stringed bowed lute probably of Middle-Eastern origin) and the *suling* (bamboo flute), are non-percussive and thought to have been a later addition, as was the introduction of vocal parts. In fact, solo playing occurs only in the context of folk music and not at the court.

The basic principle underlying all *gamelan*

trunk is the melody; and the branches, leaves and blossoms represent the delicate complexity of the ornamentation.

In Central Java, the main theme or *balungan* (skeleton) of a piece is played on the various *saron* (small to medium size metallophones with six or seven bronze keys lying over a wooden trough resonator), and on the *slentem* (metallophones with bamboo resonators). Faster variations on the *balungan* are played simultaneously on the elaborating instruments: the *bonang* (a set of small, horizontally suspended gongs), *gender* (similar to the *slentem*), *gambang* (a wooden xylophone), and *celempung* (a zither with metal strings). They, together with the *suling*, the *rebab* and the vocalists, create the complex, sensual sound that is unique to

music is that of stratification. It is essentially a technique of orchestration in which the density of notes played on each instrument is determined by its register—higher instruments play more notes than lower ones. In addition, instruments are grouped according to their function. Gongs, for example, maintain the basic structure of the music, while mid-register metallophones carry the theme and other instruments provide ornamentation. The *kendhang*, wooden drums with skins stretched over both ends, lead the orchestra by controlling the tempo of the piece. Many Indonesian musicians metaphorically compare the structure of *gamelan* music to a tree: the roots, sturdy and supportive, are the low registers; the

gamelan music.

Vocal parts in an ensemble became popular in Java only in the 19th Century, even though solo and choral singing has long been a feature of poetry recitations, folksongs and religious ceremonies. In an orchestra it is now common to have soloists as well as a chorus. These may be either female (*pesinden*) or male (*gerong*), although female singers seem to be more popular. It is important to note that the sound of voices is traditionally regarded merely as another element of

Above, the *gamelan* Kyahi Bermoro of Yogyakarta. Right, village *gamelan* in Bali. The *gamelan* orchestra has a focal role in village communities, performing in temple festivals.

294

ment in the overall texture of the orchestra and is not necessarily given prominence over the instrumental parts. Lyrics are only rarely understood, as they are normally composed in an archaic or literary language.

A common misconception of *gamelan* compositions is that they are improvised, perhaps because scores are rarely used. This is not true. Most compositions (*gendhing*) are as rigidly determined as they are lucidly performed. There are literally thousands of pieces, and every region has its favourites. Each *gendhing* has its own name and theme (*balungan*), usually corresponding to the specific *wayang* character, dance or ritual for which it is played. Special compositions were developed at the Javanese courts for every occasion, notably in the palaces of

Borneo and the Malay peninsula where it took on some Chinese characteristics, as it did in the Batavia (Jakarta) region.

Balinese *Gamelan*

Balinese *gamelan* exhibits overwhelming variety. Dozens of completely different types of ensembles exist, some of which are found all over the island, others of which are restricted to isolated areas. Given Bali's tiny size, it may seem peculiar that there should be such differentiation among districts that are virtually within walking distance of one another. But at least part of the answer lies in the topography of the island itself—Bali's many rivers and ravines subdivide the island into eight distinct regions, each of which has

Yogyakarta and Surakarta. A general distinction may be made between the metallophone-dominated "loud" style and the "soft" style of playing which emphasizes the vocals and the *rebab*. This distinction, however, is less known in the Sundanese areas of West Java, where singing, *rebab* playing and intricate drumming are almost always preferred to bronze instruments.

In addition to the regional styles of West, Central and East Java, we may distinguish the individual styles of the *pesisir* North Coastal regions: Cirebon, Semarang and Madura, which because they were cosmopolitan trading areas, absorbed a multitude of musical influences. Javanese *gamelan* music has also spread to the neighbouring shores of

developed a unique cultural persona over the centuries. In the 20th Century, the tendency is for greater eclecticism. Yet, the western Jembrana district retains its indigenous *jegog* ensemble (made up of giant bamboo tubes tuned to a unique four-tone scale), and the village of Renon, now a burgeoning administrative centre, still maintains the *gong bheri gamelan*, bossless gongs that resemble Chinese tamtams, used exclusively to accompany the rarely performed *baris cina* dance. These are just two examples, yet there are many other cases of musical traditions flourishing in unlikely places. With thousands upon thousands of *gamelans* active in Bali, exploring the musical scene can be a fascinating adventure.

One of the most frequently encountered ensembles in Bali is the *gamelan gong kebyar*. *Kebyar* refers to a particularly flashy style of music that originated in the north of the island around 1915, but the ensembles that play it have since expanded their repertoire to include other styles. In the *gong kebyar*, four different gongs mark the musical phrase. They are, in order of descending size: the *gong*, *kempur*, *kempli* and *kemong*. The melodic theme is carried by two pairs of large metallophones: the *jegogan* and *calung*. A ten-piece *gangsa* (high-pitched metallophones) section ornaments the theme, and the *reong* (Bali's version of the Javanese *bonang*) is played by four musicians who produce a rippling stream of visceral, syncopated figurations. A pair of

rehearsed by each player, have reached a zenith of complexity in Bali.

The Niceties of Tuning

The tuning of the instruments is highly complex—the idiosyncratic preferences of individual *gamelan* makers ensuring that no two sets of instruments sound quite alike. The basic schema is to have two independent tuning systems, called *slendro* and *pelog*. In the *slendro* scale, the octave is divided into five roughly equal parts, whereas in the *pelog* system, a mixture of large and small intervals is used. Javanese *pelog* commonly uses seven tones, while in Bali a five-note version is generally preferred. In Java, separate *slendro* and *pelog* sets are cast for each

kendhang drums leads the group, interlocking with each other to produce spectacular rhythms. The drummer of the lower pitched *kendhang* is generally also the leader, teacher, composer, and often choreographer for the ensemble. A set of shimmering cymbals (*cengceng*) and several bamboo flutes (*suling*) completes the orchestra.

Balinese musical performances are noted for their capriciousness, stridency, and rhythmic vitality—particularly in contrast to the slow and measured *gamelan* performances of Java. One of the chief differences is that most Balinese metallophones are struck with unpadded mallets, thus producing a much sharper tone. And the interlocking rhythms, all painstakingly memorized and

orchestra, both of which are readily accessible to the players during performances. Individual pieces are normally composed for one tuning or another. Balinese ensembles, however, never use both scales. The *kebyar* instruments, for example, are exclusively tuned to *pelog*, while the *gamelan gender wayang* (used to accompany shadow play performances) is always in *slendro*.

The unique tonality of each instrument set means that standard *pelog* and *slendro* scales do not exist. The variety of colours imparted

Above, *gamelan* instruments, referred to as early as the 10th Century, are made using time-honoured methods and craftsmanship. Right, a full *gamelan* orchestra.

to a piece by various orchestras help in part to produce stylistic differences. Balinese ensembles have the added complexity of "paired tuning" in which pairs of instruments are tuned slightly apart to produce pulsations that greatly enhance the timbre.

There are several systems of notation, yet professional musicians normally shun them. *Gamelan* musicians were traditionally trained without any reference to written scores, and by other musicians in their spare time. In the Central Javanese palaces, musicians began to receive special training for their courtly duties at the beginning of this century, but this was exceptional. Before this, and still today in Bali, musicians study and play mostly in their village, coming into the cities to perform only on special occa-

other jobs as well. In recent years, the prospects of gaining employment teaching in the music schools or of being invited to join government-sponsored cultural missions abroad have attracted many young people to pursue a musical career.

The big orchestras were and still are royal heirlooms, and the musical style of a royal house is considered to be a part of the orchestra. In Java, instrument sets are invariably a family possession, even in the villages, and are often highly decorative—a kind of status symbol. Good examples of Javanese court *gamelans* may be seen in the Sasono Budaya Museum in Yogya and the Mangkunegaran Palace in Solo. Once a year, during the Sekaten festival celebrating the Prophet Mohammed's birthday, the

sions. Since independence, however, several government music academies have been founded and students now learn the traditional arts in a more formal setting.

At the village level, it is often difficult to distinguish amateurs from professionals. Many village artists are quite expert in the music of their region and yet no special status is assigned to them, nor is any sizeable payment given for their services. Some *gamelan* musicians are itinerant, making the rounds of traditional performances, be they theatrical or ceremonial or both, including the ever-popular shadow play or *wayang kulit* circuit. There are many famous artists who lead this precarious life, but the financial rewards are minimal and most hold

court *gamelans* of Yogya and Solo are played in the mosque to an audience of thousands—in clear violation of Islamic law but testimony to the enduring eclecticism of the Javanese.

Balinese *gamelans* are normally owned and maintained cooperatively by village music clubs, (*sekaha*). The Balinese religious calendar prescribes a hectic schedule of performances for temple festivals, and the provincial government has taken an active role in preserving lesser-known musical styles that may be in danger of extinction. Island-wide inter-village musical competitions provide an impetus for composers and performers to constantly expand the expressive parameters of the music.

DANCE AND DRAMA OF INDONESIA

Dance, storytelling and theatre of one sort or another are ubiquitous in Indonesia, for they are elements in a traditional cultural life that is all-encompassing—in which the performing arts fulfil a wide variety of sacred and secular needs. Dancers, shamans, actors, puppeteers, priests, storytellers, poets and musicians are members of the community who perform vital roles in informing, entertaining, counselling and instructing their fellows in the well-worn ways of tradition. To Indonesians at least, a coherent society is utterly unthinkable without them.

There is such a variety of dance and dramatic traditions throughout the archipelago that it is impossible to speak of a single, unified tradition. Each Indonesian ethnic and linguistic group possesses its own unique complex of performing arts. Nevertheless there has been a good deal of borrowing, and all groups seem to have several things in common. Trance and ritual dancing, for example, are found everywhere, as is some form of social dancing. Storytellers, be they village elders or professional puppeteers, exist in each society, telling about the past and about the unseen world of ancestor spirits and powerful deities.

In societies that developed, historically, into hierarchical kingdoms, parallel court and village traditions have also grown up. In those areas that received strong Javanese influence (primarily on Java and Bali, but also on Sumatra, Lombok and the coast of Kalimantan), there is the entire *wayang* complex of performing arts for which Indonesia is best known: shadow plays and puppet theatres of various types, stylized poetry recitals (both oral and literary), mask dances and dance dramas, all incorporating tales from the Indian and Old Javanese epics, often accompanied by *gamelan* music and ritual offerings.

Unfortunately, very little is known about the historical development of these many forms. Knowledge and records of the enormous performance repertoire that survives in Indonesia today, much of it steadily being eroded by a modern urban mass culture, is incomplete. All we can do is provide a brief survey of Indonesia's most vital and accessible dance and dramatic arts, in the hopes that visitors will be stimulated to observe, appreciate and support them.

Dance and Ritual

Among all pre-urbanized societies in the world, it seems that dance and ritual life are inseparable. Such a connection is most evident among so-called "primitive" tribes in Indonesia, most of whom have their shaman

dances performed by priests or priestesses for purposes of exorcism and spirit propitiation. The Batak *datuk* (magician) of highland Sumatra, for example, holds a magic staff as he treads with tiny steps over a magic design he has drawn on the ground. At the climax of this dance, he hops and skips, thrusting the sharp end of his staff into an egg on the ground.

Most tribes also have their ritual group dances, performed to mark rites of passage and annual agricultural events—births, funerals, weddings, puberty, plantings, and harvests—as well as to inaugurate tribal leaders, to move villages, to undertake any new project, to exorcize sickness or evil spirits and, of course, to prepare for battle

Dance is found throughout the archipelago. Left, this Legong dancer is from Bali. Right, the *zaiwo* (men's dance) with sword and shield from Anakalang, Sumba.

and celebrate victory. Almost invariably, these involve members of one sex only, except in the case of ritualized courting dances.

Sometimes they are danced by a select group or clan only, but more often all males or females in the community are welcome to join in and the movements are easily imitated. Female movements are generally slow and deliberate, with tiny steps and graceful hand movements; while men lift their knees high and use their hands as "weapons," often in imitation of martial arts movements (*pencak silat*).

Costumes are used, and music is, of course, an important element. Accompaniment is provided by chanting, pounding the rice mortar (*lesung*), and sometimes by bam-

Barong (somewhat resembling a Chinese lion, but clearly a descendant of the Tantric *kala* heads of ancient Javanese temple sculptures, the Hindu Lord of the Woods, *Banaspati*) and the evil witch, *Rangda*.

A group of men armed with swords (*keris*) attempts to kill *Rangda*, but she possesses them and turns their swords back on themselves. They are saved only thanks to the intervention of the benevolent *Barong*. By the end of the play some of the dancers are so deeply entranced that they must be exorcized—by sacrificing a chicken over them and burning incense.

Another Balinese family of dances, the dramatic *Sanghyang* trance dances, also involve the putative possession of dancers by gods, goddesses and animal spirits. The most

boo chimes or flutes. In Islamic areas of Sumatra, West Java and Sulawesi, the *rebab* (a bowed zither), of Middle Eastern origin, is also played.

Traditionally, these group dances with their steady, rhythmic musical accompaniments often involved the entrancement and possession of some or all of the participants. The best known of these trance dances is the Balinese *Barong*, immortalized in the Margaret Mead film of the 1950s, *Trance and Dance in Bali*.

The *Barong* dance drama, now performed daily for hundreds of tourists (and still well worth seeing), is a contest between the opposing forces of good and evil in 'the universe, embodied in the good beast,

famous of these is the *Sanghyang Dedari* or "heavenly nymph" dance performed at irregular intervals to drive away disease. In it, two young girls dressed in white enter a circle of 40 to 50 chanting men, the so-called *kecak* chorus. They begin to sway in time to the chants with eyes closed, a sign that they are possessed by goddesses, and are then clothed in glittering costumes and borne aloft on the shoulders of men, making a tour of the village to drive out evil influences.

Whereas on Bali, trance ceremonies such

Left, the dance being performed by these men from Mollo, Timor, serves as one preparation for battle. Right, the Bedoyo Ketawang—Java's most sacred and secret dance.

as the *Barong* and the *Sanghyang Dedari* still retain their relevance and meaning; on Islamic Java, the trance dance has developed into something of a commercial spectacle. It is here variously known as *Kuda Kepang*, *Kuda Lumping*, *Reog* and *Jatilan* and consists of one or more riders on hobby-horses made of leather or plaited bamboo, accompanied by musicians, masked clowns and perhaps also a masked lion, tiger or crocodile similar to the *Barong*.

Such hobbyhorse troupes were once commonly seen at weekly markets and in crowded city squares during festival days, but they are now rare. The riders would begin in an orderly fashion, trotting in a circle, then one of them would become entranced and start behaving like a horse, charging back and forth wildly, neighing and eating grass or straw. The others might follow his lead, and sometimes there might be a confrontation between the masked animal and the horsemen.

Eventually the riders would be brought out of trance by their leader, and money would be collected from the assembled crowd. Similar hobbyhorse trance dances were once performed in Sumatra and Sulawesi in connection with funeral rites. The horse (sometimes also a bird) seems to function as a symbolic mount bearing human souls to and from the other world.

Central Javanese Court Dances

Before the turn of the century, all traditional Indonesian rulers of the coastal and inland kingdoms maintained palace dance and theatrical troupes. But following the Dutch conquests, most court traditions were allowed to lapse into obscurity. Only in Central Java are courtly performances, and royal patronage of dancers, actors and musicians, still found.

Java has by far the oldest attested dance and theatre traditions in Indonesia. Stone inscriptions dating from the eighth and ninth centuries A.D. frequently speak of dances, clowns, musicians and theatrical performances. And adorning the walls of the great Central Javanese temples of this period— Borobudur, Prambanan and others—are numerous reliefs depicting dancers and entainers, from lowly market minstrels and roadside revelers to sensuous court concubines and prancing princesses.

These reliefs, like modern Javanese and Balinese dance, bear a strong Indian influence. Carved on the outer face of the main balustrade at Prambanan are 62 illustrations from the classic Indian dance manual, the *Natyasastra*. In these carvings, the dancers are always depicted low to the ground, with knees bent, legs turned out, body straight, and with great emphasis on the attitude of the head and the posture of the hands. In classical Indian dance, the hands communicated literally, telling a story through a complex sign language of hand *mudras*. While in Javanese and Balinese dance the literal meanings of these hand signals have been lost, the rich expressiveness of hand gestures remains a primary element throughout Southeast Asia.

Most of the dances in Central Java today are attributed to one or another of the past rulers of Islamic dynasties, particularly their 16th to 18th Century founders. Undoubtedly the vocabulary of movements and music

employed are much older. As we know from the 19th Century, rulers frequently choreographed some dance or dramatic pieces for specific occasions. Often this meant simply that the palace dance master was instructed to concoct a particular type of piece using a certain musical composition, but several rulers were also accomplished dancers and musicians in their own right.

The most famous of all Javanese court dances is the *Bedoyo Ketawang*, performed once yearly in the Surakarta palace on the anniversary of the Susuhunan's coronation. This is a sacred and private ritual dance, said to have been instituted by Sultan Agung (he reigned 1613-45), the greatest of the Mataram kings. It celebrates a re-union between the descendant of the dynasty's founder, Senopati, and the powerful goddess of the south sea, Kyai Loro Kidul.

Nine female palace guards perform the stately *Bedoyo Ketawang* attired in royal wedding dress, and so sacred is it that they may rehearse only once every five weeks on a given day. Until recently, no outsiders were permitted to witness the performance, for it is claimed that Loro Kidul herself attends and afterwards "weds" the king. A similar *Bedoyo* dance was formerly performed in the Yogyakarta palace, but it has been discontinued. Some speculate that these dances are remnants of an ancient Javanese fertility rite.

The other important Javanese court dance, the *Serimpi*, was traditionally per-

men, such as the *Beksan Lawung*. Most of these are war or processional dances and are therefore rarely performed today. They are characterized by the use of weapons (lances, shields, swords, bows) and high-stepping, vigorous movements.

The reliefs at Borodudur, depicting popular dances and musical entertainment, suggest that dance once figured prominently in Javanese life. Today, outside of the courts, or in the Javanese villages, very little dancing remains. This is perhaps a reflection of Islam's penetration to rural areas since the 17th Century. But it is equally possible that Dutch rule and a population explosion contributed to a demise of this art form in the 19th Century.

Well into this century, however, there were

formed only by princesses or daughters of the ruling family. It portrays a duelling pair (sometimes two pairs) of Amazons who move in unison, gracefully and deliberately fighting with dainty daggers and tiny bows and arrows. Various stories are attached to this dance, and it may have antecedants in a Borobudur relief showing two female dancers in identical attitudes, and in a scene at Prambanan depicting a dancing female warrior. Following the establishment of Javanese dance schools outside of the palaces at the beginning of this century, the *Serimpi* became the standard dance taught to all young women.

There are, in addition, several Javanese court dances choreographed specifically for

commercial Javanese dance spectacles, like the *Ronggeng* street dancers, the professional *Talèdèk* dance girls and the hobbyhorse dance troupes mentioned above. All these may be echoes of earlier village dance traditions, similar perhaps to those found today in Bali.

The Splendour of Balinese Dance

The traditional Balinese polity has been described as a "theatre state." While a culture as vital and as lively as theirs has not remained immutable, there are clear indications that dance and drama have played a central role in Balinese life since time immemorial. Following the demise of Balinese kingdoms at the beginning of this century, the focus for all Balinese dance and drama shifted from the courts to the villages.

In Balinese dance a good deal of Indian influence is also evident. In fact the Balinese dancers of today resemble those depicted in ancient East Javanese temple reliefs more than the court dancers of Java do. Balinese dance costumes, with their glittering head-dresses and elaborate jewellery, are clearly of Hindu-Javanese origin. And like his Javanese counterpart, the Balinese dancer adopts the basic "Indian" stance: knees bent, legs turned out, body straight, head tilted, with highly expressive hand gestures and a fluttering of the fingers.

In other respects, though, Balinese dance imparts a very different feeling. While the

well as for the participants). The Balinese, nevertheless, distinguish among those dances that are sacred (*wali*), ceremonial (*bebali*) and simply for watching (*bali-balihan*). The last category of dances appears to have developed exclusively among the nobility, but they are now performed by villagers as part of a ceremonial repertoire.

The *Legong Keraton* (*keraton* means palace), for example, has been the most popular dance in Bali since it was first performed in the villages in the 1920s. Originally a court dance developed for royal amusement, it is now seen frequently at village temple ceremonies throughout Bali and is becoming a big hit with the tourists. Traditionally, a *Legong* was performed by

Javanese have developed slow, controlled, continuous movements performed with eyes downcast and limbs close to the body (in keeping with their aesthetic of refinement), the Balinese dancer is charged with energy, eyes agape, darting this way and that, high-stepping, arms up, moving with quick, cat-like bursts that would startle a Javanese.

All Balinese dances are connected in some way with rituals. Temple festivals in Bali always require a dance or drama of some kind as entertainment for the gods (as

Left, *wayang orang* performance at Surakarta by the Sriwedari Troupe. Right, I Nyoman Mario, the legendary dancer from the 1930s seen here performing the Kebyar.

two very young girls, introduced by a court attendant (*condong*) who sweeps the stage clean and presents the dancers with fans. Sheathed in glittering gold costumes, with headdresses crowned by frangipani blossoms, the two dancers then enact one of a dozen or so possible stories. Today, more than two women may perform the dance, and they need not be very young.

The *Baris* or warrior dances, on the other hand, seem to have developed out of old ritual battle dances. They are exciting to watch—whirlwinds of music and action. The ancient *Baris Gede* is performed by groups of men who stand poised with lances or shields, eyes wide, ready at any moment for the enemy's advance. The popular solo *Baris* uses no weapons at all—the intensity of the movements serving to forcefully communicate self-confidence and mental control. A good *Baris* performance is a true test of wits for dancers and musicians, for they must respond to each other's signals to produce the quivering bursts of synchronized energy that are the essence of the dance.

New dances are being created all the time. The powerful *Kecak* dance was adapted from the *Sanghyang Dedari* at the beginning of this century, by isolating the chorus of the latter and treating it as Hanuman's monkey army in scenes from the Ramayana. Now performed by as many as a hundred chanting and swaying men dressed only in loincloths, the *Kecak* is by far Bali's most popular tourist spectacle.

In the 1930s the legendary dancer and choreographer, I Nyoman Mario, introduced a dance known as the *Kebyar*, based upon a new type of *gamelan* music (of the same name) that had appeared in North Bali around 1915. It is performed by a virtuoso soloist, using the upper parts of his body while in a sitting position to interpret the capricious moods of this scintillating music. Mario's other creations include *Oleg Tambulillingan*, which depicts two bumblebees making love in a garden of flowers!

Traditional Balinese and Javanese Theatre

Theatre traditions in Indonesia have always been closely tied to the local music,

dance and storytelling repertoire of a particular region. In Java, for example, all theatre seems to have its roots in the *wayang* puppet theatres, among which the flat, leather shadow-puppet play, the *wayang kulit*, is pre-eminent. This is evident from the fact that all Javanese theatre, whether performed by actors or by puppets, is referred to as *wayang*, a term which means "shadow" and refers in its narrowest sense to the shadow-puppet play. Used in its wider sense, however, *wayang* refers also to forms of theatre performed by actors on a stage: *wayang topeng* (mask drama) and *wayang orang* (dance drama) being the best known. In these, many of the tales, voices, iconography and even some of the character's movements have been borrowed from the shadow play.

Of these surviving theatrical forms, the *wayang topeng* or mask drama is undoubtedly the oldest. The earliest evidence of *wayang topeng* is in East Java, where it was used, at least by the 14th Century, to enact tales from the Panji cycle of epics concerning the founding of the 13th Century *Singhasari* dynasty. These ancient performances were perhaps direct forerunners of the *gambuh* dramas of Bali, dramas that are still performed occasionally today with masks and archaic *gamelan* instruments, and with dialogue that nobody understands because it is entirely in Old Javanese.

Whereas on Bali, mask plays are still popular, on Java they lost favour at the Islamic Central Javanese courts sometime after the 16th Century, and were then preserved mainly in north coastal villages, where they barely survive today (notably in the Cirebon area). It seems that competition from other *wayang* forms, particularly dance dramas resulted in the decline.

Javanese *wayang orang* or *wayang wong* (literally: "human" *wayang*) dance dramas are said to have been created in the 18th Century by one or another of Central Java's rulers. This has become a partisan matter, in which Surakartans claim their Prince Mangkunegara I as the originator of the genre, and Yogyakartans insist that their Hamengkubuwana I created it.

Neither ruler truly invented the *wayang orang*, for dance dramas (with and without masks) existed already in Java from a much earlier time. On the other hand, both rulers were extremely active in creating new pieces and promoting their performance. A strong

Javanese theatre has its roots in puppet theatre. Left, a *wayang golek* performance. Right, students from ASTI perform a fan dance combining tradition with a modern idiom.

rivalry developed, in fact, between the several competing courts—a battle on the stage that followed hard on the heels of the fractious civil war of 1740 to 55. This rivalry intensified during the 19th Century, when Javanese rulers became more and more concerned with matters of cultural prestige, and possessed the time and the means to devote to cultural pursuits.

Wayang orang thus became a part of the state ritual of these kingdoms, performed in an open pavilion to commemorate the founding of the dynasty and the coronation of the king, as well as at lavish royal weddings. The great age of *wayang orang* was in the 1920s and 1930s, when massive productions lasting several days and employing casts of 300 to 400 actors were mounted. These performances became extremely stylized and abstract, emphasizing music and technically difficult movements over drama and dialogue.

Today, performances are smaller in scale, lasting only a few hours, in which fragments from the Ramayana or the Mahabharata are staged in a hall with props, heavy make-up, painted backdrops and proscenium lighting. There are now three commercial *wayang wong* companies in Java: Sri Wedari in Surakarta, Ngesti Pandhawa in Semarang and Bharata in Jakarta. They perform nightly, and the emphasis is on lengthy dialogues and the ever-popular comedy scenes, rather than the dance.

Modern Trends

Traditional Indonesian dance and drama is today everywhere in great danger of being swamped by modern urban entertainments: films, television, nightclubs, discos, etc. Even in the Central Javanese palaces, the financial burden of maintaining dance and musical troupes is becoming too great, and though private companies do exist, Indonesians on the whole seem less inclined to support the old "palace" arts commercially.

The government has done its best to remedy the situation by establishing performing arts academies (ASTI) in various cities. Performances, however, are infrequent and often poorly funded. And there are few careers awaiting graduates of these academies. Despite this, many dedicated students attend them, and popular interest in the traditional performing arts does survive in certain areas.

Tourism is now having a big impact by providing commercial demand for traditional dances, albeit not always in traditional settings (hotel poolsides, for instance). Bali

is exceptional, in that tourism has here stimulated dance traditions that have always been very healthy. In Bali, every village has its own dance troupe, and these now have an impetus to improve and expand their repertoire for a steady schedule of tourist performances. Dancers of the *Barong* in Batubulan village, for example, perform every morning for busloads of foreigners, then at night they often dance again in elaborate *Topeng* or *Arja* dramas before enthralled villagers at temple ceremonies.

A new generation of Indonesian choreographers, educated at the performing arts academies and familiar with western classical and modern dance, is also now at work. Since the 1950s, teachers such as Bagong Kussudiardjo in Yogya, Wayan Dibia in Bali

and Sulawesian Wiwiek Siepala in Jakarta have been adapting traditional dance work for modern audiences.

One result has been the *Sendratari* (lit. art-drama-dance), essentially a traditional dance drama minus the dialogue but incorporating some modern movements and costumes. The first *Sendratari*, an adapted version of the Javanese *wayang orang*, was staged in the early 1960s, supposedly at the urging of a Cook's-Tour operator. Today this Ramayana Ballet spectacular, with a cast of over 200, is performed over four nights around every full moon during the dry season months (June to September), on a large stage erected in front of the elegant 9th Century Prambanan temple complex.

INDONESIAN TEXTILES: THREADS OF TRADITION

Textile connoisseurs are quick to point out that Indonesia possesses the greatest diversity of traditional textiles in the world. Found among the colourful barkcloths of Borneo, Irian and Sulawesi, the plain weaves and exquisite *songket* silks of Sumatra, the beautiful *batiks* of Java and the renowned *ikats* of the eastern islands, is a variety and a technical virtuosity that is unsurpassed.

For Indonesia, fine textiles are far more than just coloured cloth. Indeed, they maintain many old and hallowed sartorial associations, symbolizing power and status and being employed as ritual objects, as gift-trade items—even as forms of accumulated wealth and currency.

Spreading the Craft

Each of Indonesia's more than 350 ethnic and linguistic groups appear to have had, at one time or another, their own distinctive textile traditions. Some of these may date back 2,000 years or more, and are preserved today in remote upriver or mountainous areas. Many have also been influenced by foreign (especially Indian) textiles. As early as the 14th Century, Indian fabrics were imported on a very large scale, and during the 16th and 17th centuries Indian *patola* cloths were particularly influential. Europeans later promoted Indian textiles here as items of trade, and the colonial presence left its mark both in patterns of textile distribution and in the use of some European motifs derived from coins and porcelains.

Migrants as well as traders have played a role in the diffusion of textile techniques and motifs. For example, the northern coasts of Ceram and Irian Jaya were home to traditional weaving communities that may have originated in the Banggai islands off the east coast of Sulawesi, and one finds here the Alune tribe (literally "the people who weave") amidst groups who are talented at making bark cloth and plaiting, but who are not traditionally weavers.

And there is a story about a princess of Wolio, the old kingdom of Buton in southeast Sulawesi, who married a sultan of Ternate (in the Moluccas) in the mid-17th Century. When she left her home of Koloncucu to cross the waters, it took three *kora-kora*—huge Moluccan out-riggers rowed by upwards of 100 men—to transport her retinue. Among them was a group of weavers, who upon their arrival in Ternate were given a plot of land. There they stayed and practised their craft for the benefit of the court. The realm of Ternate extended in those days as far north as Mindanao and as far south as Flores, and one may still find Koloncucu weavings today in Halmahera and on neighbouring islands.

The Symbolism of Textiles

The spinning and dyeing of yarns and the weaving of them into pieces of cloth was traditionally regarded as symbolic of the process of creation, and of human birth in particular. Weaving was generally an exclusively female function. Men were permitted to participate only in the dyeing of certain colours of the thread, analogous with their role in human conception. Dyeing sessions required the utmost privacy—partitions were often set up around the dyeing area. Trespassers were publicly expelled and punished by being made to taste the dye, for it was believed that otherwise the dye would spoil. Dyers were forbidden to speak of death; pregnant, menstruating or sick women were barred.

The mounting of the threads upon the loom was done on an auspicious day, for at other times the threads would break. In some coastal villages this meant a full moon and a high tide. If a death occurred in the village, the weaving would stop at once, otherwise the spirit of the departed would exact vengeance, bringing sickness upon the weaver and causing the threads to lose their strength.

A finished product was sanctified by such metaphysical and psychological associations, and this is perhaps why certain textiles were traditionally regarded as powerful objects that could protect the weaver and which were necessary for the performance of magic

opening a powerful cloth is said to bring immediate rainfall.

On many islands, specific textiles are required as payment of the bride price and on the island of Buton, small squares of cloth were used for centuries as currency.

The best-known Indonesian ritual textiles are the so-called "ship cloths" once found in several areas of south Sumatra. The motif they have in common resembles a ship, or sometimes also a bird: a central platform with one or more angularly extended arms. Human figures are generally depicted on the ships, often together with a variety of plants, animals and valuable objects—a kind of Noah's ark. This ship motif was a frequent design element in traditional Indonesian art and architecture, and not surprisingly, it

and life-cycle rituals.

An entire language of textiles developed. For example, the brown and white *ragidup* ("pattern of life") cloths of the Bataks were presented to a woman seven months pregnant with her first child, as a "soul cloth" (*ulos ni tondi*). Her in-laws would drape it around her shoulders and then the pattern would be "read" by a knowledgeable elder.

The sacred *maa* cloths of the Torajans of South Sulawesi are still necessary for the performance of all major rituals—as decorations and offerings. A divine origin is ascribed to the threads of which they are woven, and they are carefully kept in special baskets. Some *maa* are considered effective for the propitiation of fertility spirits, and

seems to be associated with concepts of change and the passage of time. Up until the 19th Century, a ship cloth was essential for the performance of all important South Sumatran life-cycle rituals: rites of birth, circumcision, marriage and death.

Certain cloths, colours and motifs were also set aside for the exclusive use of kings and nobles. Such sumptuary restrictions are a common feature of all pre-modern societies; the wearing of designer labels today can be thought of as a similar attempt to

Above, a woman "wears" the weaving loom in order to work. Right: Lembata woman spinning cotton. Far right; weaving loom with "koffo" fabric from Sangihe, northeast Sulawesi.

express class distinctions through costume. In Indonesia, not only class distinctions but also specific courtly duties were once designated by a particular fabric.

'Primitive' Textiles

Textiles from all periods of Indonesia's history are still being produced. However, these are living traditions and not fossilized relics. Textiles change, and unfortunately many traditional ones are now being lost.

The barkcloths found among upland tribes in Kalimantan (Borneo), Sulawesi (the Celebes) and Irian Jaya (New Guinea) harken back to a prehistoric development. Nevertheless, some barkcloths, particularly those of the Palu and Torajan peoples of

require a loom, and therefore fall somewhere in between the categories of weaving and basketry. Up until recently, certain tribes in Kalimantan, Flores, Sulawesi and Timor produced warrior tunics from bast (bark) fibres by twining them, a simple process in which two weft fibres are alternately wrapped above and below a passive warp.

Garments made of plaited grasses, pandanus or sago leaves, bamboo, palm, and other plant fibres are not unknown today. And more sophisticated weavings produced from wild banana and pineapple fibres are still found in northeastern Sulawesi (Minahassa) and on the nearby islands of Sangir and Talaud. The local name for these fabrics is *hote*, though they are also known as *koffo* or

central Sulawesi, display an extremely high degree of artistry.

The Torajans, for example, boiled and fermented the inner bark of pandanus, mulberry or other trees before beating the resultant pulp into extremely soft and pliable sheets with special wooden and stone mallets. This cloth (*fuya*) was then dyed, painted or stamped using natural pigments. Finally it was cut and sewn into headwraps, blouses, ponchos and bags, and then often embroidered or appliqued.

Weaving techniques were probably well developed in prehistoric times. Clues as to the nature of earlier weavings may exist in the simple vegetable fibre fabrics still found in some areas. Many of these do not even

"Manila hemp" cloths. Most are decorated with geometric patterns (diamonds, scrolls, stars) formed by dyeing short lengths of fibre and incorporating them into the weft.

Non-cotton fibres do not belong necessarily to an earlier stage of textile development. Many of the more "primitive" textiles showed an extraordinary degree of sophistication. Since cotton is used in most of the more advanced textiles, and requires cultivation, spinning and the use of a loom, it is generally thought of as a later development, though it is indigenous to the region and is grown and woven by many so-called "primitive" peoples.

The technique closely associated with the advent of cotton in Indonesia is warp *ikat*.

This is a traditional method of design in which the warp threads of a cloth are tie-dyed prior to being woven. The term *ikat* means "to tie" in many Indonesian languages, and the threads are most often patterned by tying off areas, which are not meant to absorb the dye with dye-resistant fibres. In the hands of a master weaver, the result can be intricate, detailed motifs executed in deep, rich colours.

Warp *ikat* weavings are found today mainly in the eastern islands of the Sunda archipelago (from Sumba and Flores to Timor and Tanimbar), but also in some of the more inaccessible areas of Sumatra, Borneo and Sulawesi. These textiles require tremendous patience and skill. Spinning the threads and preparing the dyes, tying the dyeing process.

The most famous warp *ikat* is the *hinggi* or mantle from the east coast of Sumba. These cloths are known for their rich colours, fine details and bold, horizontal fields of stylized human and animal figures. They are normally produced in pairs, one to wrap around the body and one to drape over the shoulders, and have served as valuable trade items for centuries. They were, for example, exported extensively by the Dutch during the 19th Century.

The tendency today is to produce large fields rather than several detailed bands, but the mass-production of *hinggi* using quick chemical dyes has resulted in a lot of inferior work. So-called "Sumba blankets" are now produced in Bali and Java for the tourist

warp threads, and then repeatedly immersing and drying them to achieve the desired colour is no less a task than the actual weaving itself.

A fine cloth produced with natural dyes used to take eight to 10 years to complete. Natural dye recipes are extremely complex, some of them requiring sophisticated carriers and mordants. Traditionally, it appears that indigo, *mengkudu* root (a red dye) and *soga* (produced from brown roots and barks) were the main dyes used, but Turkey red and cochineal were popularized by Islamic traders.

All warp *ikats* are distinguished by the grouping of motifs into horizontal or longitudinal bands, a logical outcome of the warp

trade, while the older, traditional pieces are scarce and astronomically priced.

People on the small, arid islands of Roti and Sawu (between Sumba and Timor), also produce highly distinctive warp *ikats*. The Sawu ones are recognizable by their narrow longitudinal bands, symmetrically patterned with rows of delicate flowers, stars or diamonds in white and red against a background of indigo. Roses and tulips are commonly depicted, having been copied from Dutch fabrics and porcelains. Two or more

Left, tying off the thread in the *ikat* process prior to dying. Right, *ulos ni tondi* "soul cloth" of the highland Batak tribes of north-central Sumatra.

panels are normally sewn together to form a blanket or a *sarung*, but the total number of warp stripes is always odd—a characteristic feature of Sawu cloths.

Rotinese *ikats* are similar to those of Sawu in colouring and detail, but instead of longitudinal bands they have adopted the compositional scheme of the Indian *patola* cloth—a field of many eight-pointed stars or flowers framed with striped borders and bands of triangles (*tumpal*) at either end.

A simple back-strap loom is used for warp *ikats* and indeed for all traditional weavings produced in Indonesia. There are two types—the discontinuous and continuous warp loom—and with both the warp tension is maintained by means of a strap placed around the weaver's back as she sits on the ground. String heddles are employed to create individual sheds and a bamboo comb is sometimes introduced to maintain the warp spacing.

Weft and Double *Ikats*

Weft and double *ikats* are found in only a few scattered areas and it is thought that the technique was introduced from India. The distinguishing feature of Indonesian weft *ikats*, fashioned by tie-dyeing the weft threads of a cloth before weaving, is that they are generally produced in silk. Sericulture was probably introduced from China at a fairly early date, but it was only later, after Islamic traders began to popularize silk *ikat* fabrics made in India, that Indonesians seem to have begun producing them.

Weft *ikats* occur primarily in the Islamic coastal trading areas: Palembang, Riau, Gresik and Ujung Pandang, but also on the island of Bali. The Palembang and Bangka weft *ikats* are extremely sophisticated, done on silk in rich tones of red, blue and yellow, often with supplementary gold threads in the weft. Indian, Javanese and Chinese motifs are all employed, sometimes simultaneously, reflecting the cosmopolitan milieu of these trading ports. Today, inferior examples are still produced near Palembang, and are worn on holidays and at weddings as part of a formal, ritual costume.

Tenganan Pageringsingan in eastern Bali is one of only three places in the world (the others being in India and Japan) to traditionally produce the fabulously difficult double *ikat*—fabrics decorated by tie-dyeing both warp and weft before weaving. These so-called *geringsing* cloths are dyed with indigo and *mengkudu* red, producing a reddish-purple design on a cream background. Loosely woven, some apparently

imitate the Indian *patola* (also a double *ikat*). Others are clearly indigenous in design, such as the *geringsing wayang kebo* with its symmetrical groupings of wayang figures around a central four-pointed star.

Considered by the Balinese to be the most sacred of all textiles, *geringsing* cloths are used in many important ceremonies throughout the island, including tooth-filings and cremations. Within the village of Tenganan, wearers of these cloths were once said to be protected from evil influences and illness (*geringsing* means "without sickness"), but there are reports that Tenganan residents no longer consider the cloth to the powerful.

The fact that Tenganan is one of the few *Bali Aga* (original—i.e. non-Hindu) villages

on the island is intriguing. Either the *geringsing* cloth is of very ancient, pre-Hindu origin or the production of the cloth is surrounded by certain taboos which only the *Bali Aga* disregard.

It appears that a textile revolution took place in Indonesia after the 14th Century, when Islamic (and later European) traders began to flood the archipelago with Indian textiles. Not that Indian textiles were something new—they had probably been imported for centuries for the nobility. Rather it was the scale of the trade and its impact on local textile usage that was unprecedented.

It has been argued that the use of cotton and silk was traditionally the preserve of the Indonesian aristocracy. Warp *ikats*—the indigenous cotton fabrics of Indonesia—are very time-consuming and hence expensive to produce. The same is true of silks and many vegetable fibre fabrics. In fact the production of all dyed spun-fibre textiles is extremely labour-intensive, and in a world where labour was at a premium, it is unlikely that any but the rulers or aristocrats could have possessed them.

A democratization of textiles occurred as a result of the spice trade. Traders discovered that they could obtain valuable Indonesian spices (worth their weight in gold in some corners of the globe) in exchange for Indian cottons and silks. Indonesians, meanwhile, discovered that they could have fine textiles in exchange for easily gathered cloves, nutmegs, peppers and aromatic

woods.

Perhaps the most important innovation of this period was the cotton plain weave now found throughout Indonesia and worn by a majority of people as the all-purpose *sarung* or body-wrap. Characterized by its simple striped or checked design, it was a significant advance over the cruder bark cloths and plaited vegetable fibre fabrics that the common man previously wore.

These plain weaves today go under a variety of names and are produced in or around the great coastal trading centres founded during the Islamic period—on the north coast of Java, the north and east coasts of Sumatra and in south Sulawesi. The plain weave is found inland also, for instance in

central Java where the striped *lurik* is a part of the traditional Javanese costume, and in the Minangkabau regions of west-central Sumatra.

The Indian textile revolution extended also to fabrics that were considered rare and valuable, or even magical. The Indian *patola*, a double *ikat* silk fabric produced in Gujarat, became the single most influential and widely imitated textile in Indonesia. It was incorporated into the ritual life of many peoples and became part of the costume of kings on many islands, including Java where it was known as *cinde*.

The bright, shimmering colours of the *patola* must have appeared quite unusual compared to the more somber reds, browns and blues of the native *ikats*. As fewer of the cloths were imported after about 1800, many weavers in Indonesia set about producing replicas in silk and cotton. Today the characteristic eight-pointed flower or *jilamprang* design is seen everywhere.

Another textile inspired by the flowering of trade with the Islamic world is the *songket*—weavings produced with gold- and silver-covered thread imported from India.

The most famous *songkets* are those of Palembang—with glittering gold threads woven into bright red silk to form a fine geometrical pattern that often covers the entire cloth. Unlike the plain weave, in which the warp and weft threads alternate in a regular fashion, the *songket* is produced by "floating" the metallic weft over and under a number of warp threads at a time. This is done by laboriously counting off the warp threads into individual sheds and then inserting sticks, called *lidi* to guide the weft. Traditionally, real gold-plated threads were used but now only a kind of flat tinsel is available and old gold threads are reserved for special pieces.

The Minangkabau of west Sumatra are also known for their silver-threaded *songkets*, produced against a background of wine-red silk. And in Bali a whole range of *songkets* are produced, from simple *sarungs* with small geometric gold or silver patterns, to wildly exuberant festive costumes combining gold and silver designs in silks of purple, green, yellow and blue. Some Balinese animal and wayang figures are also executed in *songket* and some years ago, an Italian designer even began to use Balinese tinsel-striped cotton *songket* fabrics in a range of disco wear.

Left, Timor cloth with characteristically bright colours. Right, the most sacred cloth in Bali—*geringsingan* cloth from Tenganan.

THE WORLD OF JAVANESE BATIK

Batik textiles are such an integral part of Javanese culture today that it is difficult to imagine a time when the Javanese did not possess them. Yet the batik process as we know it may not be very old. Scholars debate whether the wax-resist dyeing process was brought to Java from India, where it has been known for centuries, or whether it developed here independently. An antecedent for batik might be the *kain simbut* of West Java, produced by smearing rice-paste on cloth as a dye-resist. Others have said that the Javanese *kain kembangan*, pro-

pounding, of dye preparation and fixing, and a whole repertoire of elaborate motifs were necessary for Javanese batik to become what it is. Fine, tightly woven cloth was also a prerequisite to high-quality *tulis* work produced with a *canting*, and this was always imported until very recently.

The Batik Process

Some batik is produced on islands other than Java—Sumatra, Sulawesi and Bali, for example—but none can really compare.

duced by tie-dyeing, led ultimately to the use of wax and resin resists **Names** for various batik motifs have been traced to Javanese literary works dating from the 12th Century. But the fact remains that the terms *batik* and *tulis* (as applied to textile design) do not appear in Javanese court records until the Islamic period, when Indian traders were already active in the archipelago.

No one disputes, however, that Javanese batik is by far the finest in the world. The reason is that there developed in Java, possibly in the 17th or 18th Century, a tool known as the *canting*—a pen used to apply molten wax to cloth and capable of executing very fine designs. Together with this, a complex technology of wax and resin com-

The reason is quite simple: fine batik requires extraordinary patience. Beginning with a white silk or cotton cloth, the first step is to sketch a design. Areas which are not to be coloured in the first dyeing must then be covered with wax. Depending on the delicacy of the design this can take hundreds of hours of painstaking labour. The cloth is then immersed in a prepared dye solution and dried—when natural dyes were used, long repeated immersions and dryings were required and a single dyeing might take

Above, two designs from the Central Javanese court: left; royal *ceplok* motif; right, *garuda* wing motif. Near and far right, characteristic bright colours of north Javanese batik.

months. Next the cloth must be re-waxed in preparation for the second dyeing. Sometimes this is accomplished by boiling out all the wax and re-waxing the entire cloth, but sometimes it involves scraping certain areas and adding wax to others. The dyeing and re-waxing process is then repeated as many times as is necessary to produce the number of colours required.

The art of batik-making is generally assumed to have reached its zenith at the turn of this century. There are a number of explanations: the population of Java had

north coast (Indramayu, Cirebon, Tegal, Pekalongan, Demak, Kudus, Rembang, Lassem, Tuban, Gresik, Madura). In central Java, batik-making was the preserve of aristocratic women, whereas on the north coast it was an industry pursued by Chinese, Arab and even by Indo-Dutch artisans.

The differences in colouring and design were considerable. In central Java, certain motifs were set aside exclusively for the court and members of the aristocracy. These included the *kawung* (large ovals arranged in fours like leaves of a clover), the *ceplok* (an

increased dramatically during the 19th Century so that labour was abundant and cheap; secondly, there was a great demand for quality batik fabrics among affluent Javanese, Chinese, Arab and even Dutch urban residents; thirdly, there was a steady supply of fine, imported silks and cottons from abroad; and last, there were many individual artists devoted to producing the very finest possible batik.

Dragons and Clouds

The traditional designs catalogued at this time numbered over 1,000. And the regional styles numbered more than 20—primarily in central Java (Yogya and Solo) and along the

eight-pointed flower motif deriving from the Indian *patola*), the *sawat* or *garuda* wings (of a mythical Hindu bird), and the *parang rusak barong* or "broken sword" motif that consists of diagonal rows of interlocking scrolls, to name but a few.

Two primary colours were used: indigo and *soga* (a brown dye obtained from the bark of a tree) though these came in many shades and elaborate dye recipes called for the addition of substances like palm sugar, bananas, fermented cassava and chicken meat.

On the north coast, yellows, mauves, ochres, greens and pale blues were more popular and the motifs showed Chinese, European and Islamic influence. In Cirebon, a Chinese clouds motif that symbolizes mystical energy was incorporated in all of the courtly batik designs and in one of the most famous motifs, the *mega mendung* or "menacing rain clouds," they appear in bright, contrasting shades of red, blue, pink or green, like some supernatural storm. Chinese dragons and phoenixes appeared together with Hindu *nagas* and elephants and European lions, and some central Javanese motifs were executed in uncharacteristically bright colours. The most popular designs were of European origin, however: bouquets of flowers with hovering hummingbirds, or just birds alone—elegant, long-legged storks and herons.

Less well-known but interesting from a technical point of view are the related dyeing

techniques of *plangi* and *tritik*. Both are methods of tie-dyeing and are hence related to *ikat* except that the cloth is dyed *after* being woven: *plangi* is produced by tying or pinching a spot of fabric with dye-resistant fibre so that a circular pattern results; *tritik* involves stitching a cloth to create a linear pattern. The two methods are often combined with batik in a single scarf, sash or headwrap. Silk was formerly used, and several deep colours—burgundy, indigo and yellow would create shimmering, rainbow-like effects. The scarves worn by central-Javanese court dancers are fine examples of *plangi* and *tritik*, techniques also practised extensively in Bali.

It is fair to say that at the turn of the century, everyone in Java wore batik. Women wore it more than men, perhaps, because the female *sarung* and *kebaya* costume required it whereas men in important positions wore European clothes to the office. But once at home everyone would slip into a comfortable cotton *sarung*. The advent of *batik cap* (batik produced with the use of a wax stamp—*cap*) revitalized the industry during the 1890s because even the peasants were then able to afford this cruder, mass-produced product. Batik was also widely exported from Java to other islands as well as to Singapore and Malaya, where local Chinese and Malay women still wear Javanese batik.

Batik Trends

Since World War Two, the industry has experienced a series of setbacks. The unavailability of imported cotton cambrics during the Japanese occupation put a temporary halt to all batik production, a situation that was only partially alleviated during the 1950s due to persistent shortages of this key material. The rapid development of an automated weaving industry in Indonesia during the 1960s and 1970s, though providing ample supplies of fabric for batik production, has also given rise to the production of cheap synthetics and pigment-printed cloth. This competition has been disastrous for the *batik cap* industry, which is now seriously endangered. Thousands of craftsmen have been put out of work.

The finer *batik tulis*, which sells for upwards of US$20 to $100 per 2-metre (6.5-foot) length, has fared better. Recently, however, there has been competition from a new type of imitation-batik silkscreen print produced in Jakarta, which is practically indistinguishable from the real thing at a fraction of the cost. There are signs, too, that batik is simply no longer fashionable in the eyes of young Indonesians, who prefer Western-tailored clothes and wrinkle-free polyester fabrics. The two bright spots on the batik scene are the use of fine *tulis* fabrics in men's shirts and women's fashions in Jakarta and the export of modified *batik cap* cottons and rayons to Europe, Australia and America. There is no doubt, though, that the batik industry will never regain the pre-eminence it enjoyed in Java before World War Two.

Left, a Javanese batik factory. Right, batik has found a place in sophisticated fashion circles with both Western and Indonesian designers imaginatively exploiting its potential.

EVERYDAYLAND

The drab becomes delightful, the bland beautiful. The mundane becomes magical, the ordinary extraordi

THAILAND

ens only in Thailand and it starts to happen the moment you step on board your Thai International flight.

Thai
Smooth as silk.

Perfection at its best...

Discover the perfect taste
in beer. Carlsberg the best
quality beer from Denmark.
Now after more than 100 years,
Carlsberg is still brewed in the
tradition to meet the highest
degree of perfection.
Carlsberg created to fulfill
your perfect taste.

The glorious beer
from Denmark

J.C. Jacobsen (1811-1887)
Founder of Carlsberg Beer

From now on...Ask for Carlsberg

Insight Guides

"Bringing colour to the dreary world of guide books"
Popular Photography – Feb 1987

Only one family of h
offers a choice of two c
hotel in do
a tranquil
in West Ja
a 264 room hotel in the
the two be
in Bali

els in Indonesia
erent classes of
ntown Jakarta,
ach hotel

tural capital Yogyakarta,
resort hotels
and the true
meaning of
Indonesian hospitality.

Apa Maps

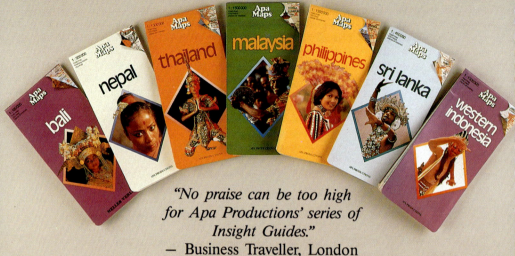

"No praise can be too high for Apa Productions' series of Insight Guides."
— Business Traveller, London

Since 1970, Insight Guides have established a milestone in travel-guide publishing. California or Korea, Mexico or Malaysia, each title in this fast-growing series will guide you with unprecedented style, inspiring as they inform.

And now a series of Apa maps also complement the Asian titles of the Insight Guides.

Two unbeatable travel companions. Go to your nearest bookshop or write to us for further information:

APA PRODUCTIONS (PTE) LTD.
3, Gul Crescent, Singapore 2262
Tel: 8612755, Fax: 8616438
Cable: APAPRODUCT, Tel: APASIN RS 36201

Insight Guides
APA PRODUCTIONS

GUIDE IN BRIEF

Prices

With a few exceptions, prices in the Guide In Brief are quoted in US dollars. Steady devaluations in the Indonesian currency have led to frequent price changes. Prices, when stated in US dollars, have remained (and are more likely to remain) relatively reliable. Despite this, any figures given in the Guide In Brief *should be treated as guidelines only*. Conversions in this edition were made at the mid-1985 rate of US$1 equals approximately Rp 1,100.

Schedules

Flight and train schedules are continually changing. The tables of information in the Guide In Brief are provided primarily as an indication of routes and frequencies. Departure and arrival times should be checked when you purchase your ticket.

Travelling to Indonesia

By Sea

If you're one of the lucky ones with plenty of time (and money), an ocean cruise to Indonesia should not be missed. Luxury cruise lines offer fly/cruise arrangements which allow you to fly to Bali and other ports where you can play in the sun, then catch your ship on the way home or vice versa. For those seeking elegance, a few ships offer cruises to Indonesia. The *Pearl of Scandinavia*, run by Mansfield Travel in Singapore (tel: 732 0088) offers a 14-day Indonesian Islands cruise, which begins and ends in Singapore, to Penang, Belawan, Sibolga, Nias, Jakarta, Padang Bay, Bali and Surabaya. Harpers Travel (in Singapore—tel: 250 8118) handles the *Coral Princess* which sails out of Hong Kong during the winter months to Bali, Jakarta, Penang and Phuket. There are many discount fares when three or more people travel and you won't just be spending long hours staring at your friends; interesting scholars, artists, writers, historians and diplomats sail as guest lecturers and sailing companions.

If you like to travel with the footloose budget travellers, you can hop on a motor launch leaving Finger Pier, Prince Edward Road in Singapore for Tanjung Pinang where you can catch the *KM Tampomas*, flagship for the Indonesian National Pelni Lines which runs weekly sailings to Medan or Jakarta. In November 1984 the service was temporarily discontinued. Ticketing agents will confirm the current situation.

There are many motor launches to Tanjung Pinang, one at 8:30 a.m. but none later then noon. Check at Finger Pier in the morning for schedules and tickets. The 5-6 hour ride costs S$65 (US$30) but a S$75 (US$35) fast boat is available. Intra Express Pte. Ltd. next to the Garuda ticketing office in Goldhill Shopping Centre (tel: 2540914) also sells tickets. It is advisable to leave Singapore two days before the *Tampomas* departs and spend time on Tanjung Pinang. *Tampomas* leaves for Jakarta every Saturday at 5 p.m. local time. It costs the same amount of money to buy a package fare from German Asian Travels in the Straits Trading Building, 14th floor, 9 Battery Road, Singapore (tel. 5335466) which includes the boat ride from Singapore, the transfer from Tanjung Pinang to the *K.M. Tampomas* by sampan and accommodation on board according to the class booked. Food and drinks can be purchased on board but may be costly. You might want to pack your own food. It is an 'unforgettable' two-day trip across the Java Sea aboard a crowded ship with primitive sanitation facilities and it's recommended only for the hardy. The ship arrives in Port Tanjung Priok. Jakarta on Monday at 5 a.m. and turns around to head back ready for embarkation at 6 a.m. Cabins must be booked one to two weeks in advance. Deck class can be obtained at short notice. (*See* Travel Advisories for custom and health formalities).

Several other big shipping companies run ships, both big and small, in and out of the hundreds of ports of Indonesia. However, most of them carry cargo with limited space for passengers and are less accommodating than the *KM Tampomas*. Check with the harbourmaster for prices. It's often cheaper to go direct to the captain himself and pay for your fare.

By Air

Coming from outside the Indonesian archipelago you have two main options: through Jakarta's new international airport at Cengkareng 20 kilometres (12.5 miles) west of Jakarta or through Ngurah Rai Airport near Denpasar on the neighbouring island of Bali with connecting flights to Yogyakarta. Airport tax on international flights is Rp. 4000. Halim international airport will continue to serve only special flights including government and state guests. A new highway links Cengkareng with Jakarta and until a railway system is completed buses will operate at regular intervals to Gambir—itself the location of a railway station and only a few minutes by road from the city.

A majority of visitors arrive in Jakarta from Singapore. Garuda and Singapore Airlines have 5-8 flights daily from Singapore to Jakarta at between US$170 and $190 for round-trip, one-month excursion fares. A one month excursion fare is available from Singapore to Bali with stops in Jakarta and Yogyakarta for approximately US$300.

Travel Advisories

Visa Regulations

All travellers to Indonesia must be in possession of a passport valid for at least six months after arrival and with proof (tickets) of onward passages.

Visas have been waived for nationals of 28 countries for a visit not exceeding two months. Those countries are:

Australia	Malaysia
Austria	Netherlands
Belgium	New Zealand
Brunei	Norway
Canada	Philippines
Denmark	Singapore
Finland	South Korea
France	Spain
Greece	Sweden
Iceland	Switzerland
Ireland	Thailand
Italy	United Kingdom
Japan	United States of America
Luxembourg	West Germany

Entry and exit must be through the air or seaports of Jakarta, Bali, Medan, Manado, Biak, Ambon, Batam, with the addition of Surabaya seaport only and Pekanbaru airport.

For other ports of arrival and departure visas are required. Visas are free also for registered delegates attending a conference which has received official approval.

For citizens of countries other than the 28 listed above, tourist visas can be obtained from any Indonesian Embassy or consulate. Two photographs are required and a small fee is charged.

Business Visas for five weeks can be obtained on application and extension is at the discretion of the immigration authorities.

An airport tax of Rp.3000 per person is required on international departures from Jakarta, Medan and Denpasar.

Surat Jalan: A *surat jalan* is a letter from the police permitting the bearer to go to certain places. It is advisable to carry one when travelling in some of the outer islands, but in Java only in such out-of-the-way places as the Ijen plateau. If in doubt check with a good travel agent. In Jakarta a *surat jalan* may be obtained in an hour or two at Police Headquarters (Markas Besar Kepolisian Republik Indonesia) in Jalan Trunojoyo (Kebayoran Baru).

Health Precautions

Be sure to have valid inoculations against smallpox and cholera, and an International Health Certificate to prove it. Yellow fever vaccination is required if you arrive within 6 days of leaving or passing through an infected area. It is also advisable to be vaccinated against typhoid and paratyphoid.

If you intend staying in Indonesia for some time, particularly outside of the big cities, gammaglobulin injections are recommended; they won't stop hepatitis, but many physicians believe that the risk of infection is greatly reduced. Diarrhea may be a problem: it can be prevented by a daily dose of Doxycycline, an antibiotic used to prevent 'traveller diarrhea.' Obtain this from your doctor at home. At the first signs of stomach discomfort, try a diet of hot tea and a little patience. Stomach reactions are often a reaction to a change in food and environment. Proprietary brands of tablets such as Lomotil and Imodium are invaluable cures. A supply of malaria-suppressant tablets is also highly recommended. Make sure the suppressants are effective against all the strains of malaria. It was recently discovered that a malaria strain was resistant to the usual malarial prophylactic (chloroquine). Consult your physician.

All water, including well water, municipal water and water used for making ice, MUST be made safe before consumption. Bringing water to a rolling boil for 10 minutes is an effective method. Iodine (Globoline) and chlorine (Halazone) may also be used to make water potable. All fruit should be carefully peeled before eaten and no raw vegetables should be eaten.

Last but not least, protect yourself against the sun. Tanning oils and creams are expensive in Indonesia, so bring your own.

Currency and Exchange

The exchange rate for a US $1 was about Rp. 1,100 in mid 1985. It is advisable not to exchange large sums of money if you plan to be in Indonesia for more than a month.

Changing Money: Foreign currency, in banknotes and travellers checks, is best exchanged at major banks or leading hotels (though hotel rates are slightly less favourable than bank rates). There are also limited numbers of registered money changers, but avoid unauthorised changers who operate illegally. Banks in many smaller towns are not necessarily conversant with all foreign banknotes, so it is advisable to change most currencies in the cities. Your *rupiah* may be freely converted to foreign currencies when you are leaving the country.

Travellers checks are a mixed blessing. Major hotels, banks and some shops will accept them, but even in the cities it can take a long time to collect your money (in small towns, it is impossible). The US dollar is recommended for travellers checks. Credit cards are usable if you stay in the big hotels. International airline offices, a few big city restaurants and art shops will accept them, but they are useless elsewhere.

Transportation

Domestic Air Travel

Indonesia, for those that can afford it, is aviation country. The national flag carrier, Garuda, serves both international as well as domestic routes. The only carrier using jet airplanes on domestic routes, it has several flights from Jakarta to all main provincial cities. Several flights daily run from Jakarta to Bali, Medan, Ujung Pandang, Manado, Balikpapan and other destinations. Shuttle flights run to Surabaya, Semarang, Bandung and Bandar Lampung.

Merpati also offers regular services to 100 destinations within Indonesia. Of special interest are the "pioneer flights" to remote areas not served by other airlines. Merpati is particularly active in eastern Indonesia, serving the small islands and interiors of Sulawesi, Kalimantan and Irian Jaya. Besides Garuda and Merpati, there are several privately owned airlines with both scheduled and charter services. Those with scheduled services include Bouraq, Mandala and Sempati. The table of flight information provides details of frequencies and costs. Prices given were correct as of July 1985. Some addresses of airline offices are given in the regional information sections. Airport taxes range between Rp.1,000 and Rp. 2,500 depending on the airport of departure.

Garuda now operates an air-travel pass. Called the "**Visit Indonesia Air Pass**," it allows for a number of flights for one payment;
- **Visit 1:** flights between five cities of your choice as long as they are completed within no more than ten nights. Price: US$300.
- **Visit 2:** flights between ten cities of your choice as long as they are completed within no more than 20 nights. Price: US$400.
- **Visit 3:** flights between 33 cities of your choice as long as they are completed within no more

than 60 nights.

The pass is operated only by Garuda and can be obtained in Japan, Australia, New Zealand, Europe and the United States. The pass is *not* for sale in Singapore. Airport tax must still be paid by the passenger.

For the Indonesian archipelago, such a travel package is invaluable. For relatively little expense you can plan an itinerary that stretches between Banda Aceh in northern Sumatra and Jayapura in Irian Jaya. More than that, it means that you can do a little island-hopping by air instead of by sea. The "Visit Indonesia Air Pass" will be especially useful for Nusa Tenggara where you can plan a route through Sumba, Sumbawa, Flores and Timor and then continue east into the Maluku archipelago.

Whether you have this air pass or not, you are likely to use the domestic air network in Indonesia. **Garuda**, **Merpati** and **Bourag** are the principal carriers, between them covering a veritable labyrinth of destinations. The travel information under the regional listings that follow includes a box selecting just a few of the flights that might come in useful. Prices are rounded up to the nearest US dollar, *but should be treated as rough guidelines only* since the companies concerned change prices at short notice. Care has been taken to select routes that relate to the locations covered in this book. If you intend travelling by plane frequently you should get a copy of the timetables and latest fares from the respective company. A seemingly endless variety of itineraries can be planned.

● **Garuda Indonesian Airways**, Head Office, Jalan Ir. H. Juanda 15, Jakarta, tel: 370709.

● **Merpati Nusantara Airlines**, Jalan Angkasa 2, Jakarta, tel: 411650.

● **Bouraq Indonesia Airlines**, Jalan Angkasa 1-3, Jakarta, tel: 655170.

Domestic Sea Travel

There are a number of inter-Indonesian shipping routes that offer an adventurous and surprisingly cheap form of transportation. Two particular ships are worth consideration; neither of them are "cruise" ships. Economy-class fares offer a viable way of spanning some of the great distances involved if you intend making some extensive journeys through the archipelago.

The KM Kerinci (pronounced ke-rin-chee) plies the route between Padang (west coast of Sumatra) to Jakarta and on to Ujung Pandang (Sulawesi). It sails from Padang every Monday evening at 22.00 and arrives in Tanjung Priok Tuesday 16.00. The second leg of the journey takes you to Ujung Pandang arriving at 13.00 Thursday. The boat "turns round" in Ujung Pandang leaving at 18.00 the same day for Jakarta again. The 42-hour return journey gets you to Jakarta at 10.00 Saturday morning. Sailing time for the final segment of the trip back to Padang is 21.00 the same day. Arrival in Padang at 06.00 Monday.

Another truly mammoth route, on the KM Kambuna starts from Belawan (Medan) and then follows this itinerary: Tanjung Priok (Jakarta), Surabaya, Ujung Pandang, Balikpapan, Bitung (Manado, North Sulawesi), Balikpapan, Ujung Pandang, Surabaya, Tanjung Priok and Belawan.

The whole round trip takes two weeks, though you should certainly consider building one or two segments into your own itinerary.

Fares* are listed below in the table (correct as quoted in January 1985). Another boat, KM Rinjani, goes all the way to Bau Bau (an island off Southeast Sulawesi) and on to Ambon and Sorong.

Tanjung Priok to:	1st Class	2nd Class	3rd Class	4th Class	Economy
Padang	48	39	31	25	21
Belawan (Medan)	72	59	47	39	31
Surabaya	34	27	23	18	15
Ujung Pandang	71	58	46	39	31
Balikpapan	74	60	49	40	34
Bitung (Manado)	132	108	86	71	58
Bau Bau	85	70	56	47	39
Ambon	115	94	75	62	51
Sorong	140	113	91	75	62

* Fares (in US$) rounded up to nearest unit and converted at rate of Rp1,100 equal US$1.

Both the *Kerinci* and the *Kambunan* are operated by the national shipping company PELNI. They can be contacted in Jakarta PT PELNI, Jalan Angkasa 18, Jakarta, telephone: 417569 or 415428.

Language

Indonesia's motto, *Bhinneka Tunggal Ika* (unity in diversity) is seen in its most driving, potent form in the world of language. Although there are over 350 distinct languages and dialects spoken in the archipelago, the one national tongue, *Bahasa Indonesia*, will take you from the northernmost tip of Sumatra through Java and across the string of islands to Irian Jaya.

Bahasa Indonesia is both an old and new language. It is based on Malay, which has been the *lingua franca* throughout much of Southeast Asia for centuries, but it has changed rapidly in the past few decades to meet the needs of a modern nation.

Although formal Indonesian is a complex language demanding serious study, the construction of basic Indonesian sentences is relatively simple. A compact and cheap book—*How to Master the Indonesian Language*, by Almatseier—is widely available in Indonesia and should prove invaluable in helping you say what you want to say. Indonesian is written in the Roman alphabet and, unlike some Asian languages, is not tonal.

Indonesians always use their language to show respect when addressing others, especially when a younger person speaks to his elders. The custom is to address an elder man as *bapak* or *'pak* (father) and an elder woman as *ibu* (mother), and even in the case of slightly younger people who are obviously VIPs, this form is suitable and correct. *Bung* (in West Java) and *mas* (in Central and East Java) roughly translate as "brother" and are used with equals, people your own age whom you don't know all that well, and with hotel clerks, taxi drivers, tour guides and waiters (it's friendly, and a few notches above "buddy" or "mate").

Travelling in Java: Introduction

Each part of the island has its own distinctive character. Central, West and East Java are only rough geographical divisions, made for administrative purposes, within which much finer local distinctions in dialect, custom and food exist.

The areas around the old court cities (Yogya, Solo and Cirebon being the main ones) are culturally much richer than other areas. In general the lowlands are very much more crowded (and hotter!) than the uplands. Bear the following in mind also:

- All of Java's many hill resorts are deliciously cool and spectacularly scenic—every major city has one.
- The only well-developed tourist beaches are found in West Java.
- For handicrafts, ancient temples, palaces, dances and wayang puppet shows, the Yogyakarta/Surakarta central Javanese heartland should not be missed.
- Java has several national parks and nature reserves, some of which have visitor facilities. (See Part IV, "Indonesia's Wildlife.")

The standard 2-week "package tour" of Indonesia has, up to now, included only Jakarta, Yogyakarta and Bali. Visitors with more time to spare generally add a few more days in Bandung, Yogya and Solo, before continuing on to Bali. Only a handful of adventurous young budget travellers explore the north coast of the island or the eastern highlands around Malang and Bromo.

Many visitors and even many tour operators are not aware that the situation has changed quite dramatically over the past few years. Domestic tourism has opened up many new areas on Java—mainly hill stations and beaches around the major cities—and these are now served by good roads, with convenient public transportation and clean, comfortable accommodation. Most medium sized cities have at least one good hotel.

Study the Java map in Part III carefully. Even better, buy a large fold-out map of Java in a bookshop or hotel and spend some time familiarizing yourself with the intricate geography of the island. Though the distances aren't very great—the island is only 1100 kms (650 miles) long—remember that roads here, though generally good, are made slow by heavy traffic.

Bus fares and schedules are too numerous to list here. Remember that buses operate on all major highways, linking together the cities in a comprehensive and inexpensive travel network. Minibuses (known here by the Mitsubishi brand-name "Colt" or the Dutch word *oplet*, which means "to flag down") ply the by-roads, providing a complementary local network of transport to and from smaller towns and villages.

Decide how much time you intend to spend in Java, then ask yourself what you most want to see and do. Compromises are unavoidable. It's easy to spend two weeks in West Java mountain climbing and hiking, or even longer just visiting temples and other sites around Yogya.

If you allot only a few days for Java and want to get on to Bali or another island, then a direct train or flight through to Yogyakarta, with connections from here on to Bali, is advisable. Assuming that you have at least two weeks on Java, you can visit Bandung and possibly the north coast, en route from Jakarta to Yogya and Solo (or vice versa).

BIMA EXPRESS TRAIN
(Jakarta-Yogyakarta-Solo-Surabaya)
1st/2nd class, air-con w/sleepers

	daily	daily	First Class Fare	Second Class Fare
Jakarta (Kota Station)	16:00	8:20		
Cirebon	19:50	4:24	US$25	US$20.50
Yogyakarta	1:40	22:00	US$25	US$20.50
Solo (Balapan Station)	3:33	20:36	US$26	US$22
Surabaya (Gubeng Station)	9:30	16:00	US$33	US$26.50

MUTIARA UTARA EXPRESS TRAIN
(Jakarta-Cirebon-Semarang-Surabaya)
1st/2nd class, air-con

	daily	daily	First Class Fare	Second Class Fare
Jakarta (Kota Station)	16:30	7:45		
Cirebon	20:20	3:40	US$17.50	US$13.30
Tegal	21:45	2:20	US$17.50	US$17.50
Pekalongan	23:03	1:17	US$17.50	US$17.50
Semarang (Tawang Station)	1:15	22:56	US$17.50	US$13.30
Surabaya (Pasar Turi Station)	8:00	16:30	US$22.00	US$15.30

The following is a review of the advantages and disadvantages of each method of travel in Java:

Air: by far the quickest and easiest way to get around the island. Numerous daily flights. You can go from Jakarta to Yogyakarta, for example, in only half-an-hour as opposed to the 10 or even 12 hours it takes by bus or train. Air tickets are invariably two or three times the price of a first-class train ticket and as much as 10 times more than the bus.

Route	Dep.	Arr.	Days	one-way economy fare US$
JKT – BDO				
Garuda	07.30	08.05	Daily	26
	10.30	11.05	Daily	
	12.30	13.05	Daily	
Merpati	06.30	07.00	Sat	21
	16.00	16.30	Wed. Fri. Sun.	
Bouraq	14.45	15.15	Daily	21
JKT – JOG				
Garuda	06.30	07.30	Daily	48
	08.30	09.30	Sat. Sun.	
	10.00	11.00	Daily	
	12.00	13.00	Sat. Sun.	
	13.30	14.30	Daily	
JKT – SUB				
Garuda	Hourly between 07.00 and 18.00 75 minute flight		Daily	70
Merpati	05.00	06.30	Daily	58
Bouraq	14.45	17.10	Daily	58
JKT – SRG				
Garuda	06.40	07.40	Daily	44
	08.40	09.40	Daily	
	10.40	11.40	Daily	
	12.40	13.40	Daily	
	13.40	14.40	Daily	
	14.40	15.40	Daily	
	15.40	16.40	Daily	
Bouraq	07.30	08.45	Daily	36
JKT – SOC				
Garuda	07.50	08.10	Daily	48
	11.15	12.20	Sun.	
	13.05	14.10	Daily	
JKT – CBN				
Merpati	07.10	08.00	Daily	27
	14.00	14.50	Daily	
JOG – SUB				
Merpati	07.00	08.10	Daily	24
SRG – SUB				
Garuda	08.30	09.15	Daily	27
	16.30	17.15	Daily	
BDO – JOG				
Bouraq	07.30	08.35	Tue. Thur. Sun.	37
BDO – SUB				
Garuda	12.00	13.20	Daily	95
Bouraq	15.40	17.10	Daily	55

CITY CODES: JKT-Jakarta: BDO-Bandung: JOG-Yogyakart: SUB-Surabaya: SRG-Semarang: SOC-Solo (Surakarta): CBN-Cirebon.

Inter-city trains: are quite comfortable, if a bit slow. First-class carriages have air-conditioning and a dining car that serves passable meals (generally a set dinner of rice, chicken and pickles with tea). Though the train equipment is imported from Germany, the service is certainly not. Javanese trains are often late—sometimes many hours late as only a single track connects many major cities, so if one train is held up, they are all late. (*See* box on previous page.)

Inter-city buses: generally faster and more punctual than trains. Considerably cheaper. Most Indonesians travel this way, and you can go across Java for as little as US$10! Long-distance express buses operate at night, leaving major cities at either end of the island in the late afternoon, stopping to pick up and discharge passengers in Central Java in the middle of the night, and arriving at the other end of the island early in the morning. Seats are narrow—six across in a bus that in the West would only seat four across. Some have air-conditioning and video movies. Bus drivers drive like maniacs, at breakneck speed with little concern for safety. Accidents are not uncommon. Definitely not a method of travel for the weak at heart.

Private rented car: you still cannot rent a car on Java without a driver (as you can in Bali), but a chauffeur is not an extravagance here. Automobiles are heavily taxed and expensive, nevertheless, and the price of renting one reflects that—US$50 a day is common, though beat up taxis and older cars can be rented for as little as US$20 a day with a driver.

Rented mini-bus ("colt"): the most comfortable and practical way to go. These can be rented for US$20 to US$30 per day including a driver. For trips out of town or across the island you need only pay for the driver's food and lodging (about US$10 a day), and you may have to buy some or all of the petrol. Still, with a group of four or five people you can go from Jakarta all the way to Yogyakarta via Bandung and the north coast in a week for about US$250—about the same cost as flying. Arrange for such a rental through your hotel in Yogyakarta or Jakarta. This may take some negotiation. Be sure that the agreement is all worked out clearly in advance, including the amount you will give the driver every day for food and lodging (tips are not expected, though of course they would be appreciated). You may have difficulty finding a driver who speaks some English, so expect to pay a premium for this. Count on one extra day's rental fee and a full tank of gas for the driver to get home.

Jakarta

There are many "musts" in Jakarta, but be forewarned about trying to do too much. Two major sights or areas of the city a day are enough. Take a siesta or a swim in between to recover from the heat. Get an early start in the cool morning hours, do your errands and sightseeing, then get in out of the noonday sun. Venture out again in the late afternoon and early evening, when the weather has cooled off and the crowds are thinner.

City Orientation

At Jakarta's centre lies **Medan Merdeka** (Freedom Square), a vast parade ground criss-crossed by broad ceremonial boulevards, with the National Monument towering in its midst. Going north, the major artery is Jl. Gajah Mada/Jl. Hayam Wuruk, two one-way roads with a canal separating them. This is the older, commercial area of town, horribly congested throughout much of the day and practically deserted at night. At the north end of this artery lies the old colonial city and the old harbour, now both major tourist sights. To the east along the coast are Ancol, a sprawling entertainment complex, and Tanjung Priok, the port.

The "mainstreet" of Jakarta is now **Jl. Thamrin/Jl. Jendral Sudirman**, which connects Medan Merdeka (the central square) with Kebayoran Baru (the new satellite suburb). Many international hotels, office buildings, theatres, restaurants and nightclubs are on this street. To the east of Jl. Thamrin lie the older colonial residential areas of **Menteng, Cikini** and **Gondangdia**, with their luxurious mansions and tidy, tree-shaded streets. **Jl. Imam Bonjol/Jl. Diponegoro** is "Embassy Row," lined with many of the finest mansions in Jakarta and worth a quick drive or walk-through. Many shops, boutiques and restaurants are in this area, as is TIM, the arts centre of Jakarta.

Arrival and Departure

There are five major train stations, one airport and three inter-city bus terminals in Jakarta. When making arrangements to leave the city, be sure to ask the name of the one you will be using.

Air: all Jakarta flights now operate to and from the new international airport at **Cengkareng**, 20kms (12 miles) to the west of the city. A new expressway links Cengkareng to the city's western edge, but from here heavy traffic can mean a ride of up to an hour to reach the central hotel districts.

Transportation to and from the new airport is made relatively expensive by the expressway's steep auto toll (US$2.50 each way) and a cab surcharge of US$3 that is tacked on to the metered fare, so expect to pay the equivalent of US$12-15 to reach your destination.

Alternatively, hop aboard a convenient air-conditioned *Damri* airport bus operating to one of several strategic points in the city (Gambir Train Station, the old Kemayoran airport and Blok M in Kebayoran, among others) for only US$2 and then catch a cab from there to your hotel. These large, cream-colored buses may be flagged down from any point in front of the terminals, though their schedule is irregular and the service stops around 8 pm.

Sea: all ocean-going vessels berth at **Tanjung Priok Harbour**, 10 kms (six miles) to the northeast of the city. Tanjung Priok is about half an hour and US$6 from the city centre by cab.

Train: there are five major train stations in Jakarta, but only two serve the First Class inter-city trains. **Kota Station** in the north of the city is the gateway for Central and East Java, whereas **Gambir Station** on the eastern side of Medan Merdeka serves trains bound for Bogor and Bandung.

Train tickets should be purchased a day in advance from Carnation Travel Agency, corner of Jl. Kebon Sirih and Jl. Menteng Raya (Jl. Menteng Raya 24, Jakarta Pusat, tel: 344027, 356728 and Jl. Kyai Maja 53, Kebayoran Baru, tel: 713943), or else on the morning of your departure from the station ticket window. Allow one hour to reach the Kota Station during business hours, because of the heavy traffic in that part of town. Most trains depart in the afternoon, although the Parahiangan trains to Bandung depart four times daily.

● **Gambir Station**, Jl. Merdeka Timur, tel: 348612, 342777.

● **Jakarta Kota Station**, Jl. Station 1, tel: 278 515, 277275.

Bus: three bus terminals for buses operating to the west, the south, and the east of Jakarta respectively. Buses to Sumatra and Java's west coast operate from **Grogol Terminal** (tel: 592274) on the western edge of Jakarta. Those to Bandung, Bogor and other points south operate from **Cililitan Terminal** (tel: 884554) just beyond the old Halim Airport. Those to Central and East Java operate from **Pulo Gadung Terminal** (tel: 881763) where Jl. Bekasi Timur Raya meets Jl. Perintis Kemerdekaan. All bus terminals are connected by local city buses to the city centre. By cab they are not more than US$4 from the city centre. Intercity buses also pick up passengers at their offices in the city, so if you know the address and don't mind getting there early and waiting on the bus as they collect passengers, you can save the trip out to the terminal.

Mini-buses/inter-city taxis: best way to get to nearby cities like Bogor, Bandung or Cirebon. They will pick you up and deliver you directly to your destination, for about the same fare as the train and slightly more than an air-conditioned bus. They do not operate directly to more distant destinations. Ask your hotel to book seats for you a day or more in advance.

● **"4848" Inter-city Taxi**, Jl. Prapatan 34, tel: 348048, 364488, 364448.

● **Media**, Jl. Kebon Sirih 32, tel: 345348.

● **Parahyangan**, Jl. Wahid Hasyim 13, tel: 353434.

● **Metro**, Jl. Kopi 2C, tel: 672827, 674585.

● **Perkasa**, Jl. Merdeka Barat 18, tel: 354497.

Getting Around Jakarta

Taxis: by far the most practical way of getting around the city. Despite a recent increase, fares remain reasonable. The flagfall is currently Rp400 or about US$0.40 for the first kilometre (0.6 miles) and Rp190 for each subsequent kilometre. It costs about US$2-5 for most cross-town journeys. Cabs are available at any hotel and easily hailed on major thoroughfares. President and

JAKARTA

Attractions
1. National Monument (Monas)
2. National Museum
3. Presidential Palace
4. Istiqlal Mosque
5. Lapangan Banteng
6. Taman Ismail Marzuki (TIM)
7. National Archives
8. Chinatown
9. Taman Fatahillah
10. Sunda Kelapa
11. Ancol
12. Ragunan Zoo

Hotels
13. Borobudur
14. Hilton
15. Horizon
16. Hyatt
17. Kartika Plaza
18. Mandarin
19. Hotel Indonesia
20. President
21. Sahid Jaya

22. Sari Pacific
23. Jalan Jaksa
24. Sabang Metropolitan

Shopping
25. Sarinah
26. Sarinah Jaya (Kebayoran)
27. Pasar Baru
28. Jl. Kebon Sirih Dalam Timur
29. Blok M (Kebayoran)
30. Batik factories

Transportation
31. Halim International Airport
32. Kemayoran Airport (Domestic)
33. Kota Train Station
34. Gambir Train Station
35. Tanjung Priok Harbor
36. Cililitan Bus Terminal
37. Grogol Bus Terminal
38. Pulo Gadung Bus Terminal
39. Cengkareng International Airport

Bluebird are the largest and generally the most reliable companies. Radio cabs may be summoned by phone. Be sure the meter is on when you get in, and that it stays on for the entire journey. Some cabbies will try and take you for a ride. It is a good idea to rent a cab by the hour if you intend making a lot of stops. Tipping is not customary, but drivers rarely have change, so carry some with you and even then be prepared to round off to the nearest Rp 500 (US$0.50).

Rental Cars: available with drivers from Avis, Hertz and President Taxi or from any major hotel. Hourly or daily rates are available within the city; trips out of town are charged on a round-trip basis according to a fixed schedule. For example, a trip to Bogor and back will cost roughly US$25 for a total distance of almost 160 kms (100 miles) and an elapsed time of between three and four hours.

- **Avis Car Rental**, Jl. Diponegoro 25, tel: 349206, 351849.
- **Bluebird Taxi**, Jl. Garuda 88, tel: 356527, 344937.
- **Hertz Car Rental**, tel: 370108.
- **President Taxi**, Jl. D/7 Pekan Raya, tel: 352634.
- **Steady Safe Taxi**, Jl. Gondangdia Lama 22.

City Buses: cheap (Rp100 fixed fare), but often crowded and sometimes dangerous as they do not stop completely when picking-up and discharging passengers. You must also beware of pickpockets, especially during peak hours. Your hotel staff can advise you which buses to take, and a bus map is sometimes available from the **Tourist Information Centre** in the **Jakarta Theatre Building** on Jl. Thamrin.

Accommodation

Jakarta has come a long way since the 1960s, when the only international-class hotel in town was the Hotel Indonesia, built by the Japanese as a war reparation. Of the older, pre-war establishments, only the Transaera and the Royal remain, but neither is truly "colonial" in ambience.

Luxury Class (above US$100 per night)

Jakarta now has three five-star hotels, with another to be completed soon. Two have extensive grounds and sports facilities: the **Borobudur Intercontinental** and the **Jakarta Hilton**. In addition to Olympic-size swimming pools, tennis courts, squash courts, health clubs, jogging tracks and spacious gardens, they also boast discos and a full complement of European and Asian restaurants. The other hotel in the same category, the **Mandarin**, is a newer "city" hotel—providing a central location and emphasizing superior service and excellent food.

- **Borobudur Inter-Continental** (866 rooms), Jl. Lapangan Banteng Selatan, P.O. Box 329, Jakarta. tel: 370108, tlx: 44150 BDO JKT.
- **Jakarta Hilton International** (396 rooms), Jl. Jendral Gatot Subroto, P.O. Box 3315, Jakarta, tel: 587981, 583051, tlx: JKT 46345-46673-46698 HILTON JAKARTA.
- **Jakarta Mandarin** (504 rooms), Jl. M.H. Thamrin, P.O. Box 3392, Jakarta, tel: 321307, tlx: MANDAJKT 45755.

First Class (US$60 to US$100 per night)

There are another half-dozen or so first-class hotels in town. The **Sari Pacific** is centrally located and has a popular coffee shop and deli. The **Hyatt** boasts an excellent French restaurant. The **Horison** and the **Sahid Jaya** have restaurants specializing in seafood. The **President Hotel** is Japanese-operated with several Japanese restaurants. And the venerable **Hotel Indonesia** has a supper club with nightly floorshows and a swimming pool garden open to the public (US$4 admission).

- **Horison Hotel** (350 rooms), Jl. Pantai Indah, Taman Impian Jaya Ancol, P.O. Box 3340, Jakarta, tel: 680008, tlx: 42824 HORIZ.
- **Hotel Indonesia** (666 rooms), Jl. M.H. Thamrin, P.O. Box 54, Jakarta, tel: 320008, 322008, tlx: 44233 HIPAJKT, 46347 HIJKT.
- **Hyatt Aryaduta** (250 rooms), Jl. Prapatan 44-46, P.O. Box 3287, Jakarta, tel: 376008, tlx: 46220 HYATT JAKARTA.
- **Kartika Chandra** (200 rooms), Jl. Gatot Subroto, Jakarta, tel: 510808, 511008, tlx: 45843 KACHA IA, 46470 KACHA JKT.
- **President Hotel** (354 rooms), Jl. M.H. Thamrin 59, tel: 320508, tlx: 46724 PREHOIA.
- **Sahid Jaya Hotel** (514 rooms), Jl. Jendral Sudirman 86, P.O. Box 41, Jakarta, tel: 584151, tlx: 46331 SAHID JKT.
- **Sari Pacific Hotel** (500 rooms), Jl. M.H. Thamrin 6, P.O. Box 3138, Jakarta, tel: 323707, tlx: HTISARIIA 44514.

Intermediate Range (US$20 to US$60 per night)

At the upper end of the moderate price range, the most centrally located hotels are the **Transaera**, the **Sabang Metropolitan**, the **Monas** and the **Asoka** (all are about US$35 and up for a double). The **Transaera** is particularly quiet, with older, spacious rooms and the **Monas** has a reputation for good service. The **Sabang Metropolitan** is convenient for business and shopping.

In Kebayoran Baru, you may choose between the **Kemang** and the **Kebayoran Inn**, both popular with frequent visitors for their reasonable prices and quiet, residential surroundings. Or try the **Interhouse**, centrally located by Kebayoran's shopping district, Blok M. There are several hotels in town providing small but clean, air-conditioned rooms for around US$25. These include the **Menteng Hotel** and the **Marco Polo**, both in Menteng.

- **Asoka Hotel** (83 rooms), Jl. M.H. Thamrin 28-30, P.O. Box 3076, Jakarta, tel: 322908, tlx: ASOKA JKT 4432.
- **City Hotel** (196 rooms), Jl. Medan Glodok, P.O. Box 1575, Jakarta, tel: 627008, tlx: CTHOTELJKT 41138.
- **Garden Hotel** (100 rooms), Jl. Kemang Raya, P.O. Box 41, Kebayoran Baru, Jakarta, tel: 715808, tlx: 47166 ADIGJKT.

- **Interhouse Hotel** (133 rooms), Jl. Melawai Raya 18-20, P.O. Box 128, Kebayoran Baru, Jakarta, tel: 716408, tlx: BAMBANG 471811A.
- **Jayakarta Tower** (435 rooms), Jl. Hayam Wuruk 126, Jakarta, tel: 624408, tlx: 41113 JAHOTELIA.
- **Kartika Plaza** (331 rooms), Jl. M.H. Thamrin 10, P.O. Box 2081, Jakarta, tel: 321008, tlx: 45843 KACHA IA, 46470 KACHA JKT.
- **Kebayoran Inn** (61 rooms), Jl. Senayan 57, Kebayoran Baru, Jakarta, tel: 716208.
- **Kemang Hotel** (100 rooms), Jl. Kemang Raya, P.O. Box 163, Kebayoran Baru, Jakarta, tel: 793208, tlx: 47145 JKT.
- **Marco Polo Hotel** (181 rooms), Jl. Teuku Cik Ditro 19, Jakarta, tel: 375409.
- **Menteng I** (82 rooms), Jl. Gondangdia Lama, Jakarta, tel: 352508.
- **Menteng II** (70 rooms), Jl. Cikini Raya 105, Jakarta, tel: 326312, 325543, 326329.
- **Monas Hotel** (50 rooms), Jl. Merdeka Barat 21, Jakarta, tel: 375208.
- **Orchid Palace** (85 rooms), Jl. Letjen S. Parman, Slipi, P.O. Box 2791, Jakarta, tel: 593115, 596911, tlx: 46631 OPHIA.
- **Putri Duyung Cottages** (102 cottages), Taman Impian Jaya Ancol, Jakarta, tel: 680611, 680108, tlx: TIJAJKT.
- **Sabang Metropolitan** (157 rooms), Jl. H.A. Salim 11, P.O. Box 2725, Jakarta, tel: 354031, 357621, tlx: 445555 SAGANGIA.
- **Transaera Hotel** (50 rooms), Jl. Merdeka Timur 16, P.O. Box 3380, Jakarta, tel: 351373, 359336, 357059.
- **Wisata International** (165 rooms), Jl. M.H. Thamrin, P.O. Box 2457, Jakarta, tel: 320308, 320408, tlx: 46787 WISATA IA.
- **Wisma Bumi Asih Guesthouse**, Jl. Solo 4, Menteng, Jakarta, tel: 350839.

Budget (under US$20 per night)

True budget travellers almost invariably stay at Jalan Jaksa No. 5 (**Wisma Delima**) or one of the other homestays on that street. Also in the US$3-to-US$5 a night category, the new **Borneo Hostel** around the corner and the **Pondok Soedibyo** are perhaps slightly cleaner. A bit more expensive at US$10 is the nearby **Bali International**, and for US$18 you get a double room with fan and breakfeast at the **Royal**. For just a little bit more, however, stay in an air-conditioned room at the **Srivijaya.**

- **Bali International** (31 rooms), Jl. K.H. Wahid Hasyim 116, tel: 345058.
- **Borneo Hostel**, Jl. Kebun Sirih Barat Dalam 35, Jakarta, tel: 320095.
- **Pondok Soedibyo**, Jl. Kebon Sirih 23, Jakarta.
- **Royal Hotel**, Jl. Juanda 14, Jakarta, tel: 362598, 348894, 357068.
- **Srivijaya Hotel**, Jl. Veteran 1, Jakarta, tel: 370409.
- **Wisma Delima**, Jl. Jaksa 5.
- **Wisma Esther**, Jl. Matraman Raya 113.

Dining Out in Jakarta

Dining in Jakarta can be a delightful experience, though on the whole restaurant meals are expensive here by Indonesian standards (about twice the price of a meal in the provinces), and the food is highly uneven in quality. Locals seek out obscure roadside stalls (*warung*) for a special *soto* or *sate* but too many visitors are hit with a stomach bug and this can ruin a week or more of your stay. It is possible to eat a good meal in a clean restaurant for US$2 and truly excellent Indonesian or Chinese food can be had for US$5 a head. With the exception of Western-style food and service, a meal at the best restaurants will rarely cost more than US$10 per person, all-inclusive. Seafood of any sort is excellent so be sure not to leave Jakarta without sampling some.

Indonesian Food

Indonesian Food is of course the smart traveller's first choice in Jakarta, particularly as one may indulge in gastronomic island-hopping on consecutive nights.

Beginning with the northern tip of Sumatra, try the Acehnese restaurant, **Sinar Medan**, conveniently located on Jl. Sabang. Acehnese food is displayed and served cold on many small plates, in the same way as Padang food, but some say it is more delicately spiced, with a wider range of flavours.

The best Padang food is found at **Roda** and **Sari Bundo**. Here, as in all Padang restaurants, between 10 and 15 spicy dishes are placed in front of you and you pay only for what you eat. For slightly more atmosphere and a view (at higher prices), try **The Pepper Pot.**

Javanese cuisine may be divided into three or four categories: Sundanese (West Javanese), Central Javanese, East Javanese and Madurese cooking. For an excellent Sundanese meal of grilled carp (*ikan mas bakar*), grilled chicken (*ayam bakar*), prawns (*udang pancet*), barbequed squid (*cumi-cumi bakar*) and a raw vegetable salad with shrimp-paste chili sauce (*lalap/sambal cobek*), try the extremely popular **Sari Kuring**. This is, incidentally, one of the best seafood places in town, and serves a deliciously cooling cucumber- and lime-juice drink.

The Central Javanese delicacies are fried chicken and *gudeg*. Javanese chickens are farmyard chickens, allowed to run free in the village. As a result they are full of flavour but very tough in comparison with factory-feed chickens in the West. The Javanese boil their chickens first in a concoction of rich spices and coconut cream for several hours, finally deep frying them for about a minute at very high temperatures to crisp the outer coating. The two famous fried chicken places in Jakarta are both in Kebayoran: **Ayam Bulungan** and **Ayam Goreng Mbok Berek**.

Gudeg is the speciality of Yogyakarta, consisting of young jackfruit boiled in coconut cream and spices, served with buffalo hide boiled in chili sauce, chicken pieces, egg and gravy. The best *gudeg* is to be had at a branch of the Yogya restaurant, **Bu Tjitro's**.

East Java and Madura are known for their soups and their *sate*. For *soto madura* (spicy chicken broth with noodles or rice), the best place is **Pondok Jawa Timur**. For chicken or mutton *sate* (barbequed meat skewers), the **Senayan Satay House** has a near monopoly on the Jakarta scene, with its three convenient locations.

- **Angin Mamiri** (Makassarese), Jl. K.H. Hasyim Ashari 49, Roxy, tel: 377241.
- **Ayam Bulungan** (Javanese Fried Chicken), Jl. Bulungan I No. 64, Kebayoran Baru, tel: 772005.
- **Ayam Goreng Mbok Berek** (Javanese Fried Chicken), Jl. Prof. Dr. Soepomo 2, Tebet, tel: 825366.
- **Ayam Goreng Mbok Berek** (Javanese Fried Chicken), Jl. Panglima Polim Raya No. 93, tel: 770652.
- **Fatahillah**, Jl. Fatahillah 14, tel: 673842.
- **Gudeg Bu Tjitro**, Jl. Cikajang 80, Blok Q2 Kebayoran Baru, tel: 713202.
- **Gudeg Bu Tjitro**, Jl. Senen Raya 25A, tel: 371197.
- **Happy** (Makassarese), Jl. Mangga Besar Raya 4C, tel: 632144.
- **Jawa Timur** (East Javanese), Jl. Jendral A. Yani 67, tel: 884197.
- **Marunda Restaurant**, Hotel Wisata International, tel: 320408, 320308.
- **Natrabu Restaurant** (Padang), Jl. H. Agus Salim 29A, tel: 371709.
- **The Pepper Pot** (Padang and Javanese), 18th floor, Wisma Metropolitan, Jl. Jendral Sudirman, tel: 584736.
- **Pondok Jawa Timur** (East Javanese), Jl. Prapanca Raya, Kebayoran.
- **Ratu Sari** (Sundanese), Glodok Plaza, Jl. Pinangsia Raya, tel: 625999, 627701.
- **Roda** (Padang), Jl. Matraman Raya 65-67, tel: 882879.
- **Sari Bundo** (Padang) Jl. Ir. H. Juanda 27, tel: 358343.
- **Sari Kuring** (Sundanese Seafood), Jl. Batu Ceper No. 55A, tel: 341542.
- **Senayan Satay House**, Jl. Pakubuwono VI/No. 6, Kebayoran Baru, tel: 715821.
- **Senayan Satay House**, Jl. Kebon Sirih 31A, tel: 326238.
- **Senayan Satay House**, Jl. Tanah Abang II/No. 76, tel: 347270.
- **Sinar Medan** (Acehnese), Jl. H.A. Salim (Sabang).
- **Tamalatea** (Makassarese), Jl. Krekot I/No. 40G, Pasar Baru, tel: 363447.
- **Tinoor Asli** (Menadonese), Jl. Gondangdia Lama 33A.

Seafood

Seafood was formerly eaten either at Tanjung Priok, near the harbour, or on Jalan Pecenongan at streetside stalls. Although these places are still popular, the prices have risen so that it is just as cheap, and far more pleasant, to eat seafood in a good restaurant. The most famous one is **Yun Njan**, formerly of Tanjung Priok. The atmosphere here is somewhat plastic and busy, but the plates of steamed, grilled or fried crab, fish, prawns and squid are unfailingly fresh. Another good place nearby is the **Sanur** which also has a full menu of Chinese delicacies. The **Sari Kuring** mentioned above and located next to Yun Njan, also has excellent seafood. More pricey but excellent Western-style seafood is to be had at the **Mirasari Restaurant** in the Sahid Jaya Hotel. The **Horison Hotel** in Ancol also has a charming seafood restaurant, right by the sea.

- **Perahu Bugis**, Horison Hotel, Ancol, tel: 680008.
- **Mirasari Restaurant**, Sahid Jaya Hotel, Jl. Jendral Sudirman 86, tel: 584151, 583981.
- **Sanur**, Jl. Ir. H. Juanda III/No. 31.
- **Sari Kuring**, Jl. Batu Ceper No. 55A, tel: 341542.
- **Yun Njan**, Jl. Batu Ceper 69, tel: 364063, 364434.

Chinese Food

Chinese Food served in Jakarta cannot compare to that in Singapore, Hong Kong or Taiwan, but it's very, very popular and compares favourably to Chinese food in the West. The premier banquet houses are the **Cahaya Kota**, the **Istana Naga** and the **Ekaria**. For northern Chinese/Mongolian cuisine, try the **Barbeque Restaurant** in Blok M, Kebayoran. For Szechuanese food, the only place is the pricey but delicious **Spice Garden** in the Mandarin Hotel.

While visiting the Chinatown/Kota area, or in fact for a light lunch anywhere, it is *de rigeur* to sample a bowl of Chinese noodles with chopped pickled vegetables and beefballs (*mee bakso*). The largest noodle house in Chinatown is **Bakmi Gajah Mada**.

- **Bakmi Gajah Mada**, Jl. Gajah Mada 92.
- **Bakmi Gajah Mada**, Jl. Melawai IV/25, Blok M, Kebayoran Baru.
- **Cahaya Kota**, Jl. Wahid Hasyim 9, tel: 356331, 354862, 353015.
- **Ekaria** (Yit Lok Yun), Jl. Hayam Wuruk (Pasar Lindeteves Bldg), tel: 621083, 626397.
- **Istana Naga**, Jl. Gatot Subroto (Kav. 12, Case building), tel: 583081, 583087, 583089.
- **Spice Garden Restaurant** (Szechuanese), Jakarta Mandarin Hotel.

European Food

If you insist on eating **European Food** in Jakarta, then the only acceptable excuse is so as to experience the colonial atmosphere (and cuisine) of Dutch Batavia. This is best done at the magnificent **Oasis Restaurant**, a turn-of-the-century mansion turned eatery. Specialities of the house include a flaming sword shishkabob and the traditional Dutch colonial *rijsttafel* ("rice table") consisting of 20 Indonesian dishes served by 16 attractive young ladies. *Rijsttafel* is also the speciality of the **Club Noordwijk**, which has a *tempo doeloe* ("olden times") atmosphere in a somewhat less regal setting. Both establishments provide nightly musical entertainment. A less expensive place for *Indische* colonial food and atmosphere is the **Arts and Curios Restaurant** and Art Shop, conveniently located near TIM, the performing arts centre of Jakarta.

For French cuisine with a local touch, many residents are devotees of Rima Melati's **Le Petit Bistro**, although the Mandarin and the Hyatt Hotels also boast fine French eateries replete with both traditional and nouvelle cuisines. The **Sari Pacific coffee shop** is the popular place for breakfast and brunch, as it serves the best breads and croissants in Jakarta, prepared by a French pastry chef. For a delicious English-style pub lunch or a pizza, it's over to the **George & Dragon** behind the hotel Indonesia, or to the **Jaya Pub**. For an evening steak, you can try **The Ponderosa**, **The Raffles Tavern** in Ratu Plaza, or **The Club Room** in the Mandarin Hotel—also **La Bodega Grill & Bar**, though it's rather far from the city. Of course, all hotels have coffee shops for breakfast and lunch—Hotel Indonesia's **Java Room** is a popular place.

There is also an Italian restaurant (**Rugantino**), and a German restaurant (**Old Heidelberg**), a Swiss fondue restaurant (**The Swiss Inn**) and a Scotch eatery (**The Thistle**), but all are somewhat disappointing and exhorbitantly priced—aimed mainly at the homesick expatriate crowd. There is even a Mexican joint, **The Green Pub**, which presents country-rock or jazz music nightly, though the food is so-so. American-style fast-food outlets like Kentucky Fried and Swensons are sprouting up everywhere now.

• **Art and Curio Restaurant** (Dutch Colonial), Jl. Kebon Binatang III/8A, Cikini, tel: 322879.
• **Brasserie Le Parisien** (French), Aryaduta Hyatt Hotel, Jl. Prapatan 44, tel: 376008 ext. 141.
• **Club Noordwijk** (Colonial/Dutch), Jl. Ir. H. Juanda 5A, tel: 353909.
• **The Club Room** (French), Jakarta Mandarin, tel: 371208.
• **George & Dragon Pub & Restaurant** (English), Jl. Telukbetung 32, tel: 345625.
• **Green Pub** (Mexican), Jakarta Theatre Bldg, Jl. M.H. Thamrin, tel: 359332, 325808.
• **Java Coffee Shop**, Hotel Indonesia, tel: 320008.
• **Jaya Pub** (sandwiches & soups), Jaya Building, Jl. M.H. Thamrin 12, tel: 327508 ext. 255.
• **Jayakarta Grill**, Sari Pacific Hotel, Jl. M.H. Thamrin 6, tel: 359141 ext. 1481.
• **La Bodega** (Continental), Caringan Shopping Centre, Cilandak, tel: 767798.
• **Le Bistro** (French), Jl. K.H. Wahid Hasyim 75, tel: 347475.
• **Oasis Restaurant** (Continental), Jl. Raden Saleh 47, tel: 326397, 327818.
• **Old Heidelberg** (German), Prince Theatre, Jl. Jendral Sudirman 3-4, tel: 586683.
• **The Ponderosa** (steaks), Widjoyo Centre, Jl. Jend. Sudirman 57, tel: 587731 ext. 251.
• **Raffles Tavern** (English), Ratu Plaza, 3rd Floor, tel: 711894.
• **Rugantino** (Italian), Jl. Melawai Raya 28, tel: 714727.

• **The Stable** (steaks), 4th floor, Wisma Hayam Wuruk, Jl. Hayam Wuruk, tel: 360200.
• **The Swiss Inn**, Arthaloka Building, Jl. Jendral Sudirman 2, tel: 583280.
• **The Thistle Bar & Restaurant** (Scotch), Wisma Metropolitan, 18th floor, Jl. Jendral Sudirman, tel: 584736.

Asian Fare

Finally, there are a handful of **Japanese**, **Korean**, **Indian** and **Thai** restaurants. The big Japanese chains are well-represented here, with the **Ginza Benkay** (President Hotel) and the **Okoh** (Horison Hotel) and the **Keio** (Borobudur Inter-Continental) all having branches with imported food, furnishing, cooks and prices. One small Japanese establishment stands out from the rest by virtue of the fact that it is the oldest in Jakarta and serves locally caught and grown delicacies at reasonable prices: the **Kikugawa**, located in a converted house near TIM. The several Korean restaurants in town, all owned by Koreans, are reasonably good. Northern Indian food is served at the **Omar Khayyam** and Thai food at the **Ayothaya Thai**.

• **Ayothaya Thai**, Jl. Ir. Juanda 35A, tel: 350921.
• **Furusatu** (Japanese), Sari Pacific Hotel, Jl. M.H. Thamrin, tel: 323707.
• **Ginza Benkay** (Japanese), President Hotel, Jl. M.H. Thamrin, tel: 320508.
• **Jakarta Okoh** (Japanese), Horison Hotel, tel: 680008 ext. 111, 129.
• **Jakarta New Hama** (Japanese), 4th floor, Ratu Plaza, Jl. Jendral Sudirman, tel: 711895, 711333.
• **Jakarta Nippon Kan** (Japanese), Jakarta Hilton, tel: 586111 ext. 627, 628.
• **Keio** (Japanese), Borobudur Intercontinental Hotel, tel: 357511 ext. 2358.
• **Kikugawa** (Japanese), Jl. Kebon Binatang III/No. 3, tel: 341808.
• **Korean International**, Jl. Melawai VI/No. 3 (Blok M), Kebayoran, tel: 713776.
• **Mitsuyo** (Japanese), Jl. Raden Saleh 44.
• **Omar Khayyam** (Indian), Jl. Antara 5-7, tel: 357705, 356719.
• **Shima** (Japanese), 17th floor, Hyatt Aryaduta Hotel, tel: 376008.
• **Yamazato** (Japanese), Hotel Indonesia, tel: 320008 ext. 176.

Shopping

Jakarta is not known as a shopper's paradise—imported goods are heavily taxed and domestic manufactures can only rarely compete in quality, though they are cheap. The good buys are hence limited mainly to two categories: handicrafts and antiques, with certain exceptions—notably pirated cassette tapes and locally produced designer clothes.

Batik

Batik Keris, with showrooms in Sarinah, has the largest selection of *batik* in Jakarta, particularly yard goods and inexpensive *kain*. Another big Solo-based batik maker, **Danar Hadi**, specializes in finer *tulis* work fabric and ready-made shirts and dresses. The **Government Batik Cooperative (GKBI)**, is rather disappointing—a place to get medium-grade Central Javanese *batik*. Connoisseurs will want to stop in at the shop of designer **Iwan Tirta**. For *batik* paintings, Yogya-based **Amri** is the best known artist. Smaller, quality boutiques selling a range of clothes and fabrics include **Srikandi** and several of the shops on Jl. Palatehan I (Blok M, Kebayoran) and in the **Hilton Bazaar**. You may also want to see *batik* being produced at one of the factories in the Palmerah area. Try Berdikari or Hayadi.

- **Amri Gallery**, Jl. Utan Kayu 66E.
- **Batik Berdikari**, Jl. Masjid Pal VII, Palmerah Barat, tel: 542814, 582814.
- **Batik Hayadi**, Jl. Palmerah Utara 46, tel: 540656, 540584.
- **Batik Keris**, Sarinah Jaya Department Store, Kebayoran Baru.
- **Batik Semar**, Jl. Tomang Raya 54, tel: 593514.
- **Danar Hadi**, Jl. Raden Saleh 1A, tel: 342390, 343712.
- **GKBI**, Indonesian Government Batik Cooperative, Jl. Jendral Sudirman 28, tel: 581022.
- **Iwan Tirta**, Jl. Panarukan 25, tel: 349122.
- **Iwan Tirta**, Borobodur Intercontinental Hotel shopping arcade.
- **Maison Young**, Jl. Palatehan I/39B, Kebayoran Baru.
- **Royal Batik Shop**, Jl. Palatehan I/41, tel: 773599.
- **Srikandi**, Jl. Melawai VI/6A, tel: 775604.
- **Srikandi**, Jl. Cikini Raya 90, tel: 354446.
- **Intisari**, Jl. Melawai V/8, Blok M Kebayoran Baru.

Handicrafts

These are produced outside of Jakarta (with the exception of cane furniture and some batik). Nevertheless all are available in the city, and short of going to the original producer, you cannot get them much cheaper elsewhere. The first stop for handicrafts of every description is the **Handicraft Centre** in the Sarinah Jaya Department Store in Kebayoran. Here you can get everything from baskets to cane chairs to leather sandals. Then for paintings, carvings, *wayang* puppets and other "art" items, spend an afternoon or evening at the **Art Market** (Pasar Seni) in Ancol, where you can observe craftsmen at work and chat with them.

The Indonesia Bazaar at the Hilton Hotel has a number of up-market boutiques selling quality *batik*, jewellery and *wayang* puppets. Many of the antique and art shops at Jl. Kebon Sirih Timur Dalam, Jl. Majapahit and Jl. Palatehan (Kebayoran) also sell handicrafts. A few shops, such as the **Irian Art and Gift Shop** specialize in tribal handicrafts and primitive art. (*See* below for shop listings.)

Antiques and Curios

These are available throughout the city, but especially on **Jl. Kebon Sirih Timur Dalam**, where there are several tiny shops with names like **Bali**, **Bima**, **Djody** and **Nasrun**—all stocked with old furniture, weavings, masks, puppets and porcelains. Nearby **Johan Art** has one of the largest collections of old Chinese porcelains; they will refund your money if later dissatisfied, a rarity in Jakarta. Farther down Jl. Wahid Hasyim is a shop specializing in pewter ware: **The Banka Tin Shop**. Several other shops are on Jl. Haji Agus Salim (Jl. Sabang). All the above are within walking distance of Sarinah or the Sari Pacific Hotel.

There are concentrations of antique and art shops in three other areas of the city:

- The **antique market** on Jl. Surabaya, near Embassy Row (Jl. Diponegoro) consists of about 20 stalls set in a row. Porcelains, puppets, tiles, brass and silver bric-a-brac, much of it new but made to look old, spill forth onto the sidewalk. Nearby, two homes houses a cache of antique Dutch furniture: Alex Papadimitriou's, and the Srirupa Shop.
- Three shops dating from the Dutch times still survive on Jl. Majapahit: **Arjuna**, **Garuda** and **Lee Cheong**. All sell quality merchandise—jewellery, furniture, masks, puppets etc.
- A new row of chic boutiques, galleries and studios catering to the foreign community and wealthy Jakartans is located in Kebayoran on **Jl. Palatehan I** (Djelita, Maison Young, Urip, Pura, Pigura, Royal, Tony's and Oet's). The new Sarinah Jaya Department Store is next door, and Aldiron Plaza/Blok M is within walking distance.
- **Alex Papadimitriou** (antiques), Jl. Pasuruan 3.
- **Ardjuna Craft Shop**, Jl. Majapahit 16A.
- **Bali Art & Curio**, Jl. Kebon Sirih·Timur Dalam 42.
- **Bandung Art Shop**, Jl. Pasar Baru 18C.
- **Bangka Tin Shop**, Jl. Wahid Hasyim 178.
- **Bima Arts & Curios**, Jl. Kebon Sirih Timur Dalam 257.
- **Djelita Art Shop**, Jl. Palatehan I/37.
- **Djody Art & Curio**, Jl. Kebon Sirih Timur Dalam 2.
- **Garuda**, Jl. Majapahit 12.
- **Irian Art and Gift Shop**, Jl. Pasar Baru 16A, tel: 343422.
- **Johan Art**, Jl. Wahid Hasyim 80.
- **Johan Art Curios**, Jl. H. Agus Salim 59A.
- **Lee Cheong**, Jl. Majapahit 32.
- **Lindungan Store**, Jl. H. Agus Salim 48.
- **Made Handicraft**, Jl. Pegangsaan Timur 2.
- **Magasin L'Art**, Jl. Cikini Raya 71.
- **Majapahit Arts & Curios**, Jl. Melawai III/4, Blok M, Kebayoran Baru.
- **Naini's Fine Arts**, Jl. Palatehan I/20, Kebayoran Baru.
- **Pigura Art & Gift Shop**, Jl. Palatehan I/41, Kebayoran Baru, tel: 773599.
- **Ramayana**, Jl. Ir. H. Juanda 14A.

- **Srirupa Shop**, Jl. Pekalongan 16.
- **Tony's Gallery**, Jl. Palatehan I/31, Kebayoran Baru.
- **Urip Store**, Jl. Palatehan I/40, Kebayoran Baru.

Jewellery

Many jewellery shops in Jakarta design and produce their own gold and silver work here. Prices are higher than in Kota Gede (Yogyakarta) and Bali, but the quality and designs are vastly superior—especially if you are interested in Indonesian gems: Borneo diamonds, purple amethyst, natural pearls and the recently-discovered West Javanese black opal. This can also be a good place to buy chains, filigree and repousse work. Labour is cheap and workmanship can be good. Check the papers for the current per gram cost of gold and silver before shopping, so you know exactly how much you are paying for workmanship and design. Most of the quality shops are in the hotels:

- **Jay's Jewellery**, Jakarta Mandarin Hotel, tel: 371208 ext. 3781.
- **Joyce Spiro**, Sari Pacific Hotel, tel: 323707.
- **Judith Tumbelaka**, Jl. H.A. Salim 94, tel: 348252.
- **Linda Spiro**, Borobudur Intercontinental, tel: 370108 ext. 2121.
- **F. Spiro Jewellers**, Jakarta Hilton Hotel, tel: 587441 ext. 618.
- **Kevin's Jewellery**, Jakarta Hilton Hotel.
- **Olislaeger Jewellers**, Jl. Ir. H. Juanda 11, tel: 341850.
- **Pelangi Jewellery**, Jakarta Hilton Hotel, tel: 587981.
- **Pelangi Opal & Jewellery Centre**, Jl. R.S. Fatmawati 42, Cilandak, tel: 7601523.
- **Sesotya**, Sahid Jaya Hotel.
- **Sri Sadono**, Hotel Indonesia.

Indonesian Paintings

These are generally of three types: traditional, modern and poster kitsch. For a look at the work of serious artists, go to the **Harris Art Gallery**. **Oet's Gallery** features the work of a different artist every few weeks. Several artists also maintain their own galleries. One example is **Adam Lay's**. Check the English language press for exhibitions of Indonesian art at TIM and in the foreign embassy cultural centres. Traditional Balinese and other paintings are to be found in the shops selling antiques and curios. The best place to see kitsch is **Taman Suropati** in Embassy Row. The **Art Market** in Ancol also has several shops where you may watch artists at work and commission a portrait. Quick portraits can be ordered from sidewalk artists in front of the General Post Office on Jl. Veteran.

- **Adam's Gallery**, Sari Pacific Shopping Arcade.
- **Harris Art Gallery**, Jl. Cipete 41, Kebayoran Baru, tel: 766660.
- **Oet's Gallery**, Jl. Palatehan I/33, Kebayoran Baru.

Cassette Tapes

Jakarta is also one of the best places in the world to feed your Walkman. Cassette supermarkets stock hundreds of titles, many of them pirates of the latest pop and classical releases, recorded on commercial production equipment using quality Maxell, BASF and TDK tapes. A 90-minute recorded pop tape costs only US $1.50; classical and copyrighted Indonesian music costs slightly more. The best shops allow you to pick tapes off the rack and provide decks with headphones so you can listen before you buy. As these shops are generally air-conditioned, this can be a pleasant way to while away the hot noonday hours. The shops on Jl. Haji Agus Salim (especially **Duta Suara**—No. 26A), are convenient and complete. Otherwise try **Duta Irama** and **Aquarius** in the Aldiron Plaza, Blok M (No. 38 ground floor, and No. 4-6 second floor).

Shopping Centres

Visit the shopping streets and big shopping centres in Jakarta, just to see what is available and to indulge in some people-watching. This is best done in the early evening when it is cool. The two best places are **Pasar Baru** ("New Market") and the more fashionable **Blok M** in Kebayoran. A visit to one of the new, air-conditioned shopping plazas like **Gajah Mada Plaza** and **Ratu Plaza** can also be a cool way to escape the noonday sun.

- **Aldiron Plaza**, Blok M, Kebayoran Baru.
- **Gajah Mada Plaza**, Jl. Gajah Mada, 10 storeys of air-conditioned shops and restaurants.
- **Glodok Shopping Centre**, 6-storeys, in the middle of Jakarta's Chinatown.
- **Glodok Plaza**, Jl. Pinangsia, 5-storeys of air-conditioned shops.
- **Hayam Wuruk Plaza**, Jl. Hayam Wuruk.
- **Pasar Baru**, several square blocks of shops, where everything and anything can be bought.
- **Ratu Plaza**, Jl. Jendral Sudirman, Senayan, one of the newest and brightest air-conditioned malls, with a supermarket, a bookstore, many electronics goods shops and restaurants, and a cinema.
- **Sarinah Department Store**, Kebayoran Baru.

Nightlife and Entertainment

Unlike most other Indonesian cities, Jakarta rages on into the night. This is perhaps one more reason to have a nap during the noonday heat, so that you can get out on the town in the evening, when a cool breeze blows in from the sea.

For culture in any form, the first place to check is **Taman Ismail Marzuki** (TIM), the cultural and performing arts centre of Jakarta. TIM hosts an eclectic variety of Indonesian dance performances, *wayang kulit* and *wayang orang* performances, singing groups, poetry readings, modern and traditional theatre productions, as well as performances of ballet, modern dance, and classical and jazz music by visiting artistes. Check at your hotel or in the English-language press for programme details.

If you are not planning to visit Central Java, then you will perhaps want to attend the popular Javanese *wayang orang* performances at **Bharata Theatre**, Jl. Pasar Senen 15. The audience is almost entirely Javanese and very appreciative of the performances—often more so than in Yogya and Solo these days, where there is rarely a good turnout and tourists often outnumber the locals. This in itself is a good reason to see *wayang orang* in Jakarta. Performances nightly between 8 p.m. and 11 p.m.

If you are truly fascinated by folk theatre, you might want to pay a visit to the **Teater Miss Tjihtjih** on Jl. Stasion Angke in a poor, western suburb of the city. It's rather dark and dingy inside, and you won't understand a word unless you speak Sundanese, but the audience seems to enjoy the traditional folktales being enacted.

Visit the **Art Market** (Pasar Seni) at Ancol, where three or four nights a week there are live, open-air performances of one sort or another, and one may walk leisurely about the pavilions inspecting the handicrafts and paintings for sale. Chat with the artists and then sit down at one of the sidewalk cafes for a tasty bowl of soup, a hamburger or a plate of noodles. Ancol is about 10 kms (six miles) or US$3 by taxi from the centre of town. Ask at your hotel or the Tourist Information Office for programme details.

Or if you enjoy comedy of the slapstick variety and don't mind not understanding the dialogue, go to the **Sri Mulat** show at the Youth centre (Taman Ria Remaja) in Slipi. The show kicks off with some rather overdressed and undertalented singers who are funny in their way without perhaps meaning to be so. This farcical overture is followed by two acts of pure hilarity—a cross between Monty Python and the popular Javanese *ketoprak* theatre. One generally depicts Javanese aristocrats and servants in absurd situations, while the other features a family of bizarrely attired transvestites. On Thursday night, it's the ever-popular Dracula show, in which Dracula is often a woman played by a man.

In addition to these are regularly scheduled performances put on by the big hotels and foreign embassies. The Hilton and the Borobudur are the most active hotels, culturally speaking, while the French, British, Dutch, American, Australian and German embassies all maintain cultural centres with frequently scheduled exhibitions, tours, films and lectures. Call them up to find out what is happening.

• **Alliance Francaise** (French Cultural Centre), Jl. Salemba Raya 25.
• **The British Council**, Jl. Jendral Sudirman 57, tel: 5874411.
• **Erasmus Huis** (Dutch Cultural Centre), Jl. Menteng Raya 25.
• **Goethe Institute**, (German Cultural Centre) Jl. Matraman Raya 23, tel: 882798.
• **Indonesia-America Friendship Society,** Jl. Pramuka Kav. 30, tel: 881241, 883536, 883867.
• **Italian Cultural Centre**, Jl. Diponegoro 45.
• **Japan Cultural Centre**, Jl. Cemara 1.

Rounding out the cultural scene, the Jakarta station of **Radio Republik Indonesia (RRI)** broadcasts live from their studios on Jl. Medan Merdeka Barat, with traditional music from all over Indonesia, classical concerts and *wayang* performances. Ask your hotel to phone RRI for details and ticket availability. Several restaurants also have live music, notably the Oasis restaurant with its band of strolling Batak players (*see* "Dining"). And on Sundays, **Taman Mini** to the south of Jakarta comes alive with traditional drama and music from many of Indonesia's 27 provinces. Also on Sunday morning, at the Wayang Museum, there is a brief puppet performance from 10 a.m. to noon.

Western style nocturnal amusements also abound in Jakarta. The disco craze hit the city a decade ago and is here to stay. Every weekend, wealthy youngsters in designer clothes pack the fashionable clubs. Two swank hotel establishments have ruled the scene for some time now: Sari Pacific's **Pitstop** and the **Oriental Club** at the Hilton. The cover is steep (about US$10 to US$15 per person), as are the drinks, but for this clientele it doesn't matter—transported to a fantasy world of plush carpeting, flashing lights and pounding rhythms, they are busy getting their money's worth. No sandals, bluejeans or T-shirts allowed, naturally.

Expatriates looking for a looser (and less expensive) atmosphere in which to unbend generally end up at **Tanamur**, Jl. Tanah Abang Timur 14, an older rock club that is a bit seedy now and smelling of beer—but the music is good, the lights are low and nobody seems to care what you wear. The **Bali International**, Jl. Wahid Hasyim 116, has opened a disco which attracts the young foreign travellers from nearby Jl. Jaksa and the local long-haired motorcycle crowd.

For a drink and a sing-a-long, it's over to the lively **Jaya Pub** piano bar on Jl. Thamrin, to Rima Melati's **Le Petit Bistro**, or to the **George & Dragon** on Jl. Telukbetung (behind the Hotel Indonesia) for a rowdy round of darts. Other popular expatriate watering holes include the **Hotmen Bar** (Menteng Hotel), the **Tankard** (Kebayoran Theatre, Blok M), and **the Club** (Jl. Hasanuddin 52, Blok M, Kebayoran). The **Green Pub** in the Jakarta Theatre has passable country/rock or jazz bands nightly. The most popular girlie bars, with attached massage parlours, are on Jl. Blora (**Aloha, Shinta, Paradise**) or try the **Columbus Bar** in the Marco Polo Hotel.

The Mandarin and Hyatt hotel bars have regularly scheduled jazz nights, and the Hotel Indonesia has a supper club, the **Nirwana Room**, with Australian and European entertainers.

For a truly bizarre night out, try one of the Chinese cabarets on Jl. Gajah Mada/Hayam Wuruk: Blue Ocean, Sky Room, Paramount, Tropicana. They serve up Chinese banquets and Taiwanese singers for the sugar daddy *cukong* crowd.

Lastly, you have your pick of grade B or C Italian and American films (generally in English with Indonesian subtitles). Check the papers for listings, but be aware that ticket prices are comparable to those in the West—about US$5 a head for an air-conditioned theatre.

Airlines (International) in Jakarta

Air India, 402 Hotel Sari Pacific, Jl M H Thamrin, Tel:325534, 325470.

Cathay Pacific, BDN Bldg, Jl M H Thamrin, Tel R:326807 Tel A:327807.

China Airlines, Blk A, 11 Komplek Duta Merlin, 3 Jl Gajah Mada, Tel R:353195, 354448.

Garuda Indonesian, Jl Angkasa Kemayoran, Tel R:414081 Tel A:417808.

Japan Airlines, 59 Jl M H Thamrin, Tel R:322207 Tel A:322726.

KLM Royal Dutch Airlines, Hotel Indonesia, Jl M H Thamrin, Tel R:320708 Tel A:334809.

Lufthansa, Panin Centre Bldg, 1 Jln Jen Sudirman, Tel R/A:710247.

Malaysian Airline System, Hotel Indonesia, Jl M H Thamrin, Tel:320909.

Philippine Airlines, G/F Borobudur Intercontinental, Jl Lapangan Banteng Selatan, Tel R:370108 Tel A:372728.

Qantas Airways, BDN Bldg, 5 Jl M H Thamrin, Tel R:327707 Tel A:326707.

Singapore Airlines, 3/F Sahid Jaya Hotel, 86 Jl Jen Sudirman, PO Box 3088. Tel R:584021/584011 Tel A:584041.

Swissair, 3/F Borobudur Intercontinental, Jl Lapangan Banteng Selatan, Tel:378006.

Thai International, 5 Jl M H Thamrin, Tel R/A:320607.

UTA French Airlines, 12 Jl M H Thamrin, Tel R:323507 Tel A:323609.

Airlines (Domestic) in Jakarta

Bouraq Indonesian Airline, Jalan Patrice Lumumba 1, tel: 354395, 357640, 357940.

Garuda Indonesian Airways (GIA), Jalan Ir. H. Juanda 15 (Head Office); tel: 370709; Kemayoran Airport, tel: 410808; Halim Perdanakusuma Airport, tel: 884156; Wisma Nusantara Building, Jalan M.H. Thamrin, tel: 373909; Hotel Borobudur Inter-Continental, tel: 359901 ext., 2116, 2117.

Mandala Airlines, Jalan Veteran 1/34, tel: 368107 (5 lines).

Merpati Nusantara Airlines (MNA), Jalan Patrice Lumumba 2, tel: 314608, 413672; Kemayoran Airport, tel: 348031, 348038.

Pelita Air Service, Jalan Abdul Muis 52, Tel: 357389.

Sempati Air Transport, Jalan Merdeka Timur 7, tel: 348760, 37911.

Foreign Missions in Jakarta

Australia, Jalan M.H. Thamrin 15, Jakarta Pusat, tel: 350511 (10 lines).

Burma, Jalan H. Agus Salim 109, Jakarta Pusat, tel: 340440, 347204.

Canada, Wisma Metropolitan 5th floor, Jalan Jend. Sudirman Kav. 29, Jakarta Pusat, P.O. Box 52/JKT, tel: 584030, 584039.

Finland, Jalan Dr. Kusuma Atmaja SH. 15-A, Jakarta Pusat, tel: 346686, 345871.

Denmark, Jalan Abdul Muis 34, Jakarta Pusat, tel: 346615.

France, Jalan M.H. Thamrin 20, Jakarta Pusat, tel: 357311, 347871, 347872, 360572.

The Federal Republic of Germany, Jalan M.H. Thamrin 1, Jakarta Pusat, tel: 323908 (5 lines).

Her Britannic Majesty's Embassy, Jalan M.H. Thamrin 75, Jakarta Pusat, tel: 341091, 341098.

Apostolic Nunciature (Holy See-Vatikan), Jalan Medan Merdeka Timur 18, Jakarta Pusat, tel: 341142, 341143.

India, Jalan Kebon Sirih 44, Jakarta Pusat, tel: 342815, 365554.

Italy, Jalan Diponegoro 45, Jakarta Pusat, tel: 348339, 347907.

Japan, Jalan M.H. Thamrin 24, Jakarta Pusat, tel: 324308, 324948, 325140, 325268.

Korea, Jalan Jenderal Gatot Subroto, Jakarta Selatan. tel: 512309 (4 lines)

Malaysia, Jalan Imam Bonjol 17, Jakarta Pusat, tel: 354945, 346770, 348243, 350176. Open: 8 a.m. to 2 p.m. Monday to Friday.

The Netherlands, Jalan H.R. Rasuna Said Kav. 5-3, tel: 511515, 361808.

New Zealand, Jalan Diponegoro 41, Jakarta Pusat. tel: 357924, 359796.

Norway, Jalan Padalarang 4, Jakarta Pusat, tel: 354556.

Papua New Guinea, Wisma Metropolitan 4th Floor, Jalan Jenderal Sudirman Kav. 29, Jakarta Pusat. tel: 584604, 584605.

The Philippines, Jalan Imam Bonjol 6-8 Jakarta Pusat. tel: 343745, 348917, 349986, 351917.

Saudi Arabia, Jalan Imam Bonjol 3 Pav. Jakarta Pusat. tel: 346342, 346343, 359838.

Singapore, Jalan Proklamasi 23 Jakarta Pusat, tel: 346046, 342885.

Spain, Wisma Kosgoro 14th Floor, Jalan M.H. Thamrin 15, Jakarta Pusat, tel: 325996, 321808 ext. 362, 322869, 322872.

Sweden, Jalan Taman Cutmutiah 12 Jakarta Pusat. tel: 349121, 346953.

Switzerland, Jalan Latuharhary SH. 23, Jakarta Pusat. tel: 347921, 347922.

Thailand, Jalan Imam Bonjol 74, Jakarta Pusat, tel: 349180, 343762, 348221.

USSR, Jalan M.H. Thamrin 13, Jakarta Pusat, tel: 351263, 351477, 342552.

The United States, Jalan Medan Merdeka Selatan 5, Jakarta Pusat, tel: 340001.

Hospitals (Rumah Sakit) in Jakarta

Cipto Mangunkusumo Hospital
Jl. Diponegoro 71; tel:343021, 882829
Fatmawati Hospital
Jl. R.S. Fatmawati; tel:760124, 764147
Gatot Subroto Hospital
Jl. Abdul Rachman Saleh 1; tel:371008
Husada Hospital
Jl. Mangga Besar 137–139; tel:620108, 622555
Islamic Hospital Jakarta
Jl. Letjen. Suprapto; tel:414208, 414989
Mintaharja Hospital
Jl. Bendungan Hilir; tel:581031
Persahabatan Hospital
Jl. Raya Persahabatan; tel:481708

Pertamina Hospital
Jl. Kyai Maja 43; tel:775890, 775891
Sint Carolus Hospital
Jl. Salemba Raya 41; tel:883091, 882401
Sumber Waras Hospital
Jl. Kyai Tapa, Grogol; tel:596011, 591646
Tjikini Hospital
Jl. Raden Saleh 40; tel:336961, 365297
Yayasan Jakarta Hospital
Jl. Jend. Sudirman; tel:582241, 584576

West Java

The Thousand Islands (Pulau Seribu)
Banten and the West Coast
Krakatau
Ujung Kulon National Park
Bogor
Puncak Pass/Cibodas/Cipanas
Pelabuhan Ratu
Bandung
The Sundanese Performing Arts
Exploring the Bandung Highlands

Thousand Islands (Pulau Seribu)

There are three groups of frequently visited islands in this 600-island chain that scatters across the Java Sea to the north of Jakarta. The first is a cluster of tiny islands located just 3 to 5 kms (2 to 3 miles) offshore, directly to the north of the city, including: Pulau Onrust, Pulau Kelor, Pulau Kahyangan, Pulau Bidadari (also known as Pulau Sakit), and Pulau Damar.

Pulau Onrust, for example, was formerly the major VOC dry-docking station for the entire Asian fleet. Captain Cook had his ship, *HMS Endeavour*, repaired here in 1770 and praised the island's caulkers and carpenters as the best in the East. Today, there are several houses dating from a later period and a fort is being slowly reconstructed as a historical monument by the Department of Museums & History.

On neighbouring **Pulau Kelor** and **Pulau Kahyangan**, the remains of Dutch forts are also visible. **Pulau Bidadari** ("Heavenly Nymph Island") was once the site of a leper colony, and **Pulau Damar** ("Torch Island") houses a powerful beacon used to guide airplanes into Jakarta at night. On the latter are also the ruins of a Japanese-style house constructed in 1685 by Governor-General Camphuijs, one of the few VOC leaders known for his intellectual endeavours.

Much farther out to sea, about 100 kms (65 miles) from Jakarta, two islands have been developed into a private scuba and skin diving resort: **Pulau Puteri** ("Princess Island") and **Pulau Melinjo**. Pulau Puteri now has 25 deluxe, air-conditioned bungalows and cottages which rent for anywhere from US$60 to US$170 per night (plus 21 per cent tax and service) during peak seasons. At other times the prices are about 25 per cent less. Neighbouring Pulau Melinjo has what is called a "divers camp"—simple thatched huts with toilets, fresh water, showers, barbeques, tables and chairs—renting for US$42 per night per hut (capable of sleeping several people; bring your own food, bedding and cooking utensils).

The main attractions on both islands are crystal-clear waters and the spectacular coral reefs offshore—teeming with a colourful assortment of tropical fish and exotic marine life. Diving equipment, food and evening entertainment are available on Pulau Puteri—on Pulau Melinjo, you're on your own, though there are resident attendants who maintain radio contact with the main island.

Large, (5-foot) black lizards inhabit these islands, but they're harmless. Be careful, however, to wear protective footwear and to avoid the razor-sharp coral when in the water. There are sea urchins and poisonous stone-fish, and cuts fester very quickly in the tropics. Bring along plenty of mosquito repellant.

Lastly there is the **Pulau Rambut** ("Hair Island") bird sanctuary, two tiny islands lying some distance to the west of Jakarta, about 15 kms (10 miles) from shore. These islands serve as a nursery for seabirds during the breeding season (March-July), and also have a large permanent population of herons, storks and cormorants. Two chalets on the island may be rented from the resident forestry guards.

Many of the Thousand Islands are crowded on weekends, though much less so during the rainy season, November to March, when the strong NW monsoon winds bring daily afternoon showers, making the return boat journey precarious. The best time to visit is thus during the dry summer months: May to Semptember.

Getting There

Motorboat launches may be hired to all the islands from the Jaya Ancol Marina, located within the vast Ancol "Dreamland" amusement park on Jakarta's northeastern shore. Pulau Onrust and the other islands closest in to the mainland are only 20 to 30 minutes away, making this an easy and relaxing day trip 'escape' from the city to the beach. Pulau Rambut is about an hour away from Ancol. The boat out to Pulau Puteri or Pulau Melinjo, takes three hours and costs US$50 per person round trip. The developers of this resort, Pulau Seribu Paradise, also provide an air charter service from Kemayoran Airport, for US$120 per person round trip.

A regular morning ferry leaves from Sanggar Bahari pier at Tanjung Priok harbour at 8 a.m. for several of the closer islands (Onrust, etc.), returning in the afternoon. For the farther islands, such as Pulau Puteri, Pulau Genteng and Opak Besar, boats leave from the Kartika Bahari pier.

Accommodation

To stay at Pulau Puteri or Pulau Melinjo, make prior bookings through any travel agent, or directly through:
● **P.T. Pulau Seribu Paradise**, Jakarta Theatre

Building, Jl. M.H. Thamrin, Jakarta, tel: 359333-359334, tlx: DARMA JKT 44122.

Don't let them tell you that you must rent one of their deluxe bungalows on Pulau Puteri if you just want to stay at the divers camp on Pulau Melinjo instead. Actually they have several other "camps" on islands besides Pulau Melinjo which may be rented by the day or by the week. This office will also book round trip transportation to the islands by air and sea (*see* above).

Banten and the West Coast

The excursion out to Java's sparsely populated west coast is made easier now that the new Jakarta-Merak expressway is (at least partially) completed. The surf and the sand are not as fine as in Bali or at Pelabuhan Ratu, but a visit to the historic ruins at Banten or the active volcano, Anak Krakatau, or the famous Ujung Kulon Nature Reserve more than makes up for this. Go during the week if possible, when the west coast is less crowded and hotels like the Carita Beach offer a discount rate.

Sights of Banten

From Serang, a town 90 kms (56 miles) due west of Jakarta, a surfaced road leads 10 kms (6 miles) north to Banten village. About 2 kms (1 mile) before the village, on the right-hand side of the road, is the tomb of Maulana Yusup, the second Muslim ruler of Banten, who died around 1590. A little farther on, on the left-hand side, are the remains of **Istana Kaibon**, the palace of Queen Aisyah, mother of Banten's last Sultan.

Crossing a narrow bridge and turning off to the left down a dirt track, you arrive after about one km (half-a-mile) at the old Banten town square. The remains of **Surasowan Palace** line the south side of the square and the recently renovated **Grand Mosque** stands to the west.

Banten used to be protected by a thick outer wall enclosing the fortified palace with the square at its centre, surrounded by a large market and a number of crowded ethnic quarters inhabited by Malay, Chinese, Gujarati, Abyssinian and Annamese traders. Recently, the palace was excavated and an elaborate four-km (2.5-mile) long system of terracotta pipes was discovered, complete with two filtering reservoirs, linking the sunken royal baths with Tasik Ardi, an artificial lake and pleasure garden, about 1 km (half a mile) to the southwest.

About one km (half-a-mile) to the northwest of the square are the ruins of **Fort Speelwijk**, built by the Dutch in 1682 and expanded in 1685 and 1731.

To the west of the fort, a paved road leads across a bridge to the red and yellow **Wan-De Yuan** temple, one of the oldest and largest Chinese temples on Java. The Goddess of Mercy, Kuan-yin or Avalokitesvara, is enshrined here along with several other deities, and a steady stream of devotees burn incense and consult the temple's fabled divination sticks.

Getting There

To visit the ruins at Banten, which are some distance from the main road, a hired car or taxi is certainly recommended. A round-trip Jakarta-Banten excursion by car will cost about US$50 and take the better part of a day (*see* "Jakarta" above for a listing of rental car and taxi companies, or inquire at your hotel, and request a driver who knows the area around Banten). Otherwise take a bus from Jakarta's Grogol Terminal to Serang (any bus bound for points west: Merak, Labuan or Sumatra will pass through Serang—fare about US$0.85) and alight at the centre of town. Then locate the small road leading north to Banten, and wait at the intersection for a local mini-bus ferrying passengers up to the village (fare: about Rp100 or US$0.10), or else walk the remaining 10 kms (6 miles). A slow, local train also operates to Serang from Jakarta's Tanah Abang Station.

A taxi or rental car all the way to the west coast beaches at Anyer or Carita will take about four hours and cost about US$60. A chartered minibus ("colt") will cost less, about US$30, and carry more people (ask someone in your hotel in Jakarta to arrange this for you). In either case you can make the detour to Banten along the way, though this should be negotiated as part of the fare in advance.

Inter-city buses operate hourly from Jakarta's Grogol Terminal to the port of Labuan on the west coast (about five hours) via the inland route through Serang and Pandeglang (fare about US$2), and from here you can then catch a "colt" going north along the coastal road to the beach areas for just a few hundred rupiah (about 20 to 50 cents, depending on your final destination). Alternatively, take the slow, local train from Tanah Abang Station in Jakarta all the way to Cilegon, and from here catch a colt on the main road going south. Remember that if you intend to visit the National Park at Ujung Kulon, you must first get your permit and make arrangements through the PPA head offices in Bogor (Department of Nature Conservation—*see* Ujung Kulon below).

Alternatively, phone the Jakarta booking office of any west coast hotel to make all the arrangements for you. They will be happy to arrange transportation (generally at a slightly higher cost than if you do it yourself), if you plan to stay at the hotel (*see* accommodation below). Private tours to Ujung Kulon, Krakatau and the west coast can also be arranged. Contact travel agents in Jakarta for details (try Vayatour, Jl. Batu Tulis 38, Jakarta, tel: 365008, 377339).

Accommodation

Serang is a fairly small town with only a few *losmen*—for more comfortable accommodation continue on to Cilegon, Merak or to the west coast beaches.

The **Krakatau Guest House** is open to the general public—air-conditioned motel-style bungalows renting for about US$20, a bit seedy now but quite inexpensive. The **Merak Beach Motel**, located right on the water just next to the Merak-

Bakauhuni ferry terminal at the far northwestern tip of the island, is clean and reasonable at US$25 to US$30 a night for an air-conditioned room (tax and service included).

The most comfortable place on the west coast beaches to the south is the **Anyer Beach Motel**. Tidy little concrete bungalows set in a grove by a broad, secluded beach here rent for US$30 on up to US$80 a night for a suite (plus 21 per cent tax and service).

Farther south around the village of Carita are two somewhat more rustic seaside establishments: the **Selat Sunda Wisata Cottages**, a small resort with several air-conditioned bungalows by the shore (US$35 per night), and the larger **Carita Krakatau Beach Hotel**—US$36 per night, plus 21 per cent tax and service.

• **Anyer Beach Motel** (30 rooms), Jl. Raya Karang Boiong, Anyer, Serang Banten, Jakarta, tel: 367594, 367838 ext. Anyer 196, 197, 198. Reservations: Gedung Patra, Jl. Jendral Gatot Subroto, Kav. 32-34, Jakarta, tel: 510322.

• **Carita Krakatau Beach Hotel** (150 rooms), Carita, Labuan, Pandeglang, West Java. Jakarta Office: Hotel Menteng (above Hero Supermarket), Jl. Gondangdia Lama 28, tel: 330846, 325208 ext. 5, P.O. Box 4507, Jakarta.

• **Guest House Krakatau Steel**, Kompleks P.T. Krakatau Steel, Kota Baja, Cilegon, Banten, West Java.

• **Merak Beach Hotel** (30 rooms), Jl. Raya Merak, Banten, West Java, tel: 15, Jakarta tel: 367838, ext. Merak 164.

• **Selat Sunda Wisata Cottage**, Cibenda, Carita Beach, Labuan, Banten, West Java. Jakarta Office: Jl. Panglima Polim Raya 21, Kebayoran Baru, tel: 714683.

Krakatau

Boats may be chartered to the four uninhabited islands of the Krakatau group from Labuan. Cost is anywhere from US$60 for a small fishing craft, on up to US$200 for a motorized fibreglass launch that carries up to 10 people. Arrangements can be made through any of the hotels listed above, or at the port. Bring along lunch and refreshments, as it is hot and there is no fresh water out there. The boat trip takes about five hours each way, so get an early start in order to have some time to explore the islands.

Most visitors land at the eastern side of Anak Krakatau and then climb up from here to the top of the first ridge for a view into the smoking crater and across to the other three islands: Sertung to the west, Small Krakatau to the east and Big Krakatau to the south. Not recommended during the rainy season, November to March, when the seas are rough.

Ujung Kulon National Park

A. Hoogerwerf's authoritative book on Ujung Kulon's floral and faunal species is recommended—available from the publisher, E.J. Brill

in Leiden. The Directorate-General of Tourism in Jakarta also publishes a very informative brochure about Ujung Kulon, and Vayatour (Jl. Batu Tulis 38, Jakarta, tel: 365008, 377339) offers a deluxe three-day deep-sea fishing tour to the park for US$375 per person, all-inclusive.

The first step is to get a permit at the head offices of the PPA (Department of Nature Conservation) at Jl. Juanda No. 9 in Bogor, just to the left of the Botanical Gardens (Kebon Raya)—an hour south of Jakarta by car or bus (*see* "Bogor" below). Bring your passport along and get there in the morning (they are open daily Mon. to Sat. from 8 a.m. to 12 noon). There are forms to fill out and a small fee to pay. Ask them to call the PPA office in Labuan while you are there, to reserve space in a guest bungalow within the park for the dates of your intended visit.

It is important to provision yourself well for the trip. The bungalows in the park do provide bedding and cooking utensils, even a cook, but you must bring all your own food. A mosquito net (available for only US$3 from any housegoods shop) and repellent are a must; you may also want to bring along your own sheets, a first aid kit and some camping supplies (if you intend to make the two day hike around the south and west coasts). Many basic provisions, such as canned foods, bottled drinks and rice can be purchased in shops in Labuan, but you may want to bring most of your supplies from Jakarta.

Once in Labuan (to get there, *see* "West Coast Beaches" above), check in at the PPA office to show them your permit and to make arrangements for a boat and a bungalow. It is a good idea to confirm all fees in advance, including payments for services provided by park staff (such as cooks and guides), and use of park equipment, such as motorboats. The government launch may be available to take you into the park, otherwise the PPA officers will help you charter a local fishing craft. Cost is about US$100 each way—be sure that you make an appointment for the boat to pick you up at a specified time and day, and if you want to detour on the way back via Krakatau for a look at the volcano, this should be negotiated in advance. If you arrive at Labuan early enough, then it may be possible to embark immediately for Ujung Kulon, otherwise spend the night at one of the hotels in nearby Carita Beach just a short distance to the north.

The park's guest bungalows are situated on two small islands. **Handeleum Island** is somewhat closer (five hours from Labuan) and has one older, two-storey bungalow that sleeps eight. **Peucang Island** (seven hours from Labuan) has two newer cabins, sleeping a total of 16 people with a comfortable lounge area. Both islands are populated by monitor lizards, wild deer and long-tailed macaques and are worth exploring in their own right. The bungalows have resident staff and small motor boats that may usually be hired to cross over the straits and motor upriver, though you may have to supply the gasoline (inquire at the PPA office about this before leaving, and purchase a few 5-litre jerry-cans in Labuan if necessary).

Bogor

Suprisingly few foreign tourists visit Bogor, despite the quick and easy connection from Jakarta. Those who finally do make it often wish they had come earlier, to spend more time in the orchid houses or in the library by the entrance to the gardens, pouring over the beautifully illustrated botanical tomes.

Another little-known feature of Bogor is that it has one of the few remaining *gamelan* foundries left on Java, and probably the only one in West Java. It's located at Jl. Pancasan 17 and the gongsmith's name is Pak Sukarna. From the centre of Bogor, go left down Jl. Empang and bear right at the next intersection. Cross over the bridge and after several hundred metres you will see carpenters working by the side of the street on the left making the frames. The foundry is across the street.

Getting There

Most Jakarta taxis will be willing to take you to Bogor and back for US$25, waiting while you spend a couple of hours in the Botanical Gardens. For a more leisurely visit, rent a car or "colt" mini-bus for the entire day.

Buses leave for Bogor very frequently from Jakarta's Cililitan Terminal (in the south of the city). Express buses marked "Jl. Tol Jagorawi—Bogor" are the fastest (one hour) and cheapest (US$0.60), dropping you at the Ciawi terminal just above the town to the south. From here, mini-buses circulate into Bogor, going right by the Kebun Raya entrance. Fare is Rp. 100.

The **Jabotabek** (JAkarta-BOgor-TAnggerang-BEKasi) commuter train is a slower but cheaper way to get there. Board the train at Gambir, Pegangsaan or Mangarai stations in Jakarta.

Accommodation

The only place worth staying is the old colonial **Hotel Salak** (54 rooms) just opposite the Presidential Summer Palace (Jl. H. Juanda 8, Bogor, tel: 22091), a bit seedy now but they have several new air-conditioned rooms in the back for US$30.

Puncak Pass/Cibodas/Cipanas

Ten kms (six miles) beyond Bogor, at Ciawi, the road splits and you must choose between the southerly route, leading through Sukabumi with a side-road to the dramatic black-sand beaches of Pelabuhan Ratu, and the easterly route, leading up over Puncak Pass to the mountain resort of Cipanas. The two routes join up again at Cianjur and continue on to Bandung.

Puncak Pass and Cipanas are quite spectacular, offering vistas that stretch across the flanks of Mts. Gede, Pangrango and Salak on a clear day. During the dry season (May-September) the mountain weather is delightful.

The Cibodas branch of the Botanical Gardens is well worth a visit (*see* Part III).

Getting There

A rental car or taxi up to Puncak Pass or Cipanas will cost up to US$50 and take two hours from Jakarta. Inter-city taxis like "4848" bound for Bandung also take this route and cost about US$6 per person (*see* Jakarta above for listings). Buses cost only about US$1.20 from Jakarta's Cililitan Terminal or US$0.60 from the Ciawi Terminal outside Bogor.

Accommodation

There are many good hotels around Puncak and Cipanas, including one that perches dramatically on the edge of the steep mountain slope just below the pass. For a group of people or a longer stay, private holiday bungalows may be rented for anywhere from US$20 to US$100 per night. Just walk around and inquire at houses that look promising. Most of them are vacant during the week. Budget travellers can stay at the new youth hostel just below the Cibodas Botanical Gardens for US$2 a night.

- **Bukit Indah** (41 rooms), Jl. Raya 116, Ciloto, Cianjur, tel: 49.
- **Bukit Raya** (92 rooms), Jl. Raya 219, Cipanas, Cianjur, tel: 2505.
- **Evergreen** (101 rooms), Jl. Raya, Puncak, Tugu, Bogor, tel: 4075.
- **Puncak Pass Hotel** (45 rooms), Jl. Raya Puncak, Sindanglaya, Cianjur, tel: 2503, 2504.
- **Sanggabuana** (29 rooms), Jl. Raya 4-6, Cipanas, Cianjur, tel: 2227, 2696.
- **Sindanglaya** (22 rooms), Jl. Raya 43, Pasekon, Cianjur, tel: 2116.
- **Tunas Kembang** (66 rooms), Jl. Raya, Cipanas SDL, Cianjur, tel: 2719.
- **USSU International** (180 rooms), Jl. Raya, Cisarua, Bogor, 4499 Gadog.
- **Wisma Remaja Youth Hostel**, Kebon Raya Cibodas, Pacet, Cianjur.

Pelabuhan Ratu

Fine black-sand beaches line this dramatic coastline for miles. Be careful of the powerful undertow; don't go in very far because the bottom drops off precipitously. Visit the fish market in the morning to see the night's catch—a fantastic variety including giant prawns and tuna. Buy some, very cheap, and have one of the little restaurants nearby grill it for you and serve it with sweet chilli sauce and rice.

Getting There

The roads to Pelabuhan Ratu are excellent—Pelabuhan Ratu can be reached in only four hours from Jakarta by car. A taxi or rental car will charge up to US$60 to take you there, and you should arrange to have them pick you up for the return journey. To get there by bus, hop on one bound for Sukabumi from either Jakarta's Cililitan Terminal or the Ciawi Terminal south of Bogor and then alight at the intersection at Ciba-

dak. From here, "colts" will take you down to
Pelabuhan Ratu.

Accommodation

One hotel, called **Bayu Amrta**, rents small
rooms perched on a cliff overlooking the sea for
US$10 a night and has bungalows sleeping up to
six people for only US$20. The place is in need of
repairs, but the beach is beautiful and they serve
very good seafood. Another place called **Karangsari** across the road is about the same price and
slightly cleaner but without the view. Even the
first-class **Samudra Beach Hotel** is not exorbitant
considering the facilities, at US$35 per night for a
standard double room (plus 21 per cent tax and
service). It is said they keep a room here for
Loro Kidal, the goddess of the South Sea. Closer
in to town, the **Pondok Dewata** offers small air-
conditioned bungalows by the sea for US$23
and larger ones (with two bedrooms and four
beds) for US$45, all inclusive.

● **Bayu Amrta** (12 rooms), Pelabuhan Ratu,
Sukabumi.

● **Karangsari**, Pelabuhan Ratu, Sukabumi.

● **Pondok Dewata Seaside Cottage** (14 rooms),
Pelabuhan Ratu, Sukabumi, tel: 22. In Jakarta,
tel: 772426 for reservations.

● **Samudra Beach Hotel** (106 rooms), Sang-
kawayana, Pelabuhan Ratu, Sukabumi, tel: 23. In
Jakarta, make reservations through the Hotel
Indonesia, tel: 322008 ext. 171, tlx: 46347 HI
JKT, 44233 HIPA JKT.

Bandung

There are two views of Bandung—either as a
charming old colonial town with a cool mountain climate, the capital of Sundanese culture—
or a bustling industrial metropolis. Certainly the
city's ambiance has suffered immensely with the
influx of industry and the dramatic increase in
population, from just 150,000 before the war to
over 1.5 million today. On the other hand, some
of the city's colonial charm is still in evidence,
and the arts are not doing too badly either.

Getting There

Bouraq, Merpati and Garuda operate frequent flights to Bandung from Jakarta (*see* box),
but it's so close and the mountain scenery is so
spectacular that it seems a pity to fly. Most Indonesians take the bus or train. The Parahiangan
Express takes just over three hours from Jakarta
to Bandung and costs about US$6 first class,
US$4.50 second class. There are four trains dai-
ly, leaving from Jakarta's Gambir Station at
5:30, 10:15, 15:15 and 18:45 respectively, with a
similar return schedule.

The next quickest way is by shared inter-city
taxi ("4848" and its equivalents—*see* "Jakarta"
for listings), a ride of four hours (generally in a
huge Holden with six other people) costing about
the same as the train (but delivering you to your
doorstep). The express bus is a bit slower, be-

cause of the stops) but cheaper, about US$3.50
for an air-conditioned express, even less for a
local. Bandung-bound buses leave from Jakarta's
Cililitan Terminal at the south of the city.

Orientation

For all sorts of information about Bandung, and
a mimeographed map, visit the **Tourist Information Kiosk** on Jl. Asia-Afrika at the north-eastern
corner of the town square (*alun-alun*), staffed by
helpful young students. They will be glad to
arrange a personal guided tour of Bandung and
transportation to fit your budget. Ask for Soenar-
dhie Yogantara or call 71724.

Any of the travel agents in Bandung listed at
the end of this section will also be happy to
arrange a guided tour of the city with a car and an
English-speaking guide for a reasonable price.

Getting Around

There are no cruising metered cabs in Bandung
as yet. You have to rent a car from your hotel or
from one of the companies listed below, by the
trip, by the hour or by the day, generally US$2 to
US$3 per hour in the city, with a two-hour mini-
mum. For excursions outside of the city, a minibus
will be cheaper and roomier, about US$30 per day
including gas and driver, a bit more or less depending on the destination.

Ask at your hotel or the Tourist Information
Kiosk how to travel around the city by bus.

Accommodation

The only international-class hotel in Bandung is
the **Panghegar** (US$45 on up for a double, plus 21
per cent tax and service). The **Savoy Homann**
(US$35 plus 21 per cent) is of a similar standard
and very charming.

Many of Bandung's hotels fall into the intermediate category. Several small guest houses are
in old Dutch mansions, including the **Soeti** and
Kwik's (both about US$20 for a double).

For a bit more money, Cisitu's newer **Sangkuriang Guesthouse** (US$30 a night plus 21 per
cent tax and service) is very pleasant—located in
a residential neighbourhood just above the ITB
university campus. The **Hotel Istana** is clean
and reasonably priced at US$25 a night for a
double (plus 21 per cent), with an excellent restaurant. The **Hotel Trio** has spotlessly clean
rooms, excellent service, a sumptuous breakfast,
free transportation to and from the airport or
train station, and free coffee and tea all for
US$30 but is usually fully-booked.

There are few good *losmen* for the budget
traveller. The cheap hotels around the train
station are rather dingy. The **Wisma Gelanggang**
youth hostel is not too bad at US$1.50 a night
for a dorm bed. For about US$12 you can get a
decent room at the **Hotel Dago** or **Hotel Lugina**.

First Class (above US$35 a night)

● **Kumala Panghegar** (65 rooms), Jl. Asia-
Afrika 140, P.O. Box 507, Bandung, tel: 52141-2,

tlx: 28276 PANGHEGAR BD.
- **New Naripan** (20 rooms), Jl. Naripan 31-33, Bandung, tel: 51167, 59383, tlx: 28274 SA BD.
- **Panghegar Hotel** (123 rooms), Jl. Merdeka 2, P.O. Box 506, Bandung, tel: 57751, 57584, tlx: 28276 PANGHEGAR BD.
- **Patra Jasa Motel** (33 rooms), Jl. Ir. H. Juanda 132, Bandung, tel: 81644, 82590.
- **Savoy Homann** (100 rooms), Jl. Asia-Afrika 112, P.O. Box 9, Bandung, tel: 58091-4, tlx: 28425 HOMANN BD.

Intermediate (US$15-30)

- **Arjuna Plaza Hotel** (30 rooms), Jl. Ciumbuleuit 128, P.O. Box 171, Bandung, tel: 81328, 84742.
- **Braga Hotel** (68 rooms), Jl. Braga 8, tel: 51685.
- **Bumi Asih** (27 rooms), Jl. Cilamaya, Bandung, tel: 50419.
- **Cisitu's International Sangkuriang Guesthouse** (44 rooms), Jl. Cisitu (Jl. Sangkuriang) 45 B, Bandung, tel: 82420, 82285-6, 84707.
- **Grand Hotel Preanger** (63 rooms), Jl. Asia Afrika 81, P.O. Box 124, Bandung, tel: 58061-3.
- **Istana Hotel** (34 rooms), Jl. Lembang 22-24, Bandung, tel: 57240, 58240.
- **Kwik's Guesthouse** (3 rooms, 2 suites w/ kitchen), Jl. Dipati Ukur 42, Bandung, tel: 81858.
- **Lugina Hotel**, Jl. Jendral Sudirman 526, Bandung, tel: 52057.
- **Pakunegara Hotel** (36 rooms), Jl. Merdeka 56, Bandung, tel: 58037.
- **Soeti Guesthouse** (15 rooms), Jl. Sumatra 52-54, Bandung, tel: 51686.
- **Trio** (89 rooms), Jl. Gardujati 55-61, Bandung, tel: 58056, 61505-9.

Budget (under US$15 per night)

- **Brawijaya**, Jl. Pungkur 28, Bandung, tel: 50673.
- **Dago**, Jl. Ir. H. Juanda 21, Bandung, tel: 58696.
- **Gania Plaza**, Jl. Bungsu 30, Bandung, tel: 56557.
- **International**, Jl. Veteran 32, Bandung.
- **Melati Baru**, Jl. Kebonjati 24, Bandung, tel: 56409.
- **Sahara**, Jl. Otto Iskandardinata 3, Bandung, tel: 51684.
- **Wisma Gelanggang Generasi Muda** (100 beds), Jl. Merdeka 64, Bandung, tel: 50155.

Dining

Tizi's (Jl. Hegarmanak 14), high up near ITB just off of Jl. Ir. H. Juanda is managed by the wife of a former Indonesian ambassador to Germany and has an open-air garden dining area, with German specialities and excellent breads and pastries. The **Sukarasa** (Jl. Tamblong 52, tel: 56968) is a more formal and expensive establishment with a French-style menu. Many westerners also patronize **The Coffee Shop** opposite the Kumala Panghegar Hotel on Jl. Asia-Afrika.
The **Braga Permai**, in the middle of Jalan Braga

(No. 58, tel: 50519) is a popular sidewalk cafe serving ice-cream, pastries, yoghurt, sandwiches and rice dishes. And no visit to Bandung is complete without a visit to the **Dago Teahouse**—turn left at the top of Jl. Ir. H. Juanda and follow a narrow winding road through the Christian university campus to the teahouse parking lot at the very end, for a lovely vista of the city.

Another of Bandung's treats is **Babakan Siliwangi**, an open-air Sundanese restaurant set amid acres of green rice paddies and large fish-ponds, below the ITB campus (Jl. Siliwangi 7, tel: 81394). Here are served all the traditional Sundanese delicacies: grilled carp (*ikan mas bakar*; barbequed chicken in sweet soya (*ayam panggang*); fish with coconut and spices wrapped in banana leaves (*ikan mas pepes*) and sour vegetable soup (*sayur asem*). Other good Sundanese restaurants are **Bale Kambang**, Jl. Bungur 2, and **Ponyo** on Jl. Malabar.

The best-known Chinese restaurants are the **Queen** (Jl. Dalem Kaum 53 A—near the *alun-alun*), the **Tjoan Kie** (Jl. Jendral Sudirman 46), and the **Trio Restaurant** (Jl. Gardujati 55-61—in the Hotel Trio).

Shopping

Bandung is a good place to buy baskets and mats (woven in nearby Tasikmalaya, an hour to the east past Garut on the Yogya highway), bamboo *angklung* instruments, *wayang golek* puppets (old and new, though most old-looking puppets are 'antiqued' by hanging them over the kitchen stove) and cassette tapes. High-quality ceramics (including many imitations of Chinese antiques) are produced in the nearby village of Plered (to the north, past Lembang) and sold in Bandung. You can have good leather shoes made in many shoestores—they will copy your favourite pair for a fraction of what you would pay at home. And the city also has many talented young artists.

The biggest souvenir shops are located on Jalan Braga—there are also many bookstores here.

For *wayang golek* puppets, try E. Sukatma Muda. For a set of *angklung* instruments, go out to Pak Udjo's Saung Angklung on the eastern edge of town. They put on frequent afternoon performances and they make the instruments here.

If you are interested in ceramics, go over to the Balai Penelitian Keramik (Ceramic Research Office), Jl. a. Yani 390, in the mornings, where you can observe the whole process and also purchase the finished products. There is a Textile Institute in the same complex.

Airline Offices (Bandung)

- **Garuda Indonesian Airways**, Jl. Asia-Afrika 73-75, tel: 51497.
- **Bourag Airlines**, Grand Hotel Preanger Arcade, Jl. Asia-Afrika 81, tel: 58061-3.
- **Merpati Nusantara Airlines**, Jl. Lembong 5, tel: 57474.
- **Merpati Nusantara Airlines**, Jl. Halimun 15, tel: 50794.

Sundanese Performing Arts

Culturally, the Sundanese are known for their folk literature (especially their sung poetry) and their music, for their *wayang golek* puppet plays and their popular dances.

Wayang Golek (*golek* means "round") are three-dimensional puppets carved from wood, painted and adorned with traditional clothing.

There is a *wayang golek* performance in Bandung each Saturday night beginning at 9 p.m. and often lasting till 4 a.m. at Yayasan Pusat Kebudayaan (the city's Cultural Centre), Jl. Naripan 7-9 (just a few doors down from Jl. Braga). The Cultural Centre also holds *jaipongan* dance evenings regularly, in which slim dance hostesses (seated along one side of the hall and dressed like brides in the traditional Sundanese *sarung kebaya*) invite the male patrons (seated along the other side of the hall and dressed in street clothing) to dance. Before they leave, the men pay a cashier in the corner who keeps rack of who he has danced with. *Jaipongan* is also held nightly at the Sanggar Tari Purwa Setra, Jl. Otto Iskandardinata 541 A.

Angklung (hand-held bamboo chime) performances are held regularly in the afternoons (generally beginning at 3:30 p.m.) at Pak Ujo's Saung Angklung, located down a narrow lane at the eastern edge of town (Jl. Padasuka 118, tel: 71714). This is both an *angklung* school and a workshop, and *wayang golek* and dance performances are also put on by request (call them to find out the schedule of events). Instrument sets may be purchased here.

The Bandung Highlands

The Tangkuban Prahu volcano, the Ciater hot springs, Lembang and the waterfall at Maribaya are all less than an hour to the north of Bandung and easily reached by renting a car or colt for a day. With a little time on your hands, you might even want to stay at one of the hotels in these hills. The colonial pavilion-style **Grand Hotel** in Lembang, for instance (Jl. Raya 228, Lembang, tel: 82393), offers spacious double rooms (a bit old and musty now) for only US$12 to US$20, including breakfast and use of the tennis courts and pool (both cracked). And the luxurious **Panorama Panghegar**, located between Lembang and Tangkuban Prahu offers horse-riding, tennis courts and a large swimming pool in a delightfully scenic location (60 rooms, make reservations through Hotel Panghegar, Bandung).

As indicated in Part III, the highlands to the south of Bandung are even more spectacular, and anyone really seriously interested in exploring them should get a copy of *Bandung and Beyond* by Richard and Shila Bennett, available for US$7 from the Bandung Man (Jl. Cihampelas 120). This little booklet has very detailed instructions on how to get to a wide variety of mountain destinations, and descriptions of what you can see there.

Java's North Coast

Cirebon
Pekalongan
Semarang
East of Semarang
Semarang to Yogya

Cirebon

Cirebon (pronounced: "Cheer-i-bon") has begun to receive a bit more attention of late from scholars and artists, mostly because of her very colourful past and her wealth of traditional performing arts and crafts. Some of the contributors to this book were in fact involved in a recent project to study Cirebon's history and culture. The result is a small bilingual booklet (English/Indonesian) entitled CERBON (Sinar Harapan/Mitra Budaya: Jakarta, 1982) that is highly recommended to all visitors and can be purchased in most bookstores in Jakarta for US$6. It has chapters on Cirebon's history, historical monuments, music, theatre, paintings, cuisine and *batik*.

Getting There

Cirebon is about four hours (260 kms [160 miles]) overland from Jakarta, only three hours by road from Bandung. There is a small airport with two weekly flights from Jakarta (*see* box for details), but trains and mini-buses are generally more convenient.

There are two air-conditioned **first class trains** operating on the Jakarta-Cirebon coastal route. On these, however, you must pay for a further destination just to occupy the seat as far as Cirebon. The Bima Express leaves Jakarta's Kota Station daily at 16:00 and arrives in Cirebon at 19:43, costing US$25 one-way (the fare to Yogya). The Mutiara Utara leaves from Kota Station at 16:30 and arrives in Cirebon at 19:45, costing US$17.50 one-way (the fare to Semarang).

Two non-airconditioned **second class trains** also serve Cirebon. The Gunung Jati makes two daily runs, leaving from Jakarta's Pasar Senen Station at 7:00 and again at 14:27 and arriving about five hours later. Tickets are US$4 one-way. The evening Senja Utama also departs from Jakarta's Gambir Station at 18:15 and arrives in Cirebon at 21:50. Tickets are US$7.50 each way (the fare to Yogya).

A more convenient way to go is by nine-seater colt mini-bus. They will fetch you in Jakarta and deliver you to your hotel in Cirebon, approximately four hours later. Departures are hourly 6 a.m. to 4 p.m. daily; the fare is only about US$6 each way. Some companies offer air-con; ask your hotel to book a seat for you one or more days in advance of departure (try **Libra Express**). Mini-buses also operate Bandung-Cirebon, and on from Cirebon to Semarang via Pekalongan. To or from Yogya you have to change in Semarang.

Numerous eastward-bound inter-city buses leave Jakarta in the late afternoon (between

3 p.m. and 5 p.m.) from Pulo Gadung Terminal, arriving in Cirebon four hours later. The fare is about US$3 one-way. From Bandung's Cicaheum Terminal, buses to Cirebon generally depart in the early evening (between 6 p.m. and 8 p.m.) and arrive two hours later. Fare is about US$1.50.

Getting Around

Everything in town is pretty much within walking distance. You can also take a pedicab (*becak*) most anywhere for Rp 300. For trips out to Gua Sunyaragi, Trusmi and Gunung Jati, you can rent a car or "colt" from your hotel (between US$20 and US$25 per day) or simply catch one of the local mini-buses headed in that direction.

Accommodation

First choice in hotels is the venerable old **Grand Hotel**, with a variety of rooms, ranging in price from the huge air-conditioned President's Suite for US$50 all the way down to a small room in the back with a fan for only US$7.50. The **Patra Jasa Motel** has more modern (but tacky) rooms for between US$30 and US$70, as do the nearby **Omega** and **Cirebon Plaza**.

Budget travellers will find a variety of accommodation in the US$3 to US$7 range right next to each other all along Jl. Siliwangi around the train station and farther down past the Grand Hotel (**Hotel Baru, Hotel Familie, Hotel Semarang, Hotel Damai,** etc.). Also around the corner along the canal on Jl. Kalibaru (**Hotel Asia**).

The Pertamina Cirebon Country Club (Ciperna) located up on the hill beyond the airport, 11 kms from Cirebon on the road to Kuningan, has an olympic-size swimming pool and an 18-hole golf course. Bungalows may also be rented here for as little as US$7 a night with a nice view of the coast.

First Class (over US$20 a night)

- **Cirebon Plaza Hotel** (34 rooms), Jl. Kartini 46, Cirebon, tel: 2061-3.
- **Grand Hotel** (66 rooms), Jl. Siliiwangi 98, Cirebon, tel: 2014-5, 2286-7.
- **Omega Hotel** (64 rooms), Jl. Tuparev 20, Cirebon, tel: 3072-3.
- **Patra Jasa Motel** (55 rooms), Jl. Tuparev 11, P.O. Box 68, Cirebon, tel: 3792-3, 3005-6, 3442.

Intermediate and Budget (under US$20 a night)

- **Hotel Asia**, Jl. Kalibaru Selatan 33, Cirebon, tel: 2183.
- **Hotel Baru**, Jl. Siliwangi 159, Cirebon, tel: 2196.
- **Hotel Cordova**, Jl. Siliwangi 75-77, Cirebon, tel: 4677.
- **Hotel Damai**, Jl. Siliwangi 130, Cirebon, tel: 3045.
- **Hotel Familie**, Jl. Siliwangi 76, Cirebon, tel: 2324.
- **Hotel Priangan**, Jl. Siliwangi 122, Cirebon, tel: 2929.
- **Hotel Semarang**, Jl. Siliwangi 132, Cirebon, tel: 3231.

Dining

Cirebon is famous for its seafood (the city's name means "shrimp river"), and the best seafood restaurant in town is **Maxim's** (Jl. Bahagia 45-7, tel: 2679, 3185)—just a short walk back along the road next to the Thay Kak Sie Chinese temple. Giant steamed crabs and prawns here are unbelievably fresh and inexpensive. They serve delicious Chinese food, too.

For spicy Padang food, there's **Sinar Budi** (Jl. Karang Getas 20, tel: 3846) not far from the Grand Hotel, where they also serve good fresh fruit drinks. For a simple lunch, try the local speciality, *nasi lengko* (rice with bits of fried *tempe*, *tahu*, vegetables and *sambal*) at the **Kopyor** across the street (Jl. Karang Getas 9, tel: 4343).

For western-style breakfast or dinner, the **Grand Hotel** or **Patra Jasa** coffee shops are adequate. Or, after a hot visit to the *kraton* and the mosque, stop in at the air-conditioned **Corner Restaurant** (Jl. Pasuketan 31 A, tel: 4375) for a cold drink and a local version of a western snack.

Shopping

To get the best *batik*, you really must visit **Ibu Masina's** studio in Trusmi, 12 kms (7 miles) to the west of Cirebon just off the Bandung road (there is a small sign marking the narrow lane in Weru where you turn off to the right from the main highway—from here it's about one km to the showroom and workshop). She has revived many of the traditional Cirebon court designs, which incorporate a variety of Chinese, Javanese, Indian, Islamic and European motifs.

For Cirebonese *topeng* masks, visit Pak Kandeg at Suranenggala Lor village about 5 kms (3 miles) north of Cirebon on the road to Gunung Jati—easily reached by hopping a colt mini-bus in front of the Grand Hotel.

Topeng masks and paintings on glass incorporating Arabic calligraphy are also produced in Palimanan and Gegesik villages to the northwest of Cirebon. They are also interesting villages for all sorts of local dance and theatre traditions, including the *sintren* trance ritual.

Pekalongan

Pekalongan is between three and four hours from Cirebon by bus or "colt." Two hours from Semarang. The best way to get around town is to walk or take a *becak*.

Accommodation

Top-of-the-line is the **Hotel Nirwana**, near the bus terminal, with air-conditioned rooms for US$25 to US$35 a night, and a large new swimming pool. More conveniently located is the **Hayam Wuruk** right on the main street, with air-conditioned double rooms for only US$15 to US$20 including breakfast. The Hayam Wuruk also has pleasant double rooms with a fan for

US$10.50, singles for US$8—breakfast, tax and service included. Cheaper accommodation across from the train station at the western edge of town include: the **Istana**, the **Gajah Mada** and the **Ramayana**.

- **Istana Hotel** (33 rooms), Jl. Gajah Mada 23-25, Pekalongan, tel: 61581.
- **Gajah Mada**, Jl. Gajah Mada 11A, Pekalongan.
- **Hayam Wuruk** (56 rooms), Jl. Hayam Wuruk 152-158, Pekalongan, tel: 41823, 21405.
- **Nirwana Hotel** (56 rooms), Jl. Dr. Wahidin 11, Pekalongan, tel: 41691, 41446.
- **Ramayana**, Jl. Gajah Mada 9, Pekalongan, tel: 21043.

Dining

Your best bet here is Chinese food, either at the **Remaja** (Jl. Dr. Cipto 20, tel: 21019), or the **Serba Ada** (Jl. Hayam Wuruk 125). For breads, ice cream and snacks, try the **Purimas** bakery on Jl. Hayam Wuruk. There is also a cafeteria next to the *alun-alun*.

Buying Batik

In addition to several shops on Jl. Hayam Wuruk and Jl. Hasanuddin where a range of fabrics is sold, seek out individual *batik* makers. **Tobal Batik** at Jl. Teratai 24, Klego, (tel: 61885) specializes in export clothing—many of the *batik* sundresses and shirts you see in boutiques in California and Australia are drawn, dyed and sewn here. While they produce to order for wholesale customers and do not normally sell individual pieces, they often have overstocks of certain items that they are happy to sell to casual visitors.

The same is true of **Ahmad Yahya** (Jl. Pesindon 221, tel: 41413—enter the small lane near the bridge on Jl. Hayam Wuruk, next to the Sederhana Restaurant). His fabrics have been selling in New York for many years, and have been used to decorate Jackie Onassis' bathroom and Farrah Fawcett-Majors' bedroom.

Achmad Said at Jl. Bandung 53 is another producer well known to foreigners, producing bold, brightly coloured *cap* fabrics under the "Zaky" label.

Salim Alaydrus (Jl. H. Agus Salim 31, tel: 41175) produces and sells some floral piece goods and often has antique fabrics for sale.

For higher-quality, hand-drawn *tulis* work, visit **Jane Hendromartono** at Jl. Blimbing 36 (tel: 1003). Her superb work is in the permanent collection of the Textile Museum in Washington D.C. as well as in many private collections around the world. She generally has a variety of original *sarung* and *kain* pieces ranging in price from US$25 up to US$100, as well as some Chinese altar cloths done in *batik* and several types of less-expensive *batik cap*.

Perhaps Pekalongan's most famous batikker is **Oey Soe Tjoen**, who bought over and continued many of the designs of the great Eliza Van Zuylen, an Indo-Dutch woman whose rare *batik*, produced in the 1920s and 1930s, now fetch thousands of dollars from avid collectors in Holland and New York. Oey Soe Tjoen's wife and son now continue the business at their home and workshop in Kedungwuni, 9 km to the south of Pekalongan (Jl. Raya 104, Kedungwuni—located just about 200 metres before the police station on the left).

Semarang

Getting There

From Jakarta, take the Mutiara Utara air-conditioned express train (leaves Kota Station at 16:30, arrives at Semarang at 1:15—fare is US$17.50), or catch a Garuda shuttle flight from Kemayoran Airport—8 daily flights, no advance bookings. Mandala also has daily flights to and from Jakarta, and Bouraq connects Semarang with Kalimantan and Sulawesi.

To get here directly from Bandung, you have to take the bus, but from Cirebon, Pekalongan, Yogya or Solo, you can travel by more comfortable and convenient inter-city "colt" instead.

Accommodation

Semarang's best hotel is the **Patra Jasa**, located up on a hill in Candi Baru overlooking the city (US$35 to US$60 for a double, plus 21 per cent tax and service). A bit closer to the city but still in the hills, the old **Candi Baru Hotel** has spacious rooms with a view for less money (US$17 to US$28 for a double; US$40 for a huge suite) and in the same area, the **Green Guest House** is a bargain at US$14 to US$18 for an air-conditioned double with breakfast (tax and service included).

Down in the centre of town, the best hotel is the **Metro Grand Park** (doubles are US$35 to US$45 plus 21 per cent). The old Dutch hostelry, the **Dibya Puri**, is just across a busy intersection from here—only US$25 for an air-conditioned double, with breakfast, tax and service included, but the place is looking (and smelling) a bit wilted these days. The **Queen Hotel** around the corner on Jl. Gajah Mada is a newer place and about the same price.

Budget travellers can check out some of the hotels on Jl. Imam Bonjol around the train station, like the **Dewa Asia**, the **Tanjung** and the **Singapore**, all with rooms in the US$5 to US$10 range. The **Nan Yon Hotel**, right in the middle of the Chinatown district, also has clean rooms for as little as US$4.50 a night including breakfast—air-conditioning for only US$14 a night, tax and service included.

First Class (US$35 and Up)

- **Metro Grand Park** (80 rooms), Jl. H. Agus Salim 2-4, Semarang, tel: 27371-7, tlx: 22332 MH DIRGA SM.
- **Patra Jasa Hotel** (72 rooms), Jl. Sisingamangaraja, P.O. Box 8, Semarang, tel: 314441-7, tlx: 22286 PATRA SM.

- **Siranda Hotel** (61 rooms), Jl. Diponegoro 1, Semarang, tel: 313271-5.
- **Sky Garden Motel** (64 rooms), Jl. Setiabudi, Grogol, Semarang, tel: 312733-6.

Intermediate (US$15-US$35)

- **Candi Baru** (23 rooms), Jl. Rinjani 21, Semarang, tel: 312981-2, 315272.
- **Candi Indah** (31 rooms), Jl. Dr. Wahidin 122, Semarang, tel: 312515, 315356.
- **Dibya Puri Hotel** (72 rooms), Jl. Pemuda 11, P.O. Box 562, Semarang, tel: 27821.
- **Green Guesthouse** (20 rooms), Jl. Kesambi 7, Candi Baru, Semarang, tel: 312528, 312787, 312642-3.
- **Merbaru Hotel** (46 rooms), Jl. Pemuda 122, Semarang, tel: 27491.
- **Queen Hotel** (24 rooms), Jl. Gajah Mada 44, Semarang, tel: 27063.
- **Telomoyo Hotel** (66 rooms), Jl. Gajah Mada 138, Semarang, tel: 25436-9k.

Budget (under US$15 a night)

- **Grand** (25 rooms), Jl. Plampitan 39, Semarang, tel: 21739.
- **Islam** (23 rooms), Jl. Pemuda 8, Semarang, tel: 20538.
- **Dewa Asia** (21 rooms), Jl. Imam Bonjol 1, Semarang, tel: 22547.
- **Nan Yon/Nendrayakti** (41 rooms), Jl. Gang Pinggir 68, Semarang, tel: 22538.
- **Rama Losmen** (16 rooms), Jl. Plampitan 37, Semarang, tel: 288951.
- **Singapore** (27 rooms), Jl. Imam Bonjol 12, Semarang, tel: 23757.
- **Tanjung** (15 rooms), Jl. Tanjung 9-11, Semarang, tel: 22612.

Dining

This town is famous for its Chinese food. The best Chinese restaurant is probably **Pringgading** (Jl. Pringgading 54, tel: 288973, 27219, 27364), though the **Gajah Mada** (Jl. Gajah Mada 43, tel: 23753) is a bit more centrally located. Also on Jl. Gajah Mada is a complex of open-air eateries known as the **Kompleks Warna Sari**, containing a wide assortment of Chinese and Indonesian restaurants. There are also many Chinese restaurants in Chinatown on **Gang Lombok**, just beside the Thay Kak Sie temple, all of them quite good.

At night, food stalls set up along both sides of **Jalan Depok** just off of Jl. Gajah Mada and this is a great place to get inexpensive seafood—grilled prawns and steamed crabs, as well as barbequed chicken and a variety of other dishes.

For Sundanese grilled fish and chicken, try **Lembur Kuring** on Jl. Gajah Mada, or for *sate* go over to **Sate Ponorogo** (Jl. Gajah Mada 107, tel: 20637).

The most notable restaurant in town, though, is **Toko Oen** (Jl. Pemuda 52, tel: 21683)—a hold-over from colonial times, with Dutch items like *Paprika Schnitzel* and *Uitsmijter Roastbeef* and *Biefstuk Compleet* on the menu. They also have an exotic assortment of ice creams—*Vruchten*

Sorbet, *Cassata* and *Oen's Symphoni*—as well as cakes, cookies and Chinese dishes.

Entertainment

Semarang residents are avid theatre goers, and this city boasts not one but three venues to watch nightly performances of the popular *wayang orang* and *ketoprak*—more troupes than in any other Javanese city!
- **Ngesti Pandowo**, Jl. Pemuda 116.
- **Sri Wanito**, Jl. Dr. Dipto.
- **Wahyu Budoyo**, Kompleks Tegal Wareng, Jl. Sriwijaya.

East of Semarang

To visit any of the towns east of Semarang—**Demak**, with its famous 16th Century mosque; **Kudus** with its old carved teakwood houses, its strange old mosque with a Hindu-Javanese minaret and its *kretek* cigarette industry; **Jepara** with its wood-working industry and **Rembang** and **Lasem** with their beautiful Chinese temples (*klenteng*)—just book a seat on a "colt" mini-bus from the Semarang central terminal on the corner of Jl. M.T. Haryono and Jl. H. Agus Salim, or else hop on an eastward-bound bus at the Terminal Bis across the street.

Accommodation

None of these places has a first-class hotel, but the **Notosari** in Kudus is not too bad. If you're visiting Rembang and Lasem, then stay in Pati. There is also a Pesanggrahan or government resthouse in Colo, 6 kms (3.5 miles) above Kudus on the slopes of Mt. Muria.
- **Air Mancur**, Jl. Pemuda 70, Kudus.
- **Anna**, Jl. Jendral Sudirman 36, Pati.
- **Duta Wisata**, Jl. Sunan Muria 194, Kudus.
- **Kurnia**, Jl. Tondonegoro 12, Pati.
- **Menno Jaya Inn**, Jl. Diponegoro 40/B, Jepara, tel: 143.
- **Mulia**, Jl. Kol. Sunandar 17, Pati, tel: 2118.
- **Notosari**, Jl. Kepodang 17, Kudus, tel: 21245.
- **Pati**, Jl. Jendral Sudirman 60, Pati.
- **Pesanggrahan Colo/Gunung Muria**, Jl. Sunan Muria, Colo, Kudus, tel: 557 Kudus.

Semarang to Yogya

This is a delightful two-hour ride over the mountains across the narrow "waist" of Java. If you have the time, spend a night halfway in the mountain resort of **Bandungan**, to see the Gedung Sanga temples—about 10 kms (6 miles) from here. Try to get up to the temples in the early morning—they are spectacular at sunrise. There are hot springs at the end of the trail beyond the temples, so bring along your swimsuit and a towel.

Getting There

Turn off to the right at the sign in the middle of

Ambarawa (or get off the bus here and wait for a mini-bus going up the hill). Bandungan is 7 kms (4 miles) above Ambarawa.

Accommodation

There are many hotels in Bandungan at the top of the road. The **Wina** and the **Gaya** are the biggest. None are expensive—US$20 a·night, tops with many rooms for less than US$10. The best place is the **Rawa Pening Hotel**—turn left at the top of the hill and continue out of Bandungan town for about 1 km—you will see and old colonial mansion with bungalows above it on your right. You can get a bungalow here for US$20 to US$25 a night, a double room for US$12.

Yogyakarta

Emerging from the shadow of an increasingly touristed Bali, it has been some years now since Yogyakarta was discovered as a tourist destination and ceased being merely a stopover on the way to Paradise. Indeed, more and more visitors are finding that Yogyakarta's majestic temples and palaces, her traditional crafts and performing arts provide a fascinating counterpoint to those of Bali. Many who have spent time in both places profess to prefer this laid-back city.

A modest tourist boom has overtaken the venerable Javanese court centre as a result: the standard and availability of hotels, restaurants, tours and other services have improved greatly over the past decade, and since 1974 the Regional Tourism Office has actively promoted local cultural events.The 10-year UNESCO-sponsored restoration of Borobudur was completed in time for the official re-opening of this 1,200-year-old monument on February 23, 1983 by President Suharto. Tourist parks are being constructed at both Borobudur and Prambanan, in order to accommodate an estimated 2 million visitors in 1985, most of them Indonesians.

Getting There

A majority of foreign visitors to Yogya arrive by air. **Garuda** has several daily flights from Jakarta's Cengkareng International Airport, and in fact it is often possible to bypass Jakarta completely—hopping on the first plane to Yogyakarta upon arrival from overseas.

The first-class **Bima Express** train that plies the Jakarta-Yogyakarta-Surabaya route nightly in either direction is Java's finest—comfortable air-conditioned sleeper cars with small two mattress bunk compartments, a sink and a table. The schedule is less than ideal, nonetheless. The Bima leaves Jakarta Kota Station at 4 p.m. and arrives in Yogya 10 hours later, which means that your sleep is interrupted and you travel by night. At US$25 one way, it's about half the price of an air-ticket. The second class **Senja Utama** and **Senja Yogya** trains from Jakarta cost much less (only US$8) but they are slower and not air-conditioned.

Inter-city buses always travel at night. The Jakarta-Yogyakarta run takes about nine hours and costs less than US$10. From Bandung it's only six hours and about US$6. The more expensive Mercedes buses are air-conditioned.

From Semarang or Solo or other nearby cities, you're better off taking a mini-bus, with services all day from dawn to dusk. Cost is only US$1.20 from Solo, US$2.50 from Semarang.

City Orientation

As described in Part III, Yogya's main street is **Jalan Malioboro**, which runs north-south from the front steps of the **Kraton** or palace all the way up to the Tugu monument that stands in the middle of the intersection with Jl. Jendral Sudirman and Jl. Diponegoro. Looking at the map, you'll see that Malioboro's northern half is now called Jalan Mangkubumi, while its southern end is known as Jl. Jendral Ahmad Yani. A rail line bisects this main street, and the **Train Station** is located here. The new inter-city **Bus terminal** is in the southeastern corner of the city, on Jl. Veteran, though you can buy tickets and board most express buses on Jl. Sosrowijayan, just off Malioboro. The "colt" offices in Yogyakarta are located on Jl. Diponegoro just to the left of the Tugu monument.

Jalan Pasar Kembang is a small street lined with inexpensive hotels and shops— once Yogya's red-light district, but now "cleaned up" and taken over by foreign budget travellers. **Jalan Sosrowijayan**, the next small street to the south also has budget hotels, as do several of the lanes connecting these two streets.

The more fashionable suburbs of Yogyakarta are located to the east of Jl. Malioboro/ Mangkubumi, across the river. From here, it is about a mile north to the new campus of **Gajah Mada University**. **Jalan Solo**, in between, has become a busy shopping area lined with stores, restaurants and hotels on both sides—almost a second Malioboro and a good place to shop for photo accessories or other necessities not available on the latter. The **Ambarrukmo Palace Hotel** and the **Adisucipto Airport** are located several miles out of town to the east along this road.

Getting Around

Rented **Taxis** and **mini-buses** have become rather expensive in Yogya because of the tourist demand. Drivers have come up with a fixed schedule of fares and most stick to it, though a few will accept less after some bargaining. Some will demand even more—be sure you fix the fare before getting in.

Most hotels, including the budget guest houses on Jl. Prawirotaman, will meet you at the airport or train station with transportation if you send them a letter or call them long distance before arrival.

From the airport, the standard fare into town is now US$5 (if you don't have much luggage, you can just walk out of the airport to the highway and flag down a passing mini-bus heading into the city—which is to the left as you come out—for only Rp 200, or about US$0.20 cents). For trips around the city, taxis now charge US$3.50 per hour (with a two-hour minimum). Out of town trips have been worked out according to the following, rather arbitrary schedule:

• Borobudur (round trip) 84 kms (52 miles) US$15.50
• Prambanan (round trip) 32 kms (20 miles) US$12.50
• Parangtritis (round trip) 56 kms (35 miles) US$14.50
• Surakarta (round trip) 130 kms (81 miles) US$22.50
• Dieng Plateau (round trip) 180 kms (112 miles) US$45.00
• Surabaya (one way) 327 kms (202 miles) US$75.00
• Bandung (one way) 425 kms (264 miles) US$125.00
• Jakarta (one way) 600 kms (372 miles) US$160.00
• Bali (one way) 720 kms (447 miles) US$190.00

Arrange for taxis (up to four persons) or mini-buses (up to 8 persons) through any hotel or travel agent or through the Tourist Information Office on Jl. Malioboro, or by going down to the taxi stand to the east of the GPO on Jl. Senopati (where you may be able to get a cheaper rate for one of the older cars).

Pedicabs (*becak*) are convenient for short distances in town. Yogyakartans use them daily to go everywhere in the city, and some tourists have taken to "chartering" one to tour around in. The problem is that *becak* drivers have gotten wise to the fact that tourists have a lot of money, don't know the fares and don't understand how to bargain. As a result, they sometimes try to charge outrageous amounts, and often won't come down to a reasonable price even if you *do* know the fares. Bargaining for *becak* rides is something of an art anyway, and this makes it doubly difficult for foreigners to use them. The key to good bargaining is to smile and joke about how high the first offer is, then to walk away once you have stated your final price. If it is reasonable, he will usually accept and call you back.

A few of the drivers who hang around Malioboro and the Kraton now understand some words of English, and several enterprising young English-speaking guides have taken up *becak*-driving in order to solicit tourists for guided tours of the city. Not a bad way to go, provided that you don't pay more than a few dollars for a morning or afternoon tour. Many of them just want to take you shopping, though, so they can get a commission. Again, be sure to establish all fees in advance.

Within the city, bright orange-coloured Mercedes **city-buses** circulate all day along eight fixed routes until 8 p.m. In addition, there is a whole fleet of smaller pick-up **micro-buses** that are perhaps more convenient, because they travel in smaller circuits. Fare is fixed at Rp 100 regardless of distance. A few of the more useful routes are:

• A **counter-clockwise circuit** (**Campus**) serves the north-eastern quadrant of town, going down Malioboro, east on Senopati and Sultan Agung, up Jl. Dr. Sutomo to Jl. Jendral Sudirman and by the university in a small detour along Jl. Cik Ditro, then down Mangkubumi/Malioboro again. Useful for getting up the university, to ASTI or to Jl. Solo.

• A **clockwise circuit**, meanwhile, goes up the western side of town along Jl. Bhayangkara to Diponegoro and then comes down Mangkubumi/Malioboro and turns west on Jl. K.H. Ahmad Dahlan.

• From Malioboro down to the Kraton or Taman Sari, you want the **Ngasem** line, that travels down around the *alun-alun* to Jl. Ngasem. To get down to the southeastern corner of town from Malioboro, take **Pojok Beteng**.

• To get out to Borobudur or Prambanan or Parangtritis via public transportation is not difficult. You simply have to study the map and ask for some advice where to get on and off the buses or mini-buses. Most people are very helpful, and if you can just pronounce the place names properly, they will indicate where to get off or where to change buses even if they speak no English. Check with someone at your hotel or with the Tourist Information Office on Jl. Malioboro to be sure of the route and method of transport for each destination.

Last but not least, you can hire an **Andong** or **Dokar** pony cart for trips into the country along scenic back roads—a very nice and slow way to get out to Kota Gede or even to Imogiri or Parangtritis. Not recommended on major highways, however. To Kota Gede, pay about Rp 500 each way, Rp 2,000 to Imogiri or Parangtritis (count on at least two hours each way). *Dokars* generally wait to the east of the post office, along Jl. Senopati, or on side roads at edge of town; villagers still use them to get to and from the city.

Tours/Travel Agents

Certainly the easiest way to see the city is by guided tour, though it can be grating to go on a large bus tour with people you don't know. For your own private tour, hire a car (US$20 to US$30 a day) and arrange for a guide (US$10 to US$20 a day) from one of the travel agencies below (or through the Tourist Information Office). Agencies like **Intan Pelangi** organize daily bus tours of the city (including a *wayang* performance, Taman Sari, the Kraton and a *batik* factory), Borobudur, Dieng and Prambanan for as little as US$7 per person. Call them or check with the Tourist Information Office (Jl. Malioboro 16) or your hotel for the latest schedules.

• **Bunda Mulya Utama**, Jl. Mangkubumi 105. Yogyakarta, tel: 3644.
• **Intan Pelangi**, Jl. Malioboro 18, Yogyakarta, tel: 3644.
• **Intrastour**, Jl. Malioboro 183, Yogyakarta, tel: 86972.
• **Natrabu**, Ambarrukmo Hotel Arcade, Jl. Adisucipto, Yogyakarta, tel: 88488.
• **Nitour**, Jl. K.H.A. Dahlan, Yogyakarta, tel: 3165, 3450.
• **Pacto**, Jl. Malioboro 72, Yogyakarta, tel: 88195, 2113-4.

YOGYAKARTA

1. Kraton Ngayogyakarta
2. Taman Sari (Water Castle)
3. Pasar Ngasem Bird Market
4. Batik Painter's Colony
5. Agastya Art Institute
6. Tirtodipuran Batik Factories
7. Diponegoro Monument
8. Dalem Pujokusuman (Mardawa Budoyo
   Dance School)
9. Sasono Suko (THR – Ramayana Ballet)
10. Sono Budoyo Museum
11. Post Office
12. Batik Research Institute
13. Benteng Budaya National Art Museum
    (Fort Vredeburgh)
14. Tourist Information Centre
15. Pasar Beringan (Central Market)
16. Garuda Airways Office
17. Asri Fine Arts Academy
18. Asti Dance Academy
19. Gajah Mada University
20. Bus Station
21. Immigration Office
22. Telephone Office
23. Bank Negara Indonesia
24. Affandi's Gallery
25. Railway Station
26. Gembiraloka Zoo
27. Ambarrukmo Palace Hotel
28. Garuda Hotel
29. Mutiara Hotel
30. Guest Houses (Jl. Prawirotaman)

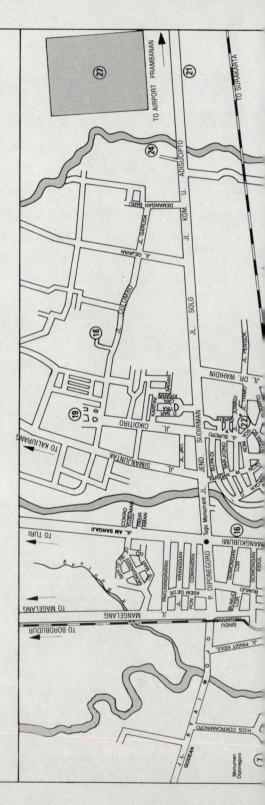

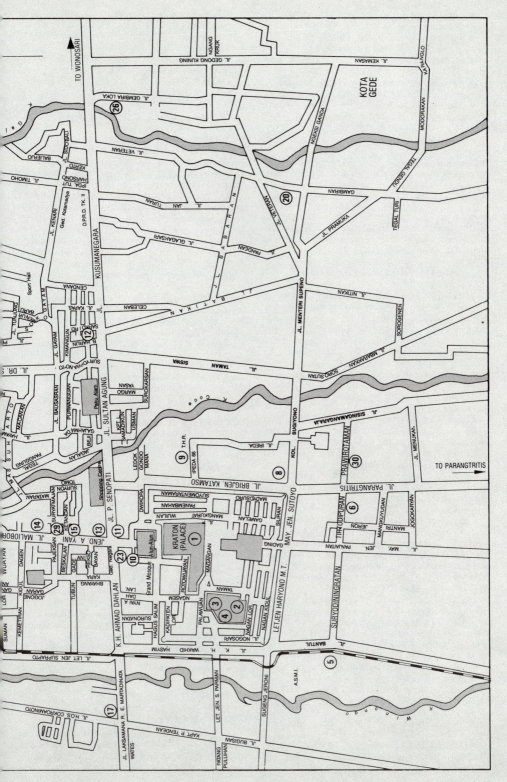

- **Royal Holiday**, Ambarrukmo Hotel Arcade, Jl. Adisucipto, Yogyakarta, tel: 88488.
- **Satriavi**, Ambarrukmo Hotel Arcade, Jl. Adisucipto, Yogyakarta, tel: 88488.
- **Sri Rama** Tours, Wisma LPP, Jl. Demangan Baru 8, Yogyakarta, tel: 88480.
- **Vayatour**, Ambarrukmo Hotel Arcade, Jl. Adisucipto, Yogyakarta, tel: 88488 ext.121.
- **Vista Express**, Ambarrukmo Hotel Arcade, Jl. Adisucipto, Yogyakarta, tel: 88488 ext.719.

Accommodation

Yogya has a room for everyone, from the US$350 a night Presidential Suite at the Ambarrukmo to the dollar a night closets at the "Home Sweet Homestay" on Gang Sosrowijayan I. There

is even one agency, Indraloka, that will place you in the home of an English or Dutch-speaking family where you share home-cooked meals and enjoy the warm hospitality of the Javanese.

First Class (US$35 and up per night)

The 4-star **Ambarrukmo Hotel**, built by the Japanese in the early 1960s, is still the only international-class luxury hotel in Yogya, with rooms going for US$65 on up (plus 21 per cent tax and service). It is symbolically situated some miles to the east of town near the airport upon the grounds of the old royal *pesanggrahan* or rest house once used to entertain visiting dignitaries to the court, and some of the old buildings survive, including the elegant *pendapa* and the *dalem agung* ceremonial chambers.

The old **Hotel Garuda** (US$35 to US$50 a night) right on Malioboro has just added a modern seven-storey wing at the back, and has up-graded their spacious colonial suites (huge rooms and bathrooms, with high ceilings and an outer sitting-room/balcony looking out onto a central courtyard). The hotel has quite a history, as it housed several government ministries during the Indonesian revolution (1946 to '49).

The newer **Mutiara Hotel** down the street is just 10 minutes' walk from the Kraton and the museum. Prices are about the same as the Garuda. Motel-style "cottage" hotels include the **Sahid Garden**, nice and thoroughly Javanese. Owned by an aristocratic Surakartan family (US$45 on up plus 21 per cent).

It's hard to beat the **Puri Artha's** friendly service and well-manicured surroundings (US$35 a night). The nearby **Sri Manganti** and the **Sriwedari** (opposite the Ambarrukmo) are about the same price. All of these hotels have pools and quiet gardens, but none is within walking distance of Malioboro, so you'll have to think about transport.

- **Ambarrukmo Palace Hotel** (240 rooms), Jl. Adisucipto, P.O. Box 10, Yogyakarta, tel: 88488, 88984, tlx: APH YOGYA 12511.
- **Hotel Garuda**, Jl. Malioboro 72, Yogyakarta, tel: 2113-4.
- **Mutiara Hotel** (170 rooms), Jl. Malioboro 18, P.O. Box 87, Yogyakarta, tel: 3272, 4530-1, tlx: 25155 MTH YK.

- **Puri Artha** (60 rooms), Jl. Cendrawasih 9, Yogyakarta, tel: 5934-5, tlx: 25147 ARTHA YK.
- **Sriwedari** (70 rooms), Jl. Adisucipto, P.O. Box 93, Yogyakarta, tel: 88288.
- **Sri Manganti** (46 rooms), Jl. Urip Sumoharjo, P.O. Box 46, Yogyakarta, tel: 2881.
- **Sahid Garden** (64 rooms), Jl. Babarsari, Yogyakarta, tel: 3697.

Intermediate (US$15-35 a night)

The above-mentioned **Indraloka Homestay Service**, founded and run by Mrs. B. Moerdiyono, currently costs US$21 a night for a double (plus 21 per cent tax and service) including breakfast. Home-cooked lunch or dinner is an additional US$6. The families are mostly headed by Dutch-educated professionals (doctors and university lecturers), and the rooms have all the western amenities and a fan. Mrs Moerdiyono also arranges tours through Java to Bali, using her network of homestays in other cities. Write to her for details. (*See* address below under Indraloka.)

Other choices depend largely on where you want to be and how much you want to pay. The **Arjuna Plaza** and the **New Batik Palace** hotels are both centrally located on Jl. Mangkubumi (US$25 to US$30 for a double, plus 21 per cent). The **Gajah Mada Guesthouse**, with air-conditioned doubles for US$24 is a quiet place located on campus in the north of town. Mrs. Sardjito, the widow of Gajah Mada University's first rector also rents rooms at her elegant home on Jl. Cik Ditiro, opposite the Indraloka office.

Many other small hotels and guesthouses cluster along **Jalan Prawirotaman** in the south of Yogya. A few of these have air-conditioned rooms in the US$15-to-US$25 range (plus 21 per cent), including breakfast. Try the **Airlangga** or the **Duta**.

- **Airlangga** (25 rooms), Jl. Prawirotaman 4, Yogyakarta, tel: 3344.
- **Arjuna Plaza** (25 rooms), Jl. Mangkubumi 48, Yogyakarta, tel: 3036, 86862.
- **Batik Palace Hotel** (26 rooms), Jl. Pasar Kembang 29, P.O. Box 115, Yogyakarta, tel: 2149.
- **Duta Guest House** (15 rooms), Jl. Prawirotaman 20, Yogyakarta, tel: 5219.
- **Indraloka Homestay** (40 rooms), Jl. Cik Ditiro 14, Yogyakarta, tel: 0274, 3614.
- **Koba Cottages** (48 rooms), Jl. Babarsari 1, Tambakbayan Baru, Yogyakarta, tel: 3697.
- **Gajah Mada Guest House** (20 rooms), Jl. Bulaksumur, Kampus Universitas Gajah Mada, Yogyakarta, tel: 88461, 88688 ext. 625.
- **New Batik Palace Hotel** (22 rooms), Jl. Mangkubumi 46, Yogyakarta, tel: 2149.
- **Wisma LPP**, Jl. Demangan Baru 8, Yogyakarta, tel: 88380.

Budget (under US$15 a night)

The guest houses along **Jalan Prawirotaman** are all converted homes—generally quiet, clean and comfortable. Cheapest rate available here for a double is US$7.50, including tax, service and breakfast, but most are in the US$10-to-US$12 a night range. Some also have air-conditioned doubles for only US$15 a night.

The many small hotels around **Jalan Pasar Kembang** (also on Jl. Sorowijayan and down the small lanes in between), are substantially cheaper and more central, but this is not as pleasant an area. Many places here have rooms for US$3 to US$5 and even less. Try the **Kota** down at the end of Jl. Pasar Kembang—very clean.

- **Asia Afrika**, Jl. Pasar Kembang 25, Yogyakarta, tel: 4489.
- **Agung Guest House**, Jl. Prawirotaman 68, Yogyakarta, tel: 2715.
- **Aziatic Hotel**, Jl. Sosrowijayan 6, Yogyakarta.
- **Kota Hotel**, Jl. Gandekan Lor 79, Yogyakarta.
- **Pura Jenggala Guest House**, Jl. Cendrawasih 2, Yogyakarta, tel: 2238, 88509.
- **Ratna Hotel**, Jl. Pasar Kembang 17 A, Yogyakarta, tel: 2654.
- **Rose Guest House**, Jl. Prawirotaman 22, Yogyakarta, tel: 2715.
- **Srivijaya Guest House**, Jl. Prawirotaman 7, Yogyakarta, tel: 2387.

Dining

The pilgrimage point for fried chicken lovers from all over Java (and all over the world now) is **Nyonya Suharti's** (also known as Ayam Goreng "Mbok Berek," after the women who invented this famous fried chicken recipe), located 7 kms (4 miles) to the east of Yogya on the road to the airport (a short distance beyond the Ambarrukmo on the same side). The recipe is one of the best-kept culinary secrets in Indonesia—the chicken is first boiled and coated in spices and coconut, then fried crisp and served with a sweet chilli sauce and rice. Excellent when accompanied by pungent *petai* beans and raw cabbage. Indonesians patronize the place in droves, and you can see Jakartans in the airport lounge clutching their take-away boxes of Nyonya Suharti's chicken for friends and family back home.

Nasi Padang fanatics also rave about the fare at **Sinar Budi Restaurant**, at Jl. Mangkubumi 41, about 500 metres north of the railway tracks on the left (opposite the cinema). Muttons brain *opor*, beef *rendang* and *gulai ayam* (chicken curry) await you at a moment's notice. Be sure to ask for their spicy potato chips (*kentang goreng*)— Sinar Budi's answer to the barbeque flavoured variety in the West.

The Yogya speciality is *gudeg*—a combination plate consisting of rice with boiled young jackfruit (*nangka muda*), a piece of chicken, egg, coconut cream gravy and spicy sauce with boiled buffalo hide (*sambal kulit*). The famous spot in Yogya for *gudeg* is **Juminten** at Jl. Asem Gede 22, Kranggan 69, just north of Jl. Diponegoro. The other *gudeg* restaurant of note is **Bu Citro's**, located just opposite the entrance to the airport out on Jl. Adisucipto (a good place to eat while waiting for a flight). Most restaurants in Yogya also serve the dish, and there is excellent *gudeg* just north of Taman Sari on the eastern side of Jl. Ngasem.

Western food is now readily available in Yogya, and not just in the large hotels. The **Legian Garden Restaurant** serves excellent steaks, chops, sautéed fish, avocado seafood cocktails, yoghurt and corn and crab soup. Everything is very reasonable, the beer is cold and the vegetables are not overcooked. Enter via a well-marked doorway around the corner from Jl. Malioboro—Jl. Perwakilan 9 (tel: 87985). The Legian Garden now has a branch, called **The Rose**, on the southern side of Jl. Solo—the same menu and prices but more atmosphere. For more money, the **Gita Buana** offers air-conditioning and low lighting at two locations: Jl. Diponegoro 52 A and out at Jl. Adisucipto 169 by the Ambarrukmo hotel. The **French Grill** in the Arjuna Plaza Hotel (Jl. Mangkubumi 48) is also good, and they have puppet and dance performances every other night. (*See* Performances below).

Many other restaurants on both sides of Jl. Malioboro cater to the young tourist crowd, offering a standard Kuta Beach menu of fruit drinks, yoghurt, sandwiches, vegetarian plates, desserts, ice cream and other western dishes, in addition to a full range of Chinese and Indonesian meals.

The most popular hang-out with the budget crowd (because it is the cheapest), is Supirman's—known to foreigners as **Superman's**—on Gang Sosrowijayan I, a narrow lane parallel to Maliboro between Jl. Pasar Kembang and Jl. Sosrowijayan.

Another favourite hang-out, with better food, is **Mama's Gado-Gado** on Jl. Pasar Kembang behind the train station. Mama holds court nightly with the aplomb of an Italian pasta queen. Papa is occasionally there too, tending his songbirds and collecting the bread. Local foreign residents like to pop in for a *nasi campur*, a fruit salad and a cold beer, and it's frequently packed. Good for breakfast too: French toast, banana pancakes with honey, fresh fruit juices and coffee with fresh milk.

There are several fine Chinese restaurants in town. The old standby and the favourite of the local Chinese community is the **Tiong San**, at Jl. Gandekan 29, a block west of Malioboro. **Moro Senang**, Jl. Solo 55 (on the north side next to Miroto's Supermarket), is also very good. The best seafood, however, and probably also the best Chinese food, is to be had at **Sintawang**, several doors north of Jl. Diponegoro at Jl. Magelang 9, on the west side of the street.

Shopping

Yogyakarta is commonly said to be a "shopper's paradise" but when you come right down to it, most of the stuff sold here is pretty tacky. Nevertheless it is all extremely cheap, and for this reason alone tourists seem to buy it. Concentrate on getting a few quality items that you will really enjoy and use.

Batik

Most tours take you down to one of the factories around **Jalan Tirtodipuran** in the south of Yogya, to observe the *batik* process and to shop in the showroom, but they don't sell much *tulis* work here—most of the *batik* is produced by the quicker copper-stamp (*batik cap*) method. They do have good yard-goods, though, including some that are on heavier cotton, to be used for curtains and upholstery.

- **Batik Gurda**, Jl. Parangtritis 77 B, Yogyakarta, tel: 5474.
- **Batik Plentong**, Jl. Tirtodipuran 28, Yogyakarta, tel: 2777.
- **Rara Djonggrang**, Jl. Tirtodipuran 6 A, Yogyakarta, tel: 2209.
- **Sumiharjo**, Jl. Mandkuyudan 15A, Yogyakarta, tel: 3061.
- **Surya Kencana**, Jl. Ngadinegaran MD VII/98, Yogyakarta, tel: 3798.
- **Tjokrosoeharto**, Jl. Panembahan 58, Yogyakarta, tel: 3208.
- **Winotosastro**, Jl. Tirtodipuran 34, Yogyakarta, tel: 2218.

For high-quality traditional Javanese *batik tulis*, try **Toko Terang Bulan** at Jl. Ahmad Yani 76, next to the central market. The prices here are fixed and reasonable. They have one of the best selections in Central Java.

Otherwise, you should seek out one of the boutiques of the better-known *batik* artists in town. Most of them produce both *batik* paintings and yard goods; many of them also teach one-week *batik* mini-courses. Some of the better known names are **Kuswadji, Amri, Sapto Hudoyo** and **Bambang Oetoro**. The dancer **Bagong Kussudiardjo** and the famous expressionist painter **Affandi** also do some *batik* paintings. Within the **Taman Sari** *batik* painters complex, the best place is **Gallery Lod,** on the western edge of the *kampung*.

- **Affandi Gallery**, next to the river off Jl. Solo, before the Ambarrukmo Hotel.
- **Agus**, Jl. Taman Siswa Mg. III/102, Yogyakarta.
- **Amri Gallery**, Jl. Gampingan 67, Yogyakarta, tel: 5135.
- **Bagong Kussudiardjo**, Jl. Singasaren 9, off Jl. Wates, Yogyakarta.
- **Bambang Oetoro**, Jl. Taman Siswa 55, Yogyakarta, tel: 2147.
- **Gallery Lod**, Taman Sari, Yogyakarta.
- **Kuswadji K.**, Jl. Alun-Alun Utara, Pojok Barat Daya, Yogyakarta, tel: 4995.
- **Sapto Hudoyo**, Jl. Solo Km 9, Maguwo, Yogyakarta, tel: 87443.

Silver

Kota Gede, to the southeast of Yogya, almost a suburb of the city now, is the centre of the silver industry. There are two major workshops, **M.D. Silver** and **Tom's Silver**, and a number of minor ones where (buying or not) you can pass an intriguing half hour watching the hammering, beating, heating, cleaning and polishing of the precious metal. Deft fingers create spider-web filigree; anvils clang till your ears ring; gentle hammer-blows tap out elegant repoussé work.

Do not be constrained to buy only what is on display. Any workshop will produce pieces to your specifications. All that is needed is a drawing or a specimen to copy. In most workshops, prices are calculated strictly according to the weight and grade of the silver used (generally either 80 per cent or sterling, 92.5 per cent), except for certain exceptional or truly original designs (almost non-existent here because they all copy one another). A good place to order, besides from the two large producers in Kota Gede, is at the home and workshop of **Tan Jam An** in Yogya (just north of the Tugu monument on the right-hand side).

- **MD Silver**, Jl. Keboan, Kota Gede, Yogyakarta, tel: 2063.
- **Sri Moeljo's Silver**, Jl. Mentri Supeno UH XII/1, Yogyakarta, tel: 88042.
- **Tan Jam An**, Jl. Mas Sangaji 2, Yogyakarta.
- **Tjokrosoeharto**, Jl. Panembahan 58, Yogyakarta, tel: 3208.
- **Tom's Silver**, Jl. Kota Gede 3-1 A, Kota Gede, Yogyakarta, tel: 3070, 2818.

Leather Goods

Yogya's buff-coloured hand-tooled suitcases, overnight bags, briefcases, pocketbooks, sandals, belts and money pouches produced from buffalo hide are slowly improving in quality, but one of the problems is that the tanning process employed here is still very crude, so they are unable to produce finer, softer grades of leather. Another problem is the finishing—flimsy brass or tin clasps and hinges, and poor stitching.

There are many shops on Malioboro, one of the better ones being **Toko Setia**. For a bit better quality, though, try **Kusuma** just off Malioboro, or **Moeljosoehardjo's** near Taman Sari.

Buffalo hide is also the starting point for making **Wayang Kulit Puppets**, though the thin, translucent *kulit* used to make them is not tanned at all and should properly be called 'parchment.' For the best quality puppets, try **Ledjar** and **Swasthigita**.

- **Aris Handicraft**, Jl. Kauman 14, Yogyakarta.
- **B.S. Store**, Jl. Ngasem 10, Yogyakarta.
- **Budi Murni**, Jl. Muja-muju 21, Yogyakarta.
- **Kusuma**, Jl. Kauman 50, Yogyakarta.
- **Ledjar**, Jl. Mataram DN I/370, Yogyakarta.
- **Moeljosoehardjo's**, Jl. Taman Sari 37 B, Yogyakarta, tel: 2873.
- **Swasthigita**, Jl. Ngadinegaran MD 7/50, Yogyakarta, tel: 4346.
- **Toko Setia**, Jl. Malioboro 79, Yogyakarta.
- **Toko Setia**, Jl. Malioboro 165, Yogyakarta.

Antiques and Curios

Hunting grounds include the many shops that line Jl. Malioboro (**Edi Store, Naga** are the best), and one more across the tracks on Jl. Mangkubumi (**Jul Shop**). Try also the streets to the south and west of the Kraton and the handful of small shops near the Ambarrukmo Palace Hotel. Most of the *batik* galleries listed above also sell antiques. Try **Ardianto** for top quality antiques, also the new and excellent art gallery on Jl. Pramuka.

Among the things that may catch your eye are carved and gilded chests for herbal medicines, or a pair of polychrome *loro blunyo*, seated wedding figures that were traditionally kept in the ceremonial chamber of an aristocratic Javanese home. A handful of 18th Century copper coins with the Dutch East India company's VOC insignia can be fashioned into interesting decorations, and all sorts of elaborately carved old Dutch and Chinese teak-wood furniture is available: roofed and walled wedding beds, gilded panels, marble-top tables, wicker chairs, massive chests and delicate vanities. Then there are *naga*-wreathed stands for *gamelan* instruments, bronze statuettes of Durga, Nandi, Siva, Ganesa, Agastya, Buddha and innumerable bodhisattvas, crude *wayang klitik* figures and antique blue-and-white Ming porcelains from Annam and China. Many of these things are cheaper and more readily available in Solo (*see* below).

- **Antiques Art Shop**, Jl. Kota Gede, Yogyakarta.
- **Ardianto**, Jl. Pejaksan 21, Yogyakarta.
- **Arjuna Art Shop**, Jl. Solo 110, Yogyakarta.
- **Asmopawiro**, Jl. Let. Jendral Haryono 20, Yogyakarta.
- **Edi Store**, Jl. Malioboro 13 A, Yogyakarta, tel: 2997.
- **Ganeda Art Shop**, Jl. Abdul Rahman 69, Yogyakarta.
- **Hastirin Store**, Jl. Malioboro 99, Yogyakarta.
- **Jul Shop**, Jl. Mangkubumi 29, Yogyakarta, tel: 2157.
- **Ken Dedes**, Jl. Sultan Agung, Yogyakarta.
- **La Gallerie**, Jl. Kota Gede, Kota Gede, Yogyakarta.
- **Mahadewa Art Shop**, Jl. Taman Garuda, Yogyakarta.
- **Pusaka Art Shop**, Jl. Taman Garuda 22, Yogyakarta.
- **Seni Jaya Art Shop**, Jl. Taman Garuda 11, Yogyakarta.
- **Sidomukti Art Shop**, Jl. Taman Kampung III/103 A, Yogyakarta.
- **The Ancient Arts**, Jl. Tirtodipuran 30, Yogyakarta.

Painting

Affandi, Indonesia's "grand old man" has a large studio-cum-gallery overlooking the river on Jl. Solo, close to the Ambarrukmo Palace Hotel. Fame has brought fortune in its wake: the starting price for an original is US$1,000, which you may consider a "bargain" by international standards. In 1973, Affandi acquired the status of "painter laureate" when his egg-shaped concrete dome received the blessing of the government as a permanent private museum (the first of its kind in Indonesia), though unhappily for the collector, most of his earlier and finer work is not for sale. The works of other artists, including his daughter **Kartika**, are also displayed.

To find out where the up-and-coming generation is moving in painting, sculpture and handicrafts, pay a visit to Yogya's **Academy of Fine Arts (ASRI)** on Jl. Gampingan. This is considered one of the two or three top art academies in the country.

Masks and Wooden Puppets

For the finest work, made by one of the few remaining craftsmen who still carves for the actors and *dalangs*, rather than for casual visitors, visit **Pak Warno Waskito** a shy, gentle old man who's been playing his craft for more than 50 years. He never went to school, and taught himself.

To reach Pak Warno's secluded hideaway, take the Bantul road south from Yogya, turn right at the 7.6 km marker, walk about 300 metres, turn left, and stop at the first house on your right. Signposts will guide you.

Pottery

On your way back to Yogya from Pak Warno (*see* above) turn left at the 6.5 km post (a sugarcane trolley track crosses the road at this point) and follow the side-road for about a kilometre. If you've admired the jauntily coloured "piggy banks" in the form of elephants, roosters, mythical beasts and mounted cavalry which can be found in Yogya, especially around Pasar Ngasem, **Kasongan** is where you can see them being modelled by hand, fired in an open blaze of roots and palm leaves, and then painted with a verve and panache that's almost Mexican in feeling. Almost every household you come to will have a potter. It is possible to have items made to order—allow up to a week or 10 days.

Performances in Yogya

There are basically two types of performances: those that are put on especially for tourists and those that are put on for and by the Javanese.

Tourist performances are not necessarily any less authentic or in any way inferior (as some people insist), even though they are frequently shortened or excerpted versions of the originals, adapted for the benefit of foreign audiences.

What they do lack, of course, is a Javanese audience, and as the audience is as much a part of most performances as the players (especially in Java), you should try if at all possible to catch a village or *kampung* shadow play or dance drama. Being here at the right time to see one is just a matter of luck. Check with the **Tourist Information Office** (Jl. Malioboro 16) and travel agencies for up-to-date information.

Gamelan

A *gamelan* orchestra is struck to accompany all of the dances and puppet shows listed below, and you can hardly avoid hearing recorded *gamelan* music everywhere you go in Yogya.

- As mentioned in Part III, visit the **Kraton Gamelan Rehearsals** on Monday and Wednesday mornings.
- Concerts are also staged at the **Pakualaman Palace** on Jl. Sultan Agung every fifth Sunday Minggu Pahing beginning at 10. No admission charge.
- And if somehow you seem to be missing all the other performances, then you can always go

over to the lobby of the Ambarrukmo Palace Hotel, where a small *gamelan* ensemble plays daily from 10:30 a.m. to 12:30 a.m., and then again from 3:30 p.m. to 5:30 p.m. No admission charge.

Wayang Kulit

This is truly the most influential Javanese art form, the one that traditionally has provided the Javanese with a framework through which to see the world and themselves. Not surprisingly, many foreigners have become fascinated with the shadow play (even if very, very few of them are able to understand the dialogue), and there is quite a voluminous literature in Dutch and English on the subject (*see* Bibliography). Traditional performances are always at night, beginning at 9 p.m. and running until dawn.

The **Agastya Art Institute** (Jl. Gedong Kiwo MD III/237), a private *dalang* (puppeteer) school, stages "rehearsal" excerpt performances for the benefit of tourists every day except Saturday, 3 p.m. to 5 p.m. US$3 admission.

Another tourist excerpt performance is at **Ambar Budaya** in the Yogyakarta Craft Centre opposite the Ambarrukmo Palace Hotel every Monday, Wednesday and Friday from 9:30 p.m. to 10:30 p.m. US$3 admission.

On the second Saturday of each month, Radio Republik Indonesia broadcasts a live all-night performance from the pavilion to the south of the Kraton, **Sasono Hinggil Dwi Abad**. This is the best regular performance. Begins at 9 p.m. No admission charge.

You can also try the **Habiranda Dalang School** at Pracimasono on the north-eastern side of the *alun-alun* town square, where there are often informal training sessions or rehearsals in the evenings, 7 p.m. to 10 p.m., except Thursday and Sunday. No admission charge. *Wayang kulit* in an air-conditioned restaurant with dinner is the latest thing at the French Grill in the **Arjuna Plaza Hotel** (Jl. Mangkubumi 48) every Tuesday and Sunday night at 7 p.m.

Wayang Golek

These are the three-dimensional round puppets that are less popular in Central Java than in West Java (*see* Bandung above). The movements, voices and staging, even much of the dialogue is similar, however, to the *wayang kulit*.

Nitour Travel Agency sponsors *wayang golek* excerpt performances daily (except Sunday) from 10 a.m. to 12 a.m. at their offices, Jl. Ahmad Dahlan 71.

The **Agastya Art Institute** (Jl. Gedong Kiwo MD III/237), a private *dalang* school located to the southwest of Taman Sari, puts on short "rehearsal" performances every Saturday from 3 p.m. to 5 p.m.

For dinner with your *wayang golek*, try the Thursday night performances at the French Grill Restaurant in the **Arjuna Plaza Hotel** (Jl. Mangkubumi 48). Begins at 7 p.m.

Javanese Dance

There is a rehearsal of the **Kraton Dancers** every Sunday from 10:30 a.m. to 12 a.m. US$0.50 admission.

The Mardawa Budaya School, one of the best in Yogya, now stages a wide selection of dance excerpts in an aristocratic **pendapa, Dalem Pujokusuman**, Jl. Brig. Jend. Katamso 45, every Monday, Wednesday and Friday evening from 8 p.m. to 10 p.m. US$3 admission.

Of course, if you happen (or plan) to be here between May and October around the full moon, don't miss the **Ramayana Ballet** at Prambanan. This is a so-called *sendratari* spectacular with a cast of thousands but without any dialogue. Get a round-trip "package" ticket out to Prambanan and back, including the US$4 admission from any travel agent or from the Tourist Information Centre on Jl. Malioboro, (about US$11).

And if you prefer comfortable, hotel surroundings with dinner and refreshments, try the nightly "cultural show" at the **Ambarrukmo Palace Hotel**.

The regular performances listed above are all excellent. You should also visit some of the schools during the day to observe how Javanese dance is taught and studied. Most of them are situated in quite interesting surroundings— what are or used to be elegant homes of members of the royal family.

- **Krido Bekso Wirama**, Dalem Tejokusuman, Jl. K.H. Wahid Hasyim. The first school to teach Javanese dance outside the Kraton.
- **Siswo Among Bekso**, Dalem Poerwodiningratan, Jl. Kadipaten Kidul 46. They have frequent student performances.
- **Mardawa Budaya**, Jl. Brig. Jen. Katamso 45. Regular tourist performances (see above).
- **Pamulangan Beksa Ngayoyakarta**.
- **Bagong Kussudiarjo**, Jl. Singosaren 9, off Jl. Wates. The best-known Javanese "modern" dancer and choreographer. He was one of the artists that helped to invent and develop the *sendratari* art-dance-drama in the 1950s. Still an energetic writer, teacher and choreographer.
- **Indonesian Dance Academy (ASTI)**. This is one of five government tertiary-level dance schools in the nation and they get all the most promising young dancers from the Yogya area. Visit the school out on Jl. Colombo (*see* map). This is where the most innovative Javanese dancing is found.

Wayang Orang/Ketoprak

Last but not least you might want to see a folk version of the courtly dance dramas. There are performances nightly at the **Taman Hiburan Rakyat (THR)**—in the "People's Amusement Park" on Jl. Brig. Jen. Katamso. US$0.50. Admission. The **Arjuna Plaza Hotel** (Jl. Mangkubumi 48) also has a *wayang orang* tourist performance in their French Grill Restaurant every Thursday night, beginning at 7 p.m.

Side Trips From Yogya

Dieng Plateau
Temples in the Vicinity of Prambanan
Kota Gede
Imogiri
Parangtritis
Kaliurang
Mt. Merapi

In addition to the better-known temple complexes like **Borobudur** and **Prambanan**, there are many other-lesser known but equally spectacular temple sites within easy reach of Yogyakarta. These include the monuments of the **Dieng Plateau**, the **Gedung Sanga** group (covered in a previous section on Java's North Coast), and a handful of sites around Prambanan: **Sewu, Plaosan, Ratu Boko, Kalasan, Sari** and **Sambisari**.

The Yogya area has more to offer than just temples, however. The expansive black-sand beaches on the southern coast at **Parangtritis** are only about an hour from the city. Along the way, you can stop at the scenic hill-top cemetery of Java's rajas at **Imogiri**, and the old silver-making town of **Kota Gede** on Yogya's outskirts.

To escape the heat, simply zip up Mt. Merapi to the nearby hill resort of **Kaliurang**. It is possible, in fact, to climb all the way up to the peak of this active volcano, for an incredible view over all of Central Java, but this is best done in the early morning from Solo, on the Boyolali-Blabak road.

The Dieng Plateau

The day-long excursion up to the Dieng Plateau (from *di-hyang* meaning "spirit place"), about 100 kms (60 miles) and three hours to the northwest of Borobudur, is a journey to a 2,000-metre (6,500-foot) mountain fastness shrouded in mists and mysteries. The final climb from **Wonosobo** to the plateau follows a narrow, twisting course.

The existence of demons, spirits and wrathful giants seems not only plausible but probable here as grey skeins of mist envelop the surrounding ridges. The temples themselves are enigmatic—thought to have been constructed in the 8th Century, though the earliest inscription found here is dated 809 A.D. It is known at least that they were built not by the Buddhist Sailendras, but by worshippers of Siva—perhaps by the descendants of Sanjaya, who ruled parts of Central Java as vassals of the Sailendras and then expelled them. Eight small stone temples have been partially restored. The foundations of others are nearby, and the remains of several wooden *pendopos* or pavilions may indicate that there was once a palace or a monastery here.

The main group of temples is now named after the heroes and heroines of the *Mahabharata*, though these names are certainly later attributions. Arjuna, Puntadewa, Srikandi and Sembadra stand in a row in the centre of a flat field, accompanied by their squat, ungainly servant, Semar. The ground around them looks firm

enough, but is mostly marshland. A millennium ago this marsh was drained by an elaborate series of tunnels cut through the hills, the entrance to which are on the northwest corner of the field.

Perhaps the real reason this area was designated a holy site, despite its remoteness, was the presence of contemplative scenery and violent volcanic activity. A walk along the wooded pathways encircling **Telaga Warna** ("Multi-coloured Lake") and **Telaga Pengilon** ("Mirror Lake") is enchantingly peaceful and beautiful. Nearby knolls and dells, straight from a Chinese brush painting, hide small grottoes—still popular as meditation retreats. Beyond the lakes, a never-ending billow of hot steam and sulphurous gas marks a dramatic fissure in the earth.

Getting There

A taxi or mini-bus seating anywhere from 1 to 8 persons may be chartered to Dieng for only US$45 (for a one day return trip—*see* Yogya: "Getting Around" above). Public inter-city buses and mini-buses operate from Yogya to Wonosobo (from the Yogya bus terminal on Jl. Veteran and the "colt" offices on Jl. Diponegoro). From here you can get a local "colt" up to Dieng. Intan Pelangi (*see* Yogya: "Tours/Travel Agents" above) offers a day-long guided bus tour to Dieng and Borobudur for only US$12 per person. Check with your hotel or directly with the agency for schedules. Check also with the Tourist Information Office, Jl. Malioboro 16, for other tours.

Accommodation

Assuming you are travelling to Dieng on your own, there are several small *losmen* and a restaurant facing right onto the central plain and temples, where you can spend the night for only a few dollars. Be sure to bring some warm clothing. Better accommodation exists in the town of Wonosobo, though there is no first-class hotel.

● **Bhima**, Jl. Ahmad Yani 5, Wonosobo, tel: 745.

● **Jawa Tengah**, Jl. Ahmad Yani 45, tel: 202.

● **Merdeka**, Jl. Sindoro 2, tel: 53.

● **Nirwana**, Jl. Tanggung 18, tel: 66.

In the Vicinity of Prambanan

Sewu and **Plaosan** are two Buddhist *candi* complexes located nearby. Sewu (the "thousand temples"), about one km (half-a-mile) to the north of Prambanan, consists of a tall central monument surrounded by 240 minor shrines. It was probably completed just before Prambanan or around 850 A.D. and almost equals the latter in its intricacy. The central temple, now undergoing reconstruction, has an unusual gallery that is reached by passing through enclosed gateways lined with Moorish-looking niches. The walls of the smaller shrines have crumbled, revealing a tantalising array of Buddhist statues.

Plaosan, about 1 km (half-a-mile) to the east of Sewu, originally consisted of two large, rectangular temples surrounded by a number of little shrines and solid *stupas*. Both major temples were two-storeyed, three-roomed buildings with windows (an unusual feature), containing a number of beautiful small Buddhas and boddhisattvas and reliefs which may depict donors, priests or pilgrims—one of whom wears a large headdress and looks almost Egyptian. This temple complex may date also from the mid-9th Century.

The remains of **Candi Ratu Boko** are up on a ridge 1.6 kms (one mile) south of Prambanan village (double back in Prambanan following the one-way traffic and instead of turning right back to Yogya, turn left), overlooking the entire valley. A steep, stairway leads up to the plateau to the left of the road opposite a 2 Yogya-18-km stone marker and a new road also comes all the way up to the temple from behind. Come here at dawn or dusk, when the valley and its temples are bathed in golden light.

Ratu Boko was probably a fortified palace built by the last of the Buddhist Sailendras and later taken over by the Hindu builders of Prambanan.

There are three more temples along the main road back to Yogyakarta. **Candi Sari**, prettily set amongst banana and coconut groves (just north of the road, 3 kms [2 miles] from Prambanan), is similar to the Plaosan temples— a Buddhist temple with two storeys, windows, and several internal chambers. Thought to have been a monastery, Sari is distinctive because of its 36 panels of heavenly beings—dancing nymphs, musicians, dragon kings and because of its heavily ornamented roof. Built by the Sailendras, perhaps in the late 8th Century.

Candi Kalasan is visible from the road, just to the west of Sari—another Buddhist shrine that may have been begun as early as 778 A.D. The outstanding feature is a huge, ornate *kala-makara* head above the southern doorway.

Finally, turn north just beyond the 10.2-km marker (from Yogya) to see **Sambisari**—a small *candi* that was discovered only in 1966 in the middle of a rice field and has now been excavated from beneath five metres (16 feet) of earth. Many of the temple's reliefs remain curiously unfinished, which has given rise to speculation that it was buried by a volcanic eruption before completed—perhaps the same eruption that buried Borobudur and also drove the Mataram kings out of Central Java.

Getting There

All of the temples can be visited in a single day, together of course with the main Loro Jonggrang complex at Prambanan. Get a few people together and rent a mini-bus for about US$20 for a 10-hour excursion. Available through any hotel. Be sure to specify: all the places you intend visiting; the price; and the number of hours before leaving. Stop on the way back at Nyonya Suharti's for her famous fried chicken dinner (*see* Yogya: "Dining").

Kota Gede

A short distance to the southeast of Yogya, the town of **Kota Gede** is famous for its silver work-

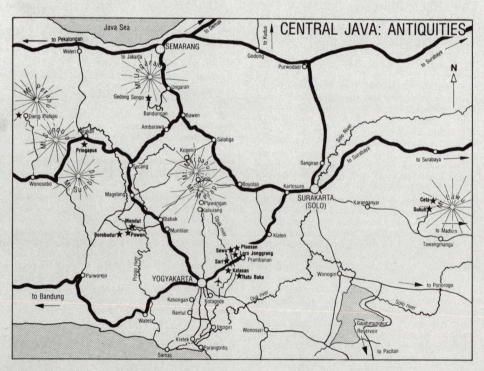

shops (*see* Yogya: "Shopping"). Kota Gede was founded around 1579 by Senopati, the illustrious founder of the New or Second Mataram dynasty to which all the present-day Central Javanese rulers belong (though Solo's Susuhunan claims, with good reason, to be the only true claimant to the Mataram throne). Kota Gede is thus much older than Yogya itself, and Senopati now lies buried in a small moss-covered graveyard only half-a-kilometre from the town's central market. A broad pathway and two enormous banyan trees herald a secluded courtyard through which a narrow pathway leads on to an ancient mosque and a maze of lesser courtyards and decorated doorways.

In the midst of this serene labyrinth lies the tiny, high-walled cemetery. Offerings of flowers, petals, incense and cigars strew the worn stone steps in front of the large, weather-grained wooden door leading to Senopati's tomb, which is opened to visitors only on Mondays, 10 a.m. to 1 p.m., and on Fridays, 1:30 p.m. to 4:30 p.m.

In the clearing outside the cemetery is a small white-washed building housing a large, polished black rock the size of a double bed. It is variously described as an executioner's stone or as Senopati's throne, but it has a Dutch inscription. In any case, it is considered to be a magically powerful *pusaka* or heirloom of the place. Next to it are three large balls of yellow stone, ranging in size from a shot-putt to a volley ball, and reputedly used for juggling. More likely, these are ancient, pre-Islamic "ancestor stones."

Royal Tombs at Imogiri

Another and more splendid link with Yogya's past is at **Imogiri**, 20 kms (13 miles) to the south along a narrow road.

Imogiri has an ancient, sturdy air about it. A little beyond the village the road ends in a tiny square containing a single *warung* and an old *pendopo*. Ahead, a broad pathway leads off through an avenue of trees, the starting point for the climb to the royal tombs.

The famous Sultan Agung was the first of his line to be buried there, interred in 1645 on the top of a small rocky outcrop. Since then almost every prince of the house of Mataram, and of the succeeding royal families of Yogyakarta and Surakarta, has been laid to rest at Imogiri.

A visit to this venerated site takes on the air of a pilgrimage (which indeed it is for many Javanese), for the 345 shallow-tread steps of the wide, formal stairway will exact considerable penance.

The tombs lie within three major courtyards at the top of the stairway: in front are those of Mataram; to the left, those of the Susuhunans of Solo; to the right, those of the Sultans of Yogya. Each great courtyard encloses smaller courts containing the memorials and tombs of the princes. Entry into the smaller courts, and viewing of the tombs, is permitted briefly only on Mondays and Fridays after noontime prayers, and you must wear formal Javanese court costume to visit them. This is less demanding than it may sound, and the necessary garments can be hired on the spot for a low fee.

Although the forecourts and inner courts are closed at other times, the long, high-walled walks along the front of each complex are always open. At each end of the front gallery an archway leads through the walls to a pathway which reaches the real summit of the hill. Open Monday 10 a.m. to 1 p.m., Friday 1:30 p.m. to 4:30 p.m.

Parangtritis

The shore at **Parangtritis** is linked with an ancient tradition which may have flourished in pre-Hindu times as a fertility cult, and which was later observed symbolically by Sultan Agung and his successors. Legends claim that Senopati, or perhaps Sultan Agung, was married in fact (not fantasy) to Raden Loro Kidul, the 'Queen of the Southern Ocean' whose domain, also known as the region of death, is beneath the waters of the Indian Ocean. Ritual observances of the marriage are still performed in the Central Javanese courts: a special dance, the *Bedoyo ketawang*, takes place in Solo on the anniversary of the *susuhunan's* accession, and until recently could be witnessed only by the *susuhunan* and the closest of his nobles, for the dance symbolises his marriage to Raden Loro Kidul. In Yogya, on the occasion of the sultan's birthday, a special *Labuhan* ceremony involves the distribution of sacred nail- and hair-clippings, together with *melati* flowers which have been offered during the year to the royal *pusakas*, at rituals held on the slopes of Gunung Merapi and Gunung Lawu, and on the shore at Parangtritis.

Raden Loro Kidul, 'Queen of the Southern Ocean', may be the consort of kings, but she has a malevolent disposition. Swimming on her rough southern coast is tantamount to entering her territory without a permit, and offenders frequently drown. She has a special predilection for young men dressed in green (her colour).

Legend or no, the rips and violent currents, and a heavy surf, make swimming dangerous on most of Java's southern coast. At Parangtritis this seascape is backed by a forbidding shoreline of jagged cliffs and dunes of shifting, iron-grey sand.

Getting There

To go directly to Parangtritis from Yogya, catch a mini-bus at Jl. Parangtritis just south of the intersection with Jl. Jendral Sutoyo. Fare as far as the river at Kretek is Rp 200. Walk or cross over and hire a pony cart or ride on a motorbike to the beach (Rp 500). Otherwise, rent a car or "colt" for the day for US$20 and go on the back road via Imogiri. There are cheap losmen and restaurants in Parangtritis, for budget travellers.

Kaliurang

Only 23 kms (14 miles) due north of Yogya, this town offers plenty of guesthouses, two swimming pools, a tiny herd of deer from Bogor and a beautiful 2.5-km (1.5-mile) lung-exercising walk to Overseer Point. The weather can be unpredictable: even if Merapi is crystal clear from the lowlands it may be shrouded in cloud by the time you reach the lookout at Plawangan.

Near the summit of Plawangan the path traverses a narrow ridge where tree-clad slopes fall away steeply on both sides, splashed with fiery red and yellow lantana blossom.

Mt. Merapi

On a clear day **Gunung Merapi** can be seen in all its glory. Watching it is a full-time job at the Plawangan seismological station where the vulcanologists, armed with binoculars and seismographs, work in month-long shifts before moving on to Gunung Kelud or Ijen or wherever else Java's crust is growing restless. Merapi is the most volatile of the island's volcanic tribe, and tops the dangerous list: the closing months of 1973 were marked by a series of minor lava flows and the ensuing (and more damaging) *lahar* streams of water, mud and ash; the last serious eruption occurred in 1954.

Another observation point is to the west of the mountain. A small side-road, well sign-posted in English, branches off the main route to Muntilan, 23 kms (14 miles) from Yogya and creeps slowly through tunnels of bamboo and tall stands of pine before revealing the ravaged western slope of the volcano, scarred and twisted by a continuing series of lava flows. At night, dull red globs of molten rock can be seen through the darkness.

To stand on the rim of Merapi, gazing down on the world from a height of 2,900 metres, and down into the Dantean crater as well, is probably the most exciting mountain experience in all of Java. Bromo, in East Java, is usually given more attention for it is easier to get to. At Bromo, you walk. At Merapi, you climb.

Surakarta (Solo)

Surakarta, or Solo as it is better known, is an easy one-hour's drive from Yogya. Although at first glance the flat, sprawling city seems even less a royal capital than its neighbour, Solo rewards patience. Its Susuhunan or ruler, as writer and *batik* artist Iwan Tirtaamidjaja has noted, "was the only Javanese to whom the Dutch paid full respect. His palace . . . was an enclave where absolute deference was awarded to ancient Javanese laws and traditions."

Partly as a result of the aristocratic emphasis on Javanese traditions and proprieties in this city, Solo is very different from Yogya—more sedate, more reserved and more refined, without the young, revolutionary undercurrent—or at least this is how the Solonese like to see themselves. Physically, the city is sleepier and smaller (in area if not in population), with less traffic, and also far fewer tourists.

Getting There

The easiest way, from Yogya, is to book a seat on an express "colt" at one of the travel offices on Jl. Diponegoro just west of the Tugu monument for US$1.20. They leave all day about every half hour and will drop you anywhere in Solo. Actually, you can flag down a bus or mini-bus heading east on Yogya's Jl. Sudirman or Jl. Solo and get to Solo for about half the price, or US$0.60, but it takes a lot longer and you get packed in with scores of other passengers.

The other alternative is to rent your own taxi or mini-bus from Yogya with up to seven other people for US$17.50 one-way, US$22.50 round trip (returning on the same day).

Solo also has its own airport, with two or three flights operating daily to and from Jakarta and Surabaya. And all trains stopping at Yogya also stop here (*see* Java: "Train Schedules" above).

City Orientation

Solo's main street is **Jalan Slamet Riyadi**, a broad boulevard which runs east-west and is a continuation of the main highway into town from Yogya. At its eastern end stands a *Tugu* monument, just in front of the northern gates leading into the *alun-alun* (town square) and the Kraton precincts. The General Post Office, government buildings, banks, the telephone office and the central market (Pasar Gede) are all nearby (*see* map). Most hotels, restaurants and shops are also within easy walking distance, on or near Jl. Slamet Riyadi, and the interesting areas of town to explore on foot are mostly centred around the two palaces—the **Kasusuhunan** and the **Mangkunegaran**. Running parallel and one block to the south of Slamet Riyadi, **Jalan Secoyudan** is the main shopping street. The travel offices are in between these two streets, on **Jalan Yos Sudarso**, and this is where you book and board an express "colt" back to Yogya. Most inter-city bus companies have offices or representatives along Jl. Veteran in the south of the city, as well as at the new **Bus Terminal** near the city "bypass" (Jl. Parman/Tendean/Haryono) in the north.

Getting Around

Almost everything is within walking distance. Otherwise take a pedicab (*becak*). *See* Yogya: "Getting Around" for tips on bargaining for *becaks*. The fares here are essentially the same, and you normally pay no more than Rp 500 to go about a mile in the centre of town. With some practice you may be able to get rides for Rp 200.

Accommodation

First Class (US$20) a night on up)

The best hotel in town is the **Kusuma Sahid Prince**, with very comfortable doubles ranging from US$24 on up to US$200 a night for an "Indraloka Suite" (plus 21 per cent tax and service). They have a good sized swimming pool, that

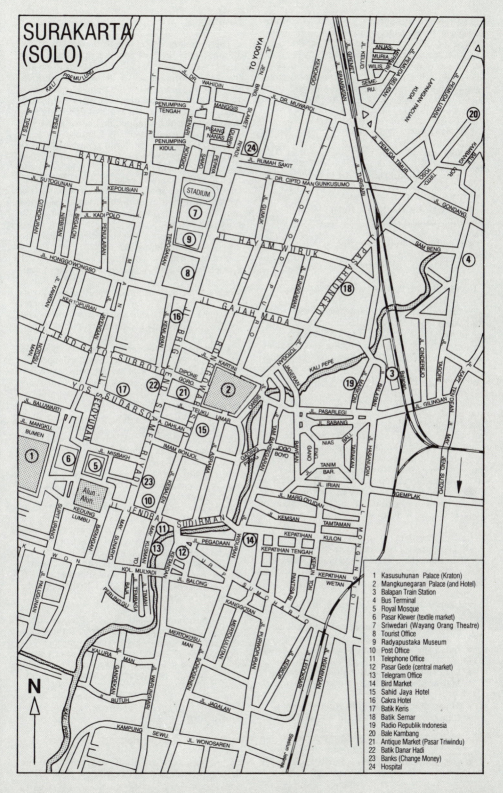

SURAKARTA (SOLO)

1 Kasusuhunan Palace (Kraton)
2 Mangkunegaran Palace (and Hotel)
3 Balapan Train Station
4 Bus Terminal
5 Royal Mosque
6 Pasar Klewer (textile market)
7 Sriwedari (Wayang Orang Theatre)
8 Tourist Office
9 Radyapustaka Museum
10 Post Office
11 Telephone Office
12 Pasar Gede (central market)
13 Telegram Office
14 Bird Market
15 Sahid Jaya Hotel
16 Cakra Hotel
17 Batik Keris
18 Batik Semar
19 Radio Republik Indonesia
20 Bale Kambang
21 Antique Market (Pasar Triwindu)
22 Batik Danar Hadi
23 Banks (Change Money)
24 Hospital

can be used by outsiders for US$1.50. The **Mangkunegaran Palace Hotel** is just nearby (same price: US$24 on up). Two other hotels in the same category, the **Cakra** and the **Solo Inn**, are similarly priced and quite adequate, but being on busy Jl. Slamet Riyadi are not as spacious or as quiet (without pools). The **Sahid Sala** is a bit older and slightly less expensive (US$20 for an air-conditioned double, plus 21 per cent).

- **Cakra Hotel** (50 rooms), Jl. Slamet Riyadi 171, Solo, tel: 5847, 7000.
- **Solo Inn** (32 rooms), Jl. Slamet Riyadi 318, Solo, tel: 6075-7.
- **Kusuma Sahid Prince Hotel** (100 rooms), Jl. Asrama 22, Solo, tel: 6356-8, 6901-2, 7022, tlx: 22274 KSPH SOLO.
- **Mangkunegaran Palace Hotel** (48 rooms), Jl. Mangkunegaran, Solo, tel: 5683, 2226, tlx: HIPA JKT 44233.
- **Sahid Sala** (40 rooms), Jl. Gajah Mada 104, Solo, tel: 3889, 5889.

Intermediate & Budget (under US$20 a night)

Your best bet in the intermediate range is the **Ramayana Guest House**, with several rooms ranging in price from US$12 up to US$22 for a large room with a fan, including breakfast. Very clean and airy, but a bit far from town. Several other guest houses nearby, like the **Sarangan** and the **Putri Ayu** in the same price category, are only slightly less comfortable.

The new **Indah Jaya** near the train station gives you good value: air-conditioning, carpeting, colour T.V. and breakfast for as little as US$15.50 a night (plus 21 per cent). The **Hotel Trio** is a centrally located Chinese-run establishment right opposite Pasar Gede with small, clean rooms in the back for US$10. They also have several large older rooms in the front that sleep three or four for the same price. The newly remodelled **Mawar Melati** has rooms with a fan and private bath for only US$8, as well as some cheaper rooms for US$3.

Budget travellers invariably stay at **Mawardi's** (also known as "**The Westerners**") in Kemlayan for US$1.50. The *becak* drivers all know the place. If they are full, try the Mawar Melati, the **Kota** or the **Central**, all nearby.

- **Central Hotel**, Jl. H.A. Dahlan, Solo, tel: 2842.
- **Dana Hotel**, Jl Slamet Riyadi 232, Solo, tel: 3890.
- **Indah Jaya**, Jl. Srambatan 13, Solo, tel: 5444, 7445.
- **Kota Hotel**, Jl. Slamet Riyadi 113, tel: 2841.
- **Mawar Melati**, Jl. Imam Bonjol 44, Solo, tel: 6434.
- **Mawardi's**, Jl. Kemlayan Kidul 11, Solo.
- **Ramayana Guest House**, Jl. Dr. Wahidin 15, Solo, tel: 2841.
- **Seribu Hotel**, Jl. Marconi 28 A, Solo, tel: 3525.
- **Trio Hotel**, Jl. Urip Sumarharjo 33, Solo, tel: 2847.

Dining

The overall best Javanese restaurant, by general consent, is the **Sari**, on the south side of Jl. Slamet Riyadi (No. 351), but it's about three kms (two miles) from the centre of town. The specialities here are *nasi liwet* (a Solonese speciality—rice cooked in coconut cream with garnishes), fried chicken and various types of *pepes* (prawns, mushrooms or fish wrapped in a banana leaf with spices and steamed or grilled). Closer to town, the original **Timlo Solo**, Jl. Urip Sumoharjo 106, is also very good. They have excellent daily specials, but also the standard Javanese fried chicken, *pecel* (boiled vegetables with peanuts sauce), *nasi gudeg* (the Yogyanese speciality) and *nasi kuning* (rice cooked in turmeric), with *tahu*, *tempe* and coconut. For the best Javanese-style fried chicken in town, try the new **Tojoyo** at Jl. Kepunton Kulon 77. That's all they serve and it goes fast (open only 6 p.m. to 9 p.m. at night).

The best Chinese restaurant is the **Orient**, Jl. Slamet Riyadi 337 A (several doors down from the Sari). Here you can order a beef hotplate, sweet & sour pork or fish (a whole *gurame*), corn and crab (or shark's fin) soup, Chinese broccoli with black beans (*kailan tausi*), and their speciality: boiled chicken with garlic, onion and ginger sauce (*ayam rebus*). The **Centrum** at Jl. Kratonan 151 is much more central and also very good—let the manager order for you. They are famous for their crab rolls (*sosis kepiting*), prawns stir-fried in butter (*udang goreng mentega*), fish with salted vegetables (*ikan sayur asin*) and fried crab claws (*kepit kepiting*).

For the best chicken and mutton *sate* in town, go over to the **Ramayana** at Jl. Ronggowarsito 2 (one block in front of the Kusuma Sahid Hotel). They also have excellent Chinese dishes such as fried spinach (*kangkong*) and deep-fried pigeon (*burung dara goreng*).

A convenient spot for a light lunch is the **Segar Ayem** restaurant on Jl. Secoyudan opposite Pasar Klewer (the central *batik* market), within walking distance of the Kraton. Excellent iced fruit drinks here, with some simple Javanese dishes like *gado-gado*, *pecel* and *nasi rames*. Another nearby luncheon spot, good for Chinese noodles of many types as well as iced fruit juices and cold beer, is **Bakso Taman Sari** on Jl. Gatot Subroto (42C) between Secoyudan and Slamet Riyadi. Another good place for Chinese noodles is **Miroso**, Jl. Imam Bonjol 10.

The best *nasi Padang* place is **Andalas**, on Jl. Ronggowarsito opposite and a bit to the east of the Mankunegaran Palace Hotel entrance.

Finally, you should sample the sweet coconut cream cakes sold from little carts all along Jl. Slamet Riyadi at night—a local speciality called *serabi*.

Shopping

Batik

Solo is known as "Batik City" and the three largest producers are all based here: **Batik Keris,**

Batik Semar and Batik Danar Hadi. Visit their showrooms. Danar Hadi has many better quality *kain* and *batik* shirts in the US$10-to-US$20 and up range. Semar aims at the mass-market, with printed *batik* dreses and shirts selling for as little as US$2. Keris is in between. For the best in Solonese *tulis* work, visit Ibu Bei Siswosugiarto (**Sidomulyo** is her label) in the south of town, where most pieces cost between US$40 and US$120. **K.R.T. Hardjonegoro**, one of Java's best-known *batik* designers also lives and has his factory here, but generally sells only through outlets in Jakarta. You might try his home though. Have a look also at the thousands of pieces for sale in **Pasar Klewer**, and wander the side streets nearby, behind the Grand Mosque, where there are several quality producers.

- **Batik Danar Hadi**, Jl. Slamet Riyadi, Solo.
- **Batik Keris**, Jl. Yos. Sudarso 37, Solo.
- **Batik Semar** (factory showroom), Jl. Pasar Nongko 132, Solo.
- **Batik Semar** (branch), Jl. Slamet Riyadi 76, Solo.
- **K.R.T. Hardjonegoro**, Jl. Kratonan 101, Solo.
- **Sidomulyo** (Ibu Bei Siswosugiarto), Jl. Dawung Wetan R.T. 53/54, Solo.

Antiques

Visit the **Pasar Triwindu** market first, to get an idea what is available and what it costs. In 1983, antique brass oil lamps were fetching between US$15 and US$50 depending on size and ornamentation (the glass is an expensive part, as few original ones are left intact). Round marble top tables with four chairs were up to US$175 (US$50 less without the marble, which is scarce here but can be easily bought in the West). And Chinese wedding beds were over US$1,000 for a good one with the gold-leaf trim intact.

Many of the vendors and dealers here also have caches of antique furniture and other valuable items at home, or they can guide you around to some of the refinishing workshops in town. No obligation to buy if you go with them, though you should pay for the *becak*. But then visit the established antique shopfronts on Slamet Riyadi and Urip Sumarharjo, where all sorts of treasures are sitting gathering dust. They are a bit more reputable and less likely to sell you fakes. But still beware and bargain hard!

- **Eka Hartono**, Jl. Dawung Tengah 11/38, Solo.
- **Mertojo "Sing Pellet"**, Jl. Kepatihan 31, Solo.
- **Mirah Delima**, Jl. Kemasan RT XI, Solo.
- **Parto Art**, Jl. slamet Riyadi 103, Solo.
- **Singo Widodo**, Jl. Urip Sumarharho 117, Solo.
- **Trisno Batik & Art Shop**, Jl. Bayangkara 2, Solo.

Keris

To buy an antique *Keris* dagger, visit Pak Suranto Atmosaputro, an English lecturer at the university, at his home just down a narrow alley across from the RRI radio studios (Jl. Kestalan III/21). He is a *keris* afficionado and a member of the "Keris-Lover's Association" of Solo, and always has pieces of his own for sale, or he can quickly round up a selection for you to examine, at prices ranging from US$30 to US$200, with many good ones in the US$75-to-US$100 range. Go with him on Sundays to watch new *keris* being forged and carved in the village of Komplang just to the north of Solo (at the home of Ki Lurah Wignyosukadgo).

Wayang Puppets

The acknowledged centre for *wayang kulit* production in Java is the village of **Manyaran**, about 35 kms (21 miles) to the south and west of Solo (take a "colt" first to Wonogiri and then change for **Manyaran**). Here the village head, **Pak Sukar Hadiprayitno** organizes the village craftsmen and sells their wares at quite reasonable fixed prices. Smaller figures cost about US$10 to US$15 while large *gunungan* go for US$50 (US$100 with gold leaf). Visit his home in Kampung Kepuhsari, Manyaran.

You can also visit the workshop of **Pak Parto** in Pajang Kampung Sogaten, RT 27, RK IV) just to the west of Solo (travel out of town on the main highway about 4 kms [2.5 miles] and turn left onto a dirt road just after the bridge and ask for directions). He produces very fine puppets (his craftsmen are all from Manyaran) for the same prices.

You can also go directly to the *dalang dalang* themselves, most of whom make their own puppets in their spare time. **Pak Soetrisno** is descended from a well-known court *dalang* family and now teaches *wayang kulit* at ASKI (he also speaks good English and spent some time in the United States.) He lives out of town and has no telephone, so get someone to call his office at the university (tel: 5260) and leave a message that you are interested in buying puppets. He generally has many nice ones for US$7.50 to US$25.

Java's most famous *dalang* is **Pak Anom Suroto** and he lives down a small lane from Jl. Slamet Riyadi. Enter from between the Danar Hadi shop and the Cakra Hotel and ask anyone where he lives. He occasionally has puppets for sale.

Gamelan

To buy a complete *gamelan* orchestra, a single instrument or just to observe these bronze metallophones being cast and forged as they have been in Indonesia for thousands of years, using hand-operated bellows, teak-wood charcoal and primitive tools, visit the *gamelan* assembly of **Pak Tentrem Sarwanto**. His family have been suppliers of instruments to the court for many generations. Located in the southeast of town: Jl. Ngepung RT 2/RK I, Semanggi, Solo.

Dancer's Requisites

Gold-spangled headdresses, gilded bracelets, painted or unpainted *topeng* masks, coloured gloves and matching tights used in various types of dance dramas in Solo are for sale at **Toko Bedoyo Serimpi** at the corner of Jl. Hayam Wuruk and Jl. Ronggowarsito. This is a real theatrical supplier, not just a souvenir shop for tourists (though many tourist now go here). Many of these items are also produced at a workshop just in back and to the left of Trisni Art Shop on Jl. Bayangkara.

The Performing Arts in Solo

Taman Sriwedari on Jl. Slamet Riyadi boasts the most accomplished *wayang orang* troupe in Java.

The **Taman Hiburan Bale Kambang** amusement park complex, located in the north-west of the city, houses two theatres. One, the popular Sri Mulat comedy theatre, presents an earthy fare of slapstick routines such as "Big, Bad Dracula" and "The Commercial Gigolo" nightly. The other offers more serious **Ketoprak** folk dramas, enactments of historical tales and legends. There are also several open-air restaurants and a billiards hall in the park, as well as a video hall. Shows begin nightly at 8 p.m. except Sundays (when there is a matinee beginning at 10 a.m.).

Side-trips

Directly to the east of Solo lies the 3,265-metre (10,700 ft) bulk of **Mount Lawu**. **Candi Sukuh**, 910 metres (3,000 ft) up on Lawu's western flank, is sometimes billed as Java's only example of erotic temple carving. The temple is worth visiting for its spectacular views out over the Solo River Valley.

About 600 metres (2,000 ft) higher up the mountain and several miles to the east, another temple known as **Candi Ceta** seems to have been built at about the same as Sukuh. Its Bima figures and numerous terraces lie beyond the village of Kemuning, reached by paved but rather badly pot-holed road.

East Java

> Surabaya
> Tretes
> Malang
> Batu/Selecta
> Byroads to Bali

Surabaya

Getting There

Convenient air services link Surabaya with almost all cities in Indonesia (no international flights as yet), with a **Garuda** (Airbus) shuttle every other hour to and from Jakarta (about US$90 one-way). Many flights bound for the northern and eastern islands stopover here.

A good number of trans-Javan express trains and buses terminate or originate in Surabaya, with many immediate onward connections (for the bus/train to Bali, *see* Bali: "Getting There" below).

City Orientation

Jalan Tunjungan/Basuki Rachmat is generally regarded as the main street, running north-south parallel to the river, roughly in the middle of town.

There are three train stations: **Pasar Turi, Semut** (also known as **Kota**) and **Gubeng**. The last is the closest to the hotel districts, if you have a choice where to alight. The **Joyoboyo Bus Terminal** is in the south of the city, just opposite the Surabaya Zoo, about two kms (one mile) south of Jl. Tunjungan. **Juanda Airport** is 15 kms (9 miles) farther south, on the road to Malang and Tretes. (So if you are going immediately to the mountains, you need not enter the city.) Inter-city bus company offices (like **Elteha**) are around Jl. Basuki Rachmat on side-lanes like Embong Sawo.

There is a **Tourist Information Office** at Jl. Pemuda 118 with many brochures and a helpful "Calendar of Events" of dates for such things as the fortnightly bull races on Madura (August/September) and the Ramayana Ballet performances at Pandaan (June to November).

Getting Around

There are as yet no metered cabs in this city of more than 3 million. Taxis may be rented by the hour (US$3 to US$4 per hour, two-hour minimum) at any hotel and at the airport. The fare from the airport to the city is US$5.

City buses and mini-buses (*bemos*) circulate throughout the city, converging on the **Joyoboyo Bus Terminal** in front of the zoo. The important lines to know are those that travel north-south between here and the old section of town through the central hotel district: Jembatan Merah ("Red Bridge")—Tunjungan-Joyoboyo and Jembatan Merah-Diponegoro-Joyoboyo. Fare is Rp 100. Ask at your hotel for details about other lines.

Tours/Travel Agents

Most travel agents will arrange a private tour of the area for any number of people, via rented taxi or mini-bus with a guide. **Turi Express** organizes excursions to Bromo and East Java's temples. The **Tourist Information Office** (Jl. Pemuda 118) will also arrange special bull races and trance dances.

Accommodation

First Class (above US$35 per night)

There is only one four-star luxury hotel—the new **Hyatt Bumi** (US$75 a night on up, plus 21 per cent tax and service). The new **Simpang**, at the corner of Jl. Tunjungan and Jl. Pemuda, costs US$64 a night (plus 21 per cent). The **Mirama** and the **Ramayana** just to the south are in the US$50 to US$60 range (plus 21 per cent), and the **Elmi** and the **Garden**, also in the same area, have rooms for a bit less.

The older **Majapahit Hotel** on Jl. Tanjungan (formerly the "Oranje"—built in 1910) is something of a historical monument, the site of the famous "flag incident" that sparked off the revolutionary battle for Surabaya. Air-conditioned rooms for US$40, non-airconditioned ones for US$24, plus 21 per cent.

- **Elmi Hotel** (74 rooms), Jl. Panglima Sudirman 42-44 Surabaya, tel: 47150-8, 45291, tlx: 31431.
- **Garden Hotel** (100 rooms), Jl. Pemuda 21, Surabaya, tel: 470000-9, tlx: 31428 GARDEN HOTEL.
- **Hyatt Bumi Surabaya** (268 rooms), Jl. Basuki Rachmat, Surabaya, tel: 470875, 470503, tlx: 31391 HYATT BUMI.
- **Majapahit Hotel** (105 rooms), Jl Tunjungan 65, P.O. Box 199, Surabaya, tel: 43351-5, 42018, 43599, tlx: 31363.
- **Mirama Hotel** (105 rooms), Jl. Raya Darmo 68-72, P.O. Box 232, Surabaya, tel: 69501-9, tlx: 31485.
- **New Grand Park** (103 rooms), Jl. Samudra 3-5, Surabaya, tel: 270004-8, 314288, tlx: 31486.
- **Patra Jasa Motel** (63 rooms), Jl. Gunung Sari, Surabaya, tel: 68681-3.
- **Ramayana Hotel** (100 rooms), Jl. Jenderal Basuki Rachmat 67-69, Surabaya, tel: 45395-6, 41746-7, 46321, tlx: 31202.
- **Simpang Hotel** (128 rooms), Jl. Pemuda 1-3, P.O. Box 36, Surabaya, tel: 42219, 42220-5, 42151-9, tlx: 31607.

Intermediate & Budget (under US$35 a night)

No guest houses here. For US$30 your best bet is the **Garden** (*see* above) or for US$22 you get a non-airconditioned room at the Majapahit (*see* above). The **Sarkies** across the street and down Jl. Embong Malang is another older hotel owned by the Majapahit, with air-conditioned rooms for US$25 to US$30. Or try the newer **Royal** and Olympic for around US$20.

Budget travellers always stay at the **Bamboe Denn/Transito Inn**, with dorm beds for US$1, singles for US$2 and doubles for US$3. They have lots of travel info here to help you get around and they serve cheap breakfasts and snacks. For a bit more (US$6 to US$8) try **Wisma Ganeca** near Gubeng Station.

- **Bamboe Denn/Transito Inn**, Jl. Pemuda 19, Surabaya, tel: 40333.
- **Cendana Hotel** (23 rooms), Jl. K.B.P. Duryat 6, Surabaya, tel: 42251-2.
- **Lasmana Hotel** (27 rooms), Jl. Bintoro 16, Surabaya, tel: 67152.
- **Olympic Hotel** (22 rooms), J. Urip Sumoharjo 65-67, Surabaya, tel: 43215-6.
- **Pregolan Hotel** (25 rooms), Jl. Pregolan 11-15, Surabaya, tel: 41251-2.
- **Royal Hotel**, Jl. Panglima Sudirman 68, Surabaya, tel: 43547-8.
- **Sarkies Hotel** (51 rooms), Jl. Embong Malang 7-11, Surabaya, tel: 44514, 43080, 40494, 40167.
- **Wisma Ganeca**, Jl. Sumatra 34 A, Surabaya.

Dining

Surabaya is well known for its Chinese food. The **Garden** (Jl. Pemuda 21) specializes in Hong Kong style Tim Sum. The best-known banquet houses are located along the river: the **Mandarin** (Jl. Genteng Kali 93) and the **Phoenix** (Jl. Genteng Kali 15). Try also the **Hoover** in the Wijaya Shopping Centre (2nd floor), and the **Oriental**, Jl. Ade Irma Suryani 37. For something less pricey, go to Chinatown: **Kiet Wan Kie** at Jl. Kembang Jepun 51 and a small hole-in-the-wall opposite the New Grand Park Hotel on Jl. Samudra (excellent fish here).

For seafood, try the **Miami Seafood Restaurant** down on Jl. Urip Sumoharjo 34.

The best-known Indonesian restaurant is **Bibi & Baba** right on Jl. Tunjungan 76. The new **Taman Sari Indah** (Jl. Taman Apsari 5), just opposite the Joko Dolog statue next to the Post Office is also very clean and good—serving *pepes* and *sate*.

Shopping

It is said you can buy cameras, tape recorders and portable electronic items here as cheaply as in Singapore. Try the shopping centre on Jl. Tunjungan or the new Wijaya Shopping Centre.

There is a whole string of antique & curios shops around the Hyatt on Jl. Basuki Rachmat. Also on Jl. Tunjungan (**Kundadas** at No. 97 and **Sarinah** at No. 7). Several more are located down on Jl. Raya Darmo (**Rochim** at No. 27 and **Bangun** at No.5).

For *batik* and hand-woven cotton textiles, the area around the Sunan Ampel mosque in the middle of the Arab quarter is best.

Entertainment

Javanese *wayang orang, ludruk* and *ketoprak* folk dramas are performed nightly at two theatres in the **People's Amusement Park** (Taman Hiburan Rakyat) on Jl. Kusuma Bangsa. There is also a hysterically funny Sri Mulat slapstick comedy troupe here featuring a whole gang of transvestites. Shows start at about 8 p.m. Tickets are cheap.

From June to November there are fortnightly (1st and 3rd Saturdays of each month) Sendratari classical Javanese dance-drama performances at the huge open-air **Candra Wilwatikta** amphitheatre in Pandaan, 45 km (28 miles) south of Surabaya on the Malang road.

The Tourist Information Office can arrange an East Javanese *kuda kepang* "hobbyhorse" trance dance performance for you given three days notice.

Regular bull races are now held monthly in the new stadium at **Bangkalan** just across the straits of Madura. Check with the Tourist Information Office for dates.

Other than this, there are many cinemas in Surabaya, and most large hotel restaurants have some form of evening entertainment or live music. Check the local papers for film listings.

Tretes

Getting There

Only an hour south of Surabaya by very good roads. The turn-off is at **Pandaan** and from here it's about 20 kms (12 miles) up the hill to this large resort. Only about US$20 by taxi or rented mini-bus. Otherwise catch any bus or mini-bus from Surabaya headed in the direction of Malang (south) and get off at the intersection in Pandaan (fare will be only Rp200 to 300). From here "colts" go up to Tretes (Rp 200).

Accommodation

The best hotel is the **Natour Bath**, with doubles starting at US$45 a night (plus 21 per cent). It has a crystal-clear swimming pool. Also with a large pool is the **Dirgahaya Indah**, with rooms for around US$20. Actually, though, you can rent an entire bungalow for only US$20 with two or more bedrooms, and a very deluxe house could be had for US$50 a night. Walk around Tretes and inquire—most bungalows are for rent during the week.

- **Dirgahaya Indah** (12 rooms), Jl. Ijen 5, Tretes, tel: (0343) 81932.
- **Natour Bath Hotel** (50 rooms), Jl. Pesanggrahan 2, Tretes, tel: (0343) 81161, 81718.
- **Pelita**, Jl. Wilis 19-21, tel: (0343) 81802.
- **Tanjung Grand Park** (62 rooms), Jl. Wilis 7, Tretes, tel: (0343) 81102, 81173.
- **Tretes Raya**, Jl. Malabar 166, Tretes tel: (0343) 81902.

Malang

Unlike many Javanese towns which lie dead straight along a dreary, shuttered, down-at-heel main street, Malang sweeps and winds over gentle ridges and gullies along the banks of the Brantas River, offering unexpected views and quiet backstreets that demand to be explored. It hasn't experienced the explosive growth of other large Javanese cities, and it remains a small, quiet town.

Getting There

Although there are local 3rd-class trains running along the old tracks from Surabaya to Malang, the new highway is much quicker—comfortably travelled by express "colt"—costs just US$2 and delivers you to your doorstep in Malang. Ask your hotel in Surabaya to book a seat for you.

Buses also leave regularly from Surabaya's Joyoboyo bus terminal and the fare is only about US$1.

Accommodation

The old colonial-style **YMCA** has huge, spotlessly clean rooms with hot water and a fan for only US$14 (including tax, service and breakfast). For a bit more money, the **Splendid Inn** is very pleasant: a spacious guesthouse with gardens. Air-conditioned rooms are US$20 to US$25 (including tax, service and breakfast). The old **Pelangi** facing the town square has many large rooms for US$10 to US$18 and some cheaper ones at the back for only US$7 (including tax and service). Budget travellers stay at the **Bamboe Denn** for US$2 and can stay for free if they attend some English classes at the language school.

- **Bamboe Denn/Transito Inn**, Jl. Semeru 35, Malang, tel: 24859.
- **Pelangi Hotel** (73 rooms), Jl. Merdeka Selatan, Malang, tel: 27456-7.
- **Santoso**, Jl. K.H. Agus Salim 24, Malang, tel: 23889.
- **Splendid Inn** (21 rooms), Jl. Majapahit 2-4, Malang, tel: 23860.
- **YMCA**, Jl. Basuki Rachmat 68-76, Malang tel: 23605.

Dining

There's good Padang food opposite the **YMCA** at the **Minang Jaya** (Jl. Basuki Rachmat 22). **Oen's** at Jl. Basuki Rachmat 5 is an old colonial place serving Dutch food like *wienerschnitsel*, *broodjes* and *uitsmijters*. For steaks and ice cream, try the new **La Vanda** ice cream parlour at Jl. Semeru 49. For Chinese food, try the **New Hongkong**, Jl. Arif Rahman Hakim.

Shopping

There are many antique & curio stores on Jl. Basuki Rachmat. Also try the antique section of the **Pasar Besar** market, on the second floor at the back left-hand corner. This can be a great place to buy old Dutch glasses, trays and silverware.

Batu/Selecta

Just above Malang, 23 kms to the west, is the hill town of **Batu** with its neighbouring colonial resort, **Selecta**. Several new motels with swimming pools have been built around here, notably the large **Songgoriti** complex located on the main road some distance past Batu. The older Dutch bungalow resort at Selecta is still very well kept, with huge suites available for only US$15.

- **Asida** (40 rooms), Jl. Panglima Sudirman 99, Batu, Malang, tel: 259.
- **Batu Hotel**, Jl. Hasanuddin 4, Batu, Malang, tel: 77, 234.
- **Libra Bungalows**, Jl. Konto 4, Batu, Malang, tel: 64.
- **Palem** (29 rooms), Jl. Trunojoyo 26, Batu, Malang, tel: 177.
- **Palem Sari** (22 rooms), Jl. Raya Punten, Batu, Malang, tel: 219.
- **Purnama** (37 rooms), Jl. Raya Selecta, Batu, Malang, tel: 195.
- **Santoso II**, Jl. Tulungrejo, Batu, Malang, tel: 25.

- **Selecta Hotel & Pool**, Jl. Tulungrejo, Batu, Malang, tel: 25.
- **Songgoriti Hotel**, Jl. Songgoriti, Batu, Malang, tel: 126.

Byroads to Bali

The following excursions can be made en route to Bali, or equally well as side-trips from Bali.
- **Bromo:** best approach is by the 20-km road which winds up from the north coast highway at Tongas, just west of Probolinggo, through Sukapura to **Ngadisari**. Lots of "colts" make this journey and you can board one at the Tongas turnoff (fare to Ngadisari is about US$0.30). From here, a newly completed cobblestone road covers the last 3 kms (two miles) up to **Cemara Lawang** on the lip of the caldera, but special permission must be sought from the police in Ngadisari to use this road (if you have your own vehicle). Otherwise, all public transport stops at the Ngadisari parking lot and you have to walk or rent a pony for the final, steep climb. Try to get up there before sunset. It takes about five hours altogether to reach the caldera's rim from Surabaya, a bit less from Tretes.

The **Bromo Permai Hotel** at Cemara Lawang sleeps 30 and usually has space available. Call the booking office in Probolinggo (Jl. Raya Panglima Sudirman 237-242, tel: 21510, 21983) if you want to be sure of accommodation, particular during the peak tourist seasons. The rooms are very basic, costing only US$4 to US$10 a night for a double, many without private bath. The hotel restaurant is quite adequate, serving coffee, tea, beer, eggs, toast and a few rice dishes. Temperatures can drop below freezing at night because of the altitude. The hotel supplies you with a thin blanket, but bring along extra covers and several layers of warm clothing.

Hire a pony to make the two-hour trek down into the caldera and across the famous "Sand Sea" to the base of Bromo. From here, a flight of steps leads up to the rim of this volcano-within-a-volcano so that you can peer down into Bromo's steaming, sulphurous pit. The horsemen like to get you up at 3 a.m. and ride you across to Bromo for the sunrise, because that way they get home by 9 a.m. while it is still cool, but this is a miserable, cold and windy journey in pitch blackness. The view of the sunrise is better from the caldera's rim anyway, just near the hotel. So watch it from here, have breakfast, and then go down to Bromo (bring some water along, because it does get hot). The horse ride normally costs US$3 to US$5 round trip.

It is also possible to continue on from Bromo across the Sand Sea in a southerly direction to the village of **Rano Pani** (about 20 kms away) and then to **Rano Kumbolo** (another 12 kms away) for the climb up Mt. Semeru, Java's highest mountain (3,676 metres/12,500 feet). You'd better be well prepared for this, though, both physically and with good camping gear. There are three beautiful lakes nestling in this highland massif, amid grassy meadows and pine forests. From Rano Pani you can descend to the west via **Ngadas** and **Gubug**

Klakah, from where there is a road leading down through Tumpang to Malang.
- **Banyuwangi:** This is the capital of eastern Java's Banyuwangi regency, just seven kms (four miles) south of the Java-Bali ferry terminal at Ketapang—the jumping-off point for visits to Ijen, Meru Betiri (Sukamade) and the Blambangan Peninsula. There are many inexpensive hotels in and around Banyuwangi, including the two-star **Manyar** located by the ferry in Ketapang (*see* listing below). You can also stay up at the hill resort of **Kaliklatak**, 15 kms (nine miles) west of Banyuwangi (*see* below).

Banyuwangi's **Tourist Information Office** at Jl. Diponegoro 2 (tel: 41761) is very helpful in advising you how to reach the places mentioned below, and the **Nitour** office at Jl. Raya 43 C will arrange guided tours to fit different budgets.
- **Manyar Hotel** (50 rooms), Jl. Situbondo, Ketapang, Banyuwangi, tel: 41741-2.
- **Banyuwangi Hotel** (20 rooms), Jl. Dr. Wahidin 10, Banyuwangi, tel: 41178.
- **Wisma Blambangan** (18 rooms), Jl. Dr. Wahidin 4, Banyuwangi, tel: 21598.

Ijen Plateau: The focal point for a visit here is the spectacular blue-green lake inside of the **Ijen Crater**, west and north of Banyuwangi. By the lake are many steaming fumeroles where labourers collect bright-yellow sulphur and then carry 60-kg loads of it in baskets along a steep trail to a processing plant at **Jambu**, 17 kms (10.5 miles) down the mountain. It's about a seven hour hike each way, though horses can be rented for the climb in Jambu, and if you have a sleeping bag you can stay overnight at the volcanology station at **Ungkup-Ungkup**, about an hour below the crater (it gets very cold).
- **Banyuwangi Selatan Reserve**: The main attraction here is the huge 10 to 20 foot rollers that come crashing onto the western shore of the narrow Blambangan Peninsula from May to July. Surfers have constructed a few crude huts here to be able to take advantage of what is said to be one of the best surfing spots in the world, at **Plengkung**. This "surfer's camp" can be reached in three ways. The first is to charter a launch directly from Bali, which is expensive (about US$100 each way). The second way is to go by road to the fishing village of **Grajagan** on the southern coast opposite Plengkung, and then charter a fishing boat from here for the crossing of Grajagan Bay. Grajagan is 52 kms (32 miles) from Banyuwangi and can be reached by *bemo*, via Benculuk and Purwoharjo. The third and most difficult route is to travel by motorcycle or jeep directly into the reserve as far as **Pancur**, and then to cover the last 10 kms (6 miles) to the camp on foot. Pancur is 60 kms from Banyuwangi, reached via Muncar and Tegallimo.
- **Meru Betiri Reserve**: This is the most exciting nature reserve on Java, second only perhaps to Ujung Kulon. Access is via **Pesanggaran**, a village 68 kms (42 miles) west and south of Banyuwangi (turn off to the south at Genteng, 35 kms (22 miles) west of Banyuwangi). From Pesanggaran a 24-km (15-mile) rutted track leads west into the reserve over rickety bridges and across several

river fords. At **Rajegwesi** there is a small guest-house that sleeps up to 6 (make prior arrangements at the PPA office in Banyuwangi).

From Rajegwesi, it's 11 kms (7 miles) further to the **Sukamade Baru** coffee estate, which has a more comfortable guest house that sleeps 30. The guest house is several kilometres inland from **Pantai Penyu** ("Turtle Beach"), which should be visited at night to observe the huge 200-kg female green and leatherback turtles laying their eggs.

Bali

| Getting There |
| Getting Around |
| Shopping |
| Performing Arts Venues |
| Nightlife |
| Sports |
| Medical Facilities |
| Airline Offices in Bali |
| Sanur |
| Kuta/Legian |
| Nusa Dua |
| Denpasar |
| Ubud |

To the Balinese, the world is their living-room and its travellers their guests. Do your best to respect their traditions and attitudes:

Settle all prices beforehand, otherwise you must pay the price demanded. Don't ask the price or make an offer unless you intend to buy.

Dress up rather than down. You are afforded special guest status as a foreigner, so don't abuse it. Old faded or torn clothes, bared thighs and excessively "native" dress are considered bad form.

Keep all valuables out of sight and preferably locked up. The Balinese have a strong sense of pride and consider temptation an affront, suspicion an insult.

Wear a temple sash whenever entering a temple, and expect to pay a token entrance fee to the custodian. Behave with reverence and deference.

Getting There

● **Air:** Bali's Ngurah Rai International Airport, which straddles the narrow Tuban Isthmus in the south of the island, is served by many daily flights from Jakarta, Yogyakarta, Surabaya and various other cities in Indonesia.

Several weekly international flights arrive directly from Sydney, Melbourne, Perth and Darwin in Australia (Qantas and Garuda). Only Garuda flies here from Europe and Singapore, always with a stopover first in Jakarta. Other international airlines fly only as far as Jakarta and you must then transfer to Garuda to reach Bali.

Flights to Bali from Jakarta's Cengkareng International Airport are frequent throughout the day, and you can generally catch a connection if you arrive before 6 p.m. See box below for domestic flight information:

Route	Dep.	Arr.	Days	one-way economy fare US$
JKT — DPS				
Garuda	06.00	07.30	Daily	83
	10.00	11.30	Daily	
	15.00	16.30	Daily	
	19.30	21.00	Daily	
JOG — DPS				
Garuda	08.20	09.35	Daily	45
	12.05	13.20	Daily	
	16.00	17.15	Daily	
SUB — DPS				
Garuda	07.00	07.50	Daily	34
	14.00	14.50	Daily	
	17.30	18.20	Daily	
Merpati	06.10	07.20	Tue. Fri. Sun.	29
	10.00	11.10	Tue. Wed. Fri. Sat. Sun.	
Bouraq	06.00	07.05	Mon. Tues. Thur. Fri. Sat.	29
	06.10	07.15	Mon. Wed. Thur. Sun.	

CITY CODES: JKT-Jakarta; DPS-Denpasar; JOG-Yogyakarta: SUB-Surabaya.

● **Train:** From Jakarta, Bandung or Yogyakarta travel first to Surabaya (see Java: "Trains" above) and change over here to the Mutiara Timur, a non-airconditioned train bound for Banyuwangi, at Java's eastern tip. Choose from two daily departures from Surabaya's Gubeng Station, at 11:00 and 21:30. Fare is just US$3.50 2nd class, US$2.50 3rd class as far as Banyuwangi (an eight hour journey). From here a bus takes you across the straits on the ferry and over to Denpasar (fare: US$1), an additional four hours.

Bus: With improvements in road conditions, the bus is now faster than the train. Air-conditioned buses from Surabaya (a 10-to-12-hour trip) to Denpasar cost about US$8, non-airconditioned buses are US$5. From Yogya (15 to 16 hours) the fare is US$9 to US$12.

Getting Around

Balinese roads are a parade ground, used for escorting village deities to the sea, for funeral cremation processions, for filing to the local temple in Sunday best, or for performances of a trans-island *barong* dance. They are also now increasingly crowded. The volume of traffic has increased dramatically over the past two decades.

In the end, the best way to see Bali is on foot. Away from the heavily travelled main roads, the island takes on an entirely different complexion.

Taxis: There is a taxi service from the airport, with fares ranging from US$3 (to nearby Kuta Beach) on up to US$10 (to Ubud). To Sanur, Denpasar and Nusa Dua costs between US$5 and US$7.

Taxis and minibuses are for hire at every hotel (and in front of the Hyatt), just with a driver, or with an English-speaking driver/guide. Rates are US$2 to US$4 per hour (two-hour minimum) and US$30 to US$40 per day, a bit more for air-conditioning, newer cars and long journeys. Often there is little difference (other than the price) between simply renting a car for a day (many drivers speak good English) and going on a professionally guided tour (see below). The following is a sampling of rates for simple one-way drop offs (you will have to negotiate a bit more for round-trip excursions with stops):

Sanur - Denpasar US$3   Sanur - Besakih US$20

Sanur - Kintamani US$18   Sanur - Ubud   US$5

Sanur - Kuta   US$5   Sanur - Uluwatu US$12

Rental Cars: The best way to get around the island independently is to rent a self-drive car, available in Kuta, Sanur or Denpasar. You must have a valid International Driving Permit. The most commonly rented vehicles are old beat-up **VW Safari** convertibles (US$30 per day/US$ 180 per week/US$240 for 10 days), although newer (sometimes air-conditioned) Suzuki Jimny's are also available for a bit more money (US$35 to US$40). You buy the gas. Buy the extra insurance also. Book a car through your hotel or from any of the companies listed below. Test-drive it before paying.

● **Bali Wisata**, Jl. Imam Bonjol, Kuta tel: 24479.

● **Bali Car Rental**, Jl. By-pass Ngurah Rai, Sanur tel: 8550, 8359.

● **Utama Motors**, Jl. Imam Bonjol, Kuta, tel: 22073.

Motorcycles: Convenient and inexpensive. Be aware that the roads are crowded and traffic is dangerous—your chances of an accident are uncomfortably high. Each year several tourists are killed in motorbike accidents, and many more injured. If you do rent a bike, ride slowly and defensively.

The cost of hiring a motorbike is usually a matter of bargaining, and varies greatly. The usual price of a 100cc or 125cc machine is US$3 to US$6 per day, or US$20 to US$30 per week (paid in advance). You provide the gas. Any hotel can arrange a rental for you, and it is a good idea to buy insurance also, so that you are not responsible for damages to the bike in case of an accident. Be sure to test-drive it.

You must have an International Driving Permit valid for motorcycles, or else spend a morning at the Denpasar Police Office (see map) to get a Temporary Permit (valid for one month only on Bali). This entails passing a driving test and paying an administrative fee of US$4. Bring along your passport and three photos, plus your own auto driving license from your home country (or a doctor's certificate indicating that you are fit to drive a vehicle). Normally the person who rents you the bike will accompany you to the police station. Get there early and practise driving slowly in small circles beforehand.

Guided Tours/Travel Agents: Expert daily bus tours, with well-informed multi-lingual guides are run by many travel agencies. They range in price from US$6 to US$7 for a half-day jaunt to Ubud or Sangeh/Mengwi, up to US$15 to US$20

for a full-day cross-island trip up to Kintamani or Besakih, including a Barong Dance in Batubulan, lunch and several stops at shops and temples.

You can also design your own private guided tour, in an air-conditioned car with a chauffeur/guide, which allows you to establish the itinerary and the amount of time spent at each stop—US$30 up to US$60. The most experienced agents for the demanding traveller are **BIL** and **Pacto. Perama's** and many others in Kuta provide a decent service for budget group tours in mini-buses.

● **Bali Holiday**, Tanjung Bungkak, Denpasar, tel: 24000.

● **Bali Indonesia Ltd.**, Hotel Tanjung, Denpasar, tel: 22634.

● **Ida's Tour**, Ida Beach Inn, Kuta, tel: 8781 ext. 44.

● **Natour**, Jl. Veteran 1, Denpasar, tel: 24161, 22619, 22408.

● **Natrabu**, Jl. Patimura 31, Denpasar, tel: 24047.

● **Nitour**, Jl. Veteran 3, Denpasar, tel: 22849, 22593.

● **Pacto**, Jl. Sanur, Sanur, tel: 8247-8.

● **Udaya Tour**, Indra Building 2nd Floor, Jl. Gajah Mada, Denpasar, tel: 8192.

● **Universal Travel Service**, Jl. Diponegoro 32, Denpasar, tel: 24305, 22110.

Public Mini-Buses/Buses: The local system of pick-ups and mini-buses (collectively known as bemos) and intra-island buses is efficient and inexpensive. You can get from one end of the island to the other for less than US$2. In addition, almost every bemo on the road in Bali may be chartered by the trip or by the day, with the driver, by telling him where you want to go and then agreeing upon a price. Most drivers are willing to go anywhere on the island for US$25 to US$30 a day (which is what they normally make hauling passengers).

There are four bus/bemo teminals in Denpasar (see below) serving points to the south, west, north and east of the city respectively.

Tegal Terminal (southwest of Denpasar)

   Kuta Rp 200

   Airport (Tuban) Rp 250

   Nusa Dua Rp 400

Ubung Terminal (northwest of Denpasar)

   Gilimanuk Rp 1650

   Singaraja Rp 1050

   Sangeh Rp 350

   Mengwi Rp 200

   Tabanan Rp 200

   Tanah Lot Rp 300

Kereneno Terminal (east of Denpasar)

   Sanur Rp 200

   Ubud Rp 250

   Kintamani Rp 1200

   Klungkung Rp 600

   Bangli Rp 600

   Padangbai Rp 800

   Amlapura Rp 1200

Suci Terminal (centre of Denpasar

   Benoa Harbour Rp 200

Note that rather than taking a taxi from the airport, you can just walk out to the road and catch a local *bemo* to Kuta (Rp 100) or Denpasar (Rp 250).

All **Inter-City Buses** leave from Suci Terminal on Jl. Hasannudin, and the bus companies have their offices here.

Shopping

Bali is a great place to shop. Hundreds of boutiques and roadside stalls have set up all over the island, and thousands of artisans, craftsmen, seamstresses, woodcarvers, painters, etc. are busy supplying the tourist demand.

Woodcarvings

You are sure to find good woodcarvings in the shops along the main roads in **Mas** (particularly well-known is Ida Bagus Tilem's Gallery and Museum). Also try the villages of **Pujung** (past Tegalalang north of Ubud), **Batuan** and **Jati**. All types of indigenous wood, ranging from the butter-coloured jackwood to inexpensive be-speckled coconut, are sculpted here in bold designs which set the standards for carvers elsewhere on the island. Woods imported from other islands—buff hibiscus, rich brown Javanese teak and black Sulawesian ebony are also hewn into delicate forms by Balinese craftsmen. Hunt for antique woodcarvings that once adorned gilded temple pavilions or royal palaces, in shops in **Kuta**, **Sanur** and on the main street of **Klungkung**.

Paintings

The artist's centre is **Ubud**, including the surrounding villages of **Pengosekan, Penestanan, Sanggingan, Peliatan, Mas** and **Batuan**. The famous **Neka Gallery** & **Museum** and the **Puri Lukisan Museum**, both in Ubud, will give you an idea of the range of styles and the artistry achieved by the best painters. Then visit some of the other galleries in the area: **Gallery Munut**, **Gallery Agung** and the gallery of the **Pengosekan Community of Artists**. Examples from every school of painting active in Bali are found here as well as canvasses of young artists portraying festivals and dancers.

For quality works of art, seek out the gallery-homes of well-known artists in Ubud such as **Antonio Blanco, Hans Snel, Wayan Rendi, Arie Smit** and the late, great **I Gusti Nyoman Lempad**. In other villages, seek out **Mokoh** and **I Made Budi** (Batuan).

For traditional astrological calendars and *ider-ider*—strips of cotton, a foot wide and 15 feet long which are suspended from the eaves of shrines during temple ceremonies—paintings in the so-called *wayang* style, visit **Kamasan**, just south of Klungkung. This style has been around for many centuries and some of the paintings are antique. Examples are found in **Klungkung** and in many antique shops.

Stone Carvings

For traditional sand-stone carvings, stop at the workshops in **Batubulan**. And **Wayan Cemul**, an Ubud stone carver with an international following, has a house full of his weird and wonderful creations.

Textiles

For *batik* clothing, try the many boutiques in **Kuta Beach**. Brocades that gleam like gold lamé, and also the simpler, handloomed *sarung* cloths, are sold in every village. **Gianyar** is the home of the handloom industry, but the villages of **Blayu, Sideman, Mengwi, Batuan, Gelgel, Tengganan** and **Ubud** all produce their own style of weavings.

Gold & Silver

The centres for metal working are **Celuk** and **Kamasan**, where all such ornaments are on sale at reasonable prices. **Kuta** is another centre for export gold and silver wares. For traditional Balinese jewellery, visit the shops on Jl. Sulawesi and Jl. Kartini in **Denpasar**.

Handicrafts

Bamboo implements, *wayang kulit* figures and ornaments made of coconut shell and teakwood are sold at most souvenir shops. Bone-carvings can be had for good prices at **Tampaksiring**, while plaited hats and baskets are the specialty of the women of **Bedulu** and **Bona**. **Sukawati** market and the row of stands opposite **Goa Gajah** are the best places to buy baskets. **Klungkung** market also has some finely worked traditional wares.

The **Handicraft Centre** (Sanggraha Karya Hasta) in Tohpati, Denpasar, has a collection of handicrafts from Bali and the other islands of Indonesia, such as baskets and weavings. Open 8 a.m. to 5 p.m. daily, closed Mondays.

The morning market at **Pasar Badung** in Denpasar is also an eye-opener. Coral-lined alleys lead to a ceremonial knick-knacks section selling baskets of every shape and size.

Antiques

Try the shopping arcades of major hotels for truly outstanding pieces (at outstanding prices). In **Kuta**, Anang's and the East West Artshop have the best collection of antiques and primitive artifacts.

In **Denpasar**, there are several antique shops along Jl. Gajah Mada up near the town square end. Also on Jl. Arjuna, Jl. Dresna, Jl. Veteran and Jl. Gianyar. In **Sanur**, the shops are along Jl. Sanur.

The many antique shops adjacent to the Kerta Gosa in **Klungkung** house collections of rare Chinese porcelains, old Kamasan *wayang* style paintings, antique jewellery and Balinese weavings. Prices are reasonable. **Singaraja** has some of the best antique shops in Bali, too. They are all on the main roads of this northern city.

Pottery

Some unusual pottery is manufactured at the village of **Pejaten** in the district of Tabanan about 20 kms (12 miles) west of Denpasar. Here, the villagers create striking figurines with twisted limbs and grotesque bodies out of terra-cotta, as they have done for many generations. Beautiful glazed ceramics are also being produced now in Batu Jimbar, **Sanur**.

Performing Arts Venues

The best way to see Balinese dances, *wayang kulit* puppet shows and *gamelan* orchestras is to attend a village temple festival. There is one going on somewhere on the island almost every day. Ask your hotel, or consult the **Bali Post Calendar**, available from most shops. In the fine print beneath are listed the names of villages having ceremonies and the type of celebration (it is not 100 per cent accurate, however).

Public performances are also given at various central locations all over the island. These are mainly for the benefit of tourists only. Some of the best dancers and musicians in Bali participate in tourist performances, and for them it's a good source of income.

Kecak Dance

- **Ayoda Pura**, Tanjung Bungkak
- **Banjar Taman**, Sanur
- **Banjar Legian Kelod**,
- **Banjar Buni**,
- **Bona**, Gianyar
- **Abian Kapas Art Centre**,

Ramayana Ballet

- **Ayoda Pura**, Tanjung Bungkak
- **Pemecutan Palace Hotel**,
- **Banjar Pengaretan**, Kuta
- **Indra Prasta**, Kuta

Barong Dance

- **Banjar Seminiyak**, Legian
- **Saha Dewa**, Batubulan

Legong Dance

- **Puri Agung**, Peliatan
- **Ayoda Pura**, Tanjung Bungkak
- **Pemecutan Palace Hotel**, Denpasar
- **Indra Prasta**, Kuta

Wayang Kulit

- **Pemecutan Palace Hotel**, Denpasar

Trance Dance/Fire-walking

- **Bona**, Gianyar

The following hotels also have regular evening dinner shows with dances:
- **Bali Hyatt Hotel**, Sanur
- **Hotel Bali Beach**, Sanur
- **Bali Seaside Cottage**, Sanur
- **Nusa Dua Hotel**, Nusa Dua
- **Sanur Beach Hotel**, Sanur

Nightlife

Nightlife on the **Sanur** side is relatively tame. There are cocktail lounges with live music at some

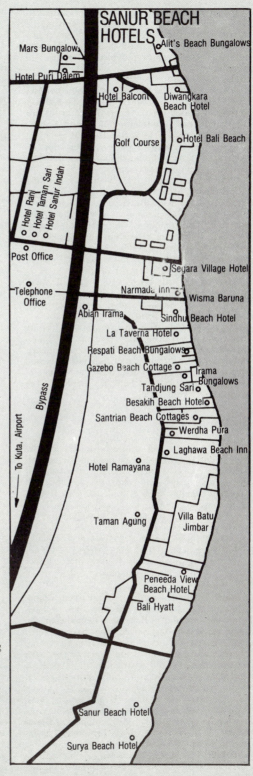

SANUR BEACH HOTELS

Mars Bungalow
Hotel Puri Dalem
Alit's Beach Bungalows
Hotel Balcont
Diwangkara Beach Hotel
Golf Course
Hotel Bali Beach
Hotel Ranj
Hotel Taman Sari
Hotel Sanur Indah
Post Office
Segara Village Hotel
Telephone Office
Narmada Inn
Wisma Baruna
Abian Irama
Sindhu Beach Hotel
La Taverna Hotel
Respati Beach Bungalows
Gazebo Beach Cottage
Irama Bungalows
Tandjung Sari
Besakih Beach Hotel
Santrian Beach Cottages
Werdha Pura
Laghawa Beach Inn
Hotel Ramayana
Villa Batu Jimbar
Taman Agung
Peneeda View Beach Hotel
Bali Hyatt
To Kuta, Airport
Bypass
Sanur Beach Hotel
Surya Beach Hotel

of the larger hotels, such as the Hotel Bali Beach, whose **Bali Hai** supper club offers razzmatazz international entertainers straight out of Vegas. The Bali Hyatt has a plush disco, the **Matahari** with deejays and music provided by Juliana's of London.

Also in Sanur, the **Karya Restaurant**, the **Purnama Terrace** (in the Bali Hyatt) and the **Kul Kul Restaurant** (book for the Frog Dance night) are the island's best venues for dinner and a show under the stars. The **Nusa Dua Hotel** at night is a spectacle in its own right—go there for its Ramayana Night and dine in opera box-like seats surrounding an open-air stage.

For hot, pulsating nightlife with loud, gyrating crowds and ear-shattering music, make your way on over to the **Kuta Beach** side. This formerly somnambulent beach village is now on the go day and night. A number of watering holes along Jalan Legian and Jalan Buni Sari stay open as long as there are people. **Casablanca** and **The Pub**, to mention just two, serve chilled Bintang beer in chilled mugs—a beer drinker's paradise.

Some of the Kuta discos keep going till dawn, after which you can go down to the beach to watch the spectacular sunrise—quite a common pasttime in Kuta. The **Sand Bar** on Jl. Legian is a popular hang-out, with an even mix of leaping locals and Australians. If you're up in Legian, then head for the **Rum Jungle**—an open-air dance floor adorned with vines and creepers and packed with gyrating bodies. Farther down, in Seminyak, the happening place on Saturday nights is **Chez Gado-Gado** by the beach.

Sports

There are two **golf** courses available on the island. The Hotel Bali Beach in Sanur has a small nine-hole course that can be used for a fee. But the serious golfer will want to visit the **Bali Handara Country Club** at Bedugal. This 18-hole championship course was designed by Peter Thompson and is perhaps the only course in the world set inside a volcano. Green fees are US$45 per day on the weekends, US$30 during the week.

For a fee ranging from US$1.50 to US$5 a per day, the **swimming** pools at most of the larger hotels may be used by non-guests.

Aquatic Sports—surfing, diving, spearfishing, wind-surfing and deep-sea fishing—have all become very popular in Bali. **Nusa Lembongan**, the small island directly opposite Sanur has developed into a haven for surfers and divers alike. Group charters and safari tours are available, together with equipment and instruction if needed. A complete scuba outfit and a ride out to the reef at Sanur can be had for as little as US$20 a person for a group of five or more (US$40 for just one). Contact Nyoman at **Bali Aquatic Sports** in Kuta (in the La Barong Bar). Also in Kuta, try **Gloria Maris** (Jl. Airport) and **Nusa Lembongan Tours** (at the Happy Restaurant.)

For the best surfing, go down to **Ulu Watu** on the eastern side of the southern Bukit Peninsula.

Medical Facilities

In the event of emergency, you can call an **Ambulance** by dialing **118**. Every village in Bali now has a small government clinic called **Puskesmas**, but for major problems visit one of the hotel clinics or one of the public hospitals in Denpasar.

Pharmacies (Apotik)

Most pharmacies are open daily 8 a.m. to 6 p.m. Late at night, on Sundays and holidays there is a rotation system in Denpasar. Check the Bali Post or ask your hotel to call.
• **Kimia Farma**, Jl. Diponegoro 43, Denpasar, tel: 22376, 22640.
• **Kosala Farma**, Jl. Kartini 106, Denpasar tel: 22301
• **Ria Farma**, Jl. Veteran 43, Denpasar, tel: 22635, 24154.
• **Bali Farma**, Jl. Melati 9, Denpasar, tel: 22878, 22918.
• **Dirga Yusa**, Jl. Surapati 23, Denpasar tel: 22267.
• **Sadha Karya**, Jl. Gajah Mada 85, Denpasar, tel: 24009.
In **Kuta**, there is an apotik on the main road to the airport. In Sanur, try **Farmasari**, Jl. Banjar Taman.

Airline Offices

• **Bouraq**, Jl. Kamboja 45, Denpasar tel: 22252.
• **Cathay Pacific**, Hotel Bali Beach, Sanur, tel: 8576.
• **Garuda**, Jl. Melati 61, Denpasar, tel: 22028.
• **Merpati**, Jl. Melati 57, Denpasar, tel: 22864.
• **Qantas**, Hotel Bali Beach, Sanur tel: 8511.
• **Sempati**, Hotel Bali Beach, Sanur tel: 8511.
• **Thai International**, Hotel Bali Beach, Sanur, tel: 8511.

Sanur

Sanur is for gracious living, peace and quiet—more international but far less cosmopolitan than frenetic Kuta. Foreigners have been staying in Sanur since the 1920s, and they know how to take care of you here. Strictly first-class. Seek out the lovely Sanur temples, particularly when they are having their anniversary ceremonies (*odalan*), every seven months.

Accommodation

There are so many excellent first-class hotels in Sanur, that you can scarely go wrong. The main choice is between the convenience and luxury of a big four-star hotel (there are three: the **Bali Beach**, the **Bali Hyatt** and the **Sanur Beach**) or the quiet and personality of a private bungalow by the sea (at two-thirds to half the price). Reservations are advisable during the peak seasons: July to September and December to January. *Prices quoted below do not include the obligatory 21 per cent tax and service surcharge.*

First Class (above US$35 per night)

For such a large luxury hotel, the new **Bali Hyatt** offers a remarkably breezy, spacious Royal Hawaiian feeling, with striking public areas, clay tennis courts and hanging Babylonian gardens. The venerable **Hotel Bali Beach** (constructed by the Japanese in the early 1960s) looks more like a traditional Miami Beach luxury hotel—a 10-storey concrete block by the sea, set amidst a golf course, bowling alleys and two swimming pools.

Last but not least of the three four-star establishments, the smaller **Sanur Beach Hotel**, owned by Garuda, claims to be the friendliest large hotel in Sanur.

Of the smaller cottage resorts, the **Tanjung Sari Hotel** is the hands down choice of frequent visitors. This was one of the island's first beach-bungalow establishments and is still its most charming and efficient. The latest addition (since the hotel's vintage Ford bus was attacked by a band of Balinese painters) is a nightclub, Rumours, which features backgammon and a well-stocked video loft.

The **Segara Village** deserves mention for its snazzy and congenial Indonesian atmosphere. **La Taverna** gets kudos for its Italian Balinesia and attractive beach-restaurant pizzeria. **Wisma Baruna**, the smallest and oldest first-class hotel in Sanur is also very cozy, with a superb breakfast pavilion overlooking the lagoon.

- **Alit's Beach Bungalow** (98 rooms), Jl. Raya Sanur, P.O. Box 102, Denpasar, tel: 8567, tlx: 35165 BALICTOT. At the north end of the beach. Cottages in a garden that borders a small road, and a beachfront packed with brightly painted sailing craft. A/c and hot water. US$35 to US$37 a night.
- **Bali Hyatt Hotel** (387 rooms), Sanur, P.O. Box 392, Denpasar, tel: 8271-7, tlx: 35127. A/c rooms and suites overlooking the sea. Several restaurants, swimming pool, discotheque, convention facilities, broad beach. US$72 to US$400 a night.
- **Bali Seaside Cottages** (111 rooms), Jl. Segara, Sanur, P.O. Box 217, Denpasar. An annex of the Hotel Bali Beach. Private beach bungalows with a/c, hot water and carpeting. Facilities include a swimming pool and 24-hour coffee shop. US$40 to US$65 a night.
- **Bali Sanur Besakih Bungalows** (50 rooms), Jl. Tanjungsari, Sanur, Denpasar, tel: 8423-4, tlx: 35178. Right on the beach. Part of the large "Bali Sanur Bungalows" group, which took over several hotels that failed in the 1970s. Each hotel thus has a different character. All bungalows with a/c and hot water. US$40 to US$45 a night.
- **Bali Sanur Penida View Bungalows** (44 rooms), Jl. Bali Hyatt, Sanur, Denpasar, tel: 8425-6, tlx: 35178. On the beach right next to the Bali Hyatt. All with a/c and hot water. US$45 to US$100 a night.
- **Bali Sanur Puri Dalem Bungalows** (44 rooms), Jl. Raya Sanur, P.O. Box 306, Denpasar, tel: 8421-2, tlx: 35187. On the main road to Denpasar, a 5-minute walk from the beach. All bungalows with a/c and hot water. US$32 to US$45 a night.
- **Gazebo Beach Cottages** (60 rooms), Jl. Tanjung Sari, Sanur, P.O. Box 134, Denpasar, tel: 8300. Private beach with cool 2-storey bungalows in a garden. All with a/c and hot water. US$35 to US$45 a night.
- **Hotel Bali Beach Intercontinental** (605 rooms), Sanur, P.O. Box 275, Denpasar, tel: 8511-7, tlx: 35133, 35129. Older 10-storey Intercontinental hotel with a new 2-storey wing. Private beach, two swimming pools, four restaurants. All rooms with a/c, carpeting, hot water. US$58 to US$180 a night.
- **Hotel Sanur Beach** (310 rooms), Sanur, P.O. Box 279, Denpasar, tel: 8011-5, tlx: 35135. Bungalows attached. All with a/c and hot water. US$55 to US$120.
- **La Taverna Bungalows** (44 rooms), Jl. Tanjungsari, Sanur, Denpasar, tel: 8497. Private beach and elegantly styled rooms. All a/c with hot water, a swimming pool, pizzeria and bar on the beach. US$50 to US$85 a night.
- **Respati Beach Bungalows** (25 rooms), Sanur, P.O. Box 223, Denpasar, tel: 8427. Cottages grouped around a small garden with a private beach. US$32 to US$40 a night.
- **Santrian Beach Hotel** (80 rooms), Jl. Tanjungsari, Sanur, P.O. Box 55, Denpasar, tel: 8181-3. Private seaside bungalows in a spacious garden. US$36 to US$40 a night.
- **Segara Village Hotel** (85 rooms), Jl. Segara, Sanur, P.O. Box 91, Denpasar, tel: 8407-8, 8021-2, tlx: 35134. Distinctive 2-storey cottages 20 metres from the beach. All with a/c and hot water. Swimming pool and tennis courts. US$42 to US$65 a night.
- **Sindhu Beach Hotel** (50 rooms), Jl. Sindhu, Sanur, P.O. Box 181, Denpasar, tel: 8351-2, tlx: 35166. Bungalow hotel on the beach. All with a/c and hot water. US$39 to US$65 a night.
- **Tanjung Sari Hotel** (24 rooms), Jl. Tanjungsari, Sanur, P.O. Box 25, Denpasar, tel: 8441, tlx: 35257 TANSARI. Serene and stylish, with private bungalows by the sea and lovely gardens. Price: US$65 to US$170 a night.
- **Wisma Baruna** (10 rooms), Jl. Sindu, Sanur, Denpasar, tel: 8546. Apartments open onto a wide grass court-yard bordering the sea. All with a/c and hot water. US$40 to US$80 a night.

Intermediate Range (US$15 to US$35 a night)

Bali Sanur Bungalows, at the upper end of the scale, are recommended. All of the other beach bungalow establishments in this category are excellent value and generally quite pleasant, the major consideration being whether you require air-conditioning or not (rooms at the lower end of the scale have only a fan).

- **Abian Irama Inn**, Jl. Tanjungsari, Sanur, Denpasar. Ten minutes from the beach. Some a/c rooms. US$15 to US$36 a night.
- **Bali Sanur Irama Bungalows** (23 rooms), Jl. Tanjungsari, Sanur, Denpasar, tel: 8423-4, tlx: 35178. Right on the beach. The least expensive of the "Bali Sanur Bungalows" group. All a/c with hot water. US$30 to US$35 a night.
- **Diwangkara Beach Hotel** (36 rooms), Jl. Pantai Sanur, Sanur, P.O. Box 120, Denpasar,

tel: 8577, 8412. Private bungalows in a secluded compound just behind the Le Mayeur museum at the north end of the beach strip. Some with a/c and hot water. Swimming pool. One minute from the beach. US$23 to US$35 a night.

- **Hotel Ramayana**, Jl. Tanjungsari, Sanur, Denpasar, tel: 664359. Five minutes from the beach. US$16 with a fan, US$20 with a/c and US$25 for a private bungalow.
- **Laghawa Beach Inn** (25 rooms), Jl. Tanjung Sari, Sanur, Denpasar, tel: 8494, 8214. Cottages with a/c and hot water in a garden. Five minutes from the beach. Good value at US$20 to US$35 a night.
- **Mars Hotel** (14 rooms), Jl. Raya Sanur, Sanur, P.O. Box 95, Denpasar. Five minutes from the beach. Bungalows in a garden. All with a/c and hot water. US$24 a night.
- **Narmada Bali Inn** (17 rooms), Jl. Sindhu, Sanur, P.O. Box 119, Denpasar, tel: 8054. Bungalows in a quiet garden. Two minutes from the beach. All with a/c and hot water. US$28 to US$35 a night.
- **Puri Mas Hotel** (16 rooms), Jl. Raya Sanur, Tanjung Bungkak, Denpasar, 3.5 kms (two miles) from Sanur Beach on the main road to Denpasar. Simple accommodation in a bungalow complex. Some with a/c and hot water. US$22 to US$30 a night.
- **Werdha Pura**, (14 rooms), Jl. Tanjungsari, Sanur, P.O. Box 24, Denpasar. A government-run tourist cottage prototype on the beach. All with a/c and hot water. Inexpensive at US$22 to US$32 a night.

Budget (under US$15 a night)

Cheapest room in Sanur is US$7 a night. Your best bet is the **Tourist Beach Inn**, just 100 metres from the beach. Three bungalow establishments opposite the Post Office—**Sanur Indah**, **Taman Sari** and **Hotel Rani**—give you a bit more space, but are farther from the beach. The **Taman Agung** is the nicest budget place, with well-kept gardens and very quiet. True budget travellers get better value for money in Kuta, however.

- **Hotel Rani**, Jl. Segara, Sanur, Denpasar. Opposite the Post Office, ten minutes from the beach. US$7 to US$15 including tax and service.
- **Hotel Sanur Indah**, Jl. Segara, Sanur, Denpasar. Several *losmen*-style rooms and more expensive bungalows. Ten minutes from the beach. US$7 to US$15 including tax and service.
- **Hotel Taman Sari**, Jl. Segara, Sanur, Denpasar. Next door and about the same as above. US$7 to US$15 including tax and service.
- **Taman Agung Beach Inn** (20 rooms), Jl. Tanjungsari, Sanur, Denpasar, tel: 8549, 8006. Very pleasant losmen-style rooms facing onto a well-kept garden. Five minutes from the beach. No a/c or hot water. US$8 to US$15 a night, including tax, service and breakfast.
- **Tourist Beach Inn** (10 rooms), Jl. Segara, Sanur, P.O. Box 42, Denpasar, tel: 8418. *Losmen*-style rooms around a central courtyard. Very close to the beach and quiet: US$8 to US$12 including tax, service and breakfast.

Dining

The **Tanjung Sari Hotel Restaurant** has a formidable reputation for Indonesian *rijsttafel* and a sublime atmosphere. A bamboo *tingklink* orchestra provides the ideal accompaniment to dinner in a cosy, antique-filled dining area by the beach. The restaurant's new menu has a more creative nouveau-Bali slant, and the famous Bar, designed by Australian artist Donald Friend, is an elevated pavilion overlooking the sea.

At **Kuri Putih**, in the Bali Sanur Irama Bungalows, chef Nyoman Sana of Ubud has at last brought his kitchen to Sanur. Try the barbequed specials from the grill and help yourself to side dishes from a tempting buffet salad bar.

Si Pino's Home of Fine Food, opposite the front gate to the Hotel Bali Beach is another Sanur institution. Mr. Pino is not only Bali's best boxing coach, but also one of its most imaginative cooks.

The **Kul Kul Restaurant** near the Hyatt has an elegant bar and serves good western, Indonesian and Chinese cuisine in its handsome garden pavilion. Book for the dinner-dance night (Batuan's famous Frog Dance troupe). The nearby **Swastika Gardens** is also a great favourite with those who are tired of paying hotel prices. The food is fair and the menu varied enough to satisfy most tastes—try the Balinese speciality, curried duck (*bebek tutu*).

Telaga Naga, opposite the Bali Hyatt, is a spectacularly stylish Szechuanese restaurant in a lake, designed by Hyatt architect Kerry Hill. The food is good and the prices are non-hotel. Try the 'Chicken With Dried Chilli Peppers," the king prawn and the duck dishes.

The best Italian food in Bali is available at **Trattoria Da Marco**, where Reno and Diddit da Marco have guarded their reputation and clientele for 15 years now. Try the grilled fish, *spaghetti carbonara*, bean salad and their steaks—truly the best in Bali.

La Taverna is part of a Hong Kong-based chain of Italian restaurants in Asia. The Sanur branch is a charming bar and open dining area on the beach, with a menu that features imported cheeses, French pepper steak, seafood and pizza from a real pizza oven.

For more local flavours, try the inexpensive **Beach Market** (on Jl. Segara right at the beach), a little outdoor restaurant run by Sanur's mayor. Great for lunch (*sate, nasi goreng* and fresh fried fish) or dinner (grilled lobster), with delicious Balinese desserts, all at unbeatable prices.

The original **Swastika I** (opposite the La Taverna) also has a domestic section, with reliable *nasi campur*, good fruit juices and a variety of Balinese dishes at local prices. Rumah Makan Mini on the by-pass has good budget meals. And the last *warung* (Mak Beng's) on the left on Jl. Raya Sanur (just north of the Bali Beach) has fantastic grilled fish.

For Javanese cuisine, seek out **Adi's Restaurant** at the Renon roundabout (on the road in to Denpasar)—a bit out of the way but worth the trip. Finally, **Meme Disco** and her basket of turtle *sate* are parked in front of the Sanur Police Station every evening from 4 p.m. to 8 p.m. And despite considerable bad press during the World Wildlife Fund's recent conference here, a packet of these grilled morsels with a gin and tonic is still one of the island's best kept culinary secrets.

Sailing

The fleet of native outrigger canoes (*jukung*) lining Sanur's beach, with their brightly coloured Bir Bintang sails, are obviously no longer used for fishing, now that the tourists have taken to chartering them for cruises across the water. The fishermen have wisely banded together into a cooperative to regularize their rates. The standard fee, for a sail around the lagoon, is US$8 regardless of the time.

Kuta Beach

Kuta in the 80s is like a malignant sea-side Carnaby Street of the 60s. Chaotic, noisy, lots of hype, but a great playground. Originally what drew visitors to Kuta was the wide beach and the surf, and it still has the best seafront on the island, now cluttered with hundreds of hotels, restaurants, bars, boutiques, travel agencies, antique shops, car and bike rentals, banks, cassette shops and wall-to-wall tourists. Though there are now many first-class hotels, the 5-km (3-mile) strip still caters best for the economy traveller who likes to be in the thick of things. The Legian end of the beach is the best place to stay for any period of time—much quieter and more relaxed.

Accommodation

Kuta Beach has so many bungalows, beach hotels and homestays (*losmen*) that no list could ever be complete, nor is a list really needed. Drop in and shop around. The difference between Kuta and Sanur is that one has far more choices in the lower price range here. Reservations are necessary for the larger hotels during July to September and December to January.

First Class (above US$35 a night)

There are two luxury class hotels on the Kuta side, the **Bali Oberoi** and **Pertamina Cottages**. The Oberoi's restaurant, Kura Kura, is excellent, and breakfast *al fresco* at the Oberoi is one of Bali's great treats. Pertamina Cottages features tennis courts and convention facilities.

There are also several comfortable first-class bungalow resorts, notably the **Kuta Beach Palace**, the **Kuta Beach Hotel** and the **Kartika Plaza**. The **Legian Beach Hotel** offers air-conditioned rooms on the beach for under US$40 a night. *Prices quoted do not include the obligatory 21 per cent tax and service surcharge.*

- **Bali Oberoi** (75 rooms), Kayu Aya, P.O. Box 351, Kuta, tel: 25581-5 tlx: 35125 OBHOTEL DPR. Away from it all at the far end of the beach. Tasteful air-conditioned beachside bungalows, in an attractive garden, with a large swimming pool. US$70 to US$250 a night.

- **Beach Hotel Kartika Plaza** (120 rooms), Kuta Beach, P.O. Box 84, Denpasar, tel: 22454, 25081-5. Beachside rooms and bungalows in a large garden. All with a/c and hot water. Swimming pool. US$40 to US$84 a night.
- **Kuta Beach Club** (83 rooms) Jl. Bakungsari, P.O. Box 226, Kuta, tel: 25056, tlx: 35138 KUTA CLUB. A bungalow-style hotel 150 metres from the beach. With a/c or fan and hot water. US$38 to US$75 a night.
- **Kuta Beach Palace** (107 rooms), Legian, Kuta, tel: 25858, tlx: 35234. Large new first-class hotel up in Legian with 3-storey wings overlooking the sea. All with a/c and hot water. Swimming pool. US$42 to US$85 a night.
- **Legian Beach Hotel** (110 rooms), Jl. Melasti, Legian, P.O. Box 308, Denpasar, tel: 26811-2, tlx: 35104. Right on the beach in the middle of Legian. Excellent value. US$36 to US$38 a night.
- **Pertamina Cottages** (156 rooms), Kuta Beach, P.O. Box 121, Kuta, tel: 23061, tlx: 35131. Facilities include several restaurants, banquet and convention halls, tennis courts and a swimming pool. All rooms a/c with carpeting and hot water. US$68 to US$620 a night.
- **Natour's Kuta Beach Hotel** (32 rooms), Jl. Pantai Kuta, P.O. Box 393, Kuta, tel: 25791. Opened in 1959 on the site of Ktut Tantri's house, it is the oldest and most spacious of Kuta's hotels. In the middle of Kuta. Quiet bungalows and rooms surrounding a patio garden by the sea. All with a/c and hot water. US$48 to US$62 a night.

Intermediate Range (US$15 to US$35 a night)

If you are willing to do without air-conditioning you can find many beautiful bungalows in the US$20-to-US$30 range. **Poppies Cottages** is one of the most popular establishments, almost always fully booked. And the **Yasa Samudra** puts you right on the beach in Kuta.

For more privacy and for longer stays, the **Legian Sunset Beach**, the **Blue Ocean** (both in Legian) and **Nova Nova** (farther down, in Seminyak) are among the favourites (with many private bungalows renting for about US$10 to US$15 a night, less by the week or the month).

- **Kuta Cottages** (40 rooms), Jl. Bakung Sari, P.O. Box 300, Kuta, tel: 24100. Small bungalows with a fan just back from the beach. US$15 to US$25 a night.
- **Sunset Beach Hotel** (16 rooms), Legian, Kuta, P.O. Box 346, Denpasar, tel: 6721 ext. 60. Right on the beach. US$24 to US$51 a night.
- **Mandara Cottages** (27 rooms), Jl. Padma, Legian, Kuta, tel: 25785. Bungalows 100 metres from the beach. Some with air-conditioning. US$22 to $35 a night.
- **Poppies Cottages** (24 rooms), Poppies Gang, Kuta, tel: 23059. 300 metres from the beach. US$24 a night.
- **Ramayana Seaside Cottages** (45 rooms), Jl. Bakung Sari, Kuta, P.O. Box 334, Denpasar, tel: 6781-5, 5058, tlx: 35149. 150 metres from the beach. Some rooms with a/c, many with fan. US$21 to US$36 a night.
- **Yasa Samudra** (34 rooms), Jl. Pantai Kuta, Kuta, P.O. Box 53, Denpasar, tel: 25305. Private

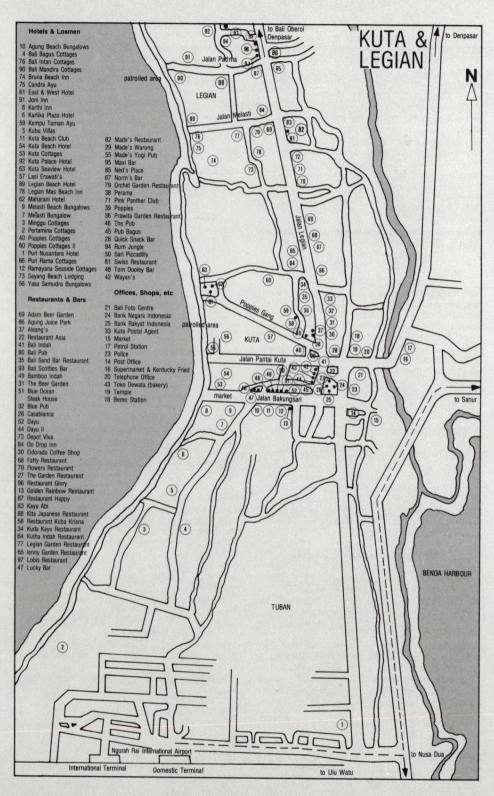

KUTA & LEGIAN

N

Hotels & Losmen

10 Agung Beach Bungalows
4 Bali Bagus Cottages
76 Bali Intan Cottages
90 Bali Mandira Cottages
74 Bruna Beach Inn
75 Candra Ayu
61 East & West Hotel
91 Joni Inn
8 Karthi Inn
6 Kartika Plaza Hotel
59 Kempu Taman Ayu
5 Kubu Villas
11 Kuta Beach Club
54 Kuta Beach Hotel
53 Kuta Cottages
92 Kuta Palace Hotel
63 Kuta Seaview Hotel
57 Lasi Erawati's
62 Legian Beach Hotel
78 Legian Mas Beach Inn
62 Maharani Hotel
9 Melasti Beach Bungalows
7 Melasti Bungalow
3 Minggu Cottages
2 Pertamina Cottages
40 Poppies Cottages
60 Poppies Cottages II
1 Puri Nusantara Hotel
66 Puri Rama Cottages
12 Ramayana Seaside Cottages
73 Sayang Beach Lodging
56 Yasa Samudra Bungalows

Restaurants & Bars

69 Adam Beer Garden
86 Agung Juice Park
37 Aleang's
22 Restaurant Asia
41 Bali Indah
80 Bali Pub
35 Bali Sand Bar Restaurant
93 Bali Scotties Bar
Bamboo Indah
31 The Beer Garden
Blue Ocean
    Steak House
32 Blue Pub
26 Casablanca
52 Dayu
44 Dayu II
Depot Viva
84 Do Drop Inn
30 Eldorado Coffee Shop
68 Fatty Restaurant
70 Flowers Restaurant
27 The Garden Restaurant
96 Restaurant Glory
13 Golden Rainbow Restaurant
87 Restaurant Happy
Kayu Abi
88 Kita Japanese Restaurant
58 Restaurant Kuba Krisna
34 Kuda Kayu Restaurant
64 Kutha Indah Restaurant
77 Legian Garden Restaurant
65 Jenny Garden Restaurant
97 Lobis Restaurant
47 Lucky Bar

82 Made's Restaurant
29 Made's Warung
55 Made's Yogi Pub
95 Maxi Bar
8 Ned's Place
67 Norm's Bar
79 Orchid Garden Restaurant
38 Perama
71 Pink Panther Club
39 Poppies
36 Prawita Garden Restaurant
46 The Pub
45 Pub Bagus
28 Quick Snack Bar
94 Rum Jungle
50 Sari Piccadilly
81 Swiss Restaurant
48 Tom Dooley Bar
42 Wayan's

Offices, Shops, etc

21 Bali Foto Centre
24 Bank Negara Indonesia
25 Bank Rakyat Indonesia
33 Kuta Postal Agent
15 Market
17 Petrol Station
23 Police
14 Post Office
16 Supermarket & Kentucky Fried
20 Telephone Office
43 Toko Dewata (bakery)
19 Temple
18 Bemo Station

to Bali Oberoi Denpasar

to Denpasar

Jalan Padma

patrolled area

LEGIAN

Jalan Melasti

Jalan Legian

Poppies Gang

patrolled area

KUTA

Jalan Pantai Kuta

Jalan Bakungsari

market

to Sanur

BENOA HARBOUR

TUBAN

Ngurah Rai International Airport

International Terminal

Domestic Terminal

to Ulu Watu

to Nusa Dua

seaside bungalows on the beach in the middle of Kuta. Dining room famed for its fresh seafood. US$27 to US$30 a night.

Budget (under US$15 a night)

There are upwards of 300 *losmen* or homestays in the Kuta-Legian area, where rooms rent for only US$2 to US$10 a night. Often you'll be approached at the airport or at the bus terminal on arrival in Bali. The best way to find a room, though, is just to walk around in any area that you fancy—whether near Kuta or Legian, near the beach, or far back in the coconut groves, away from the crowds.

Rooms are available for less than US$3 a night, just a bed and four walls, with a shared splash bath and outhouse. For US$5 to US$6 you get a private bath and a few frills. For US$10 you can get your own bungalow up in Legian or beyond with electricity and a fan. Some have luxurious garden bathrooms and second-storey sleeping lofts with bamboo staircases.

Dining

New restaurants seem to open daily in Kuta, from small fruit salad and yoghurt stands by the beach to large Chinese, French or seafood establishments. The quality of the food goes up and down as cooks come and go, so we list here only a few old standbys where you can hardly ever go wrong. Ask around though for tips on the latest "in" restaurant.

Made's Warung on Jl. Pantai hasn't missed a beat in its metamorphosis from one of only two foodstalls on the main street of a sleepy fishing village, to a hip Cafe Voltaire in the St. Tropez of the East. It has great food (spare ribs, Thai salad, escargots, turtle steaks, home-made ice cream, chocolate mousse, capuccino, fresh squeezed orange and carrot juices, breakfast specials).

Poppies, down a narrow lane, is another Kuta fixture. Avocado seafood salads, pate, tacos, grilled lobster, steaks, shishkabob and tall mixed drinks pack this garden idyll to capacity during the peak tourist seasons. Get there early to get a table.

Bali Indah and Lenny's are both first-rate for Chinese cuisine and seafood. Try the crab-in-black-bean-sauce at Bali Indah. And for fresh lobster or fried tuna fish steaks, go over to the **Yasa Samudra Hotel** (at the end of Jl. Pantai Kuta) and dine under the stars by the sea.

In Legian, the **Blue Ocean Hotel's** beach-side cafe is a popular gathering point for breakfast and lunch. And farther down, in Seminyak, **La Marmite** (also known as **Chez Gado-Gado**) serves Balinese "nouvelle cuisine" in a secluded open-air location by the beach. The after-dinner disco on Saturday nights is the happening.

The **Kura Kura** restaurant in the Bali Oberoi hotel, several kilometres beyond Legian, is perfect for that special occasion. A quiet pool-side terrace overlooking the ocean. Go there for the sunset, dinner and drinks. Very romantic. Try the pepper duck, or grilled lobster.

And Bali's only serious Japanese restaurant,

Shima, is located in the Pertamina Cottage Hotel, several kilometres south of Kuta at Tuban. Two Japanese chefs prepare a full range of Japanese dishes.

Nusa Dua

As the newcomer on the scene, Nusa Dua is at a bit of a disadvantage because it is rather isolated from the rest of Bali. On the other hand, the new hotels here have tried to make up for this by providing a "total" hotel environment—everything you could possibly ask for is available on the premises. A few restaurants and souvenir shops are sprouting up at the edges of Nusa Dua, and in a few years this area will probably become another Sanur. But in the meantime, Nusa Dua is a remarkably peaceful place.

The newly revamped **Hotel Bualu**, offers a comprehensive water sports package, lush gardens and horse-drawn buggies (*dokar*) for romantic, tropical-evening rides up and down "hotel row." And the brand new **Nusa Dua Beach Hotel** offers the ultimate in opulence—a palatial Balinese setting, a health club, squash courts, three restaurants and a discotheque.

Eleven new luxury hotels have opened in 1985 (so new that we could not get the addresses before our press deadline). There are no intermediate or budget hotels in the area.

● **Hotel Bualu** (50 rooms), Nusa Dua, tel: 71310, 71320, tlx: 35231 BUALU. Lush tropical gardens, a swimming pool and deluxe rooms. 100 metres from the beach. Sailing, scuba and skin diving, wind surfing are included. US$45 to US$85 a night.

● **Hotel Nusa Dua** (450 rooms), Nusa Dua, tel: 71210, tlx: 35206. A hotel on a scale of grandeur that even Bali's rajas never conceived of in their wildest dreams. Huge swimming pool, three restaurants, squash courts, tennis courts, health club, discotheque, large beach front. US$65 to US$500 a night.

Denpasar

Accommodation

If you really must stay in Denpasar, the old **Bali Hotel** on Jln. Veteran or the **Pemecutan Palace Hotel** are the only places to consider. The Bali Hotel was built in the early 1930s and was once the colonial oasis in Bali—the *rijsttafel* is still good and the swimming pool courtyard charming.

There are scores of other hotels in the US$3-to-US$20 category. Many are located on Jl. Diponegoro around the **Hotel Denpasar**. Two that are popular with foreigners are the **Adyasa** and the **Two Brothers Inn**.

● **Adyasa** (20 rooms), Jl. Nakula 23, Denpasar, tel: 2679. Losmen-style rooms arranged around a central garden. US$4 to US$8 including breakfast.

● **Hotel Denpasar** (78 rooms), Jl. Diponegoro 103, P.O. Box 111, Denpasar, tel: 26336, 26363. Half of the rooms have a/c and hot water. A favourite of large Indonesian tour groups from Java. US$6 to US$30 a night.

DENPASAR

1. Bus Station (Gilimanuk Singaraja Surabaya)
2. Petrol Station
3. Hospital
4. KOKAR, Conservatory of Performing Arts
5. Bank Indonesia
6. Police
7. Stadium
8. Garuda & Merpati Airline Offices
9. Radio Station
10. Telephone, Telegram & Telex Office
11. Market, Bus Station (Amlapura, Bangli, Klungkung, Ubud)
12. Abian Kapas Art Centre
13. Cinema
14. Shopping Centre, Night Market
15. Market
16. Traffic Police
17. Shopping Centre
18. Puputan Square
19. Museum Bali
20. Cinema
21. Taxi, Bus Tickets, Night Market
22. Bemo Station to Kuta
23. Cinema
24. Army Hospital
25. Petrol Station
26. Police
27. Governor's Office
28. General Post Office
29. Hospital
30. Immigration
31. Tourist Information
32. University
33. Bali Hotel
34. Puri Pemecutan Hotel

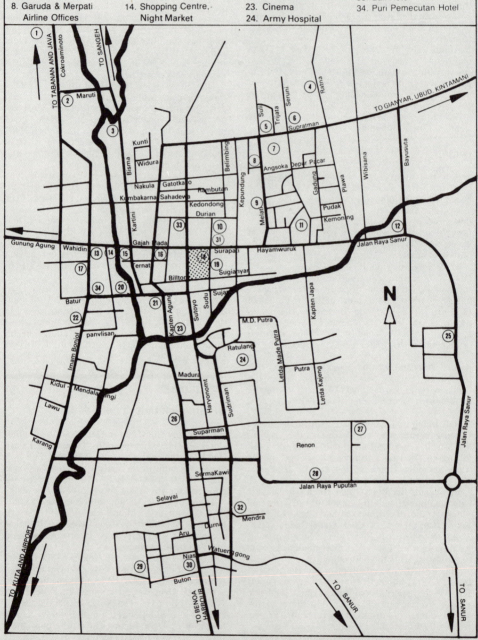

• **Hotel Pemecutan Palace** (44 rooms), Jl. Thamrin 2, Denpasar, tel: 23491. This hotel takes one side of the extensive Badung palace. Some rooms with a/c and hot water. US$15 to US$24 a night.

• **Natour's Bali Hotel** (71 rooms), Jl. Veteran 2, P.O. Box 3, Denpasar, tel: 25681-5. Centrally located in Denpasar, just a block from the main intersection and town square. Good restaurant and bar. Many rooms with a/c and hot water. US$20 to US$40 a night.

• **Two Brothers Inn**, Jl. Imam Bonjol, Gang VII/5, Denpasar. Friendly losmen for budget travellers. Near the Tegal *bemo* terminal. US$2 to US$3 a night.

Dining

Denpasar has the best Chinese and Indonesian restaurants on Bali, so if you are passing through or have errands to run here, be sure to stop in for a meal too.

A popular little streetside restaurant, half hidden from view behind an array of potted palm trees on Jl. Gajah Mada near the banks, is the **Puri Selera** serving good Chinese food, such as asparagus and crab soup, frog's legs and sweet-sour pork.

Most fun in Denpasar is the **Night Market** just off Jalan Gajah Mada where portable kitchens on wheels provide roasted satay, fried rice, noodle soup and hot drinks.

For local fare, the expatriate's favourite is **Rumah Makan Betty** on Jl. Kartini, which has a not-so-spicy menu of Javanese and Chinese dishes. Try the *tahu goreng kentang* (beancurd and potato curry), *bubur ayam* (rice porridge with chicken) and their *nasi campur*.

The Balinese favourite, meanwhile, is the **Rumah Makan Wardani** in Tapakgangsul, a modest diner serving traditional dishes (daytime only). For a full range of Indonesian chicken dishes— soups, fried chicken legs, liver *sate*, curries—visit the ever-popular **Kartini Restaurant**, diagonally opposite the Indra Cinema near the petrol pump.

The **Gajah Mada Restaurant** near the traffic lights on Jl. Gajah Mada also serves top-notch Javanese food. Their *ayam lontong* and curry dishes are a gourmet's delight.

Ubud

Accommodation

Accommodation in Ubud does not have the modern luxuries of most international hotels, but it does have a charm that you cannot find elsewhere.

• **Hotel Menara**, across the street from Ubud's art museum, is simply furnished. 9 rooms. Price: US$2 to US$10. Breakfast or all meals may be included in the tariff.

• **Hotel Mutiara**, Small and well-kept rooms surrounding a garden patio with a dining pavilion. 6 rooms. Price: US$8 to US$13 including meals.

• **Hotel Puri Saren**. Home of the Cokorda Agung, head of Ubud's royal family. Bungalows in private courtyard and gardens, are decorated with Balinese antiques. 14 bungalows. Price: US$15 to US$24 including meals.

• **Hotel Tjampuhan**. Bungalows and swimming pool beautifully located on a green hillside above the confluence of two rivers. 26 rooms. Price: US$7 including meals.

• **Hotel Uboed**. A Balinese home. Quiet bungalows around a neatly swept courtyard. 18 rooms. Price: US$5 to US$10.

• **Losmen Mustika**. Boardinghouse on the main road 200 yards from the village centre. Very simple and inexpensive furniture. You eat out and sleep in, as in the *losmen* style. 5 rooms. Price: US$1.50. Coffee or tea included.

• **Puri Saraswati**. Newly built bungalows on a lawn adjacent to Ubud's old temple and lake gardens. 6 Bungalows. Price: US$8 to US$25 including breakfast and tea.

• **Ananda Cottages**. A new hotel with 10 bungalows. The price of US$15 to US$20 includes breakfast.

• **Hans Snel's Bungalows.** Five cottages in the artist's garden home. Price: US$20 to US$30. Breakfast included.

Dining

The cuisine here, like the village itself, is Balinese and unpretentious, with meals often served on an open pavilion in a garden. Minced meat on skewers, Balinese style, along with white rice and a number of fish, meat and vegetable dishes make up the daily menu at the **Tjampuhan Hotel**.

For informal meals, the little snack bar in front of **Hotel Munara** is ever-ready with refreshments and snacks. **Hotel Uboed** and **Puri Sarawati Hotel** will prepare a local meal upon request.

At the foot of the Tjampuhan bridge stands **Murni's Warung**, the sign outside proclaiming "the best hamburgers this side of the black stump"—and so they are! Also magnificent fruit salads and yoghurt. Murni serves all kinds of excellent Western and Chinese food at reasonable prices.

The **Cafe Lotus** at Puri Saraswati in the centre of Ubud serves delicious Western and Balinese cuisine, including pasta dishes, salads, omelettes and cups of frothy capuccino. Excellent cakes also.

Lombok

If the "tourist scene" on Bali is really getting to you, then Lombok is an excellent escape. Those with only a few days on Bali should probably leave Lombok for the next trip. But if you have a month on Bali and would like to see more of Indonesia without travelling great distances, Lombok is perfect. And for the jaded expatriate Bali or Jakarta resident, Lombok is a must.

For any traveller, a three day excursion is a complete enough sampler of Lombok's attractions— all of its sights are located within an hour's drive of the old capital, Cakranegara. A week or more is needed if you intend to go diving at Gili Air or climb to the summit of Mount Rinjani.

Route	Dep.	Arr.	Days	one-way economy fare US$
DPS — AMI				
Merpati	08.15	09.45	Daily	15
	10.20	11.50	Daily	
Bouraq	07.45	09.10	Mon. Wed. Thur. Sun.	15
AMI — DPS				
Merpati	10.15	09.45	Daily	15
	14.40	14.50	Mon. Wed. Sat.	
	15.20	14.50	Tue. Thur. Fri. Sun.	
Bouraq	12.05	11.30	Mon. Wed. Thur. Sun.	15

CITY CODES: DPS-Denpasar; AMI-Mataram.

Choose between a quick 20-minute flight from Bali's Ngurah Rai to Lombok's Selaparang Airport (fare is only US$15 each way on Merpati—*see* box for schedules) or a leisurely cruise on the modern ocean ferry which shuttles between Padang Bai, on Bali's eastern coast, and the port of Lembar on Lombok's west coast. The six-hour sea passage, with the majestic volcanic peaks of Bali and Lombok in the distance, is well worth the inconvenience of travelling all the way out to and from the ports.

The ferry departs twice daily from Padang Bai (Bali) to Lembar (Lombok), at 8:30 a.m. and 1:30 p.m. From Sanur or Kuta, it takes more than two hours to get to Padang Bai by private car,

three hours or more by public transport, so get an early start. Better yet, go to East Bali the day before and spend the night in a beach bungalow at Candi Dasa, just 20 minutes from Padang Bai.

Ferry tickets are US$4 each way first class, US$3 and US$2.25, second and third class respectively. Motorcycles are charged US$3.50 and cars a rather steep US$45 for passage. There is a snack bar on board serving *nasi rawon*, soft drinks, beer, coffee and tea. Or, buy food packets from vendors at the port before departing.

The return ferry from Lembar to Padang Bai departs at 9 a.m. and 2 p.m. Strange to say, the return fares are slightly higher (only about five per cent though).

Orientation

The port of Lembar, where the ferry arrives from Bali, is located about 20 kms (12 miles) to the south of Mataram. Lombok's Selaparang Airport is right in Mataram and no more than three kms from any hotel in the city area. A daily motorboat ferry departs for Alas on Sumbawa from the port of Labuhan Lombok, on Lombok's eastern shore. A trunk highway cuts right across the island, from Ampenan to Labuhan Lombok, a distance of only 76 kms (48 miles).

The Ampenan-Mataram-Cakranegara stretch is the island's main business, administrative and shopping district. Call at the West Nusa Tenggara Regional Tourist Office (DIPARDA)—Jl. Langko 70, Ampenan, tel: 21866, 21730—for brochures and maps of the island. They haven't much info on cultural activities though.

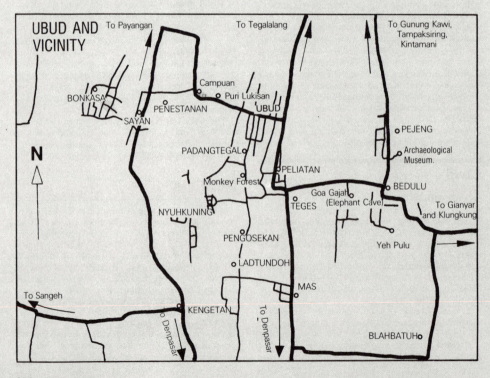

UBUD AND VICINITY

Women should be aware that naked thighs and plunging necklines are severely frowned upon, particularly by Lombok's Muslim majority (this applies particularly to towns on the eastern and southern parts of the island, where the staunchest Muslims live). Cases of harassment have been reported and women are advised not to travel alone outside of the urban areas. If you keep yourself discreetly covered, though, you should have no problems.

Getting Around

Once in Lombok, transport is easy, though it is time consuming to rely upon public transport. Taxis and mini-buses (*bemos*) are readily available for charter. You really need wheels to get around at your own pace to some of the out of the way places. Bring a motor bike from Bali on the ferry (rental cars are not supposed to leave Bali). It is possible to rent motorbikes in Ampenan and Mataram for US$4 to US$6 per day. Ask at your hotel, or at any motorcycle shop (you must have an international or Indonesian license).

Lombok's Selaparang Airport is right in Mataram, so the taxi fare to any hotel in the urban Ampenan/Mataram/Cakranegara conglomerate will be no more than US$3 (you may be able to bargain for less). Major hotels will pick you up for free. Call them from the airport or contact their representative in the arrival hall. To Suranadi, expect to pay up to US$7 with some bargaining, , up to US$10 to Tetebatu. You may charter a taxi for a day-trip around the island for between US$20 and US$30 depending on the itinerary. Do this through your hotel or get one at the airport. Try to get a Lombok Balinese driver who speaks English. The taxis here are all old cars not permitted to operate on Bali any more.

Bemo and buses service all towns on the island. Buy your *bemo* ticket at the snack bar on the ferry for the ride into Mataram from the port of Lembar (US$0.75). The central *bemo* and bus terminal is at the crossroads at Sweta, just to the east of Cakranegara and there is a signboard here displaying the official fares to all points on the island.

Ampenan to Sweta—(Rp 100)
Lembar to Sweta—(Rp 500)
Sweta to Narmada—(Rp 100)
Narmada to Suranadi—(Rp 150)
Sweta to Praya (central Lombok)—(Rp 500)
Sweta to Pemenang (northwest coast)—(Rp 500)
Sweta to Bayan (northern Lombok)—(Rp 1,250)
Sweta to Labuhan Lombok (eastern Lombok)—
    (Rp 1,250)

You can charter a *bemo* for the day for between US$15 and US$20 and they will take you anywhere on the island. *Bemos* are slow and uncomfortable, though, so you are better off paying a bit more for a taxi (perhaps with an English speaking driver).

Airlines/Travel Agents

Tours of Lombok can be arranged (try Rita Tours), but you can just as easily get one of the English speaking taxi drivers at the airport and negotiate a fee for a day-trip around the island (up to US$30). For an expedition up to the top of Mt. Rinjani, including food, tents, sleeping bags and a guide (all for US$75), contact Mr. Batubara at Wisma Triguna, on Jl. Koperasi, Ampenan. Most airlines and travel agents are close to each other on the main street (Jl. Langko) in Ampenan.

● **Bouraq Airways**, Jl. Langko, Ampenan, tel: 22670.
● **Garuda Airways**, Jl. Langko, Ampenan, tel: 23762.
● **Maju Gembira Tours & Travel**, Jl. Langko, Ampenan, tel: 23621.
● **Merpati Nusantara Airlines**, Jl. Langko, Ampenan, tel: 21757.
● **Rita Tours & Travel**, Jl. Cempaka 29A, Mataram, tel: 23998.
● **Swastika Tours & Travel**, Jl. Langko, Ampenan, tel: 21037.

Accommodation

Nestled high in the west Lombok hills, but only a 30-minute drive from the airport, is the old **Hotel Suranadi** dating from colonial times. Adjacent to the Suranadi temple and surrounded by a nature reserve, the hotel boasts spectacular views and cool, serene evenings. Its cottages wrap around a large spring-fed swimming pool and several concrete tennis courts. The pool-side restaurant, serving Chinese food, is excellent if a bit expensive. A variety of rooms are available from US$7 a night (for a single with external bath) on up to US$30 for a private air-conditioned bungalow. There is also a *losmen* nearby with rooms for only US$4.

Lombok's north-western reefs are amongst the most spectacular in the world. Aquatic enthusiasts stay at the **Sasaka Beach Hotel** at Meniting, five kms (three miles) north of Ampenan, and travel daily from here to Pantai Sira or Pantai Pemenang beaches and Pulau Gili Air island (cross to the islands from Bangkal harbour by motorboat or local sailing *prahu* for US$3). Rooms at the Sasaka Beach start at only US$10, on up to US$25 a night for an air-conditioned bungalow (plus 21 per cent tax and service—substantial discounts are available for longer stays). There are several homestays at Sira beach and on Gili Air island for US$3.50 a night including rather skimpy meals. Or stay at Pak Majid's Homestay on Gili Trawangan island for only US$3 a day with three square home-cooked meals. Bring a mosquito net.

Wisma Melati in Ampenan is the island's best hotel. Air-conditioned rooms here start at US$18 a night on up to US$30 (including tax, service and continental breakfast). The **Selaparang Hotel** in Cakranegara is also very pleasant—conveniently close to the temples and markets in Cakra. Rooms are US$7 with a fan, on up to US$17 for air-conditioning, hot water and TV. Both hotels have restaurants and they will pick you up at the airport on arrival (call them from Bali or on arrival). Just across from the Selaparang, the **Hotel Mataram** in Cakra has air-conditioned rooms for as little as US$14 (including tax, service and breakfast).

The delightful mountain resort of **Tetebatu** (Wisma Soejono) has recently added some bungalows to its restaurant complex—a much simpler mountain alternative to the Hotel Suranadi. US$7.50 a night for a double.

Air Buka, reached via Kembang Kering in central Lombok, is another very reasonably priced highland spring resort with bungalows. And there are many other *losmens* and homestays found throughout the island.

Intermediate Class (US$15 to US$35 a night)

● **Hotel Mataram** (18 rooms), Jl. Selaparang, Cakranegara, tel: 23411, 23415.
● **Sasaka Beach Hotel** (24 rooms), Jl. Meniting, Ampenan, tel: 22711.
● **Selaparang Hotel** (19 rooms), Jl. Selaparang 40-42, Cakranegara, tel: 22670, 23235.
● **Suranadi Hotel**, Suranadi, Narmada, tel: 23686.
● **Wisma Melati** (22 rooms), Jl. Langko 80, Ampenan, tel: 23780.

Budget (under US$15 a night)

● **Air Buka Homestay**, Air Buka.
● **Hotel Kertayoga**, Jl. Selaparang 82, Mataram. US$7 to US$12 with private bath, fan and breakfast.
● **Hotel Pusaka** (48 rooms), Jl. S. Hasannudin 23, Cakranegara, tel: 23119. US$5 with private bath and fan. Centrally located.
● **Hotel Tigamas**, Kampung Melayu Tengah, just off Jl. Pabean, Ampenan. US$1.50 a night.
● **Losmen Pabean**, Jl. Pabean 146, Ampenan. Right near the water front on the main street, opposite several restaurants. A popular place with budget travellers. US$2.50 a night.
● **Wisma Soejono**, Tete Batu. Several bungalows for US$7.50 a night.
● **Wisma Triguna**, Jl. Koperasi, Ampenan. A new *losmen* near the airport. US$3 for a spacious room with attached bath.

Dining

The Balinese roast suckling pig, *babi guling*, done by the Lombok Balinese beats anything on the mother island. Arrange a feast (through your hotel or driver) and ask if it can be served in one of the spacious courtyards of a Lombok Balinese home. Ask for *tuak* (palm toddy) to go with the pig, and a folk dance (also easily arranged).

The old Chinese restaurants on Jl. Pabean in Ampenan (the **Tjirebon** and the **Pabean**) are central and good, a favourite hang-out of budget travellers. The Tjirebon has cold beer and steak with chips (don't eat the salad).

The Arab restaurants of Mataram in some cases serve both Yemeni and Lombok dishes. The **Taliwang** on the main street (Jl. Pejanggik) specializes in *ayam pelicing*—the searing hot curried chicken that is Lombok's speciality. The **Garden House Restaurant** nearby serves both Indonesian and Chinese food.

In Cakranegara, there are many restaurants along Jl. Selaparang. The **Asia** and the **Harum**

serve Chinese food. The **Minang** has *nasi Padang* and the **Istimewa** and the **Hari Ini** both serve *ayam pelicing*. For western dishes, go to the **Hotel Selaparang**.

Both the **Hotel Suranadi** (in Suranadi) and the **Wisma Soejono** (in Tete Batu) enjoy good reputations for tasty, fresh fish from their icy ponds. If you are staying in town, you could go there for lunch (and for a swim, at the Suranadi).

Shopping

Traditional textiles are the best buy on the island. Visit the villages where the threads are dyed and woven by hand: **Sukarare** (for *tenun Lombok*), **Pujung** (for *kain lambung*), **Purbasari** (for *kain Purbasari*) and **Balimurti** (for the sacred *beberut* cloths). **Labuhan Lombok** on the east coast also produces fine blankets.

The best weaving factories for contemporary textiles are found in Cakranegara. Many of Bali's resident Italian couturiers buy fabrics from Pak Abdullah of **C.V. Rinjani** next door to the Hotel Selaparang (on Jl. Selaparang). His stockroom often has leftovers from bolts of top designer fabrics. His silk *sarungs* and matching *selendang* scarves are highly regarded among the rag cognescenti of Bali and Jakarta. The **Selamat Ryadi** weaving factory in the Arab quarter on Jl. Ukir Kawi (one block north and one block west of the Pura Mayura water palace) is another excellent source of yard goods. The **Balimurti** factory nearby produces weavings in the traditional Purbasari style.

Lombok's bamboo baskets are extremely fine and sturdy. Many are produced in the eastern Lombok villages of **Kotaraja** and **Loyok**. Ceramic pots and earthenwares are also beautifully crafted and elegantly shaped here. Shop for them also at the main market by the bus and *bemo* terminal in **Sweta**, or in the **Cakranegara Market** to the west of the Pura Meru temple.

There is an antique shop known as **Sudirman's**, a few hundred metres down a side lane from Jl. Pabean in Ampenan (enter across from the *bemo* station, and ask for directions). Enterprising antique merchants will often call on you in your hotel. They have old Chinese ceramics, ceremonial weavings and antique carvings. Bargain hard and nonchalantly—never appear eager or rushed.

There are a few factories in Lombok doing a booming trade in primitive bottletops, wooden spoons and carved cannisters—in some cases these are excellent reproductions of traditional pieces. Most of what you see is new and made to look antique.

The six-km (four-mile) main street running through the centre of Ampenan, Mataram and Cakranegara (Jl. Langko/Pejanggik/Selaparang) is one continuous shopping mall.

Climbing Mt. Rinjani

Lombok's central highlands, circling the upper reaches of Mt. Rinjani (Indonesia's second highest peak at 3,726 metres/12,220 ft), are sparsely populated due to the vagaries of climate and the rough terrain. Up to about 2,000 metres (6,500 ft) the mountain is covered in dense jungle and forest, but above this level, scattered stands of pine and low scrub take over. The volcano's windswept rim is quite barren, and from here you have spectacular morning views across Lombok to Bali and Sumbawa on either side. The only time to attempt the climb is during the dry season (June to October) and even then you must plan your trip to reach the top in the early morning hours, because swirling mists envelop the peak soon after 10 a.m.

Inside the vast crater is a large lake, Segara Anak ('Child of the Sea'). The steep descent from the rim down into the crater is precarious, and only possible from a single point at the northern side. Not for the timid.

It is important to have warm clothing (temperatures can drop below freezing near the summit at night), a tent, boots or sturdy shoes, a sleeping bag, a water bottle, cooking utensils and enough food for up to four days (rice, tinned meats, biscuits, bread, instant noodles, coffee, tea, sugar, spices, chocolates and fruit). Camping equipment can be rented in Ampenan from Mr. Batubara at the Wisma Triguna Hotel on Jl. Koperasi for about US$15. Cooking utensils may be borrowed or rented along with guides and porters at villages along the way, together with some snacks, but you are better off buying most of your provisions before setting out (remember to bring along extra food for the guide).

There are two principal ways of approaching the crater's rim. Many people begin from the eastern hill town of **Sapit**, which can be reached by *bemo* from the main highway at **Pringgabaya** (about 3 hours and US$1.25 altogether from the central Sweta terminal). From Sapit it is about a five-hour hike along a well-worn trail up to the villages of **Sembulan Bumbung** and **Sembulan Lawang**. You can make arrangements through the village chief of Sembulan Lawang for a guide (and porters) to the summit and spend the night here. The next, hike up to a base camp just below the rim and spend the night, so as to make the final one-hour ascent in the early morning when it is clear. Return via Sembulan Lawang and Sapit, or continue on to the north coast at Bayan.

A shorter and easier route begins from the northern village of **Bayan**, reached via the north-western coastal road by bus (a three-hour journey from Sweta costing US$1.25). From Bayan, where the bus stops, you may be able to get a lift on a truck farther on to the end of the road at **Batu Kok**, where you should contact a school teacher known as Pak Guru Bakti to make arrangments for guides and porters. If you arrive early enough in the day (before noon), you may be able to begin the ascent immediately. Otherwise spend the night with Pak Bakti. From Batu Kok it is about a six-hour hike past the traditional Sasak village of **Senaro** to a base camp just below the crater's rim. Camp overnight here, and climb up to the summit early in the morning. From this point you may want to turn back, or you can descend into the crater and spend the night comfortably by the crater lake (after soaking away some of your sore muscles in the adjacent hot springs). The return journey to Batu Kok from within the crater takes a full 12 hours and you will

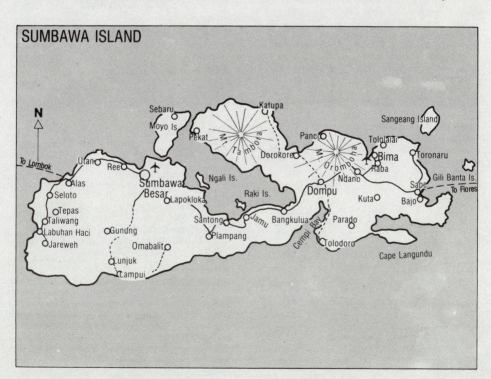

SUMBAWA ISLAND

have to spend the night here unless you have your own transportation, as the last bus leaves Bayan for Sweta at 6 p.m.

Nusa Tenggara

Sumbawa
Komodo
Sumba
Flores

Travel to Sumbawa and the islands to the east requires a rudimentary knowledge of Indonesian and a spirit of adventure—not to mention a willingness to endure physical discomforts. Over the last few years communications have improved remarkably and island-hopping has been made easier.

Hotels and *losmen* are found only in the district capitals. In **Mataram** (Lombok) and **Kupang** (West Timor) there are hotels approaching international standards at very reasonable rates. Some of the other district capitals are finishing construction of air-conditioned hotels in the US$15-to-US$25 range. *Losmen* as cheap as US$1 to US$3 per night can still be found. Once you leave the main population centres you will need to rely on the hospitality of local people.

Conservative and modest dress is very important in Nusa Tenggara. Women should be cautious and conscious of Muslim sensitivities in this respect, keeping shoulders and thighs covered.

Bank Negara Indonesia will change only US-dollar travellers' cheques. Don't consider trying to change any other currencies. It is best to carry all the cash you will need once you leave Bali or Lombok. Business hours for government offices and banks are between 8 a.m. and 1 p.m. Everything shuts at around 11 a.m. on Fridays (Muslim sabbath).

Getting There And Getting Around

● **Air:** most of the *kabupaten* (district capitals) are served by flights—from one per week to several each day. See the box of information for details of flights to and around Nusa Tenggara.

Route	Dep.	Arr.	Days	one-way economy fare US$
AMI — SWQ				
Merpati	12.20	13.00	Mon. Wed. Sat	23
AMI — BMU				
Bouraq	09.30	10.25	Mon. Wed. Thur. Sun.	37
Merpati	09.45	10.45	Tue. Thur. Fri. Sat. Sun.	
DPS — BMU				
Merpati	07.00	09.00	Wed.	53
	10.30	13.20	Tue. Thur. Fri. Sun.	

	07.50	10.45	Tue. Thur. Fri.	
	via AMI		Sat. Sun	
Bouraq	07.45	10.25	Mon. Wed.	52
	via AMI		Thur. Sun	
DPS — DIL				
Garuda	08.30	12.35	Daily	104
DPS – KOE				
Garuda	08.30	11.10	Daily	85
	09.00	11.40	Daily	
Bouraq	07.35	12.05	Mon. Thur.	76
	via MOF		Fri.	
	07.35	11.50	Tue. Sat.	
	via WGP			
DPS — MOF				
Merpati	07.35	11.05	Tue. Sat	
	10.35	13.50	Thur.	
Bouraq	07.35	10.55	Mon. Thurs. Fri.	73
DPS — WGP				
Bouraq	07.35	10.20	Tue. Sat.	68
Merpati	07.35	10.25	Wed. Fri. Sun.	
	07.30	11.30	Tue. Thur.	
	via TMC			
DPS — RTG				
Merpati	07.00	11.30	Wed.	79
	via BMU/LBJ			
DPS — LBJ				
Merpati	08.00	12.15	Sat.	
	via AMI/SWQ			
KOE — BJW				
Merpati	07.00	09.15	Sun.	43
	via ENE			
KOE — DPS				
Merpati	10.00	14.00	Thur.	
	via WGP/TMC			
MOF — KOE				
Bouraq	11.15	12.05	Mon. Thur. Fri.	29
Merpati	08.35	09.40	Fri.	
WGP — KOE				
Bouraq	10.40	11.50	Tue. Sat.	49
Merpati	14.00	15.30	Wed. Fri. Sun	
	12.00	13.35	Tue. Thur.	
	13.10	14.45	Sat.	
DPS — SWQ				
Merpati	10.20	13.00	Mon. Wed.	35
	via AMI		Sat.	
	08.00	10.25	Fri. Sat.	
	via AMI			

CITY CODES: AMI-Mataram; SWQ-Sumbawa Besar; JKT-Jakarta; WGP-Waingapu; BMU-Bima; DPS-Denpasar; DIL-Dili; KOE-Kupang; MOF-Maumere; RTG-Ruteng; LBJ-Labuhanbajo; BJW-Bajawa; ENE-Ende; TMC-Tambolaka; LKA-Larantuka.

● **Road:** the road network within the islands also links together the *kabupatens*. Improvement and upgrading of road conditions over the last few years still leaves much to be desired. Flores has perhaps the worst roads. Public transport is cramped though cheap.

● **Sea:** unscheduled cargo-and-passenger motorboats offer another alternative. Passage is strictly deck class but you might be able to bargain for the berth of one of the crew. From **Larantuka** (Flores) to points east, boats are the only means of communication though your schedule must be flexible enough to allow for delays. Ferries link all the major islands. Refer to the information under each island for details of air and sea transport throughout Nusa Tenggara.

Sumbawa

Getting There

● **Sea and Road:** a number of travellers reach Sumbawa by taking one of three daily ferries at 8 a.m., 9 a.m. and 10 a.m. from **Labuhanlombok** (Lombok) to **Alas** (western Sumbawa). The three-hour journey costs about US$3. *Bemos* meet the ferries at Alas to take passengers to either Sumbawa Besar (three hours away) or all the way to Bima (nine hours away). The fare from Alas to Sumbawa Besar is about US$2 and to Bima US$8.

● **Air: Merpati** runs a Twin-Otter flight from Denpasar to Sumbawa Besar every Sunday via Ampenan (Lombok). They also run from Denpasar to Bima every Friday; this flight continues on to Labuhanbajo and Ruteng (Flores). Other flights from Denpasar (each via Ampenan) leave on Friday and Saturday. The one-way fare to Sumbawa Besar is about US$34.

Bouraq fly from Denpasar on Monday, Wednesday, Thursday and Sunday for about US$52. **Garuda** fly to Sumbawa Besar on Monday, Wednesday and Saturday.

Check details at Bali's Ngurah Rai airport or at the office of each respective airline in Denpasar. (Merpati—Jalan Melati 57, tel: 22864. Bouraq—Jalan Kamboja 45, tel: 2252. Garuda—Jalan Melati 61.) When you check flight times remember that Lombok and points east are one hour ahead of Bali.

Sumbawa Besar

Accommodation

There are many *losmen* to choose from.
● **Hotel Suci** (Jalan Hasanudin 57, tel: 21589) with 18 rooms at about US$4.
● **Losman Saudara**, Jalan Hasanudin, tel: 21528 is in the same price range.
● **Hotel Tambora**, Jalan Kabayon, tel: 21555 is by far the best in town. Fourteen standard-sized rooms are available at US$7 (including tax and service). Another eight double-rooms with air-con are available at US$13 each. Another 12 economy-class rooms cost only US$3 a night.

Dining

You should try the **Aneka Rasa** for Chinese or local food. Bintang, Anker and San Miguel beer is served. There are a number of other local coffee shops and restaurants.

Bima

Accommodation

The new **Hotel Sangiang** is by far the best in town. Air-con rooms are available at about US$20 each. Fan-cooled rooms cost half this. All rooms have modern bathrooms with tub, shower and western-type toilets (the latter is a rarity here). Indonesian and Western food are served. The hotel's Wisata Komodo bus makes regular runs between Surabaya and Bima in 30 hours (about 22 hours from Denpasar). The Sangiang is located just around the corner from the palace of the former sultans.
● **Lila Graha**, Jalan Belakang Bioskop, tel: 740, has four rooms each with attached toilets and bath for US$5. Other rooms are available with communal bathroom facilities at US$4.50. Cold beer (not just beer with ice floating in it) is sold here.
● **Hotel Ariani**, Jalan Menginsidi 5, tel: 514 has four large rooms, each with attached bathroom, for US$4.

Plenty of other cheaper *losmen* are available for budget travellers.

Dining

Try the Rumah Makan Anda near the cinema. Serving Chinese and Indonesian food, this restaurant is also noted for its delicious crayfish.

Komodo
Getting There

● **Sea and Land:** you have a number of choices in arranging a trip to Komodo. Travel agencies in Jakarta, Bali and even Lombok can set up a tour for one or a group. Government tourist offices can supply the names of travel agents who deal specifically with Komodo. Prices of trips depend on the duration of the visit and the size of the group. Whatever the arrangements, tours such as these are inevitably expensive.

An overland trip from Bali on your own is much easier now than it used to be though you should have plenty of time on your hands.

Travel first from Bali by ferry and bus across Lombok and Sumbawa to Sape, a port on the eastern coast of Sumbawa.

From Sape you can take a third ferry to complete the journey to Labuhanbajo on the western tip of Flores. The official schedule provides for sailings from Sape on Monday, Wednesday and Saturday, and for a return trip from Labuhanbajo on Tuesday, Thursday and Sunday. One-way passage costs US$6.50. Only the Saturday and Sunday sailings call at Komodo. The Komodo "leg" of the journey is cheaper: US$2 from Labuhanbajo and US$4.50 from Sape. The duration of the crossing varies according to sea conditions but the Sape-Komodo trip usually takes eight hours, while the Komodo Labuhanbajo trip takes about three hours. The ferry leaves Sape at 9 a.m. on Mondays and Wednesdays but at 8 a.m. on Saturdays. The return ferry from Labuhanbajo starts at 8 a.m. on Sundays and 9 a.m. on Mondays and

Wednesdays. Once the ferry anchors off from Komodo, local boats will land you on the island for a small fee. For groups of 15 or more, the ferry will stop at Komodo on any of its regular runs in either direction for an extra fee of US$25 per person. All of this should be checked nearer the time of your intended journey as the schedules are always changing. When you board the ferry you should get final confirmation from the captain that the ferry will call at Komodo.

Boat charter is one way of solving the headaches that might arise on scheduled services. Both Sape and Labuhanbajo provide charter services. Because the landing point for Komodo is on the eastern side of Komodo, it is much closer to Labuhanbajo (about 50 kms [31 miles]) than to Sape (about 120 kms [72 miles]). In addition, the sea tends to be much rougher between Sape and Komodo than to the east. All this is reflected in boat charter prices. From Sape, the round trip can cost as much as US$250. From Labuhanbajo, you can get the same type of charter for US$75. Prices can be considerably lower, though this will depend as much on the condition of the boat as on your ability to bargain in Indonesian. Be sure to arrange a schedule for your voyage *both* ways when chartering.

Currents are strong in these seas though boatmen don't take unnecessary risks. Do respect departure times once you have arranged them as they depend on tides and currents.

• **Combinations of Flights, Ferries and Charters:** if time is on your side then there's nothing to stop you leaving your itinerary to chance. If this is not the case here are three itineraries for you to choose from:

1) For the fastest schedule, take a flight from **Bali** on a Friday, land in **Bima** (Sumbawa) and go straight to **Sape** for the Saturday 8 a.m. departure by ferry. Unless you plan to spend a week on Komodo, you must leave the island by ferry the next day to return to Sape on Sunday afternoon. This way you'll be able to catch a Monday flight back from Bima to Denpasar.

2) If you want to spend more time on Komodo, you could fly from **Bali** to **Labuhanbajo** on a Friday, wait for the ferry to Komodo on Sunday and return to Labuhanbajo the following Saturday or the following day to Sape. This arrangement will give you six days on Komodo.

3) A combination of chartering and flying is perhaps the best solution. As it costs only a few dollars more to fly from Bali to Labuhanbajo than to Bima, it is advisable to decide on the charter option for your final hop over to Komodo. (Remember that the cheapest boats are chartered from Labuhanbajo.) This way you could fly into Labuhanbajo on a Friday, be on your way to Komodo the same afternoon in a chartered boat and return to Labuhanbajo on Sunday morning in time to catch the 11:25 a.m. flight back to Bali. If you want to spend more time on Komodo, fly in on Sunday to Labuhanbajo and back to Bali the next Friday.

When arriving in either Sape or Labuhanbajo, you must report to the local PPA office (the initials stand for the Indonesian words meaning Directorate of National Conservation). They will call the PPA camp in Komodo by radio to advise them of your visit and to make certain that beds and food are available.

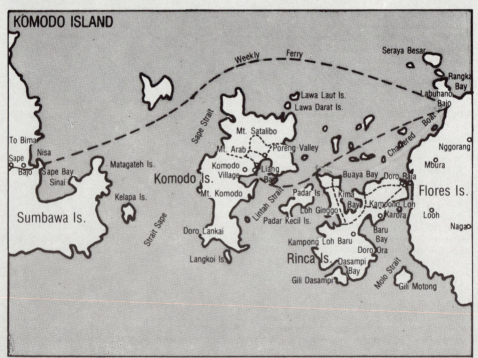

KOMODO ISLAND

Accommodation

At the PPA site in Loho Liang, there are several large and comfortable native-style cabins with a total capacity of 80 beds. Each cabin has two toilet/bath rooms and an overnight stay costs about US$4. Cheap meals of rice and fish are available.

You'll have already reported to the PPA office in either Labuhanbajo or Sape. On arriving in Komodo you must report to the PPA office in Loho Liang. There you will be required to register and pay a US$1 entrance fee. Any time you leave the PPA compound you must be accompanied by a guide (one for every three visitors) whose fee is US$2.50 per day.

Sumba

Getting There and Getting Around

- **Air:** there are five flights a week between Bali and Waingapu on **Merpati** and **Bouraq** airlines (Tuesday, Wednesday, Friday, Saturday and Sunday). On Tuesdays and Saturdays, Merpati flies Twin Otters (18 passengers) from Bali to Tambolaka (about 42 kms [26 miles] from Waikabubak). Twice a week there are flights between Tambolaka and Waingapu. The one-way fare from Denpasar to Waingapu is about US$68.
- **Sea:** West Sumba has a small harbour on the north coast at Waikelo—about 50 kms (31 miles) from Waikabubak. East Sumba has a much better and busier harbour at Waingapu. Unscheduled, small, freight-carrying motor boats call at these two ports and take deck passengers. Larger ships of the national Perintis line call twice a month at these ports on their way to and from Surabaya, and four times a month from Kupang (Timor). Passengers sleep on deck. The fare from Waikelo to Kupang (Timor) is about US$15. These ships call at several other harbours of neighbouring islands and if you have time this is an excellent way to do a little island hopping.
- **Road:** the two district capitals, Waikabubak and Waingapu, are connected by a 137-km (83-mile) road. Two buses daily cover the five-hour trip for about US$2.50. Smaller roads, mainly unpaved, provide public transport (*bemos*) to small towns and villages.

Attractions

Many traditional activities, all of which involve paying homage to spirits, take place between July and October. These include the building of *adat* houses, and burials in which sometimes hundreds of pigs, water buffalo, horses and dogs are sacrificed.

Other ceremonies include the *pajura* (traditional boxing matches), the festivals for the New Year in October and November, and horse races and ritual dances on August 17th—National Day. You should contact Pak Mude, head of the Waikabubak cultural office (Kepala Seksi Kebu-dayaan) for advice on cultural events or for the hire of a guide.

Buying Textiles

Traditional Sumbanese textiles will be top of the list of purchases for most visitors. You should shop carefully as much inferior work is sold. Look for smoothly curved lines as a sign of good work. The intricacy of the patterns is also important. Check to see if the colours are clean or if the dyes have run into each other (if there are white patches in the design they should be sharp and clean). Bargain with great determination—final prices could well be one-third the original asking price. Most *hinggi* come in pairs—one as a body-wrap and one as a shawl. Prices can range from US$10, for a mass-produced throw-away, on up to US$100 for a priceless heirloom fabric. Prailiu and Mangili (outside Waingapu) are the centres of the weaving industry. Melolo (on the southeast coast) is also a good source of old Sumban hand-woven fabrics.

Waikabubak

Accommodation

- **Hotel Rakuta**, Jalan Veteran. Managed by Heroe Nugroho, it is by far the best in town. Bathroom and toilet shared between two rooms. Double room with meals included for about US$15 per day.
- **Losmen Pelita** has 14 rooms each with between two and four beds. No interior toilet or bath. US$2.50 per night without meals or US$5 for full board.
- **Wisma Pemuda** has five rooms, two of which have clean, modern bathroom/toilets. The other three share a common bath and toilet. US$3.50 for the former and US$2.50 for the latter. Meals at US$1.

Waingapu

Accommodation

- **Elim Hotel**, Jalan Achmad Yani 35, tel: 32 or 162. Eighteen rooms each with private bath and toilet. Between US$3 and US$8 per person. Meals available.
- **Lima Saudara**, Jalan Wanggametti 2, tel: 83. Twelve rooms, some with toilet and bath. Between US$3 and US$9 per person. Meals available.
- **Surabaya Hotel**, Jalan Eltari 2, tel: 125. Seventeen rooms at between US$4 and US$8 per person.
- **Sandalwood Hotel**, Jalan Matawai, tel: 117. This is the best in town. Each of the 13 rooms with attached bath and toilet. About US$7 per person.

Dining

There are good restaurants to be found—not just in the hotels. You should try the **Rajawali**, the **Feni** (Jalan Tribrata) and the **Jakarta** (Jalan Ahmad Yani).

Flores

Getting There and Getting Around

- **Air:** air links between the centres are increasing. Labuhanbajo, Ruteng, Banjawa, Ende, Maumere and Larantuka all have airstrips. **Merpati** flies to all of them while **Bouraq** and **Garuda** serve only Maumere.

Merpati flies from Denpasar to Ruteng—via Bima (Sumbawa) and Labuhanbajo (Flores)—on Wednesdays making the return trip the same day. On Saturday they fly from Denpasar to Labuhanbajo—via Ampenan (Lombok) and Sumbawa Besar (Sumbawa)—making the return trip the same day. Bajawa, Ende, Maumere and Larantuka are served as part of more local hops. One example is a flight from Bima (Sumbawa) to Kupang (Timor)—via Bajawa and Ende—on Tuesday and Friday.

A brief summary of flight frequency throughout Flores follows:
- **Ruteng:** five flights weekly by Twin Otter from Denpasar. Air links to Ende.
- **Bajawa:** two flights weekly to ende by Twin Otter.
- **Ende:** flights to Kupang four times weekly, and to Denpasar four times weekly. Service to Waingapu (Sumba) once a week.
- **Maumere:** flights to Denpasar, Ende, Ujung Pandang (Sulawesi).
- **Larantuka:** three flights weekly to Kupang.
- **Road:** of all the major islands in Nusa Tenggara, Flores has the worst road network due to the rugged terrain. Mountains and 14 active volcanoes make for beautiful scenery and a not inconsiderable engineering headache. You can travel the length of Flores by public transport but don't be fooled by the fact that there is a 667-km (400-mile) road running the length of the island. Even for those undertaking this masochistic marathon, it will take at least four to five days as transport seldom runs at night. During the rainy season (November to May), roads between the principal towns could be cut for several days.
- **Sea:** Larantuka's port is the place to hitch or buy a ride on a boat to all points east of Flores. Plenty of unscheduled seagoing traffic to all points will enable you to do some island hopping.

Labuhanbajo

Accommodation

There are three *losmen* that you should try first: the **Mutiara** (7 rooms), the **Makmur** (7 rooms) and the **Komodo Jaya** (4 rooms).

Ruteng

Accommodation

- **Wisma Sindha**. Located in the centre of town. Twenty rooms.
- **Wisma Agung**. Fifteen rooms at between US$7 and US$12.
- **Losmen Karya**. Five rooms at US$2 per person per night.

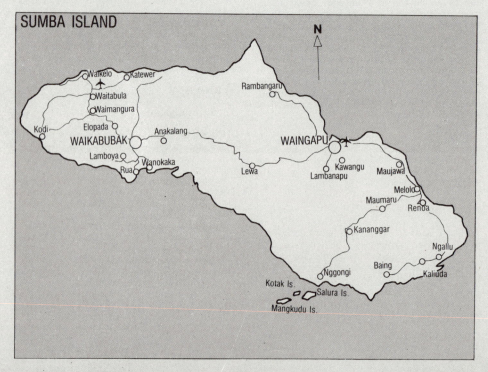

Ende

Accommodation

Small hotels with about 10 rooms each include:
- **Wisma Flores**, Jalan Jend Sudirman 18.
- **Karya**, Jalan Pelabuhan.
- **Solafide**, Jalan Onekore.
- **Wisma Melati**, Jalan Wolowona.
- **Wisma Amica**, Jalan Garuda. Six rooms at US$6 each.
- **Losmen Marga Utama**, Jalan Kelimutu. Six rooms at US$6 each.

Dining

Depot Ende and **Aneka** restaurants serve good Indonesian and Chinese food.

Maumere

Accommodation

- **Sea World Club Waiara**. Eleven bungalows at about US$30 each including meals.
- **Losmen Beng Goan**. Twenty-seven rooms. US$6 to US$7 per room.
- **Losmen Flora**. Four rooms at US$7 each.
- **Losmen Bogor**. Ten rooms at US$3 each.

Larantuka

Accommodation

- **Hotel Tresna**, Jalan Yos Sudarso. Eleven rooms. US$3 to US$6 per person.
- **Losmen Rullis**, Jalan Yos Sudarso. Eight rooms at US$6 to US$7 per person including meals.
- **Losmen Kurnia**. Six rooms. US$3 per person.

Sumatra

Medan
Banda Aceh
Brastagi
Prapat
Lake Toba
Bukittinggi
Padang
Arts and Crafts of West Sumatra
Palembang
Pekanbaru
Telukbetung
The Riau Archipelago

Getting There and Getting Around

- **Air:** Medan and Palembang are international airports with regular flights from Singapore and Malaysia. If you intend beginning your trip to Indonesia in Sumatra, then Medan is the natural point of entry. Both **Garuda** and **Malaysian Airline System** have inexpensive daily flights from Penang to Medan.

Padang is the main gateway to West Sumatra. Garuda has several flights daily from Jakarta and at least one flight daily from Medan. There are also daily flights between Singapore and Padang via Pekanbaru and Palembang making Padang a possible international gateway.

Route	Dep.	Arr.	Days	one-way economy fare US$
JKT — MES				
Garuda	06.45	08.55	Daily	127
	08.45	10.55	Daily	
	12.45	14.55	Daily	
	16.45	18.55	Daily	
Merpati	07.00	09.55	Mon. Tue. Sat. Sun.	108
	07.00	10.30	Wed. Thur. Fri.	
JKT — PDG				
Garuda	06.30	08.05	Daily	91
	07.35	10.40	Daily	
	11.05	12.40	Daily	
	14.00	15.35	Daily	
JKT — PLM				
Garuda	07.35	08.30	Daily	50
	10.00	10.55	Daily	
	13.35	14.30	Daily	
	16.00	16.55	Daily	
	17.00	17.55	Daily	
Merpati	07.00	09.35	Daily	82
MES — PDG				
Garuda	13.25	14.30	Daily	58
MES — PLM				
Garuda	13.25	16.20	Daily	96
PDG — PLM				
Garuda	15.10	16.20	Daily	58
TNJ — PDG				
Merpati	10.05	15.40	Mon. Wed. Fri.	49

CITY CODES: JKT-Jakarta; MES-Medan; PDG-Padang; PLM-Palembang; TNJ-Tanjungpinang.

- **Sea**: a ferry makes the crossing from the port of Merak on the northwest tip of Java to Panjang, near Telukbetung at the southern tip of Sumatra. The trip takes 4½ hours aboard a new ferry. Krakatau, the infamous volcanic island, can be seen off the port side of the boat in good weather.

Sibolga is the port for Nias and the 16-hour journey costs about US$5.

PELNI ships connect Medan with Jakarta, and Padang with Jakarta. See page 000.

- **Road**: the Trans-Sumatran Highway, the 2,500-km (1,550-mile) central spine of the Sumatran Highway system, has finally been completed after decades of construction. This fine road, from Tanjung Karang in the south to Banda Aceh in the north, greatly reduces the driving time between locations on its route. Other roads—except in the Medan-and-Lake-Toba area or the Padang-Bukittingi areas—are in poor condition. During the rainy season you should expect many smaller roads to be entirely impassable, while even in the dry season motoring will only be possible with a four-wheel drive vehicle.

Buses in Sumatra

Route	Distance	
	kms	miles
Medan-Bukittinggi	728	450
Medan-Bukittinggi-Padang	819	507
Medan-Bukittinggi-Pekanbaru	949	588
Padang-Bukittinggi-Pekanbaru	312	194
Bukittinggi-Pekanbaru	221	137
Padang-Pekanbaru-Dumai	498	308
Padang-Bukittinggi-Padangsidempuan-Sibolga	470	292
Bukittinggi-Sibolga-Tarutung-Parapat	552	342

The table above gives a few routes on Sumatra's bus network. Fares are low: the Bukittinggi-Pekanbaru run costs a little over US$2 and the ticket for the Medan-Bukittinggi-Pekanbaru route is less than US$10.

● **Rail**: there are three separate rail systems in Sumatra; none connects with another. In North Sumatra, a line runs from Medan north to Banda Aceh and south to Rantauprapat. In West Sumatra, there's a rail from Padang and its port of Teluk Bayur to Padangpanjang, thence north to Bukittingi and Payakumbuh, and south to Solok and Lunt. In South Sumatra, the rail line begins at Tanjung Karang and runs north to Parabumulih, east to Palembang and west to Lubulkinggau.

Medan

Accommodation

First Class (US$30 and up per night)

● **Danau Toba International**, Jalan Imam Bonjol 7, tel: 327000. US$45 to US$55 for single. US$50 to US$60 for double.
● **Garuda Plaza Hotel**, Jalan Sisingamangaraja 18, tel: 326255. Rooms between US$35 and US$40.
● **Polonia**, Jalan Jend. Sudirman 14-18, tel: 325300 (10 lines). Rooms between US$30 and US$45.

Intermediate and Budget (less than US$30)

● **Dirga Surya**, Jalan Imam Bonjol 6, tel: 321244 or 325660. Rooms up to US$30.
● **Garuda Hotel**, Jalan Sisingamangaraja 27, tel: 22775. Rooms up to US$20.
● **Garuda Motel**, Jalan Sisingamangaraja 7, tel: 22760 or 51203. Rooms up to US$20.
● **Pardede International**, Jalan Ir. H. Juanda 14, tel: 323866. Rooms up to US$28.
● **Angkasa**, Jalan Sutomo 1, tel: 321244. Rooms up to US$15.
● **Waiyat**, Jalan Asia 44, tel: 27575 or 321683. Rooms up to US$9.
● **Natour's Hotel Granada**, Jalan Jend. A. Yani VI/1, tel: 326211 or 326799 or 326344. Rooms up to US$18.

● **Sumatra**, Jalan Sisingamangaraja 21, tel: 24973. rooms up to US$12.

Dining

Medan is a good place for eating. The **Tip Top Restaurant** is noted for its excellent Padang food, curried mutton brains and extravagant choice of ice cream. The **Garuda Restaurant**, on Jalan Pemuda, serves excellent Padang food along with a thirst-quenching choice of fruit juices.

At night, one of the best places to visit is at **Selat Panjang**, an alley behind Jalan Pandu, with stalls serving Chinese food, satay and fruit juices. Another open-air eatery is at the swimming pool on Jalan Sisingamangaraja—famous for its choice of satays.

Medan is also highly regarded for its durians. August and September are the best months when street stalls offer the fruit in abundance and at just about unbeatable prices.

● **Bali Plaza**, Jalan Kumango 1A, tel: 321164 or 27757. Chinese.
● **Cafe Demarati**, Jalan Gatot Subroto, tel: 29141. European.
● **De'Bour**, Hotel Dharma Deli, Jalan Balai Kota 2, tel: 22210 or 327011. Indonesian, European, Chinese, Japanese, Seafood.
● **De'Plaza**, Hotel Garuda Plaza, Jalan Sisingamangaraja 18, tel: 326255 or 326256. Indonesian, European, Chinese.
● **Fuji Japanese**, Hotel Danau Toba Inn, Jalan Imam Bonjol 17, tel: 22700 ext.149. Japanese.
● **Garuda**, Jalan Pemuda 20 C,D, tel: 327692. Indonesian, European, Chinese.
● **Hawa Mandarin**, Jalan Mangkubumi 18. Indonesian, European, Chinese.

The **Mohammed Shariff**, Jalan Bandung 30, is another good Padang restaurant with a noisy and lively atmosphere. An excellent and cheap Indian restaurant is the **Tajmahal** on Jalan Mesjid. Other restaurants serving good quality Western food at reasonable prices include: **Lynn's Bar** on Jalan Jend. A. Yani and **Liandanis Restaurant** on Jalan Let. Jend. Suprapto 3C.

Shopping

Medan is a large trading town whose markets offer handicrafts from all over Sumatra and Java. A number of antique shops will give you a good choice of purchases. Art-and-craft-shops worth visiting are:

● **Borobodur**, Jalan Jend. A. Yani. Batak textiles, masks and statues.
● **Arafah Art Shop**, Jalan Jend. A. Yani 56. Paintings and carvings.
● **Asli Art Shop**, Jalan Jend. A. Yani 62. Paintings.
● **Rufino Art Shop**, Jalan Jend. A. Yani 64. Paintings and statues.
● **Selatan Art Shop**, Jalan Jend. A. Yani 44. Paintings.

Jalan Jend. A. Yani has a number of other souvenir shops selling a variety of arts and crafts.

For **batik** you should go to Pasar Ikan Lama located on Jalan Perniagaan between Jalan Yani and the railway tracks. Most of the souvenir shops along Jalan Jend. A. Yani sell *batik* as do some shops on Jalan Arifin. A number of shops sell *batik* by the metre or ready made; they include:

- **Batik Keris**, Jalan Arifin 200.
- **Danar Hadi**, Jalan Arifin 131-133.
- **Batik Semar**, Jalan Jend. A. Yani 128.
- **Seni Batik Indonesia** in Gedung Perisai, Jalan Pemuda 7.
- **Iwan Tirta**, Jalan Sriwijaya Ujung Utara 1.
- **Tiara Boutique**, Jalan Prof. Yamin 20C.

Banda Aceh

Getting Around

The Banda Aceh Express **bus** service connects Medan with Sumatra's northernmost city. Numbered seats, reclining chairs, fans and non-stop all-night videos, featuring *kung-fu* and Indonesian rock bands, are the norm on this route.

Other bus services, which start in the early morning and arrive mid-afternoon, connect the following destinations: Blangkeseren - Kutacane, Takingon - Bireuen, Sigli - Aceh.

Accommodation

- **Aceh**, Jalan Mohammed Jaim 1, tel: 2263. Rooms between US$5 and US$11.
- **Aceh Barat**, Jalan Sibolga 17, tel: 3278. Rooms between US$3 and US$7.
- **Ladang**, Jalan Nasional 9, tel: 2268. rooms between US$3 and US$7.
- **Masda**, Jalan K. Anwar 12. Rooms between US$2 and US$11.
- **Medan**, Jalan Jend. A. Yani 9, tel: 22636 or 21501. Rooms between US$6 and US$13.
- **Prapat**, Jalan Jend. A. Yani 11, tel: 2779. Rooms for less than US$5.

Dining

The food in Aceh is different in that it offers a chance to try something other than the ubiquitous Padang food. Aceh food is usually served with steamed rice and common dishes include: fish (*ikan panggang*), papaya flower salad (*sambal bunga kates*) and egg cooked in spinach (*sayur bayam*). Squares of twice-cooked black rice (*pulot hitam dua masak*) serve as sweets. Tea with honey, ginger and condensed milk (*serbat*) is an alternative. Batak restaurants at Kutacane serve dog curry (*cicang anjing*) and palm wine (*tuak*). Good coffee is available everywhere in Aceh: bitter coffee is *kopi tok*, and coffee with milk is *kopi susu*. a coffee with a half-boiled egg (*telur setengah malang*) is the usual breakfast fare.

- **Aroma Restaurant**, Jalan Palembang. Chinese.
- **Asia Baru**, Jalan Gutmeuda. Acehnese food.
- **Eka Daroy Coffee Shop**, Hotel Eka Daroy, Jalan Mata Ie. Chinese, Indonesian, European.

Shopping

Special items to look for in Banda Aceh include *rencong* (traditional Acehnese daggers) and deli-cate filigreed jewellery. The best place to shop for *rencong* is in the market, where you can pay anything up to US$100 for a beautiful ivory dagger. A shop on Jalan Kartini offers Acehnese and Dutch antiques for browsers and collectors.

The whole province of Aceh offers a variety of textiles with each locality having its own characteristic pattern of *kain adat* or *opo adat*.

Museums

- **Architecture Museum** at the Junongan, Jalan Teuku Umar.
- **Rumah Kuno Awe**, Jalan Mansur Sjah. Handicraft and History Museum.

Brastagi

Accommodation

- **Rudang**, Jalan Sempurna, tel: 43. US$6 for single. US$8 for double.
- **Bukit Kubu**, Jalan Sempurna 2. Rooms between US$9 and US$15.

Prapat

Accommodation

- **Natour Hotel Prapat**, Jalan Marihat 1, tel: 41012 or 41018. Rooms between US$10 and US$20.
- **Astari Hotel**, Jalan P. Samosir, tel: 41219 or 41725. Rooms for US$20 to US$28. US$24 to US$56 for bungalow.
- **Danau Toba International**, Jalan P. Samosir 17, tel: 41583 or 41719. Rooms between US$13 and US$16.
- **Danau Toba Prapat**, Jalan P. Samosir 19, tel: 49. US$13 to US$15 for single. US$15 to US$17 for double.
- **Patrajasa Prapat Hotel**, Jalan Prapat, tel: 41796. US$14 to US$25 for single. US$20 to US$34 for double.
- **Mimpin Tua**, Jalan Talun Sungkit 9. Rooms for less than US$10.

Dining
- **Tara Bunga Hotel**. Chinese, Indonesian, European.
- **Restaurant Asia**. Chinese.

Lake Toba

Accommodation

- **Pulo Tao Cottage**. US$20 to US$24 for single. US$24 to US$32 for double.
- **Toledo Inn**. US$10 for single. US$12 for double.

On the Samosir peninsula over the water from Prapat are a number of *losmen* including: **Tuk Tuk** rooms between US$5 and US$7; **Carolina** for less than US$3; and **Krista Ace**, **Bernard Ace** and **Gordin Ace** each for less than US$4. In Tomok you can try **Edison Ace** at US$1, while in Ambarita at the same price is **Rohandy Ace**.

Buying Batak Handicrafts

Fifteen years of tourism has unfortunately almost exhausted the supply of genuine antiques in the Toba and Karo districts. Reproductions of Batak calendars and buffalo-horn medicine pouches are all too common. A real antique is just as likely to turn up in Medan (try **Toko Bali** on Jalan Jend. Jani 68 or **Indonesian Art Shop** on the same street). Some Toba entrepreneurs will take visitors on "antique safaris" around the country, but prices are high. There's still good Chinese porcelain available along with Dutch silver coins. The greatest, though certainly most macabre, find is a Tungkat carved magic wand. Real wands contain a phial of slaughtered baby's blood and, because they are considered so powerful, could fetch up to US$1,000. Genuine Batak spirit figurines are still around though the mini Batak houses are invariably contemporary carvings. Batak weaving and *kain ulos* are good buys, though you should bargain very hard.

Bukittinggi

Accommodation

- **Denai**, Jalan Rivai 26, tel: 21460. Rooms between US$5 and US$8.
- **Lima's**, Jalan Kesehatan 34, tel: 22641. Rooms between US$2 and US$9.
- **Minang**, Jalan Panorama 20 A, tel: 21220 or 22638. Rooms up to US$13.
- **Surya**, Jalan A. Karim 7, tel: 2585. Rooms for less than US$2.
- **Yani**, Jalan Jend. A. Yani 101, tel: 22740.

Rooms for less than US$4.
- **Yogya**, Jalan M. Yamin S.H. 43. Rooms for less than US$5.
- **Dymen's International**, Jalan Nawawi 1-5, tel: 23781, 22702, 21015.
- **Bentung**, Jalan Benteng 1, tel: 22596 or 21115. Rooms between US$4 to US$12.

Dining

- **ACC**, Muka Jam Gudang, tel: 21631. Indonesian (Minang special).
- **Dymen's Hotel Restaurant**, Jalan Nawawi. Indonesian, European, Chinese.
- **Ria Sari**, Ngarai Sianok Shopping Centre, Jalan Jend. Sudirman 1, tel: 21503. Indonesian (Minang special).
- **Selamat**, Jalan A. Yani 19, tel: 22959. Indonesian (Minang special).
- **Simpang Raya**, Muka Jam Gadang, tel: 22585. Indonesian (Minang special).

Shopping

The two levels of the **Pasar Atas** and **Pasar Bawah** (Upper Market and Lower Market) in Bukittinggi, connected by a 40-step stairway below the Jam Gadang are crowded any day of the week and brimming to capacity on market days—Wednesday and Saturday. Besides foodstuffs, you'll find the market sells a variety of silverware from Kota Gadang, embroidery from Silungkang and brass. A number of other shops provide crafts of varying quality:
- **Aisah Chalik**, Jalan Cindur Mato 94. Paintings, carvings, batik, songket textiles, embroid-

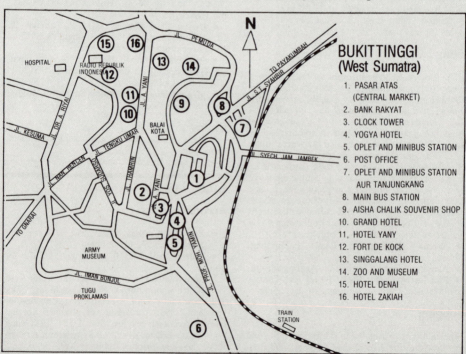

BUKITTINGGI (West Sumatra)

1. PASAR ATAS (CENTRAL MARKET)
2. BANK RAKYAT
3. CLOCK TOWER
4. YOGYA HOTEL
5. OPLET AND MINIBUS STATION
6. POST OFFICE
7. OPLET AND MINIBUS STATION AUR TANJUNGKANG
8. MAIN BUS STATION
9. AISHA CHALIK SOUVENIR SHOP
10. GRAND HOTEL
11. HOTEL YANY
12. FORT DE KOCK
13. SINGGALANG HOTEL
14. ZOO AND MUSEUM
15. HOTEL DENAI
16. HOTEL ZAKIAH

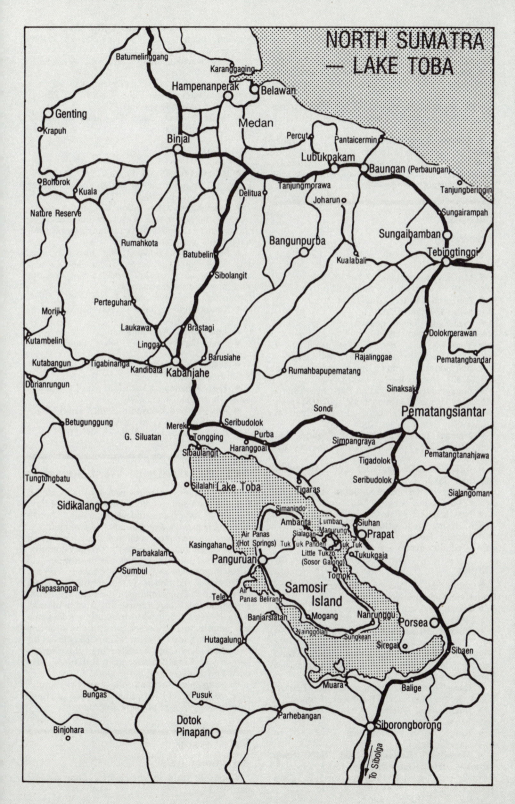

NORTH SUMATRA
— LAKE TOBA

Batumelinggang
Karanggaging
Hampenanperak
Belawan
Genting
Krapuh
Medan
Binjal
Percut
Pantaicermin
Lubukpakam
Baungan (Perbaungan)
Bohorok
Kuala
Tanjungbering
Nature Reserve
Delitua
Tanjungmorawa
Joharun
Sungairampah
Rumahkota
Sungaibamban
Batubelin
Bangunpurba
Tebingtinggi
Sibolangit
Kualabali
Moriji
Perteguhan
Dolokmerawan
Kutambelin
Laukawar
Brastagi
Pematangbandar
Lingga
Barusiahe
Rajalinggae
Kutabangun
Tigabinanga
Rumahbapupematang
Durianrungun
Kandibata
Kabahjahe
Sinaksak
Pematangsiantar
Sondi
Betugunggung
Merek
Seribudolok
Simpangraya
Pematangtanahjawa
G. Siluatan
Tongging
Purba
Sibaulangit
Haranggoal
Tigadolok
Tungtuhbatu
Silalahi
Lake Toba
Seribudolok
Sidikalang
Tigaras
Sialangoman
Simanindo
Ambarita
Lumban
Siuhan
Air Panas
Sialagan
Manrung
Prapat
(Hot Springs)
Tuk
Tuk Panden
Tuk Tuk
Kasingahan
Parbakalan
Little Tukzo
Tukukgaja
Sumbul
Panguruan
(Sosor Galong)
Napasanggar
Tomok
Air
Samosir
Tele
Panas Belirang
Island
Banjarslatan
Mogang
Nanrunggu
Porsea
Hutagalung
Nainggolan
Sungkean
Siregak
Sibaen
Muara
Balige
Bungas
Pusuk
Binjohara
Parhebangan
Siborongborong
Dotok
Pinapan
To Sibolga

ery, basket work, silver, coconut shell handicrafts and bamboo.
- **Antique Shop**, Jalan A. Yani 2, tel: 22557. Paintings, statues, *batiks*, *songket* textiles, silver.
- **Basrida**, Jalan Yos Sudarso 2. Carved design, silver, *batik*, textile embroidery and basket work.
- **H. Muchtar Is**, Jalan Minangkabau 90. Statues, carvings, *batik*, ivory and bamboo handicrafts.
- **Nuraini**, Jalan Minangkabau 25. Paintings, *batik*, *songket* textiles, basket work, silver.
- **Tiga Putra**, Jalan Minangkabau 19. carvings, embroidery, basket work, silver, coconut shell handicrafts and bamboo.

Padang

Accommodation

- **Jakarta**, Jalan Blk. Olo 55, tel: 23331. Rooms for less than US$6.
- **Minang International**, Jalan Diponegoro 17, tel: 21719. Rooms for less than US$4.
- **Pangeran's Hotel**, Jalan Dobi 3, tel: 26233. Rooms for less than US$20.
- **Tiga-Tiga**, Jalan Pemuda 31, tel: 22633. Rooms for less than US$4.
- **Yaayan's Sari**, Wisma, Jalan Sudirman 9, tel: 23555. Rooms between US$12 and US$22.
- **Benyamin**, Jalan Bgd. Azis Chan, tel: 222324. Rooms for less than US$5.
- **Bouganville**, Wisma, Jalan Bgd. Azis Chan 2, tel: 22149. Rooms between US$5 and US$13.
- **Femina**, Wisma, Jalan Bgd. Azis Chan 15, tel: 21950. Rooms for less than US$8.
- **Mariani International**, Jalan Bundo Kandung 35, tel: 22020 or 22634. Rooms for less than US$13.
- **Adilla**, Jalan Damar 2, tel: 23962. Rooms for less than US$9.
- **Natour Hotel Muara**, Jalan Gereja 34, tel: 25600. Rooms between US$9 and US$23.
- **New Kartika**, Jalan Gurun 40, tel: 23621 or 25376. Rooms for less than US$8.
- **Padang Hotel**, Jalan Bgd. Azis Chan 28, tel: 22563. Rooms for less than US$8.

Dining

- **Alima**, Jalan Pasarbaru 29, tel: 21794. Indonesian (Minang special).
- **Bopet Irama**, Jalan Prof. M. Yamin, tel: 22425.
- **Chan's Restaurant**, Jalan Pondok 94, tel: 22131. Chinese.
- **Grand Bar and Restaurant**, Grand Hotel, Jalan Pondok 84, tel: 22088 or 25888. Indonesian, European, Chinese.
- **Hang Tuan**, Hotel Hangtuah, Jalan Pemuda 1, tel: 26556. Indonesian, European, Chinese.
- **Imambonjol**, Jalan Imam Bonjol 9, tel: 26153.
- **King's**, Jalan Pondok 86B, tel: 21701. Indonesian, Chinese.
- **Macudum's Restaurant and Coffee Shop**, Hotel Macudum, Jalan Haligoo 43-45, tel: 22333 or 23997. Indonesian (Minang special), European, Chinese.

- **Mariani Restaurant and Coffee Shop**, Hotel Mariani, Jalan Bundo Kandung 35, tel: 25466. Indonesian, European, Chinese.
- **New Kartika**, Jalan Gurun 40, tel: 23621. Indonesian.
- **Phoenix**, tel: 21304. European, Chinese.
- **Roda Baru**, Jalan Pasar Raya 6, tel: 22814. Indonesian (Minang special).
- **Serba Nikmat**, Jalan H. Agus Salim 20, tel: 26210. Indonesian.

Shopping

- **H. Mochtar**, Jalan Pondok 85, tel: 25615. Paintings, statues, carved design, *batik*, basket work, silver and bamboo.
- **Silungkang**, Jalan Imam Bonjol 6A, Kompleks Nusantara Building, tel: 26426. Paintings, statues, *batiks*, basket work, silver, coconut shell handicrafts and bamboo.
- **Songket Silungkang**, Jalan Imam Bonjol, tel: 23711. Paintings, carved design, *songket* textiles, embroidery, basket work, silver, coconut shell handicrafts and bamboo.

Other handicraft shops include:
- **Toko Sartika**, Jalan Jend. Surdirman 5, tel: 22101.
- **Abu Nawas**, Airport Tabing.
- **Toko Batik Arjuna**, Jalan Pasar Raya, tel: 23253.
- **Toko Dewi**, Jalan Pasar Raya, Complex Toko Bertingkat.
- **Toko Ramona**, Jalan Pasar Raya Complex, Toko Bertingkat, tel: 22476.
- **Antique and Souvenir Shop**, Toko Atom Shopping Centre 6A, tel: 26426.
- **Batik Semar**, Jalan Hiligoo, tel: 21215.

Arts and Crafts of West Sumatra

West Sumatra is renowned for its beautiful hand-loomed *songket* cloth and fine embroidery, and for its silverwork and woodcarving. Though weaving is practised in a number of communities, the best known source is Silungkang, a small town on the Agam plateau where the brightly coloured silk *songket* sarongs, scarves and headwear—all richly interwoven with gold—are made. Another well-known and much-visited centre is **Pandai Sikat** near Padangpanjang on the main road from Padang to Bukittingi. Loomed by women in small cottage industries, it takes from a few weeks to a few months to finish a set consisting of a *sarung* and matching scarf. Pandai Sikat is also known for its embroidery and woodcarving. Silversmiths working in **Kota Gadang**, near Bukittingi, produce fine spider-web filligree work.

In **Sungaipuar**, a small village twenty minutes from Bukittingi, blacksmiths still make anything from spoons to agricultural equipment.

Palembang

Accommodation

- **Asiana**, Jalan Sudirman 45E. rooms for less than US$4.

- **Dharma Agung**, Jalan H. Barlian km 7. Rooms up to US$9.
- **Jakarta**, Jalan Sayangan 763, tel: 21737. rooms up to US$7.
- **Kenanga Inn**, Jalan Bukit Kecil 76, tel: 23491. Rooms up to US$8. US$12 to US$13 for double.
- **Leparadis**, Jalan Kapten A. Rivali 257, tel: 260707. Rooms between US$15 and US$30.

Dining

- **City Bar and Restaurant**, Jalan Jend. Sudirman 589, Makmur Store 3rd floor, tel: 26710. Indonesian, European, Chinese.
- **Coffee House Maxim**, Jalan Jend. Sudirman 304, tel: 26635. Indonesian.
- **Mandala**, Jalan Veteran 86-88, tel: 23614. Indonesian, European, Japanese, Chinese.
- **Musi**, Jalan Merdeka 252, tel: 22107. Indonesian, European, Chinese.
- **Sanjaya**, Jalan Kapten A. Rivai 6193, tel: 20272 or 20634. Indonesian, European, Chinese.

Pekanbaru

Accommodation

- **Asmar**, Jalan K.H. Agus Salim 57. Rooms for less than US$3.
- **Bunda**, Wisma, Jalan Prof. Moh. Yamin SH 104, tel: 21728 or 21175. Rooms for less than US$8.
- **Dharma Utama**, Jalan Sisingaangaraja 2. Rooms for less than US$4.
- **Kelabang Sakti**, Jalan Diponegoro 53. Rooms for less than US$7.

Dining

- **Anom**, Jalan Gatot Subroto 3, tel: 22636. Indonesian.
- **Caloca**, Jalan Diponegoro 26, tel: 22986. Indonesian, European.
- **Gelas Mas Restaurant**, Jalan H. Sulaiman, tel: 22092. European, Chinese.
- **Medan**, Jalan Ir. Juanda 28, tel: 23770. Indonesian, Chinese.
- **Rempah Sari**, Jalan Jend. A, Yani 80. Indonesian.
- **Selamat**, Jalan A. Yani 82, tel: 21081. Indonesian.
- **Tedja Restaurant**, Jalan Kampar 34, tel: 23316. Indonesian.
- **Tin Tin**, Jalan Tangkubanperahu. Indonesian.
- **Tri Ariga Baru**, Jalan Jend. Sudirman 91, Indonesian.

Telukbetung

Accommodation

- **New Jakarta Hotel**, Jalan Belanak 28. Rooms for less than US$9.
- **Pasific**, Jalan Yos Sudarso, tel: 42218 or

42334. Rooms between US$5 and US$14.
- **Shintana**, Jalan Selat Berhala 95, tel: 42941. Rooms for less than US$2.
- **Sriwijaya**, Jalan Kalimantan 30, tel: 41046 or 41284. Rooms for less than US$9.

Dining

- **Grand Park Coffee Shop**, Jalan Dr. Susilo 1A, tel: 42550. European, Chinese.
- **Hongkong**, Jalan Pangkalpinang 30, tel: 53473. Chinese.
- **Pasific Hotel**, Jalan Yos Sudarso 58, tel: 42218. Indonesian, European.

Riau Archipelago

Tanjung Pinang can be reached by sea from Jakarta, Pekanbaru, Palembang and Singapore. Once you are in Tanjung Pinang you can travel easily to neighbouring islands. For **Pulau Penyengat** and the **Snake River**, as well as a number of nearby beaches, you should charter a *prahu* from the wooden wharf (about US$20 per day).

A Singapore-based travel agent—German Asian Travels—organises two-day tours to Tanjung Pinang including excursions to Pulau Penyengat and other areas.

Pulau Batam is another island easily reached from Singapore. A country club opened recently and there are plans for hotels along some of the beachfronts. Regular boat services leave Singapore (US$50 return). A special visa is supplied by the Indonesian Embassy in Singapore for those wishing to make a short visit to this part of Indonesia only.

Kalimantan

Pontianak
Banjarmasin
Balikpapan
Samarinda
Tarakan
Kutai National Park and
Mahakam River Region
Dayak Arts and Crafts

Getting There and Getting Around

- **Air: Balikpapan** is the major gateway for flights to and within Kalimantan. From Jakarta, **Garuda** flies four times every day with an additional early morning flight on Wednesday, Friday and Sunday. There are also two flights daily from Surabaya. A one-way economy-class ticket from here costs US$82.

Merpati fly to Pontianak for US$63 from Jakarta and **Bouraq** make the trip to Banjarmasin twice a day and to Balikpapan three times a day—also from Jakarta.

There are twice-weekly flights (Fridays and Sundays) on **Bouraq** between Denpasar (Bali) and Balikpapan. Bouraq also flies daily from Ujung Pandang (Sulawesi).

Within Kalimantan there are regular direct flights on Garuda, Bouraq and Merpati between Balikpapan and Banjarmasin, Samarinda, Bontang, Tarakan and Pontianak. Oil company planes (including Pertamina) and charter flights travel regularly to these and many other small airstrips throughout the island, and if there is room, fare-paying passengers are normally allowed on these flights. (Fares can be expensive: "space-available" fare from Balikpapan to Bontang runs to about US$16.) The Missionary Air Service also often has room on trips from Samarinda to the interior.

Travellers arriving at Balikpapan's Sepinggan Airport can take a taxi to town for US$5. It's better value to walk to the airport's main gate, from where you can catch a motorbike taxi (for US$1) or an old Morris Minor for US$2.

See below for flight information.

Route	Dep.	Arr.	Days	one-way economy fare US$
JKT – BDJ				
Garuda	06.05	08.40	Daily	91
	12.45	15.20	Daily	
Bouraq	07.30	11.55	Daily	78
JKT – BPN				
Garuda	07.15	10.20	Daily	117
	09.15	12.20	Daily	
	11.15	14.20	Daily	
	13.15	16.20	Daily	
Bouraq	05.30	09.25	Daily	105
	06.00	11.10	Daily	
	07.30	13.25	Daily	
JKT – PNK				
Garuda	07.10	09.30	Daily	74
	09.00	11.20	Daily	
	13.00	15.20	Daily	
Merpati	05.30	08.40	Daily	63
BDJ – BPN				
Garuda	10.40	11.30	Wed. Fri. Sun.	42
Bouraq	09.55	10.55	Daily	38
	10.05	11.10	Daily	
	10.30	11.40	Mon. Wed. Fri. Sat.	
	12.20	13.25	Daily	
BPN – SRI				
Merpati	10.05	10.40	Mon. Tues. Thur. Sat.	21
	11.45	12.20	Tues. Fri. Sun.	
Bouraq	11.00	11.35	Daily	25
SUB – BDJ				
Garuda	06.30	08.30	Daily	55
	14.15	16.15	Daily	
Bouraq	06.00	08.30	Daily	46
	07.00	09.20	Daily	
	13.45	15.15	Daily	
SUB – BPN				
Garuda	06.00	08.30	Daily	82
	13.00	15.30	Daily	
Bouraq	06.30	09.45	Daily	73
	08.00	11.20	Tues. Fri.	
	10.00	13.15	Daily	

CITY CODES: JKT-Jakarta; BDJ-Banjarmasin; BPN-Balikpapan; SRI-Samarinda; PNK-Pontianak; SUB-Surabaya.

● **Sea:** the national shipping company's inter-Indonesian-island route takes in Balikpapan. (*See* "Transportation" under "Domestic Sea Travel" on page 324 for the full itinerary and fare structure.) Because the itinerary takes in Surabaya and Ujung Pandang before Balikpapan, travelling by sea makes more sense if you are planning to take in more than just your chosen destination in Kalimantan.

● **Inland by River:** from Banjarmasin you can trace the Barito River north to its headwaters. With a couple of weeks to spare, the whole of the river could be explored. Boats can be chartered up river as far as Mauratewe. From here it's by canoe to the headwaters. A long trek northeast (with the possibility of shortening some of the journey by road) will take you across swamps to Intu and finally to Long Iram on the Mahakam River. Long Iram is a relatively short journey upriver from Samarinda. There is a small airstrip at Melak just downstream from where you might be lucky enough to hitch a ride into Samarinda with the Missionary Air Service. The other, more adventurous, alternative on arrival in Long Iram is to boat it up the Mahakam to the Dayak villages of Longbangun, Longpakah, Longnawan and Longbawan.

● **Speedboats:** depart Samarinda daily at 6 a.m. and arrive in Bontang five hours later. The fare is about US$5. Going in the opposite direction, the time of departure and fare is the same. Water taxis take about twice as long to cover the same distance. Other speedboats travel from Samarinda to Lokh Tuan (or return) in four hours. Find an office of P.T. Kayu Mas to get more information.

● **Road:** the **Trans-Kalimantan Highway**, still under construction, extends from Batakan, south of Banjarmasin, through Balikpapan and on to Samarinda. It will soon connect to Bontang, and eventually to Tarakan. Buses run on a regular schedule from Banjarmasin to Balikpapan and Samarinda; the Balikpapan-Samarinda fare is less than US$2.

There is a reasonable road running north from Pontianak and which forks at the village of Seipenyu. Continuing north the road approaches the Sarawak border and passes through an area well known for its excellent hand-woven cloth. The right fork heads due east to Bodok after which the type of vehicle you are driving, and the weather conditions, will determine how much farther you get.

Meanwhile, logging roads provide a crude path for sturdy vehicles in some areas. There are numerous abandoned rudimentary roads. Bridges are often made of rotting logs. Erosion and mudslides create common obstacles. On dry days it may be possible to use a Jeep on these roads.

Pontianak

Accommodation

- **Orient**, Jalan Tanjungpura, tel: 2650. US$7 to US$18 for single.
- **Pondok Kapuas Permai Cottages**, Jalan Gajah Mada, tel: 4374. US$20 for one unit.
- **Pontianak City Hotel**, Jalan Pak Kasih, tel: 2496. US$16 for single. US$11 to US$18 for double.

Dining

- **City Hotel Restaurant**, Jalan Kasih 448, tel: 438. Indonesian, Chinese.
- **Hawai**, Jalan Tanjungpura 33. Indonesian, Chinese.
- **Kapuas Room**, Dharma Hotel, Jalan Imam Bonjol 555, tel: 759. Indonesian, Chinese
- **Lembur Kuring**, Jalan Ir. H. Juanda 32. Indonesian.
- **Orient Hotel Restaurant**, Orient Hotel Tanjung Pura, tel: 2650. Indonesian, Chinese.
- **Pagi Sore**, Komplek Kapuas Indah, 2nd floor. Indonesian.
- **Paradisio**, Jalan Tanjung Pura 6, tel: 428. Chinese.
- **Tahiti**, Jalan Imam Bonjol 567-569. Indonesian, European, Chinese, Japanese.

Banjarmasin

Accommodation

- **Anda**, Jalan Letjen R. Suprapto, tel: 2006. US$5 for single. US$7 to US$9 for double.
- **Banua**, Jalan Brigjen Katamso 8, tel: 3215. US$6 to US$9, US$8 to US$11.
- **Maramim**, Jalan Lambung Mangkurat 32, tel: 4958 or 4835. US$22 for single. US$30 for double.
- **Metro**, Jalan Mayjen Sutoyo 102, tel: 2427. US$6 to US$9 for single. US$7 to US$10 for double.
- **Perdana**, Jalan Brigjen Katamso 5, tel: 3276. US$6 to US$9 for single. US$8 to US$10 for double.
- **Rahmat**, Jalan Ahmad Yani 9, tel: 4322 or 4429. US$4 to US$6 for single. US$5 to US$11 for double.
- **Sabrina**, Jalan Bank Rakyat 21, tel: 4442 or 4721. US$5 to US$8 for single. US$9 to US$12 for double.
- **SAS**, Jalan Kacapiring Besar 2, tel: 3054 or 4759. US$4 to US$8 for single. US$6 to US$9
- **Sewarga**, Jalan Cempaka 1, tel: 3690. US$10 to US$14 for single.
- **New River City**, Jalan R.E. Martadinata 3, tel: 2983. US$9 for single. US$13 for double.
- **Ritta City**, Jalan R. Soeprapto 11, tel: 4785 or 2423. US$5 to US$14 for single. US$7 to US$18 for double.
- **Sempaga**, Jalan Mayjen Sutoyo S 292, tel: 2480 or 2753. US$3 to US$16 for single. US$17 for double.

- **Loktabat**, Jalan Jend. A Yani 33,5 km. tel: 84. US$12 for single. US$13 for double.
- **KI Damang**, Jalan Haryono M.T. 4, tel: 2334. US$9 to US$15 for single. US$14 to US$21 for double.

Balikpapan

Accommodation

Balikpapan's (and Kalimantan's) first five-star hotel is the new **Hotel Bena Kutai**, operated by the Beaufort International group. This is a luxury hotel with all the comforts of home, and is good value to boot: weekend discount rates (Friday through Sunday) are US$35 all-inclusive, double occupancy; midweek rates are only slightly higher. Write PO Box 200, Jalan Antasari, Balikpapan, tel: 21804 or 21813.

Other hotels in Balikpapan include:
- **Grand Park Hotel**, Jalan Pangeran Antasari, tel: 22942. Private bath, hot water air-con. US$36 for single.
- **Hotel Bahtera**, Jalan Gajah Mada SK1/47, tel: 22563. US$7 for single. US$14 for double.
- **Hotel Balikpapan**, Jalan Garuda 2, tel: 21490. US$16 for double.
- **Blue Sky**, Jalan Letjen Jenderal Suprapto 1, tel: 22267. US$8 for single. US$9 for double.
- **Benakutai**, Jalan P. Antasari, tel: 21804 or 21813. US$65 to US$75 for single. US$75 to US$85 for double.
- **Budiman**, Jalan Pangeran Antasari, tel: 581. US$9 to US$10 for single. US$10 to US$11 for double.
- **Kaltim**, Jalan Kampung Baru Tengah, US$3 for single. US$5 for double.
- **Piersa**, Jalan Gunung Bakaran. US$14 for single. US$16 for double.
- **Puri Kencana**, Jalan Gajah Mada 14. US$8 for single. US$9 for double.
- **Mirama**, Jalan Mayjen Sutoyo, tel: 22960 or 22961. US$18 to US$50 for all standard rooms.
- **Patra**, Jalan Yos Sudarso, tel: 46. US$15 to US$16 for double. Bungalows US$25 per night.
- **Tirta Plaza**, Jalan D.I. Panjaitan, tel: 22324 or 22364. US$10 for single. US$11 for double US$14 for bungalows.

Dining

- **Bahtera Restaurant and Bar**, Hotel and Bahtera, Jalan Gajah Mada 1/47. Indonesian, European, Chinese.
- **Mirama**, Hotel Mirama, Jalan Letjen Soetoyo, tel: 561 or 562. Indonesian, European, Chinese.
- **Rainbow Coffee Shop and Restaurant**. Blue Sky Hotel, Jalan Letjen Soeprapto 1, tel: 2324. European, Chinese.
- **Tenggarong**, Hotel Balikpapan, Jalan Garuda 2. Indonesian, European, Chinese.

Samarinda

Accommodation

- **Hotel Andhika**, Jalan H. Agus Salim RT. V.

37, tel: 22358. US$15 for double.

- **Holiday Inn**, Jalan Pelabuhan 29-33 and Jalan Darmaga 18-20, tel: 21185 or 21124, or 22413. Private bath, hot water, air-con, colour TV, radio. Restaurant, coffee shop, bar, barber shop, billiard room.
- **Hotel Jakarta I**, Jalan Jend. Sudirman 57, tel: 22624.
- **Hotel Jarkarta II**, Jalan Dewi Sartika, tel: 22965 or 23895.
- **Mesra International Hotel**, 1 Jalan Pahlawan, tel: 21011 or 21397. Private bath, hot water, air-con, colour TV, radio, room telephone. Coffee shop, bar, swimming pool. US$29 to US$37 for single. US$44 to US$85 for double.
- **Sewarga Indah Hotel**, Jalan Jend. Sudirman 43, tel: 22066. Air con, colour TV with video movies, radio, room telephone. Restaurant, coffee shop, bar.
- **Lamin Indah**, Jalan Bhayangkara. US$14 for single. US$16 for double.

Dining

- **Banjar**, Jalan Diponegoro 25, tel: 1586. Indonesian.
- **Gumarang**, Jalan Veteran, tel: 717. Indonesian.
- **Lezat Baru**, Jalan Mulawarman 34. Chinese.
- **Mesra**, Hotel Mesra, Jalan, Pahlawan 1, tel: 2903. Indonesian, European, Chinese.
- **Puncak Indah**, Lamin Indah Hotel, Jalan Bayangkara 57, tel: 588. Chinese.

Tarakan

Accommodation

- **Hotel Bahtera**, Jalan Sulawesi 1, tel: 298. Private bath, hot water, air-con. Coffee shop, bar, discotheque.
- **Hotel Wisata**, Jalan Jend. Sudirman 46, tel: 221. US$5 for single. US$9 for double.
- **Tarakan Plaza**, Jalan Yos Sudarso, tel: 501 or 502 or 503. US$32 for single. US$40 for double.

Kutai National Park and Mahakam River Region

Apart from the obvious rewards once you arrive in the wildlife reserve at Kutai, the journey there can often be a mini-adventure in itself. The following travel notes will show you what to expect.

- **Sea and River**: access to the east of the reserve is by boat from **Samarinda**. Regular water taxis run to **Bontang** and **Sengatta**; this journey takes 18 hours. Speed boats offer a faster alternative: from Lok Tuan to Samarinda is under four hours in a twin-engined inboard-outboard belonging to P.T. Kayu Mas. The Santan and Sengatta rivers are navigable—the latter as far as **Mentoko**. Beyond here rapids make progress difficult, particularly at low water. A speedboat trip from Bontang to the University of Washington build-

ings on the Sengatta takes 3½ hours. The best boats are powered longboats called *ketinting*. Progress is slow but steady, and underwater obstacles are easily avoided. They also have the advantage of employing an engine which is less sophisticated then the two-stroke outboard. In the west, Sedulang can be reached in one day from Samarinda by speed boat, or by water taxi in double the time. Klampa may be reached from Sedulang in four hours if the water is high though at other times the journey takes much longer.

- **Air**: Balikpapan has connecting services to Samarinda. If room is available, fare-paying passengers can travel by P.N. Pertamina aircraft from Balikpapan to one of three airstrips owned by oil companies. There are airstrips at Tanjung Santan, Bontang and Sengatta and the oil companies are prepared to allow for charter-flight landings if previous arrangements are made.
- **Road**: a number of roads exist both close to and within the reserve. The new highway linking **Balikpapan** and **Samarinda** was completed in 1977 and it is planned to extend this road as part of the Trans-Kalimantan Highway project from Banjarmasin to Tarakan, north of Samarinda. This road now reaches **Muara Badak** and it is to connect with Bontang by 1986. Logging roads exist in the south of the reserve built by P.T. Kayu Mas and extend at least 50 kms (32 miles). Another road, built by P.T. Sylvaduta from Sengatta, joins the Kayu Mas Road at KM 42 and continues in a westerly direction to KM 76.

In the Sengatta area, Pertamina has a network of roads extending about 16 kms (10 miles) to the south and then eastwards to the coast. There are numerous abandoned roads which are navigable by jeep. **Teluk Kaba** is accessible this way from Sengatta on dry days.

Dayak Arts and Crafts

The centre of attention for anybody interested in Kalimantan's arts and crafts is the culture of the Dayak tribespeople. Their work displays an extraordinarily vibrant sense of design; the characteristic flowing geometrical patterns used in portraying scenes of jungle life bear unmistakable Chinese and Hindu-Javanese influences.

Ikat, or tie-dye, is the common technique in weaving; it originally used bark fibres, natural plant dyes and earth dyes though greater use is being made of commercial yarn and dyes. Dayak cloth is as good if not better than the famous Sumban *ikat*.

More than any other ethnic group in Indonesia, the Dayaks are famed for their beadwork. Thousands of tiny glass beads are used to decorate purses, tobacco pouches, scabbards, baby carriages, basket lids, hems, caps and headbands. The Punan are famous for their yellow and black beadwork.

Yet another craft is basketry and a wide variety of work in characteristic two-tone patterns can be bought.

Sex roles differentiate most of the Dayak crafts. Men are more at home carving wood and working metal, while the women tend more to plaiting, weaving, beadwork and tatooing.

Sulawesi

Ujung Pandang
Pare Pare
Rantepau and Makale
Kendari
Palu
Manado

Getting There and Getting Around

● **Air: Garuda** has three flights a day from Jakarta to Ujung Pandang leaving at either 5 a.m.,
8:30 a.m. or 1 p.m. The journey takes 2 hours.
One way economy-class fare is US$124. **Merpati**
flies on three days a week via Surabaya and
costs about 15 per cent less.

Many of the outlying towns in Sulawesi are
served. Garuda flies to Kendari, Manado and
Palu white Merpati flies to Gorontalo and Ma-
nado. **Bouraq** makes the connection between
Ujung Pandang and Manado flying via Palu and
Gorontalo. Prices vary of course but Garuda
offer one-way economy-class Ujung Pandang to
Manado for US$91, while both Merpati and
Bouraq charge US$77.

The Manado airport, located at Mapanget, is
a good half-hour's drive from the city itself. Buses ply the route through coconut groves and past
a winding river, but they are not on a fixed
schedule. A ride on a *bemo* will cost US$6 so it
might work out cheaper sharing a taxi into town.

Route	Dep.	Arr.	Days	one-way economy fare US$
JKT – UPG				
Garuda	05.00	08.15	Daily	124
	08.30	11.45	Daily	
	13.00	16.15	Daily	
Merpati	05.00	10.00	Wed.	106
	via SUB			
	05.00	10.35	Mon. Sat.	
	via SUB			
DPS – UPG				
Garuda	06.15	08.25	Daily	58
BPN – PLW				
Bouraq	11.50	12.55	Daily	42
	13.50	14.35		
UPG – MDC				
Garuda	11.50	13.25	Daily	91
Bouraq	07.15	15.45	Daily	77
	09.00	13.35	Mon. Wed. Fri.	
UPG – PLW				
Garuda	07.00	08.05	Tue. Thur. Sat. Sun.	53
	13.35	14.40	Daily	
Bouraq	07.15	08.50	Daily	45
	09.00	10.40	Mon. Wed. Fri	
UPG – KDI				
Garuda	10.30	11.20	Daily	41

CITY CODES: JKT-Jakarta; UPG-Ujung Pan-
dang; DPS-Denpasar; MDC-Manado; PLW-
Palu; GTO-Gorontalo; KDI-Kendari; BPN-
Balikpapan.

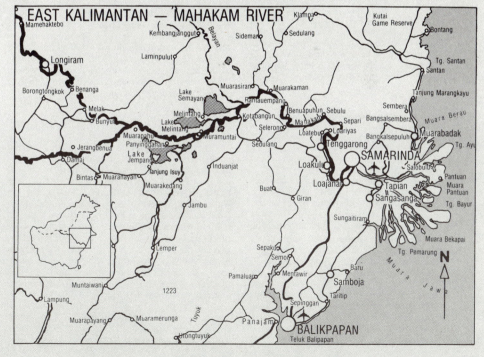

EAST KALIMANTAN — MAHAKAM RIVER

● **Sea:** the national shipping company PELNI run a passenger service throughout the archipelago. The last portion of its itinerary offers one method of access into Sulawesi and, incidentally, Kalimantan. Surabaya is the embarkation point for a passenger ship which sails to Ujung Pandang, Balikpapan (this is the Kalimantan stepping-off point), Bitung (the port for Manado in northeastern Sulawesi), and back again on the same route. Cabins are cheap so the only factor you have to take into account is time. The best place to consider this mode of transport is in Jakarta where you can visit the national shipping company's head office: PT PELNI, Jalan Angkasa 18, tel: 471569 or 415428. (*See* page 324.)

Dining

Sulawesi has a well-developed cuisine and prices are reasonable. Minahassans in particular are gourmets and gourmands. The "national food" is *tinutuan*; this is a rice porridge cooked with sundry vegetables, pieces of pumpkin and shredded maize, and eaten with salted fish and very hot chilli sauce.

Bakpiah, a big dumpling filled with meat, eggs and vegetables, is a popular treat. A fresh salad called *dabu-dabu*, made of fresh sour tomato, cucumber, onions, chillies and lemon cuy juice, accompanies any meal. Breakfast, called *smokol* (from the Dutch *smokkelen* [eating] consists of cooked banana, bolu cakes and coffee. A favourite drink is *es kacang*—cooked red beans topped with shredded ice, a splash of liquid chocolate syrup and another splash of condensed milk. It is cooling, filling and invigorating on a hot day.

For the daring, Minahassan cuisine features a number of unusual dishes—including fruitbats on the spit, field mice and snake (which, according to afficionadoes, tastes similar to eel). The greatest native delicacy is dog's meat, stewed in hot spices and peppers. The dish is called "RW," a code meaning "the pig with short hair." When in doubt, the diner can always ask to have a look at the carcasses in the kitchen; the cook will not be offended.

Ujung Pandang

Accommodation

Unlike many other large towns in East Indonesia, Ujung Pandang is a pleasant place to spend a day or two. Basing yourself in one of the hotels near the waterfront will let you walk to most places of interest and the best restaurants. The **Pantai Losari Indah** at Jalan Pasar Ikan 8 has air-conditioned rooms for US$18 and up. The more basic **Benteng** at Jalan Ujung Pandang 9, right across from Fort Rotterdam, has rooms for about US$8.

Budget travellers will find little suitable accommodation besides the **Hotel Alaska**, Jalan Saddang 52. The best deal in town is probably the **Pasangrahan Beach Hotel**, a 50-years-old white-washed structure at the far end of Jalan Somba Opu. The

rooms are small, with narrow, rickety folding beds, but all rooms face the sea and include a balcony cum sitting room, where you can enjoy the huge breakfast included in the room price.

Another possibility for those on a flying visit is the **Ramayana** on Jalan Gunung Bawakaraeng 12, which you pass coming in from the airport. Rooms are a bit expensive for what you get, but the hotel is right across the street from a Liman Express office, who will book your bus ticket to Rantepao. The Ramayana Travel agency, located in the hotel, specializes in arranging tours through Torajaland, including trekking to Mamasa. Other upmarket hotels downtown include the **Grand** and the **Victoria**.

● **Alaska Hotel**, Jalan S. Saddang 52, tel: 7138. US$2 for single. US$4 for double.
● **Benteng**, Jalan Ujung Pandang 9, tel: 22172. US$6 for single. US$7 for double.
● **Pantai Losari Indah**, Jalan Pasar Ikan 8, tel: 4363 or 6303. US$18 for single. US$20 for double.
● **Karuwisi Indah**, Jalan Urip Soemohardjo 10, tel: 28101. US$7 to US$9 for single.
● **Pessanggrahan Beach Hotel**, Jalan Somba Opu 279, tel: 4218 or 7615. US$6 to US$9 for single. US$10 to US$13 for double.
● **Ramayana**, Jalan Gunung Bawakaraeng 12, tel: 22165. US$6 to US$16 for single. US$6 to US$20 for double.
● **Rian Tira**, Jalan, Ranggong 5, tel: 4133. US$4 to US$7 for single. US$7 to US$11 for double.
● **Widhana Hotel**, Jalan Botolempangan 53, tel: 21393 or 22499. US$14 to US$16 for single. US$19 to US$23 for double.
● **Zeds Hotel**, Jalan Urip Soemohardjo 45, tel: 5725. US$12 for single. US$15 for double.
● **Grand Hotel**, Jalan Jend. A. Yani 5, tel: 5881. Rooms up to Us$60.
● **Victoria Hotel**, Jalan Jend. Sudirman 24, tel: 21428. Rooms up to US$70.

For the best in Sulawesian luxury you should stay at the Makassar Golden Hotel. Prices range from US$44 for a single to US$110 for a cottage "suite." Excellent location.

Dining

The sea-going Makassarese are famous seafood cooks using simple but delicious recipes. Their most famous dish is ikan *Bakar*, red snapper or sea bass grilled over an open flame, served with rice and spicy sambal. Though it is best eaten while sitting on the wooden benches of a waterfront *warung* in the company of Bugis sailors in town for the night, you many also sample it in the more gentile environment of the **Asia Baru Restaurant** on Jalan Salahutu 2. Other Restaurants serving a mix of Chinese, Indonesian and Western food include the **Hilman** on Jalan Jampea 2, the upmarket **Bamboo Den** on Jalan G. Latimojong, and the waterfront **Sea View** on Jalan Panghibur.

If seafood is not to your liking, another Masakarese specialty is Soto Makassar, a thick, nutritious soup made from various parts of the water buffalo. Best eaten in the afternoon, it is served at

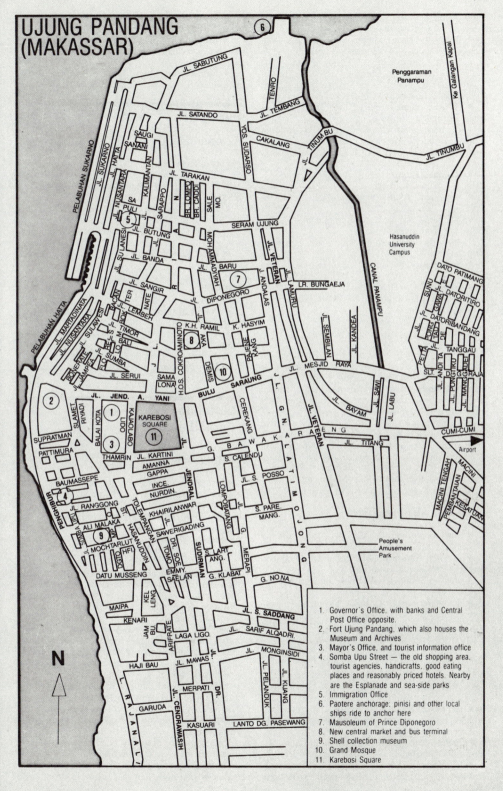

UJUNG PANDANG (MAKASSAR)

1. Governor's Office, with banks and Central Post Office opposite.
2. Fort Ujung Pandang, which also houses the Museum and Archives
3. Mayor's Office, and tourist information office
4. Somba Upu Street — the old shopping area, tourist agencies, handicrafts, good eating places and reasonably priced hotels. Nearby are the Esplanade and sea-side parks
5. Immigration Office
6. Paotere anchorage; pinisi and other local ships ride to anchor here
7. Mausoleum of Prince Diponegoro
8. New central market and bus terminal
9. Shell collection museum
10. Grand Mosque
11. Karebosi Square

N

Soto Daeng, near the Istana cinema, or at roadside *warungs* all over town.

- **Bamboo Den**, Jalan G. Latimojong, tel: 33228. Indonesian, European and Chinese.
- **Dunia Baru**, Jalan Timor Timur 71, tel: 5161. Indonesian, Chinese.
- **Happy Building**, Jalan Sulawesi, tel: 22947. Indonesian, European, Chinese.
- **Hilman**, Jalan Jampea 2, tel: 7895. Indonesian, European, Chinese.
- **Idaman**, Jalan Timor 56, tel: 3041. Indonesian, Seafood, Chinese.
- **Maranu**, Jalan Pasar Ikan 52. Indonesian, European, Chinese.
- **Raodah**, Jalan Khairil Anwar 28, Indonesian, European, Chinese.
- **Sea View**, Jalan Panghibur, tel: 22668. Indonesian, European, Chinese.
- **Widhana**, Jalan Batu Lempengan 53, Indonesian, European, Chinese.

Three other restaurants which are especially popular with locals are:

- **Sop Pangkep**, Jalan Andalas (near the church).
- **Kios Melati**, Jalan Veteran.
- **Wisma Ria**, Jalan Pasar Ikan. Indonesian, European, Chinese.

Transport

Though Merpati flies daily to Rantepao in Torajaland, most locals agree that the nine-hour bus journey is still worth taking. **Liman Express**, leaving from Jl. Laiya downtown with a scheduled stop in front of the Ramayana Hotel, has daily morning and evening buses.

For other areas of South Sulawesi, collective taxis are the best bet. **CV Taxis**, Jalan Durian 2, and **MPS**, Jalan Martadinata 142, have frequent taxis to towns on the South Coast and Watampone, the ferry terminal for Southeast Sulawesi.

- **C.V. Omega**, Jalan Hati Murni, tel: 82679.
- **Liman Express**, Jalan Laiya 25, tel: 5851.

Domestic Airline Offices

- **Garuda Indonesia Airways**, Jalan Slamet Riyadi 6, tel: 22804 or 22705 or 7746.
- **Merpati Nusantara Airlines**, Jalan G. Bawakaraeng 109, tel: 4114 or 4118.
- **Bouraq Indonesia Airlines**, Jalan Pattimura 5, tel: 5906.
- **Mandala Airlines**, Jalan Seram 62, Jalan Hasanuddin 29, tel: 7765.

Shipping Company

- **PELNI**, Jalan Martadinata, tel: 6967.

Art and Craft Shops

- **Art Shop**, Jalan Somba Opu 20. Indonesian statues, carving, batiks, sarongs, basket work and leather.
- **Asdar Art Shop**, Jalan Somba Opu 199. Paintings, carving, silk sarongs, basket work.
- **Cony Karya**, Jalan Pasar Ikan, 26. Paintings, statues, carving, porcelains, sea shells and silver.

- **Kanebo Art Shop**, Jalan Pattimura 27. Paintings, statues and sea shells.
- **Mutiara Art Shop**, Jalan Somba Opu 117A. Statues, carvings, sarongs, sea shells and animal hides.
- **Paleori Art Shop**, Jalan Somba Opu 108. Paintings, Toraja weaving and bamboo.

Pare-Pare

Accommodation

- **Gandaria Hotel**, Jalan Bau Massepe 171, tel: 21093. Rooms from US$3 to US$10.
- **Kartika**, Jalan Lompobattang 110. All rooms US$15.
- **Roxi**, Jalan Baso Dg. Patompo. Rooms for less than US$3.
- **Hotel Siswa**, centre of town, US$9 per person.
- **Hotel Bima**, Jalan Usman Isah 25. US$9 per person.

Dining

- **Angin Mamiri**, Jalan Pinggir Laut. Indonesian, Chinese.
- **Sampurna**, Jalan Bau Massepe. Indonesian, Chinese.
- **Asia**, Jalan Baso Dg. Tompo. Indonesian.
- **Kios Nirwana**, Jalan Bau Massepe 122. Indonesian.

Rantepao and Makale (Tana Toraja)

Getting Around

Most of the attractions are in the immediate vicinity of Rantepao, reachable by local transportation and much walking. Old motorcycles rent for US$10 a day, or jeeps for approx US$40. During the months of August to October, the funeral season, someone will always be organizing shared transportation to the event. Ask around.

For extended excursions through the outlying villages, you will need standard mountain trekking gear and a guide. The guide will also carry your pack—helpful if you are not used to high altitudes. Although the townfolk of Rantepao will tell you to pay for your barter goods, this is no longer the case. Villagers these days are moving into a money economy—they want cash. In each village, ask the *Kepala Desa* (village headman) to arrange for you to sleep in someone's house. If you have a guide, he will arrange it.

The treks from Rantepao involve making a loop through several villages, ending where you began. The longest and most interesting walk, however, will take you 60 kms (37 miles) to touristically virgin Mamasa.

The walk to Mamasa begins in Bituang, a four-hour *bemo* ride from Makale. You will not be alone, the path is a major trading route between Toraja and Mamasa; the walk takes up to four days. In Mamasa, stay at the **Losmen Mini**, for a few days before braving the horrendous 90-km (56-mile) ride to Polewali on the coast.

Accommodation

- **Indra**, Jalan Pasar 63, Rantepao. Rooms for less than US$7.
- **Merlin**, Jalan Pahlawan, Rantepao. Rooms for less than US$8.
- **Nirmala**, Jalan Pahlawan 118, Rantepao, tel: 60. Rooms for less than US$6.
- **Tana Bua**, Jalan Abdul Gani 43, Rantepao, tel: 61. Rooms for less than US$9.
- **Toraja Cottage**, Jalan Paku Balasara, Rantepao, tel: 84146. US$21 to US$25 for single. US$25 to US$28 for double.
- **Misiliana**, Jalan Pao, Rantepao, tel: 56. US$13 for single. US$15 for double.
- **Barana**, Mendetek, Makale. US$14 for single. US$16 for double.
- **Batupapan**, Makale. US$6 for single. US$9 for double.

Dining

- **Marlin**, Jalan Pahlawan 30C, Rantepao. Indonesian, European.
- **Misiliana**, Jalan Pahlawan 5, Rantepao. Indonesian, European, Chinese.
- **Sedia**, Jalan Irawan, Rantepao, Indonesian, European, Chinese.

Kendari

Getting There

- **Air:** Garuda flies to Kendari from Ujung Pandang once daily, while **Merpati** has flights several times a week to Kendari and Bau-Bau, though schedules on the latter are likely to be changed without notice.
- **Sea:** a ferry leaves **Bone** (Wantampone) 9 p.m. daily, arriving in Kolaka early next morning. No cabins are available. Going deck class and renting an army cot is the best alternative. There is a direct taxi connection to Kendari from the terminal. From dock to terminal is about one km, bargain hard with the *becak* driver.

Another possibility is a PELNI boat stopping once a week in Bau-Bau enroute to **Ambon** from Ujung Pandang, or vice versa. A ferry leaves Kendari every afternoon for Raha and Bau-Bau, four berths to a cabin, arriving in Raha at midnight and Bau-Bau at 3 a.m., though you can stay on board until a civilized hour.

Accommodation

Impossible to get lost in this town, it has only one main road, though it changes its name several times. The best hotel is the Kendari Beach. Other hotels are farther along the main street toward the wharves. Try **Arnin's Hotel** Jalan Jend Yani. or the Wisma Andika.

- **Arnin's Hotel**, Jalan Jendral A. Yani 55, tel: 21615. US$12 for single. US$17 for double.
- **Hamdamin**, Jalan Jendral S. Parman 62, tel: 21516. Rooms for less than Us$5.
- **Wisma Andika**, Jalan Jendral A. Yani, tel: 21651. US$7 for single. US$9 to US$14 for double.
- **Wisma Wolio**, Jalan Sultan Hasanuddin 62, tel: 21484. US$5 for single. US$6.50 for double.
- **Kendari Beach**, Jalan Hasanuddin 44. Rooms up to US$40.

Palu

Accommodation

- **Angkasa Raya**, Jalan Danau Poso. Rooms for less than US$2.
- **Astoria**, Jalan S. Parman. US$6 for single. US$10 for double.
- **Buana**, Jalan R.A. Kartini 6, tel: 21476. US$3 for single. US$6 for double.
- **Fahmil**, Jalan Jendril A. Yani I. Rooms for less than US$9.
- **Garuda**, Jalan Hasanuddin 33, tel: 48. Rooms for less than US$3.
- **Kanado**, Jalan M.T. Haryono. Rooms for less than US$6.
- **Latimojong II**, Jalan Gaja Mada. Rooms for less than Us$3.
- **Palu Beach Grand Park Hotel**, Jalan Raden Saleh 22., tel: 21126 or 21326. US$25 to US$30 for single and double.
- **Wisata**, Jalan S. Parman 39, tel: 39, tel: 379. US$8 for single. US$16 for double.

Dining

- **Dunia Baru**, Jalan Danau Lindu 14, tel: 21371.
- **Restaurant Marannu**, Jalan Setia Budi 11, tel: 21068.

Travel Agencies

- **Aksa Utama**, Jalan Yos sudarso Poso 10.
- **Ateka Sakti**, Jalan Jendral Sudirman 11, tel: 21995.
- **Bemagy Travel**, Palu Beach Hotel, Jalan Raden Saleh, tel: 21226.

Manado

Accommodation

- **Kota**, Jalan Yos Sudarso, tel: 3251. US$3 for single. US$6 for double.
- **Minahasa**, Jalan Sam Ratulangi, tel: 2059 or 2559. US$8 for single. US$10 for double.
- **Mini Cakalele**, Jalan Korengkeng 40, tel: 52942. US$8 for single. US$11 for double.
- **Mitysilna**, Jalan Sarupung, tel: 3445. US$11 for double.
- **New Garden Hotel**, Jalan Rike Atas, tel: 52688 or 21476. US$13 for single. US$15 for double.

- **Sartum Wisma**, Jalan Brigien Katamso, tel: 3375. US$5 for single. US$8 for double.
- **Tentram**, Jalan Serapung, tel: 3127. Rooms for less than US$3.
- **Yepindra**, Jalan Sam Ratulangi 37, tel: 4049. US$9 for single. US$11 for double.
- **Kawanua City Hotel**, Jalan Sam Ratulangi 1, tel: 52222. US$23 for single. US$25 for double.
- **Angkasa Raya**, Jalan Kol. Soegiono 12, tel: 2039. US$14 for double.
- **New Queen Hotel**, Jalan Wakeke 12-14, tel: 4440. US$10 for single. US$15 for double.
- **Wenang/Marannu City Hotel**, Jalan Bathseda 25, tel: 2663. US$13 for single. US$15 for double.

Dining

- **Cakalong, Kawanua City Hotel**, Jalan Sam Ratulangi 1, tel: 3771. Indonesian, European, Chinese.
- **Dua Raya**, Jalan P. Tenoban 46, tel: 2236. Chinese.
- **Jit Hien**, Jalan Panjaitan 35. Chinese.
- **Miami**, Jalan Yos Sudarso 73, tel: 3236. Indonesian, European, Chinese.
- **Lupa Lelah Club**, Jalan Letjen Soeprapto, tel: 3314. Indonesian, European, Chinese, Japanese.

Maluku

Getting There and Getting Around

- **Air: Garuda, Merpati, Bouraq** and **Mandala** airlines all have regular services to Ambon and Ternate. To Ambon, there are flights from Jakarta, Surabaya and Denpasar, either direct (daily) or via Ujung Pandang (twice daily).

Merpati flies to Ternate from the same cities as above though overnight transit in Manado is necessary. Bouraq has a direct flight from Jakarta to Ternate with intermediate stops in Balikpapan, Palu, Gorontalo and Manado.

Merpati also has a regular flight schedule from Ternate to smaller towns on Halmahera and Bachan; and from Ambon to Ceram, Banda and towns of the Southeast Moluccas. A daily "shuttle flight" connects Ambon and Ternate.

Route	Dep.	Arr.	Days	one-way economy fare US$
JKT — AMQ				
Garuda	05.00	12.00	Daily	177
	06.00	12.55	Daily	
DPS — AMQ				
Garuda	06.15 via UPG	12.00	Daily	123
	08.30	12.55	Daily	

SUB — AMQ				
Garuda	06.05	12.20	Mon. Wed. Thur. Sat.	152
	06.05 via UPG	12.00	Tue. Fri.	
	07.00 via DPS	13.10	Daily	
UPG — AMQ				
Garuda	09.20	12.00	Daily	85
MDC — TTE				
Bouraq	14.10	16.15	Mon. Wed. Fri. Sat.	36
AMQ — NDA				
Merpati	08.00	08.55	Wed. Sat.	39
AMQ — TTE				
Merpati	10.45 via MAL	13.50	Sun.	58

CITY CODE: JKT-Jakarta; AMQ-Ambon; DPS-Denpasar; UPG-Ujung Pandang; TTE-Ter-nate; MDC-Manado; NDA-Bandaneira.

Ambon airport is situated on a peninsula opposite the city. The journey by taxi to the city (32 kms [20 miles]) is expensive so it is wise to share. Alternatively, a speedboat will ferry you across the water in style.

- **Sea:** sea travel is the traditional means of transportation. Sailing vessels still carry agricultural and commercial products over long distances, and small dugouts hop from village to village to sell their wares. The deep-water harbour at Ambon is the principal port of Maluku. In addition to large commercial vessels from throughout the province, Indonesian vessels tie up at Halong and tuna boats gather at Galala.

On the east coast of Ambon island, speedboats and other motorized vessels dock at Tulehu and connect with the towns of Ceram, the Lease islands and Banda.

Check with the Ambon *Syahbandar* (harbourmaster) or PT Pelni for boats going to Banda and Ternate. A Pelni Perintis (pioneer) boat leaves Ambon twice monthly for the islands of Maluku Tenggara. The boat takes 15 days to reach the terminus at Leti, but you can save time by flying Merpati to Banda or Kai and boarding the boat there. On Leti, you might also fnd a fisherman to ferry you across to East Timor, which is now open for tourists, but don't count on it.

In Ternate's harbour there are motorboats and motorized sailing boats offering connections with the surrounding islands as far as Morotai, Tobelo and Patani on Halmahera's east coast, and Gebe and Bachan.

- **Road:** *bemos* travel the principal roads throughout the Maluku archipelago. In Ambon city and Ternate the main terminals are in the centre of town next to shopping centres. In some of the more remote areas there is nothing to stop you walking if you think you have discovered something to visit. Village hopping on the coast is easy with numerous *prahus* willing to take a passenger or two.

Dining

The Moluccan lifestyle is reflected in what is a rather basic cuisine. Sago is the staple food in the south, supplemented by sweet potatoes and cassava. Fish is the main source of protein, with meat and fowl reserved for feasts. Kanari, a nut similar to an almond, is made into a sauce for *gado-gado*-style salads. In the north, the yellow rice eaten with curries or sate is very popular.

Mixed Arab and Chinese families have more varied dishes and eat more meat. Eurasian Moluccans favour a Dutch-style cuisine with such dishes as red-bean soup with pork trotters, and fish with white sauce. Dining out is not a widespread habit though coffee houses serve lunches. To cater fo the many immigrant workers, a number of foo stalls and restaurants are beginning to appear.

Accommodation

Both Ambon and Ternate offer numerous pseudo-modern hotels. *wisma* (family hotels), and *losmen* (pensions). Prices range up to US$30 a night in a new hotel; up to US$15 (meals included) in a *wisma*; and less at a *losmen*, where rooms are clean but toilet facilities must be shared.

If you venture farther afield you should enquire about accommodation before you head off anywhere. Often you'll be offered the hospitality of a Christian mission in which case a "donation" would be a fair way of showing gratitude.

Ambon

- **Hotel Abdulali**, Jalan Sultan Baabullah, tel: 2796. US$16 for single. US$25 for double.
- **Hotel Amboina**, Jalan Kapten Ulupaha no. 5A, tel: 41725. US$20 for single. US$26 for double.
- **Hotel Beta**, Jalan Wim Reuwaru, tel: 3463. US$6 for single. US$11 for double.
- **Hotel Cendrawasih**, Jalan Tulukabessy, tel: 2487. US$22 for single. US$30 for double.
- **Hotel Eleonoor**. US$7 for single.
- **Hotel Mutiara**, Jalan Raya Pattimura, tel: 3075, 3076. US$22 for single. US$30 for double.
- **Hotel Reflany**, Jalan Wim Reuwaru, tel: 41692. US$6 for single. US$12 for double.

For cheaper rooms in Ambon, try the basic hotels and *losmen* around the teacher's college, such as the **Silalou**, Jalan Sedapmalam 41. This area is the most strategic, close to the market and Merpati and Garuda Airline offices.

Ternate

- **Hotel Anda Baru**, Jalan Ketilang 49. US$9 for single.
- **Hotel Chrysan**, Jalan Ahmad Yani, tel: 377, 210. US$11 for single. US$22 for double.
- **Hotel Indah**, Jalan Busoiri no. 3, tel: 217. US$16 for double.

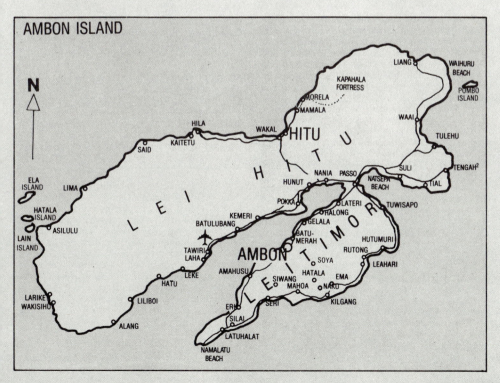

AMBON ISLAND

Irian Jaya

All visitors to Irian Jaya **must** obtain a letter of recommendation and travel clearance (*surat jalan*) from the *bupati* (provincial governor) in Jayapura before travelling to the interior. Unauthorised visitors to sensitive areas are sent back to Jayapura at their own expense. And it is not always possible to know in advance which parts of the island are considered "sensitive." For the most up-to-date information on Irian Jaya you should contact: 1) The Tourist Development Board of Irian Jaya, Bapparda, Governor's Office of Irian Jaya, PO Box 499, Jayapura, Irian Jaya; 2) Irian Jaya Promotion Board, Jalan Suwirjo 43, Jakarta, tel: 353579.

Travel agents experienced in operating tours to Irian Jaya are: **Tunas Indonesia**; and **Pacto**.

Getting There and Getting Around

● **Air: Garuda** has at least one flight daily from Jakarta to Jayapura with transfers in Ujung Pandang, Biak and Sorong. Aircraft leave the capital at 5 a.m. and arrive in Jayapura at 3:35 p.m. (some flights arrive at 5 p.m.). The fare is US$240. **Merpati** also flies from Jakarta to Biak via Surabaya and Ujung Pandang (no transfers) with connections to Jayapura twice a week. Planes leave Jakarta at 5 a.m. and arrive in Biak at 3:30 p.m. The connecting flights from Biak depart at 5 a.m. and arrive in Jayapura at 7:15 a.m. The fare is US$220.

From Jayapura and Biak, Merpati has Twin Otter flights to the following places: Sorong, Manokwari, Serui and Nabire on the north coast; Fakfak, Kaimena, Kokenau, Timika and Merauke on the south coast; and Enarotali and Wamena in the highlands. Jayapura-Wamena flights take about one hour and cost around US$29.

In addition, missionary aircraft travel to isolated settlements throughout the highlands and coastal regions. Four, missionary groups have bases at Jayapura's Sentani Airport (34 kms) [22 miles] from Jayapura): the Missionary Aviation Fellowship (MAF); the Christian and Missionary Alliance (CAMA); the Seventh Day Adventists; and Cenderawasih University's Summer Institute of Linguistics. MAF is by far the largest with 27 planes, two helicopters, 30 pilots, and seven main bases (Jayapura, Wamena, Nabire, Manokwari, Yaosakor, Bokondini and Mulia). Other missionary groups in Irian Jaya are the Australian Baptist Mission (ABMS), Asian Pacific Christian Mission (APCM), Regions Beyond Missionary Alliance (RBMU), The Evangelical Alliance Mission (TEAM), and the Unevangelised Fields Mission (UFM). Rather than fix travel plans before you arrive, it would be far better to investigate some of these organisations, ask around and find out just what you might be able to do. The possibility for getting to some of the remotest corners of the province is there and you need only use your initiative and a spirit of adventure.

Route	Dep.	Arr.	Days	one-way economy fare US$
AMQ – DJJ				
Garuda	12.30	17.00	Mon. Wed.	130
	via SOQ		Thur. Sat	
JKT – DJJ				
Garuda	05.00	15.35	Daily	279
	via UPG/BIK			
	05.00	17.00	Mon. Wed.	
	via UPG/		Thur. Sat	
	SOQ			
JKT – BKI				
Garuda	05.00	13.20	Daily	275
	via UPG			
	05.00	17.00	Mon. Wed.	
	via UPG/		Thur. Sat	
	SOQ			
Merpati	05.00	15.30	Wed.	234
	via SUB/UPG			
JKT – SOQ				
Garuda	05.00	13.30	Daily	202
UPG – DJJ				
Garuda	09.20	17.00	Mon. Wed.	213
	via SOQ		Thur. Sat.	
	09.30	15.35	Daily	
	via BIK			
DJJ – MKQ				
Garuda	07.10	08.25	Mon. Wed.	73
			Thur. Sat.	
DJJ – WMX				
Merpati	08.30	09.30	Tue. Wed. Sat.	29
	11.40	12.40	Mon. Fri.	
	09.20	10.25	Wed.	
BKI – DJJ				
Garuda	14.30	15.35	Daily	49
	14.00	16.35	Tue. Fri.	
	15.55	17.00	Mon. Wed.	
			Thur. Sat.	
Merpati	06.30	08.35	Tue. Sun	42
AMQ – FKQ				
Merpati	08.30	10.30	Tue. Sun.	70

CITY CODES: AMQ-Ambon; DJJ-Jayapura; JKT-Jakarta; BKI-Biak; UPG-Ujung Pandang; MKQ-Merauke; WMX-Wamena; FKQ-Fakfak; SOQ-Sorong.

● Sea: definitely worth trying to hitch free rides on some of the coastal steamers. The oil industry here is served by considerable sea-going traffic. On the south coast, Agats is the major port. Other vessels carry passengers though a fare is charged. If you are thinking of using the state shipping company PELNI then you should enquire in Jakarta concerning routes, schedules and fares. Planning a sea itinerary will mean travelling via the Maluku archipelago. If your sole intended destination is Irian Jaya you should stick to air travel.

Shopping

The demand for Asmat carvings has increased over the years. Simple colours—earth-red, black and white—are an Asmat trademark. The UN project (see page 275) that has been protecting the craft has restored the prestige of the master-carvers by giving them a recognised place as teachers in the education system.

Contact the **Asmat Handicraft Project** at Dinas Perindustriaan, Kotakpos 294, Jayapura if you want to buy Asmat carvings. There is also an official warehouse on **Jalan Batu Karang** outside Jayapura off the main road to Hamadi. The **Cama** shop sells carvings as does the souvenir counter at Sentani airport.

Activities

Though the government has succeeded in "set-tling" a number of tribes, there are still thousands of isolated ethnic groups in remote areas. Tours are easy to arrange. In Jayapura, guides can be hired from the Cenderawasih University anthropology department on Jalan Sentani Abepura (20 kms [12 miles] from the city). The usual rate is US$14 to US$18 a day. Guides can be hired in Wamena for less—usually US$9 to US$14 a day.

Jayapura

Accommodation

- **Hotel Dafonsoro**, Jalan Percetakan, Negara Jayapura. Air-con. US$22 for double.
- **Hotel Triton**, Jalan Achmad Yani. Air-con. US$22 for double.
- **Losmen Asia**, Jalan Pasar Sentral. Non air-con. US$11.
- **Losmen Lawu**, Dok VII. Air-con. US$14 to US$22.
- **Losmen Sederhana**, Dekat Sarinah. Air-con. US$14 to US$22.
- **Mess GKI**. Jalan Yos Sudarso. Non air-con. US$11.

A cheaper alternative to staying in Jayapura is to sleep in Sentani, 32 kms (20 miles) inland.

Dining

Jayapura has a large Bugis population, so *ikan Bakar* is the meal of choice. The alley behind the Impor-Expor Bank near the *bemo* terminal is lined with *warungs* serving *ikan akar* and *sate*.

Two recommended restaurants are **Cahaya** on Jalan Achmad Yani Jayapura and **Hawaii** on Dekat Sarinah. Both serve European and Asian food.

Wamena

Accommodation

- **Cottage Pertamina**. US$14 per person.
- **Hotel Negara**, US$12 per person.

The **Nayak Hotel** (US$26 for a double), across the road from the airport terminal, is the best value in town; it also has the best food. For accommodation outside Wamena, any village

chief will let you sleep in a communal "honnay" for Rp500 and perhaps a small gift of cigarettes or such like. The missionaries will sometimes put you up, and the Indonesians working in the villages would be honoured to have you as a house guest.

Suggested Reading

History

Boxer, C.R. *Jan Compagnie in War and Peace (1602-1799)*. Heinemann: Hong Kong, 1979.
———. *The Dutch Seaborne Empire 1600-1800*. Hutchinson: London.
———. *The Portuguese Seaborne Empire 1415-1825*. Hutchinson: London, 1969.
Day,Clive. *The Policy and Administration of the Dutch in Java*. Oxford: Kuala Lumpur, 1966.
Hall, D.G.E. *A History of Southeast Asia*. MacMillan: London, 1977.
Hanna, Willard A. *Bali Profile: People, Events, Circumstances 1901-1976*.
———. *Indonesian Banda*. ISHI: Philadelphia, 1978.
Pigeaud, T.G. Th. and De Graaf, H.J. *Islamic States in Java 1500-1700*. Martinus Nijhoff: the Hague, 1976.
Reid, Anthony. *Indonesian National Revolution 1945-50*. Longman: Hawthorn, 1974.
Ricklefs, M.C. *Jogjakarta Under Sultan Mangkubumi 1749-1792, a History of the Division of Java*. Oxford: London, 1974.
———. *A History of Modern Indonesia*. MacMillan: London, 1981.
Schnitger, F.M. *Forgotten Kingdoms in Sumatra*. E.J. Brill: Leiden, 1939.
Van Heekeren, H.R. *The Stone Age of Indonesia*. Martinus Nijhoff: The Hague, 1972.
Van Leur, J.C. *Indonesian Trade and Society*. W. van Hoeve: Bandung, 1960.

Geography and Natural History

Dobby, E.H.B. *Southeast Asia*. London, 1966.
Directorate-General of Tourism. *Indonesia: National Parks & Nature Reserves*. Jakarta, n.d.
Fisher, C.A. *Southeast Asia: A Social, Economic and Political Geography*. Methuen: London, 1964.
Wallace, Alfred Russel. *The Malay Archipelago: The Land of the Orang-utan and the Bird of Paradise*. Reprint, Graham Brash: Singapore 1983.

Society and Religion

Belo, Jane. *Trance in Bali*. Columbia University Press: New York, 1960.
Covarrubias, Miguel. *Island of Bali*. Alfred A. Knopf: New York, 1937. Oxford: Kuala Lumpur, reprint 1984.
Fox, J.J. *Indonesia: the Making of a Culture*. Australian National University: Canberra, 1980.

Geertz, Clifford. *Negara, the Theatre State in Nineteenth-Century Bali*. Princeton University Press: Princeton, 1980.

———. *The Religion of Java*. Free Press: Glencoe, 1960.

Goris, R. *Bali: Cults and Customs*. Jakarta.

Kennedy, Raymond. *Bibliography of Indonesian Peoples and Cultures*. HRAF: New Haven, 1974 (2nd revised ed.).

McVey, Ruth (ed). *Indonesia: Its People, Its Society, Its Culture*. HRAF Press: New Haven, 1963.

Mulder, Niels. *Mysticism & Everyday Life in Contemporary Java*. Singapore University Press: Singapore, 1978.

The Arts

Becker, Judith. *Traditional Music in Modern Java, Gamelan in a Changing Society*. University Press of Hawaii: Honolulu, 1980.

Brandon, James. *On Thrones of Gold: Three Javanese Shadow Plays*. Harvard University Press: Cambridge, 1967.

Elliot, Inger McCabe. *Batik, Fabled Cloth of Java*. Clarkson N. Potter: New York, 1984.

Fischer, Joseph (ed). *Threads of Tradition, Textiles of Indonesia and Sarawak*. University of California: Berkeley, 1979.

Gittinger, Mattiebelle. *Splendid Symbols: Textiles and Tradition in Indonesia*. The Textile Museum: Washington D.C., 1979.

Holt, Claire. *Art in Indonesia: Continuities and Change*. Cornell University Press: New York, 1967.

Kempers, A.J. Bernet. *Ageless Borobudur*, Servire/Wassenaar, 1976.

———. *Ancient Indonesian Art*. Harvard University Press: Cambridge, 1959.

———. *Monumental Bali: Introduction to Balinese Archaeology and Guide to the Monuments*. Van Goor Zonen: The Hague, 1977.

Kunst, Jaap. *Music in Java*. Martinus Nijhoff: The Hague, (3rd ed). 1973, 2 vols.

Soedarsono. *Dances in Indonesia*. Gunung Agung: Jakarta, 1974.

Tirtaamidjaja, N. *Batik: Pattern and Motif*. Djambatan: Jakarta, 1966.

Zoete, Beryl de and Spies, Walter. *Dance and Drama in Bali*. Faber and Faber: London, 1938.

Literature in English about Indonesia

Alberts, A. *The Islands*. trans. by Hans Koning. Univ. of Mass. Press: Amherst, 1983.

Baum, Vicki. *A Tale From Bali*. Oxford in Asia Paperbacks: Kuala Lumpur, 1973.

Breton de Nijs, E. *Faded Portraits*. trans. by Donald and Elsje Sturtevant. Univ. of Mass. Press: Amherst, 1982.

Conrad, Joseph. *Almayer's Folly: A Story of an Eastern River and Tales of Unrest*.

———. *Lord Jim*.

———. *An Outcast of the Islands*.

———. *Victory*.

Lubis, Mochtar. *Twilight in Jakarta* Hutchinson: London, 1963.

Multatuli (Eduard Douwes Dekker). *Max Havelaar, or the Coffee Auctions of the Dutch Trading Company*. trans. by Roy Edwards. Univ. of Mass. Press: Amherst, 1982.

Nieuwenhuys, Rob. *Mirror of the Indies, A History of Dutch Colonial Literature*. trans. F Frans van Rosevelt. Univ. of Mass. Press: Amherst, 1982.

Tours

The following packages are easily available through any good travel agent. If you are told that such deals are not obtainable, insist that they are recommended by a leading travel agent in Southeast Asia.

In Singapore, the schedules and prices of all the following packages can be obtained from **German Asian Travels (Pte.) Ltd.,** 9 Battery Road, #14-03 Straits Trading Building, SINGAPORE 0104. Telex: RS 21830, Cable: GERASIA, Tel: 533 5466.

Bali 4 days/3 nights

Individual tour to Bali. Tour may commence any day. Programme altered according to personal requirements. Basic programme: accommodation in Kuta Beach Club. If another hotel chosen, the difference in the respective room rate is charged. Excursions by private car.

1. day: morning dep. by Garuda via Jakarta to Denpasar. Transfer to hotel.

2. day: full day excursion. *Barong* dance, where good fights evil in an ancient Ramayana story. Then to Mas, the village of the woodcarvers, and Ubud, where many well-known painters live, Tampaksiring with its holy springs and the Elephant Cave Temple. Finally visit Kintamani with its beautiful view of the Batur volcano and its lake.

3. day: excursion along the East Coast. Visit the Palace of Justice in Klungkung, the temples of Besakih on Mt. Agung (the highest and most holy volcano of Bali), the Bat Cave Temple and the Bay of Padang.

4. day: free until early afternoon return by Garuda to Singapore.

Bali 5 days/4 nights

Individual tour to Bali. Tour may commence any day. Programme altered according to personal requirements. Basic Programme: accommodation in Kuta Beach Club. If another hotel chosen, the difference in the respective room rate is charged. Excursions by private car.

1. day: morn. dep. by Garuda via Jakarta to Denpasar. Accommodation in the hotel of your choice.

2. day: full day excursion. *Barong* dance, where good fights evil in an ancient Ramayana story. Then to Mas, the village of the woodcarvers, and Ubud, where many well-known painters live, Tampaksiring with its holy springs and the Elephant Cave Temple, finally visit Kintamani with its beautiful view of the Batur volcano and its lake.

3. day: excursion along the East Coast. Visit the Palace of Justice in Klungkung, the temples of Besakih on Mt. Agung (the highest and most holy volcano of Bali), the Bat Cave Temple and the Bay of Padang.

4. day: at leisure.

5. day: early afternoon return by Garuda to Singapore.

Bali-Yogyakarta 5 Days/4 nights.

Individual tour of Bali and Yogyakarta. This tour may start any day. Extended and altered according to your own specifications. All excursions by private car.

Basic Programme:

1. day: with Garuda via Jakarta to Yogyakarta. Immigration and customs in Jakarta. Transfer to the hotel of your choice.

2. day: morn. Excursion to Borobodur, a buddhist temple complex dating from the 8th Century. En route visit temples of Mendut and Pawon. Aft. a look at some of the art and culture that Yogya is famous for.

3. day: morning at leisure. Early afternoon transfer to airport to fly with Garuda to Denpasar. Accommodation in the hotel of your choice. Transfer not included.

4. day: full day excursion to Mas, the village of the woodcarvers, and then Ubud, where many well-known painters live, Tampaksiring with its holy springs and the Elephant Cave Temple. Finally visit Kintamani with its beautiful view of the Batur volcano and its lake.

5. day: Early afternoon return by Garuda via Jakarta to Singapore.

Excursions in Bali by Coach

Barong Dance, Art and Volcano 8 hours

Witness the colourful *Barong* and *Kris* dance then drive to Tegal Tamu, centre of the sandstone sculpturing, Celuk silver and gold working village, Mas, famous for its wood carvings, the ancient Elephant cave at Bedulu, view the rice terraces at Gunung Kawi, the pools at Tampaksiring's Holy Springs and enjoy the breathtaking view of the semi-active volcano at Mt Batur. Daily.

Sailing Tour 4 hours

Sail with the large sailing boat *Janggolan* around the harbour, then visit the village of Tandjung and Turtle Island if the tide permits, drop anchor for swimming, snorkeling, sunbathing or fishing. Wednesdays.

Excursions in Bali by Private Car

Kintamani Tour

Full-day excursion to Mas, the village of the woodcarvers, Ubud, where many well-known painters live, Tampaksiring with its springs and the Elephant Cave Temple. Finally visit Kintamani with its beautiful view of the Batur volcano and its lake.

Karangasem Tour

Full-day excursion along the East Coast. Visit the Palace of Justice in Klungkung, the temples of Besakih on Mt. Agung (the highest and most holy volcano of Bali). Visit the Bat Cave Temple and the Bay of Padang.

Excursions in Yogyakarta by Private Car

City Tour 3 hours

Tour of the town, visit the Sultan's Palace. Visit Batik factory. See the silversmith in Kota Gede.

Prambanan 3 hours

Loro Jonggrang and the complete Prambanan temple complex.

Borobodur 4 hours

Borobodur. En route visit temples of Mendut and Pawon.

Overland Jakarta — Bali

Bali-Jakarta 10 days

1. day: Bali-Tretes. Early departure for Gilimanuk to take the ferry to Java, then travel along the northern coast on to Tretes—situated in the mountains of East Java.

2. day: Surabaya Excursion. Afternoon excursion to Surabaya, Indonesia's second largest city. City sightseeing tour including a visit to the Zoo to view a prehistoric Komodo Dragon. Return to Tretes.

3. day: Tretes-Yogyakarta. Drive through the Javanese countryside with a stop for lunch. Prior to arriving at Yogyakarta, visit the famous Prambanan Temple.

4. day: morning visit a batik factory, the Sultan's Palace, the Water Castle and a silver workshop.

5. day: Yogyakarta. Today free for shopping, relaxation or for optional sightseeing.

6. day: Yogyakarta-Batu Raden. In the morning leave Yogyakarta to visit Borobodur, the magnificent Buddhist temple complex. After ample time to enjoy Borobodur to the full, proceed along the central route with stops for photos and for lunch. Overnight in Batu Raden.

7. day: Batu Raden-Bandung. Continue along the delightful scenic route with regular stops and visit to Naga Village where the villagers have retained their traditional ways. Overnight in Bandung.

8. day: Tangkuban. Excursion into the countryside to visit Tangkuban Prahu, and the active volcano. Assisted by guides to the crater. Visit a nearby hot spring, before lunch. In the afternoon return to Bandung.

9. day: Bandung-Jakarta. In the morning drive down from the highlands through the Puncak Pass to Bogor. Lunch, and visit the famous Botanical Gardens.

10. day: Jakarta. Tour arrangements end at noon.

Diving Tour 6 days/5 nights.

Service included: room rent, all meals starting with breakfast on 2nd day; dive equipment; transportation as described, guide/instructor/ two tanks each course.

1. day: arrive at Ngurah Rai Airport; transfer to hotel, Manggis Inn, located in the village.

2. day: early morning, coach eastward to Padang Bay, to start with the first dive around Gili Tepekong island group. Boxed lunch.

3. day: after breakfast, coach to Tulamben, on the east tip of the island. Shore as well as boat dives can be done. Boxed lunch. In the afternoon, drive westward along the northern road to Teluk Terima. Dinner and overnight.

4. day: after breakfast, enjoy a drive around Menjangan island group, large number of tropical fish, marine plants are the main attractions. Boxed lunch. Afternoon, back to your Inn. Dinner and overnight.

5. day: after breakfast, Tabuhan island group is the destination. Coral reefs, tropical fish and shark sites are the main diving draws. Boxed lunch. Afternoon, back to your Inn. Dinner and overnight.

6. day: after breakfast, a chance to have another dive, in a different location, yet still around the island group. Boxed lunch. In the afternoon, drive to Denpasar.

Diving Tour 14 days/13 nights

1. day: arrival at Airport and transfer to the hotel.

2. day: whole morning at leisure. Evening drive to nearby village to see the world famous *kecak* dance.

3. day: early morning, drive on a coach eastward to Gili Tepekong to start first dive. Boxed lunch. Afternoon, drive to Manggis Inn for overnight. Dinner included.

4. day: after breakfast, drive on a coach to Padang Bay to enjoy a dive. Lunch. Afternoon back to Manggis Inn. Dinner and overnight.

5. day: after breakfast, dive around Padang Bay. Lunch. Afternoon, back to Manggis Inn. Dinner and overnight.

6. day: after breakfast, drive eastward to Tulamben beach, where shore or boat dive can be done. Lunch. Afternoon, back to Manggis Inn. Dinner and overnight.

7. day: after breakfast, drive to Teluk Terima via Kintamani, Singaraja. Lunch en route, dinner and overnight at Teluk Terima.

8. day: after breakfast dive around Menjangan island group. Afternoon, back to Inn. Dinner and overnight.

9. day: after breakfast, dive around Tabuhan island group. Lunch. Afternoon back to the Inn. Dinner and overnight.

10. day: after breakfast, dive around west coast of the island. Lunch. Afternoon, back to the Inn. Dinner and overnight.

11. day: after breakfast, dive around Menjangan island group. Lunch. Afternoon, back to the Inn. Dinner and overnight.

12. day: after breakfast, transfer to Denpasar via Negara and Tabanan. Arrive at your hotel in Sanur. Lunch at hotel.

13. day: whole day at leisure.

14. day: transfer to the Airport.

Service included: Transportation as described; dive equipment; room rent/meals, except in Denpasar/Sanur; guide/instructor/two tanks each course.

East Java

Surabaya City Tour 3 hours

Surabaya, capital city of East Java Province and second largest city in Indonesia. Visit the daily activities in the harbour area, with its Bugis and Madura proas, the memorable monument and the flora market.

Bromo Tour

Mini coach, brings you to the village of Ngadisari. Then the tour will proceed on pony, riding for 1½ hours, to reach the foot of Mt. Bromo and a staircase with 245 steps to go up to the crater. From this point watch the sunrise. Departure: 11.30 p.m.

Triple Temple & Malang Tour 10 hours

Visit 3 important places in the area of Malang— the Singosari temple, the Jayagu temple and the Kidal temple. The Singosari temple believed to be the grave of King Kertanegara.

Bull Races Tour 5 hours

The only Bull Races in the world can be found on the island of Madura, just across the Strait of Madura, 3 miles.

Sukamade Experience 5 days

1. day: Surabaya - Jember. After breakfast, depart for Jember via South Semeru route, the highest still-active volcano in Java. Picnic lunch while enjoying the spectacular view of the mountain. Overnight at Safari hotel or similar.

2. day: Jember - Sukamade. Drive through the rubber estates and the Meru Betiri wild games reserve. Picnic lunch served at Rajekwesi beach. Overnight at simple Sukamade guest house. At night; The Giant Turtle Excursion. After dinner, depart for the beach, passing through the coffee estates and the jungle.

3. day: Sukamade. After breakfast, back to the beach. After lunch, explore the village.

4. day: Sukamade - Banyuwangi. After breakfast at the guesthouse, depart to Banyuwangi. Day of sunbathing and swimming.

5. day: Banyuwangi - Denpasar. After breakfast at the hotel, depart for Denpasar by crossing the Strait of Bali by ferry. En route see the terraced rice fields, view of the Indian Ocean. Arrive at Denpasar, stay at a hotel of your own choice.

Komodo

4 Days

This tour is arranged from Denpasar in conjuction with a Bali tour.

1. day: By air to Lombok. Transfer to hotel, lunch, dinner and overnight.

2. day: 07.00 leave Bali by air for Bima, arrival 09.00. Transfer by public transport to the town. Chinese lunch. Leave by road to Sape, about 2 hours away. Take a rest in Camat house. Due to the strong current the crossing can only be made at night. After dinner leave by boat for an 8 hour trip to Komodo.

3. day: Early morning arrive in Komodo. Pay respect (and money) to the village head. Here a goat is bought to be used as bait. Walk to Waing Galung to watch the giant lizards. Picnic lunch, all food is brought from Bali. Return to Komodo. Dinner on board.

4. day: 02.30 arrive in Sape. Breakfast on board, do not miss the beautiful sunrise at 04.30. Drive to Bima. Rest at the Hotel Komodo. Lunch in the Blama restaurant. Afternoon visit to town by pony cart. Then watch the sunset at Bima Beach. Dinner and overnight in the hotel.

5. day: After breakfast transfer to airport to return to Denpasar via Lombok.

Lombok

Lombok 3 days/2 nights
1. day: Transfer from the airport or ferry landing to the hotel of your choice. Rest of day at leisure to stroll through the streets and markets of Cakranegara and Ampenan.
2. day: Depart from the hotel via Cakranegara, here, visit the main market with its special bird market, to Getap, a village with a primitive smith system where knives are made and horse shoes fitted. Proceed to the weaving village of Sukarasa. From Praya, the capital of central Lombok, through the flat ricefields to Nyale Beach. On the return trip, visit a typical Sasak village.
3. day: early afternoon return by air or ferry to Bali.

High Land Trekking 8 days/7 nights
1. day: transfer from airport or ferry landing to the hotel.
2. day: after breakfast drive to Pasagulan. Start the hike by climbing through jungle to Mount Pusuk. Picnic lunch in the jungle. Enjoy the beautiful view of the high valley of Sembalun Bumbung and Sembalun Lawang. Descend to Sembalun Bumbung guesthouse for dinner and overnight.
3. day: after an early breakfast climb to Pelawangan, local lunch and dinner, watch the sunset from Pelawangan.
4. day: descend to the Segara Anak Lake to the National Park. Lunch, dinner and overnight in Segara Anak.
5. day: Climb to Pelawangan, lunch, dinner, overnight in Pelawangan.
6. day: 03.00, if weather permits, climb Mount Rinjani before breakfast to watch the sunrise. Return to Pelawangan then see the village of Sembalun Lawang. Dinner and overnight.
7. day: descend Mount Pusuk for Pasugulan, dinner and overnight.
8. day: transfer to airport or ferry landing.

Sulawesi

Toraja Land 5 days/4 nights
1. day: after arrival in Ujung Pandang drive directly through the typical Buginese and Makassarese villages, fish farms, ricefields to Tana Toraja. Lunch in Pare Pare. Coffee break with fresh fruits in Kotu Enrekang. Arrival in Tana Toraja in the late afternoon. Dinner and overnight in a hotel or guesthouse.
2. day: tour typical Toraja villages, the grave caves at Marante, the hanging grave of Lemo, the old Toraja village Palawa. Also visit the handicraft centre and souvenir shops at Kete. Lunch en route.

3. day: full day tour to explore Batutumonga, Lemo and Loko' mata, typical Toraja villages, the most scenic rice terraces in Indonesia and enjoy the panorama of southern Sulawesi. Visit the typical Toraja market and the ancient grave of Londa. Art carving houses in Siguntu and Manggala. Lunch en route.
4. day: return to Ujung Pandang. Stop for swimming on the beach of Lumpue. Seafood dinner and accommodation in Ujung Pandang.
5. day: morning sightseeing in old Makassar, Port Rotterdam and the museum, see the harbour from where the Bugis sail to all islands of Indonesia. Orchid garden and sea shell collection. Transfer to airport.

North Sumatra

Prapat—Lake Toba 4 days
1. day: after arrival transfer by bus to Prapat, passing plantation road via Tebingtinggi. Lunch at Pematangsiantar. En route to Prapat panoramic view of Lake Toba. Dinner and overnight in Hotel Danau Toba International. Prapat.
2. day: after breakfast, embark launch for cruise on Lake Toba, for a visit to Ambarita and Tomok on Samosir Island, to see the original home of the Batak people, the ancient Batak Houses, and Tombs of Batak King Sidabutar. Back to Prapat for lunch in hotel Danau Toba International. After lunch shopping in Prapat. Dinner and overnight in the Hotel.
3. day: after breakfast depart for Hotel Danau Toba International Medan. Lunch at the hotel. After lunch, City Tour visiting the Palace of Sulthan Deli, Mesjid Raya and shopping at Jalan A. Yani. Dinner at Restaurant in Medanor in Hotel. Overnight.
4. day: after breakfast, transfer to Polonia Airport.

Bohorok Orang Utan, 3 days/2 nights
1. day: Medan, transfer by bus to Hotel Danau Toba International in Medan. After lunch City Tour visiting Palace of Sulthan Deli, Mesjid Raya and shopping at Jalan A. Yani. Dinner and overnight.
2. day: after breakfast, depart for Bohorok via Binjai. Take lunch, rest at your leisure. Out of Binjai see attractive scenery with mountain ranges along the way in Langkat District. Arrive at Bukit Lawang. From Bukit Lawang by foot, pass through Stone Caves, along the river Bohorok. Reach Bohorok Apes Centre by crossing the Bohorok river in a local boat. See the animals until departure to Medan. Dinner and overnight at Hotel Danau Toba International in Medan.

ART/PHOTO CREDITS

Index